**55** *Victorian Prose Writers Before 1867,* edited by William B. Thesing (1987)

**56** *German Fiction Writers, 1914-1945,* edited by James Hardin (1987)

**57** *Victorian Prose Writers After 1867,* edited by William B. Thesing (1987)

**58** *Jacobean and Caroline Dramatists,* edited by Fredson Bowers (1987)

**59** *American Literary Critics and Scholars, 1800-1850,* edited by John W. Rathbun and Monica M. Grecu (1987)

**60** *Canadian Writers Since 1960, Second Series,* edited by W. H. New (1987)

**61** *American Writers for Children Since 1960: Poets, Illustrators, and Nonfiction Authors,* edited by Glenn E. Estes (1987)

**62** *Elizabethan Dramatists,* edited by Fredson Bowers (1987)

**63** *Modern American Critics, 1920-1955,* edited by Gregory S. Jay (1988)

**64** *American Literary Critics and Scholars, 1850-1880,* edited by John W. Rathbun and Monica M. Grecu (1988)

**65** *French Novelists, 1900-1930,* edited by Catharine Savage Brosman (1988)

**66** *German Fiction Writers, 1885-1913,* 2 parts, edited by James Hardin (1988)

**67** *Modern American Critics Since 1955,* edited by Gregory S. Jay (1988)

**68** *Canadian Writers, 1920-1959, First Series,* edited by W. H. New (1988)

**69** *Contemporary German Fiction Writers, First Series,* edited by Wolfgang D. Elfe and James Hardin (1988)

**70** *British Mystery Writers, 1860-1919,* edited by Bernard Benstock and Thomas F. Staley (1988)

**71** *American Literary Critics and Scholars, 1880-1900,* edited by John W. Rathbun and Monica M. Grecu (1988)

**72** *French Novelists, 1930-1960,* edited by Catharine Savage Brosman (1988)

**73** *American Magazine Journalists, 1741-1850,* edited by Sam G. Riley (1988)

**74** *American Short-Story Writers Before 1880,* edited by Bobby Ellen Kimbel, with the assistance of William E. Grant (1988)

**75** *Contemporary German Fiction Writers, Second Series,* edited by Wolfgang D. Elfe and James Hardin (1988)

**76** *Afro-American Writers, 1940-1955,* edited by Trudier Harris (1988)

**77** *British Mystery Writers, 1920-1939,* edited by Bernard Benstock and Thomas F. Staley (1988)

**78** *American Short-Story Writers, 1880-1910,* edited by Bobby Ellen Kimbel, with the assistance of William E. Grant (1988)

**79** *American Magazine Journalists, 1850-1900,* edited by Sam G. Riley (1988)

**80** *Restoration and Eighteenth-Century Dramatists, First Series,* edited by Paula R. Backscheider (1989)

**81** *Austrian Fiction Writers, 1875-1913,* edited by James Hardin and Donald G. Daviau (1989)

**82** *Chicano Writers, First Series,* edited by Francisco A. Lomelí and Carl R. Shirley (1989)

**83** *French Novelists Since 1960,* edited by Catharine Savage Brosman (1989)

**84** *Restoration and Eighteenth-Century Dramatists, Second Series,* edited by Paula R. Backscheider (1989)

**85** *Austrian Fiction Writers After 1914,* edited by James Hardin and Donald G. Daviau (1989)

**86** *American Short-Story Writers, 1910-1945, First Series,* edited by Bobby Ellen Kimbel (1989)

**87** *British Mystery and Thriller Writers Since 1940, First Series,* edited by Bernard Benstock and Thomas F. Staley (1989)

**88** *Canadian Writers, 1920-1959, Second Series,* edited by W. H. New (1989)

**89** *Restoration and Eighteenth-Century Dramatists, Third Series,* edited by Paula R. Backscheider (1989)

**90** *German Writers in the Age of Goethe, 1789-1832,* edited by James Hardin and Christoph E. Schweitzer (1989)

**91** *American Magazine Journalists, 1900-1960, First Series,* edited by Sam G. Riley (1990)

**92** *Canadian Writers, 1890-1920,* edited by W. H. New (1990)

**93** *British Romantic Poets, 1789-1832, First Series,* edited by John R. Greenfield (1990)

**94** *German Writers in the Age of Goethe: Sturm und Drang to Classicism,* edited by James Hardin and Christoph E. Schweitzer (1990)

**95** *Eighteenth-Century British Poets, First Series,* edited by John Sitter (1990)

**96** *British Romantic Poets, 1789-1832, Second Series,* edited by John R. Greenfield (1990)

**97** *German Writers from the Enlightenment to Sturm und Drang, 1720-1764,* edited by James Hardin and Christoph E. Schweitzer (1990)

**98** *Modern British Essayists, First Series,* edited by Robert Beum (1990)

**99** *Canadian Writers Before 1890,* edited by W. H. New (1990)

**100** *Modern British Essayists, Second Series,* edited by Robert Beum (1990)

**101** *British Prose Writers, 1660-1800, First Series,* edited by Donald T. Siebert (1991)

**102** *American Short-Story Writers, 1910-1945, Second Series,* edited by Bobby Ellen Kimbel (1991)

**103** *American Literary Biographers, First Series,* edited by Steven Serafin (1991)

**104** *British Prose Writers, 1660-1800, Second Series,* edited by Donald T. Siebert (1991)

**105** *American Poets Since World War II, Second Series,* edited by R. S. Gwynn (1991)

**106** *British Literary Publishing Houses, 1820-1880,* edited by Patricia J. Anderson and Jonathan Rose (1991)

**107** *British Romantic Prose Writers, 1789-1832, First Series,* edited by John R. Greenfield (1991)

**108** *Twentieth-Century Spanish Poets, First Series,* edited by Michael L. Perna (1991)

**109** *Eighteenth-Century British Poets, Second Series,* edited by John Sitter (1991)

**110** *British Romantic Prose Writers, 1789-1832, Second Series,* edited by John R. Greenfield (1991)

**111** *American Literary Biographers, Second Series,* edited by Steven Serafin (1991)

**112** *British Literary Publishing Houses, 1881-1965,* edited by Jonathan Rose and Patricia J. Anderson (1991)

**113** *Modern Latin-American Fiction Writers, First Series,* edited by William Luis (1992)

**114** *Twentieth-Century Italian Poets, First Series,* edited by Giovanna Wedel De Stasio, Glauco Cambon, and Antonio Illiano (1992)

**115** *Medieval Philosophers,* edi… Jeremiah H…

**116** *British* … edited … (1992)



**(Continue**

Dictionary of Literary Biography® • Volume One Hundred Fifty-Nine

# British Short-Fiction Writers, 1800–1880

Dictionary of Literary Biography® • Volume One Hundred Fifty-Nine

# British Short-Fiction Writers, 1800–1880

Edited by
John R. Greenfield
*McKendree College*

A Bruccoli Clark Layman Book
Gale Research Inc.
Detroit, Washington, D.C., London

The paper used in this publication meets the minimum requirements
of American National Standard for Information Sciences–Permanence
Paper for Printed Library Materials, ANSI Z39.48-1984. ™ ∞

*For Patrick Brantlinger and Mary Burgan and all inspiring teachers of nineteenth-century British literature*

**Library of Congress Cataloging-in-Publication Data**

British short-fiction writers, 1800–1880 / edited by John R. Greenfield.
   p. cm. – (Dictionary of literary biography; v. 159)
"A Bruccoli Clark Layman book."
Includes bibliographical references and index.
ISBN 0-8103-9354-9 (alk. paper)
1. Short stories, English – Bio-bibliography. 2. Authors, English – 19th century – Biography –
Dictionaries. 3. English fiction – 19th century – Bio-bibliography. 4. English fiction – 19th century –
Dictionaries. 5. Short stories, English – Dictionaries I. Greenfield, John R. II. Series.
PR829.B72 1995
823'.010908 – dc20
                                    95-41313
                                       CIP

10 9 8 7 6 5 4 3 2 1

# Contents

# Plan of the Series

*. . . Almost the most prodigious asset of a country, and perhaps its most precious possession, is its native literary product – when that product is fine and noble and enduring.*

Mark Twain\*

The advisory board, the editors, and the publisher of the *Dictionary of Literary Biography* are joined in endorsing Mark Twain's declaration. The literature of a nation provides an inexhaustible resource of permanent worth. We intend to make literature and its creators better understood and more accessible to students and the reading public, while satisfying the standards of teachers and scholars.

To meet these requirements, *literary biography* has been construed in terms of the author's achievement. The most important thing about a writer is his writing. Accordingly, the entries in *DLB* are career biographies, tracing the development of the author's canon and the evolution of his reputation.

The purpose of *DLB* is not only to provide reliable information in a convenient format but also to place the figures in the larger perspective of literary history and to offer appraisals of their accomplishments by qualified scholars.

The publication plan for *DLB* resulted from two years of preparation. The project was proposed to Bruccoli Clark by Frederick C. Ruffner, president of the Gale Research Company, in November 1975. After specimen entries were prepared and typeset, an advisory board was formed to refine the entry format and develop the series rationale. In meetings held during 1976, the publisher, series editors, and advisory board approved the scheme for a comprehensive biographical dictionary of persons who contributed to North American literature. Editorial work on the first volume began in January 1977, and it was published in 1978. In order to make *DLB* more than a reference tool and to compile volumes that individually have claim to status as literary history, it was decided to organize volumes by topic, period, or genre. Each of these freestanding volumes provides a biographical-bibliographical guide and overview for a particular area of literature. We are convinced that this organization – as opposed to a single alphabet method – constitutes a valuable innovation in the presentation of reference material. The volume plan necessarily requires many decisions for the placement and treatment of authors who might properly be included in two or three volumes. In some instances a major figure will be included in separate volumes, but with different entries emphasizing the aspect of his career appropriate to each volume. Ernest Hemingway, for example, is represented in *American Writers in Paris, 1920–1939* by an entry focusing on his expatriate apprenticeship; he is also in *American Novelists, 1910–1945* with an entry surveying his entire career. Each volume includes a cumulative index of the subject authors and articles. Comprehensive indexes to the entire series are planned.

With volume ten in 1982 it was decided to enlarge the scope of *DLB*. By the end of 1986 twenty-one volumes treating British literature had been published, and volumes for Commonwealth and Modern European literature were in progress. The series has been further augmented by the *DLB Yearbooks* (since 1981) which update published entries and add new entries to keep the *DLB* current with contemporary activity. There have also been *DLB Documentary Series* volumes which provide biographical and critical source materials for figures whose work is judged to have particular interest for students. One of these companion volumes is entirely devoted to Tennessee Williams.

We define literature as the *intellectual commerce of a nation:* not merely as belles lettres but as that ample and complex process by which ideas are generated, shaped, and transmitted. *DLB* entries are not limited to "creative writers" but extend to other figures who in their time and in their way influenced the mind of a people. Thus the series encompasses historians, journalists, publishers, and screenwriters. By this means readers of *DLB* may be aided to perceive literature not as cult scripture in the keeping of intellectual high

\**From an unpublished section of Mark Twain's autobiography, copyright by the Mark Twain Company* priests but firmly positioned at the center of a nation's life.

*DLB* includes the major writers appropriate to each volume and those standing in the ranks immediately behind them. Scholarly and critical counsel has been sought in deciding which minor figures to include and how full their entries should be. Wherever possible, useful references are made to figures who do not warrant separate entries.

Each *DLB* volume has a volume editor responsible for planning the volume, selecting the figures for inclusion, and assigning the entries. Volume editors are also responsible for preparing, where appropriate, appendices surveying the major periodicals and literary and intellectual movements for their volumes, as well as lists of further readings. Work on the series as a whole is coordinated at the Bruccoli Clark Layman editorial center in Columbia, South Carolina, where the editorial staff is responsible for accuracy of the published volumes.

One feature that distinguishes *DLB* is the illustration policy – its concern with the iconography of literature. Just as an author is influenced by his surroundings, so is the reader's understanding of the author enhanced by a knowledge of his environment. Therefore *DLB* volumes include not only drawings, paintings, and photographs of authors, often depicting them at various stages in their careers, but also illustrations of their families and places where they lived. Title pages are regularly reproduced in facsimile along with dust jackets for modern authors. The dust jackets are a special feature of *DLB* because they often document better than anything else the way in which an author's work was perceived in its own time. Specimens of the writers' manuscripts are included when feasible.

Samuel Johnson rightly decreed that "The chief glory of every people arises from its authors." The purpose of the *Dictionary of Literary Biography* is to compile literary history in the surest way available to us – by accurate and comprehensive treatment of the lives and work of those who contributed to it.

The *DLB* Advisory Board

# Introduction

*Dictionary of Literary Biography* volume 159 is chronologically the first in a five-part series of volumes treating the development in the British Isles of the genre of short fiction from the early nineteenth century to the latter part of the twentieth century. The time span treated by this volume encompasses the Romantic period and the early and middle Victorian period. During these eighty years England – along with Western civilization in general – underwent a transformation from a largely rural to an urban lifestyle and from an agrarian to an industrial economy. In England thousands migrated to London and to the new industrial cities, such as Birmingham, Liverpool, Manchester, and Leeds, that grew rapidly from villages. Four monarchs occupied the English throne during these years: George III from 1760 to 1820; George IV from 1820 to 1830 (after serving as prince regent during his father's infirmity from 1811 to 1820); William IV from 1830 to 1837; and Victoria from 1837 to 1901.

The year 1800 found England embroiled in the Napoleonic Wars, which had begun in 1797 and ended with Napoleon Bonaparte's defeat at Waterloo in 1815. The early days of the French Revolution, with its emphasis on democracy and equality, had been hailed by English writers such as Thomas Paine, William Godwin, Mary Wollstonecraft, William Blake, William Wordsworth, and Samuel Taylor Coleridge; but the Reign of Terror and France's transformation into an empire under Napoleon left many of these writers disillusioned about the prospect for a political revolution in England. Most English intellectuals and politicians adopted the conservative principles enunciated by Edmund Burke in *Reflections on the Revolution in France* (1792): England's definition of liberty is not social but individual and includes the property rights of landed families; the constitution is organic – capable of change, but only gradually and when conditions are right. For the first thirty years of the century the English government defended the status quo, attempting to slow political change as much as possible if it could not stop change altogether. Unrest and revolutionary stirrings occurred at various times; perhaps the most infamous example was the Peterloo Massacre on 16 August 1819, in which eleven people were killed and more than four hundred were wounded when a crowd that had assembled to hear radical speeches at St. Peter's Field in Manchester was charged by a troop of cavalry. The event was immortalized by the radical poet Percy Bysshe Shelley in *The Masque of Anarchy* (1832) and "England in 1819" (1839).

Nevertheless, the England that emerged from the Napoleonic Wars was poised to become the dominant economic and colonial power until World War I. England was a leader in the Industrial Revolution because of inventions such as the steam engine, a ready supply of workers and materials, and an entrepreneurial class with capital to invest. Furthermore, England's control of the seas, established by its naval victories over France, meant that it could transport the goods it manufactured anywhere in the world. By establishing colonies in Australia, New Zealand, Africa, and Asia and on islands scattered throughout the globe, England ensured its place as the world's foremost economic and colonial power into the twentieth century.

During the Regency period ostentatious shows of wealth and elegance were the rule. The tone was set by the Prince Regent himself and by the epitome of fashion, George Bryan "Beau" Brummell. As the Victorian period approached, however, a new moral tone began to take hold – particularly on the rising middle class: originating in Evangelicalism, specifically in Methodism, the new morality transformed the English code of behavior into one of repression of sexual desires, elaborate rules of etiquette, and a display of solid, not showy, financial well-being that included certain standards of dwelling and the employment of servants.

The main domestic political events of the period were the two Reform Bills. The first, in 1832, did not greatly enlarge the franchise, despite the agitation and fears that surrounded its passage. Chartism arose in the 1840s as a grassroots working-class movement that demanded universal suffrage; to many it seemed to threaten England's stability in the wave of European revolutions that came to a head in 1848. But England stayed the course of gradual reform by waiting until 1867 to pass the Second Reform Bill, which, although it greatly widened the franchise, still did not admit women or even all men to the electorate. In international relations England had to deal with continuing unrest in Ireland and, from 1853 to 1856, with the Crimean War. Yet none of these problems shook England's faith in its greatness. A monument to that greatness was the Great Exhibition of 1851, with its centerpiece, the Crystal Palace, constructed to display England's successes in invention, manufacturing, and trade.

The middle of the nineteenth century has been called "the age of ideology," in which various philosophical, political, and religious ideas – utilitarianism, Marxism, socialism, Tractarianism, and Darwinism, as well as the reaction against these "isms" – competed in the intellectual marketplace. The ideas of such eighteenth-century economists as Adam Smith, Thomas Malthus, David Ricardo, and the French Physiocrats were transformed by the philosopher Jeremy Bentham, along with his disciple James Mill, into utilitarianism. Utilitarianism was a hard-nosed way of deciding ethical and social issues by calculating the pain or pleasure that would be produced by alternative courses of action; the goal was to achieve "the greatest happiness for the greatest number." The major publishing outlet for the utilitarians, who were known in their own day as Philosophical Radicals, was the influential *Westminster Review,* edited by Mill's brilliant son, John Stuart Mill, who, influenced by his reading of the works of the Romantic poets Coleridge and Wordsworth, softened the rather mechanistic thinking of utilitarianism by making room for feeling and individualism. (It was also John Stuart Mill who coined the term *utilitarianism.*) The unemotional austerity of utilitarian thought was also criticized by Thomas Carlyle in his fictional autobiography *Sartor Resartus* (1834) and satirized by Charles Dickens in his novel *Hard Times* (1854).

While the Industrial Revolution resulted in increased wealth for entrepreneurs, the workers in the factories and mills suffered from low wages, long hours, and harsh working conditions. The German immigrants Karl Marx and Friedrich Engels – the latter of whom was himself the son of a factory owner – formulated a new philosophy that claimed to analyze the cause of the workers' plight: the capitalist system, they said, allowed the owners of the means of production (the "bourgeoisie") to exploit the workers (the "proletariat"). Using the reports of various government commissions as his main sources, Engels chronicled the miseries of the workers in *The Condition of the Working Class in England* (1845); Marx and Engels jointly wrote the *Manifesto of the Communist Party* (1848), calling on the workers to unite in revolution and overthrow their capitalist

masters; and Marx, working long hours in the reading room of the British Museum, worked out his massive critique of capitalism in *Das Kapital* (1867–1895). A nonrevolutionary version of socialism, more suited to the English predilection for gradual change, influenced several writers of the later Victorian period, including William Morris, George Bernard Shaw, and H. G. Wells.

Religious thought during the period ranged from Evangelicalism to the Oxford Movement to Christian socialism to agnosticism. The Oxford Movement – also called Tractarianism to reflect the many tracts that were published to explain its ideas – advocated restoring to the Church of England many of the Catholic rituals and sacraments that had been abandoned at the time of the Reformation; one of its leaders, John Henry Newman, ultimately converted to Catholicism and became a cardinal. The writer Charles Kingsley tried to show how the generosity exemplified by Christianity could be combined with socialism. But the theory of evolution posed the greatest challenge to traditional religious beliefs. Many writers – perhaps best exemplified by the poet laureate, Alfred Tennyson, in *In Memoriam* (1850) – suffered crises of faith that were at least partly attributable to discoveries in geology that seemed to contradict the account of the creation of the world in the book of Genesis and to evolutionary ideas that were already in the air even before the publication of Charles Darwin's *On the Origin of Species by Means of Natural Selection* (1859). Thomas Henry Huxley, who earned the epithet "Darwin's Bulldog" for his lively defense of the reclusive scientist's theories, coined the term *agnosticism* in 1870 to refer to those who concluded that no judgment could be arrived at as to the existence of God. Huxley championed science and practical thinking in general in a series of exchanges with the great defender of classical education and culture, Matthew Arnold. According to Arnold, who wrote *Culture and Anarchy* (1867–1868) at least partly as a response to the agitation that led up to the passage of the Second Reform Bill, culture is the last bastion of order in a society that can no longer look to religion as a unifying and ordering institution.

The first eighty years of the nineteenth century span two major literary periods, the Romantic and the Victorian. Romanticism is often contrasted with neoclassicism in art, music, and literature: while the neoclassical is marked by decorum, tradition, propriety, balance, symmetry, imitation, and rationality, the Romantic is characterized by innovation, experimentation, emotional extremes, spontaneity, organicism, individualism, originality, and imagination. In England the Romantic period is generally assumed to begin with the publication either of Blake's *Songs of Innocence* in 1789 or of Wordsworth and Coleridge's *Lyrical Ballads* in 1798. Probably the latter had more influence during the period because the two poets' volume of verse was more widely read than Blake's book, of which only a few copies were produced. Wordsworth and Coleridge, along with their literary followers (but ideological opponents) George Gordon, Lord Byron; Percy Bysshe Shelley; and John Keats, not only introduced into poetry the personal expression of feeling but also reoriented the prevailing view of the individual's relationship to God, to nature, and to society.

The poets of the early Victorian period, most notably Tennyson and Robert Browning, set out to emulate their Romantic forebears but found their own voices by altering the subject matter of their poetry to meet the challenges of their own time; and Browning developed poetic forms that stretched the limits of the forms the Romantics had created. Though the Romantic lyric continued to be produced brilliantly by poets such as Tennyson, Arnold, and, later, the Pre-Raphaelites Dante Gabriel Rossetti, his sister Christina Rossetti, and Algernon Charles Swinburne, there was — perhaps due in part to the increasing popularity of the novel — a resurgence of long narrative poetry. Such works included Tennyson's popular *Idylls of the King* (1859–1885); Swinburne's *Atalanta in Calydon* (1865); Browning's *The Ring and The Book* (1868–1869), groundbreaking in its brilliant use of multiple points of view; and William Morris's *The Earthly Paradise* (1868–1870) and *Sigurd the Volsung* (1876).

Both the Romantic and the early Victorian periods are marked by distinguished prose writers, with masters of the familiar essay such as Charles Lamb and Thomas De Quincey using many of the techniques of Romantic poetry. In the Victorian period prose writers such as Thomas Carlyle and John Ruskin innovatively combined personal observation and creative vision in addressing social, moral, and aesthetic questions. In addition to Carlyle and Ruskin, Victorian prose writers such as Newman, John Stuart Mill, and Arnold have come to be known as "sages" for their willingness to contemplate philosophical and moral issues and to prophesy the dangerous consequences of following "popular" trends.

If the poets held sway over literature in the first quarter of the nineteenth century, writers of fiction, particularly novelists, gained greater influence, prestige, and popularity in the Victorian period.

Kathryn Sutherland, in her essay " 'Events Have Made Us a World of Readers': Reader Relations 1780–1830" (1994), identifies the 1820s as the decade in which prose fiction assumed ascendancy over poetry and points to Sir Walter Scott as the prime example. Scott was a popular poet; but because he needed more money than he was earning from his poetry, he and his publisher Archibald Constable made a successful transition to producing and selling novels for the new mass market. During the mid Victorian period Tennyson, a tremendously popular poet and poet laureate, could not begin to match the sales of Dickens's novels.

The popular fiction published during this period falls into three main types: Gothic, romance, and realistic. Beginning with Horace Walpole's *The Castle of Otranto* (1765); revived in the lurid novels by Mary Wollstonecraft, Matthew Gregory "Monk" Lewis, and Ann Radcliffe in the 1790s; and continued into the early 1800s by writers such as Scott, James Hogg, Maria Edgeworth, Mary Wollstonecraft Shelley, and John Galt, Gothic literature remained a popular genre throughout the century. While Dickens, as well as many lesser-known writers, tried their hands at the Gothic, Wilkie Collins and Joseph Sheridan Le Fanu devoted themselves to the genre and excelled at it. A close cousin to the Gothic was the romance novel, which is characterized by improbable plots, exotic locales, dreamy heroines, dashing and virile heroes, broadly drawn villains, and frequent use of the past, especially the Middle Ages; the consummate master of this genre was Scott. Competing with popular Gothic and romance fiction was the realistic or "bourgeois sentimental" novel, which treated in a fairly believable way the concerns of the rising middle or professional class, the fastest-growing group of readers and one that demanded high-quality literature. During the Romantic period this kind of fiction is best represented by the carefully crafted novels of Jane Austen, though her works often have an ironic or even satiric tone. During the first two-thirds of the Victorian period the tradition of realism was carried on and modified by the great Victorian novelists, each of whom was highly successful in depicting the dynamics of a particular environment in multilayered detail: in addition to Dickens, the dominant figure of the age in popularity and influence, the major realistic writers include William Makepeace Thackeray, who depicted London high society; George Eliot, who portrayed life in the rural areas and small towns that were being changed by the Industrial Revolution; Elizabeth Cleghorn Gaskell, who examined the working-class milieu; Anthony Trollope, who wrote about the lives of villagers and the rural gentry; and George Meredith, who dealt with questions of gender and class. The Brontë sisters, Charlotte, Emily, and Anne, blended strains of romance, Gothic, and realistic fiction to produce some of the most exciting and innovative fiction of the period. All of these novelists wrote at least some short fiction as well.

In the early 1800s three venues of publication developed through which readers could have access to an increasing variety of fiction: expensive multivolume novels, or "triple deckers"; relatively inexpensive chapbooks, so called because they were often sold by chapmen, street peddlers who traded in a variety of goods; and periodicals. In the early years of the century books were still expensive and slow to produce; but with the advent of the steam printing press books could be produced quickly, cheaply, and in large quantities to meet the demand of the burgeoning mass reading public. Circulating libraries became increasingly popular as a means of acquiring inexpensive reading material. As literacy increased throughout the century, a myriad of newspapers and magazines were founded. Many of these periodicals published serialized novels, which not only made the works more affordable for readers but heightened their excitement as they waited for succeeding installments to appear. Periodicals also became an outlet for shorter forms of fiction. Literary journals included *Blackwood's Edinburgh Magazine,* probably the single most important outlet for short fiction during the first half of the nineteenth century; *Bentley's Miscellany, Fraser's Magazine,* the *Dublin University Magazine,* and the *New Monthly Magazine.* Dickens's literary magazines, *Household Words* and later *All the Year Round,* provided outlets for his own serialized novels and short fiction and also for that of writers such as Gaskell and Collins, and the prestigious *Cornhill Magazine* included fiction by Thackeray and Trollope. These literary journals achieved circulations in six figures for at least short intervals during their heydays. In addition to the magazines and newspapers that published works of fiction, there were also literary reviews that criticized such works. The *Edinburgh Review,* founded in 1802, set the standards for the many such periodicals that were to follow, among them *The Quarterly Review, The Monthly Review, The Critical Review,* and *The Examiner.* Often these publications were highly politicized, so that it became common for reviewers to criticize or praise writers on the basis of their political orientations rather than on their literary merits. By the mid Victorian period total circulation for

the many literary periodicals had reached more than a million in London alone.

Short fiction has existed since ancient times; the earliest examples may be Theophrastus's studies of character types in the late fourth and early third centuries B.C. The medieval Breton *lai,* a genre perfected by Marie de France, is, however, closer to the modern conception of a short narrative form. In the fourteenth century the one hundred *novelle* that comprise *The Decameron* (1351–1353) of Giovanni Boccaccio and the twenty-four tales of Geoffrey Chaucer's *Canterbury Tales* (circa 1387–1400) – though the latter are in verse – demonstrate the development, popularity, and versatility of the short form. In the sixteenth century Margaret de Navarre, in the *Heptaméron,* followed the pattern established by Boccaccio of a series of tales linked by the framing device of a group of narrators taking turns. The Elizabethan period was marked by the appearance of "jestbooks," collections of tales that attained a degree of popularity. Samuel Butler, a seventeenth-century successor to Theophrastus, wrote a series of character sketches that were finally published as *Characters* in 1749. In the eighteenth century the advent of magazines provided an outlet for the short narrative form. Daniel Defoe, who published short fiction in his *Journal,* is usually given credit for writing the first ghost story: "A True Relation of the Apparition of Mrs. Veal, the Next Day after Her Death, to One Mrs. Bargrave at Canterbury, the 8th of September, 1705" (1706). A further development in the eighteenth century was the appearance of the oriental tale. At the end of the century Hannah More produced *Repository Tracts* (1797), didactic moral treatises in fictional form.

It was not until the nineteenth century, however, that the short story began to take shape as a distinct, important, and popular genre. The reasons for this development were at least threefold: the rapid expansion of the mass reading public, particularly among the middle and working classes and including, for the first time, a significant and growing number of women; the corresponding proliferation of popular magazines and newspapers, which especially lent themselves to short narrative forms; and the advent of miscellanies and annuals, which also lent themselves to short fiction, including novellas ranging from five thousand to twelve thousand words. Distinct subgenres of short fiction began to emerge: the Gothic tale, which may or may not include supernatural occurrences but creates an atmosphere of surprise and is at least suggestive of the supernatural; the sentimental romance or melodrama, the nineteenth-century equivalent of the twentieth-century romance novel or soap opera; the realistic story, often dealing with social problems, which gained in popularity from midcentury onward; the detective story; the adventure tale; and the humorous sketch, particularly identified with the magazine *Punch,* founded in 1841.

The authors included in this volume all made unique contributions to the short-fiction form, even though none of them probably would have identified himself or herself as primarily a writer of short fiction. Most of the contributors to the short form during the Romantic period were Irish or Scottish, perhaps because the rich folklore traditions of those countries have provided a wealth of source material. In his "Tales from Big House and Cabin: The Nineteenth Century" (1984), Gregory Schirmer divides the early-nineteenth-century Irish short-fiction writers into two groups: the Anglo-Irish Protestant gentry – Maria Edgeworth, George Croly, Anna Maria Hall, and Joseph Sheridan Le Fanu – writers of "the big house"; and the rural Catholic peasant writers John and Michael Banim, Gerald Griffin, William Carleton, and Samuel Lover, writers of "the cabin." Schirmer believes that the success of Edgeworth's novelette *Castle Rackrent* (1800), along with Charles Maturin's *Melmoth the Wanderer* (1820), had a profound influence not only on Irish writers but on the popular use of Gothic themes and trappings by many other writers. The Irish writers, whether Protestant or Catholic, had in common that they were writing primarily for English audiences. Even the Protestant gentry writers such as Edgeworth and Hall took a critical view of the English landlord system in Ireland. Hall's two series of *Sketches of Irish Character,* published in 1829 and 1831, present a picture of Irish life at all levels of the social scale. In the mid Victorian period the most significant Anglo-Irish writer was Le Fanu, who edited the *Dublin University Magazine* between 1861 and 1869. Though he wrote some comic and historical stories, Le Fanu is mainly known for his contributions to the Gothic: his novel *Uncle Silas* (1864), along with stories such as "Green Tea" (1869) and "Carmilla" (1871–1872) – the latter of which was probably an inspiration for Bram Stoker's *Dracula* (1897) – are considered classics of the genre.

The brothers John and Michael Banim are at the forefront of writers in the rural Irish Catholic tradition. The two series of *Tales by the O'Hara Family* (1825, 1826), according to Schirmer, "brought to the English reader's attention for the first time the singular mixture of broad humor and lawlessness that characterized Irish cabin life at the beginning of the nineteenth century." Despite some melodra-

matic scenes and Gothic trappings, the tales convey a realistic view of the harshness of Irish rural life at the time. Griffin began as an apprentice to John Banim, but, not wanting to be too dependent on Banim, rejected an offer to contribute a story to the second series of *Tales by the O'Hara Family* and brought out a collection of his own stories, *Holland-Tide; or, Munster Popular Tales* (1827). Because of his superior skill in writing Irish dialect, handling narrative voice, using irony and humor, and treating the Irish peasantry realistically, Carleton's many Irish tales and sketches of the 1830s and 1840s mark an advance over previous efforts in these genres. Though his contribution to short fiction is not as prodigious as Carleton's, Lover, a cofounder of the *Dublin University Magazine,* published *Legends and Stories of Ireland* (1831–1834), which are predominantly in the comic mode but which also treat the problem of Anglo-Irish relations. Ireland's relationship to England is always at least implicit, and sometimes explicit, in nearly all of the nineteenth-century writers from Ireland.

While Sir Walter Scott was enormously popular because of his skill in using medieval and Gothic settings and themes, he acknowledged his debt to Edgeworth in his preface to the *Waverley Novels* (1829–1833): "I felt that something might be attempted for my own country, of the same kind with that which Miss Edgeworth so fortunately achieved for Ireland." Though Scott did not write many short stories, and most of those that he did write are incorporated in his novels (such as "Wandering Willie's Tale" in *Redgauntlet* [1824]), he was capable of creating lasting work in the short-fiction genre. For example, "The Two Drovers," one of three stories in *Chronicles of the Canongate* (1827), is still considered an important contribution because of Scott's skill in dramatizing the conflict between the Highland and Lowland cultures.

Within the Scottish milieu James Hogg, "the Ettrick Shepherd," holds a similar position to that of Carleton in Irish literature – that of an untutored genius. Best known for his psychological Gothic novel *The Private Memoirs and Confessions of a Justified Sinner* (1824), Hogg used *Blackwood's* as an outlet for many of his stories about dogs, lasses, and the supernatural that were later collected in *Winter Evening Tales* (1820) and *The Shepherd's Calendar* (1829). Hogg became one of *Blackwood's* "Noctes Ambrosianae," a group of writers portrayed as uncouth peasants. Though John Galt's *Annals of the Parish* (1821), a series of incidents purporting to come from the diary of the Rev. Micah Balwhidder, has been seen by some as a novel, Galt discouraged this opinion, averring that "when it was written, I had no idea it would ever have been received as a novel." Jane and Anna Maria Porter drew their material from contemporary life, history, and legend to write stories and novels involving moral examples, romance, and adventure. The stories in Anna Maria's *Artless Tales* (1795, 1798) are early examples of the medieval romance tale, while those in her *Tales of Pity* take a didactic approach to instruct young readers in the need for compassion. *Tales round a Winter Hearth* (1826), a collection of mostly sentimental romance tales endowed with moral lessons, is deemed the sisters' most important contribution to the short genre.

English writers who contributed to the short-fiction genre during the Romantic period include Amelia Opie and Mary Wollstonecraft Shelley. Opie is noteworthy for exploring emotional subjectivity in some of her tales rather than concentrating on external action or moral didacticism. She published four collections: *Simple Tales* (1806), *Tales of Real Life* (1813), *New Tales* (1818), and *Tales of the Heart* (1820). Though her reputation rests on her novel *Frankenstein* (1818), Shelley also wrote stories in the Gothic and romance modes. Her favorite venue of publication for these stories was the annual *Keepsake* volumes of the late 1820s and early 1830s. In her later years Shelley cultivated a friendship with Caroline Norton, a feminist who contributed short fiction to periodicals as well as producing novels and poetry.

The early Victorian period is marked by an increase in the amount of fiction appearing in periodicals. The Gothic mode continued to be popular, but satiric and humorous stories gained in prominence. William Mudford excelled in the Gothic horror genre and contributed many such tales to *Blackwood's, Bentley's Miscellany,* and *Fraser's* in the late 1820s and the 1830s; his "The Iron Shroud" (1830) may have influenced Edgar Allan Poe's "The Pit and the Pendulum" (1843). William Maginn, one of the founders of *Fraser's,* contributed a variety of Gothic, humorous, and satiric tales to that magazine as well as to *Blackwood's* and *Bentley's Miscellany.* Douglas Jerrold published Gothic and humorous tales in *Blackwood's* and the *New Monthly Magazine* in the 1830s and 1840s. Harriet Martineau, though remembered today principally as a feminist author, produced several collections of instructive tales for children, including *Illustrations of Political Economy* (1832–1834), *Poor Laws and Paupers Illustrated* (1833–1834), *Illustrations of Taxation* (1834), and *Forest and Game Law Tales* (1845–1846).

During the mid Victorian period, from the 1840s to the 1880s, the most significant contribu-

tions to the short genres came from writers whose considerable reputations rest on their novels. Charlotte Brontë's relationship to the genre is unique in that it consists of her youthful efforts at creating fantasy worlds such as Angria, the raw materials of which she would later mold into her great novels, such as *Jane Eyre* (1847). Charles Dickens's *Sketches by Boz* (1836–1837) imbued the tale, traditionally defined as a story of unspecified time and place, with specific details for satiric purposes. Dickens also excelled in the subgenre of the Christmas story with classics such as *A Christmas Carol* (1843), *The Chimes* (1844), and *The Cricket on the Hearth* (1846). Wendell V. Harris regards *Cranford,* a series of stories of rural life that appeared in *Household Words* from 1851 to 1853, as Elizabeth Cleghorn Gaskell's most important contribution to short fiction; she also wrote ghost, murder, and romance stories. In both his novels and his short fiction Wilkie Collins is a master at building suspense. In his detective, Gothic, and mystery stories, many of which were first published in Dickens's magazines, Collins experiments with multiple and unreliable narrators.

The prolific novelists Thackeray, Trollope, Meredith, and Oliphant contributed a wide variety of short fiction – ghost, adventure, humorous, and realistic stories – much of it first published in periodicals. Meredith and Oliphant, drawing from their own painful experiences and writing during a period when realism had become the dominant mode in fiction, made great strides toward the realistic treatment of relationships between men and women. Meredith is also noteworthy for abandoning the standard notion of fixed characters to experiment with shifting character identities and for his compressed style.

While the authors treated in this volume demonstrated an adaptability that allowed them to meet the growing demands of a rapidly increasing mass reading public, especially women readers who demanded shorter fiction that was designed primarily to entertain, few of the efforts at short fiction by the writers treated in this volume fulfill the standard of the tightly wrought short story that achieves a unity of effect. Though there are individual examples of well-told tales, especially in the Gothic, mystery, and humorous sketch or anecdote genres, the real flowering of short fiction as an independent art form – rather than as filler for periodicals or as a way for writers to earn extra income – did not occur until the last two decades of the nineteenth century, when writers such as Robert Louis Stevenson, Thomas Hardy, Henry James, Arthur Conan Doyle, Rudyard Kipling, George Gissing, and H. G.

Wells took the art of the short story and novella to a new level.

I would like to especially thank William Thesing, who has coordinated the whole five-volume *DLB* series on the development of short fiction in English literature from 1800 to the present. He has also been helpful in drawing up the table of contents and in securing contributors for this volume. To those contributors — from the United States, Canada, and Great Britain — who have met their deadlines, completed revisions, and shown forbearance, I owe a debt of gratitude. Two secretaries at McKendree College, Naomia Severs and Linda Gordon, deserve special thanks for the help they gave me in handling the correspondence associated with this volume. I would like to also thank Mary Lampman, who served as an editorial assistant for this volume under the auspices of the McKendree internship program, and Sharol Walthes, who assisted with the proofreading.

*— John R. Greenfield*

## Acknowledgments

This book was produced by Bruccoli Clark Layman, Inc. Karen L. Rood is senior editor for the *Dictionary of Literary Biography* series. Philip B. Dematteis was the in-house editor.

Production coordinator is James W. Hipp. Photography editor is Bruce Andrew Bowlin. Photographic copy work was performed by Joseph M. Bruccoli. Layout and graphics supervisor is Penney L. Haughton. Copyediting supervisor is Laurel M. Gladden. Typesetting supervisor is Kathleen M. Flanagan. Systems manager is George F. Dodge. Julie E. Frick is editorial associate. The production staff includes Phyllis A. Avant, Charles D. Brower, Ann M. Cheschi, Melody W. Clegg, Patricia Coate, Joyce Fowler, Stephanie C. Hatchell, Rebecca Mayo, Margaret Meriwether, Kathy Lawler Merlette, Jeff Miller, Pamela D. Norton, Delores Plastow, Laura Pleicones, Emily R. Sharpe, William L. Thomas Jr., Allison Trussell, Jonathan B. Watterson, and Jane M. J. Williamson.

Walter W. Ross and Robert S. McConnell did library research. They were assisted by the following librarians at the Thomas Cooper Library of the University of South Carolina: Linda Holderfield and the interlibrary-loan staff; reference-department head Virginia Weathers; reference librarians Marilee Birchfield, Stefanie Buck, Cathy Eckman, Rebecca Feind, Jill Holman, Karen Joseph, Jean Rhyne, Kwamine Washington, and Connie Widney; circulation-department head Caroline Taylor; and acquisitions-searching supervisor David Haggard.

The publishers acknowledge the generous assistance of William R. Cagle, director of the Lilly Library, Indiana University, and his staff, who provided many of the illustrations in this volume. Their work represents the highest standards of librarianship and research.

# British Short-Fiction Writers, 1800–1880

# Dictionary of Literary Biography

# William Edmondstoune Aytoun

*(21 June 1813 – 4 August 1865)*

Thomas L. Cooksey
*Armstrong State College*

See also the Aytoun entry in *DLB 32: Victorian Poets Before 1850.*

BOOKS: *Poland, Homer, and Other Poems,* anonymous (London: Longman, Rees, Orme, Brown, Green & Longman, 1832);

*The Life and Times of Richard the First, surnamed Coeur-de-Lion, King of England* (London: Tegg, 1840);

*Our Zion: or Presbyterian Popery,* as Ane of that Ilk (Edinburgh: Constable, 1840);

*The Drummond Schism Examined and Exposed,* as A Layman of the Church (Edinburgh: Grant, 1842);

*The Book of Ballads,* by Aytoun and Theodore Martin, as Bon Gaultier (London: Orr, 1845; New York: Redfield, 1852; revised edition, Edinburgh & London: Blackwood, 1857);

*Lays of the Scottish Cavaliers, and Other Poems* (Edinburgh & London: Blackwood, 1849; New York: Redfield, 1852);

*Firmilian; or, The Student of Badajoz: A Spasmodic Tragedy,* as T. Percy Jones (Edinburgh & London: Blackwood, 1854; New York: Redfield, 1854);

*Bothwell: A Poem* (Edinburgh & London: Blackwood, 1856; Boston: Ticknor & Fields, 1856; revised edition, London & Edinburgh: Blackwood, 1858);

*Inaugural Address to the Associated Societies of the University of Edinburgh on the Occasion of His Installation as Their Honorary President* (Edinburgh: Blackwood, 1861);

*Norman Sinclair: A Novel,* 3 volumes (Edinburgh: Blackwood, 1861);

*Nuptial Ode on the Marriage of His Royal Highness the Prince of Wales* (Edinburgh: Blackwood, 1863).

*William Edmondstoune Aytoun ( photograph by T. Moffat, Edinburgh)*

Collections: *Poems of William Edmondstoune Aytoun,* edited by Frederick Page (London & New York: Oxford University Press, 1921);

*Stories and Verse,* edited by W. L. Renwick (Edinburgh: Edinburgh University Press, 1964).

3

OTHER: *The Ballads of Scotland,* 2 volumes, edited by Aytoun (Edinburgh & London: Blackwood, 1858);

Johann Wolfgang von Goethe, *Poems and Ballads of Goethe,* translated by Aytoun and Theodore Martin (Edinburgh: Blackwood, 1859; New York: Holt & Williams, 1871);

"Endymion; or, A Family Party of Olympus," in *Ixion in Heaven and Endymion: Disraeli's Skit and Aytoun's Burlesque,* edited by Eric Partridge (Freeport, N.Y.: Books for Libraries, 1927; London: Scholartis, 1927).

SELECTED PERIODICAL PUBLICATIONS – UNCOLLECTED: "My First Spec in the Biggleswades," *Blackwood's Edinburgh Magazine,* 57 (May 1845): 549–560;

"Advice to an Intending Serialist," *Blackwood's Edinburgh Magazine,* 60 (November 1846): 590–605;

"The Inca and His Bride," *Blackwood's Edinburgh Magazine,* 63 (June 1848): 750–766;

"Additional Chapters for the History of John Bull," *Blackwood's Edinburgh Magazine,* 69 (January 1851): 69–88;

"Meditations on Dyspepsia No. 1, The Malady," *Blackwood's Edinburgh Magazine,* 90 (September 1861): 302–322;

"Meditations on Dyspepsia No. 2, The Cure," *Blackwood's Edinburgh Magazine,* 90 (October 1861): 406–419.

William Edmondstoune Aytoun "seemed born for" humor, recalled his friend and collaborator Theodore Martin. Even at the height of a busy career as a poet, lawyer, professor of rhetoric and belles lettres, and active staff member of *Blackwood's Edinburgh Magazine,* Aytoun remained good tempered, marked by a dry wit and a vivid sense of fun and of the ludicrous. His stories, essays, and ballads, as well as the full-length burlesque *Firmilian; or, The Student of Badajoz* (1854), poke fun at smug pretensions in politics, literature, social relations, and finance. In his works one glimpses, suggests Eric Partridge, "something of Aytoun, who possessing a magnificent head, had ample brains inside it; whose heart was warm, speech vivid, and touch satirical as well as poetical." He was, W. L. Renwick says, at his best when he was least serious.

Writing mostly between the Reform Bill of 1832 and the Crimean War of 1853, between the Romantics and the Victorians, Aytoun has largely fallen into obscurity. James Hannay noted that Aytoun, along with Thomas Love Peacock and the

Reverend Frank Mahony ("Father Prout"), was among the class of writers who are admired by the cultivated but do not become universally popular. "Every generation has writers of this peculiar type," Hannay explains, "writers often of higher powers and attainments than many who are better known, – but who, somehow, never pass the line which divides those who are distinguished from those who are famous." While Aytoun was a skilled craftsman, possessing a good eye and an accurate ear, he was not profound in his meditations, cultivating a conservative mistrust of change and a conventional acceptance of the status quo. Despite these limitations, Aytoun's prose was, says Partridge, "a source of deep pleasure to the readers of *Blackwood's* in the eighteen-forties and fifties," and his satires on life and letters still retain a wit and even a relevance that keep them surprising and fresh.

Aytoun was born in Edinburgh on 21 June 1813, the youngest of three children. His father, Roger Aytoun, a successful lawyer, came from an old Scottish family that boasted a poet in the court of James I. The elder Aytoun's firm, Younger, Aytoun, and Rutherford, were solicitors and legal agents for Archibald Hamilton, Ninth Duke of Hamilton, a prominent Whig politician. His mother, Joan Keir, a staunch Jacobite, came from an equally old Scottish family and was the childhood friend of Sir Walter Scott's sister Anne. Aytoun enjoyed the double blessing of being both the youngest child and only son, receiving the best education available. After private tutoring between 1821 and 1824 Aytoun became a member of the first class of the Edinburgh Academy and was present at its inauguration on 1 October 1824, a ceremony presided over by the cream of Scottish letters, including Scott; Henry Mackenzie, author of *The Man of Feeling* (1771); and Francis Jeffrey, the editor of *The Edinburgh Review.* Anticipating the reforms later advocated by Dr. Thomas Arnold and his son Matthew Arnold, the Edinburgh Academy included the study of English literature and composition as well as the more conventional classical curriculum. As a student there Aytoun showed an early aptitude for recitation and the composition of poetry.

Aytoun entered Edinburgh University in 1828. His autobiographical novel, *Norman Sinclair* (1861), suggests that he had little enthusiasm for his formal studies, though he enjoyed a wide if desultory reading. Writing under the influence of Percy Bysshe Shelley and George Gordon, Lord Byron, the seventeen-year-old Aytoun completed his first volume of poetry, *Poland, Homer, and Other Poems,* which was published anonymously in 1832. While the book received favorable notices, it did not sell widely, and Aytoun later dismissed the poems and their radical political sentiments with some embarrassment.

Uncertain about a career on leaving the university in 1832, Aytoun entered his father's firm as a chartered clerk. His duties involved him in the passage of the first Reform Bill and took him to London to study parliamentary procedure. Inspired by the "Germanizing" efforts of Thomas Carlyle and others, he took up residence in Aschaffenburg am Main for seven months to study German language and literature. He developed an enthusiasm for Johann Wolfgang von Goethe, laboring over a verse translation of *Faust* (1808, 1852). Although this enthusiasm eventually waned, he continued to enjoy German literature and would produce several translations over the years. While in Germany he contemplated a career in literature, even dreaming of becoming a professor of belles lettres. Since no such prospects were on the immediate horizon, Aytoun returned to Scotland in April 1834, resigning himself to an apprenticeship with his father's firm. What Aytoun may have lacked in enthusiasm for the law, he soon made up for with industry. He was called to the bar as an advocate in 1840 and by 1852 had one of the largest criminal-law practices in Scotland. He satirized his early experiences as an advocate in his story "The Emerald Studs" (1847). He would practice law throughout his life, shifting from criminal to the nineteenth-century version of corporate law as he represented clients before parliamentary committees, especially regarding railroad bills.

Aytoun submitted some poetry to *Blackwood's Edinburgh Magazine* in February 1836. *Blackwood's* was the conservative counterpart of and competitor to the Whig *Edinburgh Review* and was noted for its attacks on literary figures, such as John Gibson Lockhart's assault on Leigh Hunt and "the Cockney School of Poetry" and the savaging of Samuel Taylor Coleridge by "Christopher North" (John Wilson). William Blackwood accepted Aytoun's submission, "Ballads from Uhland" (March 1836), initiating a happy collaboration that would last until Aytoun's death and would include the publication of some 190 poems, translations, essays, reviews, and stories. In 1844 Aytoun became a member of the magazine's staff.

Aytoun's early literary efforts focused on his love of courtly romance and Scottish balladry, a taste that was instilled and nurtured by his mother. Thus, many of his early contributions were ballads in imitation of Scott and others. While these efforts reflected a serious interest in the ballad and romance, Aytoun was aware that the forms were easily subject to exaggeration and burlesque. A short story for *Blackwood's,* "The Surveyor's Tale" (April 1846), touches on this concern. The narrator records a dinner conversation with a gaunt engineer, a sort of Don Quixote figure, who soon identifies himself with the old Scottish nobility and begins to regale his auditors with his adventures in Austria. The narrator finally cuts the story short, recognizing the engineer's tales as a pastiche of Scott. More important, however, Aytoun's love of balladry and parody led to his collaboration with Martin on the highly successful *Book of Ballads* (1845), published under the pseudonym Bon Gaultier, the Old French equivalent of *bon vivant* and derived from the prologue of the first book of François Rabelais's *Gargantua et Pantagruel* (1532–1564): "A moy n'est que honneur et gloire d'estre dict et repute Bon Gaultier et bon compaignon" (To me, that spells honor and glory to be a jolly man and a good companion). The allusion hints at the tone, object, and methods of the book. Martin and Aytoun composed a series of exuberant verse parodies, satirizing what they took to be the obscurity, impiety, egotism, and extravagance of many contemporary poets. Targets ranged from the old Hunt to the young Alfred Tennyson. *The Book of Ballads* was an immediate success and would go through some sixteen editions by 1903.

In no small measure because of the success of *The Book of Ballads,* Aytoun was appointed to the chair of rhetoric and belles lettres at the University of Edinburgh in 1845. His duties were limited to four lectures a week, six months a year. When he took up his position the course was moribund, with only thirty students, and the commissioners of the university had contemplated abolishing it. While not a rigorous or systematic scholar, Aytoun was a diligent teacher, a popular lecturer, and an academic innovator. In his first six sessions he had 24 to 44 students, by the seventh he had 72, and he would eventually have 150. At his recommendation the chair was reconstituted as one in rhetoric and English literature, and English literature became a requirement for graduation in the liberal arts. Aytoun's efforts, along with those of Thomas and Matthew Arnold, played a crucial role in introducing the study of modern literature to the British university system.

Aytoun's views on literature are found both in his lectures and in his many reviews in *Blackwood's,* and they illuminate his stories and poetic parodies. He had a profound admiration for what he termed "primitive" poetry, an admiration derived in part from his love of the Scottish ballad and informed by his studies of German classical scholarship. What "primitive" poetry might lack in polish and sophistication, it made up in naturalness, simplicity, and vigor. Thus, in ancient literature he admired Homer and the German *Nibelungenlied* (Song of the Nibelungs, circa 1200), as well as *Beowulf* (circa 900–1000 or circa 790–825) and the Icelandic and Norse sagas. Among more contemporary poets he praised Robert Burns, William Cowper, and, of course, Scott. Thomas Percy's *Reliques of Ancient English Poetry* (1765), he suggested, taught "that the natural, simple, and genuine language of passion, even though the verse be rude, has a charm which no artificial polish, or artistical numbers can convey." By "natural," Aytoun did not mean naturalism. The characters in his stories were based on a commonsense conception of the norm; violators of that norm were eyed with suspicion, often becoming the focus of satire and ridicule. By contrast, he disparaged Alexander Pope and the Augustans for their artificiality and unnaturalness. In a similar fashion, though he admired Elizabethan drama, he was uncomfortable with what he took to be "excess enthusiasm" in its verse, singling out Edmund Spenser's *Faerie Queene* (1590, 1596) for censure. His distaste for the artificial, the unnatural, or the extravagant shaped his reception of contemporary writers, especially his criticism of Tennyson, Elizabeth Barrett Browning, and the "Spasmodic" poets. He was also unhappy with writers such as Charles Dickens and George Eliot, though he liked Eliot's *Adam Bede* (1859). In his humorous essay "Advice to an Intending Serialist" (November 1846) he complained of the contemporary fashion for underworld characters such as those found in Dickens's *Oliver Twist* (1838): "It seems difficult to imagine what kind of pleasure can be derived from the description of a scene, which, if actually contemplated by the reader, would inspire disgust, or from conversations in which the brutal alternates with the positive obscene."

In 1849 Blackwood published Aytoun's *Lays of the Scottish Cavaliers, and Other Poems* in imitation of Thomas Babington Macaulay's *Lays of Ancient Rome* (1842). Like the Bon Gaultier ballads, the book was an immediate best-seller, going through some thirty-two editions. Having thus successfully established himself in law, academia, and letters, on 11 April 1849 Aytoun married Jane Emily Wilson, the youngest daughter of John Wilson, Aytoun's colleague both at *Blackwood's* and the University of Edinburgh, where he held the chair of moral philosophy.

Aytoun's best-known satire began as a joke. In the May 1854 issue of *Blackwood's* he reviewed, with extended extracts, the dramatic poem *Firmilian – A Tragedy,* by one T. Percy Jones. Jones was identified as the brightest exponent of the "Spasmodic" school of poetry and compared favorably to other contemporary poets such as Philip James Bailey, Alexander Smith, and Sydney Dobell. In reality, the review was a hoax. Jones, like the term *Spasmodic School,* was Aytoun's invention, and the extracts from *Firmilian* were burlesques of the lyrical excesses of Bailey, Smith, and Dobell. Many readers took Aytoun seriously, however, supposing that Jones existed and that the Spasmodics represented a real literary movement. Amused by this reaction, Aytoun expanded the "extracts" into a full-length work, *Firmilian; or, The Student of Badajoz: A Spasmodic Tragedy.* A parody of Goethe's *Faust* and the Byronic hero, *Firmilian* satirizes the latent ultra-Romanticism of poets such as Bailey, Smith, and Dobell. The title is a pun on the color vermilion, symbolic of "purple" verse, and on the name of George Gilfillan, a critic who regularly praised and advocated the work of Bailey and company. The designation *Spasmodic School* soon extended beyond this circle to embrace what Aytoun took to be the unhealthy extremes in Tennyson's *Maud* (1855), Henry Wadsworth Longfellow's *Golden Legend* (1856), and Elizabeth Barrett Browning's *Aurora Leigh* (1856). He also looked at John Ruskin and Carlyle as "prose Spasmodics." The satire hit its intended targets, and Aytoun's efforts were effective in deflating the aesthetic pretensions of Bailey, Smith, and Dobell and in curbing the ultra-Romantic tendencies in Tennyson and Browning.

After the publication of *Firmilian,* Aytoun turned to the long-gestating project of a serious "lyric epic" on Mary, Queen of Scots. The long poem developed into a dramatic monologue in six cantos and aspired to exemplify an anti-Spasmodic verse. Published in 1856 as *Bothwell: A Poem,* the work received mixed notices, most reviewers being more concerned with the historical accuracy of Aytoun's vision of a spotless Mary than with the poetry itself.

Jane Aytoun's health was precarious, and she died on 15 April 1859. "Aytoun was left," Martin recalled, "a childless, lonely, and shattered man." "His health," observed Hannay, "failed, not abruptly, but gradually; and he seemed to lose his relish for society, and his interest in human pursuits. His characteristic face, with its yellowish beard, and the deep seated twinkle of fun in his eyes, retained its interest; but he looked thin and feeble about the legs, and walked without vigor or decision of stride." In part as therapy, Aytoun composed his autobiographical novel, *Norman Sinclair*. He also continued to contribute stories and essays to *Blackwood's,* including two humorous essays, "Meditations on Dyspepsia No. 1, The Malady" in September 1861 and "Meditations on Dyspepsia No. 2, The Cure" in October 1861, on the debilitating dyspepsia that plagued his later years. He also managed a poem commemorating the marriage of the Prince of Wales to Princess Alexandra of Denmark (1863). Finally rallying his spirits, Aytoun remarried, to Fearne Jemima Kinnear, on Christmas Eve, 1863. His health continued to decline, however, and he died on 4 August 1865 at the age of fifty-two.

Between 1845 and 1853 Aytoun wrote and published in *Blackwood's* ten stories, all of which were reprinted in *Tales from Blackwood's* (1858–1861) except "My First Spec in the Biggleswades" (May 1845). As with his satiric poetry, Aytoun's stories tended to be topical, responding to current events or fashions. Mark A. Weinstein divides them into four categories: the first, pure humor, comprises "How I Became a Yeoman" (September 1846), "The Emerald Studs" (August 1847), and "The Raid of Arnaboll" (August 1851). The second, literary, comprises "The Surveyor's Tale." The third, stories focusing on social and financial problems, consists of "My First Spec in the Biggleswades," "How We Got up the Glenmutchkin Railway and How We Got out of It" (October 1845), "The Congress and the Agapedome" (September 1851), and "Rapping the Question" (December 1853). The final category, political, comprises "How I Stood for the Dreepdaily Burghs" (September 1847) and "How We Got Possession of the Tuilleries" (April 1848).

All of Aytoun's stories reflect his conservative politics to some degree, though in the more purely humorous pieces he is primarily concerned with good-natured fun at the expense of human foibles. In "How I Became a Yeoman" the narrator joins the local yeoman cavalry to impress a lady friend with his uniform, but his inability to ride a horse soon undercuts any favorable effect the uniform might have produced. Similarly, in "The Raid of Arnaboll" a young man stages a raid of Highland brigands so that he might fight them off and thereby win the favor of his love's father, a rich Manchester merchant who styles himself the Laird of Arnaboll because he has bought the old Arnaboll estate. While taking a few jabs at the pretensions of the Whig magnates, Aytoun paints his humor with

broad strokes, occasionally approaching the slapstick.

More explicitly political is "How We Got Possession of the Tuilleries," Aytoun's comic explanation of the fall of Louis-Philippe in the February Revolution of 1848. Aytoun attributed the uprising to the fulminations of French intellectuals, represented in the story by the Count of Monte Cristo. The narrator, Augustus Dunshunner, a frequent figure in Aytoun's stories, and a Mr. Bagsby, a Socialist follower of Richard Cobden, find themselves caught up in the action and trapped in the Tuilleries with a group of revolutionary communards. Only at the last moment is Bagsby rescued from a compulsory marriage to a revolutionary fisherwoman who has taken a fancy to him. "The Congress and the Agapedome" extends Aytoun's mistrust of intellectuals and bohemians, as the narrator and a friend follow the friend's rich uncle to Homburg for an international peace conference that soon degenerates into factional warfare. The uncle, under the sway of an American feminist, Miss Lavinia Latchley, is swept off to the Agapedome, a sort of religious commune and matchmaking establishment run by Aaron B. Hyams. The anti-Semitic stereotype of the Jewish charlatan hints at Aytoun's discomfort with Benjamin Disraeli, the Tory prime minister. In his short story "Endymion; or, A Family Party of Olympus," not published until 1927, Aytoun satirized Disraeli's skit "Ixion in Heaven" (1833) — a burlesque of a burlesque.

Critics agree that "How We Got up the Glenmutchkin Railway and How We Got out of It" and "How I Stood for the Dreepdaily Burghs" are Aytoun's best stories. Hannay offers a fair assessment when he writes that they are representative of Aytoun's comic talent: "It was a talent quite inferior to Thackeray's in insight, delicacy, and edge, but it was a genuine gift of his own, — depending for its effect, not on style . . . but on its intrinsic force of humorous character." It was, Hannay concludes, a humor that was broad and "required plenty of elbow-room." Each of the stories is narrated by Augustus Dunshunner, an amiable young scoundrel, a sort of amoral Bertie Wooster without the wholesome moderating influence of a Jeeves (the characters created by P. G. Wodehouse). Dunshunner represents Aytoun's conception of a Whig opportunist, a disciple of Adam Smith and free trade. Both stories are organized according to the principles of Aristophanic comedy, beginning with the "happy idea," shifting to its implementation, and concluded by working out its implications. In "How We Got up the Glenmutchkin Railway and How We Got out of It" the impecunious Dunshunner and his pal, Bob M'Corkindale, decide to solve their money problems by using the principles of political economy. Drawing up a prospectus, they elicit a series of partners, form a stock company, and put shares on the market for the purpose of building a railroad through a sparsely inhabited stretch of the Highlands. Through a series of stock manipulations and sales Dunshunner and M'Corkindale rake in a tidy profit before the bubble bursts and the railroad, which exists only on paper, collapses. The story was a success, and *Glenmutchkin* became a synonym for worthless, fraudulent projects. Underlying Aytoun's story was his experience as a lawyer during the craze for railroad building and other speculative ventures. Informing his satire was his conservative mistrust of a political economy that focused on speculation and the creation of capital at the expense of the production of goods and services.

In "How I Stood for the Dreepdaily Burghs" Dunshunner and M'Corkindale, again in serious debt, run Dunshunner for Parliament: parliamentary immunity would protect him from his creditors, and the office would enable him to advocate policies that would be advantageous to their speculative enterprises. Dunshunner decides to stand for the Highland Burghs of Dreepdaily, since they seem easy to contest. Publishing a slate of anachronistic Whig principles in the local paper, he travels to the burghs to canvass votes and ingratiate himself with the mysterious "clique" that supposedly controls local politics. By hinting that he might marry the daughter of one of the clique, a girl who sings Highland ballads about stock speculations, Dunshunner gains their support. The clique turns out to be three drunken shopkeepers who in the end cannot deliver the election, which is won handily by the conservative candidate. Dunshunner and M'Corkindale decide to visit the Continent to lecture on political economy and avoid their creditors. As in "How We Got up the Glenmutchkin Railway . . . ," Aytoun satirizes the Whig opportunism and disingenuousness he observed during and after the passage of the Reform Bill. By narrating the stories through Dunshunner, Aytoun lets his characters condemn themselves through their amiable immorality, a strategy that he uses in all of his satirical writings. Rather than denouncing folly, he parodies his opponents, thereby drawing attention to the folly and letting it undercut itself.

The nineteenth century was the great age of parody, according to George Kitchin: it represented a literary fashion particularly congenial to those uncomfortable with change or the unusual; it provided a way of mocking what was different and deflating what seemed threatening. "Parody is for the man of medium taste," Kitchin explains, "and is often a source of annoyance to exceptional people – to transcendentalists, mystics, lofty romantics, Utopians, primitives, and so on. The history of nineteenth-century parody is a constant tale of the normal man's dislike of these things." Kitchin's remarks pertain to all of Aytoun's humorous writings, from the Bon Gaultier ballads to *Firmilian,* and especially to the short stories. Aytoun wrote for the medium taste, the voice of common sense. His humor was always good-natured, occasionally self-deprecating, refraining from bitter diatribes or moral didacticism. He saw himself as the defender of a conservative norm in a world of cant, fraud, and pretension. The "transcendentalists, mystics, lofty romantics, Utopians" of his day were the targets of Aytoun's suspicions, and it is because such people still exist to be doubted and deflated that Aytoun's tales are capable of speaking to readers today.

**Biographies:**
Theodore Martin, *Memoir of William Edmondstoune Aytoun* (Edinburgh & London: Blackwood, 1867);
Rosaline Masson, *Pollok and Aytoun* (New York: Scribners, 1898).

**References:**
Erik Frykman, *W. E. Aytoun, Pioneer Professor of English at Edinburgh* (Göteborg: Almquist & Wiksell, 1963);
James Hannay, "Recent Humorists: Aytoun, Peacock, Prout," *North British Review,* 45 (September 1866): 75–104;
George Kitchin, *A Survey of Burlesque and Parody in English* (New York: Russell & Russell, 1967);
J. H. Millar, "William Edmondstoune Aytoun," *New Review,* 14 (1896): 103–112;
Mark A. Weinstein, *William Edmondstoune Aytoun and the Spasmodic Controversy* (New Haven: Yale University Press, 1968).

**Papers:**
The bulk of William Edmondstoune Aytoun's letters, university lectures, and notes are in the Edinburgh University Library.

# Michael Banim

*(5 August 1796 – 30 August 1874)*
and

# John Banim

*(3 April 1798 – 13 August 1842)*

Richard D. McGhee
*Arkansas State University*

See also the John Banim entry in *DLB 116: British Romantic Novelists, 1789–1832* and the Michael and John Banim entry in *DLB 158: British Reform Writers, 1789–1832.*

BOOKS: *The Celt's Paradise: In Four Duans,* by John Banim (London: Warren, 1821; New York: Sadlier, 1869);

*Damon and Pythias: A Tragedy, in Five Acts,* by John Banim, revised by Richard Lalor Sheil (London: Warren, 1821; New York: Murden & Thomson, 1821);

*A Letter to the Committee Appointed to Appropriate a Fund for a National Testimonial, Commemorative of His Majesty's First Visit to Ireland,* by John Banim (Dublin: Millikin, 1822);

*The Sergeant's Wife: A Drama in Two Acts,* by John Banim (London: Lacy, 1824);

*Revelations of the Dead-Alive,* anonymous, by John Banim (London: Printed for W. Simpkin & R. Marshall, 1824); republished as *London and Its Eccentricities in the Year 2023: Or Revelations of the Dead Alive,* by the Author of "Boyne Water," "Anglo-Irish," etc. (London: Simpkin, Marshall/Newman, 1845);

*Tales, by the O'Hara Family: Containing Crohoore of the Bill-Hook, The Fetches, and John Doe,* 3 volumes, by John and Michael Banim (London: Simpkin & Marshall, 1825);

*Tales by the O'Hara Family. Second Series. Comprising The Nowlans, and Peter of the Castle,* 3 volumes, by John and Michael Banim (London: Colburn, 1826);

*The Boyne Water: A Tale, by the O'Hara Family,* 3 volumes, by John Banim (London: Simpkin & Marshall, 1826; republished, with introduction and notes by Michael Banim, New York: Sadlier, 1866);

*John Banim*

*The Anglo-Irish of the Nineteenth Century: A Novel,* 3 volumes, anonymous, by John Banim (London: Colburn, 1828);

*The Croppy: A Tale of 1798. By the Authors of the "O'Hara Tales," "The Nowlans" and "The Boyne Water,"* by Michael Banim (3 volumes, London: Colburn, 1828; 2 volumes, Philadelphia: Carey & Hart, 1839);

*The Denounced. By the authors of "Tales of the O'Hara Family,"* by John Banim (3 volumes, London: Colburn & Bentley, 1830; 1 volume, New York: Printed by J. & J. Harper, 1830) — comprises "The Last Baron of Crana" and "The Conformists"; republished as *The Denounced; or, The Last Baron of Crana,* with introduction and notes by Michael Banim (New York: Sadlier, 1865; Dublin: Duffy, 1866);

*The Smuggler: A Tale, by the author of "Tales of the O'Hara Family," "The Denounced," &c.,* 3 volumes, by John Banim (London: Colburn & Bentley, 1831);

*The Chaunt of the Cholera: Songs for Ireland. By the Authors of "The O'Hara Tales," "The Smuggler," &c. etc.,* by John Banim (London: Cochrane, 1831);

*The Ghost-Hunter and His Family. By the O'Hara Family,* by Michael Banim (London: Smith, Elder, 1833; Philadelphia: Carey, Lea & Blanchard, 1833);

*The Mayor of Wind-Gap* [by Michael Banim] *and Canvassing* [by Harriet Letitia Martin], *by the O'Hara Family,* 3 volumes (London: Saunders & Otley, 1835); Banim work republished alone as *The Mayor of Wind-Gap. By the O'Hara Family* (New York: Harper, 1835);

*The Bit O'Writin' and Other Tales. By the O'Hara Family,* by John Banim (3 volumes, London: Saunders & Otley, 1838; 2 volumes: Philadelphia: Carey & Hart, 1838);

*Father Connell, by the O'Hara Family,* 3 volumes, by John and Michael Banim (London: T. C. Newby and T. & W. Boone, 1842);

*The Town of the Cascades,* 2 volumes, by Michael Banim (London: Chapman & Hall, 1864).

**Editions:** *Tales, by the O'Hara Family,* edited by Robert Lee Wolff, Ireland, from the Act of Union, 1800, to the Death of Parnell, 1891, volume 21 (New York: Garland, 1978);

*The Ghost-Hunter and His Family,* edited by Wolff, Ireland, from the Act of Union, 1800, to the Death of Parnell, 1891, volume 22 (New York: Garland, 1978);

*The Mayor of Wind-Gap and Canvassing,* edited by Wolff, Ireland, from the Act of Union, 1800, to the Death of Parnell, 1891, volume 23 (New York: Garland, 1978);

*The Bit O'Writin' and Other Tales,* edited by Wolff, Ireland, from the Act of Union, 1800, to the Death of Parnell, 1891, volume 24 (New York: Garland, 1978).

PLAY PRODUCTIONS: *Damon and Pythias,* London, Theatre Royal, Covent Garden, 28 May 1821;

*The Sergeant's Wife* and *The Sister of Charity,* Dublin, Theatre Royal, 21 July 1835;

*Sylla,* Dublin, Theatre Royal, June 1837.

In July 1835, at age thirty-seven, John Banim had been paralyzed for nearly twenty years by a spinal disease; he was devastated by the death of his four-year-old son; and he was impoverished. Yet when he returned to Ireland after seven years in London and six years in France, he found himself a celebrated author whose writings were beloved by many. Arriving with his wife and daughter in Dublin on their way to Kilkenny, his hometown, he was met by his older brother, Michael, and they all enjoyed a benefit performance of dramatizations of two of John's stories. When they reached Kilkenny in September, the Banims again heard friends and neighbors praising John as they welcomed him home. Thanking them he explained that his stories had been "inspired simply by a devoted love of our country" and that they were his way of making "fiction the vehicle of fact" as he intended to "paint his country's claims with filial pride." His historical novels, from *The Boyne Water* in 1826 to "The Conformists" in 1830, had earned him the attention and applause he received on his return to Ireland; but he would be celebrated into the twentieth century as one of "the O'Hara Family," authors of powerful tales of Irish life and history.

Michael and John Banim were born in Kilkenny to Michael and Joannah Carroll Banim, Michael on 5 August 1796 and John on 3 April 1798. Both attended the local English Academy conducted by George Charles Buchanan, which they would describe comically in *Father Connell* (1842). Michael began to study law in 1814, but when his father experienced financial difficulties he left school to work in the family sporting-goods store.

John Banim attended Buchanan's academy for five years, spent a year in a Roman Catholic seminary, and in 1810 became a student at the academy of one of the best-known teachers in the area, Terence Doyle, who encouraged his aspirations to become a writer. From that period survive manuscripts for what Banim's biographer, Patrick Joseph Murray, calls "a romance in two thick volumes" and a poem "extending to over a thousand lines, entitled 'Hibernia.' " In 1811 Banim entered one of the most prestigious schools in Ireland: the Protestant College of St. John, also known as Kilkenny College. He would memorialize his residence at the college in the opening of "The Fetches" in *Tales, by the O'Hara Family* (1825). From 1813 to 1815 he studied drawing at the Academy of the Royal Dublin Society, then returned to Kilkenny to teach. He met a seventeen-year-old girl who has been identified only as Anne D— and sought to marry her, but her father refused his consent. Soon afterward Anne died, and Banim spent the year 1818 to 1819 in grief and dissipation.

He returned to Dublin in 1820 and found employment as a reporter for *The Limerick Evening Post,* for which he wrote articles signed "A Traveller." He composed a poem, "Ossian's Paradise," and sent the manuscript to Sir Walter Scott, who wrote him mild encouragement. The most important influence in his life, however, was the dramatist, attorney, and rising politician Richard Lalor Sheil. On Sheil's advice Banim had the poem published as *The Celt's Paradise* in February 1821. Also with Sheil's support and encouragement – and some believe collaboration – he composed a drama, *Damon and Pythias,* which was produced at the Theatre Royal in Covent Garden, London, on 28 May. He used the money he made from this production to repay debts he had left in Kilkenny, where he made a brief visit in September. While there, he prepared a letter he intended to publish when he returned to Dublin. A committee had been formed to raise funds for a testimonial commemorating the first visit of King George IV to Ireland, and Banim wanted to seize the moment to raise interest in Irish art. This letter was published as a pamphlet in January 1822.

At this time John and Michael Banim began to plan a series of stories that would realistically portray the Irish people and seek to explain, and even vindicate, their history of resorting to violence to achieve emancipation of the Catholic Church from the restrictive laws that had been in effect for almost a century. Spokesmen for the cause of emancipation included John's new friend Sheil and the "Great Liberator," Daniel O'Connell, who founded the Catholic Association in 1823. Their stories would be published under the joint pseudonym "The O'Hara Family"; John would call himself "Abel O'Hara," and Michael would be "Barnes O'Hara."

John married Ellen Ruth, the daughter of a Kilkenny farmer, on 27 February 1822 and left with his new bride for London on 13 March. While he tried to build a reputation as a dramatist, he earned a living by writing for newspapers and magazines. In July 1822 he joined the staff of a newly launched weekly paper, *The Literary Register,* and also began making the contacts he would need to get into the theatrical world. In November 1822 the couple's

first child was born dead, and, soon after, John experienced an attack of the spinal disease that would afflict him for the rest of his life. To add to his problems, the paper for which he worked did not last through the end of 1823. On the brighter side, his drama *The Prodigal* was accepted and scheduled for production at Drury Lane Theatre. He also composed some operatic pieces for the English Opera House.

Meanwhile, Michael Banim, in Kilkenny, was writing the first of the "O'Hara Family" stories, "Crohoore of the Bill-Hook." He sent the first version of the story to John for comment at the end of 1823, and John sent his stories "The Fetches" and "John Doe" for Michael to read. John Banim, as the dominant force in the "O'Hara Family" collaboration, often wrote instructions for composition in his letters to Michael. In a long letter, dated 2 May 1824 to 4 June 1824, he wrote: "Aim at distinctness and at individuality of character. . . . thus will you dramatize your tale, and faithful drama is the life and soul of novel-writing. Plot is an inferior consideration to drama, though still it is a main consideration." He advises Michael to take notes while reading novels by others and to study their methods.

Production of *The Prodigal* fell through when one of the actors withdrew; the play was never produced, and the text has disappeared. Desperate for money, John Banim sold for thirty guineas a series of essays he had written; published as *Revelations of the Dead-Alive* (1824), they satirize topics of the day, especially the fashionable interest in phrenology. The financial pressures on Banim were increased when his wife's physicians recommended that she spend some time in France for her health. On 7 April 1825, during her absence, *Tales, by the O'Hara Family* appeared.

Michael's story "Crohoore of the Bill-Hook" opens on an evening in the home of a happy eighteenth-century Irish Catholic farming family, the Doolings; their servant, Crohoore, is sharpening his billhook in the shadows cast by a peat fire. The next morning dawns on a scene of bloody mayhem: Dooling and his wife have been murdered, and Crohoore and their daughter, Ally, are missing. Believing that Crohoore is the murderer and has kidnapped Ally, a group of neighbors led by Pierce Shea, who loves Ally, hunts for them in the wild hills of the Kilkenny countryside. A jealous rival for Ally's affections, Jack Doran, tries to cast suspicion on Shea and nearly succeeds. Doran is a leader of the "whiteboys," one of the many gangs of peasants who ravaged their oppressors throughout the eighteenth and nineteenth centuries in Ireland. One gruesome scene, based on stories the Banim brothers had heard many times in Kilkenny, is the torture of a tithe-proctor, Peery Clancy. Tithe-proctors were agents who collected tithes from the Catholics for support of their English and Ascendancy masters' hated established church, the Protestant Church of Ireland. The whiteboys kidnap Clancy, parade him into a field to the cheers and celebration of all who see, and then bury him up to his neck. One of the "boys," Yemen O'Nase, sharpens his knife, echoing Crohoore's actions in the opening scene, and slices off Clancy's ears. More violence follows before Ally is rescued and reunited with Shea, and Doran is discovered to be the leader of the gang that murdered her parents. Crohoore, it turns out, is her brother and was protecting her from their parents' murderers. The plot is sensational, but it was close to the reality of life in eighteenth- and nineteenth-century Ireland, and the characters – peasants, schoolmasters, and farmers – are powerfully drawn.

The title of John Banim's "The Fetches" refers to ghostlike images whose appearance foretells the deaths of those whose likeness they are. In the last scene of the story the lovers Tresham and Anna recognize their fate in their fetches: they are on a ledge over a waterfall of the River Nore when Tresham dies after seeing something in the water; Anna pulls his body with her as she leaps to her death. The tragedy is witnessed by their three horrified and uncomprehending friends. With this fantastic tale of superstition Banim tried to understand the psychology of love and, perhaps, also sought to analyze the fate of a nation whose origins lie deep in the mysterious past.

In "John Doe" (retitled "Peep O'Day" in later collections) fighting almost seems to be an end in itself. The opening chapter, written by Michael Banim, describes a country feast that ends in a fight between factions that seem to have no other reason to fight than love of violence: it is the sort of "ferocious encounter" to which the Irish are devoted, the narrator proclaims, as drinking and dancing produce "a scene of truly astounding and appalling uproar." The rest of the story was written by John Banim, whose objective was to explain his people to their English masters; this goal may have led him to temper some of his hatred for England. Thus, the protagonists of "John Doe" are two young English lieutenants, Howard and Graham, assigned to duty in Munster, County Tipperary. They are puzzled by much they witness as they search for "John Doe," the leader of the local whiteboys. One of the soldiers falls in love with a local girl and learns

more about Irish ways as he courts her; he is Protestant and she Catholic, a situation that repeatedly intrigues Banim in his fiction. At the end of the tale "John Doe's" motives for violence are explained, and he promises to leave Ireland.

In May 1825 John Banim returned to Ireland to explore the countryside of Derry, Coleraine, and the Boyne River valley as research for his next piece of fiction, to be based on the Battle of the Boyne in 1690. He also visited his family in Kilkenny, where he began writing *The Boyne Water* in July. He remained until 24 August, when he went to France to pick up Ellen and then went back to London. By the end of the year he had completed the novel, which was published in three volumes in early 1826. Though English critics treated the historical romance harshly, it was popular with Irish readers who were preoccupied with efforts to free Irish Catholics from the laws that had been enacted since the battle his novel described.

John had asked Michael to extend his research by exploring the countryside around Limerick to gather information about the battlefield there. While doing so Michael met a family whose concern for an ill son provided an idea that John used in his next story, "The Nowlans," one of his most powerful tales. Michael, who may have participated in the writing of the story, visited John in London while it was being composed in the summer of 1826. He was shaken by John's much-deteriorated appearance: he looked forty, though he was only twenty-eight. John's story "Peter of the Castle" seems to have been started while Michael was in London; six weeks after his return to Kilkenny, in August, Michael was reviewing the manuscript, which he had just received from John. "The Nowlans" and "Peter of the Castle" appeared in the second series of *Tales, by the O'Hara Family*, published in November. Critical response was strongly positive, especially for "The Nowlans."

The story is marked by forcefully rendered characters from all walks of life. The socially ambitious, prosperous Nowlans have a mixed marriage: the husband is Catholic while the wife is a Protestant from an Ascendancy family. They want their son, John, to benefit from the wealth of his wasteful and licentious Uncle Aby, a colorful and engaging character. They send John to live with Aby, and the young man learns much about life from his cousin Maggy, whose sexual passion for him is uncompromisingly described. John resists her advances, even though he is strongly attracted to her; obeying his parents' and uncle's wishes, he enters the priesthood. This decision proves to be a tragic mistake, for John does not have a true vocation for the church. Often in doubt about his vows, he falls in love with and marries Letitia "Letty" Adams, a Protestant. Because John is a priest, he has committed a sin by marrying. She cannot understand John's agony of spirit, as he cannot understand her failure to sympathize with it. When she dies in childbirth John goes insane, wandering the highways while his family believes him to be dead. The episode is drawn from John Banim's frenzied reaction to the death of Anne D– in 1818. This lurid plot is interwoven with another, involving John's sweet, innocent sister and Letty's brother, a liar, thief, and murderer. John finally returns home, and as the story ends his parents and sisters are tending him in his illness. It was at this point that the story had opened, and returning to it at the end provides a realistic frame for the fantastic adventures between.

In "Peter of the Castle" John Banim loses the concentration of dark passion that drove "The Nowlans." Redmond, a brooding young man, discovers that his father may have been a ruthless outlaw rather than an aristocrat; there is an element of allegory here, with Redmond representing the young Irishman who discovers, like John Banim himself, that there are unsavory persons and dark powers in the history of his people. Redmond, however, does not struggle to understand and learn from his past, and the story degenerates into a series of incidents involving brotherly deception, mysterious Spaniards, lost children, and long years of repentance. Banim achieves neither intensity nor illumination in this story, as he had done so well in "The Nowlans."

At the time he was finishing "The Nowlans" and "Peter of the Castle" John Banim was also at work on a tragedy, *Sylla.* He finished it in January 1827, but it would not be produced for another decade – and then it would be as a benefit for the crippled author. Ellen Banim gave birth to a daughter, Mary, on 22 July 1827. Michael visited them in August 1827, and again he was struck by his brother's physical deterioration: John seemed to have aged another twenty years. Nevertheless, he had begun writing *The Anglo-Irish of the Nineteenth Century: A Novel,* which was published anonymously in 1828. After returning home Michael received letters from John urging him to write a novel based on the lives of their mother's family; Michael would do so with *The Ghost-Hunter and His Family* (1833). The title of Michael's historical romance about the insurrection of 1798, *The Croppy* (1828), refers to a contemptuous expression used by Orangemen for the men of the

United Irishman movement who cropped their hair in imitation of the French revolutionaries.

John wrote his brother in August 1829 that his physicians had persuaded him to move to France; before leaving for Boulogne, he began writing a story called "The Dwarf Bride"; but his publisher lost the manuscript during bankruptcy proceedings, and it was never recovered. When their mother died in June 1830, John was paralyzed and unable to attend the funeral.

*The Denounced* is the collective title for two novels by John Banim, "The Last Baron of Crana" and "The Conformists," that were published together in 1830. Both works deal with the Irish penal laws enacted in the eighteenth century. Banim had written the novels before Catholic Emancipation in 1829 and revised them before publication, apparently believing that the original texts might harm prospects for successful implementation of the more liberal laws. The works suffer from strong didactic, even propagandistic, tendencies.

John and Ellen Banim had a son in 1831. John was eking out a small living from sales of pieces to magazines and from commissions for operatic pieces, some of which were adapted from the stories, such as *The Death Fetch; or, the Student of Goettingen,* which seems to have been successful at the English Opera House in 1832. But debts were increasing faster than income, so Banim wrote a letter of appeal to "a Dublin friend," most probably Sheil, who immediately began to raise money for the Banim family. A public appeal on Banim's behalf appeared in January 1833 in *The Times* of London, leading to a meeting over which the lord mayor presided on 31 January 1833 and where many, including Sheil, moved resolutions of appreciation for Banim and his writings.

At the end of 1833 Banim and his family moved to Paris, where the son died of croup. Devastated by his son's death, Banim decided to return to Ireland. In July 1835 John, Ellen, and Mary arrived in Dublin, where Michael met them. John's friends arranged a benefit performance of his *The Sergeant's Wife* and *The Sister of Charity,* at the Theatre Royal on 21 July. In September the Banims went to Kilkenny, where friends met John with proclamations of appreciation, plans for a benefit performance of *Damon and Pythias,* and subscriptions of money for a house, Windgap Cottage, located in a spot that John had loved since his childhood and that was commemorated by Michael in his novel *The Mayor of Wind-Gap* (1835).

In 1838 John collected pieces he had written over several years for various annuals as *The Bit*

*O'Writin' and Other Tales*. He and Michael collaborated on *Father Connell,* based on people they knew while growing up in Kilkenny. John Banim died on 13 August 1842 and was buried in the cemetery of St. John's Chapel, Kilkenny. His daughter was sent to a convent school at Waterford, where she died of tuberculosis in June 1844. She was survived by her mother, who received a small annuity upon the recommendation of British prime minister Robert Peel.

Michael Banim, who had married Catherine O'Dwyer in 1840, became postmaster of Kilkenny in 1852. He wrote one more novel, *The Town of the Cascades* (1864). He died on 30 August 1874 at Booterstown, County Dublin, where he had retired after resigning as postmaster in 1873.

The Banim brothers, as "The O'Hara Family," developed their narrative art together, although John has received most of the attention and credit for their work. As the one with formal training, John provided his brother with theory and instruction, but Michael could write passionately and forcefully of life among the common people. John's interest in drama, as well as his love of the fiction of Scott, led him to emphasize character over plot, a characteristic that can be seen in the fiction of both brothers. Their devotion to the cause of Catholic Emancipation sometimes led them to moderate the tone of their writing, but they could not always restrain their anger over wrongs both ancient and current. The fiction of "The O'Hara Family" was widely celebrated as a vehicle for presenting the "facts" of Irish life and history.

**Biography:**

Patrick Joseph Murray, *The Life of John Banim, the Irish Novelist* (London: Lay, 1857; New York & London: Garland, 1978).

**References:**

James M. Cahalan, "Beginnings: The Banims," in his *Great Hatred and Little Room: The Irish Historical Novel* (Syracuse, N.Y.: Syracuse University Press, 1983), pp. 43–66;

Thomas Flanagan, "Irish Peasants and English Readers" and "The Historical Novel," in his *The Irish Novelists 1800–1850* (New York: Columbia University Press, 1959), pp. 167–202;

Barton R. Friedman, "Fabricating History, or John Banim Refights the Boyne," *Eire-Ireland,* 17 (Spring 1982): 39–56;

Mark Hawthorne, *John and Michael Banim (The "O'Hara Brothers"): A Study in the Early Development of the Anglo-Irish Novel* (Salzburg: Institut für Englische Sprache und Literatur, 1975);

Anna Steger, *John Banim, ein Nachahmer Walter Scott* (Erlangen: Döres, 1935).

# Richard Harris Barham
## (Thomas Ingoldsby)
### (6 December 1788 – 17 June 1845)

Martin A. Cavanaugh
*Washington University*

BOOKS: *Verses Spoken at St. Paul's School, on the Public Celebrations, May the 1st, 1806, and April the 30th, 1807* (London: Printed by C. Spilsbury, 1807);

*Baldwin; or, a Miser's Heir,* 2 volumes, as George Hector Epaminondas (London: Minerva, 1820);

*The Ingoldsby Legends, or Mirth and Marvels,* as Thomas Ingoldsby (London: Bentley, 1840);

*Some Account of My Cousin Nicholas; To Which Is Added, The Rubber of Life,* 3 volumes, as Ingoldsby (London: Bentley, 1841); republished as *My Cousin Nicholas,* 1 volume (London & New York: Routledge, 1856);

*The Ingoldsby Legends, or Mirth and Marvels: Second Series,* as Ingoldsby (London: Bentley, 1842);

*The Ingoldsby Legends, or Mirth and Marvels: Third Series,* edited, with "Memoir of Rev. Richard Harris Barham," by Richard Harris Dalton Barham (London: Bentley, 1847; Philadelphia, 1847);

*The Garrick Club: Notices of One Hundred and Thirty-Five of Its Former Members* (New York: Privately printed, 1896).

**Editions:** *The Ingoldsby Legends, or Mirth and Marvels,* 2 volumes, edited by Richard Harris Dalton Barham (London: Bentley, 1870);

*The Ingoldsby Lyrics,* edited by Richard Harris Dalton Barham (London: Bentley, 1881);

*The Ingoldsby Legends; or, Mirth and Marvels,* 3 volumes, edited by Mrs. Edward A. [Caroline Francis Barham] Bond (London: Bentley, 1894);

*The Ingoldsby Legends: or, Mirth and Marvels,* 3 volumes, edited by J. B. Atlay (London: Methuen, 1903);

*The Ingoldsby Legends; or, Mirth and Marvels,* edited by John Tanfield and Guy Boas (London: Macmillan, 1951);

*Richard Harris Barham*

*The Ingoldsby Legends; or, Mirth and Marvels,* edited by D. C. Browning (London: Dent, 1960; New York: Dutton, 1960).

Richard Harris Barham, divinity lecturer and minor canon at St. Paul's Cathedral, is known for a series of tales that appeared serially under his pseudonym, Thomas Ingoldsby, from 1831 until his death in 1845. The first collection of the tales was published in 1840 as *The Ingoldsby Legends, or Mirth and Marvels,* with a second series following in 1842; Barham's son, Richard Harris Dalton Barham, collected and published a third series in 1847. Many reprints and editions of *The Ingoldsby Legends* have appeared since then.

Richard Harris Barham was born in Canterbury on 6 December 1788 to Richard Harris Barham, an alderman who had inherited substantial land holdings south of Canterbury, and Elizabeth Fox, the elder Barham's housekeeper. The Barhams claimed to be able to trace their Kentish roots back to the eleventh century. The family seat, Tappington Everard, between Folkestone and Canterbury, is frequently mentioned in *The Ingoldsby Legends*. Barham's father died in 1795; his will placed the child's property in the care of three guardians. Barham registered at St. Paul's School, London, in November 1800. While at St. Paul's he began composing verses, some of which would be published in the *Gentleman's Magazine* in 1808. One of his schoolmates was the future publisher Richard Bentley, in whose *Miscellany* many of Barham's Ingoldsby Legends would appear.

In 1807 Barham entered Brasenose College, Oxford. Among his friends there was Theodore Hook, future novelist, dramatist, and editor of the periodicals *John Bull* and *New Monthly Magazine*. After graduating in 1811, Barham briefly studied law, then returned to Canterbury to ponder his future. Ultimately he chose a vocation as a clergyman in the Church of England. His first appointment was as curate in Ashford, in east Kent, in 1813; after a year there he took over the parish of Westwell, a few miles to the north. On 30 September 1814 he married Caroline Smart, whom he had met in Ashford. Their first child, Richard Harris Dalton Barham, was born in 1815. By 1817 Barham had accepted the positions of rector at Snargate and curate at Warehorne. Snargate and Warehorne, about two and a half miles apart, are in the Romney Marsh region, the setting for many of Barham's Ingoldsby Legends. While the Barhams were living in Warehorne their second child, Henry, died at seven weeks of age. In 1818 a daughter, Charlotte Maria, was born. During these years Barham was immersed in the duties of a parish priest and had little time for writing, but on 13 May 1819 he suffered a broken leg in a road accident. Confined to bed during a long period of recuperation, he wrote a novel, *Baldwin; or, a Miser's Heir* (1820), and began another, *Some Account of My Cousin Nicholas; To Which Is Added, The Rubber of Life* (1841). The novel, however, did not prove to be Barham's métier; *Baldwin* failed to excite the public after its publication.

In 1821 Barham resigned his positions in Snargate and Warehorne and moved his family to London, where he hoped to secure a more suitable position. Shortly after his arrival he was on his way to obtain medicine for one of his ailing children when he met an old friend, the Reverend Christopher Packe, who was just about to mail a letter inviting another friend to apply for a minor canonry at St. Paul's Cathedral. Barham persuaded Packe not to mail the letter, applied for the position himself, and was accepted.

Shortly after assuming the minor canonry at St. Paul's, Barham began contributing theatrical and literary reviews to *John Bull, The Literary Gazette, The Globe and Traveller,* and *Blackwood's Edinburgh Magazine*. For a brief time before its end in April 1823 Barham also edited the *London Chronicle*. In three issues in October 1822 he published his story "The Ghost," the first appearance of a tale that would later become part of the Ingoldsby Legends. "The Ghost" is a verse story, Barham's favorite form. Nick Mason, a cobbler, returns home late one evening after listening to ghost stories at the pub and is beaten by his wife. He is awakened in the middle of the night by an apparition who leads him to a mysterious iron ring, " – no doubt of some trap door, / 'Neath which the old dead Miser kept his store." To mark the spot so that he can return in the morning, Nick sticks an awl in the wall; but he is dreaming, and he actually stabs his wife in her posterior. The tale ends with Nick enduring his neighbors' ridicule:

> And still he listens with averted eye,
>     When gibing neighbors make "the Ghost" their
>         theme;
> While ever from that hour they declare
> That Mrs. Mason use a cushion in her chair!

In 1824 Barham became rector of the united parishes of St. Mary Magdalene and St. Gregory; the parish church is about a tenth of a mile south of the cathedral. Also in 1824 he was appointed a priest in ordinary of the Chapels Royal, in which capacity he ministered to the royal family. At this time he moved to a residence in Amen Court, a few hundred yards from St. Paul's Cathedral, which would remain his home for the rest of his life.

The move to London not only reunited Barham with his school friends Hook and Bentley but also gave him the opportunity to make new acquaintances with people involved in the literary and artistic scene. He was one of the founding members of the Garrick Club, whose other members included the actors Charles Kemble and William Charles Macready, the comedian Charles Mathews, the poet Samuel Rogers, the publishers Bentley and John Murray, and the authors Charles Dickens and William Makepeace Thackeray. Sidney Smith, one of the founders of the *Edinburgh Review,* became a residentiary canon at St. Paul's in 1831, furnishing the two literary churchmen opportunities to converse regularly.

Barham had begun publication of the tales that became known as the Ingoldsby Legends with the serialization of "The Ghost" in the *London Chronicle* in 1822, but the pseudonym "Thomas Ingoldsby" did not appear until the publication of "The Spectre of Tappington" in the February 1837 issue of *Bentley's Miscellany*. When the three series of *The Ingoldsby Legends* were published in 1840, 1842, and 1847, some of Barham's earlier tales were overlooked; later editions included those that had been neglected. The seventy tales that comprise the definitive corpus of the Ingoldsby Legends were established by Barham's son, Richard Harris Dalton Barham, in his 1870 edition.

The next appearance of a Barham tale after "The Ghost" was in the April 1831 issue of *Blackwood's*. "A Singular Passage in the Life of the Late Henry Harris, D.D." is the first of only six prose tales included in the Ingoldsby Legends. The narrator, the executor of Harris's estate, reproduces Harris's notes counseling of a young woman, Mary Graham, who was tormented by vivid images of physical and mental torture at the hands of her fiancé, Francis Somers, who had recently left the country to study medicine at the University of Leyden; coincidentally, Harris's grandson, Frederick, was also studying there. The medical doctor in attendance believed Mary to be suffering from simple nightmares, but her sister was not convinced; Harris did not know what to believe. Eventually Mary died. Harris learned the next month that his grandson had been killed in a duel. He rushed to Leyden to attend to the deceased, only to discover that not only did his grandson's room match the vivid description of Mary's vision but also that it contained a locket with her picture and a lock of her hair. Harris went into seizures at the revelation and soon died. No one ever discovered the identity of the mysterious scoundrel, for there had never been a student at the University of Leyden named Francis Somers.

The first two stories exhibit the type and style of many of the tales that make up the Ingoldsby Legends. Supernatural occurrences play a major part: ghosts command the human characters to do their bidding; animals take on human attributes and habits; grotesque features frighten the characters and readers.

In addition to his assignments to the Chapels Royal and the parish of St. Mary Magdalene and St. Gregory, in 1834 Barham was elected to the chaplaincy of the Vintners' Company, one of the many City livery companies, or guilds, that regulated trade; its members were the wine importers and inn-

keepers. In January 1837 Barham's "The 'Monstre' Balloon" appeared in the inaugural issue of *Bentley's Miscellany*, edited by Dickens. Bentley had entered the periodical field hoping to capitalize on the increasing popularity of Dickens, whose *Pickwick Papers* had just begun to appear in installments. Bentley also recognized the popularity of Barham's earlier tales and wanted to include him among the regular contributors to the magazine. Barham's biographer William G. Lane attributes much of the success of *Bentley's Miscellany* to Barham's tales. The novelist Thomas Hughes said in his *Memoir of a Brother* (1873) that "of all the magazines, and they were much fewer in those days, Bentley's was the favorite; chiefly, I think, because of the 'Ingoldsby Legends,' which were then coming out in it." Two years after the first issue of *Bentley's Miscellany* appeared, Bentley and Dickens parted company; Barham remained with Bentley, and between 1837 and 1843 more than forty of his tales would appear in *Bentley's Miscellany*. The remainder of the legends would be published in the *New Monthly Magazine and Humorist* between 1843 and 1845.

It was with his second tale in *Bentley's Miscellany*, "The Spectre of Tappington," that Barham began to link the stories together by introducing his first-person narrator Thomas Ingoldsby, the Ingoldsby clan, and their manor house, Tappington Everard, in the eastern division of the county of Kent. In "The Spectre of Tappington," another of the six prose stories that are included in the Ingoldsby Legends, Charles Seaforth, a cousin of Thomas Ingoldsby, returns to England from military service in India and stops for a visit at Tappington Everard. On three successive mornings he awakens to find that a pair of his trousers has disappeared. Seaforth claims that each night he has seen the ghost of Sir Giles, an Ingoldsby ancestor, sneak into his room and remove the pants but was powerless to stop the theft. Thomas hides in his guest's chamber and observes him sleepwalking, carrying another pair of his trousers. Outside, Seaforth grabs a shovel and buries the pants. Thomas awakens him, and the household enjoys a laugh. Seaforth marries Caroline Ingoldsby, and they live happily ever after.

"The Legend of Hamilton Tighe," in ballad form, is the story of a handsome young British naval officer who, after being murdered by his jealous stepmother, her lover, and a fellow sailor, returns to haunt the three conspirators. In "Grey Dolphin," one of his most popular stories, Barham returns to prose. As in many of his stories, the connection of seemingly unrelated events is not revealed

*"The Apparition paused, and would have spoke, / Pointing to what Nick thought an iron ring": illustration by John Leech for Barham's "The Ghost"*

identified elderly lady conducting a tour of the castle and condemning the sin of ingratitude.

"The Jackdaw of Rheims" is based on an old Catholic legend. An impudent crow invades a monastery dining room. After perching on just about everything and everyone, he finally alights on the cardinal archbishop's chair:

> And he peer'd in the face  Of his Lordship's Grace,
> With a satisfied look, as if he would say,
> "We two are the greatest folks here to-day!"
>     And the priests, with awe,  As such freaks they saw,
> Said, "The Devil must be in that little Jackdaw!"

When the cardinal removes his ring to wash his hands after dinner, the jackdaw makes off with it. The discovery that the ring is missing throws the group into an uproar:

> There's a cry and a shout,  And a deuce of a rout,
> And nobody seems to know what they're about,
> But the monks have their pockets all turn'd inside out;
>     The friars are kneeling,  And hunting, and feeling
> The carpet, the floor, and the walls, and the ceiling.

The search produces nothing, and the abbot concludes that the ring has been stolen. The cardinal, in a most dignified manner, pronounces an extended curse on whoever has stolen the ring, yet "nobody seem'd one penny the worse!" The fruitless search continues until dawn, when the jackdaw limps into the room "on crumpled claw": the curse had the desired effect. The contrite jackdaw leads the monks to his nest, in which the ring is hidden. The cardinal removes the curse, the jackdaw's health immediately returns, and he becomes such a pious bird that at his death the priests of the monastery declare him a saint.

"The Leech of Folkestone," which appeared in the July 1837 issue of *Bentley's Miscellany,* is an adaptation of a popular tale of bewitchment and black magic set in the coastal town of Folkestone on the edge of Romney Marsh during the early seventeenth century. Master Thomas Marsh of Marston-Hall, a patient of Master Erasmus Buckthorne, the local apothecary, suffers from a mysterious malady. Marsh departs on horseback accompanied by one of his servants. While Marsh is gone, Buckthorne and Mrs. Marsh, a woman of Spanish descent, secretly consult. The Marshes' daughter, Marian, discovers a doll with pins stuck in it; when she extracts some of the pins, Thomas Marsh, miles away, feels relief. At a town fair he meets Dr. Aldrovando, who warns

until the end. A medieval knight, Baron Robert de Shurland, kills a monk for no reason. All the forces of church and state are allied against de Shurland until the king, who had gone on a Crusade with the knight, grants him a royal pardon. An unidentified old woman curses de Shurland and foretells that his death will be caused by his faithful horse, Grey Dolphin. The knight immediately kills the horse. Three years later, when de Shurland returns home after serving in battle with the king, he sees the old woman sitting on a rock on the beach. He runs over to confront her, but she disappears. The "rock" on which she was sitting is the whitened skull of his dead horse. He kicks it and feels a sharp pain; on returning to his castle he discovers that one of the horse's teeth is embedded in his foot, and he dies of gangrene. "Grey Dolphin" is loosely tied to the Ingoldsby family story by Margaret, the knight's daughter, who visits her father on his deathbed accompanied by Master Ingoldsby, a German cousin on her mother's side, whom she later marries. Her portrait, the narrator says, still hangs in the gallery of the manor house at Tappington Everard. The story ends with an un-

Marsh that he is in grave danger and invites him to come to Aldrovando's home that night. When Marsh arrives Aldrovando draws a magic bath into which Marsh lowers himself. Aldrovando conjures up a vision of Marston Hall in which Marsh's wife, her servant José, and Buckthorne are seen gathered around the doll. As attacks are made on the doll, Aldrovando commands March to submerge himself in the water. In the vision Buckthorne fires a gun at close range at the doll and collapses, and Marsh faints. He is awakened the next morning by his servant at their lodging, having no idea how he got there. They return home to find the household in an uproar and the three conspirators missing. Many people believe that Marsh was drunk and dreamed his experience. Years later, when the building is razed, a skeleton is discovered that is thought to be that of Buckthorne. Marian inherits the estate and marries a member of the Ingoldsby clan.

"The Lady Rohesia," in the January 1838 issue of *Bentley's Miscellany,* is set in the early sixteenth century. Lady Rohesia, the sister of Sir Everard Ingoldsby, is dying. Her priest claims to have heard a deathbed bequest of a small fortune for his parish, which disheartens the future widower, Sir Guy de Montgomeri. As Sir Guy is consoled by Lady Rohesia's servant, Beatrice Grey, while they are sitting on his current wife's deathbed, it dawns on him that Beatrice would make an excellent wife, and he proposes to her. As the newly betrothed couple are enjoying an embrace, Sir Guy is struck on the head. The two are shocked to see a miraculously recovered Rohesia sitting upright in bed with a staff in her hand. Sir Guy quickly revises his plans and is last seen boarding a boat bound for Virginia.

Between 1839 and 1841 Barham held various positions at Sion College, an institution founded in 1623 as a society for London's Anglican clergy. He was elected to a one-year term as president of Sion in 1842. Also in 1842 he was appointed as divinity lecturer at St. Paul's, and he exchanged his rectorship at St. Mary Magdalene and St. Gregory for the vicarship of the united parish of St. Augustine and St. Faith, adjacent to St. Paul's Cathedral. These joint appointments decreased his workload and increased his income.

Barham's prose tale "Jerry Jarvis's Wig" appeared in *Bentley's Miscellany* in May 1843. In mid-eighteenth-century Appledore, a village in Romney Marsh, Joseph Washford, the gardener of Jeremiah Jarvis, the local attorney, is planting celery in his employer's garden on a hot, sunny day. Jarvis forces Washford to wear a wig to protect his balding head; Washford, who would have preferred a glass of beer, only accepts the wig out of deference to his employer. The wig does protect him from the sun, but it also has another, unnatural, effect: while toiling in the garden within sight of a luscious apple tree, Washford hears a "still small voice" enticing him to take just one apple to satisfy his hunger. He is progressively led down a slippery slope of crime, finally committing a murder. He pleads guilty and is hanged, but the fate of the wig is unknown. It is rumored that it was last seen directing a firestorm across the local marsh.

Barham was an antiquarian scholar, an avocation that contributed the background for many of the tales with medieval settings. Friends and acquaintances also gave him suggestions. Mary Ann Hughes, wife of the Reverend Thomas Hughes, a residentiary canon at St. Paul's (not to be confused with the novelist Thomas Hughes), conversed regularly with Barham; after the Hugheses left London, Barham and Mrs. Hughes corresponded frequently until Barham's death. Mrs. Hughes is credited with giving Barham suggestions for several of his legends.

In October 1844, after viewing an outdoor procession of Queen Victoria, Barham developed a severe cold and a seriously inflamed throat. During the next several months his health fluctuated, and he died on 17 June 1845. He was buried at the church of St. Mary Magdalene and St. Gregory. When the church was destroyed in 1886, his remains were moved to Kensal Green Cemetery, London.

The Ingoldsby Legends enjoyed great popularity when they appeared in *Bentley's Miscellany* and even greater popularity after their publication in the three collected volumes. During the second half of the nineteenth century they were frequently reprinted. The collections published in the 1840s included illustrations by George Cruikshank, George Du Maurier, John Leech, and John Tenniel; later editions were illustrated by Arthur Rackham, Herbert Cole, Gordon Browne, and Harry George Theaker. The popularity of the stories continued into the twentieth century, with both complete collections and editions of selected and individual legends.

Barham's work is recognized as having contributed to the development of English short fiction. Wendell V. Harris says, "Many a good story and tale are scattered through the corpus of English fiction prior to the 1830s, but it is not, I think, an exaggeration to claim Barham as the first consistent English writer of the true short story." Harris echoes the sentiments of Richard Garnett, who said almost a century earlier in the *Dictionary of National Biography* (1885): "Barham owes his honourable rank among English humourists to his having done one thing supremely well."

**Biographies:**
Richard Harris Dalton Barham, ed., *The Life and Letters of the Rev. Richard Harris Barham, Author of The Ingoldsby Legends,* 2 volumes (London: Bentley, 1870);
William G. Lane, *Richard Harris Barham* (Columbia: University of Missouri Press, 1967).

**References:**
Stephen Bann, "Defences against Irony: Barham, Ruskin, Fox, Talbot," in his *Clothing of Clio* (Cambridge: Cambridge University Press, 1984), pp. 112–137;
Mortimer Collins, "Ingoldsby," *British Quarterly Review,* 53 (April 1871): 391–408;
John Doran, "Richard Harris Barham – 'Ingoldsby,' " *Temple Bar,* 31 (December 1870): 61–73;
Malcolm Elwin, "Wallflower the Third: 'Ingoldsby,' " in his *Victorian Wallflowers* (London: Cape, 1934), pp. 128–153;
Royal A. Gettmann, "Barham and Bentley," *Journal of English and Germanic Philology,* 56 (July 1957): 337–346;
Charles George Harper, *Ingoldsby Country: Literary Landmarks of the "Ingoldsby Legends,"* (London: Black, 1904);
Wendell V. Harris, *British Short Fiction in the Nineteenth Century* (Detroit: Wayne State University Press, 1979);
Richard H. Horne, "Thomas Ingoldsby," in his *New Spirit of the Age,* 2 volumes (London: Smith, Elder, 1844), I: 127–150;
John Hughes, "Sketch of the Late Rev. R. H. Barham, with a Few Lines to his Memory,"

*New Monthly Magazine,* 74 (August 1845): 526–532;
William G. Lane, "The Primitive Muse of Thomas Ingoldsby," *Harvard Library Bulletin,* 12 (1958): 47–83, 220–241;
Lane, "R. H. Barham and Dickens' Clergyman of 'Oliver Twist,' " *Nineteenth-Century Fiction,* 10 (September 1955): 159–162;
"The Rev. Richard Harris Barham," *Bentley's Miscellany,* 17 (August 1845): 198–202;
George Saintsbury, "Three Humorists: Hook, Barham, Maginn," *Macmillan's Magazine,* 69 (December 1893): 105–115;
"Thomas Ingoldsby (Barham)," *Fraser's Magazine,* 83 (March 1871): 302–316;
Edmund Wilson, "The Devils and Canon Barham," *New Yorker,* 46 (21 November 1970): 206–224;
David J. Winslow, "Richard Harris Barham and His Use of Folklore," *New York Folklore Quarterly,* 27 (1971): 370–384.

**Papers:**
The largest collection of Richard Harris Barham's papers is in the Henry W. and Albert A. Berg Collection of the New York Public Library; the collection includes six notebooks, correspondence, drafts, and corrected page proofs of some of the stories. As of 1967 a sizable collection of materials was in the possession of Barham's great-grandsons, Commodore T. E. Barham Howe and Mr. Edward Platt. This collection included legal documents, family records, four notebooks, and miscellaneous letters. About two hundred items and four volumes of Barham materials are at Houghton Library, Harvard University. This collection includes about 190 letters from Barham (1825–1843), drafts of writings, and notebooks. Several miscellaneous papers are at the British Library.

# Charlotte Brontë

*(21 April 1816 – 31 March 1855)*

Toni Louise Oplt

See also the Brontë entry in *DLB 21: Victorian Novelists Before 1885.*

BOOKS: *Poems by Currer, Ellis and Acton Bell,* by Charlotte, Emily, and Anne Brontë (London: Aylott & Jones, 1846; Philadelphia: Lea & Blanchard, 1848);

*Jane Eyre: An Autobiography,* as Currer Bell (3 volumes, London: Smith, Elder, 1847; 1 volume, New York: Harper, 1847);

*Shirley: A Tale,* as Currer Bell (3 volumes, London: Smith, Elder, 1849; 1 volume, New York: Harper, 1850);

*Villette,* as Currer Bell (3 volumes, London: Smith, Elder, 1853; 1 volume, New York: Harper, 1853);

*The Professor: A Tale,* as Currer Bell (2 volumes, London: Smith, Elder, 1857; 1 volume, New York: Harper, 1857);

*The Twelve Adventurers and Other Stories,* edited by C. K. Shorter and C. W. Hatfield (London: Hodder & Stoughton, 1925);

*Legends of Angria: Compiled from the Early Writings of Charlotte Brontë,* edited by Fannie E. Ratchford and William Clyde De Vane (New Haven: Yale University Press, 1933);

*Five Novelettes,* edited by Winifred Gérin (London: Folio Press, 1971);

*The Secret & Lily Hart: Two Tales by Charlotte Brontë,* edited by William Holtz (Columbia: University of Missouri Press, 1979);

*An Edition of the Early Writings of Charlotte Brontë,* 3 volumes, edited by Christine Alexander (Oxford: Blackwell, 1987–1991; New York: Blackwell, 1987–1991).

**Collections:** *The Life and Works of Charlotte Brontë and Her Sisters,* Haworth Edition, 7 volumes, edited by Mrs. Humphry Ward and C. K. Shorter (London: Smith, Elder, 1899–1900);

*The Shakespeare Head Brontë,* 19 volumes, edited by T. J. Wise and J. A. Symington (Oxford: Blackwell, 1931–1938);

*Jane Eyre,* edited by Jane Jack and Margaret Smith, The Clarendon Edition of the Novels of the

*Charlotte Brontë; portrait by George Richmond, 1850 (National Portrait Gallery, London)*

Brontës (Oxford: Oxford University Press, 1969);

*Shirley,* edited by Herbert Rosengarten and Smith, The Clarendon Edition of the Novels of the Brontës (Oxford: Clarendon Press / New York: Oxford University Press, 1979);

*Villette,* edited by Rosengarten and Smith, The Clarendon Edition of the Novels of the Brontës (Oxford: Clarendon Press, 1984);

*The Poems of Charlotte Brontë: A New, Annotated, and Enlarged Edition of the Shakespeare Head Brontë,* edited by Tom Winnifrith (Oxford & New York: Blackwell, 1984);

*The Professor,* edited by Smith and Rosengarten, The Clarendon Edition of the Novels of the

Brontës (Oxford: Clarendon Press / New York: Oxford University Press, 1987).

Charlotte Brontë's short fiction comprises the profuse writings that she produced – in collaboration with her brother, Branwell, and their sisters, Emily and Anne – during their sheltered childhoods at Haworth Parsonage. Until the publication of Christine Alexander's *An Edition of the Early Writings of Charlotte Brontë* (1987–1991) less than half of these works were available to general readership. Apart from Fannie E. Ratchford and William Clyde De Vane's collection *Legends of Angria* (1933), Ratchford's study *The Brontë's Web of Childhood* (1941), and Winifred Gérin's biography *Charlotte Brontë: The Evolution of Genius* (1967) and collection *Five Novelettes* (1971), major attention has been denied to the Brontë juvenilia.

The first to recognize Brontë's juvenilia as a part of her development as a writer was Elizabeth Cleghorn Gaskell, during her research for *The Life of Charlotte Brontë* (1857). During her visit with Brontë's father, the Reverend Patrick Brontë, shortly after Charlotte's death, Gaskell had "a curious packet confided to me, containing an immense amount of manuscript, in an inconceivably small space; tales, dramas, poems, romances, written principally by Charlotte, in a hand which it is almost impossible to decipher without the aid of a magnifying glass." A few samples are included in Gaskell's biography "as a curious proof how early the rage for literary composition had seized upon" Brontë, but they are not given serious consideration as literature. Gaskell says that of Brontë's "imaginative writings" that "run riot, sometimes to the borders of apparent delirium . . . a single example will suffice"; but she offers her readers a passage that, in Alexander's opinion, may have been written mostly by Branwell. Gaskell could not read all the manuscripts and was, therefore, unaware of their interconnection or their true literary worth.

In 1859, as he was compiling material for his *The Brontës: Life and Letters* (1908), Clement Shorter visited Brontë's widower, Arthur Bell Nicholls, at his home in Ireland. Among the papers Nicholls gave Shorter were "countless manuscripts written in childhood," which he had found "in the bottom of a cupboard tied up in newspaper where they had lain for nearly 30 years" and where, Nicholls assured Shorter, " 'they must have remained during my lifetime, and most likely afterwards have been destroyed,' " but for Shorter's timely inquiry. Shorter turned the manuscripts over to Thomas James Wise, who published many of them privately. As Alexander notes, the tendency in the case of Wise and later editors has been to "improve upon" the originals; thus, "heavily abridged and inaccurately transcribed" limited editions abound. Many of the manuscripts were taken apart and sold off to Brontë collectors, some pages being lost along the way. Thus, simply locating Brontë's juvenilia and assigning some modicum of order to it has proved a momentous task.

Another major problem is the poor condition of the original texts. Most of the works were written in minuscule printed script on pieces of paper that usually measure about 5 by 3.5 centimeters, with more than one hundred words crammed on a page. The tiny size, poor paper quality, and the occasional inkblot have rendered some passages illegible. A shortage of paper accounts in great part for the appearance of the children's writings. Scholars, however, also point to an unusual need for privacy among the young Brontës; even when paper was more plentiful, Charlotte's habit of writing in minuscule script continued.

Because Charlotte wrote in close collaboration with her siblings, especially Branwell, authorship is questionable in many cases. The signatures "UT" (Us Two) and "WT" (We Two) after many of the pieces have left scholars with the problem of how much was written by Charlotte and how much by her brother. It is generally accepted that while Branwell developed most of the political plots and military exploits in the land of Angria, Charlotte focused on bedroom politics, romance, and family conflicts. Alexander believes that Charlotte may have written at least eleven juvenile works that had been attributed to both herself and Branwell. Still, many writings were completely the product of collaboration. By 1833, even texts written separately by Charlotte and Branwell include thoroughly consistent references to places, people, and political events.

Charlotte Brontë, the third child of the Reverend Patrick Brontë, an Irishman who had changed his surname from Brunty, and Maria Branwell Brontë, was born on 21 April 1816 in Thornton in the West Riding of Yorkshire. Maria had been born in 1813 and Elizabeth in 1815; Patrick Branwell followed Charlotte in 1817, Emily Jane in 1818, and Anne in 1820. In the latter year Mr. Brontë was appointed perpetual curate at St. Michael's Church in Haworth, and the family moved into the parsonage atop the windswept Yorkshire hills. The children, socially separated by their father's position in the community as well as by their home's location at the edge of town, had to rely on each other for companionship. The wildly beautiful moors became their playground and sanctuary.

Their feeling of isolation intensified with the illness of their mother. Gaskell reports that in the year preceding her death in 1821, Mrs. Brontë was reluctant to spend any time with her children, and "so the little things clung quietly together, for their father was busy in his study and in his parish, or with their mother, and they took their meals alone; sat reading, or whispering low in the 'children's study' or wandered out on the hillside, hand in hand." Charlotte seems to have been profoundly affected by her mother's death: her novels are populated by motherless women who must make their own way in the world, and many of her Angria tales also show a preoccupation with the loss of a parent, which is often accompanied by loss of family identity and respect.

After Mrs. Brontë's death her sister, Elizabeth Branwell, came to supervise the household. Aunt Branwell, as the children called her, was a stern and distant woman who displayed little affection. In losing their mother, however, the children gained a pathway to creativity: as long as they obeyed the household rules set down by Aunt Branwell and were conscientious about their religious studies, they were free to imagine and indulge in make-believe as they wished.

The strongest influence on the children was their father. Though he maintained an emotional distance from his children, he welcomed them into his study for conversations on current affairs, the classics, contemporary literature, and history, and he read to them from the *Leeds Intelligencer,* the *Leeds Mercury,* and *Blackwood's Edinburgh Magazine.* Mr. Brontë's heroes – especially Arthur Wellesley, first duke of Wellington – became his children's heroes; his Tory loyalties became their loyalties; the Celtic fairy tales and legends he imparted to them fed their imaginations. Furthermore, his love of Romantic literature allowed them access to the works of writers such as George Gordon, Lord Byron; Percy Bysshe Shelley; Samuel Taylor Coleridge; and Sir Walter Scott – not the usual literary diet of Victorian children. He did not require his children to agree with his views but engaged them in dialogue, fostering in them the capacity for independent thought.

In July 1824 Mr. Brontë sent Maria and Elizabeth to the Clergy Daughters' School at Cowan Bridge, near Tunstall in Lancashire, to begin preparing for careers as governesses, a position befitting their station in life. Charlotte joined her sisters in August, and Emily followed in November. Gérin notes that the "mental freedom of their early childhood – a freedom hardly ever enjoyed by girls of the period – could only be measured by its sudden loss on their being sent away to school." The long, cold walks to church in inadequate clothing, the abominable food, the tyranny of older students, the caustic comments of the teachers, and the unsanitary conditions are faithfully recorded in Charlotte's novel *Jane Eyre* (1847). Maria became ill and was sent home in February 1825; she died of tuberculosis on 6 May. Shortly after Maria's death Elizabeth contracted typhoid fever and was also sent home; she died on 15 June. Mr. Brontë immediately brought Charlotte and Emily back to Haworth, where they remained for the next six years under the guidance of their father, Aunt Branwell, and Tabitha Ackroyd, an elderly woman who was hired as housekeeper. "Experience had taught [the Brontë children] to expect the worst of an alien and hostile world," writes Helen Moglen. "Never after would they be able to meet strangers with anything less than suspicion. Agonizingly shy and withdrawn, they clung together, drawing a circle round themselves." They sank deeper into their own world – the "world below," as Charlotte would call it – and out of their isolation grew the fantastic stories of Angria, a magical land in Africa where genii ruled and brave men fought off exotic natives to build the Great Glass Town Confederation.

On 12 March 1826 Mr. Brontë returned from Leeds with a bundle of toys for his children. Among them were twelve toy soldiers for Branwell. The event is recorded in Charlotte's "The History of the Year" (1829) as she explains the origin of the children's first collaborative effort, the play "Young Men": "When Papa came home it was night and we were in bed, so next morning Branwell came to our door with a box of soldiers. Emily and I jumped out of bed and I snatched up one and exclaimed, 'This is the Duke of Wellington! It shall be mine!' When I said this, Emily likewise took one and said it should be hers. When Anne came down she took one also. Mine was the prettiest of the whole and perfect in every part. . . . Branwell chose 'Bonaparte.' "

Charlotte and Branwell had chosen to name their toys after two men who had been bitter enemies. Though Charlotte's and Branwell's Angria writings would evolve in different ways, one theme that would remain constant would be antagonism between Charlotte's fictionalized version of the duke – and, later, the duke's son Arthur – and Branwell's various versions of the duke's rival. Branwell would play the conflict out on the battlefield and in the parliament, while Charlotte would bring the conflict into the relationships of family members and lovers. Charlotte's "History of the Year" mentions two other plays: "Our Fellows," which was started in July 1827 and appears to have been abandoned almost immediately, and "Islanders," begun in December 1827, which served as the threshold to the Angria saga. While Emily and Anne must have contributed to these early works, nothing of their contribution remains. They eventually broke from the direction of their older siblings and wrote an entirely different fantasy about a land called Gondal.

Charlotte's next composition, written on 15 April 1829, was "A Romantic Tale" (called "The Twelve Adventurers" in her "Catalogue of My Books" [1830]); it was followed on 28 April by "An Adventure In Ireland," and the two stories were then combined as "Two Romantic Tales." The first tale lays the historical groundwork for "Young Men" and "Tales of the Islanders"; the second introduces fairy-tale and Gothic elements that would remain an important ingredient in Brontë's adult works.

"A Romantic Tale" begins with the voyage of the twelve Young Men on the *Invincible* in 1793; Brontë changes the names of all of the twelve from the play "Young Men" except one: Arthur Wellesley. The Young Men are washed ashore on the west coast of Africa after many harrowing adventures at sea. They battle a native tribe, the Ashantee, whom they force to sign a treaty advantageous to the Young Men. The building of their city, Glass Town, is completed in an amazingly short time; the Young Men realize that the four major genii who rule the land – Branii (representing Branwell), Tallii (Charlotte), Emii (Emily), and Anii (Anne) – have helped them. Twenty years have passed by the end of "A Romantic Tale": Wellington has enlisted the genii's help to return to England, defeat Napoleon, and sail back to Glass Town a hero, ready to become its king.

In "An Adventure in Ireland" an anonymous narrator spending the night in a haunted castle is awakened by a "skeleton wrapped in a white sheet" and commanded to rise and see the "world's wonders." The theme of being transported by fairy magic is common among these early stories, and Gothic elements such as ghosts, subterranean vaults or passageways, and moonlit graveyards appear with increased frequency. Sent below the ocean and then into a barren desert where a lion is waiting, the narrator wakes up just before the lion pounces.

"An Adventure in Ireland" was one of several miscellaneous stories written between 1829 and 1832 that do not fit into the developing saga of Angria, though some of their characters also appear in Angria stories. "The Enfant" (May or June 1829),

"The Keep of the Bridge" (May 1829), "The Search after Happiness" (July 1829), "The Silver Cup" (October 1829), "The Adventures of Monsieur Edouard de Crack" (February 1830), and "The Adventures of Ernest Alembert" (May 1830) are fairy tales that include magic objects or deal with the protagonist's transportation into the fairy realm. They also share the theme of the discovery that happiness lies in home and family rather than in adventure, travel, expensive possessions, or fame. In "The Enfant," for instance, an abandoned child is forced into labor by the infamous Pigtail, a monstrous, child-abusing invention of Branwell's, but is rescued by a stranger who turns out to be the child's true father. Edouard de Crack, also an orphan, seeks his fortune in Paris and runs afoul of a frightening "Tavern Master." In "The Silver Cup" an expensive cup reeks havoc on a family, threatening the relationship of parent and child until the object is discovered to be possessed by genii and is destroyed; then all live happily ever after.

In January 1829 Branwell created "Branwell's Blackwood's Magazine," and the children filled it with essays, stories, histories, poems, and songs "by" and about Glass Town residents. Charlotte took over the editorship in August, changed the periodical's name to "Blackwood's Young Men's Magazine," and began pursuing her own interests in its pages. Writing as either herself or Captain Tree, the noted Glass Town author, Charlotte created little plays called "Military Conversations," poems and stories celebrating Glass Town and its society, critiques of Glass Town painters and poets, and stories about her favorite hero, the duke of Wellington. Charlotte produced five more issues for 1829, then picked up the magazine again in August 1830 and continued it for another six issues.

Increasingly, the topic that commanded Charlotte's imagination was the duke and his political opponents and colleagues, which she explored most fully in the four volumes of "Tales of the Islanders." Of all her writings during this time, this collection of stories is the most important because it sets the stage for an extended, cohesive story line about the land of Angria and its many inhabitants. Charlotte leaves the genii to minor roles and devises new protectors for the duke: the Little King and Queens are the new representations of the Brontë children; they are still all-powerful and slightly haughty, but they are diminutive creatures – more like the children they symbolized – and their place in the central action of the tales is much larger and more interactive than the genii's role.

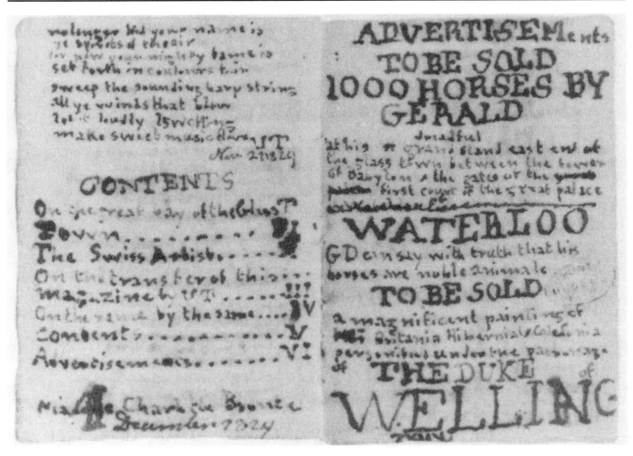

Pages from the December 1829 number of Charlotte and Branwell Brontë's handwritten "Blackwood's Young Men's Magazine," the first written by Charlotte Brontë after she took it over from her brother, Branwell (© Brontë Society)

The action begins on Vision Island, which resembles the fairy realm of Charlotte's other tales. Charlotte and her sisters devised a palace school for the royal children of the island, and Charlotte takes great care in describing its lovely gardens and romantic landscape. Side by side with this feast of beautiful description, however, lurks a darker side of Charlotte's imagination: behind a statue in the "Hall of the Fountains" is "a small door, over which is drawn a curtain of white silk. This door, when opened discovers a small apartment at the farther end of which is a very large, iron door, which leads to a long dark passage, at the end of which is a flight of steps leading to a subterranean dungeon...." Below the delightful surface of Vision Island is a dungeon where bad little girls and boys meet their cruel fates, "so far down in the earth that the loudest shriek could not be heard by any inhabitant of the upper world." Using Gothic description at its best, Charlotte is beginning to toy with the idea of evil lurking beneath a lovely surface. Later she will explore the evil in the personalities of her characters.

The Little King and Queens choose the duke as ruler of Vision Island and governor of the school (under themselves, of course), but he sends a regretful apology, explaining that he is too busy with politics in England – in particular, with the Catholic Emancipation Act, which occupied the interests of the entire Brontë family for months at this time – to accept their offer. His sons, Arthur and Charles, take his place. At Strathfieldsay, an estate that sometimes appears in Africa and sometimes in England, the duke is the victim of a poisoning plot and is saved only through the magic of one of the genii. The poisoner is Raton, a character based on Edward Raton, editor of the *Leeds Mercury*. This attempt on the life of Charlotte's duke symbolizes the Whig newspaper's attacks on the real Wellington as Tory prime minister and as an opponent, at that time, of Catholic Emancipation.

At the beginning of volume two, written in October 1829, four months have passed since the end of volume one. During that time "Parliament was opened and the great Catholic Question was brought forward and the Duke's measures were disclosed and all was slander, violence, party spirit and confusion. Oh, those 3 months, from the time of the King's speech to the end! Nobody could think, speak or write on anything but the Catholic Question and the Duke of Wellington or Mr [Sir Robert] Peel." The Little King and Queens have followed the duke to England to be present at these momentous events. A message arrives from Charles that a rebellion has broken out at the school; the students are divided into four parties but united in the cause of overthrowing the authority of Arthur and Charles. The rebellion represents the various alliances and factions that formed preceding the Catholic Emancipation Act: it is led by Prince George (George IV, who opposed the bill and Wellington) and Polignes (Prince Jules de Polignac, a French ambassador to London who created friction between the duke of Wellington and George IV). The duke and the Little King and Queens hurry back, expel all the children, and leave the island to the fairies.

The rest of the stories in the last three volumes are mostly set in England. Charlotte's hero is still the duke of Wellington, but her loyalties are moving from him to his sons. She establishes the characters of Arthur and Charles, along with those of Arthur's primary villainous rival, Branwell's Alexander Rogue, and other important Glass Town inhabitants in "Characters of the Celebrated Men of the Present Time" (December 1829). Arthur, now twenty-two, is Brontë's earliest conception of Byron ⇥ a romantic, handsome youth; throughout the juvenilia she quotes from his *Childe Harold's Pilgrimage* (1812–1818), *Manfred* (1817), and *Cain* (1821). As the tales develop Arthur takes center stage, becoming first the marquis of Douro, then the duke of Zamorna, and finally the king of Angria. His Byronism changes, as well: Arthur evolves from a melancholy, pensive youth given to romance into a military giant who thrives on the conquest of his enemies and his women. By the end of the Angria saga, Arthur will acquire three wives and many mistresses; in true Byronic form, he will never feel the least guilt for anything he does, including the seduction of his young ward, Caroline Vernon.

Lord Charles Wellesley also goes through a series of changes as the Angria saga continues. When Charles is first introduced he is devoted to his older brother. Like Arthur, he is a writer; but Charles writes with "light and airy magnificence," while his brother favors mournful songs and descriptions of storms. Arthur is an "aeolian harp," says Brontë, and Charles is a merry "dulcimer." Through him, Brontë explores the use and the limi-

tations of a first-person narrator; as she does so, Charles turns from lighthearted youth to jealous, cynical, and bitter younger brother. He never misses a chance to spread evil gossip about people of Glass Town, and he taunts his brother about the latter's love interests. Eventually, his name changes to Charles Townsend, and he brings out the worst in all he sees. Rogue, the third male lead in the Angria saga, evolves also, but he is a villain from start to finish. Brontë says that he is "rather polished and gentlemanly, but his mind is deceitful, bloody, and cruel." Rogue, who will become Alexander Percy, earl of Northangerland, is the worst of Byronism. He will instigate a rebellion against Arthur, become a pirate in his exile, and return to Angria as the husband of Lady Zenobia, herself a study in uncontrolled passion and immorality.

"Albion and Marina" (October 1830) centers on the love of Arthur, thinly disguised as Albion, and his soon-to-be bride, Marian Hume, represented by Marina, rather than the duke of Wellington and his political escapades. The "author" of "Albion and Marina" is Lord Charles Wellesley, who says in the preface that he has "written this tale out of malignity for the injuries that have lately [been] offered to me" and confesses that "the conclusion is wholly destitute of any foundation in truth, and I did it out of revenge." The young Albion, marquis of Tagus, falls in love with the beautiful Marina, the daughter of his father's physician; she is based on Hume, Arthur's "real-life" love. Here is the high-born youth and his lower-class love, a relationship that would frequently occupy Brontë's interest. (The story probably has its source in the real duke of Wellington's fourteen-year-old son's affair with Elizabeth Hume, daughter of the duke's surgeon; the romance was encouraged by Lady Wellington, but the duke ended it after several years.) Lord Cornelius (Charles) warns his older brother of the "folly" of falling in love with someone below his rank, but Albion will not heed his advice. Their father, the duke of Strathelleraye, feels that the lovers are too young for an immediate commitment. He decides to move his family to Africa, so that he can see that wonder of wonders, The Great Glass Town, and so that his son will have time to think about his relationship with Marina. On their return to England, the duke promises Albion, Marina may be his bride if he still chooses.

Circumstances change when the young marquis gets a taste of Glass Town high society. Albion "attracted considerable attention wherever he went, and in a short period he had won and attached many faithful friends of the highest rank and abilities." Most important among these acquaintances is the Lady Zelzia Ellrington, who will become Zenobia in subsequent tales. Zelzia is the perfect foil to Marina: she is a sophisticated society girl whose "features were regular and finely formed; her full and brilliant eyes jetty black, as were the luxuriant tresses of her richly curled hair. Her dark, glowing complexion was set off by a robe of crimson velvet trimmed with ermine, and a nodding plume of black ostrich feathers. . . ." The physical contrast of the two women resembles that between Rowena and Rebecca in Scott's *Ivanhoe* (1819). Scott was one of the most important sources for the later juvenilia.

As Albion compares Marina and Zelzia in his mind, "he could hardly tell which to give the preference to, for though he still almost idolized Marina, yet an absence of four years had considerably deadened his remembrance of her person." At that moment "a soft but mournful voice" whispers his name, and Marina appears as an apparition: "he stretched out his hand but she eluded his grasp, and slowly gliding away, said, 'Do not forget me; I shall be happy when you return.'" Albion immediately sails for England but finds that Marina died at the precise moment of her spiritual visitation to him. Albion is crushed, and after several days of mourning by her graveside he disappears, never to be heard from again. As Charles made clear in his preface, this is not the "true" outcome. The romance started in "Albion and Marina" would become a vicious love triangle involving Arthur, Marian Hume, and the exotic and dangerous Lady Zenobia.

In December 1830 Brontë wrote "Visits in Verreopolis"; the purported author, Lord Charles Wellesley, explains in the preface that "Verreopolis means the Glass Town, being compounded of a Greek and French word to that effect." In the story itself, and in later stories, the name is given as Verdopolis. The story includes an untitled verse drama told to Lord Charles Wellesley by Captain Bud, who is often the original teller of Charles's tales. In the drama, which is usually referred to as "The Rivals," Marian is engaged to Arthur. She is still the pure and innocent maid of "Albion and Marina," dressed in green, her hair wreathed in a garland of flowers; likewise, Zenobia continues to wear crimson and black and to exude sexuality. Based on the historical Zenobia, queen of Palmyra and the East, as described in Edward Gibbon's *The History of the Decline and Fall of the Roman Empire* (1776–1788), she is known throughout Verdopolis as "a Latin beauty of bad morals." Marian and Zenobia encounter one another in the woods; learning Marian's identity, Zenobia cries out "Ha! My rival!" and seizes her,

exclaiming "Wretch, I could kill thee!" Arthur calls to Marian from within the forest that he has a rose to give her. She tries to go to him, but Zenobia holds her firmly "as grim death." On Arthur's approach Zenobia reveals the obsessive quality of her love for him and how easily it destroys her pride:

Give me the rose, Lord Arthur, for methinks
I merit it more than my girlish rival;
I pray thee now grant my request, and place
That rose upon my forehead, not on hers;
Then will I serve thee all my after-days
As thy poor handmaid, as thy humblest slave,
Happy to kiss the dust beneath thy tread,
To kneel submissive in thy lordly presence.
Oh! turn thine eyes from her and look on me
As I lie here imploring at thy feet,
Supremely blest if but a single glance
Could tell me that thou art not wholly deaf
To my petition, earnestly preferred.

Arthur tells her to stop her ravings; he does give Zenobia the rose, however, and she runs away screaming, "now I have triumphed!" To Marian, who has uttered a "suppressed scream" and fallen into a swoon at this action, he gives a ring, assuring her that its permanence is the true sign of his love. In "Albion and Marina" and "The Rivals" Brontë has begun to deconstruct her perfect leading man. He is still the romantic youth, but his attitude toward women is changing. As time goes on, they will become possessions, their value constantly weighed one against the other.

In January 1831 Brontë was sent to Roe Head, a small private school, and her writings came to a halt; Branwell's work appears to have gone on hiatus as well, inspiration only striking him when he visited Charlotte at school or when she returned home on holidays. Charlotte suffered acute homesickness, and she was behind the other students in her studies, but under the direction of Miss Margaret Wooler and her sisters, who were more attuned to the needs of a sensitive young girl than the fanatical William Carus Wilson, headmaster of the Clergy Daughters' School, had been, Brontë proved an able student. Seeing how distressed Brontë became at the thought of being placed in a lower class, Wooler allowed her to work in private study to make up for her deficiencies. Having received the money for school from her godparents, the Atkinsons, Brontë felt an enormous responsibility to do well so that she would be able to tutor her younger sisters. Also, there was only one son in the Brontë family, and all of the father's hopes and dreams rested on Branwell's shoulders. Aunt Branwell contributed from her small savings to her nephew's education, and Charlotte, Emily, and Anne would devote much of their lives to securing Branwell's future by taking on the occupation of governesses – a role Charlotte despised.

While on Christmas holiday in 1831 Brontë wrote the poem "The Trumpet Hath Sounded." Critics disagree on the meaning of this poem, which seems to foretell the destruction of Glass Town and the end of Brontë's literary aspirations; by this time she must have come to realize that while she and her sisters might dream of becoming writers, only Branwell was in any real position to pursue such a career. But after she left Roe Head and returned to Haworth in 1832, Branwell insisted on reviving his stories of war and soldiers, and she found herself once again caught up in the "world below."

Though brother and sister continued to share plots and characters, Charlotte's stories show a sophistication in character development that Branwell's tales of the factions of the Glass Town Confederacy never achieved. The rebellions, bloody confrontations, and same old crew of soldiers that fill his pages make for tiresome, repetitive reading compared with Charlotte's new emphasis on romantic relationships and fiery love triangles. Branwell invented only one character who figured prominently in the remainder of Charlotte's juvenile writings: Rogue/Percy/Northangerland will be Charlotte's foil to Arthur Wellesley, the Marquis of Douro, and the main villain of the later juvenilia.

For her first serious attempt at writing after Roe Head, Brontë returned to "Albion and Marina" and "The Rivals." Unsatisfied with the way she had left her characters, she wrote "The Bridal" (July 1832) to offer a "true" version of the events free of Charles's satire and bitterness. She begins with a poem that retells "Albion and Marina," this time ending with the marriage of the lovers. The story continues in prose form to pick up the plot of "The Rivals," featuring Arthur Wellesley and Marian Hume. Here Zenobia is taken to the brink of insanity in her desperate attempts to win Arthur's love before he marries Marian. Returning from a day of hunting at his country palace, Arthur is confronted by Zenobia, who has traveled from Verdopolis. Her "head was bare, her tall person was enveloped in the tattered remnants of a dark velvet mantle. Her dishevelled hair hung in wild elf-locks over her face, neck and shoulders, almost concealing her features, which were emaciated and pale as death." The similarity between this portrait of Zenobia and Brontë's later creation, Bertha Antoinette Mason Rochester in *Jane Eyre,* is hard to miss. When her hysterical entreaties have no effect on the marquis's plan to

marry Marian, Zenobia graduates from simple rival to evil witch. Moved to ecstasy on hearing Arthur's denunciation of Rogue at the Glass Town Tribunal, where other women also faint in response to his eloquence, Zenobia lures him to a "subterraneous grotto," where she enlists the help of an evil genius named Danhasch to win his love. A friendly spirit whispers a warning in his ear, Zenobia's plot fails, and Arthur and Marian are married.

Brontë began her writings of 1833 by creating rather intricate and confusing pasts for her main characters, presumably to keep her stories up-to-date with Branwell's. In "Something about Arthur" Lord Charles Wellesley relates an incident that occurred during Arthur's fifteenth year. Arthur's love of horses led him into the company of the Verdopolitan libertine Colonel George Frederick, Baron of Caversham. Caversham dared Arthur to enter his prize stallion, Thunderbolt, in the grand Verdopolitan horse race but secretly struck a deal with the jockey to assure Thunderbolt's loss. Mortified when his horse lost, Arthur shot Thunderbolt in the name of honor. He then enlisted the aid of Ned Laury in seeking revenge on Caversham. Ned gathered a group of lads together and tried several wild plots, in the course of which Arthur was shot. Ned took Arthur to his cabin in the woods, where the young marquis was nursed back to health by Ned's daughter Mina – another lowborn girl. Arthur asked Ned for his daughter's hand in marriage, but the duke of Wellington arrived and put an end to the affair. Mina fainted as Arthur was taken back to the duke's estate and continued to pine away until her father was sure that she would die. Arthur was also gloomy for quite some time, but Marian came along to help him forget his suffering. Lady Wellington rescued Mina from her grief and brought her to the palace, where she became Marian's favorite handmaid. She would be Arthur's one permanent mistress, though many others would come and go through the years. From this point, although Arthur would be at the center of all that Brontë wrote until she permanently left Angria behind, increasingly her attention would be drawn to the women who fall under the spell of her hero. Only one, Elizabeth Hastings, will retain her identity and her pride; yet Elizabeth would be the one heroine to whom love is ultimately denied.

In "The Foundling" (May and June 1833) a new character, Edward Sydney, is found as an infant by a kindly country couple and raised by them with the help of a rich guardian, Mr. Hasleden of Oakwood Hall. He travels to Verdopolis to seek his fortune after Hasleden's death. Arthur Wellesley,

Marquis of Douro, has Sydney imprisoned in Waterloo Palace until Sydney agrees to become a member of Parliament and an opponent of Arthur's archrival, Rogue. From Sydney's point of view, Brontë gives her reader a panoramic view of Verdopolis's grand buildings, social structure, history, and politics. Here her cooperation with Branwell is fruitful, as old characters are recalled and the old Glass Town merges with the new Verdopolis. She also reveals more about Arthur's deteriorating personality. At Waterloo Palace, Sydney is waited on by Finic, a mute dwarf servant who is revealed to be the illegitimate offspring of Arthur's affair with Sofala, a native woman. There are also rumors of an earlier wife, but no one knows for sure how many women the marquis has seduced. Sydney also meets the marquis's young niece, Lady Julia Wellesley. He pleads with her to set him free, but like most women associated with Arthur she is totally under the marquis's power, although he continually belittles her. Sydney falls in love with Julia, but she is betrothed to someone else. When it is discovered that Sydney is actually Prince Edward of York, son of Frederick the Great, king of the twelve Young Men who formed the Glass Town Confederacy, however, the marquis, anxious to please this useful ally, takes Julia from her fiancé and gives her to Sydney. Through their marriage Brontë will explore, in other tales, a rather comic side of marital strife.

The other interesting relationship explored in "The Foundling" is that of Zenobia and Rogue, who is now Lord Ellrington. Zenobia has married Rogue and bestowed her name on him; but she continually mourns for the man she cannot possess, often scorning Rogue and irritating him beyond endurance. Their relationship overflows with sexual violence. At one point Rogue commands: "kneel at my feet this instant, and humbly and submissively ask pardon for all past offences. . . ." She declares that she will never degrade herself in such a manner (although she has performed just such a degrading act for Arthur). Rogue draws his sword, grabs Zenobia by "her thick black hair," and is about to strike her as she lies "unresisting and motionless" when he is stopped by one of his coconspirators. Brontë has moved the gory battles off the fields of Angria and into its bedrooms.

In September 1833 Brontë wrote "The Green Dwarf: A Tale of the Perfect Tense." Captain Bud is the storyteller and Lord Charles is his eager audience for this examination of the past of Alexander Percy, as Alexander Rogue is now called. In this younger version of her archvillain Brontë explores

*Pencil drawing, attributed to Brontë, of her main protagonist, Arthur Wellesley, Marquis of Douro and Duke of Zamorna (Brontë Society)*

her fascination with evil just below an inviting surface, a fascination that she will later apply to Arthur in his role as duke of Zamorna. Percy is a charioteer in the African Olympic Games, a play on the medieval tournaments of *Ivanhoe*. He is tall and handsome, but there is, "in the expression of his blue sparkling, but sinister, eyes and of the smile that ever played round his deceitful-looking mouth, a spirit of deep, restless villainy which warned the penetrating observer that all was not as fair within as without. . . ." Percy abducts Lady Emily Charlesworth and takes her to a deserted castle, where a hag named Bertha has been imprisoned in the attic for nearly sixty years. Quashia Quamina, an Ashantee orphan adopted by the duke of Wellington, rises up to wage the first of many attacks on the Glass Town Federation, thereby fulfilling the prophecy of his dying mother in Brontë's poem "The African Queen's Lament" (February 1833). Percy joins him and is exiled for treason. For sixteen years he roams the world as a pirate and bandit.

From this point Brontë's childhood fairy tales provide her with symbolic images for exploring sexual situations in her adolescence. In "The Secret"

(November 1833) Percy reappears to torture Marian. But the instigator of the trouble is Miss Foxley, Marian's former governess and another rival for Arthur. Arthur had begun to court Marian when she was fourteen, but Miss Foxley had been "prompted by her unextinguishable vanity to imagine that she yet possessed charms potent enough to attract the admiration of a handsome and high-born nobleman." When the marquis did not respond to her advances, "she vowed mentally to make him regret his cold and scornful rejection, and thenceforth set herself sedulously to work in order to prevent his union with her beautiful and youthful rival." Foxley has now returned to make good on her vow. She tells Marian that Marian's former fiancé, Henry Percy, the son of Alexander Percy, is still alive, and that Alexander Percy, her husband's worst enemy, is also Marian's real father. This awful secret will be destroyed by burning the paper on which it is recorded if Marian will spend the night with Alexander Percy, who has teamed with Foxley in hopes of attacking Arthur through his wife. Percy spends the night torturing Marian with "keen taunts, false insinuations, and detested gallantry." This idea of using women to "get back at one's enemies" will continue with Arthur's next wife, Mary, the real daughter of Alexander Percy.

The manuscript for "The Secret" is contained in a sixteen-page booklet that also includes the story "Lily Hart." The leading character is not Arthur but his friend John Sneachie, duke of Fidena, and the ending, unlike that of most of the other love stories Brontë wrote at this time, is quite happy. During the Great Insurrection, an uprising contrived by Branwell and led by Rogue (as Percy was then known), Fidena is wounded and is cared for by the lowly seamstress Lily and her mother. There is a strong attraction between Fidena and Lily, but Fidena, who has disguised himself as "Mr. Seymour" for military security, suddenly disappears. He has gone off to defend his country, but this is only one reason for his abrupt departure: the philosophical Fidena is determined to avoid love and passion, and his feelings for Lily have frightened him away. Lily, like many of Brontë's characters, becomes an orphan and falls on hard times. One night, as she is crying by her mother's grave, Fidena appears and begs her to marry him. She consents, and he is overcome with joy: "She saw at her feet the grave, philosophical Mr Seymour, he who seemed to have subdued all the turbulent passions which agitate other men. She beheld him changed for her sake into a mere mortal lover." The setting of their reunion, the graveside, becomes an impor-

tant symbol for Brontë as a place where marriage and death are intricately linked. Later, in "Henry Hastings," Elizabeth Hastings will be confronted with a proposal in such a setting; the proposal and the outcome, however, will be quite different.

In "The Spell, An Extravaganza" (July 1834) Marian has died of consumption and has been succeeded as Arthur's wife by Mary Henrietta Percy, daughter of Alexander Percy. Arthur wins new territories, and the two are subsequently referred to as the duke and duchess of Zamorna. Mary will remain Arthur's wife for four years, but his repeated absences and his womanizing will not make for a happy marriage. Mary is jealous and, like Arthur's other women, completely possessed by her love for Arthur. In one of Brontë's most complicated and extravagant plots, Mary must deal with not one but two Arthurs — Brontë's literal interpretation of his dual personality. Arthur has a twin brother; a spell placed on the twins at birth means that if they are seen together, or if more than twelve people know of their mutual existence, Arthur will die. The twins have kept their lives separate, but Mary's jealousy brings them close to doom. While passion and even adultery escape consequences in Brontë's writings, jealousy is always destructive. The tale is presented as a fabrication of Lord Charles Wellesley's; he is determined to show "that there is one person at least in Verdopolis thoroughly acquainted with all the depths, false or true, of [Arthur's] double-dealing, hypocritical, close, dark, secret, half-insane, character."

As the stories progress Arthur continues his conquests, and with Percy's help he becomes king of Angria. But the alliance does not last. Arthur denounces Percy in "An Address to the Angrians" (September 1834), accusing him of treason. Just as the action in Angria reached its peak, however, the brother-sister team was severed once again. In July 1835 Charlotte returned to Roe Head as a teacher; Emily went with her. Branwell went off to the Royal Academy of Arts in London, but he drank away his money and never appeared at the academy to present his work. Returning to Haworth with a half-baked tale of having been robbed, he continued to fail at each new venture he tried. Meanwhile, Charlotte despised her duties at Roe Head and longed for Angria and the chance to finish the story of Mary, a heroine who had been her favorite for some time. In her journal she wonders "if Branwell has really killed the Duchess. Is she dead: Is she buried? Is she alone in the cold earth on this dreary night with the ponderous coffin plate on her breast under the black pavement of a church in a vault closed up with lime and mortar. . . ? I hope she's alive still partly because I can't abide to think how hopelessly and cheerlessly she must have died. . . ."

It was only during holidays between 1836 and 1838 and, afterward, during interludes before and after her three months as governess for the Sidgwick family of Stonegappe, near Lothersdale, beginning in May 1839, that Brontë found the time to continue her Angrian tales. She took up the story of Arthur and Mary in the summer of 1836 in "Zamorna's Exile." The narrative poem in seventy-two stanzas is a soliloquy by Arthur as he is carried into exile, having been finally defeated by Percy, the earl of Northangerland. Even though she was beginning to move away from Branwell's influence, Brontë maintained the conflict between her two male protagonists: Arthur and Percy have a strong love-hate relationship that is complicated by Arthur's marriage to Percy's daughter, which keeps the conflict within one family and creates incestuous implications. Both men feed on political and sexual power, but Percy serves as a father figure for Arthur, as well: Arthur desires Percy's approval and love while, at the same time, wishing to destroy him.

In "Zamorna's Exile" Mary is the pawn in Arthur's plan of revenge on Percy. On his way to Ascension Isle aboard the *Rover,* Arthur traces the events leading to his exile and contemplates the fate of his wife, who lies dying at home. But it is a fate he has manufactured by rejecting her: "and then I've pledged my faith / To break her father's heart by Mary's death!" To the absent Percy he cries: "And so, my lord, if you have ruined me, / And ruined all the hopes I ever cherished, / I've paid you back, and that abundantly: / You'll feel it when that flower of yours has perished. . . ." Mina Laury, the patient and obedient mistress who accepts Arthur's love on any terms he chooses to set, steals aboard the ship to be by his side. "I cannot spurn her, though my wife is dying / Cheerless and desolate in solitude; / This moment, like a faithful dog, she's lying / Crouched at my feet, for with a sad, subdued, / Untiring constancy she's ever trying / To gain one word, or even one look, imbued / With some slight touch of kindness; There, then take / A brief caress, for all thy labour's sake."

Brontë concluded the Angrian cycle with "Passing Events" (April 1836), "Julia" (June 1837), "Mina Laury" (January 1838), "Henry Hastings" (February and March 1839), and "Caroline Vernon" (July to December 1839). "Passing Events" and "Julia" are series of stories, some related to Brontë's central characters and some tangential.

Mary does not die, and Zamorna returns from exile to triumph once again; but though Mary feels that "her happiness, her god, her heaven" are merged when he is once more at her side, it will always be "with a sensation of pleasurable terror" that she finds "herself . . . alone with the duke." In "Mina Laury" Arthur's control over his faithful mistress, and his ever-growing evil, are seen in a test he provides for Mina. Lord Hartford loves Mina and asks her to marry him, offering her a legitimate way of life. She, of course, refuses. Hartford then challenges Arthur to a duel and is nearly killed. Arthur knew that Mina would not consider Hartford's proposal, yet his arrogance compels him to test her. He tells her that he has a reward for her loyalty, and that reward is a husband, Lord Hartford. Saying that she cannot bear this new twist of events, "with a deep short sob, she turned white, and fell, close by the duke, her head against his foot." The narrator, Lord Charles Wellesley, notes that "I suppose Zamorna's first feeling when she fell was horror, but his next, I am tolerably certain, was intense gratification." Mina's story "uncovers not so much the particular problems of sexual and social non-conformity," says John Maynard, "as the universal danger of losing the self in the process of full sexual commitment." As Maynard points out, while she exhibits a fearlessness that allows her to follow her lover on military campaigns and into exile, and while she can inspect the accounts of Zamorna's estates with "businesslike sharpness and strictness" and command the respect of "haughty Aristocrats" with her cleverness, she cannot free herself from Arthur's power to negate her as a human being: "here she was weak as a child – she lost her identity – her very way of life swallowed up in that of another."

"Henry Hastings" and "Caroline Vernon" are stories of emerging female sexuality that explore two quite different possibilities for women. Brontë's writing style and use of fairy-tale motifs and romantic landscapes become finely tuned in these last two tales, where Africa seems to melt away into the familiar moors and country houses of England. Henry Hastings was created by Branwell, on his return from London in 1837, as another of his many soldiers, but with a significant difference: Henry is a "dissipated and drunken mushroom." As Moglen points out, Branwell projected onto Henry's own "growing guilt and impotence as well as his alienation from his family."

Like *her* creator, Elizabeth Hastings is young "but not handsome," with "a fair, rather wan complexion, dark hair smoothly combed in two plain folds from her forehead. . . ." Her expression is "fixed and dreamy." Her state of mind is mirrored in the painting of the Sleeping Beauty, a device that Brontë also uses in *Jane Eyre*. Elizabeth is as devoted to her degenerate brother as any of Zamorna's women are to him, but Elizabeth makes a decision to help her brother; she is not driven to do so by an uncontrollable passion. Henry is Branwell, the brother for whom everything is sacrificed: "The man had wasted his vigour and his youth in vice, there was more to repel than charm in the dark fiery eye stuck far below the brow, an aspect marked with the various lines of suffering, passion, and profligacy. Yet there were the remnants of a strong and steady young frame, a bold martial bearing in proud, confident, and ready action, which in better days had won him smiles from eyes he adored like a fanatic." William Percy, the son of Alexander Percy, one of the men who is pursuing Henry for deserting the army, is surprised and upset by his attraction to Elizabeth; she is too plain to warrant such feelings. When Henry is captured, Elizabeth pleads for his pardon; but Henry informs on his fellow deserters and is reinstated into the army as a private. Elizabeth opens a school that becomes successful, but she still thinks of William and he of her. Finally he contrives to meet her "accidentally." On a mild afternoon Elizabeth takes a walk in the country, as she does quite often. She is as "happy as she was capable of being except when now and then scared by hearing the remote and angry low of a great Girnington bull which haunted these parts. . . . By the gate post lay a gentlemanly-looking hat and a pair of gloves, with a spaniel coiled up beside them, as if keeping guard." Maynard points out the sexual implications of the juxtaposition of images: the bull and the gentleman can be seen as one.

She meets William and consents to walk with him. They come to the graveyard at Scar Church, where they confess their feelings for each other. But instead of proposing marriage, William asks Elizabeth to be his mistress; she refuses. The lovers come to the grave of Lady Rosamund, a former ward of Arthur's who became his mistress, was spurned by him, and is believed to have killed herself. The only readable word on her headstone is *RESURGAM*. It is a warning that Elizabeth should not love as Lady Rosamund did: "not wisely, but too well." She flees William, leaving him alone with "church and graves and tree, all mute as death, Lady Rosamund's tomb alone proclaiming in the moonlight, 'I shall rise.' "

The ending of "Henry Hastings" returns the reader to the elite of Angrian society. Zenobia com-

plains about Alexander Percy's affairs, and Mary is once again fooled by her husband into believing that he is hers alone. While unity of plot is sacrificed, unity of theme is not. Elizabeth escaped the clutches of William Percy through her personal integrity, but the rest of the characters continue to wallow in the mire of sexual power and its opposite, complete submission.

The themes of awakening passion and of the exploitation of passion are never more clearly seen in Brontë's early writings than they are in the last of them, "Caroline Vernon," a story with overtly sexual symbolism. Caroline Vernon was introduced to the duke of Zamorna in "Julia" as an eleven-year-old with a "foreign wildness." Now, at fifteen, she is a budding beauty and his ward. Her father, Alexander Percy, has taken little interest in his illegitimate offspring, but when Quashia Quamina writes to ask for her hand in marriage he decides to visit Arthur and his other daughter, Mary, at their country estate. His intention is to establish Caroline in sophisticated society by sending her to France for an education.

Zamorna retains his Byronic qualities in this story, but his evil nature is intensified. He still looks at women as prizes, but Northangerland's plans for Caroline upset him: "If your fear is that Caroline will not have beauty sufficient to attract licentiousness, & imagination warm enough to understand approaches – to meet them & kindle at them, & a mind & passions strong enough to carry her a long way in the career of dissipation if she once enters it – set yourself at rest, for she is or will be fit for all this & much more." Caroline is on the verge of womanhood, and the tale, which uses symbolism based on the story of Eve's temptation in the Book of Genesis, is the story of her fall: "Oh, human nature! human nature! & Oh, inexperience! in what an obscure, dim unconscious dream Miss Vernon was enveloped – How little she knew of herself – However, time is advancing & the hours, those 'wild-eyed Charioteers' as Shelley calls them – are driving on – She will gather knowledge by degrees – She is one of the Gleaners of Grapes in that Vineyard – where all man & woman-kind – have been plucking fruit since the world began, the Vineyard of Experience."

In Paris Caroline learns the true reputation of her guardian, and she longs to see him again. After about four months, she returns to Verdopolis, where her father sets her up in the symbolically named Eden Cottage. She writes to Arthur, hoping that he will rescue her from her boredom. His reception of her letter is a good example of Brontë's

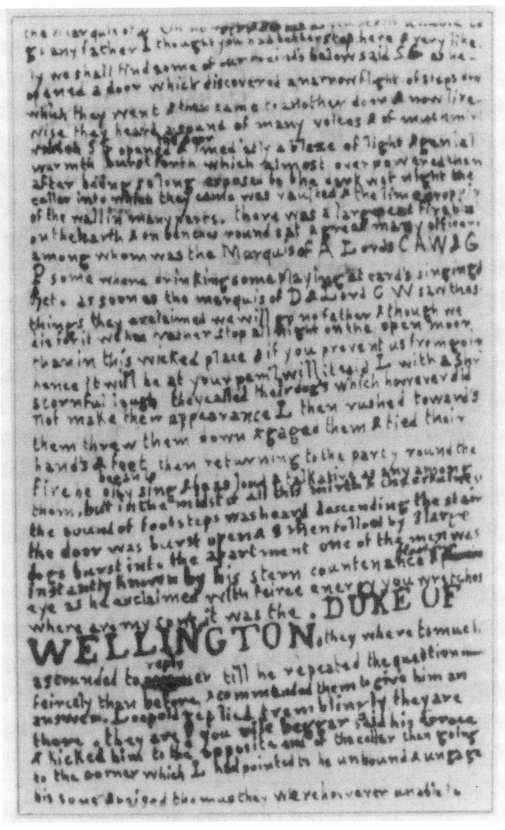

*Page from the manuscript for chapter 4 of the first volume of Brontë's "Tales of the Islanders" (Henry W. and Albert A. Berg Collection, New York Public Library, Astor, Lenox and Tilden Foundations)*

developing mastery of symbol: "He turned it over & examined the superscription & seal – it was a prettily-folded, satin-paper production – nicely addressed & sealed with the impression of a Cameo – His Grace cracked the pretty classic head – unfolded the document & read." The broken (maiden)head foreshadows Caroline's fate.

Caroline, waiting for his reply, is becoming painfully aware of her growing love for him: "I can't go to sleep, I'm so hot and restless – I could bear now to see a spirit come to my bed-side and ask me what I wanted – wicked or not wicked, I would tell all – and beg it to give me the power to make Duke of Zamorna like me better than ever he liked any body in the world before. . . ." His letter finally arrives, with an invitation to write to him again if she is indeed so miserable. Instead, she boards a coach headed for Zamorna's estate. At Wood-house-Cliff, Zamorna appears before her as "Satan's eldest Son" and says: "If I were a bearded Turk, Caroline, I would take you to my Harem." Though she is frightened, Caroline cannot pull away from her pursuer; as he caresses her and plays with the dark curls at her neck, "Caroline began to feel a new impression – She no longer wished to leave him, she clung to his side – infatuation was stealing over her – The thought of separation or a return to Eden was dreadful. . . ." Caroline agrees to accompany Arthur to a "hidden retreat" in Angria whose outside is plain but whose inside has "rooms . . . as splendid as any saloon in Victoria-Square." Arthur calls it his "treasure-house": Caroline is now another of his possessions.

In March 1839 Brontë received a proposal of marriage from Henry Nussey, a curate in Sussex and the brother of her friend from Roe Head School, Ellen Nussey. She refused him, explaining to Ellen Nussey in words that could have been spoken by Mary Wellesley or Mina Laury: "I had a kindly leaning towards him, because he is an amiable and well-disposed man. Yet I had not, and could not have, that intense attachment which would make me willing to die for him; and if ever I marry, it must be in that light of adoration that I will regard my husband." Brontë's advice to Ellen on the latter's impending marriage, only a year after her own refusal of Ellen's brother, takes the opposite view: "No young woman should fall in love till the offer has been made, accepted – the marriage ceremony performed and the first half year of wedded life passed away – a woman may then begin to love, but with great precaution – very cooly – very moderately – very rationally – if she ever loves so much that a harsh word or a cold look from her husband

cuts her to the heart – she is a fool – if she ever loves so much that her husband's will is her law – and that she has got into a habit of watching his looks in order that she may anticipate his wishes she will soon be a neglected fool. . . ." What reality presented for women in marriage and what Brontë demanded were clearly different. She must have realized that it was impossible both to feel unbridled passion and to maintain one's individuality, yet she was obsessed by the idea and continued to write about it throughout her adult life. In August 1839 James Bryce, an Irish curate "fresh from Dublin University," proposed to Brontë shortly after their first meeting. She rejected this proposal, also; she had resigned herself to being an old maid.

At the end of 1839 Brontë wrote what critics refer to as her "Farewell to Angria." The piece expresses her determination to move forward as a writer and "quit for awhile that burning clime where we have sojourned too long – its skies flame – the glow of sunset is always upon it – the mind would cease from excitement and turn now to a cooler region where the dawn breaks grey and sober, and the coming day for a time at least is subdued by clouds." She pleads with her imaginary reader not to "urge me too fast: it is not easy to dismiss from my imagination the images which have filled it so long; they were my friends and my intimate acquaintances . . . who peopled my thoughts by day, and not seldom stole strangely even into my dreams by night." Some critics say that guilt motivated her to dismiss Angria; others hold that she was running from a dangerous obsession; but most simply see in this decision the natural progression of a writer who chooses to move on to more profitable material.

Soon after completing "Caroline Vernon," Brontë began "Ashworth," a story reminiscent of the juvenilia. Here Alexander Percy becomes Alexander Ashworth, a Yorkshire industrialist. His sons, Edward and William, who have been disowned by their father, have disparate personalities that foreshadow the Crimsworth brothers of *The Professor* (1857). The plot of "Ashworth" takes a turn at the end of chapter 2, focusing on Alexander Ashworth's daughter Mary's school in London rather than on the Ashworth men. Autobiography plays a major role as Brontë recalls her days at Roe Head; the result is a more realistic portrait than any in the juvenilia.

Only four chapters of "Ashworth" exist. In April 1840 Brontë wrote to Hartley Coleridge, asking for his advice on her work. His reply must have been sobering. She answered him on 10 December

1840, saying that she would write no more until she had something specific to say.

In March 1841 Brontë became governess for Mr. and Mrs. John White of Rawdon. In December she came back to Haworth to plan a school that she, Emily, and Anne had been talking about for some time. With financial help from Aunt Branwell, Charlotte and Emily went off to the Pensionnat Heger in Brussels to improve their foreign-language skills. Teaching was the fate of unmarried women with little money, but with a school of their own the Brontës might finally become their own masters and less of a burden to their family. Emily never felt at home in the Hegers' school, but Charlotte found great joy in being a "schoolgirl" again and soon won the respect and affection of Mme Claire Zoé Parent Heger, the school's headmistress, and her husband, Constantin, who taught many of Charlotte's classes. The Hegers offered the Brontë sisters extra schooling in exchange for teaching services: Emily would teach music, and Charlotte would teach English. What was for Charlotte an extremely satisfying arrangement came to an abrupt end in October 1842: Aunt Branwell had died, and the girls were summoned home. Charlotte returned alone to Brussels in January 1843.

Having no sisterly companionship, Brontë spent more time with M. Heger, giving him private lessons in English; Heger, impressed by her intelligence and dedication, showed her a great deal of affection. While Brontë's strict Christian upbringing would not have allowed her even to contemplate an affair with a married man, she may have begun to fantasize about Heger, bestowing on him the qualities she found so irresistible in her hero Arthur Wellesley, duke of Zamorna. Mme Heger did not view the relationship as innocent, however; she became cold and formal toward Brontë and reduced the latter's interaction with her husband. Brontë, feeling the intense loneliness that would later plague her heroine Lucy Snowe, began to escape back into that "world below." She returned home in January 1844. For the next two years she wrote to Heger, begging for some correspondence as a sign that he still cared for her. The letters ring with obsession and echoes of her own Angrian heroines. Meanwhile, her father had become increasingly dependent on her as his eyesight failed and his health deteriorated; her brother, so full of promise during their childhood, had continued to decline, becoming an alcoholic and a drug addict – a constant burden on the family. The Brontë sisters resurrected their plan of opening a school and began seeking potential pupils in July 1844, but when no students had

inquired by the end of the year they abandoned the idea.

In the fall of 1845 Charlotte came across some poems written by Emily; Anne, she soon discovered, had also been writing poetry. Using part of their inheritance from Aunt Branwell, the sisters paid the London publishing firm Aylott and Jones £36 10s. to cover the costs of paper, printing, and advertising *Poems by Currer, Ellis and Acton Bell* (1846). The book sold only two copies by 1847, but its publication had inspired the three women to pursue writing careers. In 1846 each sister wrote a novel: Charlotte, *The Professor;* Emily, *Wuthering Heights;* and Anne, *Agnes Grey*. Their intention was to present the three works to publishers as a set, a popular format at that time. In July 1847, however, Thomas Cautley Newby agreed to publish only two of them; *The Professor* was rejected and would not appear in print during Charlotte's lifetime.

*The Professor* is filled with Angrian elements: there are the rival brothers, Edward and William Crimsworth; the male narrator; and the orphaned child. Scenes of romance and seduction are set in gardens, paralleling the garden scenes and biblical overtones of temptation and fall in "Henry Hastings" and "Caroline Vernon." The character Zoraide Reuter is a version of Zenobia. Hoping to capture William's heart, Zoraide leads him to a garden and offers herself in the same way Zenobia tried to win Arthur in "The Rivals": "There was at once a sort of low gratification in receiving this luscious incense from an attractive and still young worshipper; and an irritating sense of degradation in the very experience of the pleasure. When she stole about me with the soft step of a slave, I felt at once barbarous and sensual as a pasha." Critics cite awkwardness of plot and lack of action as main flaws in *The Professor,* but as Margaret Blom points out, "the amazing thing is not . . . that Charlotte failed at this stage of her career to smooth out the rough edges as she struggled to join Angria and reality, but that she was able to use remnants of the Angrian saga as effectively as she did to illuminate psychological truth."

While *The Professor* was making its unsuccessful rounds of the publishers, Charlotte accompanied her father to Manchester, where he was to undergo cataract surgery. There she filled three lonely and depressing weeks by writing *Jane Eyre*. Familiar Angrian characters return once again: Elizabeth Hastings becomes Jane Eyre; the duke of Zamorna is toned down a bit into Edward Rochester, who is humanized by his need for love and forgiveness near the novel's end; and Bertha Rochester is a combination of Zenobia and the imprisoned hag in "The Green Dwarf." Here Brontë explored again the relationship between men and women of different social classes — one of the most disturbing elements to her contemporary audience — and the power of uncontrolled and controlling passion. Jane could become Rochester's possession if she marries him on his first proposal, just as Mina Laury and Caroline Vernon became Zamorna's. Jane's need to retain her identity is a common struggle for Brontë heroines. Unlike Elizabeth Hastings, however, who must reach an "either/or" decision, Jane is able to reject a life without love and passion offered by St. James Rivers, a later version of Fidena of "Lily Hart," and form a partnership with Rochester in which she is more his keeper than his wife.

Still using the pseudonym Currer Bell, Brontë sent her manuscript to William Smith Williams, reader for Smith, Elder of London, who hurried it to press with great enthusiasm. Positive response to *Jane Eyre* was immediate on its publication in October 1847. Yet, as was always the case in the lives of the Brontës, happiness was short-lived. On 24 September 1848 Branwell died; Emily fell ill after attending her brother's funeral in a cold, heavy rain and died on 19 December. Exhibiting symptoms similar to her sister's, Anne was seen by a doctor in January 1849 and pronounced fatally ill. In an attempt to cheer her, Charlotte and Ellen Nussey took her to Scarborough, where she died on 28 May. Her second novel, *The Tenant of Wildfell Hall*, was published the following month.

Charlotte's next novel was published by Smith, Elder on 26 October 1849. *Shirley* brings recent history, current politics, and shadows of Angria together in the story of Caroline Helstone and Shirley Keeldar. As industrialization comes to the mill towns of Yorkshire, Brontë's heroines struggle, as always, with unrequited love, debilitating passion, and the danger of losing their identities through their love for the men who wish to control them. According to Gaskell, Brontë "fancied that there were fewer traces of a female pen in [*Shirley*] than in *Jane Eyre*; thus, when the earliest reviews were published and asserted that the mysterious writer must be a woman, she was much disappointed. She especially disliked the lowering of the standard by which to judge a work of fiction, if it proceeded from a feminine pen; and praise mingled with pseudo-gallant allusion to her sex mortified her far more than actual blame." In the end, a man who had grown up in Haworth published in a Liverpool newspaper his deduction that Charlotte Brontë was Currer Bell. Ironically, just as in her stories, a man was destroying a woman's identity against her will — even if that identity was a falsely masculine one.

On visits to her publishers in London between 1849 to 1851 Brontë met William Makepeace Thackeray, to whom she dedicated the second edition of *Jane Eyre;* Harriet Martineau; Matthew Arnold; and her future biographer, Gaskell. She attended lectures and went to the theater, but as she wrote to Nussey: "You seem to think me in such a happy, enviable position; pleasant moments I have, but it is usually a pleasure I am obliged to repel and check, which cannot benefit the future, but only add to its solitude, which is no more to be relied on than the sunshine of one summer's day. I pass portions of many a night in extreme sadness." In Haworth she fulfilled her commitment to her publishers for another novel by writing *Villette,* which is now considered her masterpiece. During this time there was a marriage proposal from James Taylor, an employee of the Smith, Elder firm, but she rejected him as she had the others. *Villette* chronicles the life of Lucy Snowe from her fourteenth year through her adult life as she becomes a teacher at the Pensionnat de Demoiselles and eventually has her own school. There are hints of Zenobia in Madame Beck; of Mary Percy, Elizabeth Hastings, or even the cynical social critic Charles Townsend (the former Lord Charles Wellesley) in Lucy herself; of Caroline Vernon in Paulina Home; and of the duke of Zamorna in John Graham. But the "burning clime" of Brontë's childhood imagination is further removed. Emotions that were acted out in high drama and even violent action in the tales of Angria are tamed and crafted in *Villette*. Brontë's world of Angria has been transformed into a precise study of the inner and outer worlds of Lucy Snowe.

Writing *Villette* was an emotional strain for Brontë because it forced her to engage in so much self-exploration, but also because it was the first book she wrote totally alone. None of the other Brontë children were left to be her audience; the circle they "drew around themselves" was broken. Also, though *Villette* was a success on its publication on 28 January 1853, it caused a cooling of Brontë's relationship with her publisher, George Smith. She had used Smith and his mother as models for two major characters, Dr. John Bretton and his mother; Smith had requested that Brontë alter the work, but she had refused.

Unrelated to the publication of *Villette* was a new problem in Brontë's life: yet another suitor was asking for her hand in marriage. Nicholls, an Irish curate under her father's direction, had proposed in

*Pencil drawing by Brontë, circa 1836, of Mary Henrietta Percy, Duchess of Zamorna, at her country estate, Alnwick*
*(Brontë Society)*

December 1852. The proposal placed Brontë in somewhat the same predicament as that of one of her favorite Angrian heroines, Mary Percy: Mr. Brontë was enraged by the proposal. For that reason, and because she did not love him as she believed a woman should love the man she marries, she rejected Nicholls's proposal; but as he left the parsonage after giving Mr. Brontë his resignation, Charlotte was moved by his apparent suffering to agree to correspond with him behind her father's back — the first time that she had ever committed such an act of deception. Thus, as Mary Percy strove to keep peace between Northangerland and Zamorna, Brontë tried to keep both her father and Nicholls satisfied, at great expense to her own peace of mind.

In 1853 Brontë began two books, neither of which she finished. "The Story of Willie Ellin" returns to the theme of rival brothers, one good, one bad; "Emma" returns to the setting of a girls' boarding school. Both fragments contain the ever-present theme of the orphaned child struggling with loss of identity. "Emma" would be published posthumously in the *Cornhill Magazine* in April 1860.

In April 1854 Brontë and Nicholls announced their engagement. Mr. Brontë, however reluctantly,

gave his consent, and Charlotte and Nicholls were married on 29 June 1854; the ceremony was small and quiet, at Charlotte's request. After a brief honeymoon in Wales and Ireland, the couple returned to Haworth. Nicholls continued as Mr. Brontë's curate, and Charlotte kept house for both men. As time passed, Charlotte warmed to the stern Irish curate who had fallen in love with her. Long-term happiness, however, was to elude her, as it had all her life. On a cold, wet walk with her husband in January 1855 she caught a cold that soon developed into "perpetual nausea, and ever-recurring faintness." Scholars assume from the doctor's diagnosis of "a natural cause" that she was in the early stages of pregnancy. Her fragile constitution could not tolerate the combined stresses of illness and pregnancy, and by March she was drifting in and out of a stupor; in a fleeting lucid moment she heard her husband praying for God to spare her and remarked: "Oh! I am not going to die, am I? He will not separate us, we have been so happy." She died on 31 March 1855, Easter eve.

Nicholls remained at Haworth to look after Charlotte's father and to carry on his duties at the church. When Mr. Brontë died in June 1861, Nicholls returned to his native Ireland, where he remarried in 1864. When Nicholls died on 2 December 1906 his wife had his coffin placed beneath the portrait of Charlotte by George Richmond (now in the National Gallery), which had hung in his house since his return from Haworth.

Charlotte Brontë will be remembered as a novelist; *Jane Eyre* and *Villette* will remain her crowning achievements. Some critics, such as Ratchford, contend that Brontë merely revised her early stories to create her great novels. Others, such as Kathleen Tillotson, see the Angria writings as an obsession with fantasy that had to be overcome before it became all-consuming. Tom Winnifrith regards the juvenilia as simply bad, childish writing and any attempt to bring it into the realm of literary criticism as unwarranted and unnecessary. But Brontë's short early writings are important, if for no other reason, William Holtz explains, than that "as we contemplate . . . the achieved power of *Jane Eyre* and *Villette,* we must recognize that they did not spring unprecedented from a mind turned late to fiction. Rather they are the culmination of a passionate life of writing," casting "long shadows forward toward her mature works."

**Letters:**

*The Brontës: Life and Letters,* 2 volumes, edited by Clement Shorter (London: Hodder & Stoughton, 1908; New York: Haskell House, 1969);
*The Brontës: Their Lives, Friendships and Correspondence,* 4 volumes, edited by Thomas J. Wise and John A. Symington (Oxford: Blackwell, 1932);
*The Letters of the Brontës: A Selection,* edited by Muriel Spark (Norman: University of Oklahoma Press, 1954).

**Bibliographies:**

Thomas J. Wise, *A Bibliography of the Writings in Prose and Verse of the Members of the Brontë Family* (London: Clay, 1917);
G. Anthony Yablon and John R. Turner, *A Brontë Bibliography* (London: Hodgkins, 1978; Westport, Conn.: Meckler, 1978);
R. W. Crump, *Charlotte and Emily Brontë, 1846–1915: A Reference Guide* (Boston: G. K. Hall, 1982).

**Biographies:**

Elizabeth Cleghorn Gaskell, *The Life of Charlotte Brontë,* third edition, revised, 2 volumes (London: Smith, Elder, 1857);

Winifred Gérin, *Charlotte Brontë: The Evolution of Genius* (Oxford: Clarendon Press, 1967);
Rebecca Fraser, *The Brontës: Charlotte Brontë and Her Family* (New York: Crown, 1988);
Lyndall Gordon, *Charlotte Brontë: A Passionate Life* (London: Chatto & Windus, 1994; New York: Norton, 1995);
Juliet Barker, *The Brontës* (New York: St. Martin's Press, 1995).

**References:**

Christine Alexander, *The Early Writings of Charlotte Brontë* (Oxford: Blackwell, 1983);
Phyllis Bentley, *The Brontës and Their World* (London: Thames & Hudson, 1969);
Margaret Blom, *Charlotte Brontë* (Boston: Twayne, 1977);
Sandra M. Gilbert and Susan Gubar, *The Madwoman in the Attic: The Woman Writer and the Nineteenth-Century Literary Imagination* (New Haven: Yale University Press, 1984);
John Maynard, *Charlotte Brontë and Sexuality* (New York: Cambridge University Press, 1984);
Helen Moglen, *Charlotte Brontë: The Self Conceived* (New York: Norton, 1976);
Fannie E. Ratchford, *The Brontës' Web of Childhood* (New York: Columbia University Press, 1941);
Philip Rhodes, "A Medical Appraisal of the Brontës," *Brontë Society Transactions,* 16, no. 2 (1972): 101–109;
Kathleen Tillotson, *Novels of the Eighteen-Forties* (Oxford: Clarendon Press, 1954);
Tom Winnifrith, *The Brontës and Their Background: Romance and Reality* (London: Macmillan, 1973).

**Papers:**

Important manuscript holdings of Charlotte Brontë's prose writings are at the British Library; the Brontë Parsonage Museum, Haworth; Harvard College Library; the Harry Ransom Humanities Research Center, University of Texas at Austin; the Huntington Library, San Marino, California; the New York Public Library; Princeton University Library; the Pierpont Morgan Library, New York City; the University of Missouri at Columbia Library; and the Brotherton Library, Leeds.

# William Carleton

*(4 March 1794 – 30 January 1869)*

Thomas L. Blanton
*Central Washington University*

BOOKS: *Father Butler; The Lough Dearg Pilgrim: Being Sketches of Irish Manners,* anonymous (Dublin: Curry, 1829); republished as *Father Butler, Or Sketches of Irish Manners* (Philadelphia: Latimer, 1834);

*Traits and Stories of the Irish Peasantry,* anonymous, 2 volumes (Dublin: Curry, 1830; revised edition, Dublin: Curry / London: Simpkin & Marshall / Edinburgh: Oliver & Boyd, 1832); republished as *Traits and Stories of the Irish Peasantry: First Series* (Philadelphia & Baltimore: Carey & Hart, 1833; revised edition, Dublin: Wakeman / London: Simpkin & Marshall and Rich. Groombridge, 1834); republished as *Traits and Stories of the Irish Peasantry. In Two Volumes. By William Carleton. Fourth Edition, Corrected* (Dublin: Wakeman / London: Simpkin & Marshall and Rich. Groombridge, 1835);

*Traits and Stories of the Irish Peasantry: Second Series,* anonymous, 3 volumes (Dublin: Wakeman / London: Simpkin & Marshall and R. Groombridge, 1833; Philadelphia: Carey & Hart / Baltimore: Carey, Hart, 1833);

*Tales of Ireland,* as the Author of "Traits and Stories of the Irish Peasantry" (Dublin: Curry / London: Simpkin & Marshall, 1834);

*Popular Tales and Legends of the Irish Peasantry,* by Carleton, Anna Maria Hall, and "Denis O'Donoho" (Dublin: Wakeman, 1834) – includes Carleton's "Laying a Ghost" and "Alley Sheridan, or the Runaway Marriage";

*Traits and Stories of the Irish Peasantry: Fourth Edition,* 5 volumes (London: Baldwin & Cradock / Dublin: Wakeman, 1836);

*Fardorougha the Miser; or, The Convicts of Lisnamona* (Dublin: Curry, 1839); republished as *The Miser; or, The Convicts of Lisnamona,* 2 volumes (Philadelphia: Carey & Hart, 1840);

*Neal Malone, and Other Tales of Ireland,* 2 volumes (Philadelphia: Carey & Hart, 1839);

*Characteristic Sketches of Ireland and the Irish: By Carleton, Lover, and Mrs. Hall,* by Carleton, Hall,

*William Carleton; detail from a painting in the possession of his family (Hulton Deutsch Collection)*

and Samuel Lover (Dublin: Hardy & Walker / London: Ball, Arnold, 1840); republished as *Tales and Stories of Ireland. By Carleton, Lover and Mrs. Hall* (Halifax: Milner & Sowerby, 1852);

*The Fawn of Spring-Vale, The Clarionet, And Other Tales,* 3 volumes (Dublin: Curry / London: Longmans, 1841); republished as *Jane Sinclair; or, The Fawn of Spring-Vale, The Clarionet, and Other Tales,* 3 volumes (Dublin: Curry / London: Routledge, 1843); republished as *Jane Sinclair; or, The Fawn of Spring-Vale; and the Dark Day* (London: Routledge, 1849); republished as *Jane Sinclair, Neal Malone, &c. &c.* (London: Routledge, 1850);

*Traits and Stories of the Irish Peasantry: A New Edition. With an Autobiographical Introduction, Illustrative Notes and Graphic Illustrations, on Wood and Steel by Phiz., Harvey, MacManus and Franklin* (23 parts, Dublin: Curry, 1842–1844; republished in 2 volumes, 1843, 1844);

*Valentine M'Clutchy, The Irish Agent: or, Chronicles of the Castle Cumber Property,* 3 volumes (Dublin: Duffy / London: Chapman & Hall, 1845; New York: Sadlier, 1846; Edinburgh: Oliver & Boyd, 1846); republished as *Valentine M'Clutchy, The Irish Agent; or, The Chronicles of Castle Cumber; Together With the Pious Aspirations, Permissions, Vouch-safements, and Other Sanctified Privileges of Solomon M'Slime, A Religious Attorney,* 1 volume (Dublin: Duffy, 1847; New York & Montreal: Sadlier, 1876);

*Denis O'Shaughnessy Going to Maynooth* (London: Routledge, 1845);

*Tales and Sketches, Illustrating the Character, Usages, Traditions, Sports and Pastimes of the Irish Peasantry* (Dublin: Duffy, 1845); republished as *Tales and Stories of the Irish Peasantry* (Dublin: Duffy, 1846; New York & Boston: Sadlier, 1860);

*Art Maguire; or, The Broken Pledge: A Narrative* (Dublin: Duffy, 1845; New York & Montreal: Sadlier, 1846);

*Rody the Rover; or, the Ribbonman* (Dublin: Duffy, 1845; New York: Beadle & Adams, 1881);

*Parra Sastha; or, the History of Paddy Go-easy and His Wife Nancy* (Dublin: Duffy, 1845; Boston: Donahoe, 1865); enlarged as *Parra Sastha; or, the History of Paddy Go-easy and His Wife Nancy. To Which Is Added Rose Moan, The Irish Midwife* (Dublin: Duffy, n.d.);

*The Black Prophet: A Tale of Irish Famine* (London: Simms & M'Intyre, 1847; New York: Burgess, Stringer, 1847);

*The Poor Scholar: A Pathetic Story of Irish Life* (New York: Wilkinson, 1847); republished as *The Poor Scholar and Other Tales of Irish Life* (New York, Boston & Montreal: Sadlier, 1854);

*The Emigrants of Ahadarra: A Tale of Irish Life* (London & Belfast: Simms and M'Intyre, 1848); republished as *The Emigrants: A Tale of Irish Life* (London & New York: Routledge, 1857);

*The Tithe Proctor: A Novel. Being a Tale of the Tithe Rebellion in Ireland* (London & Belfast: Simms & M'Intyre, 1849); republished as *The Tithe-Proctor: A Novel* (London & New York: Routledge, 1857);

*The Clarionet, the Dead Boxer, and Barney Branaghan* (London: Routledge, 1850);

*The Squanders of Castle Squander,* 2 volumes (London: Office of the Illustrated London Library, 1852);

*Red Hall; or, The Baronet's Daughter,* 3 volumes (London: Saunders & Otley, 1852); republished as *The Black Baronet: or, The Chronicles of Ballytrain*

(Dublin: Duffy, 1858; Boston: Donahoe, 1869);

*Willy Reilly and His Dear Coleen Bawn: A Tale, Founded upon Fact,* 3 volumes (London: Hope, 1855; Boston: Moore, 1856);

*Alley Sheridan, and Other Stories* (Dublin: Hardy, 1857);

*The Evil Eye; or, the Black Spectre: A Romance* (Dublin: Duffy, 1860; New York & Montreal: Sadlier, 1875);

*The Double Prophecy; or, Trials of the Heart,* 2 volumes (London & Dublin: Duffy, 1862);

*Redmond Count O'Hanlon, the Irish Rapparee, An Historical Tale* (Dublin & London: Duffy, 1862; New York & Montreal: Sadlier, 1875);

*The Silver Acre, and Other Tales* (London: Ward & Lock, 1862);

*Tales and Stories of the Irish Peasantry* (New York, Boston & Montreal: Sadlier, 1864);

*Tubber Derg; or, the Red Well, and Other Tales of Irish Life* (New York, Boston & Montreal: Sadlier, 1866);

*The Poor Scholar, Frank Martin and the Fairies, The Country Dancing Master, and Other Irish Tales* (Dublin & London: Duffy, 1869);

*Barney Brady's Goose; The Hedge School; The Three Tasks, and Other Irish Tales* (Dublin & London: Duffy, 1869);

*Tubber Derg; or, The Red Well; Party Fight and Funeral; Dandy Kehoe's Christening, and Other Irish Tales* (Dublin & London: Duffy, 1869);

*The Fair of Emyvale, and the Master and Scholar: Tales* (London: Ward, Lock & Tyler, 1870);

*The Works of William Carleton* (3 volumes, New York: Collier, 1881; reprinted, 2 volumes, New York: Books for Libraries Press, 1970);

*Amusing Irish Tales* (London: Hamilton, Adams / Glasgow: Morison, 1889);

*The Red-Haired Man's Wife* (Dublin: Sealy, Bryers & Walker / London: Simpkin, Marshall, 1889);

*Stories from Carleton: With an Introduction by W. B. Yeats* (London: Walter Scott / New York & Toronto: Gage, 1889);

*The Life of William Carleton: Being His Autobiography and Letters; and an Account of His Life and Writings, From the Point at Which the Autobiography Breaks Off, by David J. O'Donoghue. With an Introduction by Mrs. Cashel Hoey,* 2 volumes (London: Downey, 1896);

*Irish Tales by William Carleton. With a Biographical Introduction by W. B. Yeats* (New York & London: Putnam, 1904).

**Editions:** *The Autobiography of William Carleton,* preface by Patrick Kavanagh (London: Mac-Gibbon & Kee, 1968);

*Father Butler; The Lough Dearg Pilgrim* (New York & London: Garland, 1979);

*Traits and Stories of the Irish Peasantry,* 2 volumes (New York & London: Garland, 1979);

*Traits and Stories of the Irish Peasantry: Second Series,* 3 volumes (New York & London: Garland, 1979);

*Tales of Ireland* (New York: Garland, 1979);

*Fardorougha the Miser* (New York & London: Garland, 1979);

*The Fawn of Spring-Vale,* 3 volumes (New York & London: Garland, 1979);

*Valentine M'Clutchy, the Irish Agent* (New York & London: Garland, 1979);

*The Black Prophet* (New York & London: Garland, 1979);

*The Emigrants of Ahadarra* (New York & London: Garland, 1979);

*The Tithe Proctor* (New York & London: Garland, 1979);

*Tales and Sketches Illustrating the Character of the Irish Peasantry* (New York & London: Garland, 1980);

*Traits and Stories of the Irish Peasantry,* 2 volumes (Gerrards Cross: Smythe / New York: Barnes & Noble, 1990).

William Carleton was a storyteller first and last. Unlike other Irish literary nationalists of the nineteenth century, he did not look for his true subject in the distant past — in nostalgia or in the rich folklore and mythology of an ancient island culture. Nor was his voice simply that of the traditional Gaelic *seannachie* (teller of old tales and traditions). More literary journalist than ethnographer, he sought in his stories to re-create the rural Ireland of his youth. His artistic creed was realism, which for him meant the faithful and authentic portrayal of the people, places, and activities of a world that, by the time he began to write, was already disappearing. In re-creating his own life in story he found the surest way to preserve that vanishing world for the future.

In his autobiography (1896) Carleton recalls the time in his youth when, on a visit to his eldest sister, his fortune was told by a "Scotch gipsy": "She was cunning enough to draw from my sister . . . all the information she could gain respecting my prospects in life, and so learned that I was intended for the priesthood. . . . I remember the words as distinctly as if I had heard them only yesterday. 'He will never be a priest,' said she, 'he will love the

girls too well; but when he grows up, he will go to Dublin, and become a great man.' "

The youngest of fourteen children, Carleton was born on 4 March 1794 in the Clogher Valley in Prillisk, County Tyrone, Northern Ireland. His parents, James Carleton and Mary Kelly, poor Catholics, were able to offer him no hope for a future beyond the impoverished life of the Irish peasantry. They did, however, give him nonmaterial gifts that would enable him to rise from rural poverty to the genteel poverty of a writer in Dublin and to fame as one of Ireland's best-known and most widely read writers of the day. From his parents he gained a love for the Irish language during a childhood of listening to the stories and songs of his people. Carleton would leave his rural home; but unlike Jonathan Swift, who left Ireland to become part of the London literary scene, Carleton would never leave his homeland. Like Swift, Carleton would address the plight of the Irish poor; but while Swift's writing reflected his moral outrage, Carleton's motivation for writing about his own people would never be so clear or so selfless. At different times he would attack both Catholics and Protestants, both Irish nationalism and British rule. He writes that his father had a prodigious memory that was "a perfect storehouse, and a rich one, of all that the social antiquary, the man of letters, the poet, or the musician, would consider valuable. As a teller of old tales, legends, and historical anecdotes he was unrivaled, and his stock of them was inexhaustible. He spoke the Irish and English languages with nearly equal fluency. With all kinds of charms, old ranns, or poems, old prophecies, religious superstitions, tales of pilgrims, miracles, and pilgrimages, anecdotes of blessed priests and friars, revelations from ghosts and fairies, was he thoroughly acquainted." All of these Carleton "heard . . . as often in the Irish language as in the English, if not oftener: a circumstance which enabled me in my writings to transfer the genius, the idiomatic peculiarity and conversational spirit of one language into the other, precisely as the people themselves do in their dialogues, whenever the heart or imagination happens to be moved by the darker or better passions."

His mother "possessed the sweetest and most exquisite of voices" and was someone "whose presence at a wake, dance, or other festive occasion, was sure to attract crowds of persons . . . in order to hear from her lips the touching old airs of their country." She was not as fluent in English as her husband was, "and for this reason, among others, she generally gave the old Irish versions of the songs in question, rather than the English ones."

She was directly a part of the native lyric tradition since "some of her immediate ancestors composed in the Irish tongue, several fine old songs, in the same manner as Carolan did. . . . For this reason she had many old compositions that were almost peculiar to our family." In addition to her renown as a singer of "the old sacred songs and airs of Ireland," she was famous for "giving the Irish cry," or keen for the dead.

In contrast to the "domestic advantages" provided him by his parents is the story Carleton tells of his frustration at not being able to receive the education his family desired for him. As the family moved from place to place Carleton would begin school, only to have the opportunity terminated by the abrupt departure of the schoolmaster or the closing of the school. Carleton began his education in a "hedge school" — so named for its temporary location at a roadside or in a farmer's barn — near Prillisk. There followed a succession of rural schools, with gaps of two or three years between periods of attendance. In spite of this discontinuity, Carleton acquired, along with academic knowledge, an education in the religious and political conflicts of his country. He recalls in his autobiography the party fights between Protestants and Catholics and especially the intimidating night raids on Catholic households by militant members of the Orange Society.

His first schoolmaster, Carleton writes, "was the celebrated Pat Frayne, a Connaught man . . . who afterwards sat for the picture of the redoubtable Mat Kavanagh in my sketch of 'The Hedge School.' " In relating an anecdote about Frayne and his charges Carleton introduces the real-life Ned McKeown who at the time "had been reduced to the condition of an egg merchant." It is McKeown whose hearthside provides the setting for the storytelling in the first five stories of Carleton's *Traits and Stories of the Irish Peasantry* (1830). In a note to one of these stories, "The Three Tasks," Carleton observes that "Ned M'Keown was certainly a very remarkable individual, and became, in consequence of his appearance in these pages, a person of considerable notoriety during the latter years of his life. His general character, and the nature of his unsuccessful speculations, I have drawn with great truth. There is only one point alone in which I have done him injustice, and that is in depicting him as a henpecked husband." Carleton explains that his departure from the truth was in retaliation for Ned's not allowing him to join in the athletic activities in the roadway before Ned's house: "For this reason then, and remembering all the vexatious privations of my favourite sports which he occasioned me, I resolved to turn the laugh against him, which I did effectually, by bringing him out in the character of a henpecked husband, which was indeed very decidedly opposed to his real one."

The events behind Carleton's story "The Funeral and Party Fight," which appears in the second volume of *Traits and Stories of the Irish Peasantry,* are from the period following the Irish Rebellion of 1798 and reflect his own experience, as a boy of nine, in witnessing such conflicts between Protestants and Catholics. In his autobiography he relates an anecdote about a performance of *The Battle of Aughrim,* a political play that, like others of its ilk, "inflamed political feeling very much." In Augher "this stupid play was acted by Catholics and Protestants, each part of course sustaining their own principles. The consequence was, that when they came to the conflict with which the play is made to close, armed as they were on both sides with real swords, political and religious resentment could not be restrained, and they would have hacked each other's souls out had not the audience interfered and prevented them. . . . I am now writing not only that which is known to be historical truth, but that which I have witnessed with my own eyes." His story "The Funeral and Party Fight" concludes, "The 'Party Fight,' described in the foregoing sketch, is unhappily no fiction, and it is certain that there are thousands still alive who have good reason to remember it. . . . This tremendous conflict, of which I was an eye-witness, — being then but about twelve years of age — took place in the town or rather city, of Clogher, in my native country of Tyrone. . . . The fair day on which it occurred is known simply as 'the Day of the great Fight.' "

At about seventeen Carleton experienced "the two bitterest calamities" of his early life: the marriage of Anne Duffy, with whom he had fallen in love but whom he could only worship from a distance, and the death of his father. With the loss of his father, his family was "soon on the decline." Feeling "exceedingly anxious to acquire classical knowledge in order to prepare myself for life," he decided to go to Munster as a "poor scholar" and prepare for the Catholic priesthood — the only career that seemed to be available to him. This experience became the basis for his story "The Poor Scholar" (1833). From his time at a "classical school" in Tulnavert he had, in his teacher, a model for the "heartless tyrant" of the story; James Donnelly of his home parish provided the original of the poor scholar. Certain scenes, such as the would-be scholar's separation from his family, are transcriptions of his own experience. For that reason Carleton refers the reader of his autobiography to the story to avoid the need to repeat the details. In the story Carleton explains that "When a lad from the humblest classes resolves to Munster as a poor scholar, there is but one course to be pursued in preparing his outlet. This is by a collection at the chapel among the parishioners, to whom the matter is made known by the priest, from the altar, some Sunday previous to his departure." His journey south, as he relates it, came to an abrupt halt following a dream he interpreted as a sign that he lacked a priestly vocation.

After his abortive journey south he tried to continue his education on his own. In 1814 he went to Glasslough, County Monaghan, where for the next two years he attended a school run by his second cousin, a priest, depending on relatives and friends for lodging and money. Also during this period he joined — without enthusiasm, he insists — the Ribbon Society, a secret Catholic organization.

Having become proficient in Latin, he decided to open his own classical school but abandoned the scheme when it became clear that he could attract only a handful of students. At this time he acquired a local reputation as an athlete, dancer, and "scholar." His scholarship, like that of many of the characters in the stories he would write, was expressed as mock-serious pedantry, delivered histrionically and designed to impress an uneducated — especially female — audience. He describes himself strutting about and "uttering such sesquipedalian and stilted nonsense as was never heard," giving "the girls pompous specimens of my wonderful and profound learning, by repeating for their edification quotations from Greek and Latin, which I translate for them into wrong meanings, indicating a slight but rather significant appreciation on my part of their comeliness and beauty."

His father had frequently entertained the family on winter evenings with stories of "the far-famed purgatory of St. Patrick called Lough Dearg, or the Red Lake, situated in the county of Donegal." In midsummer 1817 Carleton resolved to make a pilgrimage to the lake; in his autobiography he describes his story "The Lough Dearg Pilgrim" (1829) as resembling a "coloured photograph [of his actual journey] more than anything else." He declares that "there is not a fact or incident, or a single penal step of duty . . . which is not detailed with the minuteness of the strictest truth and authenticity." He quotes liberally from the story in the autobiography, including the conclusion, where the narrator discovers that an old woman with whom he was

traveling has taken his clothes and emptied his purse. At that point Carleton asks the reader of the autobiography "whether this does not look very like fiction . . . [since] I daresay it will be considered as such." The fact is, however, that "there is not . . . one syllable of fiction in it," and to prove his point he identifies the old woman as a notorious "shuler," Nell McCallum, who in 1817 lived near Armagh. Carleton is not arguing for the "truth of the imagination" but is insisting that the seemingly fictional characters and incidents deserve the reader's attention because they are literally true. Carleton's insistence on "authenticity" may seem as simplistic today as do the claims of early writers of novels that their works were "true history," but his claim draws attention to his strengths as a writer: his skill at depicting real-life situations, his minute attention to the details of Irish country life, and especially his recreation of what he declares to be the actual speech of the Irish people.

After his return from his pilgrimage his family's fortunes declined to the point where the members were forced to disperse. Following the breakup Carleton remained dependent on his family for support, and his preference for dancing over learning the stonecutting trade finally led to conflict with his brother-in-law and his decision to go on the road. He had recently read Alain René Lesage's picaresque novel *Histoire de Gil Blas de Santillane* (1715–1735). At the time he did not recognize it as fiction "but took for granted that all the adventures were true." Its effect was "to fill my imagination with such a romantic love of adventure, as made me wish myself a thousand times the hero of some that might resemble those [adventures]." After being rebuffed by his brother-in-law over a request for money, "From that spot I started with a bitter and indignant heart, without one moment's preparation, friendless, moneyless and alone — but not without hope, for I had read *Gil Blas.*"

The hero of *Gil Blas* was Carleton's model on his travels. He writes, clearly with a sense of himself as a comic character, "Should I, like Gil Blas, have an adventure? When was I likely to procure my dinner?" When he literally lost his shirt to a crafty widow who operated a lodging house, he plucked up his courage by remembering "worse cases in *Gil Blas.*" When the widow ordered him to leave on threat of summoning the police, he began, however, to have doubts about his hero: "I was beginning to lose a great deal of my relish, not only for the adventures of Gil Blas — whom I cursed in my heart — but for my own, which certainly were at strong variance with romance."

*Page from the manuscript for Carleton's "National Literature and Mr. Lever," an article attacking his fellow Irish writer Charles Lever that appeared in the Dublin periodical* The Nation *on 7 October 1843 (Pierpont Morgan Library; from the Collection of Gordon N. Ray)*

His experiences as a traveler were varied. Among them was the discovery of the bagged corpse of a murderer hanging from a gibbet. On inquiry he learned of the "inhuman and hellish tragedy" for which the man was responsible, which he later related, in grisly detail, in his story "Wildgoose Lodge" in the second series of *Traits and Stories of the Irish Peasantry* (1833). On the lasting value of his travels, Carleton declares "that there never was any man of letters who had an opportunity of knowing and describing the manners of the Irish people so thoroughly as I had. I was one of themselves, and mingled in all those sports and pastimes in which their characters are most clearly developed."

By the time he reached County Louth, Carleton had discovered that he was not only "becoming acquainted with the manners and habits of the people" but was also developing a fondness for the people. He found that he could return their hospitality by telling tales by the fireside in the evening. He offered his willing listeners "the narrative of the old classical legends," which he "transmogrified and changed into an incredible variety of shapes." He avoided Irish legends and tales because such material would not display his learning. In need of fresh material, he "took to inventing original narratives, and was surprised at the facility with which I succeeded." He quickly acquired local fame as a storyteller, and soon people were coming from considerable distances to hear his tales; he had become a "regular *improvisatore.*" It seemed to him that he was "then in the highest position" he would attain in life.

By 1819, after two years of wandering, Carleton was as far south as County Kildare, where he was courteously received by the clergy at Clongowes, a Jesuit college, and at the Catholic seminary in Maynooth. No employment was available for him, however. By his own account the "most original character" he met at Maynooth was Judy Byrne, fruit woman to the college.

His account of his last adventure on the road to Dublin, an attempt at being a "hedge schoolmaster" at Newcastle that quickly ended in failure, is followed by these reflections: "I started for the great city with two-and-ninepence in my pocket. Now one would naturally imagine that after the severe and almost hopeless experience . . . it would have been little short of insanity for any young fellow in my position and circumstance to take such a step. I myself can only account for it by the feeling – derived from *Gil Blas* – which urged me on to ascertain . . . that after struggles and ad-

ventures, I might, like him, come to a calm and safe harbour at last."

The *Gil Blas* parallel is important for another reason. In a telling portion of an analysis of the Irish character in his "Autobiographical Introduction" to the 1843–1844 edition of *Traits and Stories of the Irish Peasantry* Carleton writes:

> It has been said that the Irish, notwithstanding a deep susceptibility of sorrow, are a light-hearted people; and this is strictly true. What, however, is the one fact but a natural consequence of the other? No man for instance ever possessed a high order of humour, whose temperament was not naturally melancholy, and no country in the world more clearly establishes that point than Ireland. Here the melancholy and mirth are not simply in a proximate state, but frequently flash together, and again separate so quickly, that the alternation or blending, as the case may be, whilst it is felt by the spectators, yet stands beyond all known rules of philosophy to solve it. Any one at all acquainted with Ireland, knows that in no country is mirth lighter, or sorrow deeper, or the smile and the tear seen more frequently on the face at the same moment. Their mirth, however is not levity, not their sorrow gloom. . . .

Furthermore,

> Fun, or the love of it, to be sure, is an essential principle in the Irish character; and nothing that can happen, no matter how solemn or how sorrowful it may be, is allowed to proceed without it. In Ireland the house of death is sure to be the merriest one in the neighbourhood; but here the mirth is kindly and considerately introduced, from motives of sympathy – in other words, for the alleviation of the mourners' sorrow. The same thing may be said of its association with religion. Whoever has witnessed a Station in Ireland made at some blessed lake or holy well, will understand this. At such places it is quite usual to see young men and women devoutly circumambulating the well or lake on their bare knees with all the marks of penitence and contrition strongly impressed upon their faces; whilst again, after an hour or two, the same individuals may be found in a tent dancing with ecstatic vehemence to the music of the bagpipe or fiddle.

A better explanation is unlikely for the blend of pathos and comedy that is the distinctive tone of the autobiography and is also evident throughout Carleton's stories.

Finally in Dublin, Carleton, still the picaresque adventurer, led a hand-to-mouth existence as he searched for lodging and employment. He found himself among a new cast of characters as he came to know the city's street people. In a memorable passage he describes an overnight stay with a crowd of beggars in a cellar, compared to which "Dante's Inferno was paradise":

> I must confess that the scene which burst upon me that night stands beyond anything the highest flights of my imagination could have conceived without my having an opportunity of seeing it.... My eyes then ran ... over the scene about me, but how to describe it is the difficulty. It resembled nothing I ever saw either before or since. The inmates were mostly in bed, both men and women, but still a good number of them were up, and indulging in liquors of every description, from strong whisky downwards.... There were the lame, the blind, the dumb, and all who suffered from actual and natural infirmity; but in addition to these, there was every variety of imposter about me.... This, I understood afterwards, was one of cellars to which these persons resorted at night, and there they flung off all the restraints imposed on them during the course of the day.... Crutches, wooden legs, artificial cancers, scrofulous necks, artificial wens, sore legs, and a vast variety of similar complaints, were hung up upon the walls of the cellars, and made me reflect upon the degree of perverted talent and ingenuity that must have been necessary to sustain such a mighty mass of imposture.

Characteristically, Carleton was struck by their language: "The songs and the gestures were infamous, but if one thing puzzled me more than another, it was the fluency and the originality of blackguardism as expressed in language. In fact these people possessed an indecent slang, which constituted a kind of language known only to themselves, and was never spoken except at such orgies as I am describing." He advises the reader not to expect additional accounts of what he discovered about the misery of Dublin's wretched or about his own experiences of suffering and deprivation.

He continued to live by his wits and depended on handouts from sympathetic acquaintances, and even strangers, until he was employed by a Mr. Fox, an evangelist, to tutor Fox's son. While living with the Foxes for more than two years, he fell in love with Jane Anderson, Fox's niece. They were married in 1822 and continued to live with the Foxes for several months, until Carleton, who had converted from Roman Catholicism to Anglicanism and had been employed as a clerk by the Protestant Sunday School Society, lost that job and was evicted by his father-in-law, who locked the pregnant Jane in her room. Carleton, in an escapade worthy of any hero of romance, vaulted a garden wall at night, joined in fisticuffs with his wife's father and a half-dozen watchmen, rushed to his darling's room, embraced her as she weepingly entreated him to take her away, and, after a second battle with "about a dozen watchmen," was induced to

surrender before being "brought away to the watchhouse, where I remained for the rest of the night." The next day he was reunited with his wife through the efforts of his sympathetic mother-in-law and released. His wife soon gave birth to their first child.

William Sisson, librarian at Marsh's library, where Carleton frequently went to read, had provided him with lodging when he was forcibly separated from his wife; Sisson was also one of the first to recognize Carleton's potential as a writer. Carleton had shown Sisson some essays he had written "after the manner of [Joseph] Addison in *The Spectator*." Carleton himself had been astonished by how rapidly he was able to compose them, but it took Sisson, who "actually appeared to be thunderstruck by them," to make him think that they might be worthy of publication. Through Sisson he met Dr. Wilson, a clergyman who echoed Sisson's encouragement and, in a more immediately practical display of patronage, helped Carleton achieve a teaching position at a Protestant school in Mullingar. Though he was disappointed in the assignment from the first day, he and his growing family remained for two years, returning to Dublin after Carleton was jailed for debt. Again through Dr. Wilson's influence, Carleton was assigned to a Protestant school in Carlow.

Carleton's stay in Carlow appears to have been brief, although nothing is known about his departure from there or about his life in Dublin until 1828, when his stories began to appear in the *Christian Examiner and Church of Ireland Magazine,* a journal founded in 1825 to attack Catholicism. Caesar Otway, cofounder of the publication, was the mentor who, over the four years of their association, oversaw Carleton's apprenticeship as a periodical writer. Using various pseudonyms Carleton contributed thirteen stories to the *Christian Examiner* between 1828 and 1831: "A Pilgrimage to Patrick's Purgatory" (April–May 1828), "The Broken Oath" (June–July 1828), "Father Butler" (August–December 1828), "The Station" (January–March 1829), "The Death of a Devotee" (October 1829), "The Priest's Funeral" (January–February 1830), "The Brothers" (March–June 1830), "Lachlin Murray and the Blessed Candle" (August 1830), "The Lianhan Shee" (November 1830), "The Illicit Distiller" (December 1830), "The History of a Chimney Sweep" (April 1831), "The Materialist" (July 1831), and "Dennis O'Shaughnessy Going to Maynooth" (September–November 1831).

In the introduction to the 1842–1844 edition of *Traits and Stories of the Irish Peasantry,* Carleton praised Otway for having, in his own writing, thrown light on the Irish character – Carleton's declared aim in publishing his stories. Further, at the beginning of "The Lough Dearg Pilgrim" in the 1842–1844 edition Carleton wrote that Otway "was a true friend in every sense of the word. . . . In a literary point of view I am under the deepest obligations to his excellent judgment and good taste. Indeed were it not for him, I never could have struggled my way through the severe difficulties with which in my early career I was beset." Yet commentators since David J. O'Donoghue, Carleton's nineteenth-century biographer, have insisted that Otway not only gave Carleton his start by asking him for a narrative of his Lough Derg pilgrimage but also was the evil genius responsible for inspiring the anti-Catholic propaganda in this and Carleton's other *Christian Examiner* stories. Some even credit Otway as co-author, with writing much of it. Referring to "A Pilgrimage to Patrick's Purgatory," Eileen Sullivan argues that "Most probably, Reverend Caesar Otway wrote the polemic anti-Catholic passages ridiculing Catholic dogma while Carleton composed the anecdotes of the pilgrimage. . . ." Fifteen years after its original publication, when the story appeared in the 1842–1844 edition of *Traits and Stories of the Irish Peasantry* with the title "The Lough Dearg Pilgrim" (the title he had given it in 1829 for inclusion in his first published book), Carleton deleted some of the anti-Catholic passages. The 1842–1844 edition also included three other stories from the *Christian Examiner* that Carleton revised for this publication. These revisions suggest that conflict between Otway's polemical aims and Carleton's instincts as a budding writer made inevitable Carleton's break with his first editor.

A contrary view, also based on a close study of the many revisions, deletions, and additions Carleton made as he prepared his periodical stories for book publication, is expressed by Barbara Hayley: "It is generally taken for granted . . . that Carleton was influenced by a rabidly anti-Papist Caesar Otway, who insisted that he write virulently anti-Catholic propaganda for his *Christian Examiner* and fell out with him for moderating his venom." She points out, however, that "the *Christian Examiner,* though full-bloodedly sectarian, was no more so than its contemporaries, Catholic and Protestant alike, and was a good deal more literary than its predecessors." In addition, "Otway founded numerous other non-sectarian magazines, for which Carleton wrote non-sectarian stories." She further argues that rather than rejecting "his anti-Catholic views when freed from the editorial domination of

Otway," Carleton included his most anti-Catholic *Christian Examiner* stories in *Tales of Ireland* (1834) when he was a successful author, and retained many of the propaganda passages in *Traits and Stories of the Irish Peasantry* until the edition of 1842–1844. "Even more startlingly," she writes, "he actually added anti-Catholic passages to some of his *Christian Examiner* pieces for book publication." In 1849, long after his *Christian Examiner* days, Carleton would vehemently attack Catholicism and the Irish nationalist movement in his novel *The Tithe Proctor* – whereas in the earlier novel *Valentine M'Clutchy* (1845) he would attack the Protestant clergy and the English government. These inconsistencies likely have less to do with Carleton's evolution as a writer than they do with his volatile and unpredictable nature.

"The Death of a Devotee" exemplifies the style and subject matter of Carleton's *Christian Examiner* tales. It is the story of a struggle between faith in Christ and a religion of superstition and ritual for the soul of a dying man. As a story of guilt and secret sin reminiscent of some of Nathaniel Hawthorne's tales, it has its significance less in external events and details than in the inner realm of the spirit. Some complexity is achieved in the parallel between the private struggle of a priest with his own doubts and his conflict with a dying parishioner over the kind of forgiveness in death the latter seeks. In this as in other tales, Carleton depends on characterization, setting, incident, and atmosphere rather than on plot. The story is narrated by an unnamed character who is aware of the struggle of the priest, Father Moyle, as well as the broader significance of the conflict between the priest and the devotee. The story includes excellent descriptive passages – especially of a raging hurricane in the dark of the night – some of which have symbolic value. The priest and the dying man meet in the latter's simple home. The devotee's body is literally wrapped in an object of devotion, as his soul has been ensnared by a religion of superstition and ritual:

> A wooden crucifix was placed at the foot of the bed. . . . Along with the large scapular which invested him, he had bound round his body many folds of hard whipcord, knotted in several places, to render the wearing of it more efficacious and penitential. This was called the order of St. Francis, and every one knows that the Scapular is the order of the Blessed Virgin. Around his neck, there was also a small four-cornered bit of black cloth, like a flat pin-cushion, which contained several written charms against sudden death, and the dangers of fire and water. . . .

The devotee calls on the priest to save him by keeping an earlier promise that the narrator never explains. He asks for absolution, but the priest replies, "There is none but God who can give you absolution." He calls on the dying man to repent and to believe that repentance and faith will save him. The dying man cannot comprehend the priest's earnest plea and curses him for his refusal to administer the sacrament. At this point some country folk, including the dying man's brother, attack the priest verbally "in the language of anger and exasperation." The brother, as spokesman for the people, delivers an ultimatum: " 'It's no use in spakin' any more about it: this door is now bolted . . . and out of this house you will not go, if you don't give that dyin' man the rites of the church. . . .' " The old priest falls into a stupor. The story ends with his curate arriving in time to perform the last rites to the satisfaction of the ritual-bound country folk. "The Death of a Devotee" is saved from being mere Protestant polemic by its dramatic power, its descriptions and symbolism, and, above all, by the effective presentation of Father Moyle and the dying devotee. The pathos of the tormented priest is balanced by the caricature of the zealot, suggesting the blend of the serious and the comic or grotesque typical of Carleton's fiction. In this story Carleton makes effective use of his detailed knowledge of the customs, social practices, folklore, and language of the people of rural Ireland; regardless of the editorial aim of the periodical, he had found the formula he would perfect as he developed into one of Ireland's best-known writers.

Carleton's first book, *Father Butler; The Lough Dearg Pilgrim: Being Sketches of Irish Manners,* was published in Dublin in 1829. The next year *Traits and Stories of the Irish Peasantry* appeared in two volumes. It included eight stories: "Ned M'Keown – Introductory," "The Three Tasks, or the Little House Under the Hill, A Legend," "Shane Fadh's Wedding," "Larry M'Farland's Wake," "The Battle of the Factions," "The Funeral and Party Fight," "The Hedge School and the Abduction of Mat Kavanagh," and "The Station." "Ned M'Keown" and the following four stories form a series of related "Fireside Stories" told by the members of a group of country people who gather in the evening around the fireplace at Ned's public house. The narrative structure of a frame enclosing separate tales is similar to that of Geoffrey Chaucer's *The Canterbury Tales* (circa 1387–1400) and Giovanni Boccaccio's *The Decameron* (1351–1353), although there is no suggestion of influence from these literary antecedents. The stories treat various aspects of country life: weddings, wakes, schools, religion. The names of the characters are those of people Carleton knew from County Tyrone. Ned tells the story in "The Three Tasks," a folktale about Jack Magennis, who is given three impossible tasks by a satanic figure and accomplishes them with the help of a beautiful woman who possesses magical power. Jack's "adventure" turns out to have been a dream when he is awakened by his mother, but the story ends with a final twist in which the hero is as rich as he had become in his dream. Ned's story is interrupted throughout by his listeners, whose banter with the storyteller provides comic effect. In the next story Shane Fadh tells about his own wedding. Tom M'Roarkin's story is about the deaths of a drunken Larry M'Farland and his feckless wife, Sally, followed by a lengthy, detailed account – again with interplay between storyteller and listeners – of the games and sports that take place through the night of a "merry wake." The next story abandons the frame by having the narrator, Pat Frayne, protest that he is "not bright . . . at oral relation"; he has "accordingly composed into narrative" a tale "which is appellated 'The Battle of the Factions.' " In a note following the story in the 1843, 1844 edition Carleton offers an explanation for not continuing the original frame-tale scheme with multiple storytellers and an audience: "It was the original intention of the author to have made every man in the humble group about Ned M'Keown's hearth narrate a story illustrating Irish life, feeling, and manners; but on looking into the matter more closely, he had reason to think that such a plan, however agreeable for a time, would ultimately narrow the sphere of his work, and perhaps fatigue the reader by a superfluity of Irish dialogue and its peculiarities of phraseology. He resolved therefore . . . to abandon his original design, and leave himself more room for description and observation."

The story Frayne relates, concerning the feuding O'Hallaghans and O'Callaghans and the star-crossed love of John O'Callaghan and Rose O'Hallaghan, ends tragically in the murder of John by Rose's brother, Rose's killing of her lover's murderer without knowing his identity, and her subsequent life of silent suffering. By eliminating the frame, with its lively exchanges between characters, Carleton has allowed for greater attention to the story itself. Narrated in the first person by a speaker identified by Frayne only as the grandson of Connor O'Callaghan, the story may be seen as a transition from the "Fireside Stories" to those that follow. In giving himself "more room for description and

48

observation" Carleton has complicated the relationship of author and narrator and the relationship of both to a given story with its individual cast of characters. As Hayley writes, "From now on, in the *Traits and Stories,* the 'I' becomes a variable character instead of a neutral reporter who merely sets the scene for the fireside narratives."

In "The Funeral and Party Fights" Carleton treats a large-scale conflict between Protestant Orangemen and Catholic Ribbonmen, a subject his autobiography reveals he knew intimately. "The Hedge School," which is related closely enough in subject matter to be a sequel to the previous story, describes and satirizes hedge schools and schoolmasters in general and offers a detailed portrait of the pretentious and mean-spirited Mat Kavanagh as well as scenes from his schoolroom. The story ends with a seriocomic resolution. As a realistic view of the state of education in rural Ireland it is one of Carleton's most successful stories. "The Station," concerned with a priest's visit to the house of a parishioner to hear confessions and say mass – first published in the *Christian Examiner* – is the only reprinted story in the volume. Carleton revised the story for the book version, but it retains its anti-Catholic bias. Nevertheless, it is a characteristic Carleton story in its blend of comedy and denunciation, its dependence on dialogue, its descriptive passages, and its memorable characters, especially Father Philemy M'Guirk and his parishioner Phaddhy Sheemus Phaddhy.

A second edition of *Traits and Stories of the Irish Peasantry,* with corrections, was printed in 1832 in one volume. In it "The Funeral and Party Fight" was retitled "The Party Fight and Funeral." An American edition of 1833 included the designation *First Series* in the title. In early 1833 Carleton, seeking an audience beyond the readership of the *Christian Examiner,* began to have his stories published in the newly founded *Dublin University Magazine;* later his character sketches would be published in the *Irish Penny Journal* and he would be a contributor, as well, to the *Nation.* A third edition of *Traits and Stories of the Irish Peasantry,* with corrections, was published in two volumes in 1834; the fourth, in 1836, was the first to carry Carleton's name on the title page. Meanwhile, a "Second Series" of *Traits and Stories of the Irish Peasantry* was published in 1833 in three volumes. It comprised a preface and eleven stories: "The Midnight Mass," "The Donagh; or the Horse Stealers," "Phil Purcell, the Pig-Driver," "An Essay on Irish Swearing," "The Geography of an Irish Oath," "The Lianhan Shee," "The Poor Scholar," "Wildgoose Lodge," "Tubber Derg, or

the Red Well," "Denis O'Shaughnessy Going to Maynooth," and "Phelim O'Toole's Courtship." A second edition, with the same contents, was published in 1834 and a third in 1835; Carleton's name did not appear on the title page of any of these editions.

The stories of the second series, of which two had been previously published in the *Christian Examiner* and three others in the *Dublin Literary Gazette* and its successor, the *National Magazine,* show Carleton's willingness to capitalize on what had been successful in the first series. The new stories are memorable for characters, scenes, and episodes from country life; comedy (as in "Phil Purcell, the Pig-Driver"); violence (as in "Wildgoose Lodge"); satire, parody and romance (as in "Denis O'Shaughnessy Going to Maynooth"); and pathos (as in "The Poor Scholar").

*Tales of Ireland* was published in 1834. It included "The Death of a Devotee" and four other stories originally published in the *Christian Examiner,* as well as two additional stories, including "Neal Malone," which had been published originally in January 1833 in the *Dublin University Review and Quarterly Magazine.* The title page does not give Carleton's name but says that the work is "By the Author of 'Traits and Stories of the Irish Peasantry.' " In 1836 the fourth edition of the first series and the second edition of the second series of *Traits and Stories of the Irish Peasantry* were republished together in five volumes. In 1839 Carleton's first novel, *Fardorougha the Miser,* was published. His only play, *The Irish Manufacturer; or, Bob Gawley's Project,* closed shortly after it opened on 25 March 1841.

In 1842, when Carleton was planning a definitive edition of *Traits and Stories of the Irish Peasantry,* he wrote an autobiographical introduction to the collection. This essay is Carleton's most important piece of self-criticism, especially for its emphasis on the relationship between his early life and his stories about rural Ireland and its people. The central portion of the introduction is an autobiographical sketch beginning with his birth and ending with his arrival in Dublin, material that he would develop at much greater length twenty-five years later in the first twelve chapters of his autobiography. In addition, the essay treats the emergence of an Irish national literature, as opposed to an Anglo-Irish one, as well as the "moral and physical condition" of the Irish people. The autobiographical account sets out his qualifications to write as an Irish nationalist who knows, because of his origin and his experience, the truth about the Irish people and their singular world.

*Carleton, age forty-six; portrait by Charles Grey (from* The Life of William Carleton, *1896; courtesy of the Lilly Library, Indiana University)*

That he meant the introduction for foreign readers – especially those in England and Scotland – Carleton makes clear by observing that a work of fiction exclusively devoted to "the Irish peasantry" requires that he prepare the reader by explaining the "general character, habits of thought, and modes of feeling" of these people "as they exist and are depicted" in the stories to follow. Further, he intends such preparation "to aid in removing many absurd prejudices which have existed for time immemorial against" the Irish. In English literature from William Shakespeare to the present, he writes, the "character of an Irishman has been . . . uniformly associated with the idea of something usually ridiculous," a stereotype that was most evident in the language Irish people spoke – "an absurd *congeries* of brogue and blunder." The speech of the conventional stage and fictional "Paddy," filled with "bulls and blunders," bears no resemblance to the actual speech of the Irish. It is not difficult, he concludes, to find the sources of this error in the unhappy relationship over the centuries of the English and Irish peoples.

To understand the status of their language is to understand the Irish people, Carleton maintains.

The language of the Irish has evolved, he explains, to the extent that "the English tongue is gradually superseding the Irish." In his native County Tyrone, for example, "there is not by any means so much Irish spoken now, as there was about twenty or five-and-twenty years ago." The "wild Irishman," as perceived by hostile or uninformed foreigners, understandably seems clumsy of speech as he attempts to master a foreign tongue, often impressing "the idiom of his own language upon one with which he was not familiar."

A literature in which the Irish were consistently stereotyped was a reflection of the political attitudes and conditions of the time. It reinforced the notion that the Irish were inferior or, at best, capable only of clever knavery. Such prejudice, he observes, "is fast disappearing," and, just as literature had sustained prejudice, it is now, given its "quick and powerful influence over the minds of men," capable of expressing "the truthful experience of life." He cites Maria Edgeworth, John Banim, Gerald Griffin, Lady Sydney Morgan, and Anna Maria Hall as writers of "national works, at once so healthful and so true, produced by those who knew the country. . . ."

Carleton does not fail to call attention to his own part – if not his central role – in the Irish literary renaissance, both as a writer of fiction and as a contributor to the newly founded Irish literary periodicals. He observes that until "the last ten or twelve years an Irish author never thought of publishing in his own country," with the result that "our literary men followed the example of our great landlords" in becoming absentees, draining "the country of its intellectual wealth precisely as the others exhausted it of its rents." The country was "precisely in this state. . . . when the two first volumes of 'Traits and Stories of the Irish Peasantry' were given to the public" by his Dublin publisher. Before their publication, he admits, he expected little interest on the part of readers in England and Scotland, notwithstanding his conviction that what he had written was a faithful depiction of "the manners, and language, and feelings of the [Irish] people." The second series, he notes, even surpassed the popularity of the first.

Having thus placed himself and his *Traits and Stories of the Irish Peasantry* in the context of a developing Irish literature, Carleton's next task in the introduction was to educate his non-Irish readers about the "condition and character of the peasantry of Ireland." To do so, however, he needed to establish his credibility as an interpreter of Irish life by outlining the first twenty-odd years of his own life among the rural population of his native County Tyrone. He argues that the account he will offer the reader will provide the "proofs" that his "exhibitions of Irish peasant life, in its most comprehensive sense, may be relied on as truthful and authentic." He implicitly identifies himself with the writers he mentioned earlier, whose works had thrown "much light . . . on the Irish character." Furthermore, having grown up among the people of rural Ireland, he approached the task of describing "the Irish peasantry as they are. . . . with advantages of knowing them, which perhaps few other Irish writers ever possessed; *and this is the only merit which I claim.*"

Of this claim, and of the autobiographical introduction in general, Hayley writes that

> throughout . . . Carleton projects himself as a spokesman for Ireland, his books as symbols of Irish literature, "written by a peasant's son," and even his periodical contributions as helping the advancement of Irish literature and thereby Ireland herself. . . . Carleton's General Introduction is significant as a brief history of the first Irish literary revival of the nineteenth century: Carleton was a product and also an agent of that revival. It was largely the sustained success of his Dublin-produced books throughout the 1830s that built up the Irish publishing trade, allied with the new literary periodicals in which he also played an important part. He was right to see himself as a pioneer of the new Irish tradition.

The definitive edition of *Traits and Stories of the Irish Peasantry* appeared between August 1842 and June 1844 in twenty-three paperbound parts and in two volumes in 1843 and 1844. This edition includes the stories of the first and second series, with "An Essay on Irish Swearing" and "The Geography of An Irish Oath" combined under the latter title and the title "Denis O'Shaughnessy Going to Maynooth" contracted to "Going to Maynooth." Added are the previously published "The Lough Dearg Pilgrim" and "Neal Malone," as well as the newly written "Autobiographical Introduction." Hayley describes this edition, the last prepared by Carleton himself, as "two volumes lavishly decorated and spaciously set, with illustrated title headings and tailpieces, woodcut illustrations within the text, engraved and tinted title plates and frontispieces, and thirty-six etched plates from illustrations by eight eminent artists – a handsome publication that ran to nearly twenty 'editions,' or more precisely new impressions." The edition is available in a 1990 reprint.

Carleton's use of dialogue, including dialect, is as complex an issue as is the history of his revisions of his stories from one edition to another. Hayley

observes that "There are two kinds of language in *Traits and Stories of the Irish Peasantry:* the author's English, which Carleton tries to establish as authoritative, educated and gentlemanly, and the peasant speech." During the fifteen years between the earliest publication on his stories to the 1843–1844 edition of *Traits and Stories of the Irish Peasantry* Carleton continually revised the speech of his characters in an effort to achieve authenticity and to avoid the parody of Irish speech he found so offensive in other writers' works. There is, in addition to "peasant speech," a mock-learned, mock-Latin pattern that by some characters is used as self-consciously as Carleton described himself as using it as a young wag; at other times this language is a reflection of a character's pedantry or pretension or illiteracy. Carleton's stories are polyphonic, and the many voices speak in a wide variety of ways. About the "peasant voice" in the first series, Hayley concludes,

> Carleton was obviously concerned about his characters' speech. . . . He was mediating between ear and eye, trying to express outlandish sounds in not too outlandish letters. He was often reporting speech within speech within speech, a taxing task for one who had been writing for little more than a year. And he was trying to use dialect not just as a wash of local colour but to differentiate between his characters. That he was not entirely satisfied with his efforts is clear from the number of alterations he made in subsequent editions.

One of the two tales Carleton added to the 1843–1844 edition of *Traits and Stories of the Irish Peasantry,* "The Lough Dearg Pilgrim," is his most thoroughly autobiographical story. As he makes clear in the "Autobiographical Introduction" and later in his autobiography, the principal events of the story are those of his own pilgrimage to the shrine at age nineteen. The work had special significance for him in that his disillusioning experience on the pilgrimage led him to abandon the thought of becoming a priest and, eventually, to break with Catholicism altogether. It was also his first published story and was, in his view, "probably one of the most extraordinary productions that ever appeared in any literature. . . . There is not a fact or incident, or a single penal step of duty . . . which is not detailed with the minuteness of the strictest truth and authenticity."

In the original version the story began with an essaylike introduction about superstition and blind devotion that identifies Lough Derg as Ireland's most famous – or notorious – locale where the misguided practices of the Roman Church were carried on. The version in the 1843–1844 edition begins with an account of the composition of the story. Carleton explains that Otway had asked him, as a former pilgrim to the lough, to compose "the Sketch of the Lough Dearg Pilgrim as it now appears." Carleton quotes Otway's description of the lake and island and concludes the introduction with a passage from "Bishop Henry Jones's account [of Saint Patrick's Purgatory], published in 1647." The earlier anti-Catholic polemic, having nothing directly to do with the narrative, has been replaced in the revision by topographical description and an identification of the author with the subject. The first sentence of the introduction to the story reveals that one of Carleton's purposes is to convey a sense of place as well as a portrait of the Irish people who travel there: "In describing the habits, superstitions, and feelings of the Irish people, it would be impossible to overlook a place which occupies so prominent a position in their religious usages, as the celebrated Purgatory of St. Patrick, situated in a lake that lies among the bleak and desolate mountains of Donegal."

Carleton's other purpose is to narrate a young man's pilgrimage. The narrative begins: "I was at the time of performing this station, in the middle of my nineteenth year – of quick perception – warm imagination – a mind peculiarly romantic – a morbid turn for devotion, and a candidate for the priesthood. . . ." The self-characterization continues, now with a comic touch, in the description of the narrator's attempt (also reported by Carleton in his autobiography) to prepare for the worst in the journey to come by duplicating on his father's pond the miracle of a priest who saved himself from death in a sinking boat by walking on water. Low comedy over, the narrative of the journey begins on "a delightful morning in the pleasant month of July."

What plot the story has is simply that the incidents follow one another as the journey unfolds. After walking alone for a while the narrator overtakes – with some difficulty – two women, whom he discovers to be fellow pilgrims. The older woman mistakes him for a priest. His mistaken perception of the women will take longer to be evident. He is impressed with their physical endurance and asks how they could walk at such a rate without displaying fatigue: " 'Musha!' said she, 'but your Reverence ought to know that.' – I felt puzzled at this: 'How should I know it?' said I. 'I'm sure,' she continued, 'you couldn't expect a poor ould crathur o'sixty to travel at this rate, at all, at all; except for raisons, your Reverence.' " Her reasons are unnamed, but the narrator, convinced that she refers

to the faith she carries with her, piously observes: " 'I hope you understand the nature of what you *are* carrying – and in a proper manner, too, for you that's the chief point.' 'Why, Father dear, I do my best avourneen; an' I ought of a sartinty to know it bekase blessed Friar Hagan spent three days instructin' Mat and myself in it; an' more betoken, that Mat sent him a sack o'phaties, an' a bag of oats for his trouble, not forgettin' the goose he got from myself, the Micklemas afther. . . .' " She then recites the prayer she had been given, "a beautiful Irish prayer to the Blessed Virgin, of which that beginning with 'Hail holy Queen!' in the Roman Catholic prayer books is a translation, or perhaps the original. While she was repeating the prayer, I observed her hand in her bosom, apparently extricating something, which, on being brought out, proved to be a scapular; she held it up, that I might see it: 'Your Reverence,' said she, 'this is the ninth journey of the kind I made; but you don't wonder *now*, I bleeve, how stoutly I'm able to stump it.' " The comic aspects of the scene nearly mask the religious satire on superstition and misguided devotion, which had been delivered as a direct diatribe in the opening paragraphs of the original version. In addition, the dramatic irony restricts the nineteen-year-old pilgrim to the role of observer and reporter at this point in the story.

The three stop at an inn, where the women cleverly allow the narrator to pay for their breakfast. After meeting more pilgrims they arrive at Petigo, a town near the lake. The narrator takes note of the religious acts and devotions of those he encounters, sensing that his own efforts at devotion are thwarted by his "villainous curiosity" about the people he is encountering as well as about the place itself. He asks, "How, for instance, was it possible for me to register the transgressions of my whole life, heading them under the 'seven deadly sins,' with such a prospect before me as the beautiful waters and shores of Lough Erne?"

The pilgrims are a varied lot, and the narrator's portrayal of them ranges from the comic and satiric to the sympathetic. An instance of the last is his response to a lovely young woman whose honest and passionate prayer, depending on "neither books nor beads," sharply contrasts with "the calm, unconscious, and insipid mummer" in the rest of the room. The pilgrims are taken to beds of stone spikes, on which they walk while reciting prayers. After the "best part of a July day" the narrator's feet are "flayed." Later, the pilgrims perform their devotions in "the dim religious" twilight of a dismal assembly hall called the "Prison," during which an unhappy pilgrim either throws himself or falls to his death from a gallery. The pilgrims are prevented from sleeping by persons who wander about rapping the drowsy with rods. The account turns grotesquely satiric when the narrator (now, obviously, Carleton the satirist) describes a "fellow with a hare-lip" who attempts to lead prayers: "The organs of his speech seemed to have been transferred from his mouth to his nose, and although Irish was his vernacular language, either some fool or knave had taught him to say his prayers in English: and you may take this as an observation founded on fact, that the language which a Roman Catholic of the lower class does not understand, is the one in which he is disposed to pray."

As the "station" approaches its conclusion the narrator meets Sol Donnel, a "pilgrim by profession," who in a comic scene instructs the neophyte in "prayer swapping." The passage displays Carleton's genius for developing a character through dialogue. Soon the narrator is once again in the company of the two women he had met at the beginning as he starts his homeward journey. The events of the final night and next morning are those Carleton reports in his autobiography, ending with the narrator's discovery that his clothing and money have been stolen by the old woman. A sadder and wiser young man, the narrator, "a goose stripped of my feathers; a dupe beknaved and beplundered – having been almost starved to death in the 'island,' and nearly cudgelled by one of the priests," returns home. As he crosses the threshold, the members of his family fall to their knees and ask for his blessing, as do those who crowd around him at mass the next day. He tells his story to the priest, who laughingly replies, " 'So . . . you have fallen foul of Nell McCollum, the most notorious shuler in the province! a gipsy, a fortune-teller, and a tinker's widow; but rest contented, you are not the first she has gulled – but beware the next time.' " The story ends with the young man's resolve: " 'There is no danger of that,' said I, with peculiar emphasis." Carleton's story is effective as a tale of a young pilgrim's adventure and, as Carleton repeatedly claimed, it is convincing, as well, as a representation of a famous religious place and a portrayal of those drawn to it.

Reviewers of *Traits and Stories of the Irish Peasantry* from the first edition of 1830 to the edition of 1843–1844 usually acknowledged his own claim for the authenticity of his stories and often praised him for it. In a *Blackwood's Edinburgh Magazine* review of May 1830, "Christopher North" (John Wilson) and "The Ettrick Shepherd" (James Hogg) dis-

cuss the recently published first edition, with North observing that the book is "Truly, intensely, Irish. The whole book has the brogue – never were the outrageous whimsicalities of that strange, wild, imaginative people so characteristically displayed; nor, in the midst of all the fun, frolic, and folly, is there any dearth of poetry, pathos, and passion. . . ."

Carleton's stories appeared subsequently in many editions published in Ireland, England, and the United States under various titles. The only important new collection following the 1842–1844 *Traits and Stories of the Irish Peasantry* was *Tales and Sketches, Illustrating the Character, Usages, Traditions, Sports and Pastimes of the Irish Peasantry,* published in Dublin in 1845. This one-volume work included twenty-one pieces, most of which had been published in the *Irish Penny Journal* in 1840–1841. As described by Sullivan, these works "are generally of shorter length than the tales in *Traits and Stories.* 'Rose Moan the Irish Mid-Wife,' 'Frank Finnegan the Foster-Brother,' and 'Mary Murray the Irish Match-Maker' represent the spirit of the character sketches in *Tales and Sketches.* . . . These three tales and the others in *Tales and Sketches* are like mirrors, reflecting diverse scenes of country life. The stories re-create a particular segment of a past culture to a perfection unequaled by other Irish writers of the period."

In 1845 Carleton also had four novels published. *The Black Prophet,* a novel of complex human relations set against the backdrop of the Irish famine, was published in 1847. Carleton considered it his best novel.

Carleton's bibliographer, Hayley, observes that the two series of *Traits and Stories of the Irish Peasantry* "were well received, going into four and three editions respectively." Between 1839 and 1862 Carleton had thirteen novels published, "mainly," Hayley notes, "to critical and public acclaim," with most of the novels appearing in seven or more editions and *Willy Reilly and His Dear Coleen Bawn* (1855) in at least thirty. While he had completed the bulk of his writing, including his best work, by 1850, he continued to write and to publish up to his death two decades later.

Hopelessly incapable of managing his finances or his literary interests, including the retention of the copyright of his works, Carleton – in spite of his success as a writer of fiction – spent much of his adult life in financial difficulty. According to Sullivan, "He earned at the maximum about £150 per year for his work during his lifetime, an incredible fact considering the quantity of his literary creations and the many editions of his popular works. Maria Edgeworth and Tom Moore, for instance, earned more than £1,000 for one of their popular works." In 1848 Carleton was granted a state pension of £200 a year, but this income did not put an end to his financial distress.

Carleton met Thomas Carlyle in 1847, and in 1850 he went to London, where he met William Makepeace Thackeray and Leigh Hunt. He failed then, and in subsequent attempts, to meet or establish contact with Charles Dickens. Following the departure of three of his daughters to Canada, he considered emigrating but rejected the plan. His money worries continued into the 1860s, adding to the general gloom and despondency of a man who had long passed the zenith of his career. Yet, in the final months of his life, he turned once again to his youth, clearly a golden age for him, and wrote his last story – his own. In August 1868, when he began to compose his autobiography, he was nearly blind and was suffering from a painful terminal illness. Yet in those few months before his death on 30 January 1869 he produced one of his most important works – second only, perhaps, to *Traits and Stories of the Irish Peasantry*. His final book re-creates in detail the portion of his life that had made possible his greatest work as a writer.

The autobiography ends abruptly and is obviously unfinished, but Carleton did complete a detailed account of his early life from childhood through young adulthood, ending with what was clearly both a nadir and a turning point in his life. His story is one of privation and disappointment, of a life seemingly doomed to failure. The opening paragraph of the autobiography announces this theme: "Alas! it is a melancholy task which I propose to execute – the narrative of such a continued and unbroken series of struggle, difficulty, suffering and sorrow as has seldom fallen to the lot of a literary man." His fate was "peculiarly calamitous" and ironic "because it was to a disaster, which would have ruined the hopes and prospects of any other man" that he owed his fame.

Chapter 19 ends with Carleton, his wife, and their two infant daughters in rural Carlow, inhabiting a wretched room heated only by burning life-threatening sulphur coal: "The place was not habitable; not only we ourselves, but our children became ill, and I found that to live there was only another word for death." With this portrait of suffering, Carleton the storyteller had reached the point he had promised the reader at the beginning, when the narrative would turn, like a romance, from disaster to renewal and a new life.

Carleton prided himself on his accurate memory, and his ability to recall the past, record it accurately, and at the same time tell a good story sustained him in old age as a writer of autobiography as it had in his prime as a writer of fiction. Throughout the autobiography Carleton reminds the reader that the life he depicts in his fiction is no less authentic and true than the narrative of his own life. Carleton and his contemporary William Wordsworth were similar in the importance each gave to the writer's early life, and to childhood in particular, as well as to the importance of memory in the creative process.

In Sullivan's view Carleton's autobiography reads "like an odyssey of the human spirit," with Carleton "on stage, playing a heroic role," from the first chapter to the last. Without a doubt Carleton is both the youthful protagonist as well as the ever-present elderly storyteller and interpreter in his autobiography, but if the work has heroic qualities they are of the order Carleton himself observed when he wrote, toward the end of the work, "I have often thought that man's life is divided or separated into a series of small epics; not epics that are closed by happiness, however, but by pain."

Over his long career Carleton contributed more than seventy stories, poems, and articles to a dozen Irish periodicals. In addition, five of his novels first appeared serially. As he explains in the "Autobiographical Introduction" to the 1843–1844 *Traits and Stories of the Irish Peasantry,* he saw his own entry into the Dublin literary scene around 1830 as coinciding with the early and fitful stages of an Irish literary revival which itself had been signaled by the founding of several literary periodicals:

> About this time the literary taste of the metropolis began to feel the first symptoms of life. . . . Two or three periodicals were attempted, and though of very considerable merit, . . . all perished in their infancy. . . . To every one of these the author contributed, and he has the satisfaction of being able to say that there has been no publication projected purely for the advancement of literature in his own country, to which he has not given the aid of his pen . . . such as it was, and this whether he received remuneration or not.

The tonal range of Carleton's writing – in particular, its blend of humor and pathos, the dark and the light – was frequently praised by contemporary reviewers. He is credited with skill as a descriptive writer, especially in his depiction of nature. There is less agreement about his representation of Irish speech, and some critics, usually Irish ones, found his Irish "peasants" representative of the northern

Irish and not of the people as a whole. The most sharply contrasting criticism, however, pertained to Carleton's treatment of religion, especially the Catholic church and its clergy.

By the 1843–1844 edition of *Traits and Stories of the Irish Peasantry* Carleton, in review after review, had been praised as a writer with the stature and national significance for Ireland that Sir Walter Scott had for Scotland. In the autobiography Carleton cites Patrick Joseph Murray's 1852 assessment in the *Edinburgh Review:*

> The primary and essential value of Mr. Carleton's sketches of Irish peasant life and character unquestionably consists in this – that they are true, and *so* true to nature. . . . In Ireland, since our author's youth, changes rapid and deep have taken place. . . . [He] stands alone as the exhibiter of the inward and external, the constitutional and the accidental, the life, the feelings, the ways, the customs, and the language of the Irish peasant. . . . Unless another master hand should appear, like his, or abler than his, it is in his pages, and in his alone, that future generations must look for the truest and fullest – though still far from complete – picture of those, who will ere long have passed away from that troubled land, from the records of history, and from the memory of men for ever.

Echoing this view more than one hundred years later in his preface to a 1968 edition of Carleton's autobiography, the Irish poet Patrick Kavanagh – whose native County Monaghan adjoins the area where Carleton was born and spent his early years – praised *Traits and Stories of the Irish Peasantry* for its "authentic dialect" and "racy dialogue, which reads like a translation direct from the necessities of early nineteenth-century Irish life." For him "Carleton was parochial, not provincial. In this he was not unlike [James] Joyce, though Joyce, with his legends and daring language, had a strong strain of pretension in him. Carleton instead wrote the lives of the obscure and the humble, and he recorded the lives of his own people with a fidelity that preserves for us the culture of pre-famine Ireland."

Kavanagh affirms what Carleton himself had claimed as a critic of his own writing and what the *Dublin University Magazine* (January 1841) had declared about Carleton as a unique Irish writer whose only subject was his own nation and its people:

> Whatever be his faults or merits, he is alone. Of all who have written on the fruitful theme of Irish life and manners, there is none with whom we can compare him. He has copied no one, and no one rivals him; his style and his subjects are alike his own. Irish, intensely Irish indeed his stories are, but utterly unlike any thing that ever before them had been given to the public under the name of Irish stories. . . . [He] stands alone as the portrayer of the manners and customs of our people – as the man who has unlocked the secrets of the Irish heart, and described the Irish character, without caricature or exaggeration, by that mighty power of genius which portrays reality while it frames its own creations – and produces those wonderful conceptions, which are at once fiction and truth.

### Bibliography:

Barbara Hayley, *A Bibliography of the Writings of William Carleton* (Gerrards Cross: Smythe, 1985).

### References:

Barbara Hayley, *Carleton's "Traits and Stories And the 19th Century Anglo-Irish Tradition"* (Gerrards Cross: Smythe, 1983);

Benedict Kiely, *Modern Irish Fiction* (Dublin: Golden Eagle, 1950);

Kiely, *Poor Scholar* (New York: Sheed & Ward, 1948);

Patrick Joseph Murray, "Traits of the Irish Peasantry," *Edinburgh Review,* 96 (October 1852): 384–403;

Harold Orel, "William Carleton: Elements of the Folk Tradition," in his *The Victorian Short Story: Development and Triumph of a Literary Genre* (Cambridge: Cambridge University Press, 1986), pp. 14–32;

Eileen A. Sullivan, *William Carleton* (Boston: G. K. Hall, 1983);

Robert Lee Wolff, *William Carleton: Irish Peasant Novelist. A Preface to His Fiction* (New York & London: Garland, 1980).

### Papers:

The D. J. O'Donoghue collection in the New York Public Library includes items related to William Carleton.

# Wilkie Collins

*(8 January 1824 – 23 September 1889)*

LynnDianne Beene
*University of New Mexico*

See also the Collins entries in *DLB 18: Victorian Novelists After 1885* and *DLB 70: British Mystery Writers, 1860–1919.*

BOOKS: *Memoirs of the Life of William Collins, Esq., R.A., with Selections from His Journals and Correspondence,* 2 volumes (London: Longman, Brown, Green & Longmans, 1848);

*Antonina; or, The Fall of Rome: A Romance of the Fifth Century* (3 volumes, London: Bentley, 1850; 1 volume, New York: Harper, 1850);

*Rambles beyond Railways; or, Notes in Cornwall Taken A-foot* (London: Bentley, 1851);

*Mr. Wray's Cash-Box; or, the Mask and the Mystery: A Christmas Sketch* (London: Bentley, 1852); republished as *The Stolen Mask; or, The Mysterious Cash-Box* (Columbia, S.C.: De Fontaine, 1864);

*Basil: A Story of Modern Life* (3 volumes, London: Bentley, 1852; 1 volume, New York: Appleton, 1853; revised edition, London: Sampson Low, 1862);

*Hide and Seek,* 3 volumes (London: Bentley, 1854); revised as *Hide and Seek; or, The Mystery of Mary Grice,* 1 volume (London: Sampson Low, 1861; Philadelphia: Peterson, 1862);

*The Holly-Tree Inn,* by Collins and Charles Dickens (New York: Dix & Edwards, 1855);

*After Dark,* by Collins and Dickens (London: Smith & Elder, 1856; New York: Dick & Fitzgerald, 1856) – includes, by Collins, "Leaves from Leah's Diary," "The Traveler's Story of a Terribly Strange Bed," "The Lawyer's Story of a Stolen Letter," "The French Governess's Story of Sister Rose," "The Nun's Story of Gabriel's Marriage," "The Professor's Story of the Yellow Mask," "The Angler's Story of the Lady of Glenwith Grange,""Last Leaves from Leah's Diary";

*The Wreck of the Golden Mary,* by Collins and Dickens (London: Bradbury & Evans, 1856);

*Wilkie Collins*

*The Two Apprentices: With a History of Their Lazy Tour,* by Collins and Dickens (Philadelphia: Peterson, 1857);

*The Queen of Hearts* (3 volumes, London: Hurst & Blackett, 1859; 1 volume, New York: Harper, 1859) – comprises "The Queen of Hearts," "Brother Owen's Story of the Black Cottage," "Brother Griffith's Story of the Family Secret," "Brother Morgan's Story of the Dream Woman," "Brother Griffith's Story of Mad Monkton," "Brother Morgan's Story of the Dead Hand," "Brother Griffith's Story of the

Biter Bit," "Brother Owen's Story of the Parson's Scruple," "Brother Griffith's Story of a Plot in Private Life," "Brother Morgan's Story of Fauntleroy," "Brother Owen's Story of Anne Rodway";

*The Woman in White* (3 volumes, London: Sampson Low, 1860; 1 volume, New York: Harper, 1860);

*A Message from the Sea: A Drama in Three Acts,* by Collins, Dickens, and others (London: Halsworth, 1861);

*No Name* (3 volumes, London: Sampson Low, 1862; 2 volumes, Boston: Fuller, 1863);

*No Name: A Drama in Five Acts* (London: Halsworth, 1863);

*My Miscellanies* (2 volumes, London: Sampson Low, 1863; 1 volume, New York: Harper, 1874);

*Armadale* (2 volumes, London: Smith, Elder, 1866; 1 volume, New York: Harper, 1866);

*Armadale: A Drama in Three Acts* (London: Smith, Elder, 1866);

*No Thoroughfare: A Drama in Five Acts,* by Collins, Dickens, and Charles Fechter (London: Office of All the Year Round, 1867; New York: De Witt, n.d.);

*The Moonstone: A Romance* (3 volumes, London: Tinsley, 1868; 1 volume, New York: Harper, 1868);

*Black and White: A Love Story in Three Acts,* by Collins and Fechter (London: Whiting, 1869);

*Man and Wife. A Novel* (3 volumes, London: Ellis, 1870; New York: Harper, 1870);

*Poor Miss Finch: A Novel* (3 volumes, London: Bentley, 1872; 1 volume, New York: Harper, 1872);

*The New Magdalen: A Novel* (2 volumes, London: Bentley, 1873; 1 volume, New York: Harper, 1873);

*Miss or Mrs.?: And Other Stories in Outline* (London: Bentley, 1873; revised edition, London: Chatto & Windus, 1877) – comprises "Miss or Mrs.?," "Blow up the Brig!," "The Fatal Cradle," "A Mad Marriage";

*The Frozen Deep and Other Stories,* 2 volumes (London: Bentley, 1874); republished as *The Dead Alive,* 1 volume (Boston: Shepard & Gill, 1874) – comprises "The Frozen Deep," "The Dream Woman," "John Jago's Ghost or The Dead Alive";

*The Law and the Lady* (3 volumes, London: Chatto & Windus, 1875; 1 volume, New York: Harper, 1875);

*The Two Destinies: A Romance* (2 volumes, London: Chatto & Windus, 1876; 1 volume, New York: Harper, 1876);

*The Haunted Hotel, a Mystery of Modern Venice* (Toronto: Rose-Belford, 1878); republished as *The Haunted Hotel, a Mystery of Modern Venice, to Which Is Added: My Lady's Money,* 2 volumes (London: Chatto & Windus, 1879);

*A Rogue's Life: From His Birth to His Marriage* (London: Bentley, 1879; New York: Appleton, 1879);

*The Fallen Leaves* (3 volumes, London: Chatto & Windus, 1879; 1 volume, Chicago: Rose-Belford, 1879);

*Jezebel's Daughter* (3 volumes, London: Chatto & Windus, 1880; 1 volume, New York: Munro, 1880);

*The Black Robe* (3 volumes, London: Chatto & Windus, 1881; 1 volume, New York: Munro, 1881);

*Heart and Science: A Story of the Present Time* (New York: Munro, 1883; 3 volumes, London: Chatto & Windus, 1883);

*"I Say No"; or, The Love-Letter Answered* (New York: Harper, 1884); republished as *"I Say No,"* 3 volumes (London: Chatto & Windus, 1884) – comprises " 'I Say No'; or, The Love-Letter Answered," "The Ghost's Touch," "My Lady's Money: An Episode in the Life of a Young Girl," "Percy and the Prophet: Events in the Lives of a Lady and Her Lovers";

*The Evil Genius: A Domestic Story* (3 volumes, London: Chatto & Windus, 1886; 1 volume, New York: Harper, 1886);

*The Guilty River: A Story* (Bristol: Arrowsmith, 1886; New York: Harper, 1886);

*Little Novels* (3 volumes, London: Chatto & Windus, 1887; 1 volume, New York: Dover, 1977) – comprises "Mrs. Zant and the Ghost," "Miss Morris and the Stranger," "Mr. Cosway and the Landlady," "Mr. Medhurst and the Princess," "Mr. Lismore and the Widow," "Miss Jéromette and the Clergyman," "Miss Mina and the Groom," "Mr. Lepel and the Housekeeper," "Mr. Captain and the Nymph," "Mr. Marmaduke and the Minister," "Mr. Percy and the Prophet," "Miss Bertha and the Yankee," "Miss Dulane and My Lord," "Mr. Policeman and the Cook";

*The Legacy of Cain* (New York: Harper, 1888; 3 volumes, London: Chatto & Windus, 1889);

*Blind Love,* completed by Walter Besant (3 volumes, London: Chatto & Windus, 1890; 1 volume, New York: Appleton, 1890);

*The Dead Secret,* 2 volumes (London: Chatto & Windus, 1899; New York: Fifth Avenue Publishing, 1900);

*The Lazy Tour of Two Idle Apprentices; No Thoroughfare; The Perils of Certain English Prisoners,* by Collins and Dickens (London: Chapman & Hall, 1890);

*Under the Management of Mr. Charles Dickens: His Production of "The Frozen Deep,"* by Collins and Dickens, edited by Robert Louis Brannan (Ithaca, N.Y.: Cornell University Press, 1966).

**Editions:** *The Moonstone,* introduction by T. S. Eliot (Oxford: Oxford University Press, 1928);

*After Dark, and Other Stories* (Freeport, N.Y.: Books for Libraries Press, 1972) – comprises "Leaves from Leah's Diary," "The Traveler's Story of a Terribly Strange Bed," "The Lawyer's Story of a Stolen Letter," "The French Governess's Story of Sister Rose," "The Nun's Story of Gabriel's Marriage," "The Professor's Story of the Yellow Mask," "The Angler's Story of the Lady of Glenwith Grange," "Miss or Mrs.?," "The Dead Alive," "The Fatal Cradle, Otherwise, the Heart-rending Story of Mr. Heavysides," " 'Blow up with the Brig!' A Sailor's Story," "The Frozen Deep," "Fatal Fortune," "Last Leaves from Leah's Diary."

PLAY PRODUCTIONS: *A Court Duel,* London, Miss Kelly's Soho Theatre, 26 February 1850;

*The Lighthouse,* by Collins and Charles Dickens, London, Tavistock House, 16 June 1855;

*The Frozen Deep,* by Collins and Dickens, London, Tavistock House, 6 January 1857;

*The Red Vial,* London, Olympic Theatre, 11 October 1858;

*No Thoroughfare,* by Collins, Dickens, and Charles Fechter, London, Adelphi Theatre, 26 December 1867;

*Black and White,* by Collins and Fechter, London, Adelphi Theatre, 29 March 1869;

*The Woman in White,* London, Olympic Theatre, 9 October 1871;

*Man and Wife,* London, Prince of Wales's Theatre, 22 February 1873;

*Miss Gwilt,* London, Globe Theatre, 15 April 1876;

*The Moonstone,* London, Olympic Theatre, 17 September 1877;

*Rags and Riches,* London, Adelphi Theatre, 9 June 1883.

Victorian fiction writer, essayist, and social commentator Wilkie Collins continues to perplex critics and entertain readers. Critics, pointing to his stereotyped characters, melodramatic plots, sometimes unsophisticated approaches to social issues, and repetitious subjects and story lines, hold that his contemporaries Charles Dickens, George Eliot, George Meredith, William Makepeace Thackeray, and Anthony Trollope eclipse Collins's contributions to British fiction. T. S. Eliot judged him a minor figure who contented himself with artful, albeit melodramatic plots and one whose talent exceeded his genius and artistic reach. Such appraisals, however, ignore Collins's abiding popularity, social protest, and literary innovations. Several of his novels, including *The Woman in White* (1860) and *The Moonstone* (1868), have remained in print almost continuously since their first publication, and many of his stories are still anthologized and enjoyed. It is true that he could write cloying sentimental tales at a rapid pace, and in all of his short fiction complexities are resolved, conventional marriages unite appropriate couples, and worthy offspring inherit their just rewards from devoted parents who, to outsiders, seem to be vicious. Yet this type of story was the norm for his age, and, judged by this standard, Collins's work is significant. During the last half of the nineteenth century writers enjoyed a burgeoning audience of middle-class readers whose demands fit the instability of the times. Because of the challenges offered the Victorians by scientific discoveries and the Industrial Revolution, readers wanted realistic affirmations of Britain's conservative moral orthodoxy. At the same time, they devoured escape fiction that obscured social upheaval. As the prefaces to his novels and several of his essays attest, Collins wrote with this dual charge in mind. His greatest attribute as a fiction writer is that he could provide what the public wanted far better than most of his contemporaries.

Collins's accomplishments, however, go beyond satisfying popular demand. He saw himself as a social critic who presented values that were often at odds with those held by his readers; read closely, his stories decry censorship, unfair laws, and discriminatory practices. His characters come from all classes and defy formulaic classification; comical servants have good hearts, intuitive detectives struggle to make rationality work, upstanding citizens are condemned for their pettiness and intolerance, prostitutes – "Jezebels" – are presented as strong-minded individuals who gain moral dignity and respectability because they, like their creator, censure injustice and inhumanity. The critic Arthur Compton-Rickett summarizes Collins's primary talents as "technical dexterity as a story-teller," "sense of dramatic effect," and "faculty for pictorial suggestion." While these are the skills by which Collins captured a considerable reading audience during his lifetime and has held it ever since, readers come away from his stories a little more tolerant of human idiosyncrasies and a little less of injustice.

Equally important is the long-term impact Collins had on British genre literature. In his time popular fiction was denigrated as "women's literature"; such works were filled with titillation, one-dimensional characters, and narrative inconsistencies. While he wrote to please the largest audience, Collins intuitively sought ways to enrich Gothic sensationalism and mystery fiction. He experimented with existing genres by introducing to mystery fiction the principle of fair play with the reader, the formula of the least likely suspect being the criminal, multiple narrative styles, the crime as flowing naturally from the personality of the criminal, and the eccentric detective, accompanied by a faithful chronicler, who succeeds through rational methods where the police have failed.

William Wilkie Collins was born on 8 January 1824 at his parents' house at 11 New Cavendish Street, Tavistock Square, London. He was the son of the Scots-Irish landscape painter William Collins, R.A., and Harriet Geddes Collins, the sister of the painters Andrew and Sarah Geddes; his middle name was chosen to honor his father's friend, the painter Sir David Wilkie. Early in the century William Collins had struggled to establish himself; but during the 1820s he began to sell his portraits to such noble patrons as Sir Robert Peel and Robert Banks Jenkinson, Second Earl of Liverpool, and by spring 1826 he could move his family to Pond Street, near Hampstead Heath. There, when Wilkie Collins was four years old, his brother, Charles Allston (Charley), was born. The Collins home was filled with artists and literary people; Wilkie Collins was particularly impressed by Samuel Taylor Coleridge, who commissioned William Collins to paint his daughter's portrait but continued to visit on a social basis. Even as a child, Wilkie Collins recalled later, he saw in Coleridge's anguish the power opium could hold over a person.

In the summer of 1830 financial concerns prompted William Collins to move his family to Porchester Terrace, Bayswater, from which Wilkie watched the Hyde Park demonstrations against the First Reform Bill. William Collins set Wilkie and Charley to a schedule of home education and visits to art galleries; for escape, Wilkie read his mother's library of Gothic novels and moved on to the adventure stories of Frederick Marryat and Sir Walter Scott. He also read poetry by William Shakespeare, Alexander Pope, Percy Bysshe Shelley, and George Gordon, Lord Byron. In 1833 he was enrolled at the Maida Hill Academy.

An inheritance following the deaths of his brother Frank to typhus and, two months later, of his mother enabled William Collins to take his family on a tour of Italy from 1836 to 1838. Dorothy L. Sayers speculates that during this time Wilkie Collins read about bizarre murder cases – including those of an impoverished monk tried for killing a woman for her money and a priest accused of hiring a barber to murder his mistress's husband – that he later re-created in his stories. After the family returned from Italy, Collins was enrolled at the Reverend Henry Cole's boarding school at Highbury, where his slight physique, protruding forehead, and bad eyesight made him an easy target for bullies. To save himself from abuse, he became the school's prize storyteller and so learned the value of capturing and holding an audience's attention.

In 1841 Collins was apprenticed to the tea merchants Antrobus and Company, but he was inclined more toward daydreaming than invoicing. He made several trips to Europe, some with his family and some with friends, and began his first novel, a Tahitian shocker that he abandoned but probably reused in "The Captain's Last Love" (1876).

His first literary success came in August 1843, when Douglas Jerrold published "The Last Stage Coachman" in the *Illuminated Magazine*. This short fantasy illustrates a central problem in Collins studies: what is and what is not short fiction in Collins's oeuvre? "The Last Stage Coachman" is a melodramatic essay protesting the railways' encroachment on stagecoaches, but it is replete with the sort of descriptions, settings, nightmarish fantasy, and undisguised social protest that characterize his best mature fiction. An account of an "oastler" (hostler) killed when he tries to save an aged coach horse from an oncoming train, "The Last Stage Coachman" condemns the Industrial Revolution for robbing individuals of their humanity. But its method is that of fiction: the narrator – the ghost of the last coachman – paces "the worn and weedy pavement" of a abandoned inn yard as he laments the unwarranted death of the oastler and listens fearfully to the groans from steam-engine inventor James Watt and the curses from "the invisible insides" of the carriage.

"The Last Stage Coachman" also illustrates Collins's strategy of expanding, condensing, and reshaping his stories for later publication. Features of "The Last Stage Coachman" show up in other stories, including one with a particularly telling publi-

*Caricature of Collins by Adriano Cecioni in* Vanity Fair
*(February 1872)*

cation history. The December 1855 issue of Dickens's periodical *Household Words* would include Collins's "The Ostler's Story," an eerie mystery story reminiscent of the atmosphere and descriptions in "The Last Stage Coachman." The hostler, "Unlucky Issac" Scatchard, is saved by an apparition who warns him that his wife intends to murder him. In 1859 "The Ostler's Story" would be republished as "Brother Morgan's Story of the Dream Woman" in Collins's second collection of short stories, *The Queen of Hearts*. Eight years later Collins would adapt the tale for a public-speaking tour in America, and in 1874 he would expand it into the novella "The Dream Woman: A Mystery in Four Narratives" for another collection, *The Frozen Deep and Other Stories*. Hence, "The Last Stage Coachman" shows how Collins revised and textured his fiction; it also illustrates the taxonomic nightmare of deciding what counts as fiction in Collins's works and by what title a given work should be known.

During the five years after the publication of "The Last Stage Coachman" Collins wrote much but published little. In 1846 William Collins made his last attempt to settle his elder son by enrolling him in Lincoln College to study law. Wilkie Collins found the subject tedious and realized that he was

temperamentally ill-suited for a legal career. Nonetheless, Lincoln taught him much about the value of rationality, the intricacies of the legal system, and the inequities in British law in regard to marriage, property, and inheritance. By this time he was working on a novel, *Antonina; or, The Fall of Rome,* but before the work was half finished William Collins died of heart disease on 17 February 1847. At that point Wilkie Collins temporarily abandoned his Roman romance to write a two-volume biography of his father, *Memoirs of the Life of William Collins, Esq., R.A.* Completed in six months, Collins's first published book suggests that his father's lyrical paintings steered him toward atmosphere and mood as vehicles for character and narrative. After her husband's death Harriet Collins moved the family to a small, unpretentious house on Blandford Square. Her new home was a meeting place for students, writers, lawyers, and artists, and she staged small theatrical productions in which Wilkie Collins participated as an actor, director, producer, and writer.

In 1851 a family friend, Augustus Egg, introduced Collins to Dickens, who was searching for someone to play his valet in the Guild of Literature and Art's production of Edward Bulwer-Lytton's *Not So Bad as We Seem* (1851). Dickens had recently left the editorship of *Bentley's Miscellany* to launch *Household Words,* his entry into the lucrative periodical market. From their first meeting until Dickens's death in 1870 the two would be nearly inseparable. A youthful dandy, Collins gave Dickens ribald companionship and insights into social strata that were new to Dickens; an obsessive perfectionist, Dickens went over the younger writer's work meticulously, critiqued his story lines, and kept his attention focused on fiction rather than drama or other literary forms. Critics point to Dickens's death as the turning point in Collins's career because, with few exceptions, after Dickens died Collins's writing never achieved the artistic levels it reached during the years of their friendship.

Although neither work has much to recommend it, the differences between Collins's short story "The Twin Sisters, A True Story," published in the *International Magazine* in March 1851, and his first novella, *Mr. Wray's Cash-Box* (1852), attest to Dickens's positive influence. "The Twin Sisters" melodramatically chronicles the near tragedy of two lovers and includes favorite Collins themes of doubles and mistaken identities. Clumsily written, with an obvious plot, "The Twin Sisters" sets the nadir for Collins's short fiction. *Mr. Wray's Cash-Box,* on the other hand, shows Collins revamping the highly successful formula Dickens used for the Christmas issues of *Household Words*. Eccentric characters, drawn mostly from a middle-class stratum, engage in melodramatic misadventures based on factual reports; and virtue, though rewarded, is sorely tried. Reuben Wray, a retired Shakespearean bit player, secretly makes a bust of Shakespeare and hides it in a cash box that is stolen by thieves. Wray believes that if the thieves destroy the bust they will destroy his sense of identity. Wray's granddaughter, Annie, retrieves the bust and sets matters to rights. Collins directs his satiric humor at the social scorn Wray suffers, but he makes sure that the story ends on a sentimental note: Wray and his family and friends enjoy a sumptuous Christmas dinner.

Dickensian touches also appear in "A Passage in the Life of Perugino Potts," published in *Bentley's* in February 1852. The first-person narrative chronicles the misadventures of a painter, based on Charley Collins and later recast as Blyth in *Hide and Seek* (1854) and as Pesca in *The Woman in White,* who is commissioned to produce a portrait of a narcissistic cleric, robbed by his model, ignored by the Florence officials, and pursued across Europe by the lovesick, overweight daughter of a marchesa; stylistically, the story spoofs Collins's own biography of his father.

In addition to writing for *Bentley's,* Collins contributed essays and reviews to George Henry Lewes and Thornton Hunt's magazine *The Leader.* The hard work he put into his writing contrasted with his casual attitude toward the profession of law. On 21 November 1852 he was called to the bar, even though he had neither studied for nor passed the examinations. At the time he was working on several short stories, finishing *Mr. Wray's Cash-Box,* touring in *Not So Bad as We Seem,* and revising the first volume of his new novel, *Basil.*

Dickens rejected Collins's first story for *Household Words,* "The Monktons of Wincot Abbey," because he felt that its subject, hereditary insanity, would distress many of his magazine's readers; the story was serialized in November and December 1855 in a rival magazine, *Fraser's.* Dickens's conservatism was *Fraser's* gain: "The Monktons of Wincot Abbey" is a meticulously structured, complex suspense tale; uncertain situations, skillful manipulation of atmosphere and setting, and the narrator's rational view of the events heighten the tension. As the date of his marriage approaches, Alfred Monkton hastens to Naples to seek information about his estranged Uncle Stephen's fatal duel. To most people, except for the narrator and Alfred's fiancée, Alfred seems insane. What Alfred fears is a prophecy that should a Monkton lie "graveless under open sky," the "race shall pass away." The narrator – and the reader – become increasingly drawn into Alfred's desperate search. Using rationality and compassion, the narrator finds Stephen's body resting on trestles in an outer room of a Capuchin monastery, outside the abbey vaults. Although he and Alfred arrange to have the body returned to England, the coffin is lost in a storm, and Alfred soon fulfills the prophecy by dying of fever. Honoring her true love, Alfred's fiancée never marries. Drippingly sentimental by modern standards, "The Monktons of Wincot Abbey" shows Collins's increasing artistic control and growing attachment to deduction as a pivotal story element. The story's narrator is the first in a long line of Collins's amateur detectives. Collins even manages to weave touches of unforced humor into the story in his descriptions of the monastery's vain monk.

Dickens published Collins's "A Terribly Strange Bed" in the 24 April 1852 issue of *Household Words.* Perhaps the most anthologized of all Collins's tales, "A Terribly Strange Bed" falls short of the closely knit plot, shrewd characterization, and intricately drawn atmosphere of "The Monktons of Wincot Abbey." In this tale, set during the French Revolution, a young Englishman named Faulkner spends the night alone in a disreputable gaming house rather than risk his life and winnings on Paris's unfamiliar streets. Trying to sleep in "a thorough clumsy British four-poster" bed, Faulkner notices that the picture on the opposite wall is disappearing from view and realizes that the bed's canopy is descending on him; he rolls off the bed just in time to escape suffocation. Here Collins turns an innocuous Victorian image, a four-poster bed, into a death machine, elevating the mundane to the gruesome. The story clearly anticipates the 1860s vogue for Gothic fiction.

Collins's first collaboration with Dickens was a connected seven-tale series, "The Seven Poor Travellers," that appeared in the Christmas 1854 issue of *Household Words.* Critics disagree on how many of the tales Collins wrote: some credit him with "The Story of the Second Poor Traveller" because of its similarity to "The Last Stage Coachman," "The Story of the Fifth Poor Traveller" because of its fluent French and sympathetic picture of a deformed child, and "The Story of the Sixth Poor Traveller" because of its detective plot and fair presentation of evidence to the reader. "The Story of the Fourth Poor Traveller" was reprinted in Collins's collection *After Dark* (1856) as "The Lawyer's Story of a Stolen Letter," making it undeniably Collins's work. This story begs comparison with Edgar Allan Poe's "The Purloined Letter" (1845); the tale is different enough, however, to suggest that Collins admired rather than imitated Poe's stories. The narrator-protagonist of Collins's story is a brash young lawyer – not the cool C. Auguste Dupin of Poe's tale – who helps his imprudent friend shield his fiancée from a blackmailer, "the ugliest and dirtiest blackguard" one can imagine, by finding an incriminating letter hidden in the villain's lodgings. In many ways the young lawyer prefigures Sir Arthur Conan Doyle's Sherlock Holmes: he combines keen intuition, deductive abilities, and eagerness to defeat a worthy opponent. He poses questions, then cuts his respondents short by answering them himself. He flies about, leaving his friend dumbfounded. Baffled by a cryptic memorandum, he spots the necessary clue at the last minute. Dickens was obviously taken with the character, for he bears a striking resemblance to Jaggers, the lawyer who provides Pip with his fortune in *Great Expectations* (1860). Collins's story, however, contains little hint of the bitter social satire that is threaded through Dickens's novel.

In 1856 Collins collected his stories from *Household Words* in *After Dark*. "A Terribly Strange Bed" was the first story in the book, under the title "The Traveller's Story of a Terribly Strange Bed." After "The Lawyer's Story of a Stolen Letter" the collection includes the novella "The French Governess's Story of Sister Rose," from the 7 to 28 April 1855 issues; "The Nun's Story of Gabriel's Marriage," from the 16 and 23 April 1853 issues; and "The Professor's Story of the Yellow Mask," from the 7 to 28 July 1855 issues. Collins added the previously unpublished "The Angler's Story of the Lady of Glenwith Grange," which Dickens relied on when creating Miss Haversham in *Great Expectations,* and the volume's frame stories, "Leaves from Leah's Diary" and "Last Leaves from Leah's Diary."

Appropriated from a sort of French Newgate Calendar Collins discovered in Paris, "The French Governess's Story of Sister Rose" is a tale of duplicity set during the French Revolution. Charles Danville, a former aristocrat, betrays his innocent wife, Rose, and her brother Louis Trudaine, a chemist who has tried to protect his sister from Charles's brutality, by denouncing them to the revolutionary tribunal. They are saved from the guillotine by Danville's land steward, Lomaque, a character Dickens remodeled as Sydney Carton in *A Tale of Two Cities* (1859). Despite her superior social status, Rose has always treated Lomaque with respect;

Lomaque, a member of the secret police, repays her by erasing her and Louis's names from the execution list. Rose and Louis, presumed dead, come out of hiding to denounce Danville when the Reign of Terror ends. His cowardice and disloyalty revealed, Danville dies in a duel with his bride's father. Despite the sometimes clumsy writing, the novella is a vast improvement over Collins's work before he met Dickens. Collins weaves into a complex narrative stark dramatic irony with subtle social protest, particularly in his sentimental portrayals of women. Rose Danville fits popular genre requirements: despite overwhelming pressure, she stands by her family, particularly her loving brother, and her egalitarian social principles. At her trial she eloquently presents her defense not directly to the tribunal but to an audience Collins suggests is more important – the women, "all sitting together on forms, knitting, shirt-mending, and baby-linen-making, as coolly as if they were at home." Their quiet strength prevents this oppressive social system from tyrannizing them.

The remaining stories in *After Dark* are of uneven quality, but taken together they attest to Collins's growing competence with short fiction. "The Nun's Story of Gabriel's Marriage," a romance set in a Breton fishing community during the Reign of Terror, mixes Gothic eeriness with the pathos of a son's reconciliation with his father. Collins goes against the grain of popular fiction by presenting readers with a perceptive female who narrates Gabriel's hardships and expiation. "The Professor's Story of the Yellow Mask," a thriller set in eighteenth-century Italy, advances middle-class Protestant ethics within the context of a tale of imaginative horror à la Poe and Matthew Lewis. Father Rocco is anything but a stock villain, and Brigida is Collins's most believable "Jezebel." Beloved by the poor of Pisa for his generosity and humility, Father Rocco plots with Brigida against the young nobleman Fabio and his lover, Nanina, a poor artist's model, not for personal gain but to restore to the church property seized by Fabio's ancestors. Revealed, Father Rocco accepts his punishment and encourages Fabio's and Nanina's true love. Brigida, "a tall woman, with bold black eyes, a reckless manner," and "the gait of a tragedy-queen crossing the stage," brazenly pursues Fabio but, failing in her ploy to win his love, accepts voluntary banishment. Another female character, as determined as Brigida and Rose Danville but far more eccentric, is Ida Welwyn, the protagonist of "The Angler's Story of the Lady of Glenwith Grange," who remains a spinster so that she can keep her home as a macabre monument to a forgotten past. Her younger sister, Rosamond, imprudently marries the criminal Monbrun, who poses as the "rich nobleman of France, Baron Franval." Monbrun is unmasked by a courteous and efficient *agent de police,* a character type that was beginning to appear more frequently in Collins's fiction.

To tie the stories in *After Dark* together – and to delight his mother – Collins created the frame narratives "Leaves from Leah's Diary" and "Last Leaves from Leah's Diary." Leah writes that the tales were originally told to her husband, William Kerby, a painter, by his models to pass the time during their sittings. Unable to support his family because of his temporary blindness, William wants to market these stories but cannot write them down. Grudgingly, he agrees to let his wife write and sell the stories he dictates. She writes after her household chores – "after dark" – producing a diary that both serves immediate economic needs and allows her to pass on to her daughter a sense of the creativeness female narratives can have. With this frame Collins makes a more provocative statement about the value of women's narratives than many critics have acknowledged.

Second only in importance to his association with Dickens were Collins's liaisons with Elizabeth Caroline Compton Graves and Martha Rudd. As reported by his imaginative friend John G. Millais, his meeting with Graves could have come from one of his tales; in fact, it became the first chapter of *The Woman in White*. Millais records that late in the summer of 1855 he and Charley and Wilkie Collins were strolling to Millais's studio in north London when they heard a scream and saw "a young and very beautiful woman dressed in flowing white robes that shone in the moonlight" running from the garden of a nearby house. Wilkie Collins gave chase; when he returned the next day he claimed that he had rescued the woman from a nameless man who had imprisoned her by "threats and mesmeric influence." Millais probably embellished the event, but whatever actually happened, the meeting coupled Graves and Collins in a relationship that became the major curiosity of Collins's life. The daughter of a gentleman and the widow of an army officer, George Robert Graves, Elizabeth Graves, who was always "Caroline" to Collins, was barely supporting herself and her daughter, Elizabeth Harriet ("Carrie"), as a pawnbroker when she met Collins. Collins romanced Graves from their first meeting but refused to marry her. He lived openly with her from 1859 until Caroline, exasperated with their unorthodox relationship, wed the much youn-

ger Joseph Charles Clow; according to church records, Collins was present at the 29 October 1868 ceremony. Carrie continued to live with Collins, and by 1870 Caroline had left her unsuccessful marriage and returned to Collins and her daughter.

Some time before Graves married Clow, Collins began a romance with Rudd; how they met is unknown. Whereas Graves influenced *The Woman in White,* the uneducated but intelligent and self-sufficient Rudd was the model for the wronged women in Collins's stories. At the time of Graves's marriage, Rudd was pregnant with her and Collins's first child, Marian, who was born in 1869. Even after Graves returned to him, Collins continued to maintain a household with Rudd, who bore him two more children: Harriet Constance in 1871 and William Charles in 1874. Collins educated his three children and Carrie and made them, Graves, and Rudd the primary beneficiaries of his estate.

It is not known why Collins never married either of the two women in his life. In "Bold Words by a Bachelor," in the 13 December 1856 issue of *Household Words,* he lists several reasons for avoiding marriage, including the problem of a spouse coming ahead of one's friends. Some scholars believe that he did not marry Graves because his mother disapproved of her; but this obstacle was removed in 1868 when Harriet Collins died. Another possibility is Collins's lifelong commitment to social protest: he may have decided to flout Britain's laws, which discriminated against women in matters of divorce and inheritance, by living out of wedlock. On the other hand, he upheld the ideal of marriage in his stories, and he never took an active political interest in the issue of women's rights. What is most likely is simply that Collins was financially capable of keeping two households and chose to do so.

The novella *A Rogue's Life* was serialized in *Household Words* from 1 to 29 March 1856. *A Rogue's Life* was a departure for Collins in its episodic style but not in its melodramatic tone; complex plotting; strong female characters; mystery elements, including archvillains (here, the rather affable Dr. Dulcifer); decorous love relationships; and touches of social protest. The narrator, Frank Softly, reveals himself as an impudent, irresponsible but likable scoundrel. Attracted to adventure, he has turned to fraudulent intrigues to make his living. He finds that he is not suited to his father's profession, medicine, but does have a knack for counterfeiting. Softly ends up in Australia, "a convict aristocrat – a prosperous, wealthy, highly respectable mercantile man." Collins makes the point that Softly is treated more poorly by society than he treats his "marks."

In October 1856 Collins's finances improved markedly when Dickens put him on the staff of *Household Words*; in 1857 Dickens promoted him to associate editor. For the next three years, until *Household Words* ended publication, Collins wrote primarily according to the magazine's (that is, Dickens's) strictures and for a fickle readership. The position offered him a regular salary, but it required him to produce more nonfiction than he would have liked and also meant that others, in particular Dickens, would receive credit for his work. He sought his own byline and permission to publish at least one novel a year serially in the magazine; although Dickens had doubts about the value novels held for subscriptions, he agreed to the latter request, providing that the novel ran no longer than half the year. To some extent, Dickens was correct: during Collins's time with *Household Words,* his greater contribution was his shorter writings.

The first product of Collins's new job was *The Wreck of the Golden Mary,* a novella he and Dickens wrote for the magazine's 1856 Christmas issue. *The Wreck of the Golden Mary* is far from a seamless collaboration; its style varies widely. The sections more likely attributable to Collins are those that include independent "Jezebels," portraitlike settings, methodical plotting, and reliance on rationality. *The Wreck of the Golden Mary* illustrates how easily an uninterested Collins could confirm his second-rate reputation; other of his collaborations with Dickens fared better.

In 1857 Dickens arranged for a professional staging of Collins's play *The Frozen Deep;* during the first rehearsal the forty-five-year-old Dickens put further strain on his already disagreeable home life by falling in love with an eighteen-year-old actress, Ellen Ternan. One of the more noteworthy pieces to arise from Collins's collaboration with Dickens resulted from Dickens's attempt to escape his domestic turmoil: he suggested to Collins that the two take a walking tour of Cumberland, Lancashire, and Yorkshire. The trip inspired "The Lazy Tour of Two Idle Apprentices," which appeared serially in the October 1857 issues of *Household Words.* The Christmas number for 1857 consisted of "The Perils of Certain English Prisoners," which illustrates the method of composition of most of Collins and Dickens's collaborations: Dickens outlined the work and wrote chapters 1 and 3, while Collins wrote the long middle chapter, titled "The Prison in the Woods." Dickens's writing is more exuberant and his characters are more idiosyncratic; Collins is concerned with intricate plotting and vivid descriptions.

By December 1858 Collins was earning more than a living at *Household Words.* In that year he wrote nearly two dozen pieces and collaborated with Dickens on the Christmas issue, "A House to Let," which relies on a frame concerning an elderly gentleman's interest in a nearby house that has a history of unfortunate tenants.

Dickens and his wife, Catherine, had separated in May 1858; Dickens discontinued *Household Words* in May 1859 when his publisher, Bradbury and Evans, refused to print his explanation of the breakup in *Punch.* He quickly inaugurated a new magazine, *All the Year Round,* bringing Collins with him as a member of the staff. The first number, for 30 April 1859, carried the opening of Dickens's *A Tale of Two Cities* and several stories that were included in Collins's next collection.

Like *After Dark,* Collins's second collection of short fiction, *The Queen of Hearts* links previously published stories and novellas by means of a newly composed frame story. In that story, from which the volume takes its name, young Jessie Yelverton hears the other stories because of a clever though sentimental ruse. Three old brothers seek to delay her until George, the son of one of them, can arrive and propose. The three – a clergyman, a doctor, and a lawyer – narrate tales drawn from their professional experiences and, between tales, gossip in ways that build a sense of expectation about the romance of Jessie and George. *The Queen of Hearts* aptly illustrates Collins's attitude toward fiction: stories should entertain not with "outbursts of eloquence, and large-minded philanthropy, and graphic descriptions, and unsparing anatomy of the human heart" but with something that keeps the audience "reading, reading, reading, in a breathless state to find out the end."

Each story in *The Queen of Hearts* deals with love and honor. "Brother Morgan's Story of the Dream Woman" is "The Ostler's Story" from 1855, and "Brother Griffith's Story of Mad Monkton" is a retitling of "The Monktons of Wincot Abbey" from the same year; both stories are exemplary sensational fiction. In "Brother Owen's Story of the Black Cottage" (which had originally appeared in *Harper's New Monthly Magazine* in February 1857 as "The Siege of the Black Cottage") a young girl, honor bound to protect her father's property, faces down the petty thieves Shifty Dick and Jerry. The narrator of "Brother Griffith's Story of the Family Secret" (which was first published in *The National Magazine* in New York in May 1857 as "Uncle George; or, The Family Mystery") learns more slowly than readers that his beloved Uncle George, a doctor, acting on the narrator's "Jezebel" mother's instructions, inadvertently killed the narrator's sister during delicate cosmetic surgery. Devastated by the death and its potential impact on his nephew, George disappears rather than cause further misery. The narrator of "Brother Morgan's Story of Fauntleroy" (which had appeared as "A Paradoxical Experience" in the 13 November 1858 issue of *Household Words*) is a businessman Henry Fauntleroy unselfishly encouraged; the narrator defends his benefactor as a loyal man of integrity even as he acknowledges Fauntleroy's forgeries. The "paradox" is that Fauntleroy would help someone he barely knows and yet, without reflection, betray the trust of investors who were his friends. The maudlin "Brother Owen's Story of the Parson's Scruple" (which was titled "A New Mind" in the 1 January 1859 issue of *Household Words* — the last story Collins published in the magazine before its demise the following May) attacks England's restrictive divorce laws. Alfred Carling, the middle-aged rector of Penliddy, rejects his bride-to-be, Emily Harriet, when he discovers that she is a divorcée. Later the rector reads in the *Times* about the "discreditable anomaly in the administration of justice" that allows England to stand "alone as the one civilized country in the world having a divorce law for the husband which was not also a divorce law for the wife."

*The Queen of Hearts* also reprints a sophisticated sensational tale, two mystery stories, and a novella whose theme Collins later used in *The Woman in White* and *The Moonstone*. "Brother Morgan's Story of the Dead Hand" (which appeared as "The Dead Hand" in the 10 October 1857 issue of *Household Words*) is second only to "The Traveller's Tale of a Terribly Strange Bed" as a first-rate terror story. At the Two Robins Inn, a place other travelers wisely decline to enter, Arthur Holliday agrees to share a room with a medical student who, the innkeeper ironically assures him, is "the quietest man I ever came across." As it turns out, the student is dead; but at midnight, Holliday sees the corpse's hand move. Unnerved, he calls for a doctor — the narrator — to revive the man. The final twist comes when the man turns out to be Arthur's illegitimate brother and Arthur's fiancée's first love. Shielding his identity from Arthur, the nameless traveler withdraws and is only heard from again many years later when he unsuspectingly secures employment with the narrator. "Brother Morgan's Story of the Dead Hand" is Collins at his best; it sets up its persuasively eerie atmosphere through coincidence and reason, not spiritual interventions.

*Collins, circa 1851; oil painting by J. E. Millais (National Portrait Gallery, London)*

"Brother Griffith's Story of the Biter Bit" and "Brother Owen's Story of Anne Rodway" are enduring experiments in detective fiction. "Brother Griffith's Story of the Biter Bit" (which first appeared as "Who Is the Thief ?" in the April 1858 issue of *The Atlantic Monthly*) purports to be a collection of letters of Chief Inspector Theakstone, Sergeant Bulmer, and the amateur detective Matthew Sharpin concerning Sharpin's first and only investigation. Foisted off on the department, Sharpin bungles an easy burglary case by failing to put painfully obvious clues together correctly. He follows false trails with vigor, argues for the significance of irrelevant evidence, concludes that the least likely suspect is the criminal, and sets up an elopement that backfires. As he would do in *The Moonstone*, Collins reports the amateur's miscues and the professionals' increasing aggravation in letters that humorously satirize each character. Sharpin is smugly incompetent; he makes a travesty of rationality and antagonizes the police officials, who just want this interfering outsider to go away — but he always acts consistently, showing clearly how Collins makes actions grow out of character. In many ways, Collins never equaled "Brother Griffith's Story of the Biter Bit" in any other detective story.

Collins's first true murder mystery, "Brother Owen's Story of Anne Rodway" (which was originally published in the 13 November 1858 issue of *Household Words* as "The Diary of Anne Rodway"), introduced elements into detective fiction that set the genre's pattern for decades to come. Anne is an impoverished seamstress who doubts the official verdict that her friend Mary Mallinson's death was accidental. Working from the slight evidence – "a very old, rotten, dingy strip of black silk, with thin lilac lines, all blurred and deadened with dirt" – her stoic intelligence, and her own unwavering faith in her friend, Anne proves that the drunkard Noah Truscott murdered Mary. The portrait Collins draws of lower-class life and its brutality rivals any social satire Dickens wrote. Collins attacks the unstated conventions that perpetuate class distinctions: Anne struggles to get just less than three pounds to pay for Mary's funeral because the church will not "do without so many small charges for burying poor people"; her landlord brands her a fool for spending money on a funeral when Mary "died in my debt"; a clergyman preaches to her that "all things were ordered for the best" and that Anne should accept her and Mary's fate because "we are put into the stations in life that are properest for us."

Finally, "Brother Griffith's Story of a Plot in Private Life" (which appeared as "A Marriage Tragedy" in the February 1858 issue of *Harper's New Monthly Magazine*) deftly presents a complicated family conspiracy with plot elements reminiscent of *The Woman in White* and *The Moonstone*. James Smith, an early version of Percival Glyde in *The Woman in White*, disappears after being exposed as a bigamist; all that is left is a bloodstained nightgown. The piece's "Jezebel," the quadroon maid Josephine, falsely implicates Smith's servant, William, and Smith's rich young wife in Smith's supposed murder. Mr. Dark, a suspicious lawyer-detective, launches a counterplot that brings Smith out of hiding for William and Mrs. Smith's trial and confirms that Smith bloodied the nightgown when he shaved off his beard in an attempt to disguise himself.

In the stories in *After Dark* and *The Queen of Hearts* Collins had found the narrative skills that had been lacking in his early, unreadable novels and became a master storyteller. He had learned how to create believable characters, to thread rational processes into sensational and detective fiction, and to blend social satire with humor. He

could manipulate plots as adroitly as Dickens and was recognized by his peers as the leader of the sensational school. Although he continued to write some short fiction, for the next three decades Collins turned primarily to drama and novels. When Dickens called on his protégé to contribute a novel to be serialized in *All the Year Round*, Collins, though ill and under considerable strain from his brother's health and mental problems, delivered *The Woman in White*, which ran from 26 November 1859 to 25 August 1860. A runaway bestseller, *The Woman in White* paid Collins so handsomely that in January 1861 he resigned from the staff of *All the Year Round* and turned his attention to his next novel, *No Name* (1862), which first appeared serially in Dickens's magazine, and a collection of his nonfiction, *My Miscellanies* (1863).

"Picking up Waifs at Sea," published in the Christmas 1861 issue of *All the Year Round*, pokes fun at cherished Victorian ideas. Two babies born simultaneously at sea, one in first class and the other in less opulent circumstances, are switched at birth; thus, an accident, not individual talent or industry, elevates one to riches and keeps the other poor. When the mothers discover that they have the wrong children, they both say that they are satisfied because "the Voice of Nature" directed each to the correct child.

Dr. Francis Carr Beard, Dickens's physician, had been treating Collins since 1859 for "rheumatic gout," but by 1863 Collins's enigmatic condition had become true gout in his right foot. With the onset of acute symptoms Beard prescribed regular doses of laudanum, the century's medicine of choice for the condition; as a result, Collins began an addiction to opium that he never escaped. In search of a cure for his gout he traveled to Europe with Graves and Carrie and tried Turkish baths, quinine, potassium, and restrictive diets but got only moderate relief. When he returned to England in 1864, following a year and a half of what he called "total literary abstinence," he began work in earnest on *Armadale* (1866), his fourth novel. The novel was a success, with the serialized version saving *Harper's Monthly Magazine* and securing Collins's already favorable financial relationship with the Harper publishing firm. Recognizing that the vogue for sensational fiction was waning, he set out to write a novel that subverted the genre. *The Moonstone*, which ran from 4 January to 8 August 1868, increased the sales of *All the Year Round* more than any other serialized novel and created what is regarded today as classic detective fiction.

The early 1870s brought Collins his greatest success as a playwright. He adapted *The Woman in*

*White* for a stage production that opened on 9 October 1871 to an appreciative audience at the Olympic Theatre. Collins wanted to join the touring company, but increasing ill health made it impossible for him to do so. Despite a severe attack of gout in the summer of 1871, Collins completed the novella "Miss or Mrs.?" for the Christmas issue of the *London Graphic Illustrated Newspaper*. Written with limited settings and with strategic entrances and exits, the work seems designed for eventual stage production; but it was deemed to be too scandalous for the public. "Miss or Mrs.?" repeats the contrived, overemotional love triangle of *Basil*. The prosperous merchant Richard Turlington hides his suspicious past to woo Natalie Graybrooke, the daughter of the wealthy Sir Joseph Graybrooke and a Martinique Creole, but fails to win her or her money. In a rage exceptional in Collins's fiction, Turlington plots to murder Graybrooke but, ironically, kills himself when he looks down the barrel of his gun to find out why it misfired.

In 1873 Collins collected "The Fatal Cradle" ("Picking up Waifs at Sea" under a new title), " 'Blow up the Brig!,' " and "A Mad Marriage" with the novella "Miss or Mrs.?" as *Miss or Mrs.?: And Other Stories in Outline*. Late in 1873 Collins embarked on a six-month tour of the United States, reading a much-expanded version of "The Dream Woman" to audiences eager to meet the popular novelist and close friend of the late Dickens. Collins admired America's openness and informality and savored New England's dry, cold climate. The tour, however, further damaged his health and made Collins only a fraction of the money Dickens had received on similar trips. Collins planned, but never made, a tour of England.

In 1874 Collins collected three previously published stories as *The Frozen Deep and Other Stories*. Here "The Dream Woman," an even more expanded version of his American reading text, becomes a complex, multiple-narrator tale with a new opening and closing. The title character's past, though still obscure, is integrated into the ostler's recurrent dream; the 1855 story's mood of horror and chance are moderated and blended into the characterization and dialogue. In "The Frozen Deep," adapted from Collins's 1857 play, weakly portrayed characters search for love. And "John Jago's Ghost" turns an actual 1819 Vermont legal dispute into an effective, dark melodrama comparable to Dickens's unfinished *The Mystery of Edwin Drood* (1870).

Collins attempted to tap into public tastes with his mid- to late-century stories. "The Clergyman's

Confession," in *The Canadian Monthly* (August–September 1875), is a venture into the occult weakened by thin characterization and an unconvincing atmosphere. "The Captain's Last Love," in *The Spirit of the Times* (23 December 1876), arose from Collins's first, unpublished Tahitian novel and would best have remained unpublished. It is a far-fetched, overly sentimentalized tale of a ship's captain who loses his beautiful love and her holy father when he violates her island home and sets off a volcanic eruption. When Charles Dickens Jr. asked Collins to write a story for the 2 July 1877 issue of *All the Year Round,* Collins obliged with "Percy and the Prophet," a somewhat better story than "The Captain's Lost Love" but far from Collins's best. As in *Armadale,* a fortune teller warns the title character of a vision that comes all too true. "My Lady's Money," written for the 1877 Christmas edition of *The Illustrated London News,* is clumsily written but is noteworthy as one of the first detective stories to contain openly derogatory remarks about incompetent, inflexible police detectives. Even though it steals its central theme, plot, and reliance on ghostly ornamentation from "Percy and the Prophet," "The Duel in Herne Wood," which appeared in *The Spirit of the Times* (22 December 1877), is a far superior tale with multiple narrators and a clever trick whereby a less-skilled combatant gains the advantage over an opponent. Collins also wrote an intriguing first-person narrative, "A Shocking Story," which appeared in a New York magazine, *The International Review* (2 November 1878), and a lighthearted love story, "The Mystery of Marmaduke," for *The Spirit of the Times* (28 December 1878). He could produce a ridiculously sentimental tale such as "She Loves and Lies" for *The Spirit of the Times* (22 December 1883); on the other hand, he also wrote some groundbreaking psychological detective fiction such as "Who Killed Zebedee?," published in *The Seaside Library* (26 January 1881), and a fine portrait of a young woman's mind, "How I Married Him," which appeared in *The Spirit of the Times* (24 December 1881).

Fourteen of Collins's late stories were republished under new titles in the three-volume collection *Little Novels* (1887), where "The Clergyman's Confession" became "Miss Jéromette and the Clergyman"; "The Captain's Last Love" appeared as "The Captain and the Nymph"; "Percy and the Prophet" was renamed "Mr. Percy and the Prophet"; "The Duel in Herne Wood" was published as "Miss Bertha and the Yankee"; "A Shocking Story" was retitled "Miss Mina and the Groom"; "The Mystery of Marmaduke" appeared as "Mr. Marmaduke and the Minister"; "She Loves and Lies" was retitled "Mr. Lismore and the Widow"; "Who Killed Zebedee?" was transformed into "Mr. Policeman and the Crook"; and "How I Married Him" became "Miss Morris and the Stranger." Early in 1889 an attack of bronchitis forced Collins to ask *The Illustrated London News* for an extension of the deadline for his new novel, *Blind Love,* which was to start serialization in June. Collins had carefully outlined the novel and had written sufficient installments to take him through October, but on 30 June he had a stroke and could no longer work. He asked Walter Besant, a novelist with a similar approach to literature, to finish the novel. In September Collins was again stricken with bronchitis; he died on 23 September.

In *An Autobiography* (1883) Collins's friend Anthony Trollope wrote that Collins outstripped all his contemporaries "in a certain most difficult branch of his art": he could construct fiction down to the minutest detail so that each element dovetailed with absolute accuracy. But, since Trollope could not "lose the taste of the construction," he wrote, "such work gives me no pleasure." Critical disdain for Collins's work continues; at his worst, his stories are overplotted and repetitive. But even this flaw fits his convictions about what interested audiences. He consistently held what he called an "old-fashioned view that the primary object of a work of fiction should be to tell a story" as dramatically and convincingly as possible. At his best, Collins imbued popular genres with realism and vivid characterization; unfortunately, his best came irregularly. While he showed Dickens the value of a good plot, he never invented characters as memorable as Wilkins Micawber, Uriah Heep, Martin Chuzzlewit, Ebenezer Scrooge, or Jack Dawkins, the Artful Dodger. Frequently in poor health and always contending with restrictive deadlines, Collins wrote uneven work that leads critics to label him a lesser Dickens. Yet for his skillful narrative technique, ingenious plotting, romanticism blended with realism, and economical description, Collins deserves recognition as one of the better minor Victorian writers.

## Bibliographies:

R. V. Andrew, "A Wilkie Collins Check-List," *English Studies in Africa,* 3 (March 1960): 79–98;

Kirk H. Beetz, *Wilkie Collins: An Annotated Bibliography, 1889–1976* (Metuchen, N.J. & London: Scarecrow Press, 1978).

## Biography:

Catherine Peters, *The King of Inventors: A Life of Wilkie Collins* (London: Secker & Warburg, 1991).

## References:

R. V. Andrew, "Wilkie Collins: A Critical Survey of His Prose Fiction with Bibliography," M.A. thesis, Potchefstroom University, 1959;

Robert Ashley, *Wilkie Collins* (London: Barker, 1952);

Ashley, "Wilkie Collins and the Detective Story," *Nineteenth-Century Fiction,* 6 ( June 1951): 47–60;

Bradford A. Booth, "Wilkie Collins and the Art of Fiction," *Nineteenth-Century Fiction,* 6 (September 1951): 131–143;

Arthur Compton-Rickett, "Wilkie Collins," *Bookman,* 42 ( June 1912): 109–111;

T. S. Eliot, "Wilkie Collins and Dickens," in his *Selected Essays* (London: Faber & Faber, 1932), pp. 460–470;

Sue Lonoff, "Charles Dickens and Wilkie Collins," *Nineteenth-Century Fiction,* 35 (September 1980): 150–170;

William H. Marshall, *Wilkie Collins* (New York: Twayne, 1970);

John G. Millais, *The Life and Letters of Sir John Everett Millais,* 2 volumes (London: Methuen, 1899);

C. H. Muller, "Victorian Sensationalism: The Short Stories of Wilkie Collins," *Unisa English Studies,* 11, no. 1 (1973): 12–24;

Norman Page, ed., *Wilkie Collins: The Critical Heritage* (London: Routledge & Kegan Paul, 1974);

Charles Rycroft, "A Detective Story: Psychoanalytic Observations," *Psychoanalytic Quarterly,* 26 (1957): 229–245;

Dorothy L. Sayers, *Wilkie Collins: A Critical and Biographical Study,* edited by E. R. Gregory (Toledo, Ohio: Friends of the University of Toledo Libraries, 1977);

Anthony Trollope, *An Autobiography* (2 volumes, Edinburgh & London: Blackwood, 1883; 1 volume, New York: Harper, 1883).

## Papers:

Letters, manuscripts, and other papers of Wilkie Collins are in the Princeton University Library.

# George Croly

*(17 August 1780 – 24 November 1860)*

David C. Hanson
*Southeastern Louisiana University*

BOOKS: *Paris in 1815: A Poem,* anonymous (London: John Murray, 1817);

*Lines on the Death of Her Royal Highness the Princess Charlotte* (London: John Murray, 1818);

*The Angel of the World, an Arabian Tale; Sebastian, a Spanish Tale; with Other Poems,* anonymous (London: Warren, 1820; New York: Morris, Willis, 1844);

*The Coronation: Observations on the Public Life of the King* (London: Warren / Edinburgh: Blackwood, 1821);

*Paris in 1815; with Other Poems* (London: Warren, 1821);

*Catiline: A Tragedy, in Five Acts; with Other Poems* (London: Hurst, Robinson / Edinburgh: Constable, 1822);

*Gems, Principally from the Antique, Drawn and Etched by Richard Dagley . . . with Illustrations in Verse, by the Rev. George Croly* (London: Hurst, Robinson / Edinburgh: Constable, 1822);

*Pride Shall Have a Fall: A Comedy, in Five Acts – with Songs,* anonymous [also attributed to George Soane] (London: Hurst, Robinson, 1824; New York: Wiley, 1824);

*Popery and the Popish Question: Being an Exposition of the Political and Doctrinal Opinions of Messrs. O'Connell, Keogh, Dromgole, Gandolphy, &c. &c.* (London: Printed for G. B. Whittaker, 1825);

*May Fair: In Four Cantos,* anonymous [also attributed to Henry Luttrell] (London: Ainsworth, 1827);

*The Apocalypse of St. John, or Prophecy of the Rise, Progress, and Fall of the Church of Rome; the Inquisition; the Revolution of France; the Universal War; and the Final Triumph of Christianity: Being a New Interpretation* (London: Printed for C. & J. Rivington, 1827; Philadelphia: Littell / New York: Carvill, 1827; revised edition, London: Rivington, 1828; revised and enlarged, 1838); preface republished as *The Englishman's Polar Star!! Or, a Deeply Interesting, and Highly Important View of Unquestioned Historical Facts, as Connected with the Honour and Safety of the British Empire; Being a Preface to a New Interpretation of the*

*Apocalypse of St. John. With Introductory and Concluding Remarks, by R. H. M.* (Preston: Printed and sold by E. Moreland, 1828); republished without remarks by R. H. M. as *Protestantism the Polar Star of England* (London: Wakefield, 1829); and as *England the Fortress of Christianity* (London: Protestant Association, 1837); and as *England the Fathers of Christianity* (N.p., 1840);

*Salathiel: A Story of the Past, the Present, and the Future,* anonymous (3 volumes, London: Colburn, 1828; 2 volumes, New York: Carvill / Philadelphia: Carey, Lea & Carey, 1828); revised as *Salathiel, the Immortal: A History* (London: Published for H. Colburn by Hurst & Blackett, 1855; London & New York: Routledge, 1858); republished as *Tarry Thou Till I Come; Or, Salathiel, the Wandering Jew,* edited by Isaac K. Funk, with introductory letter by Gen. Lewis Wallace (New York & London: Funk & Wagnalls, 1901);

*Tales of the Great St. Bernard,* anonymous (3 volumes, London: Colburn, 1828; 2 volumes, New York: Printed by J. & J. Harper, 1829); republished as volumes 22–24 of *English and Foreign National Tales and Novels, by Distinguished Authors* (London: Colburn / Dublin: Cumming, 1838);

*The Poetical Works of the Rev. George Croly,* 2 volumes (London: Colburn & Bentley, 1830);

*The Life and Times of His Late Majesty George the Fourth: With Anecdotes of Distinguished Persons of the Last Fifty Years* (London: Duncan, 1830; revised edition, New York: Harper, 1831); republished as *The Personal History of His Late Majesty George the Fourth: With Anecdotes of Distinguished Persons of the Last Fifty Years,* 2 volumes (London: Colburn, 1841);

*The Society for the Propagation of the Gospel in Foreign Parts: A Sermon Preached in Pursuance of the King's Letter . . . in Aid of the Funds of the Above Institution. With a Brief Memoir of the Society* (London: Duncan, 1831);

*The Year of Liberation: A Journal of the Defence of Hamburgh against the French Army under Marshal Davoust, in 1813, with Sketches of the Battles of Lutzen, Bautzen, &c. &c.,* anonymous, 2 volumes (London: Duncan, 1832);

*Divine Providence; or, The Three Cycles of Revelation, Showing the Parallelism of the Patriarchal, Jewish, and Christian Dispensations; Being a New Evidence of the Divine Origin of Christianity,* 3 volumes (London: Duncan, 1834);

*The Spread of the Gospel the Safeguard of England!: A Sermon, Preached . . . on Sunday, October 4, 1835, Being the Tercentenary of the Translation of the Whole Bible into the English Language* (London: Duncan, 1835); revised and enlarged as *The Bible: The Restorer of Christianity: A Sermon on the First Printing of the Whole Bible in Our Language* (London: Kendrick, 1849);

*The Divine Origin, Appointment, and Obligation of Marriage: A Sermon, Preached on Sunday, March 20,* *1836, in the Church of St. Stephen's, Walbrook* (London: Duncan, 1836);

*Roman Catholic Pledges, and Protestant Securities Speech* (N.p., 1837);

*The Reformation a Direct Gift of Divine Providence: A Sermon, Preached in St. Paul's Cathedral, on . . . October 8, 1838, the Triennial Visitation of the Rt. Hon. and Rt. Rev. Charles James, Lord Bishop of London* (London: Duncan, 1838; revised edition, London: Protestant Association, 1839);

*A Memoir of the Political Life of the Right Honourable Edmund Burke: With Extracts from His Writings,* 2 volumes (Edinburgh: Blackwood / London: Cadell, 1840);

*Historical Sketches, Speeches, and Characters* (London: Seeley & Burnside, 1842);

*The Holy Land, Syria, Idumea, Arabia, Egypt and Nubia: From Drawings Made on the Spot by David Roberts, R. A., with Historical Descriptions, by the Rev$^d$. George Croly,* by Croly and William Brockedon (5 volumes, London: Moon, 1842–1849; 2 volumes, New York: Appleton, n.d.);

*The Universal Kingdom: A Sermon, Preached at the Request of the Protestant Association of London, May 4, 1843* (London: Duncan & Malcolm, 1843);

*Marston; or, The Memoirs of a Statesman* (Philadelphia: Lea & Blanchard, 1845); republished as *Marston; or, the Soldier and Statesman,* 3 volumes (London: Colburn, 1846);

*Letters on the Affairs of the Parish of Walbrook* (N.p., 1845);

*The Maynooth Grant: The Substance of a Speech, Delivered at the Great Protestant Meeting in London, April 14th, 1845* (London: Rivington, 1845);

*The Modern Orlando: Cantos I to VII,* anonymous (London: Colburn, 1846);

*The Divine Origin and Obligation of Marriage: A Sermon* (London: Kendrick, 1848);

*The Claims of the Jews Incompatible with the National Profession of Christianity* (London: Seeleys, 1848);

*National Diseases, Divine Judgments: A Sermon on the Approach of the Cholera Preached in the Church of St. Stephen, Walbrook* (London: Kendrick, 1848);

*The French Revolution, of 1848: A Sermon* (London: Kendrick, 1848);

*Popery the Antichrist: A Sermon, Preached in the Church of St. Stephen, Walbrook* (London: Kendrick, 1848);

*Sermons Preached in the Chapel of the Foundling Hospital, with Others Preached in St. Stephen's, Walbrook, in 1847* (London: Smith, Elder, 1848);

*The Year of Revolutions: A Sermon, Preached on the Last Day of the Year 1848* (London: Kendrick, 1849);

*Marriage with the Sister of a Deceased Wife Injurious to Morals, and Unauthorized by Holy Scripture* (N.p., 1849);

*Papal Rome: The Principles and Practises of Rome Alike Condemned by the Gospel: A Sermon* (London: Kendrick, 1849);

*National Knowledge, National Power: An Address Delivered at the Conversazione of the City of London Literary and Scientific Institution, December 5th, 1849* (London: Kendrick, 1850);

*The Divine Origin and Obligation of the Sabbath: A Sermon* (London: Kendrick, 1850);

*The Theory of Baptism: The Regeneration of Infants in Baptism Vindicated on the Testimony of Holy Scripture, Christian Antiquity, and the Church of England* (London: Rivington, 1850);

*Infant Regeneration, the Doctrine of Holy Scripture and of the Church of England: A Sermon* (London: Kendrick, 1850);

*The Popish Primacy: Two Sermons on the Conversions to Popery. And the Coming Trial of Nations* (London: Kendrick, 1850);

*The Theory of the Lord's Supper: A Sermon* (London: Kendrick, 1851);

*The Closing of the Exhibition: Extracts from a Sermon* (London: Kendrick, 1851);

*Scenes from Scripture, with Other Poems* (London: Colburn, 1851);

*The Miracles of Scripture Contrasted with the Fictions of Popery: Five Sermons, Preached in the Church of Saint Stephen, Walbrook, in October and November, 1851* (London: Kendrick, 1852);

*Public Worship a Divine Obligation: A Sermon* (London: Teape, 1852);

*A Sermon on the Death of the Duke of Wellington* (London: Seeleys, 1852);

*Irish Eloquence, as Illustrated in the Speeches of Curran: Lectures Delivered before the Young Men's Christian Association, in Exeter Hall, from November 1852 to February 1853* (London: Nisbet, 1853);

*The Church of England, Founded on Scripture, and Essential to the Constitution: A Sermon* (London: Seeleys, 1853);

*National Defence Essential to National Safety, and Justified by Holy Scripture: A Sermon* (London: Seeleys, 1853);

*England, Turkey, and Russia: A Sermon, Preached on the Embarkation of the Guards for the East* (London: Seeleys, 1854);

*The Dealings of God with Nations* (London, 1854);

*Psalms and Hymns for Public Worship: Written, and Compiled by George Croly* (London: Kendrick, 1854);

*Observations on the Character and Conduct of the Prince Consort, in Reference to the Aspersions on His Royal Highness,* anonymous (London: Bentley, 1854);

*The Past Year, 1855: A Sermon* (N.p., 1856);

*The Threescore and Ten: Symposium, or Literary Reunion, Held at the Bedford Hotel, Brighton, on Tuesday, November 22, 1859, When the Following Original Lines Were Read by a Distinguished Author, on Proposing the Health of the Senior Member in the Chair* (N.p., 1860?);

*Divine Providence: A Sermon* (London: Bell & Daldy, 1860);

*The Book of Job, by the Late Rev. George Croly . . . with a Biographical Sketch of the Author by His Son* (Edinburgh & London: Blackwood, 1863).

PLAY PRODUCTIONS: *Pride Shall Have a Fall,* London, Theatre Royal, Covent Garden, 11 March 1824;

*Lucius Catiline, the Roman Traitor,* adapted by H. M. Milner, London, Royal Coburg Theatre, 4 June 1827.

OTHER: *The Graces, or Literary Souvenir for 1824,* edited by Croly (London: Hurst, Robinson, 1824);

*The Beauties of the British Poets: With a Few Introductory Observations,* compiled by Croly (London: Seeley & Burnside, 1828; enlarged edition, New York: Wells, 1831);

"Il Vesuviano: A Neapolitan Tale," in *Friendship's Offering for 1830: A Literary Album and Annual Remembrancer* (London: Smith, Elder, 1829);

Joseph Butler, *The Analogy of Religion, Natural and Revealed to the Constitution and Course of Nature: To Which Are Added Two Brief Dissertations: I. On Personal Identity. II. On the Nature of Virtue,* memoir of Butler by Croly, Sacred Classics, volume 8 (London: Hatchard, 1834);

*The Works of Alexander Pope; With a Memoir of the Author, Notes, and Critical Notices on Each Poem,* 4 volumes, edited by Croly (London: Valpy, 1835);

George Gordon, Lord Byron, *Opere complete di Lord Byron, voltate dall'originale inglese in prosa italiana da Carlo Rusconi, . . . con note ed illustrazioni del volgarizzatore nonchè dei signori Moore . . . Croly . . . ,* 2 volumes (Padua, 1842);

"The Cultivation of the Intellect, a Divine Duty of Man," in *Hints on the Culture of Character,* edited by James Hogg (London: Hogg, 1855);

Richard Herring, *Paper and Paper-Making, Ancient and Modern,* introduction by Croly (London, 1855);

"A View of the Reformation in England," in *The Life of Luther,* by Heinrich Gelzer, introduction by Croly (London, 1858 [i.e., 1857]);

"The Intercession of Christ," in *Nineteen Sermons, Preached in St. Ann's Church, Manchester, during the Season of the Manchester Art Treasures Exhibition 1857* (London & Edinburgh, 1858);

"Antonio di Carara: A Paduan Tale," in *Tales from Blackwood,* first series, 12 volumes (London: Blackwood, 1858–1861), X: 1–79;

"The Pandour and His Princess: A Hungarian Sketch," in *Tales from Blackwood,* IX: 1–64;

"The Natolian Story-Teller," in *Tales from Blackwood,* XI: 1–69;

"The Premier and His Wife: A Story of the Great World," in *Tales from Blackwood,* XII: 57–94;

Jeremy Taylor, *The Rule and Exercises of Holy Living,* life of Taylor by Croly (Philadelphia: Evans, 1859);

"Traditions of the Rabbins," in *The Avenger, a Narrative; and Other Papers,* by Thomas De Quincey [Croly piece misattributed to De Quincey] (Boston: Ticknor & Fields, 1859).

SELECTED PERIODICAL PUBLICATIONS –
UNCOLLECTED: "A Spanish Tale," *Blackwood's Edinburgh Magazine,* 11 (April 1822): 403–419; revised as "The Locked-Up Beauty," in Croly's *Tales of the Great St. Bernard,* anonymous (3 volumes, London: Colburn, 1828; 2 volumes, New York: Printed by J. & J. Harper, 1829);

"The Enchanter Faustus and Queen Elizabeth," attributed to Croly, *Blackwood's Edinburgh Magazine,* 12 (August 1822): 230–234;

"The Tertulla (A Spanish Conversazione)," *Blackwood's Edinburgh Magazine,* 13 (May 1823): 518–527;

"The Antonias: A Story of the South," *Blackwood's Edinburgh Magazine,* 18 (November 1825): 601–620; revised as "The Patron Saint," in *Tales of the Great St. Bernard;*

"The Carbonaro: A Sicilian Story," *Blackwood's Edinburgh Magazine,* 20 (September 1826): 494–504; revised as "The Conspirator," in *Tales of the Great St. Bernard;*

"Convent of St. Bernard," *New Monthly Magazine and Literary Journal,* 25 (May 1829): 452–458;

"The Aga of the Janizaries," *Blackwood's Edinburgh Magazine,* 31 (February 1832): 239–254;

"The Castle of the Isle of Rugen," *Blackwood's Edinburgh Magazine,* 31 (May 1832): 790–806;

"Calaspo, the Republican," *Blackwood's Edinburgh Magazine,* 31 (June 1832): 928–943;

"Eliezer the Sage, and Eliezer the Simple," *Blackwood's Edinburgh Magazine,* 32 (August 1832): 193–214;

"The Conde de Ildefonzo: A Tale of the Spanish Revolution," *Blackwood's Edinburgh Magazine,* 35 (May 1834): 756–775; 36 (July 1834): 48–65;

"Carlo Sebastiani, the Aid-de-Camp," *Blackwood's Edinburgh Magazine,* 47 (April 1840): 497–511; (May 1840): 650–661; (June 1840): 739–752;

"De Walstein, the Enthusiast: A Tale of the French Revolution," *Blackwood's Edinburgh Magazine,* 48 (September 1840): 338–354.

George Croly was noted for his versatility and productivity even in his own time, the period from the second generation of English Romanticism through high Victorianism, when prolific authorship was the rule. He invented short tales as easily as he turned out plays, novels, poetry of many kinds, and editions of the works of other poets; journalistic essays on a wide range of topics; and theological works and sermons. His tales formed a substantial contribution to the fiction in *Blackwood's Edinburgh Magazine,* which, in turn, provided one of the earliest and steadiest models for British nineteenth-century short-fiction writing. Croly also promulgated the *Blackwood's* political cause: through nearly three hundred articles during more than three decades he was among the magazine's most vehement and unwavering spokesmen for "Ultra-Toryism" or Anglican "Ultra-Protestantism" – beliefs that pervade all of his work, including his tales.

Croly was born in Dublin on 17 August 1780; his father was a physician. At fifteen he entered Trinity College, and in 1804 he took his M.A. with distinction and was ordained in the Protestant Church of Ireland. He would always resist appointments to obscure parishes, and he escaped his first curacy in a remote northern Ireland parish by moving to London in 1810 with his widowed mother, two unmarried sisters, and a brother who was in the military. There he was neglected by the Anglican Church despite his militant dedication to its causes. At first this neglect resulted from an unfortunate coincidence: he was recommended to the lord chancellor, John Scott, First Earl of Eldon, by the editor William Jerdan; but his name was confused with that of another priest who was a convert from Roman Catholicism and who was, therefore – ironically – deemed ineligible by Croly's own party. It was no accident, however, that the neglect continued for more than twenty years: Croly was disliked for his outspokenness and for his Irish heritage. Thus, he was forced to depend for survival on journalism and popular literature, requiring a rapid facility that may account for the blemishes even in his best tales.

Croly's ferocity qualified him for the slashing journalism that was acceptable at the time. Henry Crabb Robinson, having met the young clergyman in 1813, refers to his "vehement tone of conversation" that reminds one of "a bandit of the Radcliffe school." That judgment recurs in subsequent memoirs – except in those by Croly's son Frederick W. Croly (included in George Croly's *The Book of Job*, 1863) and by Richard Herring, which were authorized by the family; even the respectful Archibald Alison recalls in his autobiography (1883) that Croly "was entirely without fear in delivering his opinions either in public or private." Most accounts include comments on his rather formidable appearance: he had an imposingly bulky figure, with a large face, possibly pock-marked, and eyes that flashed beneath shaggy eyebrows. Nonetheless, behind his fierce mien may have lain a shy awkwardness, as suggested by John Wilson Croker, who claimed to have known Croly "*longer*," yet, tellingly, "*less* than anybody." In a February 1835 letter recalling Croly in earlier years, Croker portrays a "shy reserved man . . . stiff and ungainly."

In April 1813 Robinson primed Croly to step into his position as foreign correspondent to *The Times*, though whether Croly was sent to Hamburg or Paris is unclear. At this time Croly was already working for *The Times* as a drama critic. He continued reviewing theater after his return, at some point becoming the drama critic for the rival *New Times*, which was published from 1817 to 1828. When Jerdan took over the editorship of *The Literary Gazette* in 1817 he brought Croly with him as a major contributor, especially of poetry and criticism. Whether Croly also contributed tales cannot be determined, since his poems, identifiable only by their reprintings in his *Poetical Works* (1830), are signed in *The Literary Gazette* with constantly changing pen names. Croly's association with this popular magazine shows his attitude toward tales and verse, which he regarded as lending piquancy to the lighter miscellanies such as *The Literary Gazette* or as leavening the weightier material in quarterlies such as *Blackwood's* (he would frequently cajole the dignified *Blackwood's*, as in a characteristic letter of 30 July 1838, to take some "compassion for the tastes of that immense multitude who prefer being amused to being taught, & . . . would rather laugh than think").

As a clergyman, Croly gained a reputation as a "political preacher," a view Frederick W. Croly attempts to refute; however, James Grant more convincingly characterizes Croly's preaching as promulgating ecclesiastical – that is, political – rather than doctrinal or devotional opinions. The same is true of the fiction, though here Croly is less explicitly partisan in his support of Anglicanism and restricts his criticisms to denigrating Roman Catholicism, Islam, and "atheist" democracies. At the same time, though, Croly's fiction is strangely absorbed in a sensationalized treatment of the movements that he abhorred. For example, while "The Antonias: A Story of the South" (*Blackwood's*, November 1825) prophesies the overthrow of Catholicism, the narrator temporizes by admitting that "men shall long speak of it, as the richest device of the working of man's mind." Similarly, despite his politics, Croly modeled his style on that of the liberal poet George Gordon, Lord Byron. Indeed, Croly's sisters boasted to Bryan Waller Procter ("Barry Cornwall") "that George was destined to push Lord Byron from his throne." Croly made his first sensation with *Paris in 1815*, published in two parts in 1817 and 1821, a travelogue poem that imitates Byron's *Childe Harold's Pilgrimage* (1812–1818) but that, unlike Byron, dwells on the horrors of revolution. In a review of the poem in the *Quarterly Review* (April–July 1817) Croker lauded Croly's adaptation of Byronism to "a union, unhappily too rare, of piety and poetry, of what is right in politics, respectable in morals, correct in taste, and splendid in imagination." This appropriation of Byronism to Tory purposes should be borne in mind when one reads the best-known critical judgment of Croly, Byron's lampoon in the eleventh canto (1823) of *Don Juan* (1819–1824):

> Sir Walter reign'd before me; Moore and Campbell
> Before and after; but now grown more holy,
> The Muses upon Sion's hill must ramble
> With poets almost clergymen, or wholly;
> And Pegasus hath a psalmodic amble
> Beneath the very Reverend Rowley Powley,
> Who shoes the glorious animal with stilts,
> A modern Ancient Pistol – by the hilts!

Croly may well have deserved comparison with the bombastic braggart Pistol in William Shakespeare's *Henry IV*, part 2 (circa 1597), *The Merry Wives of Windsor* (1597), and *Henry V* (1599?), but Byron's sarcasm was incited by the political and religious opposition's having appropriated his manner.

In 1819 Croly married Margaret Helen Begbie, a fellow contributor to *The Literary Gazette.* Accounts differ as to the number of their children. If they had two daughters, the eldest was the future Helen Croly Webster, on whose behalf Croly would submit tales to *Blackwood's;* their youngest child was a daughter who died in childhood. They also had five sons.

In 1819–1820 Croly edited a new Tory weekly, *The Constitution.* In leading articles for the paper and in various writings – including fiction – for *Blackwood's,* which he joined in 1820, Croly advanced "Ultra-Toryism," a political philosophy that claimed intellectual parentage in Edmund Burke (on whom Croly wrote extensively); that was shared, though with reservations, by such writers as William Wordsworth, Robert Southey, Thomas De Quincey, Samuel Taylor Coleridge, and John Ruskin; and that qualified Croly to be a founding member of the Royal Society of Literature, established by George IV in 1823. The Ultra-Tories advocated a constitutional government in which Parliament, the aristocracy, and the crown checked each other, and the Anglican Church upheld the balanced privileges of these institutions; all other denominations were viewed as alien threats to the constitution. Thus, while more-moderate Tory leaders were working out political compromises such as the admission of Roman Catholics to Parliament in 1829 or the repeal in 1846 of the Corn Laws, which had served the interests of aristocratic landholders, the Ultras opposed these accommodations as dismantling the balanced structure of government and society. This political philosophy explains the persistent attacks Croly made in his fiction on whatever challenged the English establishment – especially Roman Catholicism and Continental political revolution – though it does not excuse his xenophobic vituperation of everything non-British.

The sketchiness of information about Croly's personal life points up a contradiction in his writing career: he shunned public notoriety yet courted popularity. On the one hand, he safeguarded his anonymity well beyond the journalistic conventions of the age, to the extent that whatever tales of his were published outside of *Blackwood's* may never be identified. In correspondence with *Blackwood's* Croly urged that the secrecy of the identities of contributors be maintained by burning all their letters – advice that was, fortunately for literary historians, ignored by the editor, William Blackwood. When Samuel Carter Hall requested autobiographical details, Croly rebuffed him so violently that Hall took his revenge in his *Book of Memories of Great Men and*

*Women of the Age, from Personal Acquaintance* (1877) by reprinting Croly's rude refusal. On the other hand, Croly was so wily about pouncing on popular literary fashions that Robinson, in a September 1854 journal entry, summed him up as a "literary adventurer." Anonymously Croly unleashed the scrappiness typical of a political journalist while publicly he upheld the dignity expected of a clergyman. He hoped to be remembered for his theological works, while he kept his name off of – and at least pretended contempt for – his tales and other popular periodical writings. These conflicting attitudes seem to reflect his transitional place between the sensationalism of Byronic Romanticism and the propriety of Victorianism.

Croly's verse tragedy of 1822, *Catiline,* was staged in 1827 but failed; his 1824 comedy *Pride Shall Have a Fall,* however, enjoyed a highly successful run. In these early London years Croly hobnobbed with theater people, some of whom would remember him sourly in their memoirs (one referring to his comedy as "Croly Shall Have a Fall, by the Reverend George Pride"). Such spite might have been provoked by his drama criticism, which would retain its notoriety for its severity even in Croly's obituaries – and justly so, if his tone is measured by his "Remarks on Shelley's *Adonais*" in *Blackwood's* (December 1821), which Alan Lang Strout considers the most objectionable of all early-nineteenth-century book reviews.

Croly's theatrical experiences left their mark on his tales, which owe their more lurid scenes to melodrama, and several of which sympathetically portray actors. In "The Married Actress," in *Tales of the Great St. Bernard* (1828), a successful actress, maliciously goaded by a rival actress, talks herself into marriage by execrating every aspect of the stage; then, after her marriage, she lauds what she had condemned and returns to the boards. Also connected with Croly's theatrical background are sketches that use dramatic techniques; "The Tertulla (A Spanish Conversazione)" (1823), for example, relies entirely on dialogue to satirize fashionable wit and Roman Catholic superstition. Later, satiric *conversazioni* are embedded as set pieces in longer tales such as "Hebe" in *Tales of the Great St. Bernard.*

As an editor of fashionable literature, Croly oversaw *The Universal Review,* a short-lived miscellany of 1824–1825, and *The Graces,* a gift annual for 1824 that includes an unattributed "Spanish Tale" that differs from Croly's April 1822 *Blackwood's* tale of the same title. According to James Grant, Croly also edited the *Monthly Magazine;* Grant doubtless means the *New Monthly Magazine and Literary Journal,* an anti-Jacobin journal at its inception and later a less political miscellany. No source besides Grant confirms Croly's connection with this periodical, however.

Such publications drew the contempt of many important authors, so Croly felt compelled to make a show of indifference. When Croly's story "The Red-Nosed Lieutenant" in *Forget-me-not, a Christmas and New Year's Present for 1826,* was favorably noticed in *Blackwood's,* Croly confided his authorship to Blackwood in a letter of 8 January 1827 but urged secrecy, grumbling that, much as he disliked such "scribblings," he found it easier to write them than to put off "teasing" letters from editors. He was equally embarrassed by his "trifles" for *Blackwood's* itself, since, as he pointed out to Blackwood in a letter of 5 March 1822, a reputation for tale writing gained no "advantageous result." Croly was apparently afraid that his lighter writing might compromise his clerical reputation and undermine his chances of preferment in the church. Yet, since he withheld his name even in the company of such respectably religious versifiers as Felicia Hemans and the Reverend Thomas Dale – who, unlike Croly, consented to the policy of signing contributions to Alaric Watts's *Literary Souvenir* (1827) – Croly's precautions suggest either an exaggerated affectation of contempt for his craft or outright paranoia. His desire for secrecy was also related to his political activity. Croly warned Blackwood in a letter of 5 December 1820 not to reveal his authorship of *Catiline* because "the play would be hissed for the sake of the party" at the same time, he worried (in letters of 26 December 1825 and 13 December 1827) that his political writing would be restrained by literary fame or would involve him in a "paper war."

Croly's first tales, Byronic in manner, are in verse: "Angel of the World, an Arabian Tale" and "Sebastian, a Spanish Tale," which were published together in 1820. Their strategies are carried over to his earliest identifiable prose tales, those published in *Blackwood's.* The prose narrative "A Spanish Tale" resembles "Sebastian" in that both begin with a dramatic, picturesque vignette and then proceed episodically. The plots of both Spanish tales and of "The Antonias" ring changes on a wistful heroine secretly nursing an infatuation for a dashing hero, with suspense provided by hidden identities. This basic plot is indefinitely expandable, since the heroine's secret is withheld until the end, when her devotion resurrects the hero from apparent death caused by a desperate struggle. In fact, Croly

left decisions about the compression or expansion of such tales to Blackwood's editorial needs, as his letter of 8 September 1825 suggests.

Despite the crudeness of this narrative structure, Croly excels in the episodic moment – particularly in openings handled like genre paintings. All characters' eyes are directed to an object or an incident – an overturned ferry in "A Spanish Tale," a diligence in the act of overturning in "The Antonias." Moving from observer to observer, the narrator records each characteristic response: the peasant's gawking, the aristocrat's hauteur, the officer's flirtation, the girl's blushes, the scholar-poet's rhapsodizing, and – Croly never missing an opportunity for anti-Catholic commentary – the monk's superstition and hypocrisy. This genre-painting treatment may be meant to complement engravings of sentimental gazers in the gift annuals; but the reader wearies of the wooden posing of observers and spectacles, which makes up the whole of some earlier tales.

This technique is retained throughout the 1820s, but Croly's descriptions become augmented with "all sorts of display" – his criterion for the choice of a fictional subject, as expressed in a letter to Blackwood of 9 November 1827. By 1825, in "The Antonias," a recognizable voice has emerged that augments each spectacle with florid rhetoric, relying on exotically named objects and places in its bid to display knowledge of foreign local color. In an 1826 essay William Hazlitt mocked Croly's "*auctioneer*-poetry about curtains, and palls, and sceptres, and precious stones"; the same criticism can be made of the fiction, which hawks a clutter of paraphernalia in endlessly piled compound phrases and parallel relative clauses. One feels that these exotic terms, especially the "oriental" touches, have been culled from dilettante reading; the *Eclectic Review* (January–June 1821) scoffed at Croly's "Angel of the World" for its pretense of erudition. When he is not being pedantic, however, Croly shows a pleasing affection for the objects in his colorfully strewn vignettes.

Besides inflating his voice with ornament and knowledge, the narrator readily descends to satire – often an almost bitter censoriousness – which he directs invariably against "papists," "revolutionaries," non-European "barbarians," and the manners of nations swayed by those horrors, but also against English foibles. Satire and florid language are used in the dialogue as well as in the narrative passages, imparting a uniform wry glibness to all characters, regardless of their ranks and vocations. George Gilfillan, himself a florid writer and one who was generally impressed by Croly's "loftiness," complained that the prose "wants repose" and "loves the magnificent too exclusively." In an 1854 article he quipped that Croly's "excited" characters are "cool enough" even "in their wildest vagaries" to "declaim ... their speeches trippingly on the tongue." Croly apparently never attempted dialect and never wrote a regional tale, although critics placed him in the tradition of Irish eloquence. He even crossed out the "Scotticisms" in his review copy of Alison's monumental Tory history of the French Revolution (1833). Presumably, regional differences could not be tolerated if they overshadowed Croly's national constitutionalist position, yet the universalized eloquence in the stories undercuts the class distinctions on which that position relies.

Giving free rein to this voice, the earlier tales show less concern with plot than with loosely unifying narrative devices that allow the narrator to follow any digression offering "display." "The Antonias" is unified only by the boy-hero's calling on an admired girl's name like a patron saint as he is carried through an improbable series of scrapes. "The Carbonaro" (*Blackwood's*, September 1826) is framed by a storm, the eruption of Mount Etna, and the succeeding calm — events that are irrelevant to the tale. Also for the sake of display, characters are developed in wild and contradictory directions: they suddenly acquire talents as painters or conjurers, for example, or avail themselves of unlikely disguises. Coherence is sacrificed to a prose version of Childe Harold's "intensity."

Later stories have tighter narrative structures; but Croly always remains committed to the showy episode, which he justifies with consistent critical principles. According to his 11 April 1821 comments to Blackwood on John Gibson Lockhart's *Valerius* (1821), historical fiction should be judged by its setting in a sublime transitional moment in history. That standard would still hold in his 1842–1843 letters to Blackwood's sons on his own historical novel *Marston; or, The Memoirs of a Statesman* (1845): he disdains "too much of *consecutive* story," which the Blackwoods had requested to fill up "pauses" that "check" the narrative; rather, he prefers "bold scenes, a *theatric* sketch of men and things, starts and plunges from one great event to another, leaving the reader to fill up the chasms between."

Two major fiction works of 1828 prove that while Croly lacked a feel for the appropriate length and pitch of eloquence, his rhetorical and episodic technique could be exploited and controlled in a judiciously chosen short form. The longer work, *Salathiel*, arose from Croly's theological work of the previous year, *The Apocalypse of St. John*, one of the many eschatological speculations by various authors inspired by the turmoil of the French Revolution and the Napoleonic Wars. The novel opens on the day of the Crucifixion — the choice of a sublime transitional moment meeting Croly's own test for historical fiction — when the Messiah dooms a mocker to become the deathless "Wandering Jew," condemned to roam the earth until the Apocalypse. Gilfillan said that more people had heard of *Salathiel* than had read it, since its "massive" descriptions and incidents could only be appreciated in occasional sittings. Nonetheless, the novel proved to be Croly's most lasting success. At the turn of the twentieth century Lew Wallace, the author of *Ben-Hur* (1880), included *Salathiel* on his quirky list of the six greatest English novels, proclaiming its opening scenic and historical panoramas as "without parallel in the language." To the modern reader, however, the style seems relentlessly exaggerated, and one may be grateful that Croly never executed the plan, which he announced to William Blackwood on 9 November 1827, to drive the Wandering Jew through at least nine volumes and the whole of recorded history. (He did begin this sequel in 1838–1839, according to letters to Blackwood.)

Croly's other major publication of 1828, the three-volume *Tales of the Great St. Bernard* — in which some tales are reprinted, with stylistic revisions, from earlier periodical appearances — is unified by a framing device: an avalanche in the pass of St. Bernard maroons travelers of various nationalities in the famous convent, where each traveler, like Geoffrey Chaucer's Canterbury pilgrims, is afforded a prologue and tale. Allowing space for grandeur of effect, a single story, "Hebe," spans a volume and a half. A historical tale like *Salathiel*, "Hebe" is set during the Napoleonic era and concerns the Balkan intrigues and Greek rebellions against the Turks. But where *Salathiel* draws its grand effects from the Crucifixion as the watershed of history, "Hebe" depends on a transitional place: Bucharest, "a half oriental, half European city — a border receptacle for the oddities, extravagances, and pomps of East and West in one." This collision of cultures provides a full palette for description and satire, colors that are toned down as the protagonists are carried westward to a Periclean representation of Greece and raised to a glare as they move eastward to Constantinople. But if transitional places allow Croly to broaden the range of his satire, they also allow him to flirt with the ideological enemy. The Greek insurrections form the one revolutionary movement acceptable to Croly (he had written admiringly of the Greek cause in essays for *Blackwood's* in 1826), partly out of respect for the Greeks' ancient heritage and partly in honor of Byron, who had died in 1824 while aiding the Greek insurgents.

As a counterweight to the use of transitional elements in "Hebe," Croly relies on the certitude of Providence – another influence of his apocalyptic theology on his fiction. By "permission" of Providence, secrets are disclosed by a specter. This is one of Croly's few uses of the supernatural. The plot turns on the pious fortitude of the Wallachian boyar Cantacuzene and of his adopted Greek daughter Hebe, both of whom call on Providence as they quest for one another's happiness and preservation. Hebe is the main human agent of the providential plot because, as a woman, she holds the "inextinguishable principle" of "true passion," which, "as wisdom or weakness guides," makes her a "moral volcano, whose fire may be the hidden fount of luxuriance and beauty to all upon the surface, or may display its wild strength in consuming and turning it into barrenness for ever." Finally, the tale aspires to providential history as the "mystery of . . . disposal of kingdoms" is prophesied to bring about the regeneration of Constantinople and to account for its present crimes – a degeneracy compounded, in Croly's imagination, of indolence, ignorance, cruelty, opulence, vastness, and secrecy. This providential history, not surprisingly, bears out Ultra-Tory principles, since the divine plan authorizes the foiling of degenerate oriental tyrants by responsible aristocrats such as Cantacuzene, whose "manly" virtues guarantee the stability of a class-structured, agrarian-based society.

While these apocalyptic effects help to justify the length of "Hebe," otherwise the tale only multiplies the episodic devices of Croly's earlier stories with its interminable crises. The reviewer for *The Athenaeum* (19 November 1828), while praising *Tales of the Great St. Bernard,* advised that such an eloquent writer as Croly "may feel secure of popularity without" introducing "a new . . . catastrophe in every page." In fact, Croly may have needed to rely on frequency of effect since, while he did have an eye for grand images, he shows surprisingly few resources for developing and sustaining the sublime. One scene of a mountain cloudburst suggests the influence of the apocalyptic painter John Martin (whose *Fall of Nineveh* was reviewed by Croly for *Blackwood's* in July 1828), the immensity of the natural forces measured by the dwarfishness and inundation of the victims. But in most cases Croly fails effectively to move the reader's eye around a vast

scene or through time, unless he can use an individual human drama to choreograph and sustain movement – as, for example, in "Hebe," when a maddened and bloodied pasha makes his last stand against insurrection by cutting his way, scimitar whirling, through his defeated janissaries into the swarming rebels.

More promisingly, *Tales of the Great St. Bernard* includes Croly's first use of a plot that disciplines his eloquence to a coherent design. Mustapha's narratives in "Hebe" and "The Woes of Wealth" are cynical tales of worldly ambition that form controlled, extended crescendos. In "The Woes of Wealth" the speaker bemoans his elevation, initiated by an unexpected and undesired inheritance, to wealth, title, and political prominence, since these reward him only with the loss of peace and old friendships and with the endangering of family and property. *The Literary Gazette* (8 November 1828) considered this the finest tale in the collection, likening its plot to that of Theodore Hook's "Danvers," in the first series of his highly popular *Sayings and Doings* (1824). But Croly improves on Hook by replacing the farcically duped protagonist of "Danvers" with a beleaguered ironist. The consistently ironic point of view improves on the incoherence of earlier tales by providing an outlet for Croly's characteristic sarcasm and by channeling his "auctioneer" descriptions into sarcastic inventories of the hero's rise in status.

Despite his increasingly dark and sardonic tone, Croly was uncertain about his place in the literary market. In letters to William Blackwood of 5 February 1821 and 30 January 1828 he spurned "puffery" (promotionalism) as "unworthy of a gentleman" and set his own "principled" writing apart from hackwork, yet he was a crafty self-publicist. Although *Tales of the Great St. Bernard* was published anonymously, the favorable reviewers had been made aware of Croly's authorship. The review in *The Gentleman's Magazine* ( July–December 1828) is so adulatory and so solicitous in recommending Croly for a church post that it must be a deliberate "puff." Croly himself probably wrote an article about the St. Bernard convent that appeared in the *New Monthly Magazine* in May 1829: the sketch is addressed to "lovers of works of fiction" who are currently admiring *Tales of the Great St. Bernard.* As a result, the book sold steadily, and new editions were published in 1829 and 1838. (The 1858 "revised edition" listed in the 1940 and 1969 editions of the *Cambridge Bibliography of English Literature* is a misidentification probably arising from confusion with the 1858 *Tales from Blackwood.*)

From early 1829 until "The Premier and His Wife: A Story of the Great World" appeared in January 1832, Croly's steady output for *Blackwood's* ceased. William Ross Thompson conjectures that Croly was offended with Blackwood for failing to review *Salathiel*. On 17 April 1828 Croly had pleaded "that upon success [of *Salathiel*] depends a great deal of my future scribbling. If it should be unknown, I shall probably give up . . . & delve in Theology . . . until somebody delve a location for me where men write no more, & turn their moral uses into . . . cabbages & cauliflowers." Despite Blackwood's obdurateness, *Salathiel* did well, and Croly's letters to Blackwood resumed in 1832 with no hint of rancor. Whatever the cause of his silence, his return to *Blackwood's* inaugurated an almost monthly series of tales for 1832. Their openings, which comment on foreign manners, suggest that Croly may have been traveling extensively in the interim.

In a briefer version of the plot of "The Woes of Wealth," in "The Premier and His Wife" the penalty of the politician's ambition is paid by his long-suffering lady (in "The Woes of Wealth" the wife's and daughters' social climbing spurs the reluctant squire). Although "The Premier and His Wife" is less piquant and riotous than "The Woes of Wealth," the lord's advancement is more economically indicated by constant references to the wife's countenance – from the ingenue's rosiness to the lady's magnificence that cannot disguise the pallor of "secret grief."

Since both "The Woes of Wealth" and "The Premier and His Wife" conclude with the politicians retiring from the great world to the tranquillity of domestic life, Croly seems to be moving in these tales from Byronism toward a Victorian complacency; but he appears to have become arrested in the transition between Romanticism and Victorianism. The tales of ambition end in praise of domesticity, but the peaceful home depends on the renunciation of public life and cannot serve, as it would for the Victorians, as a wellspring of virtues to be carried back into public affairs. Rather than exemplifying Victorian earnestness, the narrators are cynical – doubtless because Croly was, as Herring admits, a "disappointed man," disillusioned by his unrewarded political zealotry. At the same time, while the tales of ambition suggest a provisional Victorianism, they betray the pull of the Regency. The squire in "The Woes of Wealth" is inconsistently characterized as now reclusive, now garrulously social, and his praise of domestic retirement seems irreconcilable with his obvious relish for describing, however sarcastically, the ambitions of the

beau monde and public life – just as Croly himself badgered the editors of *Blackwood's* into letting him write what amounted to London gossip columns. In Croly, the air of the Regency "swell" still hung about the Victorian domestic patriarch.

Other stories of 1832 are divided into European tales and oriental tales. The European tales, which Blackwood preferred, are built on tediously conventional romance plots. In "The Castle of the Isle of Rugen" (May), Croly's only Gothic tale, a manhunt leads through ghostly phenomena that, in the end, are ascribed to rational causes; along the way the Gothic effects are drained of menace by the narrator's irony.

All the European tales open with desultory travel notes that a modern reader might consider bigoted and inferior to Croly's earlier vignette-style opening. These essaylike openings seem to reflect a deliberate blurring of the boundaries between fiction and nonfiction; ambiguous about what kind of writing will follow, they alert the reader to the mixture of fictional narration and chronicling of recent history that characterizes several of the tales. Two tales, for example, chronicle the French Republican campaigns in Italy (upheavals enhanced by descriptions of the sublimities of the Alpine passes): "Calaspo, the Republican" (June) concerns the young Napoleon's 1793 invasion of Piedmont; "Antonio di Carara: A Paduan Tale" (October) climaxes with Napoleon's 1800 Lombard victory, the Battle of Marengo, whose horrors are described in startling detail.

"Antonio di Carara" relies on Victorian prejudices about Italy. Antonio is aroused from his Italian "torpor" by a lively officer in the Austrian imperial service; but the officer turns out to be Antonio's disguised enemy, driven by that other Italian foible, a thirst for revenge. The officer, who has vowed to risk his own life to take Antonio's, entices Antonio into practicing forbidden arts, which causes Antonio's imprisonment, then exposes him to an avalanche, dangerous company, and finally the Battle of Marengo – where the dying officer confesses his perfidy after saving Antonio's life. The story is an interesting variation on the Faustian theme of temptation and quest; but the exposition is awkward, and incident is allowed to govern character development.

In "Antonio di Carara" Croly advances beyond his florid but quickly exhausted descriptive writing of the 1820s by attempting longer word paintings, especially of Alpine scenery; likewise, in "Calaspo, the Republican" he makes effective use of a mountain tempest. A Piedmontese marquis and his daughter, forced out of the Parisian diplomatic service by the Terror of 1793, journey to their native mountains. During a storm the daughter is saved from a collapsing bridge by the mountaineer Calaspo. Calaspo is taken into the nobleman's service; but when the château is overrun by Napoleon, circumstantial evidence points to the mountaineer's treason, and he is repudiated by the family. Later, Calaspo's actions prove his integrity. In this tale Croly put aside satire to give his clearest illustration of noblesse oblige complemented by deferential but sturdily independent peasantry; both attitudes are shown to be undermined by republicanism, which Croly defines as mere property theft disguised as liberty. This message, however, is sacrificed to a sentimental ending: to work out the love story between Calaspo and the marquis's daughter, the peasant's concealed aristocratic heritage is revealed, and to empower Calaspo to release the family from prison, he is catapulted to a generalship in the Republican army.

Two other tales of 1832, in which Croly returns to his fascination with the boundaries between European and oriental cultures, attempt interesting narrative experiments. The structure of "The Pandour and His Princess: A Hungarian Sketch" (July) aggressively realizes Croly's preference for transitionless jumps and starts. A series of apparently disconnected events – including the thwarted assassination of the Austrian emperor, a princess's unwilling betrothal to a coxcomb nobleman, and an ambush of a Turkish emissary by Hungarian highwaymen – is presented, each separated only by ellipses. Each adventure involves the same heroic pandour, (a Croatian soldier retained in the imperial service to clear the Turkish frontier of bandits), invisible or disguised, who reveals himself and his benevolent intentions in the end. Croly's clues make sense only in retrospect, but he succeeds in teasing the reader with clever, if superficial, links between the parts of the story, such as a stolen watch that comes into the possession of various characters.

Another semioriental tale that reserves the connection between parts until the end is "The Aga of the Janizaries" (February), in which two separate narratives, one about a fierce Ottoman military leader and the other about a violently passionate Genoese, turn out to concern the same person. By this time Croly had worked in London for twenty-two years without a permanent church post; if "The Woes of Wealth" and "The Premier and His Wife" vent his cynicism about ambition, "The Aga of the Janizaries" is a visceral fantasy of self-actualization. The hero, like Croly himself, is violently courageous and incisively sarcastic, and he crushes cring-

ing sycophants on his way to the top of the Ottoman command.

Croly's most seasoned thought about ambition is reflected in the two most successful tales of 1832, both modeled on the eighteenth-century oriental didactic tale. In the amusing "Eliezer the Sage, and Eliezer the Simple" (August) – which Croly declared "the very best tale I have done for a long time" in a 2 August 1832 letter to William Blackwood – the Jewish philosopher Eliezer learns humility from his unassuming young friend, simple Eliezer. Croly here reveals a rare self-irony, since the sagacious Eliezer's great stumbling blocks are verbosity and elaborate knowledge that get him into farcical scrapes, from which he must be rescued by his friend's timely common sense and terse proverbial wisdom. Thus Croly adopts the new Victorian value of earnest simplicity. The freshness of "Eliezer the Sage, and Eliezer the Simple," however, is offset by failures in consistency: the elder Eliezer's rescue is made to depend on the younger's eloquence, not on his simplicity. To close the tale, Croly desperately resorts to unmasking the young Eliezer as the elder's female beloved.

Croly's most ambitious meditation on ambition is the didactic tale "The Natolian Story-Teller" (December). The story uses a frame narration to reintroduce the theme of transitional cultures: a first narrator encounters a second storyteller in Nadoly, Homer's region of Asia Minor, where, as in "Hebe," Greek nobility is hemmed in by degenerate orientalism. The situation is emblematized by a Greek ruin festooned as a Turkish pavilion, in which reclines, statuelike, a languid but volatile Greek boy: Greece will regenerate! Besides delivering this political message, the half-Western, half-oriental setting of the frame is used to evoke the ambiguous settings of eighteenth-century didactic fables such as the Abyssinia of Samuel Johnson's *Rasselas* (1759). This neoclassical genre suggests another home for Croly: for all his sensational Byronism and tentative Victorianism, he may have been an Augustan at heart, like the temple beneath the oriental hangings. Herring says that Croly was "styled the Dr. Johnson of his day"; and Grant implies the Augustan rationalism in Croly when he passes a Victorian evangelical judgment on Croly's preaching, which, Grant says, substituted "intellect, eloquent language, and mere morality, for the vital truths of the gospel." Still, "The Natolian Story-Teller" is a classical apologue with a Victorian moral.

Like Johnson's protagonist Rasselas, Croly's Natolian hero Hamet ben Hamet is led on a quest for happiness. Unlike Rasselas, Hamet does not begin his quest by exposing the shallow complacency surrounding him; rather, Hamet is himself a hypocrite, philosophically declaring his wretchedness while reclining in luxury. A pilgrim appears who wields strange power over Hamet and entices him into proposing a journey to prove human futility. As the companions traverse Africa and the Mediterranean, Croly builds a crescendo of natural and civic catastrophes, similar in structure to the earlier tales of ambition, "The Woes of Wealth" and "The Premier and His Wife." In this case Croly's weakness in narrative structure is actually an advantage: the oriental apologue conventionally allows for episodic quests, relying on the didactic aim to impose unity. The pilgrim's goal is to humiliate Hamet and teach him to subordinate his philosophy to a trust in Providence. Repenting his impiety while in the throes of a violent death, Hamet wakes to discover that he has dreamed it all; but Croly encourages the reader to regard the pilgrim as genuinely supernatural, an agent of Providence like the specter in "Hebe."

"The Natolian Story-Teller" replaces Johnson's Christian stoicism with a more conventional providential piety. At the same time, just as Johnson refuses to explain away human suffering, Croly's narrative of increasing disaster appears at odds with the pilgrim's exhortations to quietism: if the events cure Hamet of philosophizing by truly giving him something to complain about, they also justify his original view of human wretchedness. This simultaneous expression and pacification of doubt may be the clearest sign of the emerging Victorian in Croly. More searching than the domestic resolutions of the earlier tales of ambition, the unresolved contradiction in "The Natolian Story-Teller" recalls Alfred Tennyson's *In Memoriam* (1850), another journey to resigned contentment, in which even more devastating despair is contained within, but not canceled by, the framing lyrics on providential assurance.

Just when these reflections on happiness had been prodded by Croly's ill fortune, he began to gain church preferment. From 1832 to 1835 he filled a temporary rectorship in Romford parish, Essex, then was presented with the living of Bondleigh. Typically, after visiting the "wildness and desolation" of this edge of Dartmoor in Devon, he declined the parish rather than retire to isolation, just as years earlier he had broken away from remote northern Ireland to the metropolis. It was in London that he finally found contentment, with his appointment in 1835 to the combined parish of St. Benet's and St. Stephen's, which he held until his death. Ironically, he obtained this living not in rec-

ognition of his Tory Anglicanism but through the intercession of Henry Peter, First Baron Brougham, one of the hated Whigs but also a distant relative of Mrs. Croly. Still, as Frederick W. Croly comments, the parish was suitable, "being very small, and most of the parishioners non-resident," and "the new rector could still devote a large portion of his time to general literature." One suspects also that a city church – its pulpit within earshot of newspaper reporters yet distant from the intimate relations of a village parish – comported with Croly's curiously mixed penchant for popularity and anonymity. Finally, Croly must have regarded the handsome Christopher Wren church of St. Stephen's as appropriate to a man of his merits – someone who, having been awarded in 1831 an honorary LL.D. by the University of Dublin, must henceforth, he insisted, be addressed as "Dr. Croly."

The living was not lucrative, according to Grant, who estimates it at £550 per year, including the use of the house. Although many incumbents earned far less and did not enjoy free housing, Croly's large family may have needed the continued income from his writing. When, in October 1834, a month after William Blackwood's death, Blackwood's son Alexander had dared to return a submission to Croly, the indignant writer had fumed that he could make no other use of the piece, since he maintained no connections with other periodicals. While this may have been true at the time, he was soon writing for several periodicals besides *Blackwood's*. Between 1839 and 1846 he wrote leading articles for the Tory newspaper *Britannia*, edited by Hall, and probably contributed to two other conservative papers, the *Morning Herald* and *Standard*. He also made important contributions, Grant says, to the *Church Quarterly Review*. Somewhat later he sent lighter travel sketches to *Bentley's Miscellany*.

Croly steadily produced essays but comparatively little short fiction for *Blackwood's* after the outpouring of 1832, perhaps because he feared risking his new advancement in the church. In the year before ascending to St. Stephen's he seems to have flung away his excessive Byronisms in one last gala, "The Conde de Ildefonzo: A Tale of the Spanish Revolution" (May and July 1834) – a tale so shapeless with incendiary peasant rebellions, devotions to high-minded women, revolutionary and loyalist cabals, secret dungeons, and moving statues that one cannot tell by reading it that its third and concluding part was never published. In this story Croly's greatest hatreds – Catholicism, revolution, and Mediterranean indolence – are allied in one grand travesty, at one point even suggesting an absurd analogy between modern revolutionaries and torturers during the Inquisition.

No more Croly stories appeared in *Blackwood's* until two historical tales of 1840, "Carlo Sebastiani, the Aid-de-Camp" (April, May, and June) and "De Walstein, the Enthusiast: A Tale of the French Revolution" (September). These works point the way to *Marston,* Croly's historical romance about the French Revolution, and are illuminated by Croly's letters to *Blackwood's* (1 October 1842 and 12 May and 11 July 1843) sketching his intentions for that work. He planned a crime novel incorporating political commentary, in the style of William Godwin's *Things as They Are; or, The Adventures of Caleb Williams* (1794), but he eschewed two modern variants of this form. On the one hand, he abhorred the descent into the criminal underworld in Charles Dickens's *Oliver Twist* (1838) and William Harrison Ainsworth's *Jack Sheppard* (1839). Decorum was better served, he thought, by a "stern picture of men & manners with occasional softenings from the gentler scenes of Society." But, on the other hand, he dismissed the tale of crime and fashionable life, such as Edward Bulwer-Lytton's *Pelham, or the Adventures of a Gentleman* (1828), with its "dandyism" and "languid frippery." Rather, his hero Marston would exhibit "a manly vein of strong character, strongly tried, powerfully excited – & *desperately* undone in the end."

Like Pelham, both Carlo Sebastiani and Count De Walstein move amid fashionable life. But Carlo takes his chances as a rough common soldier in the Austrian resistance to Napoleon of 1796, rather than acceding to dull safety in the diplomatic corps. Owing to his rashness, he is prosecuted on charges trumped up by an ambitious spy. He redeems his honor and proves the value of skilled soldiership over court intrigues by saving a major campaign. De Walstein also flees the Austrian imperial court, and his only crime, like Carlo's, is rash "enthusiasm," which leads him to be mistaken for a Republican in the storming of the Bastille. Then, moved by a revolutionary play, De Walstein is actually converted to the role of a Republican orator in Paris (although at this point the reader does not know that De Walstein and the orator "Regnier" are one and the same person). Only when leading citizens to arrest the royal family does he regain his Tory respect for nobility – while managing also, like Carlo, to save the aristocratic girl he loves. This device of resuscitating the hero in a totally new semihistorical character, the identity of the two guises being withheld until the end, had already been used by Croly with less skill in "The Aga of

the Janizaries." There, the opening Ottoman section of the story seemed indistinguishable from Croly's nonfictional biographical sketches for *Blackwood's* and stylistically disconnected from the second half. In these later stories, the shifts between history and fiction and between characters' guises are handled smoothly.

Croly had mixed fictional characters with historical figures in "Hebe," which includes an operatic portrayal of the Greek patriot Konstantinos Rhigas. In "Carlo Sebastiani" and "De Walstein" the Republican and imperial celebrities make pithier speeches, but the characters only parrot Croly's characteristic aphoristic pronouncements: "'I,' said Sieyes," in "De Walstein," " 'am a Republican, but no Revolutionist.' 'I,' said Talleyrand, 'am a Revolutionist, but no Republican.' " Although Croly undeservedly claimed a measure of originality by making his heroes converse with historical figures – Sir Walter Scott's novels had already included such conversations – he does skillfully achieve what, speaking of *Marston,* he called the hero's "*personal view of time*" – that it is "*not a history*" (here he may be thinking of Bulwer-Lytton) "but the sort of view which the individual might take from personal knowledge mingled with personal adventures of all mixed kinds." Carlo takes a plausible part in the campaigns of 1796 while acting out his own romantic tale.

In "De Walstein" Croly still fixes on spectacular turning points of history, as he did in "Hebe" and *Salathiel:* the count arrives in Paris, for example, precisely in time to be unwillingly caught up in the crowd storming the Bastille. This spectacle reveals what is finally most attractive and most problematic about Croly as a writer of historical short fiction. De Walstein is carrying on his shoulders a wounded Bastille guard whom he has rescued, when the door before him is broken in by the rioters: "It was the picture of the Revolution in all its wild grandeur, its sanguinary horrors, and its colossal power." As if to point out the oafishness of the sublime insurrection, De Walstein is mistaken for a Bastille prisoner who has slain his oppressor and is marched to freedom as a hero. For all its splendidly compact sensationalism, the scene reduces history to a set of ironic emblems.

After the completion of *Marston* Croly apparently stopped writing fiction. Although he continued to produce essays for *Blackwood's* and wrote a few more volumes of poetry, he devoted his remaining fifteen years primarily to the religious writing that he had always held in highest esteem. This channeling of his talents may be connected to a heavy toll of personal grief that only religion could comfort. In 1845 his twenty-three-year-old eldest son, George, was killed in the second Kabul campaign. During the mid 1840s he was embroiled in proceedings against a dishonest but powerful churchwarden of St. Stephen's, and in 1847 he indignantly resigned from an appointment as preacher to the Foundling Hospital when his sermons were criticized as too abstruse for the children. In 1851 he lost both his wife and a nine-year-old daughter.

Croly's sensational style was falling into disrepute as the new age emerged. John Ruskin, as a boy, had admired Croly's tale "Il Vesuviano: A Neapolitan Tale (1829) with almost as much enthusiasm as he gazed at the tale's accompanying engraving by J. M. W. Turner of Mount Vesuvius erupting. As a youth, Ruskin borrowed Croly's frame device in *Tales of the Great St. Bernard* for his own unfinished stories, "Chronicles of St. Bernard" (1836?). After Ruskin himself, like Croly, earned a reputation as a purple-prose writer with the publication of *Modern Painters* (1843), Croly advised him to "make a sensation." In a 2 November 1845 letter discussing Croly's fiction, the younger writer spurned this advice, however, and opted for the new age by scorning Croly's "want of earnestness" and his aim to be "fine" or "startling" instead of using eloquence in the service of reform.

In a letter of 22 March 1858 Croly, saying that he had learned from "an Advertisement" that the Blackwood firm was "about to republish a number of 'Tales'" — the first series of *Tales from Blackwood* in twelve volumes (1858–1861) — begged that any reprinted tales by him "should remain *anonymous,* as . . . the *Name* was never intended to be known, & . . . it would be unpleasant & even inconvenient to *me* — that my name should appear." In his next letter, on 27 March, he justified his reticence by his distaste for such writing: he claimed that he "forgot [the tales] altogether" but supposed them "equally good, or *bad* — . The only thing I care about is keeping the *Authorship* — (if that is not too lofty a name for such things) to *yourself.*" The affectation of contempt was nothing new and, in this case, surely disingenuous, since in letters of 24 and 28 December 1846 he had made his own proposal to the Blackwood brothers for a multivolume reprinting of his uncollected tales and essays. Moreover, *Tales from Blackwood* included — besides "Antonio di Carara," "The Pandour and His Princess," and "The Premier and His Wife" — "The Natolian Story-Teller," an ambitious tale that he is not likely to have forgotten. His insouciance, one suspects,

was a gentlemanly bid for payment, since the collected works had not materialized: "If you make the forty or fifty, *thousand* pounds by [*Tales from Blackwood*]" he goes on, "remember their writer to the extent of any poundage in the power of your prosperity."

According to Frederick W. Croly, Croly's closing years were spent happily and actively. He died unexpectedly on 24 November 1860 and was buried in his own church, St. Stephen's, where he was memorialized by a series of windows and a bust sculpted in 1857 by William Behnes. By the end of the century, his oriental and rhetorical splendor had come to appear an unoriginal imitation of Byron and Thomas Moore — poets who were, themselves, by then regarded as "unreal" and "meretricious," according to the entries on Croly by Richard Garnett in the *Dictionary of National Biography* (1888) and by Charles Dudley Warner in *A Library of the World's Best Literature* (1897). When Byron and Moore returned to favor, Croly remained in obscurity, doubtless because his poetry is inferior to theirs. But his short fiction shows that he may also have been overlooked because he fits neatly into no single category: Augustan, Romantic, and Victorian all apply, yet none completely. Croly deserves study as a transitional figure, and his fiction merits reading as exploring the transitions between cultures, regions, epochs, and, ultimately, between the values of the earlier and later nineteenth century.

**Letters:**
"The Letters of George Croly to William Blackwood and His Sons," 2 volumes, edited by William Ross Thompson, dissertation, Texas Technological College, 1957.

**Biography:**
Richard Herring, *A Few Personal Recollections of the Late Rev. George Croly, LL.D. . . . with Extracts from His Speeches and Writings* (London: Longman, Green, Longmans & Roberts, 1861).

**References:**
Sir Archibald Alison, *Some Account of My Life and Writings: An Autobiography,* 2 volumes (Edinburgh & London: Blackwood, 1883), II: 272–273;

Josephine Bauer, *The London Magazine, 1820–1829,* edited by Torsten Dahl, Kemp Malone, and Geoffrey Tillotson, Anglistica, volume 1 (Copenhagen: Rosenkilde & Bagger, 1953);

A. Boyle, "Portraiture in 'Lavengro,'" *Notes and Queries,* 196 (27 October 1951): 477–479;

Myron Brightfield, *Theodore Hook and His Novels* (Cambridge, Mass.: Harvard University Press, 1928);

John Wilson Croker, *The Correspondence and Diaries,* 2 volumes, edited by Louis J. Jennings (New York: Scribners, 1884), I: 87–90; II: 59–61;

George Gilfillan, "Dr. Croly," *Littell's Living Age,* 42 (July–September 1854): 318–321;

Gilfillan, "Dr. George Croly," in his *Modern Literature and Literary Men: Being a Second Gallery of Literary Portraits,* third edition (New York: D. Appleton, 1859), pp. 133–146;

Gilfillan, "Edward Irving, and the Preachers of the Day," in his *Sketches of Modern Literature, and Eminent Literary Men (Being a Gallery of Literary Portraits),* 2 volumes (New York: D. Appleton / Philadelphia: G. Appleton, 1846), I: 231–237;

James Grant, *The Metropolitan Pulpit; or, Sketches of the Most Popular Preachers in London* (New York: D. Appleton, 1839), pp. 144–153;

Samuel Carter Hall, *A Book of Memories of Great Men and Women of the Age, from Personal Acquaintance,* second edition (London: Virtue, 1877), pp. 232–233;

Wendell V. Harris, *British Short Fiction in the Nineteenth Century: A Literary and Bibliographic Guide* (Detroit: Wayne State University Press, 1979);

William Hazlitt, "On Envy (A Dialogue)," in *The Complete Works of William Hazlitt,* volume 12, edited by P. P. Howe (New York: Dent, 1931), pp. 104–105;

William Jerdan, *Autobiography,* 4 volumes (London: Hall, Virtue, 1852);

K. G. McWatters, "Encore du faux Stendhal: Autour de Stendhal, Foscolo, George Croly et quelques revues anglaises et francaises," *Stendhal Club,* 19 (15 October 1976): 62–78;

Margaret Oliphant, *Annals of a Publishing House: William Blackwood and His Sons, Their Magazine, and Friends,* 2 volumes (Edinburgh: Blackwood, 1897), I: 478–482;

James Robinson Planché, *Recollections and Reflections,* revised edition (London: Sampson Low, Marston, n.d.), pp. 67–68;

Bryan Waller Procter, *The Literary Recollections of Barry Cornwall,* edited by Richard Willard Armour (Boston: Meador, 1936), pp. 28–33;

"Rev. George Croly, LL.D.," *Gentleman's Magazine and Historical Review,* new series 10 (January–June 1861): 104–107;

Henry Crabb Robinson, *On Books and Their Writers,* 3 volumes, edited by Edith J. Morley (London: Dent, 1938), I: 121–122; II: 745;

John Ruskin, "Chronicles of St. Bernard," in *Works of John Ruskin,* 39 volumes, edited by E. T. Cook and Alexander Wedderburn, (London: George Allen, 1903–1912), I: 522–551;

Ruskin, *Letters to a College Friend,* in *Works of John Ruskin,* I: 445;

Ruskin, *Praeterita,* in *Works of John Ruskin,* XXXV: 140–141;

Ruskin, *Ruskin in Italy: Letters to His Parents, 1845,* edited by Harold I. Shapiro (Oxford: Clarendon Press, 1972), pp. 240–242;

G. S. Simes, "The Ultra Tories in British Politics, 1824–1834," dissertation, University of Oxford, 1974;

Alan Lang Strout, "George Croly and *Blackwood's Magazine,*" *Times Literary Supplement,* 6 October 1850, p. 636;

Strout, "Some Unpublished Letters of John Gibson Lockhart to John Wilson Croker," *Notes and Queries,* 185 (11 September 1943): 152–157;

Ann Blaisdell Tracey, *Patterns of Fear in the Gothic Novel, 1790–1830,* Gothic Studies and Dissertations (New York: Arno, 1980).

**Papers:**

The correspondence of George Croly with the Blackwood firm is held by the National Library of Scotland. A collection of letters to William Jerdan at the Bodleian Library, Oxford, may include Croly among its two hundred correspondents.

# Charles Dickens

*(7 February 1812 – 9 June 1870)*

Ruth Glancy
*Concordia College*

See also the Dickens entries in *DLB 21: Victorian Novelists Before 1885, DLB 55: Victorian Prose Writers Before 1867,* and *DLB 70: British Mystery Writers, 1860–1919.*

BOOKS: *Sketches by Boz, Illustrative of Every-Day Life, and Every-Day People* (first series, 2 volumes, London: Macrone, 1836; second series, London: Macrone, 1837); republished as *Watkins Tottle and Other Sketches Illustrative of Every-Day Life and Every-Day People,* 2 volumes (Philadelphia: Carey, Lea & Blanchard, 1837) and *The Tuggs's at Ramsgate and Other Sketches Illustrative of Every-Day Life and Every-Day People* (Philadelphia: Carey, Lea & Blanchard, 1837);

*The Village Coquettes: A Comic Opera in Two Acts,* as "Boz," music by John Hullah (London: Bentley, 1836);

*The Posthumous Papers of the Pickwick Club, Edited by "Boz"* (20 monthly parts, London: Chapman & Hall, 1836–1837; 26 monthly parts, New York: Turney, 1836–1838);

*The Strange Gentleman: A Comic Burletta, in Two Acts,* as "Boz" (London: Chapman & Hall, 1837);

*The Life and Adventures of Nicholas Nickleby,* 20 monthly parts (London: Chapman & Hall, 1838–1839; Philadelphia: Lea & Blanchard, 1839);

*Sketches of Young Gentlemen, Dedicated to the Young Ladies* (London: Chapman & Hall, 1838);

*Memoirs of Joseph Grimaldi, Edited by "Boz,"* 2 volumes (London: Bentley, 1838; Philadelphia: Carey, Lea & Blanchard, 1838);

*Oliver Twist; or, The Parish Boy's Progress, by "Boz"* (3 volumes, London: Bentley, 1838; 2 volumes, Philadelphia: Carey, Lea & Blanchard, 1839);

*Sketches of Young Couples, with an Urgent Remonstrance to the Gentlemen of England (Being Bachelors or Widowers), on the Present Alarming Crisis* (London: Chapman & Hall, 1840);

*Master Humphrey's Clock,* 88 weekly parts (London: Chapman & Hall, 1840–1841) – includes *The*

*Charles Dickens*

*Old Curiosity Shop,* republished as *The Old Curiosity Shop* (2 volumes, London: Chapman & Hall, 1841; 1 volume, Philadelphia: Lea & Blanchard, 1841), and *Barnaby Rudge,* republished as *Barnaby Rudge: A Tale of the Riots of 'Eighty* (London: Chapman & Hall, 1841; Philadelphia: Lea & Blanchard, 1841);

*American Notes for General Circulation* (2 volumes, London: Chapman & Hall, 1842; 1 volume, New York: Harper, 1842);

*The Life and Adventures of Martin Chuzzlewit* (20 monthly parts, London: Chapman & Hall,

1842–1844; 1 volume, New York: Harper, 1844);

*A Christmas Carol, in Prose: Being a Ghost Story of Christmas* (London: Chapman & Hall, 1843; Philadelphia: Carey & Hart, 1844);

*The Chimes: A Goblin Story of Some Bells That Rang an Old Year Out and a New Year In* (London: Chapman & Hall, 1845 [i.e., 1844]; Philadelphia: Lea & Blanchard, 1845);

*The Cricket on the Hearth: A Fairy Tale of Home* (London: Bradbury & Evans, 1846 [i.e., 1845]; New York: Harper, 1846);

*Pictures from Italy* (London: Bradbury & Evans, 1846); republished as *Travelling Letters Written on the Road* (New York: Wiley & Putnam, 1846);

*The Battle of Life: A Love Story* (London: Bradbury & Evans, 1846; New York: Harper, 1847);

*Dealings with the Firm of Dombey and Son, Wholesale, Retail, and for Exportation* (20 monthly parts, London: Bradbury & Evans, 1846–1848; 19 monthly parts, parts 1–17, New York: Wiley & Putnam, 1846–1847; parts 18–19, New York: Wiley, 1848);

*The Haunted Man and the Ghost's Bargain: A Fancy for Christmas-time* (London: Bradbury & Evans, 1848; New York: Harper, 1849);

*The Personal History of David Copperfield* (20 monthly parts, London: Bradbury & Evans, 1849–1850; Philadelphia: Lea & Blanchard, 1851);

*A Child's History of England* (3 volumes, London: Bradbury & Evans, 1852–1854; 2 volumes, New York: Harper, 1853–1854);

*Bleak House* (20 monthly parts, London: Bradbury & Evans, 1852–1853; 1 volume, New York: Harper, 1853);

*Hard Times: For These Times* (London: Bradbury & Evans, 1854; New York: McElrath, 1854);

*Little Dorrit* (20 monthly parts, London: Bradbury & Evans, 1855–1857; 1 volume, Philadelphia: Peterson, 1857);

*The Wreck of the Golden Mary,* by Dickens and Wilkie Collins (London: Bradbury & Evans, 1856);

*The Two Apprentices: With a History of Their Lazy Tour,* by Dickens and Collins (Philadelphia: Peterson, 1857);

*A Tale of Two Cities* (London: Chapman & Hall, 1859; Philadelphia: Peterson, 1859);

*Great Expectations* (3 volumes, London: Chapman & Hall, 1861; 1 volume, Philadelphia: Peterson, 1861);

*The Uncommercial Traveller* (London: Chapman & Hall, 1861; New York: Sheldon, 1865);

*Our Mutual Friend* (20 monthly parts, London: Chapman & Hall, 1864–1865; 1 volume, New York: Harper, 1865);

*Reprinted Pieces* (New York: Hearst's International Library, 1867);

*The Uncommercial Traveller and Additional Christmas Stories,* Diamond Edition (Boston: Ticknor & Fields, 1867);

*Hunted Down: A Story, with Some Account of Thomas Griffiths Wainewright, The Poisoner* (London: Hotten, 1870; Philadelphia: Peterson, 1870);

*The Mystery of Edwin Drood* (6 monthly parts, London: Chapman & Hall, 1870; 1 volume, Boston: Fields, Osgood, 1870);

*A Child's Dream of a Star* (Boston: Fields, Osgood, 1871);

*Is She His Wife?, or, Something Singular: A Comic Burletta in One Act* (Boston: Osgood, 1877);

*The Lazy Tour of Two Idle Apprentices. No Thoroughfare. The Perils of Certain English Prisoners,* by Dickens, Wilkie Collins, and Charles Fechter (London: Chapman & Hall, 1934);

*The Life of Our Lord* (New York: Simon & Schuster, 1934);

*The Speeches of Charles Dickens,* edited by K. J. Fielding (Oxford: Clarendon Press, 1960);

*Uncollected Writings from Household Words, 1850–1859,* edited by Harry Stone, 2 volumes (Bloomington: Indiana University Press, 1968; London: Allen Lane, 1969);

*Charles Dickens: The Public Readings,* edited by Philip Collins (Oxford: Clarendon Press, 1975);

*No Thoroughfare: A Drama in Five Acts,* by Dickens, Wilkie Collins, and Fechter (New York: DeWitt, n.d.).

**Editions and Collections:** *Cheap Edition of the Works of Mr. Charles Dickens* (12 volumes, London: Chapman & Hall, 1847–1852; 3 volumes, London: Bradbury & Evans, 1858);

*Christmas Books* (London: Chapman & Hall, 1852);

*Christmas Stories from the Household Words* (London: Chapman & Hall, 1859);

The Charles Dickens Edition, 21 volumes (London: Chapman & Hall, 1867–1875);

*The Nine Christmas Numbers of All the Year Round* (London: Office of *All the Year Round* and Chapman & Hall, 1868);

*The Plays and Poems of Charles Dickens,* 2 volumes, edited by Richard Herne Shepherd (London: W. H. Allen, 1882);

*The Works of Charles Dickens,* 21 volumes (London: Macmillan, 1892–1925);

*The Works of Charles Dickens,* Gadshill Edition, 36
    volumes (London: Chapman & Hall / New
    York: Scribners, 1897–1908);
The Nonesuch Edition, 23 volumes, edited by Ar-
    thur Waugh and others (London: Nonesuch
    Press, 1937–1938);
*The New Oxford Illustrated Dickens,* 21 volumes (Ox-
    ford: Oxford University Press, 1947–1958);
*The Clarendon Dickens,* 7 volumes published, edited
    by Kathleen Tillotson and others (Oxford:
    Clarendon Press, 1966– );
*Charles Dickens: Christmas Books,* 2 volumes, edited by
    Michael Slater (Harmondsworth: Penguin,
    1971);
*Charles Dickens: Selected Short Fiction,* edited by Debo-
    rah A. Thomas (Harmondsworth: Penguin,
    1976);
*The Cricket on the Hearth,* edited by Andrew Sanders
    (London: Genesis Publications, 1981).

OTHER: *The Pic-Nic Papers by Various Hands,* 3 vol-
    umes, edited by Dickens (London: Colburn,
    1841).

From the appearance of his first full-length
work of prose fiction, *The Posthumous Papers of the
Pickwick Club,* in 1836–1837, Charles Dickens has retained his place as one of the best-loved and most
widely read novelists in the world. Not so well
known is his contribution to the short-story genre,
although Dickens's stories had a profound influence
on Victorian publishing as well as on the development of his own art. If they are overlooked today, it
is primarily because many of them were originally
published within novels or other frameworks, and
much of their appeal is lost when they are considered apart from those contexts. For Dickens the
short story was not a complete and distinct work of
art; it was, instead, one element in a ritual of storytelling that included the teller, the listener, and the
story itself, a ritual as old as the fairy tales on which
Dickens's philosophy of storytelling was based.

The second of eight children of John and Elizabeth Barrow Dickens, Charles John Huffam Dickens was born on 7 February 1812 in Portsmouth,
Hampshire, where his father, a clerk in the navy
pay office, was employed in the dockyard. The family moved to London when Dickens was two; two
years later they moved to Chatham, Kent. For the
rest of his life Dickens would recall his seven years
in Chatham as an idyllic time when his imagination
was nurtured by acting in children's plays and by
the stories of his childhood: fairy tales; horror stories told by his nurse; collections such as *The Ara-*

*bian Nights' Entertainments;* and picaresque novels,
with their rambling plots and short, interpolated
tales. His father was recalled to London in the winter of 1822–1823. Dickens's hopes of "growing up
to be a learned and distinguished man," as he described his early dreams in an autobiographical
fragment many years later, were crushed when his
father, faced with financial ruin, postponed Dickens's education, putting him to work pasting labels
on bottles of shoe polish in a blacking warehouse.
Dickens would later see this episode as a turning
point in his life, a crisis that could have led him to
become "a little robber or a little vagabond." That
such a downfall did not occur Dickens attributed to
the power of his early reading that, as his character
David Copperfield would explain, "kept alive my
fancy, and my hope of something beyond that place
and time." "Fancy" for Dickens represented all that
was most valuable in human thought – the creative,
imaginative aspect of the child's mind, which too
often became dulled or even destroyed by the pragmatic idea of education that would be exemplified
by the teacher Mr. M'Choakumchild in Dickens's
novel *Hard Times: For These Times* (1854). Dickens's
belief in the moral power of "fancy," as evidenced
in his own life, became the foundation of his social
philosophy. Imagination was both the victim of,
and the solution to, the mental oppression produced
by such bullies as Mr. Murdstone in *The Personal
History of David Copperfield* (1849–1850) or by the
mechanization of industrial society seen in the
Coketown of *Hard Times.*

The tales of Dickens's childhood reading were
weapons against pragmatism, and throughout his
life they would provide the imagery for his fight
against unimaginative thinking. In an 1853 essay,
"Frauds on the Fairies," published in *Uncollected
Writings from Household Words, 1850–1859* (1968), he
would attack the artist George Cruikshank for
using the fairy tale to promote temperance; and
"Mr. Barlow," which would appear in Dickens's
journal *All the Year Round* on 16 January 1869, is a
remonstrance with the pedantic tutor in the standard textbook of the time, Thomas Day's *The History of Sandford and Merton* (1783–1789). Mr. Barlow
doubted the story of Sinbad the Sailor; he would
have trimmed Aladdin's lamp while lecturing on the
qualities of sperm oil and whale fisheries; he would
have proved geographically that Casgar and Tart-
ary did not exist; he would have demonstrated scientifically the impossibility of lowering a hunch-
back down an Eastern chimney on a cord.

Of the traditional tales that enriched his childhood, the most important for Dickens was Mr.

Barlow's detested *Arabian Nights' Entertainments,* partly because of its fairy-tale content but also because of its frame story, Schaherezade's nightly struggle to save her life by entertaining the sultan with her tales. Dickens felt a similar need to sustain his imaginative life, and he "kept alive" his fancy by narrating the stories of his early reading to the uneducated boys in the blacking warehouse – an experience that would become David Copperfield's nightly telling of the same books to the boys at Salem House School. Through his role as storyteller David gains influence and status, and he even becomes important in the great Steerforth's eyes. Gaining such admiration was one of Dickens's main motives in his own storytelling – storytelling that would culminate in his Christmas stories and public readings.

After a few months at the blacking warehouse Dickens resumed his education, enrolling at Wellington House Academy. He left school in 1827 and went to work, first as an office boy and then as a shorthand writer for the lawyers in Doctors' Commons. Soon his proficiency at shorthand led him to a position as a parliamentary reporter, where his surroundings and associates provided him with ample material for his first sketches and tales.

Dickens's first published story, "A Dinner at Poplar Walk," was printed in the December 1833 issue of the *Monthly Magazine.* The immediate success of this story and the ones that rapidly followed it has been overshadowed by the tremendous reception given to *The Pickwick Papers,* the novel that came after them. But Dickens's friend and biographer John Forster pointed out that when these early stories were collected in *Sketches by Boz, Illustrative of Every-Day Life and Every-Day People* (1836–1837) they were "more talked about" than the first two or three numbers of *The Pickwick Papers* and that *Sketches by Boz* "is a book that might have stood its ground, even if it had stood alone."

Like the tales that followed it in the *Monthly Magazine,* "A Dinner at Poplar Walk" (renamed "Mr. Minns and His Cousin" when it was republished in *Sketches by Boz*) is slight in plot and characterization, its success lying in its close and comic observation of human nature. When Dickens collected these twelve stories in *Sketches by Boz* under the heading "Tales" he was using the designation *tale* satirically. A tale is traditionally without roots in real life, usually set in an unspecified place (a "distant land") and time ("once upon a time.") Dickens's "tales" are specific, focusing on insignificant urban villas such as Amelia Cottage or Minerva House as Dickens satirizes the social-climbing lower middle classes of Victorian London.

Dickens's satiric use of the word *tale* draws attention also to the pretentiousness of the characters' language and behavior as they engage in trivial social situations, such as a steamboat excursion or a ball. The stories are presented in the mock-heroic mode, with introductory descriptions of each character and, in most cases, a final summing up of the events. The structure itself makes fun of the desperate attempts of the characters to rise in social status, leaving themselves open to being duped by clever impostors. Such comic deceptions were the stock in trade of the contemporary theater, and the tales are theatrical in many of their effects: characters talk at cross purposes, hide behind curtains, are mistaken for each other, end up marrying the wrong person, or otherwise engage in the farcical situations of comic opera or theater. The theatrical emphasis in the tales on role-playing, deception, and the uncovering of fraud was intended, like the mock-heroic style of the tales, to point up the artificiality of middle-class life. Other popular writers of the time, such as John Poole, similarly satirized the snobbish new middle class and its pretensions to an equally hollow and trivial higher society.

In the preface to an 1850 edition of *Sketches by Boz* Dickens dismissed his early tales as "often being extremely crude and ill-considered, and bearing obvious marks of haste and inexperience." While this criticism is true in part, the tales were received at the time as brilliantly accurate comments on London life; and later readers can see in the portraits of grumpy misanthropes, charming swindlers, and aspiring young men who would rather be "Cymon" than "Simon" the germs of characters whose vitality is still the main reason for Dickens's popularity.

"A Dinner at Poplar Walk" was followed in the *Monthly Magazine* by "Mrs. Joseph Porter, 'Over the Way' " in January 1834, "Horatio Sparkins" in February, "The Bloomsbury Christening" in April, and "The Boarding House" in May and August; "Sentiment" appeared in *Bell's Weekly Magazine* in June; "The Steam Excursion" was published in the *Monthly Magazine* in October, and "A Passage in the Life of Mr. Watkins Tottle" in January and February 1835. "The Black Veil" and "The Great Winglebury Duel" were written for the first series of *Sketches by Boz* in 1836. "The Tuggs's at Ramsgate" appeared in the *Library of Fiction* in April 1836, and "The Drunkard's Death" was written for the second series of *Sketches by Boz* in 1837. The two noncomic tales, "The Black Veil" and "The Drunkard's Death," are characteristic of Dickens's interest in death and are marred by a heavy-handed prose that affected his style throughout his career when dealing with serious topics. The influence of Edgar Allan Poe and Nathaniel Hawthorne can be seen in both tales: in "The Black Veil" a woman seeks a doctor to attend her son, who is to be hanged the following day; "The Drunkard's Death" depicts the gradual dissolution of a man whose drunkenness destroys his family and leads to his suicide. The latter story's interest lies in Dickens's portrayal of the drunkard's state of mind at the moment of death, when his descent into the river awakens in him, too late, the desire to live.

With the success of *Sketches by Boz* Dickens was commissioned to write articles to accompany a series of comic sporting prints by the artist Robert Seymour. He immediately took control of the project, turning it into a loosely organized novel instead of a series of sketches. On 2 April 1836 Dickens married Catherine Hogarth, and *The Pickwick Papers* began publication in monthly parts shortly thereafter. Dickens inserts nine short stories into the novel as the hero travels from place to place and encounters a variety of unusual people, each with a tale to tell. The interpolated stories have sometimes been criticized as not being thematically integrated into the novel, and much has been written about their introduction of death, madness, and murder into a generally comic work. But *The Pickwick Papers* itself becomes increasingly serious with Mr. Pickwick's arrest for breach of promise and incarceration in the Fleet Prison, where he encounters the seamier side of society. Many critics have regarded the tales as autobiographical, betraying the dark side of Dickens's nature that he repressed beneath a comic mask, and more-recent criticism has related the stories to the language or themes of the novel as a whole. But while it is possible to regard the stories as having been included for a specific purpose, such as to provide thematic parallels or contrasts, they are essentially experiments with different kinds of storytelling.

Dickens's first storyteller is Dismal Jemmy, a strolling actor with a gaunt face and unnaturally bright and piercing eyes, who half-reads, half-extemporizes in labored and melodramatic prose "The Stroller's Tale," a grim story about his vigil at the deathbed of a fellow actor. Jemmy's central metaphor, that life mirrors the pantomime in its frequent disparity between appearance and reality, is shown most horrifyingly in the dying clown, who is, outwardly, still a comic entertainer. It was to become a favorite metaphor for Dickens.

Another *Pickwick Papers* storyteller, Jack Bamber, is an equally grotesque character, with "a strange, wild slyness in his leer, quite repulsive to behold." In Bamber's "Tale about the Queer Client" a young couple, the Heylings, have been imprisoned for debt at the instigation of the wife's father; after the death of the wife and their child, Mr. Heyling becomes the "queer client" of a rascally lawyer as he relentlessly pursues his father-in-law to his own death. The story's unrelieved recital of cruelty and suffering includes the description of the queer client's delirious visions of vindictive murder. The story relates closely to Mr. Pickwick's troublesome dealings with the legal system in the novel.

The third "dark" tale, "The Convict's Return," is a melodramatic story of a prodigal son that resembles "The Drunkard's Death" and is narrated by an old clergyman of Dingley Dell. More interesting is another story provided by the old clergyman, "A Madman's Manuscript." The "confession" would be one of the major uses to which Dickens would put the short-story form in later years, achieving psychological intensity through the narrowing of the perspective to the narrator's point of view. Even this early story, by being purportedly placed in a manuscript, gives the sense that it is the pure recollection of a disordered mind, undiluted by the perspective of an independent narrator. The madman glories in his belief that he is fooling the world by disguising the madness he thinks he has inherited, and he revels in his mental isolation and superiority. While echoes of Poe are strong, in his self-congratulation the madman is also akin to the narrator of Fyodor Dostoyevsky's *Notes from Underground* (1864). Dickens was to use the confession to great effect in *Little Dorrit* (1855–1857), where Miss Wade's history reveals the distortions suffered by a mind out of touch with reality.

The comic stories of *The Pickwick Papers* are presented not as personal confessions but as tales that have often been repeated. "The Legend of Prince Bladud" is a fable told in a manuscript that Mr. Pickwick discovers in a desk in his rooming house in Bath. The fable is about the founding of the city of Bath and it satirizes the devices of myth. Mr. Pickwick's retelling of Sam Weller's story, "The Parish Clerk," is a gentle parody of a traditional love story. But the most successful of the comic stories are parodies of fairy tales told by a good-humored "bagman" (traveling salesman). In the first, "The Bagman's Story," he defends Tom Smart's account of a talking chair against the charge that Tom was drunk: Tom and the bagman's uncle both said it was all true, and "they must have been very nice men, both of 'em." The second, "The Story of the Bagman's Wife," satirizes the language and plot of the traditional fairy tale as the bagman's uncle unwillingly becomes knight errant to a beautiful lady in a romantic adventure on a stagecoach. The most important of the fairy tales is "The Story of the Goblins who Stole a Sexton," which is told by Mr. Wardle and contains the germ of *A Christmas Carol* (1843) in the reformation of a misanthrope through the visions of happy family life forced on him by goblins. Like Tom Smart and the bagman's uncle, Gabriel Grub is suspected by disbelievers of having been drunk when he had his supernatural experience. Although the fairy-tale experiences are explained away as dreams, the frame stories validate those experiences by returning each protagonist to a reality that has been transformed by his fantasy: encouraged by the talking chair's advice, Tom Smart proposes to a widow; the bagman's uncle resolves never to marry; and Gabriel Grub loses his misanthropy.

In January 1837 Dickens became editor of a monthly magazine, *Bentley's Miscellany,* for which he wrote *Oliver Twist* (February 1837–March 1839) while still working on *The Pickwick Papers;* at the conclusion of *Oliver Twist* he resigned from the editorship of *Bentley's Miscellany.* Before finishing *Oliver Twist* he began *The Life and Adventures of Nicholas Nickleby,* which appeared in monthly parts from April 1838 to October 1839. Early in *Nicholas Nickleby* Dickens incorporates two short tales into the narrative; although neither tale has any particular relevance to the novel as a whole, they are carefully placed in their immediate context, and for the first time the relationship between narrator and story is essential. The coach taking Squeers and Nicholas to Yorkshire overturns, and the passengers are stranded at an inn. After the punch has been served, the travelers form a storytelling club that first hears "The Five Sisters of York," narrated by a middle-aged, gray-haired gentleman who is dressed in mourning. His story, set in the fifteenth century, is about five sisters who are weaving tapestries that, their mother told them, would remind them of their carefree youth if they ever became separated and unhappy. A monk who disapproves of their work warns them that "the memory of earthly things is charged, in after life, with bitter disappointment, affliction, death; with dreary change and wasting sorrow" and that the tapestries will someday "tear open deep wounds"; but the youngest sister, Alice, reminds the others of their mother's words. Later, after Alice's death, the other four sisters return to York after lives filled with trouble and suffering. The monk urges them to enter a convent, but the tapestries remind the sisters of Alice's insistence that they must never renounce

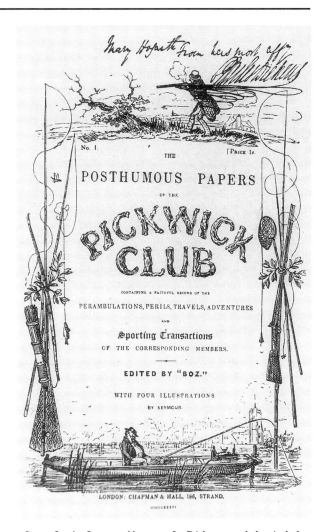

*Cover for the first monthly part of a Dickens novel that includes short stories told by various characters. The inscription at the top is from Dickens to his sister-in-law. (Dickens Fellowship)*

the active life. The remembrance of her brings them comfort, not grief. The gray-haired narrator, unnaturally aged by some trial in his early life, asks, "If, while our bodies grow old and withered, our hearts could but retain their early youth and freshness, of what avail would be our sorrows and sufferings?" At the end of the story he and a "merry-faced gentleman" discuss the value of memory, and the gray-haired man concludes that "memory, however sad, is the best and purest link between this world and a better."

The merry-faced gentleman then narrates the story of the Baron of Grogswig, who, like the storyteller, is optimistic and kindhearted, a believer in the active life. But when his shrewish wife, her mother, and his large family put an end to his amusements he sinks into despondency. He is about to kill himself when he is confronted by the Genius of Despair and Suicide, whose miserable pessimism shows him the value of his own good nature. He resolves to make the most of his cheerful disposition and, after converting his wife to a similar attitude, lives happily ever after, having learned that "nothing is too bad to be retrieved." The story illustrates the outlook of its teller, just as the subdued gravity of the gray-haired man's story matches its narrator's philosophy.

In 1839 Dickens suggested to the publishers Edward Chapman and William Hall that he edit a new periodical, *Master Humphrey's Clock,* in the tradition of *The Tatler, The Spectator,* and Oliver Goldsmith's *Bee.* It would feature, as he explained to Forster, a "little club or knot of characters," including Mr. Pickwick and Sam Weller, whose histories and day-to-day lives would comprise part of the contents; it would also include stories, sketches, letters, and essays on current events. Master Humphrey is a gentle old man with an ancient clock in which "he has kept odd manuscripts in the old, deep, dark, silent closet where the weights are; and taken them from thence to read." In these manuscripts he and his friends have woven bright autobiographical stories from their past sufferings, just as the butterflies "have sprung for the first time into light and sunshine from some dark corner of these old walls." Dickens's grief at the loss of his beloved sister-in-law, Mary Hogarth, in 1837 no doubt partly accounts for his obsessive need to find strength and consolation in painful memories.

Gog and Magog, the mythical guardians of London, are introduced in the first number of the magazine, which appeared on 4 April 1840. They amuse each other in their nightly vigil by telling tales about what they have observed in the city over the centuries. Their first story, a historical romance about sixteenth-century London, was in many ways similar to the novel *Barnaby Rudge* (1841), which Dickens had started writing in 1836 but had postponed. The story resembles the novel in its dual structure: the domestic love story that forms the first half gives way to the public events of the second. The mob scenes of the novel are foreshadowed in the crowd's protection of the apprentice, Hugh, after he murders a nobleman who has eloped with the master's daughter. The story also looks forward to *A Tale of Two Cities* (1859), which places a domestic love story within the setting of the French Revolution.

The next story, "A Confession Found in a Prison in the Time of Charles the Second," like "A Madman's Manuscript," is a first-person revelation of a deranged mind, the type of confessional story

to which Dickens would return throughout his career. The narrator is a lieutenant in the time of Charles II who is condemned to be executed the next day. He and his brother, different in every respect, had married sisters, and the brother's wife understood all of the narrator's secrets: "I was afraid of her; she haunted me; her fixed and steady look comes back upon me now, like the memory of a dark dream, and makes my blood run cold." When his brother and sister-in-law died, he inherited their son. The boy seemed to have the same power the mother had; the lieutenant feared the boy's gaze, which seemed to penetrate his innermost thoughts. He finally killed the child; and at the moment of death the mother's ghost looked from the boy's eyes, and suddenly "there were eyes in everything. The whole great universe of light was there to see the murder done." Having buried the boy, the lieutenant was obsessed by fear that the crime would be discovered; he dreamed of the reappearance of a hand or foot from the grave. By ceaselessly watching the grave, the lieutenant eventually led the authorities to it. An important early attempt on Dickens's part to explore the monomania of the criminal, the story is reminiscent of Poe, who described it in a review in *Graham's Magazine* (May 1841) as "a paper of remarkable power."

The third story, "Mr. Pickwick's Tale," is set in the time of King James I. Will Marks discovers that the supposed witches at a gibbet are women mourning for their hanged relative. They lead him to a tenement, where a masked cavalier pays him to transport the body secretly to the church where it is to be buried. Will makes his way through the plague-ridden squalor and violence of the London streets, the setting out of which the Gordon riots spring in *Barnaby Rudge.* The madness of the villagers' eagerness to find a witch in every old woman is indicative of the greater madness of the government that hangs and the mob that follows blindly, madness that forms the theme of *Barnaby Rudge.*

When Master Humphrey's short autobiography, "The Old Curiosity Shop," proved popular, Dickens abandoned the original plan for a periodical and turned the short tale into a novel published in weekly parts; it was followed by *Barnaby Rudge. Master Humphrey's Clock* concludes at the end of *Barnaby Rudge* with the death of Master Humphrey. The short stories are not well known today, because after *The Old Curiosity Shop* and *Barnaby Rudge* were published separately the rest of *Master Humphrey's Clock* was consigned, as Dickens said, to the trunk maker and the butterman. They were later included in collected editions of Dickens's works, but only "A Confession Found in a Prison in the Time of Charles the Second" has been frequently republished since.

After concluding *Master Humphrey's Clock* Dickens toured North America, giving his impressions in *American Notes for General Circulation* (1842). He then began *The Life and Adventures of Martin Chuzzlewit* (January 1842–July 1844). Toward the end of 1843 he decided to write a long story for the Christmas market; partly inspired by a visit to the Cornish tin mines, where he saw children working under appalling conditions, he threw himself into *A Christmas Carol,* which was published at Christmas 1843. In *A Christmas Carol* Dickens attacks the prevalent economic theories of the day that held that anyone who was not self-supporting had no right to live. Ebenezer Scrooge is converted from miser to benefactor by visits from a series of ghosts: the ghost of his former partner, Marley, shows Scrooge the error of shutting out the world and living for oneself; the Ghost of Christmas Past reminds him of the affectionate, generous boy he once was and how the pursuit of money hardened him; having recovered his better self through the memory of his childhood, Scrooge is able to appreciate the lesson taught by the Ghost of Christmas Present, who reiterates Marley's warning by showing Scrooge loving families, rich in spirit if not in material wealth. The Ghost of Christmas Yet to Come shows him that if he fails to change his ways he will die unloved and unmourned. Scrooge's conversion was accepted by Victorian readers as a parable about their materialistic society, and *A Christmas Carol* inspired the foundation of "Tiny Tim" beds – named for the crippled son of Scrooge's employee, Bob Cratchit – for disadvantaged children in London hospitals. Dickens raised money for such hospitals by giving readings of a shortened version of *A Christmas Carol,* the success of which led to the lucrative but physically demanding reading tours he made in the last twenty years of his life.

The four succeeding Christmas books, published from 1844 to 1848 with a gap in 1847, are less well known now but were immensely popular at the time. In each, a central character who has lost faith in humanity is brought to a realization of the generosity of the human spirit; with the exception of the 1846 book, *The Battle of Life,* in each case the cynic is reformed through supernatural means. By calling the Christmas-book form "a whimsical kind of masque" in the preface to the first collected edition of the books (1852), Dickens tried to excuse his use of the supernatural; but according to Forster he "had a secret delight" in giving the nursery tales he had enjoyed as a child "a higher form." *The Chimes* (published in late 1844 but dated 1845) was written in Italy, where Dickens spent the winter of 1844, but it is one of his most powerful evocations of the foggy, cold streets of London in January. According to his 8 October 1844 letter to Forster, Dickens intended the book as a "great blow for the poor," again attacking contemporary utilitarian philosophy and economic theory. The person to be reformed is Toby Veck, a ticket porter, or licensed messenger on foot in the city of London, who loses faith in his own class when he comes to believe the accusations of government, the law, and the aristocracy that the poor have only themselves to blame for their plight. Contemporaries recognized at once the dignitaries who were being satirized in the book, such as Sir Peter Laurie, a magistrate known for passing harsh sentences on starving women who attempted suicide. As in *A Christmas Carol,* the conversion of the protagonist is brought about by fairy-tale means: the goblins who live among the church bells teach Toby to believe in the goodness and moral strength of his daughter and his class. But many readers regret that the cruel and canting political economists remain unpunished in the book, while the kindly ticket porter is taught a frightening lesson when he is shown a possible future in which his daughter is driven to the verge of suicide. Even though he awakes to his daughter's joyful New Year's Day marriage breakfast, the shadow cast by the dream vision is not wholly dispelled at the end of the book, making it less popular than the more joyful *A Christmas Carol.* As social criticism, however, *The Chimes* remains, with *Hard Times,* one of Dickens's most accurate portrayals of the prevalent attitudes of powerful Victorians in the 1840s.

Dickens's next Christmas book, *The Cricket on the Hearth* (published in 1845 but dated 1846), leaves strident social criticism behind. Considered sentimental by many readers today, *The Cricket on the Hearth* was a huge success at the time, especially on the stage, where dramatizations of it appeared in seventeen theaters in London alone during the Christmas season of 1845. This "fairy tale of home," as the subtitle calls it, includes an "ogre" in the curmudgeonly toy maker Tackleton and an idealized heroine in the sugary Dot Peerybingle. Dot's husband, John, who is some years older than his wife, fears that she is in love with another man; on the point of killing his rival he is stopped by fairy crickets who bring back memories of his wife's goodness. But whereas Scrooge and Toby are made to realize the value of what they had distrusted,

John is led by the fairies not to believe in his wife's fidelity but to accept her apparent desire for a man her own age. He begins to see his marriage as a selfish one, and resolves to set Dot free from an unequal union. His sacrifice is, of course, unnecessary; the supposed lover turns out to be the suitor of Dot's friend May. Themes of deception and blindness are realized, respectively, in the toys that mimic real life and in Bertha Plummer, a blind girl who falls in love with the villain Tackleton because her father, Caleb, has portrayed him as a generous friend (May's lover turns out to be the long-lost brother of Bertha and son of Caleb). The story's only weakness is Tackleton's sudden transformation from misanthrope to jovial benefactor.

In 1846 Dickens was in Switzerland, working on *Dealings with the Firm of Dombey and Son, Wholesale, Retail, and for Exportation* (1846–1848), when he devised what he called "a pretty story, with some delicate notions in it agreeably presented, and with a good human Christmas groundwork." According to the book itself, *The Battle of Life* is a tale of the "quiet victories and struggles, great sacrifices of self, and noble acts of heroism . . . done every day in nooks and corners, and in little households, and in men's and women's hearts." The Christmas-book conversion takes place in Doctor Jeddler, who considers life a joke and human cares and sufferings trivial. His change of heart is brought about not by supernatural means but by the example of his two daughters, each of whom unselfishly hides her love for their friend Alfred so that he will turn to the other. Working out the story within the scope of a Christmas book and without supernatural means proved to be a mistake, as Dickens realized too late; the most glaring improbability in the plot is one sister's exile to her aunt's house for six years, while her family thinks that she has eloped. *The Battle of Life* was successful despite its flaws, selling twenty-three thousand copies on the first day and far outselling its predecessors by the end of January; a stage adaptation was also popular.

The difficulty of writing a Christmas book concurrently with a novel discouraged Dickens from producing one the following year, when *Dombey and Son* was still in progress, even though he was "loathe to lose the money. And still more to leave any gap at Christmas firesides which I ought to fill," according to his 19 September 1847 letter to Forster. In 1848 he returned to the structure of *A Christmas Carol* in *The Haunted Man and the Ghost's Bargain*. Mr. Redlaw, a chemist, is embittered by regrets and the memory of past injustices. When a phantom offers him the gift of forgetfulness he ac-

cepts eagerly, unaware that in giving up his sad memories he also has to relinquish the "intertwisted chain of feelings and associations, each in its turn dependent on, and nourished by, the banished recollections." Without such human feeling Redlaw is unable to appreciate beauty, music, or kindness, and he is doomed to pass this curse on to everyone he meets. Only a neglected waif, incapable of human feeling because of his deprivation, is immune to Redlaw's evil influence. Redlaw's change of heart is brought about through seeing the effects of the curse and through the example of Milly, a young woman whose compassion springs from her remembrance of losing her own child. Redlaw learns the lesson taught by the gray-haired narrator of "The Five Sisters of York," which was to be reiterated in many of Dickens's short stories: without the remembrance of suffering, joy is impossible.

Most critics agree with Forster that the "turning point" in Dickens's career lay in the years when he wrote the Christmas books, the years between the loosely structured *Martin Chuzzlewit* and the carefully planned *Dombey and Son*. In producing the Christmas books Dickens learned not only to construct a plot before beginning the writing of a work but also how to indicate growth and development in his characters. *Dombey and Son* is the first of his novels to be unified by a sequence of related and significant events. The memory-haunted Christmas books were largely responsible for the striking improvement in Dickens's artistry during these years.

The Christmas books — attractive small volumes designed for gift giving, with pictures by some of the best illustrators of the day, such as John Leech, Clarkson Stanfield, and Daniel Maclise — inspired a host of similar publications for the Christmas market by well-known writers including Wilkie Collins, Elizabeth Cleghorn Gaskell, and Anthony Trollope; William Makepeace Thackeray was the most successful rival to Dickens with his satiric offerings during the 1840s. The cult of the Christmas book led Dickens to search for another form that would "awaken some loving and forbearing thoughts," as he described the purpose of the books in the preface to the collected edition. For the next seventeen years Dickens worked to make the Christmas story accessible to a wider audience, and the somber tone of *The Haunted Man* was replaced by the gentler voice of Dickens himself.

In January 1850 Dickens launched *Household Words*, a weekly magazine. While many writers contributed to it, Dickens edited every item to ensure that the magazine would "tenderly cherish that light of Fancy which is inherent in the human breast," as his opening statement in the first issue declared. The issue for Christmas week the first year was a collection of sketches on Christmas customs in various places, opening with Dickens's "A Christmas Tree," in which the memory of "telling Winter Stories – Ghost Stories . . . round the Christmas fire" provides the framework for a series of tales of murders and foreshadowed death. The following year the Christmas issue appeared separately as the "Extra Number for Christmas"; it was the same length as a regular number – twenty-four pages – and there was no frame story, but the sketches were unified under the topic "What Christmas Is." Dickens's contribution, "What Christmas Is as We Grow Older," was a sequel to "A Christmas Tree."

The following year Dickens set out a framework for the Christmas number that required stories rather than sketches: the issue was titled *A Round of Stories by the Christmas Fire,* and the length was increased to thirty-six pages, which from then on was the standard for the Christmas number of *Household Words.* The stories were not connected by a linking narrative, but the most successful contributions made use of the "round of stories" framework by making the point of the tale depend on the character of the narrator. Dickens's "The Poor Relation's Story," which opened the issue, is the revelation of a secret world known only to the narrator. The poor relation, in the reticent style of such a member of the family, describes his life as people know it: his failure in business and in love because of his honest and trusting nature, his poverty resulting from his unworldly attitude, and his daily routine of escaping from his lodgings to the coffeehouses of the city and the counting houses of his relatives, where he whiles away the hours until he can finally go home to bed. But, he assures his listeners, they are wrong in thinking of him as a failed man living a solitary life: he did well in business and is surrounded in his pleasant home by a faithful wife and loving children and grandchildren. But, though his home is his castle, his castle is in the air: the poor relation is surrounded by dream children who vanish at the end of his narration, and through his story the agony of disappointed hopes and dreams is most poignantly told.

Dickens's "The Child's Story," which followed "The Poor Relation's Story" in the 1852 Christmas number, is a perfect parable, narrating in biblical language the passage of a man's life from childhood to old age. Opening with the fairy-tale phrase "Once upon a time," the story tells of a traveler who sets out on a "magic journey" during which he meets in succession a child, an adolescent, a young man, a middle-aged gentleman, and an old man. The story achieves a cumulative effect through the repetition of a similar refrain at each stage of the journey, from the child's "I am always at play. Come and play with me!" to the final climax in the old man's "I am always remembering. Come and remember with me!" Dickens here allegorizes his own spiritual passage from disillusionment and loss to the recognition of the importance of memory. The child's picture books are *The Arabian Nights' Entertainments,* James Ridley's *Tales of the Genii* (1764), and other nursery stories Dickens had read as a child. The middle-aged man is accompanied by his wife and children, but one by one they leave the path – one to sea, one to India, one to heaven (Dickens's baby Dora Annie had died in 1851), and he is alone until he becomes an old man and the figures return to him through his memory.

The Christmas number of *Household Words* was the most important and carefully planned issue of the year. Percy Fitzgerald described the status of being a favored contributor: "The time when 'the Christmas Number' had to be got ready was always one of pleasant alacrity. It was an object for all to have a seat in 'a vehicle' which travelled every road and reached the houses of a quarter of a million persons."

In 1853 Dickens wrote two ghost stories for the annual *The Keepsake.* The stories are contained in a frame titled "To Be Read at Dusk," which had been suggested by Dickens's 1846 visit to the St. Bernard Hospice in the Great Bernard Pass between Switzerland and Italy. He had been fascinated by the remote setting of the monks' mountain retreat and by the shed beside the hospice, where the bodies of lost travelers lay frozen and uncorrupted in the permanent snows. The stories are overheard by the narrator as he listens to the evening conversation of the guides at the hospice. In the first story, which was suggested to Dickens by Gaskell, one of the guides tells of his experience as courier for an English couple honeymooning at a gloomy old palace near Genoa. Before her marriage the young wife had dreamed repeatedly of a face "looking at her fixedly, out of darkness." She has nearly overcome her dread that the face will materialize at the palace when a stranger appears; she recognizes him as the dream vision. In spite of her terror her husband forces her to accept their new friend. One night she disappears and is seen for the last time at a posthouse, crouching in the corner of the stranger's carriage. The guide implies that the bride went against her inclination, but, nevertheless, willingly; he has already noted that she would look at the stranger

*Illustration by "Phiz" (Hablôt Browne) for one of the tales in* The Pickwick Papers

"with a terrified and fascinated glance, as if his presence had some evil influence or power upon her."

In the second story, told by the German guide, a man sees his brother in a vision just before the latter's death. Dickens told Gaskell in a 25 November 1851 letter that he believed the story to be "in the slightest incident, perfectly true." Although Dickens disapproved of spiritualism and made fun of mediums, he enjoyed ghost stories that dramatized the power and mystery of the human psyche under stressful conditions.

Dickens was in Italy when he planned the 1853 Christmas number, *Another Round of Stories by the Christmas Fire.* His own contributions opened and closed the issue. Part of the appeal of the opening piece, "The Schoolboy's Story," is achieved through the schoolboy's style as he tells of Old Cheeseman, a misunderstood schoolmate and later a revered schoolmaster. The number concluded with "Nobody's Story," a war cry on behalf of the poor, in which Dickens summarizes the wrongs that he returned to again and again in the regular numbers of *Household Words.* "Nobody" cannot understand why there are statues and memorials to kings and statesmen, when inventors and philanthropists are ig-

nored. He asks for education for his children; he asks for better living conditions so that cholera, which raged for five years before the government took steps to combat it, can be abated. The Bigwig family argue among themselves and finally do nothing. "So Nobody lived and died in the old, old, old way; and this, in the main, is the whole of Nobody's story . . . the story of the rank and file of the earth."

The frame story for the 1854 Christmas number, *The Seven Poor Travellers,* is set at Richard Watts's charity hostel for poor travelers in Rochester, which Dickens visited with Mark Lemon in May. The narrator goes to the hostel one Christmas Eve to learn what lies behind the inscription over the door, which is dated 1579: "Six poor Travellers, who not being ROGUES, or PROCTORS, May receive gratis for one Night, Lodging, Entertainment, and Four pence each." Discovering that the money left by Watts for the support of the hostel has been almost wholly used up, the narrator provides the six travelers with a Christmas dinner and then invites each to tell a story. The narrator himself begins the evening with the sentimental story of Richard Doubledick, a young relative who had rested at the hostel in 1799 on his way to enlist in the cavalry. As with many Dickens characters, Doubledick's "heart was in the right place, but it was sealed up," rejection by the woman he loved having driven him to dissipation and despair. Through the example of a captain, Doubledick becomes a hero; he survives his war wounds to regain and marry his lost love and to learn forgiveness. Dickens prepared a public reading of the story, which he performed some thirty times. According to Charles Kent, who saw him read it, Dickens was particularly impressive as Captain Taunton.

The frame story for the 1855 Christmas number, *The Holly-Tree Inn,* tells of a traveler who, finding himself snowed in at an inn, overcomes his timidity sufficiently to ask the other guests about their histories. For this number Dickens also wrote "The Boots," about the elopement of eight-year-old Master Harry Walmers with his seven-year-old sweetheart, Norah. The story has been viewed in the twentieth century as indicating an unhealthy interest in childhood sexuality, but it was popular in Dickens's time. Dickens made a successful public reading of the story, in which the comic voice of the narrator, Cobbs, the "boots" or general servant at the inn, relieved the sentimentality of the story.

In May 1858 Dickens separated from his wife and set up his own home with his children: Mary, Kate, Walter, Francis, Alfred, Sydney, Henry, and Edward — all except the oldest, Charlie; his sister-in-law, Georgina Hogarth, moved in with Dickens as his housekeeper. One of his main emotional supports at this time was Wilkie Collins, a rising young writer who had proved himself a capable contributor to *Household Words*. Dickens and Collins were intrigued with the friendship of the explorers Sir John Franklin and Sir John Richardson, who had disappeared on an expedition to the Northwest Passage in 1845; in a letter to Forster, Dickens spoke of "Richardson's manly friendship, and love of Franklin" as "one of the noblest things I ever knew in my life. It makes one's heart beat high, with a sort of sacred joy." The explorers' names became Frank Aldersley and Richard Wardour in Collins's play about an Arctic expedition, *The Frozen Deep,* in 1857. On the stage Dickens played Wardour, the disappointed lover who sacrifices his own life to carry his weaker rival, Aldersley, played by Collins, to safety after resisting the chance to kill him in the frozen wastes.

Heroic friendship was the theme of the frame story of the 1856 Christmas number of *Household Words,* which was titled *The Wreck of the Golden Mary.* The story has two narrators – Captain Ravender and the mate, John Steadiman, whose parts were written by Dickens and Collins, respectively – who are in charge of two lifeboats after the wreck of their ship. Other contributors were employed in the central section, "Beguilement in the Boats," in which the passengers try to keep up their flagging spirits by telling stories to each other. In the frame story Dickens developed some of his favorite themes. The spiritual center of the desperate party is a golden-haired child, Lucy, who was based on Dickens's childhood friend Lucy Stroughill and would reappear as Lucie Manette in *A Tale of Two Cities.* Lucy, whose name is derived from the Latin for "light," symbolizes religious faith in opposition to the selfish superstition of an old man in the boat. Lucy dies, but she has taught the others that they all retain the essential innocence and purity of childhood within them: Captain Ravender narrates that "The purest part of our lives will not desert us at the pass to which all of us here present are gliding. What we were then, will be as much in existence before Him, as what we are now." Dickens upheld the purity of the child, an idea shared earlier in the century by the Romantic poets, in opposition to the widely held belief in the corruption of the child by original sin. At the end of the frame story the mate relates the rescue of the survivors by a passing ship; the captain has collapsed from exhaustion.

Performances of *The Frozen Deep* occupied Dickens and Collins through the spring and summer of 1857. When the play's run ended, Dickens proposed to Collins that they go on a walking tour of Cumberland and write a fictionalized account of it for *Household Words.* "The Lazy Tour of Two Idle Apprentices," which appeared in five installments from 3 October to 31 October, is a comic account of the attempts of Francis Goodchild (based on Dickens) to goad his reluctant friend Thomas Idle (Collins) into activity. The word *idle* is used ironically throughout the piece to describe Goodchild's feverish inability to rest, with Idle's genuine laziness acting as a comic foil. Goodchild insists on climbing Carrock Fell one wet afternoon; the exhausted Idle, after dragging his weary, reluctant, and incapable body some distance behind the exuberant Goodchild, sprains his ankle on the descent and has to be carried down by his friend. During Idle's convalescence each of the friends tells a story. Goodchild's story, written by Dickens, relates an incident that occurred when he and Idle were staying at an inn in Lancaster. They saw six identical ghostly old men ascending the stairs, and later that night they were confronted by one of them,

> a chilled, slow, earthy, fixed old man. A cadaverous old man of measured speech. An old man who seemed as unable to wink, as if his eyelids had been nailed to his forehead. An old man whose eyes – two spots of fire – had no more motion than if they had been connected with the back of his skull by screws driven through it, and rivetted and bolted outside, among his grey hair. . . . He was an old man of a swollen character of face, and his nose was immovably hitched up on one side, as if by a little hook inserted in that nostril.

The ghost fixed Goodchild and Idle with his riveting eyes and told them the history of the "Bride's Chamber," in which they were sitting. The guardian of a young heiress attained mastery over her weak will, married her, and slowly killed her by telling her to die. Having gained her money through what he believed to be a perfect crime, he discovered that a secret admirer of his wife had witnessed the murder, and he was forced to kill the admirer and risk detection after all. Fear that the admirer's body would be discovered obsessed the murderer and prevented his enjoyment of his new wealth. The crime was, indeed, found out, and the murderer was hanged. At this point the old man revealed that he was the murderer, doomed to a perpetual ghostly life by the bride's constant injunction: "live." Each year, in the month of his death, he had to leave the bride's chamber to haunt the room in which he had feared discovery, appearing hourly in as many forms as the clock strikes. To remove the curse, he had to tell his story to two men simultaneously; but one man always fell asleep. Goodchild then found that he alone had been riveted to the old man by "threads of fire" stretching from the ghost's eyes to his own; Idle was sound asleep. Dickens here parodies the ghost-story conventions used by contributors to the Christmas numbers of *Household Words;* but the story is also about the action of the will, a subject that interested him greatly and that would reach its fullest expression in the relationship between Miss Havisham and Estella in *Great Expectations* (1861).

The 1857 Christmas number, *The Perils of Certain English Prisoners,* dispensed with the format of incorporating stories by various contributors within a frame story by Dickens (or by Dickens and Collins); instead, it was written as a continuous narrative, in three chapters, by Dickens and Collins alone. The story was based on the recent Indian Mutiny and Cawnpore massacre, but Dickens avoided the political issues involved by setting his story in South America. Gill Davis, an illiterate soldier, narrates the story while the aristocratic Marion writes it down. Davis relates that he was at first a self-pitying and jealous private; but he was taught by the selfless example of the gentlemen he resented to accept his social inferiority. Foreshadowing Lucie Manette and Sydney Carton in *A Tale of Two Cities,* Marion is an unattainable angel who inspires her dissipated admirer to heroic action. In his early frustration and anger at his inferiority Gill lays the foundation for Pip in *Great Expectations;* but, unlike Pip, Gill does not become educated and so must remain unequal to his ideal lady, who marries a captain.

Collins had a large hand in the 1858 Christmas number, *A House to Let,* to which Dickens contributed the lively sketch "Going into Society." Toby Magsman, a showman, relates the story of his friend Chops the Dwarf's discovery that "society" is just another fairground: " 'Magsman,' he says, and he seemed to myself to get wiser as he got hoarser; 'Society, taken in the lump, is all dwarfs. At the court of Saint James's, they was all a doin my old business. . . . Everywheres, the sarser was a goin round. Magsman, the sarser is the uniwersal Institution!' " Dickens considered saving his story of Chops the Dwarf for a novel, but while this type of comic character had been a large part of Dickens's early novels, it no longer belonged in the more unified and artistic later works.

In June 1858, against the advice of his friends, Dickens had published a public statement in *Household Words* about the breakup of his marriage, hoping to scotch the rumors — which were, in fact, true —

that he had taken up with Ellen Ternan, a young actress from the cast of *The Frozen Deep.* When William Bradbury and Frederick Evans, the publishers of *Household Words,* refused to run the statement in their comic paper *Punch,* Dickens took their refusal as a personal betrayal and canceled *Household Words* in May 1859, establishing a new journal, *All the Year Round,* with his old publishers, Chapman and Hall. He carried over the tradition of the extra Christmas number to the new magazine, increasing the length to forty-eight pages. The first such issue, for 1859, was titled *The Haunted House* and included stories about the ghostly visitations that occurred in each bedroom of the house during the night. Dickens's frame story attacks spiritualism, which Dickens considered fraudulent and antithetical to true religious belief. The narrator recounts an argument Dickens had held with a well-known spiritualist, William Howitt, about the existence of ghosts. Howitt wrote a long objection to *The Haunted House* in *The Critic,* calling Dickens un-Christian. Dickens did not reply, but other writers came in on both sides of the argument in various journals.

Dickens's contribution to the framed tales, "The Ghost in Master B.'s Room," reveals that the ghost haunting the narrator's room is the ghost of his own childhood, with which he is destined to live all his life. The ghost represents memory, the link connecting the present with the past: "No other ghost has haunted the boy's room, my friends, since I have occupied it, than the ghost of my own childhood, the ghost of my own innocence, the ghost of my own airy belief. Many a time have I pursued the phantom: never with this man's stride of mine to come up with it, never with these man's hands of mine to touch it, never more to this man's heart of mine to hold it in its purity." The narrator recalls being wrenched, as a child, from the sympathetic surroundings of a country town to the impersonality of London, where his bed was auctioned "for a song," and he wonders "what song, and thought what a dismal song it must have been to sing!"

Dickens wrote "Hunted Down" for Robert Bonner's story paper, *The New York Ledger,* where it appeared on 20 and 27 August and 3 September 1859; it was also published in *All the Year Round* in August. Bonner paid for the story of Julius Slinkton, a clever murderer based on the poisoner Thomas Griffiths Wainewright, whom Dickens had visited in Newgate prison in 1838 or 1839. The story resembles "The Bride's Chamber" in *The Lazy Tour of Two Idle Apprentices* in Slinkton's slow murder of a young woman by willing her to death to inherit her money. The murderer is found out by the girl's lover, who hunts the unsuspecting killer down.

Dickens and Collins visited Devon in November 1860 to work on the frame story for *A Message from the Sea,* the 1860 Christmas number. The story tells of a young fisherman who finds an almost obliterated message in a bottle; the message was apparently written and thrown into the sea by the fisherman's brother before his death in a shipwreck, and it suggests that their father had been involved in a theft some years previously. Searching for the truth, the brother travels to Langrean, where a storytelling club is meeting at the local inn – a device that allows for the introduction of the contributed tales. The frame story, which has a happy ending that is brought about by a blustery American sea captain, was immediately pirated for the stage, but when Dickens threatened to serve an injunction the play was withdrawn at the last minute. It appeared a week later, with Dickens's permission, and there were other successful stage adaptations.

The frame for the 1861 Christmas number, *Tom Tiddler's Ground,* was suggested to Dickens by a visit with James Lucas, a hermit living in lonely squalor near Stevenage. Mr. Traveller, the narrator, criticizes the hermit for being "a slothful, unsavoury, nasty reversal of the laws of human nature." The hermit's visitors tell him stories based on their own experience, and Mr. Traveller is sure that they will show the hermit the harmfulness of isolation and the necessity for human sympathy and interdependence: " 'Come!' apostrophising the gate. 'Open Sesame! Show his eyes and grieve his heart! I don't care who comes, for I know what must come of it!' " Many of the contributed stories did not suit the theme, but Dickens's own contribution, "Picking up Miss Kimmeens," illustrates Mr. Traveller's point in its description of a good-natured girl who, finding herself becoming morose and self-pitying when she is left alone in the schoolhouse, goes out to find companionship.

With the 1862 Christmas number of *All the Year Round* Dickens ceased his practice of making the narrator of the frame story his own alter ego and threw himself into the comic possibilities of the frame tale. *Somebody's Luggage* began the "character" stories that attained success even with critics who had failed to appreciate the philosophical importance of the earlier stories. Dickens's genius with character was allowed to blossom in these stories, starting in 1862 with Christopher the waiter. The frame for the contributed stories is provided by Christopher's opening "somebody's luggage" that has been lying under a bed in the hotel for six years,

having been left till called for. The waiter discovers manuscripts stuffed in the unknown former guest's boots, hatbox, umbrella, and other articles; the contributed stories are named for the objects in which the manuscripts were concealed. The success of the frame lies in Christopher's comic descriptions of a waiter's trade, the hardships of his life, and the public's misunderstanding of its servants. Dickens contributed two of his most characteristic stories to *Somebody's Luggage.* "His Boots" is set in France, where he was staying at the time; after publication he wrote to his friend Thomas Beard on 24 December 1862 of the immense success of the number, which by that date had sold 185,000 copies, concluding: "I wonder how many people among those purchasers have an idea of the number of steamboat, railway train, dusty French walk, and looking out of window, boiled down in His Boots?" The French corporal Theophile's devotion to an orphan girl is observed by Mr. Langley, a stuffy Englishman who, like Mr. Dombey, has disowned his daughter and her child and has fortified himself against calls on his sympathy. But like Scrooge and Redlaw, he discovers that memory can be suppressed but not denied, and the memory of his early love for his daughter is renewed by the corporal's example. When Theophile is killed, Mr. Langley adopts the child. The second story, "His Brownpaper Parcel," is so unlike Dickens's "Christmas style" that the critic for the *Saturday Review* (20 December 1862) believed that it had been written by one of his contributors; but it is unmistakably in the tradition of Dickens's "confession" stories, which depend on the narrators' sense that they are misunderstood. The narrator of this story is a street artist who, rather than suffer the humiliation of sitting on the pavement begging, rents his pictures to poor misfits who pose as the painter and make alterations to the pictures to impress passers-by with their skill. His companions, not realizing that he drew the pictures, interpret his pained expression at the inept attempts to improve his work as jealousy. He allows his friends to cast him off, letting the reader into the secret of his identity only at the end.

The sophistication of Dickens's use of the short-story form, evident in his contributions to *Somebody's Luggage,* was rare in 1862. The other contributors had problems adjusting to the length; again and again their stories began well, but bad planning resulted in a sudden and often feeble ending when the writer found the last page coming up all too soon. The *Times* critic noted the fault on 4 December 1862 but excused the contributors by describing them as restricted novelists rather than story writers: the contributed stories "are slight in texture, and it must be remembered that they occupy each but four or five pages. What is a tale-writer to do in four or five pages? Think what the first chapter of a novel is – how dull it is generally. Here is a series of first chapters, on which we really wonder at the skill of half-a-dozen writers in making their subjects interesting." That a *Times* critic could have such a false expectation of the short-story form in 1862 is indicative of how far Dickens had progressed in the genre. The frame narratives of the Christmas numbers increasingly took over from the included stories because of the poor quality and lack of cohesiveness of the contributions. Each year Dickens spelled out to his contributors the theme that he wished the whole number to convey, but each year the contributions fell short of his expectations. Reluctant to abandon the *Arabian Nights* format, he counterbalanced the poor quality of the other stories by putting even greater effort into the frames; he achieved success at the expense of the unity of the Christmas numbers by making the frame a complete story in itself.

The frame stories of the 1863 and 1864 numbers are narrated by Mrs. Lirriper, the immortal landlady of number 81 Norfolk Street Strand, whose fame rests primarily on her exuberant and uncontrollable flow of words, largely unencumbered by punctuation (although extra punctuation was added, to the detriment of the effect, for the collected edition of the Christmas stories). In Mrs. Lirriper, Dickens perfected the stream-of-consciousness technique, which was to become a hallmark of twentieth-century writing. Like Christopher the waiter, Mrs. Lirriper expounds on the hardships of her occupation – her dealings with lodgers, servants, and the rival landlady down the street. Complaining of servants, Mrs. Lirriper laments, "Girls as I was beginning to remark are one of your first and your lasting troubles, being like your teeth which begin with convulsions and never cease tormenting you from the time you cut them till they cut you, and then you don't want to part with them which seems hard but we must all succumb or buy artificial, and even where you get a will nine times out of ten you'll get a dirty face with it and naturally lodgers do not like good society to be shown in with a smear of black across the nose or a smudgy eyebrow."

The frame stories of the 1863 and 1864 numbers, "Mrs. Lirriper's Lodgings" and "Mrs. Lirriper's Legacy," are similar to "A House to Let," but the unsavory nature of that piece, influenced by Collins, is replaced in the Lirriper tales by the moral affirmation more typical of a Christmas number. In the first story a young, pregnant woman living at Mrs. Lirriper's house is deserted by her husband. The kindly landlady prevents the woman from committing suicide, then adopts her baby when the woman dies in childbirth. The two stories then relate the growth of young Jemmy under the loving care of Mrs. Lirriper and her faithful friend and lodger, Major Jackman. In "Mrs. Lirriper's Legacy" the three travel to France, where they find Jemmy's father on the verge of a miserable death as a result of his profligacy. The child innocently brings about his father's reformation and Mrs. Lirriper's forgiveness of the father. Jemmy tells two concluding fairy tales about his own life that show the power of such tales to raise a sordid or commonplace event to a level of religious significance.

By this time many periodicals and individual writers were devising frames to unify their short stories into special numbers or books, as in Collins's *After Dark* (1856) and Gaskell's *Round the Sofa* (1858). While praising Mrs. Lirriper, E. S. Dallas criticized the imitators of the form in a review in *The Times* on 3 December 1863: "These connecting halters do not show the horses to advantage, and we believe that most readers would enjoy the tales more if they made no pretence of unity." Dickens's Christmas numbers continued to be popular, however, because of the strength of the frames. Dickens wrote to Collins on 24 January 1864 that *Mrs. Lirriper's Lodgings* "has been the greatest success of all; has shot ahead of last year; has sold about two hundred and twenty thousand; and has made the name of Mrs. Lirriper so swiftly and domestically famous as never was. I had a very strong belief in her when I wrote about her, finding that she made a great effect upon me; but she certainly has gone beyond my hopes."

The disparity between the entertainer's outward appearance and inner emotions, the subject of "The Stroller's Tale" in *The Pickwick Papers* so many years before, is also the theme of the frame of the 1865 Christmas number, *Doctor Marigold's Prescriptions.* Doctor Marigold, a cheapjack who amuses his small-town customers with his patter, is another downtrodden entertainer who is aware, like Chops the Dwarf in "Going into Society" from *A House to Let,* of the similarity between his profession and some of the more prestigious positions of "society": "I have measured myself against other public speakers, – Members of Parliament, Platforms, Pulpits, Counsel learned in the law. . . . Where's the difference betwixt us? Except that we are Cheap Jacks, and they are Dear Jacks, *I* don't see any difference but what's in our favour." Marigold is alone in the world after the deaths of his cruel wife and his beloved child, who dies in his arms while he is entertaining an audience. When he finds Sophy, a neglected deaf girl with whom he discovers the true communication of kindness and sympathy, his verbal fluency as a cheapjack is shown not to be communication at all but a mask that has hidden his real character from his audience.

Dickens found the writing of the stories of Mrs. Lirriper and Doctor Marigold easy and refreshing after the labors of *Our Mutual Friend* (1864–1865), his first long novel in seven years, as he explained to Forster in a September 1865 letter: "Tired with *Our Mutual,* I sat down to cast about for an idea, with a depressing notion that I was, for the moment, over-worked. Suddenly, the little character that you will see, and all belonging to it, came flashing up in the most cheerful manner, and I had only to look on and leisurely describe it." *Doctor Marigold's Prescriptions* was a favorite of the writers Edward Bulwer-Lytton and George Gissing as well as with the public, with the issue selling more than 250,000 copies in the first week. The story was also warmly received when Dickens included it in his 1866 public reading tour.

The stories that form Doctor Marigold's "prescriptions" are introduced as the contents of a book the cheapjack makes up for Sophy when she returns from two years at school. Dickens found it troublesome to edit the stories, complaining to Fitzgerald in a 13 November 1865 letter that "the difficulty of fitting and adjusting this annual job is hardly to be imagined without trying it." Dickens wrote one of his most successful ghost stories for the number; titled "To Be Taken with a Grain of Salt," it was reprinted as the first of "Two Ghost Stories" in collected editions of the Christmas stories. The narrator is the only person who can see the ghost of a murdered man pursuing his killer along Piccadilly, in the narrator's own lodgings, and, finally, during the trial of the accused murderer, at which the narrator is the foreman of the jury. Dickens achieved a "shiver up the back," as he told Mary Boyle on 6 January 1866, at the end of the story when the convicted man declares that he knew he would be found guilty because an apparition of the foreman of the jury had appeared to him in the middle of the night and put a noose around his neck.

On 9 June 1865 the train in which Dickens was traveling to London from the south coast was derailed at Staplehurst, and Dickens spent several hours helping tend to the injured and dying passengers. Already in poor health from the punishing

*Dickens in 1839; painting by Daniel Maclise (National Portrait Gallery, London)*

schedules of his public-reading tours, he was severely affected by the accident for the rest of his life. Not surprisingly, a railway was the subject of the 1866 Christmas number, *Mugby Junction,* which achieved Dickens's long-sought-after goal of thematic unity. Also for the first time, the contributors' names appeared on the front cover. The framework story of Mr. Barbox and his spiritual journey from the barren isolation of middle age back to the spontaneous warmth of his childhood is the culmination of Dickens's Christmas short stories. Barbox, a lonely and disappointed man, finds himself alone on the platform at Mugby Junction in the middle of a rainy night. Barbox is a compound of Scrooge, Redlaw, and Mr. Langley: he is haunted by an unhappy childhood under repressive and cruel guardians, and his profession of usurer has forced him into isolation and griping meanness. At the junction Barbox meets Phoebe, a crippled girl, and her father, Lamps. Barbox instinctively values Phoebe's generosity and selflessness, and he learns from her to interest himself in other people. The second stage in Barbox's redemption repeats the plot of *The Haunted Man:* he meets his former love and her husband, his best friend, who is now near death; he has been brought to them by their young daughter, Polly, whose innocence and spontaneity enable

Barbox to overcome his repression. Like Redlaw, he is allowed to remember past suffering and forgive those who caused it; in that forgiveness lies his redemption.

The included stories are presented as experiences that Barbox has at the junction. The first of Dickens's two contributions is a comic monologue, "The Boy at Mugby," about the trials and tribulations of the boy who works at the station refreshment room. The second, "The Signal-Man," one of Dickens's best-known stories, was republished as the second of "Two Ghost Stories" in collected editions of the Christmas stories. It was clearly inspired by the Staplehurst accident, which occurred through the misreading of a timetable by the foreman of the crew repairing a bridge. Barbox encounters a signalman who has received ghostly warnings of an impending disaster on his line and is obsessed by fear of an accident that he is powerless to prevent. A sense of fatalism hangs over the story: the signalman has been a student of natural philosophy, "but he had run wild, misused his opportunities, gone down, and never risen again. He had no complaint to offer about that. He had made his bed, and he lay upon it." Charles Kent, writing in the *Sun* on 7 December 1866, said that "The Signal-Man" was "the finest Tale of Presentiment that has ever yet been told." Dickens's contributions to *Mugby Junction* have received more critical attention than most of his other Christmas stories, with "The Signal-Man" receiving particular praise.

The Christmas numbers came to an end the following year with *No Thoroughfare,* an adventure story by Dickens and Collins that did not employ introduced stories but resembled *A Message from the Sea* in its elaborate plot involving the covering up of an illegitimate birth, the revelation of which leads from London to Switzerland and a dramatic confrontation between the hero and the villain in the Alps in winter. Dickens wrote to Collins on 23 August 1867, "Let us get into all the horrors and dangers of such an adventure under the most terrific circumstances . . . we shall get a very Avalanche of power out of it, and thunder it down on the readers' heads." The story – or "performance," as Dickens referred to it – was written with an eye to the stage, with "Acts" rather than chapters, and a dramatic version was composed almost immediately by Collins and the actor Charles Fechter; Dickens was in America on a reading tour at the time. The play was performed successfully in London and in Paris.

Dickens abandoned the Christmas numbers after *No Thoroughfare* because, as he admitted to James T. Fields on 30 October 1868, he was tired of his writing being "swamped" by the inferior work of his contributors. While there were many fine contributed stories by writers such as Gaskell, the overall results were usually not what Dickens had intended. He complained to his subeditor, W. H. Wills, on 26 July 1868, "I have invented so many of these Christmas Nos. and they are so profoundly unsatisfactory after all with the introduced stories and their want of cohesion or originality, that I fear I am sick of the thing." Also, like the Christmas books, the annual Christmas number was imitated by so many contemporary magazines that Dickens saw his original idea dissolve into mass journalism. In *The Times* for 5 December 1866 Dallas compared *All the Year Round* to the proliferation of other Christmas numbers:

> Regularly as the year draws to a close we are inundated with a peculiar class of books which are supposed to be appropriate to the goodwill and joviality of the season. Most of these publications are quickly forgotten; and, indeed, are so full of display that they deserve no better fate. But amid the crowd of ostentatious and ephemeral works there appears an unpretending little brochure. The plainest, the homeliest, the cheapest, the least promising of the Christmas books – it is the best of all, the liveliest, the longest-lived, and the most successful. It is so because it is instinct with the fine spirit and the rare genius of the most popular of English authors.

In 1867 Dickens wrote *Holiday Romance. In Four Parts* for the American children's magazine *Our Young Folks,* published in Boston by his friend James T. Fields; the parts appeared in January, March, April, and May 1868 and in *All the Year Round* from January to April. The work is narrated by children who tell fairy tales that make fun of the traditional form. On 2 July 1867 Dickens wrote of the story to Forster: "I hope it is droll, and very child-like; though the joke is a grown-up one besides." Part 2 has been reprinted many times as "The Magic Fishbone," and part 3, a pirate story in which the child hero overcomes the villainous Latin grammar master, as "Captain Boldheart."

Dickens's last story, "George Silverman's Explanation," appeared in America in the *Atlantic Monthly* in January, February, and March 1868 and in *All the Year Round* in February. In a letter to his friend W. H. Wills on 28 June, Dickens commented, "Upon myself, it has made the strangest impression of reality and originality! And I feel as if I had read something (by somebody else) which I should never get out of my head!! The main idea of the narrator's position towards the other people, was the idea I *had* for my next novel in *A.Y.R.* But it is very curious that I did not in the least see how to begin his state of mind, until I walked into Hoghton Towers one bright April day." Like the narrator of "The Five Sisters of York" and his successors Redlaw and Barbox, George Silverman is prematurely gray, a disappointed man writing his autobiography for his own relief. George's tone is similar to those of other withdrawn narrators, such as Master Humphrey, the guest at the Holly-Tree Inn, the poor relation, the street artist, and Doctor Marigold. But in his inability to "come out" as Mr. Traveller had advised, he is the culmination of the confessional writers, beginning with the madman in *The Pickwick Papers,* whose attitudes to the outside world make it impossible for them to extricate themselves from their mental isolation.

George was born in a cellar in Preston and knew only deprivation for the first few years of his life. Accused of being worldly when he asked for food, he began a lifelong habit of self-sacrifice that has led only to misunderstanding. When he avoided the company of the people who took him in so that other children would not catch an infection he had, he was accused of being morose. He fell in love, but believing that he was not worthy of the girl, he brought about her marriage to another man, only to have her mother accuse him of doing so for financial gain. Thus a broken man, he continues in his solitary and useful life as a tutor and clergyman, struggling to make sense of his past. Critics have been divided on the value of Silverman's last sacrifice, Freudians arguing that it is evidence of his egotism and the split between idealistic and physical love, others seeing him as compulsive – even neurotic and self-centered – rather than noble. But Dickens shows that Adelina's marriage to George's rival is the right choice, and George's sacrifice thus becomes the expression of his innate moral sense. According to conventional thinking, a child brought up as George was should, like Martin Chuzzlewit, become selfish; but in his last story Dickens asserts his belief in the power of the good person's nature to endure misunderstanding and unhappiness.

The poignancy of George's position lies in his exclusion from the fireside circle of *Master Humphrey's Clock* and the Christmas numbers. Barbox shared George's orphan background and the repressive, isolating influence of an unsympathetic upbringing, but through Phoebe he learned to extricate himself from his past. After reading *The Old Curiosity Shop* to his friends, Master Humphrey had "felt that in living through the past again, and communicating to others the lesson it had helped to teach me, I had been a happier man," but without such an audience George is unable to find enlighten-

ment. He confesses at the end that he writes for the relief of his own mind, "not foreseeing whether or no it will ever have a reader." The story thus exemplifies Dickens's often reiterated belief in the necessity for human contact, but it is also his final statement about the power of the human spirit to sustain itself in spite of deprivation and suffering. The cruelty of a world that cast him out and misunderstood his actions turned the creative remembrances of Master Humphrey into the introspective and self-defeating memories of the lonely clergyman, but George is still uncorrupted by the behavior of those around him. Dickens's short stories have gone full circle, and Silverman is the gray-haired narrator at the inn in Yorkshire, waiting for a merry-faced gentleman to teach him the importance of storytelling in transforming the memory of suffering into a greater joy and understanding.

"George Silverman's Explanation" was the last complete work that Dickens wrote. Exhausted by the physical and mental strain of public readings, he collapsed and died on 9 June 1870; the novel *The Mystery of Edwin Drood* (1870) was left in progress on his desk in his garden chalet. He was buried in Westminster Abbey.

Dickens's short stories spanned the thirty-five years of his writing career. His influence on the development of the short-story form was great not only because of his own stories but also because of his strength as an editor of the works of others. Contemporaries such as Gissing and Algernon Charles Swinburne regarded all of Dickens's stories highly, but in the twentieth century many of them have been dismissed as Victorian potboilers written in a sentimental vein for an uncritical Christmas audience. The critic Edmund Wilson, for example, regarded the stories as "silly little episodes in the bad sentimental taste of the period which Dickens had done so much to popularize." J. B. Priestley suggested that while the Christmas stories were probably Dickens's most loved works in his own age, now "only the very old turn to them." Wilson did admit the excellence of the character monologues, however, and Mrs. Lirriper, Christopher the waiter, and Doctor Marigold continue to receive positive critical attention. Equally valued are the supernatural stories from *To Be Read at Dusk* and the Christmas numbers, which have guaranteed Dickens's reputation as a major writer in the ghost-story genre.

Louis Cazamian, in 1903, was one of the first to recognize that "the whole of Dickens's social message is contained in the Christmas books." More recently, with the proliferation of critical work on Dickens, including a book-length study of the sto-

Page from the manuscript for Dickens's A Christmas Carol *(Pierpont Morgan Library, MA 97)*

ries by Deborah A. Thomas in 1982, the short stories have begun to be valued not just for the skill with which Dickens experimented with narrative voice and compression but also for the light that they shed on his work as a social critic and as a novelist. Today they are seen not just as Dickens's "philosophy of Christmas" but as vital and significant expressions of his understanding of the workings of the mind, both for humor in Mrs. Lirriper and for psychological insight in the narrations of his isolated minds, his madmen, and his murderers. Even the seemingly sentimental stories cannot be dismissed as insincere offerings to an adoring Christmas audience, because an examination of their development reveals a profound and sustained interest in the themes that also dominate the novels: the need for human contact, the importance of the imagination in fostering a moral sense, and the role of memory in keeping alive in the adult the child's superior imaginative power. Through storytelling Dickens was able to explore the sources of his own creative springs. As Fitzgerald wrote of the major stories in *The Life of Charles Dickens as Revealed in His Writings* (1905): "How far off now seem the days when Boz, so full of fancy and spirit, his imagination at work, touched off those delightful sketches of his, the "Christmas 'Numbers'... into which he really put − hence their value − his whole personality and feelings."

**Letters:**

*The Letters of Charles Dickens,* Nonesuch Edition, edited by Walter Dexter, 3 volumes (Bloomsbury: Nonesuch Press, 1938);

*The Heart of Charles Dickens. As Revealed in His Letters to Angela Burdett-Coutts,* edited by Edgar Johnson (New York: Duell, Sloan & Pearce / Boston: Little, Brown, 1952);

*The Letters of Charles Dickens,* Pilgrim Edition, 7 volumes published, edited by Madeline House, Graham Storey, and Kathleen Tillotson (Oxford: Clarendon Press, 1965–  ).

**Bibliographies:**

James Cook, *Bibliography of the Writings of Charles Dickens, with Many Curious and Interesting Particulars Relating to His Work* (London: Kerslake, 1879);

Frederic G. Kitton, *The Minor Writings of Charles Dickens. A Bibliography and Sketch* (London: Stock, 1900);

Joseph Gold, *The Stature of Dickens: A Centenary Bibliography* (Toronto: University of Toronto Press, 1971);

Philip Collins, "Charles Dickens," in *Victorian Fiction: A Second Guide to Research,* edited by George H. Ford (New York: Modern Language Association, 1978), pp. 34–114;

Ruth Glancy, *Dickens's Christmas Books, Christmas Stories, and Other Short Fiction: An Annotated Bibliography* (New York: Garland, 1985).

**Biographies:**

John Forster, *The Life of Charles Dickens* (3 volumes, London: Chapman & Hall, 1872–1874; 2 volumes, New York: Scribners, 1905); 2 volumes, edited by J. W. T. Ley (London: Cecil Palmer, 1928); edited by A. J. Hoppé (London: Dent, 1966);

Edgar Johnson, *Charles Dickens: His Tragedy and Triumph* (2 volumes, Boston: Little, Brown / London: Hamish Hamilton, 1952; revised and abridged edition, 1 volume, New York: Viking, 1977; London: Allen Lane, 1977);

Norman MacKenzie and Jeanne MacKenzie, *Dickens: A Life* (New York: Oxford University Press, 1979);

Fred Kaplan, *Dickens: A Biography* (New York: Morrow, 1988);

Peter Ackroyd, *Dickens* (London: Sinclair-Stevenson, 1990).

**References:**

M. L. Allen, "The Black Veil: Three Versions of a Symbol," *English Studies,* 47 (1966): 286–289;

Barry D. Bart, "George Silverman's Explanation," *Dickensian,* 60 (Winter 1964): 48–51;

Richard F. Batterson, "The Manuscript and Text of Dickens's 'George Silverman's Explanation,'" *Papers of the Bibliographical Society of America,* 73, no. 4 (1979): 473–476;

M. K. Bradby, "An Explanation of *George Silverman's Explanation, Dickensian,"* 36 (Winter 1939–1940): 13–18;

Joel J. Brattin, "From Drama into Fiction: *The Lamplighter* and 'The Lamplighter's Story,'" *Dickensian,* 85 (Autumn 1989): 131–139;

John Butt, "Dickens's Christmas Books," in his *Pope, Dickens, and Others* (Edinburgh: Edinburgh University Press, 1969), pp. 127–148;

Butt and Kathleen Tillotson, "*Sketches by Boz*: Collection and Revision," in their *Dickens at Work* (London: Methuen, 1957), pp. 35–61;

R. D. Butterworth, "Hoghton Tower and the Picaresque of 'George Silverman's Explanation,'" *Dickensian,* 86 (Summer 1990): 93–104;

John Carey, *The Violent Effigy: A Study of Dickens' Imagination* (London: Faber & Faber, 1973);

Katherine Carolan, "*The Battle of Life,* a Love Story," *Dickensian,* 69 (May 1973): 105–110;

Louis Cazamian, "Dickens: The Philosophy of Christmas," in his *The Social Novel in England 1830–1850: Dickens, Disraeli, Mrs. Gaskell, Kingsley,* edited and translated by Martin Fido (London & Boston: Routledge & Kegan Paul, 1973), pp. 117–147;

G. K. Chesterton, *Charles Dickens* (London: Methuen, 1906; New York: Dodd, Mead, 1906);

Philip Collins, " '*Carol* Philosophy, Cheerful Views,' " *Etudes Anglaises,* 23 (April–June 1970): 158–167;

Wilkie Collins, *Under the Management of Mr. Charles Dickens: His Production of "The Frozen Deep,"* edited by Robert Louis Brannan (Ithaca, N.Y.: Cornell University Press, 1966);

Gary H. Day, "The Relevance of the Nickleby Stories," *Dickensian,* 81 (Spring 1985): 52–56;

Carol de Saint Victor, "*Master Humphrey's Clock.* Dickens' 'Lost' Book," *Texas Studies in Literature and Language,* 10, no. 4 (Winter 1969): 569–584;

Duane DeVries, *Dickens's Apprentice Years: The Making of a Novelist* (New York: Harvester Press, 1976);

Percy Fitzgerald, "Charles Dickens in the Editor's Chair," *Gentleman's Magazine,* 250 (June 1881): 725–742;

Fitzgerald, *The Life of Charles Dickens as Revealed in His Writings,* 2 volumes (London: Chatto & Windus, 1905);

Fitzgerald, *Memories of Charles Dickens: With an Account of "Household Words" and "All the Year Round" and of the Contributors Thereto* (Bristol: Arrowsmith, 1913);

Dudley Flamm, "The Prosecutor Within: Dickens's Final Explanation," *Dickensian,* 66 (Winter 1970): 16–23;

Ruth Glancy, "Dickens and Christmas: His Framed-Tale Themes," *Nineteenth-Century Fiction,* 35 (June 1980): 53–72;

Glancy, "Dickens at Work on *The Haunted Man,*" *Dickens Studies Annual,* 15 (1986): 65–85;

Glancy, "The Shaping of *The Battle of Life:* Dickens' Manuscript Revisions," *Dickens Studies Annual,* 17 (1989): 67–89;

Glancy, "The Significance of the Nickleby Stories," *Dickensian,* 75 (Spring 1979): 12–15;

Glancy, "To Be Read at Dusk," *Dickensian,* 83 (Spring 1987): 40–47;

Michael Goldberg, "A Philosophy of Christmas: *A Christmas Carol* and *The Chimes,*" in his *Carlyle*

*and Dickens* (Athens: University of Georgia Press, 1972), pp. 32–44;

David J. Greenman, "Dickens's Ultimate Achievements in the Ghost Story: 'To Be Taken with a Grain of Salt' and 'The Signalman,' " *Dickensian,* 85 (Spring 1989): 40–47;

Philip Hobsbaum, *A Reader's Guide to Charles Dickens* (London: Thames & Hudson, 1972);

Humphry House, *The Dickens World* (London: Oxford University Press, 1941);

Charles Kent, *Charles Dickens as a Reader* (London: Chapman & Hall / Philadelphia: Lippincott, 1872);

H. M. Levy Jr. and William Ruff, "Who Tells the Story of a Queer Client?," *Dickensian,* 64 (Winter 1968): 19–21;

Anne Lohrli, ed., *"Household Words." A Weekly Journal, 1850–1859. Conducted by Charles Dickens. Table of Contents. List of Contributors and their Contributions Based on the "Household Words" Office Book in the Morris L. Parrish Collection of Victorian Novelists* (Toronto & Buffalo: University of Toronto Press, 1973);

Sylvia Manning, "Dickens, January, and May," *Dickensian,* 71 (Spring 1975): 67–74;

Juliet McMaster, "Who *Is* Jack Bamber: More about the Old Man and the Queer Client," *Dickensian,* 81 (Summer 1985): 105–108;

Ewald Mengel, "The Structure and Meaning of Dickens's 'The Signalman,' " *Studies in Short Fiction,* 20 (Fall 1983): 271–280;

J. Hillis Miller, "Sketches by Boz, *Oliver Twist* and Cruikshank's Illustrations," in *Dickens Centennial Essays,* edited by Ada Nisbet and Blake Nevius (Berkeley & Los Angeles: University of California Press, 1971);

William E. Morris, "The Conversion of Scrooge: A Defense of That Good Man's Motivation," *Studies in Short Fiction,* 3 (Fall 1965): 46–55;

William Oddie, *Dickens and Carlyle: The Question of Influence* (London: Centenary Press, 1972);

Oddie, "Dickens and the Indian Mutiny," *Dickensian,* 68 (Winter 1972): 3–15;

Robert L. Patten, "The Art of *Pickwick's* Interpolated Tales," *English Literary History,* 34 (September 1967): 349–366;

Patten, *Dickens and His Publishers* (Oxford: Clarendon Press, 1979);

Patten, "Dickens Time and Again," *Dickens Studies Annual,* 2 (1972): 163–196;

J. B. Priestley, *Charles Dickens and his World* (London: Thames & Hudson, 1961);

Heinz Reinhold, " 'The Stroller's Tale' in *Pickwick,*" *Dickensian,* 64 (September 1968): 141–151;

Michael Seed, "Mystery in Everyday Things: Charles Dickens' 'Signalman,' " *Criticism,* 23 (Winter 1981): 42–57;

Susan Shatto, "Miss Havisham and Mr. Mopes the Hermit: Dickens and the Mentally Ill," *Dickens Quarterly,* 2 ( June 1985): 43–49; (September 1985): 79–83;

Michael Shelden, "Dickens, 'The Chimes,' and the Anti-Corn Law League," *Victorian Studies,* 25 (Spring 1982): 328–353;

Michael Slater, "Carlyle and Jerrold into Dickens: A Study of *The Chimes,*" *Nineteenth Century Fiction,* 24 (March 1970): 506–526;

Slater, "Dickens (and Forster) at Work on *The Chimes,*" *Dickens Studies,* 2 (September 1966): 106–140;

Slater, "Dickens's Tract for the Times," in *Dickens 1970,* edited by Slater (London: Chapman & Hall, 1970), pp. 99–123;

Gordon Spence, "The Haunted Man and Barbox Brothers," *Dickensian,* 76 (Autumn 1980): 150–157;

John Daniel Stahl, "The Source and Significance of the Revenant in Dickens's 'The Signal-Man,' " *Dickens Studies Newsletter,* 11 (December 1980): 98–101;

Harry Stone, "The Christmas Books: 'Giving Nursery Tales a Higher Form,' " in his *Dickens and the Invisible World: Fairy Tales, Fantasy, and Novel-Making* (Bloomington: Indiana University Press, 1979; London: Macmillan, 1980), pp. 119–145;

Stone, "Dickens Rediscovered: Some Lost Writings Retrieved," in *Dickens Centennial Essays,* edited by Nisbet and Nevius (Berkeley & Los Angeles: University of California Press, 1971);

Stone, "Dickens's Artistry and *The Haunted Man,*" *South Atlantic Quarterly,* 61 (Autumn 1962): 492–505;

Stone, "Dickens's Tragic Universe: 'George Silverman's Explanation,' " *Studies in Philology,* 55 ( January 1958): 86–97;

Stone, "The Unknown Dickens: With a Sampling of Uncollected Writings," *Dickens Studies Annual,* 1 (1970): 1–22;

Rodger L. Tarr, "Dickens' Debt to Carlyle's 'Justice Metaphor' in *The Chimes,*" *Nineteenth Century Fiction,* 27 (September 1972): 208–215;

Deborah A. Thomas, *Dickens and the Short Story* (Philadelphia: University of Pennsylvania Press, 1982; London: Batsford Academic and Educational, 1982);

Thomas, "Dickens' Mrs. Lirriper and the Evolution of a Feminine Stereotype," *Dickens Studies Annual,* 6 (1977): 154–166;

Thomas, "The Equivocal Explanation of Dickens' George Silverman," *Dickens Studies Annual,* 3 (1974): 134–143;

Kathleen Tillotson, "The Middle Years from the *Carol* to *Copperfield,*" *Dickens Memorial Lectures 1970, Dickensian,* 65, supplement (September 1970): 7–19;

Michael A. Ullman, "Where George Stopped Growing: Dickens's 'George Silverman's Explanation,' " *Ariel,* 10 ( January 1979): 11–23;

Angus Wilson, *The World of Charles Dickens* (London: Secker & Warburg, 1970; New York: Viking, 1970);

Edmund Wilson, "Dickens: The Two Scrooges," in his *The Wound and the Bow: Seven Studies in Literature* (Boston: Houghton Mifflin, 1941; London: Secker & Warburg, 1942), pp. 1–104.

**Papers:**

The manuscripts for Charles Dickens's *A Christmas Carol, The Cricket on the Hearth, The Battle of Life, Hunted Down,* and *Holiday Romance* are in the Pierpont Morgan Library, New York. The manuscript for *The Chimes* is in the Forster Collection of the Victoria and Albert Museum, London, which is the holder of most of Dickens's manuscripts. The manuscript for *The Haunted Man* is in the Pforzheimer Library, New York. The manuscript for *George Silverman's Explanation* is in the Houghton Library, Harvard University. The manuscript for *To Be Read at Dusk* is in the Royal Library, Windsor, England. There are few extant manuscripts for the stories Dickens wrote for the Christmas numbers of his journals, but several drafts of his instructions for prospective contributors to the Christmas numbers are in the Huntington Library, San Marino, California. Dickens's letters are widely scattered, with major holdings at the Pierpont Morgan Library, the Dickens House in London, and the Berg Collection at the New York Public Library, which also holds Dickens's "Book of Memoranda," in which he made notes for his writings.

# Maria Edgeworth

*(1 January 1768 – 22 May 1849)*

Kathryn Ledbetter
*Oklahoma Baptist University*

See also the Edgeworth entry in *DLB 116: British Romantic Novelists, 1789–1832.*

BOOKS: *Letters for Literary Ladies, to Which Is Added an Essay on the Noble Science of Self-Justification* (London: Printed for J. Johnson, 1795; second edition, corrected and enlarged, 1799; George Town: Published by Joseph Milligan, W. Cooper, printer, 1810);

*The Parent's Assistant; or, Stories for Children* (3 volumes, London: Printed for J. Johnson, 1796; expanded edition, 6 volumes, London: Printed for J. Johnson by G. Woodfall, 1800; 3 volumes, George Town: Published by Joseph Milligan, Dinsmore & Cooper, printers, 1809);

*Practical Education,* 2 volumes, by Maria Edgeworth and Richard Lovell Edgeworth (London: Printed for J. Johnson, 1798; New York: Printed for G. F. Hopkins and Brown & Stansbury, 1801); revised, 3 volumes (London: Printed for J. Johnson, 1801); republished as *Essays on Practical Education,* 2 volumes (London: Printed for J. Johnson, 1811);

*Castle Rackrent: An Hibernian Tale; Taken from the Facts, and from the Manners of the Irish Squires, before the Year 1782* (London: Printed for J. Johnson, 1800; third edition, revised, 1801; Boston: Printed & published by T. B. Wait & Sons, 1814);

*Early Lessons,* 10 parts in 5 volumes (London: Printed for J. Johnson, 1801–1802): *Harry and Lucy,* parts 1–2; *Rosamond,* parts 3–5; *Frank,* parts 6–9; "The Little Dog Trusty," "The Orange Man," and "The Cherry Orchard," part 10; 4 volumes (Philadelphia: Printed for J. Maxwell, 1821);

*Moral Tales for Young People,* 5 volumes (London: Printed for J. Johnson, 1801; New York: Printed for W. B. Gilley, 1810);

*Belinda,* 3 volumes (London: Printed for J. Johnson, 1801); revised edition, in *British Novelists,* edited by Anna Laetitia Barbauld, volumes 49

*Maria Edgeworth*

and 50 (London: Printed for F. C. & J. Rivington, 1810; 2 volumes, Boston: Printed for Wells & Lilly, 1814; fourth edition, corrected and improved, London: Printed for R. Hunter, 1821);

*Essays on Irish Bulls,* by Maria Edgeworth and Richard Lovell Edgeworth (London: Printed for J. Johnson, 1802; New York: Printed by J. Sevaine, 1803; fourth edition, London: Printed for R. Hunter, 1815);

*Popular Tales* (3 volumes, London: Printed for J. Johnson by C. Mercer, 1804; 2 volumes, Philadelphia: Printed & sold by James Humphreys, 1804);

*The Modern Griselda: A Tale* (London: Printed for J. Johnson, 1805; second edition, corrected, London: Printed for J. Johnson, 1805; George Town: Published by Joseph Milligan, W. Cooper, printer, 1810; third edition, corrected, London: Printed for J. Johnson, 1813; fourth edition, corrected, London: Printed for R. Hunter, 1819);

*Leonora,* 2 volumes (London: Printed for J. Johnson, 1806; New York: I. Riley & Co., 1806);

*Essays on Professional Education,* by Maria Edgeworth and Richard Lovell Edgeworth (London: Printed for J. Johnson, 1809);

*Tales of Fashionable Life,* 6 volumes; volumes 1–3: "Ennui," "Almeria," "Madame de Fleury," "The Dun," and "Manoeuvring" (London: Printed for J. Johnson, 1809; 2 volumes, George Town: Printed for Joseph Milligan, 1809); volumes 4–6: "Vivian," "Emilie de Coulanges," and "The Absentee" (London: Printed for J. Johnson, 1812);

*Patronage* (4 volumes, London: Printed for J. Johnson, 1814 [i.e., 1813]; 3 volumes, Philadelphia: Published by Moses Thomas, J. Maxwell, printer, 1814); revised edition, in volumes 11 and 12 of *Tales and Miscellaneous Pieces,* 14 volumes (London: Printed for R. Hunter and Baldwin, Cradock & Joy, 1825);

*Continuation of Early Lessons,* 2 volumes (London: Printed for J. Johnson, 1814; Boston: Printed for Bradford & Read, 1815);

*Comic Dramas in Three Acts* (London: Printed for R. Hunter, 1817; second edition, 1817; Philadelphia: Thomas Dobson & Son, 1817) – comprises *Love and Law; The Two Guardians; The Rose, The Thistle, and the Shamrock;*

*Harrington: A Tale* and *Ormond: A Tale* (3 volumes, London: Printed for R. Hunter and Baldwin, Cradock & Joy, 1817; 2 volumes, New York: Printed for Kirk & Mercein, 1817; Philadelphia: Published by Moses Thomas and Van Winkle & Wiley, New York, 1817; second edition, corrected, London: Printed for R. Hunter and Baldwin, Cradock & Joy, 1817);

*Rosamond: A Sequel to Early Lessons,* 2 volumes (London: Printed for R. Hunter, 1821; Philadelphia: Printed for J. Maxwell, 1821);

*Frank: A Sequel to Frank in Early Lessons* (3 volumes, London: Printed for R. Hunter, 1822; 2 volumes, New York: Printed for William B. Gilley, 1822);

*Harry and Lucy Concluded: Being the Last Part of Early Lessons* (4 volumes, London: Printed for R. Hunter and Baldwin, Cradock & Joy, 1825; 3

volumes, Boston: Printed for Munroe & Francis, 1825; second edition, corrected, 4 volumes, London: Printed for R. Hunter and Baldwin, Cradock & Joy, 1827; third edition, revised and corrected, London: Printed for R. Hunter and Baldwin, Cradock & Joy, 1837);

*Little Plays for Children,* volume 7 of *The Parent's Assistant* (London: Printed for R. Hunter, 1827); republished as *Little Plays . . . Being an Additional Volume of The Parent's Assistant* (Philadelphia: Thomas T. Ash, 1827) – comprises *The Grinding Organ, Dumb Andy, The Dame School Holiday;*

*Garry Owen: or, The Snow-Woman* (Salem, Mass.: John M. and W. & S. B. Ives, 1829); republished with *Poor Bob the Chimney-sweeper* (London: Printed for John Murray, 1832);

*Helen: A Tale* (3 volumes, London: Printed for R. Bentley, 1834; 2 volumes, Philadelphia: Carey, Lea & Blanchard / Boston: Allen & Ticknor, 1834);

*Orlandino,* in Chambers' Library for Young People (Edinburgh: Printed for W. & R. Chambers, 1848; Boston: Gould, Kendall & Lincoln, 1848);

*The Most Unfortunate Day of My Life: Being a Hitherto Unpublished Story, Together with the Purple Jar and Other Stories* (London: Cobden-Sanderson, 1931).

**Editions:** *Tales and Miscellaneous Pieces,* 14 volumes (London: Printed for R. Hunter and Baldwin, Cradock & Joy, 1825);

*Tales and Novels* (18 volumes, London: Printed for Baldwin & Cradock, 1832–1833; 9 volumes, New York: Harper, 1832–1834);

*Tales and Novels* (9 volumes, London: Printed for Whitaker, Simpkin, Marshall, 1848; 10 volumes, New York: Harper, 1852);

*Tales and Novels,* 10 volumes (London: Routledge, 1893).

OTHER: "The Mental Thermometer," in *The Juvenile Library,* volume 2 (London: Printed for T. Hurst, 1801), pp. 378–384;

"Little Dominick," in *Wild Roses; or, Cottage Tales* (London: Printed for T. Marden, 1807), pp. 53–60;

Mary Leadbeater, *Cottage Dialogues Among the Irish Peasantry, with Notes and a Preface by Maria Edgeworth* (London: Printed for J. Johnson, 1811);

Charles Sneyd Edgeworth, *Memoirs of the Abbé Edgeworth; Continuing His Narrative of the Last Hours of Louis XVI,* revised by Maria Edgeworth (London: Printed for R. Hunter, 1815);

Richard Lovell Edgeworth, *Readings on Poetry,* preface and last chapter by Maria Edgeworth (London: Printed for R. Hunter, 1816; second edition, corrected, London: Printed for R. Hunter, 1816; Boston: Published by Wells & Lilly and sold by Van Winkle & Wiley, New York, and by M. Carey, Philadelphia, 1816);

*Memoirs of Richard Lovell Edgeworth, Esq.; Begun by Himself and Concluded by His Daughter, Maria Edgeworth,* 2 volumes, volume 2 by Maria Edgeworth (London: Printed for R. Hunter, 1820; second edition, corrected, London: Printed for R. Hunter, 1821; Boston: Wells & Lilly, 1821);

*Garry-Owen; or, The Snow-Woman,* in *The Christmas Box,* edited by T. Crofton Croker (London: Ebers / Edinburgh: Blackwood, 1829).

On a literary tour in 1813, Maria Edgeworth was recognized by literary celebrities in London and Paris as one of the most important authors in the English-speaking world. Her only rival in popularity was Sir Walter Scott, who credited Edgeworth's tales of Irish life for inspiring him to begin writing the Waverley novels. Her novels and tales were so popular that collected editions of her works appeared in her lifetime in England and the United States; her books for children have been reprinted in various forms and in many languages. Although she is seldom read today, literary historians are quick to acknowledge Edgeworth's influence on the development of the novel and short fiction. Ivan Turgenev, James Fenimore Cooper, and Jane Austen looked to Edgeworth as the originator of the regional novel. John Ruskin copied her children's stories. Austen sent *Emma* (1816) to Edgeworth upon its first appearance for her approval. In the twentieth century William Butler Yeats acclaimed her as the first serious novelist from the upper class in Ireland; indeed, the Anglo-Irish tradition began with Edgeworth's *Castle Rackrent: An Hibernian Tale* (1800). Contemporary reviewers compared her novels with Miguel de Cervantes's *Don Quixote* (1605, 1615) and Alain René Lesage's *Histoire de Gil Blas de Santillane* (1715, 1724, 1735); Francis Jeffrey of the *Edinburgh Review* wrote in July 1812 that "she has combined more solid instruction with more universal entertainment, and given more practical lessons of wisdom, with less tediousness and less pretension, than any other writer with whom we are acquainted." As a writer of didactic, realistic short fiction, Edgeworth was an ingenious inventor of tales written specifically for children, an audience unrecognized before writers such as Edgeworth and Anna

Laetitia Barbauld. Edgeworth was also one of the first authors to target audiences from the middle and lower classes.

Edgeworth was born at her mother's family home in Black Bourton, Oxfordshire, on 1 January 1768, the third child of Richard Lovell Edgeworth and Anna Maria Elers Edgeworth. The marriage was an intellectual mismatch and an unfortunate mistake; Maria spent her infancy at Black Bourton, where she remembered her mother crying while her father left them to join friends who shared his scientific and intellectual interests. Edgeworth was a member of the "Lunar Group" of scientists, including Joseph Priestley, zoologist Erasmus Darwin, and theorist Thomas Day. Her mother died in 1773, when Maria was five years old, of puerperal fever, ten days after giving birth to her fifth child.

Four months after Edgeworth's mother's death, her father married Honora Sneyd, a friend of the poet Anna Seward from Lichfield. Her father was a powerful, personable character, and his new wife had high standards for raising children. Their deep passion for one another had been ignited long before her mother's death, and their love must have seemed an insurmountable barrier to the attention Maria desperately needed when her father took his new wife, along with his children from the former marriage, to their new home in England. Grieving deeply for her mother, Maria became a problem child in the eyes of her new stepmother, who neglected to see her as anything but naughty. Her father began to realize mistakes he had made by his own past negligence, but the problems of a small child were insignificant in his egocentric world.

Troublesome incidents began to occur as Maria tried to express her anger and grief by trampling on hotbed frames to break the glass and cutting out the squares of her aunt's checked sofa pillows. Often reflecting on these early years as the most miserable of her life, Edgeworth later remembered wishing she could die. In 1775, when she was seven years old, her father and stepmother sent her to a private school in Derby; she did not come home for three years. When the family moved to a house at Northchurch, near Berkhampstead, Hertfordshire, Maria could now visit her father at Christmas. She stayed at Derby until 1780, when she was sent to another private school at Upper Wimpole Street, London. Here she learned social graces, languages, and literature. She also learned how to be submissive.

Small in stature (she was never taller than four feet, seven inches), Maria suffered from attempts by school mistresses to stretch her body with mechani-

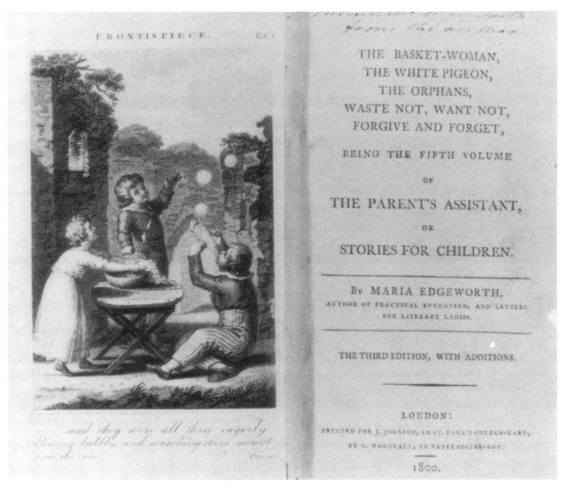

THE BASKET-WOMAN,
THE WHITE PIGEON,
THE ORPHANS,
WASTE NOT, WANT NOT,
FORGIVE AND FORGET,

BEING THE FIFTH VOLUME

OF

THE PARENT'S ASSISTANT,

OR

STORIES FOR CHILDREN.

BY MARIA EDGEWORTH,
AUTHOR OF PRACTICAL EDUCATION, AND LETTERS
FOR LITERARY LADIES.

THE THIRD EDITION, WITH ADDITIONS.

LONDON:
PRINTED FOR J. JOHNSON, IN ST. PAUL'S CHURCH-YARD,
BY G. WOODFALL, IN PATERNOSTER-ROW.

1800.

*Frontispiece and title page for a volume of the enlarged edition of Edgeworth's children's stories*

cal devices that hung her by the neck. When she complained of an eye infection, her father's friend Day dosed her with tar water for the eye inflammation. In spite of her physical and emotional deprivations, she developed a creative mind and became the school's favorite storyteller, although she made few close friends there. She had little comfort from her busy father, who was obsessed with developing theories of education with his second wife and their new children. He had raised his first son, Richard, according to Jean-Jacques Rousseau's idealistic philosophy, but he considered the experiment a failure because Richard became a wanderer at sea and was frequently in debt. He thought it was too late to save the children from his first marriage, but with his wife's guidance and companionship he managed to become a loving, though self-centered, father with the rest of his children. The improvement he saw in Maria's behavior impressed him, and he began corresponding with her at school, giving her written work to do when she was eleven to improve

the intimacy and purpose of their letters. The first project was an Arabian fable she was to finish; later he asked her to write a story on the theme of generosity.

A deep need for affection became the driving force influencing the development and indeed the entire focus of Edgeworth's life. Insecurities from childhood abandonment stimulated a desire to be loved by her father that controlled her life and artistic production. Her sole purpose in writing stories and novels was to please her father. Little of what she wrote in her life escaped his critical eye – not because he demanded it, but because she wished to get his approval. Only *Castle Rackrent* was published anonymously, without her father's consent. That this was her most successful work has prompted critics to claim that his role as adviser and collaborator in her work was a tiresome interference and that the bad parts of her fiction, such as its didacticism, were written in by him, but biographer Marilyn Butler provides convincing evidence that he did nothing more than make suggestions, which she chose to take or not, and that it was she who was didactic, with her father encouraging her to include more romance and feeling.

When her stepmother died in the spring of 1780, Edgeworth's father was thirty-six years old and the father of six children. As Honora had suggested before her death, he married her sister Elizabeth Sneyd eight months after Honora's death, although he said that no other woman could ever take Honora's place. Two years later he sent for Maria to join them at his Ireland estate. This was the start of a happy, productive era for Edgeworth, because she could spend much time with her father. He taught her how to keep accounts, assigning her the job of dealing with his tenants and educating his children. At fourteen she was the eldest child at home, and she happily embraced her new responsibilities as she rode with her father on the estate and learned the business affairs. He told stories about the tenantry to amuse the family, which she wrote down. The tales became known as "The Freeman Family" and later became the basis for her longest novel, *Patronage* (1814). Her experience with the Irish peasantry and the local gentry gave her rich details to use in her later fiction.

At her father's suggestion, Edgeworth began translating Stéphanie Félicité Brulart de Genlis's *Adèle et Théodore* (1782); but she completed only one volume, and the translation was never published. In 1791 she began writing children's stories from the educational theories her father and his second wife had developed. His theory included the idea that children's literature should be written for different ages and that the stories should aim for the characters to grow older from one part to the next, as the reader's maturity increases with the characters. Edgeworth tested this idea on her stepsisters and stepbrothers; she often entertained them by writing stories on a slate and read aloud to them at night. Later she collected their favorites and published her second book, *The Parent's Assistant; or, Stories for Children* (1796).

Edgeworth's first publication resulted from a letter written to her father by Day discouraging him from allowing her to become a writer. Day felt it was improper for women to be novelists or to receive educations; she wrote *Letters for Literary Ladies, to Which Is Added an Essay on the Noble Science of Self-Justification* (1795) in a defense of female education based on the correspondence between the two men. The following year *The Parent's Assistant* appeared in three volumes. These were stories children could read themselves under parents' supervision. Edge-

worth wanted the book to be called *The Parent's Friend,* but publisher Joseph Johnson changed its name, giving her £120 for a full copyright to the collection. The selection of tales differed with each new edition of *The Parent's Assistant,* and some stories were also published separately later. The stories typically bear titles that give clues about the lesson involved in the tale, such as "Simple Susan," "The Little Merchants," "The Orphans," "Lazy Lawrence," "The False Key," "The White Pigeon," "The Birthday Present," "Forgive and Forget," "Waste Not, Want Not; or, Two Strings to Your Bow," and "The Bracelets." The concept of each lesson is more important than the characters and the circumstances, although Edgeworth is a master at dialogue, especially with local dialects and manners of the servant classes she knew intimately.

Designed to teach skills for living, the stories pose situations that challenge two different types of children as they work through the moral possibilities; the reader learns the lesson through the contrast between the methods used by each child to handle the situation. Cleanliness and moral virtue become synonymous in "Lazy Lawrence," in which an elderly lady, Preston, makes a living from flowers in her garden; her cottage is always clean and her garden free of weeds, demonstrating how hard work and personal pride redeem a poor person. Edgeworth is quick to demonstrate in most of her stories, especially those for children, how simple people can survive poverty and life in the lower class by being honest, thrifty, and industrious. Preston's son, Jem, who is busy with his work selling fossils, meets Lawrence, who eats up his money with gambling rather than work. Lawrence falls in with bad company and is blamed for stealing because he is idle rather than industrious like Jem. After a month in prison for theft, Lawrence sees the error of his ways and decides to become industrious; his model for virtue, Jem, stays busy with productive routine that sacrifices fast cash for steady employment. Through Lawrence's example the reader sees what happens to people who are lazy.

Each story deals with a different virtue. In "The Orphans" the children are rewarded for their honesty; in "Simple Susan" one sees how people of the aristocratic class reward humble, honest lower classes for telling the truth. Class differences are upheld, as noble landowners appear frequently in the stories as benevolent caretakers of innocent workers. Bad servants are destructive in "The Birthday Present," in which Rosamond learns about respect and generosity as she chooses the proper birthday present for Bell, a boy who has been spoiled by the bad company of the servants who raised him. Edgeworth warns her readers that "the habits of tyranny, meanness, and falsehood, which children acquire from living with bad servants, are scarcely ever conquered in the whole course of their future lives." She knew from experience with her own servants how influential they could be with children.

In "Waste Not, Want Not; or, Two Strings to Your Bow" Hal and Benjamin are ten-year-old boys who learn that "economy ensures independence, and sometimes puts it in the power of those who are not very rich to be very generous." A Bristol merchant wants to adopt one of his relatives, but he wants to judge their dispositions before he decides between the two. Hal is an impatient, self-centered braggart, but Ben is careful, conservative, and caring. Because he had saved a cord that tied a parcel, Ben wins a bow-and-arrow contest, but Hal had wastefully cut his cord, preventing his participation in the contest when the remaining string breaks. Ben, of course, receives the golden reward from the merchant. Stories such as "Waste Not, Want Not" were extremely popular throughout the nineteenth century and often used as teaching tools.

In 1798 Edgeworth and her father published the two-volume *Practical Education.* These essays set forth his theories on education, which were a modification of Rousseau's ideas adopted by him and Day. With these theories firmly established in the family, Edgeworth had only to write her own series of tales to demonstrate these theories in the raising of children. All her work, including these stories and novels written for juveniles and adults, had an instructive purpose; the moral of the story was its reason for being, and all characterization and plot were secondary to this purpose.

Also in 1798, six months after the death of Elizabeth, Edgeworth's father married Frances Anna Beaufort, the daughter of an old family friend. An Anglo-Irishwoman a year younger than Maria Edgeworth, she had illustrated *The Parent's Assistant.* Jealous for her father's attention, Edgeworth was revolted by the idea of her fifty-four-year-old father marrying again, but she soon befriended "Fanny," and they were close confidantes for fifty-one years. Fanny and Edgeworth's father added six children to the family that crowded around Edgeworth nightly in a sitting room with a table in the corner, where she wrote all her works. The family took on the job of editing and proofreading her writing, making each work a group production.

At the time Edgeworth began writing novels with *Castle Rackrent,* it was a popular idea that the writing of novels was a frivolous endeavor. There-

fore, she was forbidden to read Fanny Burney's *Cecilia* (1782) because it was feared she would be tempted toward being overemotional in a home that was strictly utilitarian. She circumvented criticism of novel writing by calling all her works "tales" that promoted her father's political and social theories, since moral tales were at the height of their popularity in England. When *Castle Rackrent* was published, however, she achieved international fame as a regional novelist in spite of her protestations. Her unique narrative technique in *Castle Rackrent* was innovative because the story was told by a passive onlooker, the Rackrent family servant Thady. Based on her own family history, the tale is highly ironic not only because of the gap between Thady's simple adulation of the family and their despotism but also because of the additional voice of a sophisticated, enlightened English editor who claims the story is about the past, when landlords such as the Rackrents still existed in Ireland at the time of the novel's publication. Thady's naiveté parallels with the editor's, making for a brilliant combination of irony and humor.

Regardless of the overwhelming success of *Castle Rackrent,* Edgeworth continued to prefer educational stories more than novels, and she began to publish a series of tales for different age groups in accordance with her father's theories. *Early Lessons* (1801–1802) was a continuation of a series of stories called "Harry and Lucy" begun by her father and his second wife when she was still in school. Edgeworth would work on this series throughout most of her career, adding lessons until the final collection, *Harry and Lucy Concluded: Being the Last Part of Early Lessons,* was published in 1825. Using Day's three-volume *The History of Sandford and Merton* (1783–1789) as a model, she produced didactic short fiction illustrating practical lessons about life. The formula remained that of *The Parent's Assistant:* a boy, or a girl such as Rosamund, has to choose between beautiful but impractical objects and useful ones. Often a wise adult participates in the training process by giving insufficient or misleading answers to lead the child into making his or her own conclusions about the lessons. Intended for young children, the stories were read and cherished by children for many generations. John Ruskin reported that he learned how to write his own "Harry and Lucy" stories from the Edgeworth models when he was only eight years old.

Aimed at adolescents, Edgeworth's *Moral Tales for Young People* (1801) continued this tendency by providing instructive lessons, which were the basis for stories tested on children gathered in the Edgeworth household. Stories such as "Forester," "The Prussian Vase," and "The Good Aunt" were first intended as sequels to *The Parent's Assistant*. She began many of them in 1796, asking her cousin Sophy Ruxton for anecdotes about children from the ages of five to fifteen. Reviewers praised the collection highly. However, plots often surrender to moralization, making her purpose transparent. She covers up these faults with memorable character sketches developed through dialogue rather than description. Upon the book's publication she earned £200 for the copyright.

"Angelina; or, L'Amie Inconnue" demonstrates the results of an overly romantic sensibility. Reacting to the Edgeworth family's rejection of late-eighteenth-century literature characterized by highly emotional novels such as those of Ann Radcliffe, Edgeworth makes Angelina a comic portrayal of melodrama. Angelina has "an ungovernable propensity to make a display of sensibility; a fine theatrical scene upon every occasion; a propensity which she had acquired from novel reading." The clash of literary generations is easily seen here, as Edgeworth makes fun of domestic novels and novelists. "Angelina" is as cleverly written and finely crafted as *Castle Rackrent*, but its value is hidden in a volume of mediocre tales. Other selections in *Moral Tales for Young People* revert to the Edgeworth formula: "Forester," "The Prussian Vase," "The Good Aunt," "The Good French Governess," and "Mademoiselle Panache" are irregular but entertaining.

In 1802 Edgeworth's father decided to take the family abroad in an effort to find husbands for his eligible daughters, including the thirty-four-year-old Edgeworth. The trip was a highly successful literary tour, as she became a celebrity in London in the spring of 1803. In Paris she met inventor and diplomat Abraham Niclas Clewberg-Edelcrantz, a forty-six-year-old bachelor commissioned by the king of Sweden to look for inventions in Europe. After a short courtship, Clewberg-Edelcrantz proposed marriage; her father tried to talk her into accepting, but she did not want to leave her family to go to Sweden, even though she probably knew that this would be her last opportunity for marriage.

On her return to Edgeworthstown in 1803 Edgeworth resumed her project of composing children's stories intended to teach thrift, sobriety, honesty, and personal success. In *Popular Tales* (1804) her father wrote a preface stating her intention to write for the middle and lower classes. Written in the language of ordinary people, these stories were specifically meant to teach them the wisdom of accepting their status in life with grace while learning how to communicate with those of higher classes. As he wrote in the preface, he hoped they would "be current beyond circles which are sometimes exclusively considered as polite." Francis Jeffrey, in the July 1804 *Edinburgh Review,* praised the plan, suggesting that the examples would serve to make the working classes "proud of their independence, and cheerful in their submissions, and to point out the happiness which is placed within the reach of all who are industrious and affectionate." The eleven tales in the collection include "Lame Jervas," "The Will," "The Limerick Gloves," "Out of Debt Out of Danger," "The Lottery," "Rosanna," "Murad the Unlucky," "The Manufacturers," "The Grateful Negro," "To-morrow," and "The Contrast."

Again Edgeworth juxtaposes vice and virtue in parallel characters in the stories. Honesty, sobriety, thrift, and good manners triumph, while gambling, drinking, indolence, dishonesty, and prejudice cause destruction. Through the misfortunes of the "bad" characters, the "good" characters are able to teach new ways of living by their example. In "The Manufacturers" two nephews are joined in partnership with a cotton manufacturer. William is active and cheerful, and glories in his work, while Charles considers tradesmen and manufacturers disgraceful to polite society, caring only about how he appears to others. Charles makes a fool of himself by entering a bad marriage with a vain woman who desires to improve her social status; she teaches their children "equivocation, falsehood, envy, jealousy, and every fault of temper which could render them unsupportable to themselves, and odious to others." By comparison, William marries well within his station, has a sense of his own value, and now can save Charles from ruin with the great wealth he has amassed through hard work.

Honest people from lower classes often suffer from insensitive rich landlords in stories such as "The Contrast." The steadfast Farmer Frankland family is compared to their unhappy Bettesworth neighbors, who have names such as Idle Isaac, Wild Will, Bullying Bob, Saucy Sally, and Jilting Jessy. Because of a thoughtless, extravagant landlord who will not renew the Frankland lease, the Franklands are thrown off the farm. The well-taught Frankland children do well, of course, taking various jobs that become profitable because they are honest. The Bettesworths are conniving, jealous, and vain, which defeats every attempt at success. This pattern is repeated in other stories in *Popular Tales*.

*Sections from a draft for Edgeworth's story "Lame Jervas," which appeared in her* Popular Tales *(Pierpont Morgan Library, MA 893)*

"The Grateful Negro" presents an interesting variation. Two planters in Jamaica have different methods of managing their slaves and are surprised by the results. Jefferies considers Negroes an "inferior species, incapable of gratitude, disposed to treachery, and to be roused from their natural indolence only by force." Edwards treats his slaves with humanity and kindness, opposing slavery but sure that sudden emancipation would be harmful to them. When a Negro conspiracy threatens to overthrow the island, Edward's kindness is rewarded, while Jefferies is ruined and returns to England "railing at the treachery of the whole race of slaves." Edgeworth was aware of antislavery campaigns, but as a member of the Anglo-Irish gentry she was conservative in her views about their freedom.

In 1809 the publication of the first three volumes of *Tales of Fashionable Life* permanently secured Edgeworth's reputation. Many of the tales included in the first three volumes and in an additional three volumes published in 1812 were short novels such as "Ennui," "Vivian," and perhaps her best-known regional novel besides *Castle Rackrent*, "The Absentee." The six volumes cost thirty-nine shillings, and she was paid almost £2,000 for the entire set. The collection was an immediate success, but John Wilson Croker in the *Quarterly Review*, while placing her in the "first rank of modern novelists," criticized her for unrealistic portrayals of events. In another piece in *Quarterly Review* H. J. Stephen and William Gifford wished that she would deviate "a little from her rigid realities, and concede to the corrupted taste of her readers some petty sprinkling of romantic feeling and extraordinary incident." Her didacticism was beginning to wear thin in a society becoming accustomed to a different novelistic aesthetic.

While improving her craft, Edgeworth also began to write longer tales; many of those in *Tales of Fashionable Life* are long enough to be considered novels. Several of these represent her best work, yet the familiar moral lessons remain. "The Modern Griselda," "The Absentee," "Vivian," and "Ennui" are included as tales, but critics, including Butler, tend to refer to them as novels. Shorter selections include "Almeria," "Madame de Fleury," "The Dun," "Manoeuvering," and "Emilie de Coulanges." The responsibilities of the rich to educate children and the poor are investigated in "Madame de Fleury." Power, rank, and decorations grant the rich superiority, giving them advantages in education; in turn, a responsible rich person takes the opportunities to form the habits of "temper, truth, honesty, order, and industry" in the less fortunate classes. Madame de Fleury's example shows that the gift of education is better than the gift of money to the poor, as she descends from her coach in a bad part of Paris to investigate the cries of children who have been locked up by their working mother. In response to what she finds, she opens a school for girls to teach them practical lessons of survival in society. She does not encourage the writing of poetry or frivolous activities. The girls are educated to be useful, happy members of the working world. The story also involves the political intrigue of the French Revolution, which Edgeworth sees as useless violence. Her family had experienced violent rebellion in Ireland firsthand; their conservative political views were founded on more than philosophical ideas.

In 1813 the family took another trip abroad, during which Edgeworth was sought after at all the social functions of the London calendar. She met George Gordon, Lord Byron, who was impressed with her but thought her father a bore. She also developed friendships with notables such as play-wright and poet Joanna Baillie and poet Sydney Smith.

From 1814 Edgeworth's father's health was in decline, and she made sure that he was closely involved in everything she wrote. He was busy writing his own memoirs while she prepared two novellas, *Harrington: A Tale* and *Ormond: A Tale*, published together in June 1817. He intended for her to finish his memoirs after his death; he had completed 480 pages when he died on 13 June 1817. She found writing difficult for many months after the loss of her literary partner. Even reading novels was painful, and she worried that she would never be creative again. Indeed, after his death she wrote only children's tales with the exception of her last novel, *Helen: A Tale* (1834). She completed his plan for children's books with several more volumes in the *Early Lessons* series (1821, 1822, 1825) and a scientific textbook. She also persisted in her attempts to edit and complete her father's memoirs, which she considered a great responsibility. When the book finally appeared in 1820, some critics took the opportunity to vent their disgust with a man they saw as an egotistical bore who interfered with the talents of a great writer.

After the loss of her literary adviser, Edgeworth often turned to Scott for guidance on story ideas and details. She visited Edinburgh and Abbotsford in 1823, and in 1825 she received him in Ireland, where they took a trip together to Killarney. A matronly figure in her later years, she assumed the role of head of the family along with her stepmother. During hard financial times of the 1820s they kept the estate solvent; with the help of her literary earnings, she saved it from debts accumulated by Honora's son, Lovell, who had run up debts of £26,000. Edgeworth experienced another surprising development after her father's death: she transformed into a witty conversationalist. The meek, obedient daughter turned into a confident woman accustomed to social triumph as she traveled freely about the Continent visiting old friends. John Wilson ("Christopher North") wrote about the new Edgeworth in his posthumously edited *Memoir* (1862): "Miss Edgeworth is at Abbotsford, and has been for some time; a little, dark, bearded, sharp, withered, active, laughing, talking, impudent, fearless, outspoken, honest, whiggish, unchristian, good-tempered, kindly, ultra-Irish body. I like her on one day, and damn her to perdition the next."

Edgeworth became confident enough to begin working on another novel in 1830; it was to be less didactic, concentrating on human relationships. *Helen: A Tale* appeared in 1834 when she was sixty-six years old. It soon was published in a second edition, but the book was not as critically successful as her earlier stories because her style had yielded to the fashions of the "silver-fork" or "fashionable novels," which celebrated the upper classes then in vogue.

Maintaining a steady correspondence, Edgeworth spent her last years living peacefully at her home in Edgeworthstown, where she died in the arms of her friend and stepmother, Fanny, on 22 May 1849 at age eighty-one. Considering the enormous responsibilities she successfully fulfilled in her life – the education and raising of seventeen children, the realization of a rich career as a writer, and the management of a huge estate – Edgeworth was tough despite her short stature. In June 1849 the *Dublin University Magazine* evaluated her services to literature and assured its readers that future generations would remember her for "combining ethics with entertainment, suited to attract the young, and teaching the language of truth and virtue, in its alphabet." Future generations, however, if they have remembered Edgeworth for this achievement, have not always praised her.

**Letters:**

*A Memoir of Maria Edgeworth, with a Selection from Her Letters,* 3 volumes, edited by Frances Edgeworth and others (London: Printed by Joseph Masters & Son, 1867);

*The Life and Letters of Maria Edgeworth,* 2 volumes, edited by Augustus J. C. Hare (London: Arnold, 1894);

*The Black Book of Edgeworthstown, 1585–1817,* edited by Harold E. Butler and Jessie H. Butler (London: Faber & Gwyer, 1927);

*Maria Edgeworth: Letters from England, 1813–1844,* edited by Christina Colvin (Oxford: Clarendon Press, 1971);

*The Education of the Heart: The Correspondence of Rachel Mordecai Lazarus and Maria Edgeworth,* edited by Edgar E. MacDonald (Chapel Hill: University of North Carolina Press, 1977);

*Maria Edgeworth in France and Switzerland: Selections from the Edgeworth Family Letters,* edited by Colvin (Oxford: Clarendon Press, 1979).

**Bibliography:**

Bertha Coolidge Slade, *Maria Edgeworth, 1767–1849: A Bibliographical Tribute* (London: Constable, 1937).

**Biography:**

Marilyn Butler, *Maria Edgeworth: A Literary Biography* (Oxford: Clarendon Press, 1972).

**References:**

Elizabeth Harden, *Maria Edgeworth* (Boston: Twayne, 1984);

Harden, *Maria Edgeworth's Art of Prose Fiction* (The Hague: Mouton, 1971);

Mark D. Hawthorne, *Doubt and Dogma in Maria Edgeworth* (Gainesville: University of Florida Press, 1967);

Michael Hurst, *Maria Edgeworth and the Public Scene* (Coral Gables: University of Miami Press, 1969);

Maggie Lane, *Literary Daughters* (New York: St. Martin's Press, 1989);

Patrick Murray, *Maria Edgeworth: A Study of the Novelist* (Cork: Mercier Press, 1971);

Percy Howard Newby, *Maria Edgeworth* (Denver: Swallow, 1950);

James Newcomer, *Maria Edgeworth the Novelist* (Fort Worth: Texas Christian University Press, 1967);

Alice Paterson, *The Edgeworths: A Study of Later Eighteenth Century Education* (London: University Tutorial Press, 1914).

**Papers:**

Maria Edgeworth materials are scattered among private collections and libraries. Principal manuscript and correspondence sources are located at the National Library of Ireland, Dublin; Trinity College, Dublin; the British Museum, London; the Bodleian Library, Oxford; Bibliothèque Publique et Universitaire, Geneva; University College, London; the National Library of Scotland, Edinburgh; and the Huntington Library, San Marino, California.

# John Galt

## (2 May 1779 – 11 April 1839)

### Elton Edward Smith
*University of South Florida*

See also the Galt entries in *DLB 99: Canadian Writers Before 1890* and *DLB 116: British Romantic Novelists, 1789–1832.*

BOOKS: *The Battle of Largs: A Gothic Poem, with Several Miscellaneous Pieces* (London: Printed by C. Whittingham for S. Highley, 1804);

*Voyages and Travels in the Years 1809, 1810, and 1811; Containing Statistical, Commercial, and Miscellaneous Observations on Gibralter, Sardinia, Sicily, Malta, Serigo, and Turkey* (London: Printed for T. Cadell & W. Davies, 1812);

*Cursory Reflections on Political and Commercial Topics, as Reflected by the Regent's Accession to the Royal Authority* (London: Barrington, 1812);

*The Tragedies of Maddalen, Agamemnon, Lady Macbeth, Antonia and Clytemnestra* (London: Printed for T. Cadell & W. Davies, 1812);

*The Life and Administration of Cardinal Wolsey* (London: Printed for T. Cadell & W. Davies by Nichols, Son & Bentley, 1812); republished as *The Life of Cardinal Wolsey* (London: D. Bogue/T. C. Savill, 1846);

*Letters from the Levant; Containing Views of the State of Society, Manners, Opinions, and Commerce in Greece and Several of the Principal Islands of the Archipelago* (London: Printed for T. Cadell & W. Davies, 1813);

*The Life and Studies of Benjamin West, Esq. President of the Royal Academy of London, Prior to His Arrival in England* (London: Printed by Nichols, Son & Bentley for T. Cadell & W. Davies, 1816; Philadelphia: Moses Thomas, J. Maxwell, printer, 1816);

*The Crusade – A Poem,* anonymous (Edinburgh, 1816);

*The Majolo: A Tale,* 2 volumes (London: Printed by W. Smith for T. Faulkner, 1816);

*The Appeal: A Tragedy in Three Acts: As Performed at the Theatre-Royal, Edinburgh,* anonymous (Edinburgh: Printed for Archibald Constable and

*John Galt; portrait by Charles Grey (Scottish National Portrait Gallery)*

Longman, Rees, Orme, & Brown, London, 1818);

*Glenfell; or, MacDonalds and Campbells, an Edinburgh Tale of the Nineteenth Century* (London: Printed for Sir Richard Phillips & sold by W. Sams, 1820);

*The Life, Studies, and Works of Benjamin West, Esq. President of the Royal Academy of London* (London: Printed for T. Cadell & W. Davies, 1820);

*All the Voyages round the World: From the First by Magellan in 1520, to That of Krusenstern in 1807,* as Capt. Samuel Prior (London: Printed by W. Lewis for Sir Richard Phillips, 1820); republished as *All the Voyages round the World from the*

*First by Magellan in 1520 to That of Freycinet in 1820,* as Prior (London, 1827; New York: Colyer, 1840);

*The Wandering Jew; or, The Travels and Observations of Hareach the Prolonged,* as the Rev. T. Clark (London: Printed for John Souter, 1820);

*George the Third, His Court, and Family,* anonymous, 2 volumes (volume 1, London: Printed for Henry Colburn, 1820; volume 2, London: Printed by B. Clarke, 1820);

*A Tour of Europe and Asia,* as Clark, 2 volumes (London: Souter, 1820);

*The Earthquake: A Tale,* anonymous (3 volumes, Edinburgh: Printed for W. Blackwood and T. Cadell & W. Davies, London, by W. Smith, 1820; 2 volumes, New York: Van Winkle, 1821; New York: Gilley, 1821);

*Annals of the Parish; or, The Chronicle of Dalmailing during the Ministry of the Rev. Micah Balwhidder, Written by Himself,* as the Rev. Micah Balwhidder (Edinburgh: Printed for W. Blackwood & T. Cadell, London, by J. Ballantyne, 1821; Philadelphia: Carey, 1821);

*The Ayrshire Legatees; or, the Pringle Family,* anonymous (Edinburgh: Printed for William Blackwood & T. Cadell, London, by James Ballantyne, 1821; New York: Gilley, 1823);

*Pictures, Historical and Biographical; Drawn from English, Scottish, and Irish History,* 2 volumes (London: Printed by W. Lewis for Sir Richard Phillips, 1821);

*The National Reader,* as Clark (London: Souter, 1821);

*The National Spelling Book,* as Clark (London: Souter, 1821);

*Sir Andrew Wylie, of That Ilk,* anonymous (3 volumes, Edinburgh: Printed for W. Blackwood & T. Cadell, London, 1822; 2 volumes, New York: Printed for the Booksellers by W. Gratton, 1822);

*The Provost,* anonymous (Edinburgh: Printed for W. Blackwood & T. Cadell, London, 1822; New York: Published by E. Duyckinck and nine others, printed by J. & J. Harper, 1822);

*The Steam-boat,* as Thomas Duffle (Edinburgh: Blackwood / London: Cadell, 1822; New York: Printed by J. & J. Harper for S. Campbell & Son and eight others, 1823);

*A New General School Atlas,* as Clark (London: Souter, 1822);

*The English Mother's First Catechism for Her Children: Containing Those Things Most Necessary to Be Known at an Early Age,* as Clark (London: Printed for J. Souter, 1822);

*Passages in the Life of Adam Blair* (Boston, 1822);

*The Entail: or, The Lairds of Grippy,* anonymous (3 volumes, Edinburgh: Blackwood & T. Cadell, London, 1823 [i.e., 1822]; 2 volumes, New York: Printed by J. & J. Harper for S. Campbell & Son and eight others, 1823);

*The Gathering of the West,* anonymous (Edinburgh: Printed for William Blackwood & T. Cadell, London, by George Ramsay, 1823);

*Ringan Gilhaize; or, The Covenanters,* anonymous (3 volumes, Edinburgh: Printed by & for Oliver & Boyd / London: G. & W. B. Whittaker, London, 1823; 2 volumes, New York: Duyckinck, 1823);

*The Spaewife: A Tale of the Scottish Chronicles,* anonymous (3 volumes, Edinburgh: Printed & published by Oliver & Boyd and G. & W. B. Whittaker, London, 1823; 2 volumes, Philadelphia: Carey & Lea, 1824);

*The Bachelor's Wife; A Selection of Curious and Interesting Extracts, with Cursory Observations* (Edinburgh: Printed & published by Oliver & Boyd and G. & W. B. Whittaker, London, 1824);

*Rothelan: A Romance of the English Histories,* anonymous (3 volumes, Edinburgh: Printed & published by Oliver & Boyd and Geo. B. Whittaker, London, 1824; 2 volumes, New York: Published by Collins & Hannay, 1825);

*The Omen,* anonymous (Edinburgh: Printed for W. Blackwood & T. Cadell, London, by A. & R. Spottiswoode, London, 1825 [i.e., 1826]);

*The Last of the Lairds; or, The Life and Opinions of Malachi Mailings, Esq. of Auldbiggings,* anonymous (Edinburgh: Printed for W. Blackwood & T. Cadell, London, by James Ballantyne, 1826; New York: Printed by J. & J. Harper, 1827);

*Lawrie Todd; or, The Settlers in the Woods* (3 volumes, London: Colburn & Bentley, 1830; 2 volumes, New York: Printed by J. & J. Harper, 1830);

*Southennan* (3 volumes, London: Colburn & Bentley, 1830; 2 volumes, New York: Printed by J. & J. Harper, 1830);

*The Life of Lord Byron* (London: Colburn & Bentley / Edinburgh: Bell & Bradfute / Dublin: Cumming, 1830; New York: Printed by J. & J. Harper, 1830);

*Bogle Corbet; or, The Emigrants,* 3 volumes (London: Colburn & Bentley, 1831);

*The Lives of the Players,* 2 volumes (London: Colburn & Bentley, 1831; Boston: Hill, 1831);

*Stanley Buxton; or, The Schoolfellows* (3 volumes, London: Colburn & Bentley, 1832; 2 volumes,

Philadelphia & Baltimore: Carey & Hart, 1833);

*The Member: An Autobiography,* as Archibald Jobbry (London: Fraser, 1832);

*The Radical: An Autobiography,* as Nathan Butt (London: Fraser, 1832);

*The Stolen Child: A Tale of the Town, Founded on a Certain Interesting Fact* (London: Smith, Elder, 1833; Philadelphia: Carey, Lea & Blanchard, 1833);

*Eben Erskine; or, The Traveller* (3 volumes, London: Bentley, 1833; 2 volumes, Philadelphia: Carey, Lea & Blanchard, 1833);

*Poems* (London: Cochrane & McCrone, 1833);

*The Autobiography of John Galt,* 2 volumes (London: Cochrane & McCrone, 1833);

*The Ouranologos; or, The Celestial Volume* (Edinburgh: W. Blackwood & T. Cadell, London, 1833);

*Stories of the Study,* 3 volumes (London: Cochrane & McCrone, 1833);

*The Literary Life, and Miscellanies,* 3 volumes (Edinburgh: Blackwood / London: Cadell, 1834);

*Efforts. By an Invalid,* anonymous (Greenock: Printed for the author by John Mennons, 1835); republished as *Efforts of an Invalid* (London: Fraser, 1835);

*The Demon of Destiny; and Other Poems* (Greenock: Printed by W. Johnston & Son, 1839);

*The Howdie and Other Tales,* edited by William Roughead (Edinburgh & London: Foulis, 1923);

*A Rich Man and Other Stories,* edited by Roughead (London & Edinburgh: Foulis, 1925).

**Edition:** *Works of John Galt,* 8 volumes, edited by D. Storrer Meldrum (Edinburgh: Blackwood, 1895; Boston: Roberts, 1895–1896); enlarged and reedited by Meldrum and William Roughead, 10 volumes (Edinburgh: Grant, 1936).

OTHER: *The New British Theatre: A Selection of Original Dramas, Not Yet Acted; Some of Which Have Been Offered for Representation, but Not Accepted,* 4 volumes, edited by Galt (London: Colburn, 1814–1815).

John Galt was born in Irvine, in the county of Ayrshire, Scotland, on 2 May 1779. His father, also named John, was master of a West Indian trading vessel; Galt described him as remarkably handsome, easygoing, and trustworthy but of only modest ability. His father had no particular influence on the boy, but his mother, Jean Tilloch Galt, was a major influence. He described his mother as "a very singular person, possessing a masculine strength of character, with great natural humor, and a keen relish of the ridiculous in others." Some of these qualities were characteristic of Galt himself, as were her tendencies to use striking metaphors and her virtuoso command of Scottish dialect. The boy had heard about the charismatic Buchanites – described as heretics in *Annals of the Parish* (1821) – and when they were expelled from town loudly shouting psalms, as do the Covenanters in Galt's *Ringan Gilhaize* (1823), young Galt was saved from marching along with them only by his mother's vigilance. In *The Autobiography of John Galt* (1833) Galt says that his mother was the original of Mrs. Pringle in his novel *The Ayrshire Legatees; or, the Pringle Family* (1821).

Galt was a frail, sickly child, much given to reading and working in his mother's garden. At six the boy was composing couplets on the deaths of two larks and praying that his work might someday rival Alexander Pope's verse transcription of the *Iliad* (1715–1720). When he was ten the family moved to Greenock, where William Spence was his flute instructor and James Park his inspirer and critic at rhyming.

At twenty-five Galt moved to London. There he first took as a business partner a young man whom he later found to be insolvent. Next he reluctantly entered into a mercantile enterprise with his younger brother, Tom, but only until Tom went off to Honduras and left Galt free to enter Lincoln's Inn to study for the bar. Between 1804 and 1809 he published the octosyllabic *The Battle of Largs* (1804), an antiquarian poem, and composed a commercial treatise on underwriting as well as a history of English commerce until the reign of Edward III. He also became a master of heraldry and genealogy and worked out a new theory of crimes and punishments.

Galt departed on his three-year tour abroad only after he had completed his research at Jesus College, Oxford, for his biography of Cardinal Thomas Wolsey (1812). The itinerary of his tour he described at length in *Voyages and Travels in the Years 1809, 1810, and 1811* (1812), *Letters from the Levant* (1813), and his autobiography. He met George Gordon, Lord Byron, when the two took ship for Sardinia, a tour immortalized in cantos 1 and 2 of Byron's *Childe Harold's Pilgrimage* (1812). Galt went on to Sicily, Malta, and Corinth before renewing his acquaintance with Byron at Rome. A commercial scheme with Struthers, Kennedy and Company led him to rent a large building on the isle of Mykonos and thus become suspect as a political agent on a secret mission. He enlivened his subsequent quarantine at Messina by translating works by Conte Vittorio Alfieri for amusement, although he would include one drama – *Love, Honour, and Interest* – in *The New British Theatre* (1814–1815) when he edited those volumes.

By the end of 1811 Galt was back in London, and his Mediterranean commercial scheme never accomplished anything except to abort his study of law and interrupt his literary career. A scheme to smuggle British goods into Spain also collapsed with the triumphant entrance of Arthur Wellesley, First Duke of Wellington, into Madrid. The restoration of Louis XVIII led Galt on explorations of France, Belgium, and Holland with hopes for some possible commercial exploitation, but, finding no opportunities, he returned to London.

Thrown back on literature and assisted by Dr. Tilloch, editor of *The Philosophic Magazine* and proprietor of the *Star* newspaper, Galt prepared *Voyages and Travels* for publication. On 20 April 1813 he married Dr. Tilloch's daughter Elizabeth. For a short time he edited the *Political Review,* and he persuaded Henry Colburn to publish his plays and those of others in *The New British Theatre*; its subtitle explains the aim that Galt, as editor, had for it – to publish *A Selection of Original Dramas, Not Yet Acted; Some of Which Have Been Offered for Representation, But Not Accepted.*

A biography, *The Life and Studies of Benjamin West* (1816), was followed by a long poem, *The Crusade* (1816); Galt's first novel, *The Majolo;* and other incidental works. Then, in 1821, episodes of *The Ayrshire Legatees* began appearing in *Blackwood's Edinburgh Magazine,* and Galt had found his métier. Its success revived editorial interest in a manuscript rejected ten years earlier, *The Annals of the Parish.* This narrative of events during the years 1760 to 1796 in the Dalmailing parish of a Scottish minister, the Reverend Micah Balwhidder, is better conceived as a series of loosely related short stories than a unified novel. Although Galt's later works – *Sir Andrew Wylie, of That Ilk* (1822), *The Provost* (1822), *The Entail* (1823), and *The Last of the Lairds* (1826) – were somewhat more tightly structured, his narratives' anecdotes continued to be strung on the slender cord of a single character, and their milieu remained that of Scottish life, character, speech, and humor.

*Ringan Gilhaize,* which some critics consider his best, and others his worst, work, is possibly an answer to Sir Walter Scott's *Old Mortality* (1816), a novel in which Galt felt that Scott had treated the Scottish Covenanters unjustly. *The Spaewife* (1823), a fictional biography of King James I of Scotland,

was widely popular, but *Rothelan* (1824) had to be written and concluded in haste because of commercial opportunities in Canada – where Galt's other interests lay. Just when his literary career was prospering, his restless desire to be a man of commercial and colonial affairs lured him to the Canadian enterprise that would wreck his fortune and reputation.

Between the publication of *The Entail* and *Rothelan,* Galt received letters appointing him agent for Canadians seeking reimbursement from the United States for losses sustained during the War of 1812. From this prolonged civil suit developed the Canada Company, with Galt as secretary and one of the commissioners whom the government sent to evaluate provincial properties in Upper Canada. Here at last was the great work for which he felt destined. Taking his family along, he founded Guelph in what is now Ontario. Although he threw himself and all his resources into the task with great energy, the Canada Company did not show an immediate profit; its stock declined in value; and when Galt quarreled with Lt. Gov. Sir Peregrine Maitland, he was dismissed. He returned to England with heavy debts. Unable to pay tuition of eighty pounds for the education of his sons, Galt was imprisoned, and his health began to decline. Nevertheless, the family was held in such high esteem in Canada that one son, Thomas, would become a judge and another, Sir Alexander Tilloch Galt, would become the nation's prime minister.

Within six months of each other Galt published *Lawrie Todd; or, The Settlers in the Woods* (1830), based on conversations with a seed merchant he had met during his American travels, and *Southennan* (1830), a three-volume novel based on his Scottish youth but set in the reign of Queen Mary. In the same year his biography of Lord Byron appeared, exposing Galt to both satire and criticism for a work "which," he said, "I regard as the worst paid and the most abused, and yet among the most meritorious of all my productions."

Galt moved into Barnes Cottage, Old Brompton, where he wrote *The Lives of the Players* (1831), *Bogle Corbet; or, The Emigrants* (1831), and many periodical articles. A spinal condition thickened Galt's speech and made writing and walking difficult, but Galt continued doggedly to write: in 1833 alone *The Stolen Child, Eben Erskine,* his autobiography, and *Stories of the Study* were published. He traveled to London to oversee publication of *The Literary Life, and Miscellanies* (1834), which he had received permission to dedicate to King William IV. He died on 11 April 1839.

As ephemeral as Galt's literary production is, its mass remains impressive. Such worthy works as *The Ayrshire Legatees, Annals of the Parish, The Provost, Sir Andrew Wylie, The Entail, Ringan Gilhaize,* and *The Last of the Lairds* depict generally the same periods, share similar settings, and emphasize the same Scottish idiom and customs as Scott's Waverley novels. As one of the editors of his works, D. Storrer Meldrum, has said, however, "Galt's best books do not contain even the rudiments of a plot." In contrast to Scott, there is no adventure, no blood spilled. A first group of what Galt called "Tales of the West" – referring to that corner of Scotland bounded by the Clyde River and the towns of Irvine, Greenock, and Glasgow – were written primarily for serial publication in *Blackwood's Edinburgh Magazine.* Brief, episodic, and often topical, they are so loosely constructed that the periodical reader could pick up and read any installment without any knowledge of what had transpired in preceding installments. Their format qualifies them as loosely related short stories. This classification includes *The Ayrshire Legatees* (serialized from June 1820 to February 1821), *The Steam-boat* (February to December 1821), and *The Gathering of the West* (December 1822). Another group of one-volume novels shows greater coherence: *Annals of the Parish, The Provost,* and *The Last of the Lairds.* But even here each chapter is a report of the major events of one year, and simple chronology rather than development rules the chapter divisions.

A fragment, "The Howdie: An Autobiography" was destined for *Tait's Edinburgh Magazine* but got sidetracked by Galt's many commercial and literary projects; it was first published in 1923. The heroine, Mrs. Blithe, is a midwife whose antecedent is Daniel Defoe's Mrs. B––, who aided Moll Flanders in *The Fortunes and Misfortunes of the Famous Moll Flanders* (1722), and whose successor in the tradition is Charles Dickens's Mrs. Gamp in *Martin Chuzzlewit* (1843–1844). The warm-hearted and gossipy commentary of Mrs. Blithe makes the reader regret that Galt did not complete the tale.

"Sawney at Doncaster," in *Blackwood's Edinburgh Magazine* (October 1823), is a local-color, dialect narrative presenting an ongoing debate between a Scot and a Yorkshireman about which is the better horse trader. This pleasant trifle was written in the same year as *The Entail* and *Ringan Gilhaize,* when Galt was at the height of his creative powers.

"The Aunt in Virginia" appeared in *Blackwood's* in January and February 1833. The story's major character, the somewhat disreputable barrister Mr. Threeper, had already appeared in *The Entail.* In the matrimonial merry-go-round one of the funniest scenes has Mrs. Clatterpenny masquerading in Threeper's wig and robe – a stock pattern in farce on the London stage.

"The Joke," in *Fraser's Magazine* (September 1833), goes through the genealogies of two families before reaching the long-planned wedding of Elina, daughter of Sir Robert Merrywell, and Rupert Bragly, son of a bankrupt merchant who has recouped his fortunes in the West Indies. All goes as planned except for the public attentions paid by the groom's father to Mrs. Kittle, the landlady to Rupert Bragly. Having been originally attracted to Rupert, she is much better pleased with the prospect of a baronet.

In 1876 *Blackwood's* editor John Wilson, under the pseudonym Christopher North, had praised Galt's great powers "in the humble, the homely-pathetic." "My Father's House" (*Fraser's Magazine,* October 1833) is a superb example of this mood, as the soldier boy Dick returns with one empty sleeve to his doting Goody Gleanings. His early promise unfulfilled, his confidence in his physical abilities blasted, and his youthful innocence replaced by dissolution and idleness, the son of the decent mother ends as "an old grey-headed beggarman."

An additional portrait for the *Annals of the Parish* appeared in *Fraser's Magazine* for August 1834: "The Mem: From the papers of the late Rev. MICAH BALWIDDER of Dalmailing." Peerie, the schoolmistress, is the beautiful daughter of a learned father: "Greek and Latin were her household words, and she could read Hebrew as easily as if it had been the A B C." Her father dies; her mother pines away with sorrow; her fiancé, Peter Rawlings, mate of the *Sea Flower,* drowns; a suitor, Colin Pennyton, is attracted by stories of her hidden wealth but gives up his pursuit in discouragement. Actually penniless, Miss Peerie is advised by the minister's officious wife to offer to the local farmers' daughters lessons in Greek and Hebrew, "things which were greatly wanted among them." With quiet good sense she instead opens a school to train young women in plain sewing. For the rest of her life she lives blamelessly and usefully but barely subsists on a meager income, attracting from the community a combination of general goodwill and neglect. Galt asks the unanswerable questions: what became of the roses in her cheeks; the sparkle in her eye; the learning in Latin, Hebrew, Greek, and French; and all the early promise life held for her?

In "The Metropolitan Emigrant," in *Fraser's Magazine* (September 1835), Galt no longer exults in the golden dreams of colonial greatness that he had once shared. Instead, the failures and disappointments of the London haberdasher Stephen Needles may mirror Galt's thoughts on his own Canadian experience, which left him broken in health, impoverished, and distracted from the literary work that might have brought him fame. Needles is remarkably responsive to suggestion: his cousin Barbara Putty suggests marriage to Amelia Sprat, and forthwith they are married. An overheard conversation convinces him that tradesmen should seek their fortunes in the "States of the Canadas." After buying worsted from a visitor to his shop, Needles packs up his wife and stock for a miserable seven-week voyage intensified by seasickness on a ship bound for lower Canada and ironically named *Providence*. Snakes, mosquitoes, bears, owls, bitter winters, the necessity of carrying credit accounts, and the practical jokes of settlers ultimately drive them to return to London, "having experienced in Canada the folly of emigration."

Before Scott and Galt, stories for the London market that were set in Scotland and used Scottish dialect were almost exclusively transcriptions of oral folktales. In the eighteenth century Allan Ramsay, Robert Fergusson, and Robert Burns had aroused great interest in Scottish verse; Scott and Galt produced a similar wave of interest in Scottish narrative fiction. Indeed, they provided their late-nineteenth-century successor, Robert Louis Stevenson, with the Scottish dialect his characters speak in *Kidnapped* (1886), set in eighteenth-century Scotland.

Literary critics have traditionally discussed Galt's fiction as "secondary Scottish novels" or "regional" fiction and have appreciated the comedy of its dialect or its documentation of the social history of Scotland. More-recent critics take his work more seriously. They see Galt as a representative of the Enlightenment, a sympathetic expositor of Scottish Calvinism, a writer of fiction acquainted with the great intellectual ferment wrought by the work of Adam Smith and Adam Ferguson. Galt's late short fiction published in *Fraser's Magazine* and *Tait's Edinburgh Magazine* shows stirrings of exploration and imagination at which his earlier novels only hint.

## Bibliographies:

Harry Lumsden, "The Bibliography of John Galt," *Records of the Glasgow Bibliography Society,* 9 (1931): 1–41;

Bradford A. Booth, "A Bibliography of John Galt," *Bulletin of Bibliography,* 16 (September–December 1936): 7–9.

## Biographies:

D. M. Moir, *Biographical Memoir of John Galt* (Edinburgh: Ballantyne, 1841);

R. K. Gordon, *John Galt* (Toronto: University of Toronto Press, 1920);

Jennie W. Aberdein, *John Galt* (London: Oxford University Press, 1936);

Ian A. Gordon, *John Galt: The Life of a Writer* (Edinburgh: Oliver & Boyd, 1972; Toronto: University of Toronto Press, 1972).

## References:

Ruth I. Aldrich, *John Galt* (Boston: Twayne, 1978);

A. J. Ashley, "Coleridge on Galt," *Times Literary Supplement,* 25 September 1930, p. 757;

James Bridie, *The Scottish Character as It Was Viewed by Scottish Authors from Galt to Barrie* (Greenock: Greenock Philosophical Society, 1937);

W. M. Brownlie, *John Galt, Social Historian* (Greenock: Greenock Philosophical Society, 1952);

Keith Costain, "The Spirit of the Age and the Scottish Fiction of John Galt," *Wordsworth Circle,* 11 (Spring 1980): 98–106;

W. Croft Dickinson, *John Galt, "The Provost" and the Burgh* (Greenock: Greenock Philosophical Society, 1954);

Erik Frykman, *John Galt and the Eighteenth Century Scottish Philosophy* (Greenock: Greenock Philosophical Society, 1954);

George V. Griffith, "John Galt's Short Fiction Series," *Studies in Short Fiction,* 17 (Fall 1980): 455–462.

## Papers:

Manuscripts and letters of John Galt are in the National Library of Scotland; Edinburgh University Library; the James Watt Library, Greenock; the Bodleian Library, Oxford; the Public Archives of Canada, Ottawa; the Public Record Office, State Papers for Upper Canada; the Baldwin Room, Toronto Public Library; and the Irvine Public Library.

# Elizabeth Cleghorn Gaskell

*(29 September 1810 – 12 November 1865)*

Maureen T. Reddy
*Rhode Island College*

See also the Gaskell entries in *DLB 21: Victorian Novelists Before 1885* and *DLB 144: Nineteenth-Century British Literary Biographers.*

BOOKS: *Mary Barton: A Tale of Manchester Life,* anonymous (2 volumes, London: Chapman & Hall, 1848; 1 volume, New York: Harper, 1848);

*Libbie Marsh's Three Eras: A Lancashire Tale,* as Cotton Mather Mills, Esquire (London: Hamilton, Adams, 1850);

*Lizzie Leigh: A Domestic Tale, from "Household Words,"* attributed to Charles Dickens (New York: De Witt & Davenport, 1850);

*The Moorland Cottage,* anonymous (London: Chapman & Hall, 1850; New York: Harper, 1851);

*Ruth: A Novel,* anonymous (3 volumes, London: Chapman & Hall, 1853; 1 volume, Boston: Ticknor, Reed & Fields, 1853);

*Cranford,* anonymous (London: Chapman & Hall, 1853; New York: Harper, 1853);

*Lizzie Leigh and Other Tales,* anonymous (London: Chapman & Hall, 1855; Philadelphia: Hardy, 1869);

*Hands and Heart and Bessie's Troubles at Home,* anonymous (London: Chapman & Hall, 1855);

*North and South,* anonymous (2 volumes, London: Chapman & Hall, 1855; 1 volume, New York: Harper, 1855);

*The Life of Charlotte Brontë, Author of "Jane Eyre," "Shirley," "Villette," etc.,* 2 volumes (London: Smith, Elder, 1857; revised, 1857; New York: Appleton, 1857);

*My Lady Ludlow: A Novel* (New York: Harper, 1858); republished as *Round the Sofa* (2 volumes, London: Low, 1858; London & New York: Oxford University Press, 1913);

*My Lady Ludlow and Other Tales* (London: Smith, Elder, 1859);

*Right at Last, and Other Tales* (London: Low, 1860; New York: Harper, 1860);

*Elizabeth Cleghorn Gaskell*

*Lois the Witch and Other Tales* (Leipzig: Tauchnitz, 1861);

*Sylvia's Lovers* (3 volumes, London: Smith, Elder, 1863; 1 volume, New York: Dutton, 1863);

*A Dark Night's Work* (London: Smith, Elder, 1863; New York: Harper, 1863);

*Cousin Phillis: A Tale* (New York: Harper, 1864);

*Cousin Phillis and Other Tales* (London: Smith, Elder, 1865);

*The Grey Woman and Other Tales* (London: Smith, Elder, 1865; Philadelphia: Peterson, 1865);

*Wives and Daughters: An Every Day Story* (2 volumes, London: Smith, Elder, 1866; 1 volume, New York: Harper, 1866);

*"My Diary": The Early Years of My Daughter Marianne* (London: Privately printed by Clement Shorter, 1923).

**Collections:** *The Works of Mrs. Gaskell,* Knutsford Edition, 8 volumes, edited by A. W. Ward (London: Smith, Elder, 1906–1911);

*The Novels and Tales of Mrs. Gaskell,* 11 volumes, edited by Clement K. Shorter (Oxford: Oxford University Press, 1906–1919).

OTHER: "Clopton House," in *Visits to Remarkable Places, Old Halls, Battlefields, and Scenes Illustrative of Striking Passages in English History and Poetry,* by William Howitt (London: Longmans, 1840).

SELECTED PERIODICAL PUBLICATION –
UNCOLLECTED: "Sketches among the Poor," *Blackwood's Edinburgh Magazine,* 1 (January 1837): 48–50.

For some critics Elizabeth Gaskell was a conventional, middle-class Victorian wife and mother who accepted the values of her world and who also happened to write books – a feminine dove among literary eagles Charlotte Brontë and George Eliot, to borrow Lord David Cecil's suggestive phrase. These critics, whose views predominated from the waning years of the nineteenth century until the 1950s, tended to see *Cranford* (1853) as her most representative and important work. In her own time and for two decades after her death Gaskell was known mainly as the author of *Mary Barton: A Tale of Manchester Life* (1848), which achieved immediate success upon its publication. In the 1950s Marxist critics rediscovered this Gaskell, the social-problem novelist whose most characteristic work engages issues of industrialization, urbanization, class hostility, and both political and social change. She was seen by these critics as an incisive social critic who used fiction as a vehicle to expose the gross inequalities of class from which all Victorian social problems were perceived to have grown. More recently feminist critics have drawn attention to Gaskell's intense, ongoing interest in women's position in society, and especially in motherhood as both institution and practice. For this group of critics, who usually identify *Wives and Daughters: An Every Day Story* (1866) as her greatest achievement, Gaskell was an unconventional, complicated person, a serious artist who strove to articulate in all of her writings what

she understood to be the truth of women's lot – very far indeed from the contented, minor, feminine dove of earlier views.

Critics of various schools have made different cases for Gaskell as a major novelist, but few critics of any persuasion have paid much attention to her short fiction, focusing instead on her better-known novels and on *The Life of Charlotte Brontë, Author of "Jane Eyre," "Shirley," "Villette," etc.* (1857). One reason for the comparatively little attention given to Gaskell's short fiction is the small amount of critical interest in short fiction of her period. In the middle of the nineteenth century, when Gaskell began writing, the novel dominated. Like many other writers of this period she wrote short fiction for the increasingly popular periodicals – most notably Charles Dickens's two weeklies, *Household Words* and *All the Year Round* – but did not produce many pieces that could be described as true short stories by standard definitions. Further, much of her best short fiction, such as "Lois the Witch" (*All the Year Round,* October 1859), "The Grey Woman" (*All the Year Round,* January 1861), and "Cousin Phillis" (*Cornhill Magazine,* November 1863–February 1864), called "nouvelles" by Edgar Wright, is lengthier than what would currently be called short stories. The dominance of the novel, the embryonic state of the short story as a distinct genre, the lengthy pieces Gaskell wrote, and the false albeit widely accepted view of Gaskell as a minor writer, which has persisted through shifts in critical methods, have together diverted critical attention from her short fiction. Few critics have taken note of her experiments within the shorter forms of fiction, and those who have often seem to miss the significance of these experiments. Persistent devaluation of Gaskell's stories serves to obscure her real achievements and to keep her work from being read. All but a dozen or so of her thirty short stories remain out of print.

Born on 29 September 1810 in London's Chelsea section to Elizabeth Holland Stevenson and William Stevenson, a Unitarian minister, Elizabeth Cleghorn Stevenson was their second child. Her father had earlier come to believe that a paid ministry was morally wrong and therefore had turned to various other employments, including writing for several journals; at the time of Elizabeth's birth he was keeper of the records of the treasury. She spent most of her youth in the small country village of Knutsford in Cheshire, the model for Cranford, where she was sent to live with an aunt, always called "Aunt Lumb," after her mother's death in 1811. Her father remarried in 1814, but she never lived with him and his second wife for more than brief periods, staying instead in Knutsford with Aunt Lumb and later attending Avonbank, a school for young ladies in Stratford. According to Wright, Avonbank provided a higher quality of education than was usually given girls, with a broader curriculum (which included Latin and Italian as well as French) and a more liberal philosophy than most schools for young ladies. In 1827, the same year her elder brother, John, disappeared at sea, she left Avonbank. After returning to Knutsford she visited London, where she stayed with her father and stepmother – with whom she did not get along – until her father's death in 1829. She then traveled, visiting friends and relations, to Newcastle, Edinburgh, and Manchester.

In Manchester she met William Gaskell, a Unitarian minister, whom she married on 30 August 1832; she settled permanently with him in Manchester. Appointed assistant minister of Cross Street Chapel not long before their marriage, he became an important figure in the Unitarian community, of which the chapel was a center. For the next fifteen years, as he solidified his public position, she devoted most of her time to a busy domestic life, including work that fell to her as the wife of a minister. The Gaskells had four daughters – Marianne (born in 1834), Margaret (always called Meta, born in 1837), Florence (born in 1842), and Julia (born in 1846) – who survived infancy after their first daughter was stillborn in 1833, and one son, William, who died in 1845 at nine months from scarlet fever. During this period Gaskell also suffered the loss of her Aunt Lumb, who died in 1837.

In Manchester, Gaskell observed and tried to ameliorate through charity work the problems besetting modern industrial cities. Knutsford was only fifteen miles away but a world away in spirit, a sleepy country town that contrasted sharply with the bustle, crowds, and dirt of Manchester. The contrast between these two most important places in her life must have sparked Gaskell's imagination, as she later often drew on it in her writing. Although she attempted some short pieces both alone and with her husband, she did not turn to writing as a profession until her husband suggested writing as a way of getting through her grief over the death of her son.

In some ways Gaskell led a highly conventional life: she married and had children, involved herself in charitable activities, ran a busy household with frequent guests, and claimed in letters to accept the view that a woman could find her greatest fulfillment only in motherhood. On the other hand, she earned and controlled her own money, negoti-

ated for herself in business affairs, traveled throughout Europe without her husband, and included in her fiction critiques of the limited roles available to women. From her conventionally "feminine" beginning as a writer – writing a novel at her husband's suggestion as an escape from grief, publishing anonymously or using a masculine pseudonym (Cotton Mather Mills) in order to avoid drawing attention to herself, turning the payments for her writing over to her husband – Gaskell quickly moved to a highly unconventional position. She dropped the pseudonym almost immediately and by 1857 affixed her own name to her works, except for those that appeared in periodicals that used no authors' names. She took control of her own finances, using the money she earned to take trips with her daughters and even saving enough to buy a house without her husband's knowledge. Most important, Gaskell began to view herself as a professional writer, displaying an interest in formal publishing agreements and advertising arrangements and taking her own writing seriously.

Gaskell's self-confidence was at the root of her many troubles with Dickens, who found her maddeningly impervious to his suggestions for her work, which in fact were often wrongheaded. Following the great success of *Mary Barton,* Dickens asked Gaskell to contribute to the journal he was just beginning, *Household Words.* She wrote "Lizzie Leigh," a highly melodramatic tale of a young woman's sexual fall and eventual redemption with which Dickens led off the opening number of his weekly in March–April 1850. This was the beginning of a sometimes rocky thirteen-year association between Gaskell and Dickens, during which he published twenty of her short stories and serialized *Cranford* and *North and South* (1855).

Dickens often reacted to Gaskell not as writer to writer or as editor to contributor but as (dominant) man to (submissive) woman, as his self-revealing comment about her in an 1854 letter to his subeditor, Wilkie Collins, shows: "Were I Mr. G. Oh heaven how I would beat her!" In his letters to Gaskell Dickens is unfailingly gallant, addressing her as "My Dear Scheherazade" and flattering her shamelessly. In letters to others, however, he consistently denigrates her work, comparing her unfavorably with long, varying lists of her male contemporaries. The discrepancy between what Dickens paid Gaskell and what he paid other writers – for instance, he paid Edward Bulwer-Lytton nearly four times what he paid Gaskell for pieces of the same length published at the same period in *All the Year Round* – indicates his real attitude toward Gaskell. Gaskell seems to have sensed his hypocrisy, which may be why she paid little attention either to his compliments or to his advice. Dickens once appropriated a story he had heard Gaskell tell, writing it up as "To be Read at Dusk," which suggests yet another reason for Gaskell's ambivalent attitude toward him.

On the other hand, Dickens was among the first to recognize and to laud Gaskell's tremendous storytelling talent, which he also encouraged her to develop. Without Dickens there would be no *Cranford* and probably not much of the short fiction she produced with his prompting. Gaskell wrote "Our Society at Cranford" for the December 1851 *Household Words,* fictionalizing an essay, "The Last Generation in England," she had published in the July 1849 *Sartain's Union Magazine.* Dickens asked for more and for the next two years persistently pressed Gaskell to return to the Cranfordian characters. By May 1853 Gaskell had written eight more Cranford episodes for Dickens, which she then gathered as the novel *Cranford.*

Many Gaskell critics have maintained that once George Smith established the monthly *Cornhill Magazine* in 1860, Gaskell reserved her best work for him. This belief probably began with Gaskell's own comments, such as an 1860 letter to Smith in which she describes a story – probably "A Dark Night's Work," published in *All the Year Round* ( January–March 1861) – as *"not good enough for the CM* – I am the best judge of that please – but [it] might be good enough" for Dickens. Gaskell, however, continued to send Dickens her essays and short fiction, including "The Grey Woman," published in the January 1861 *All the Year Round,* which is certainly among her best stories.

Nearly every critic who mentions the troubled professional association between Gaskell and Dickens seems surprised that she was not more grateful for or receptive to his editorial suggestions; modern critics often are quite sympathetic to his anger that she would not alter her work in accordance with his ideas. Some, including biographer Winifred Gérin, quote the "Were I Mr. G" remark with sympathy, seemingly oblivious to the light in which it places Dickens. Yet Dickens's advice was often inappropriate, and the changes he made in her work seldom improved it. For example, Dickens inserted the word "dark" into the title of a story Gaskell sent him about an accidental killing and its aftermath in the lives of the killer and his daughter, turning "A Night's Work" into "A Dark Night's Work" and thereby emphasizing a sense of melodrama that the story in fact minimizes. Dickens seems not to have understood Gaskell's aims. For instance, when she

*Elizabeth Cleghorn Stevenson shortly before her marriage to the Reverend William Gaskell in 1832 (Manchester University Library)*

sent him "The Old Nurse's Story" in 1852 – it appeared in the December 1852 *Household Words* – he responded with enthusiasm but added a suggestion for a new ending that he thought would be "very new" and "very terrific" but that in fact would have muddied the story's central theme while recapitulating the endings of more-traditional ghost stories.

There is little evidence that Dickens influenced Gaskell's short fiction apart from the incentive he provided as a publisher who paid decently and printed virtually everything Gaskell sent him. Angus Easson notes a Dickensian influence in "Mr. Harrison's Confessions," published in the February–April 1851 *Ladies' Companion,* in which the plot largely relies on misunderstood conversations, but Gaskell's humor tends to be gentler than Dickens's, even in this highly satiric story.

On the whole, there was certainly more mutual sympathy between Gaskell and Smith than between Gaskell and Dickens. Furthermore, the monthly publication of the *Cornhill Magazine* suited her better than did the weekly schedule of *Household Words* and later *All the Year Round.* Her association with Smith, who was Charlotte Brontë's publisher, began when she agreed in 1855 to write a biography of Brontë, who had been Gaskell's friend from 1850 until her death in 1855. Shortly after Gaskell completed *The Life of Charlotte Brontë* in 1857, Smith asked her to do a second biography. In her letter of refusal she wrote, "I like to write about character, and the manners of a particular period . . . but I cannot manage politics." This comment perceptively identifies two of her strengths and by omission implies a weakness in plotting, which irked Dickens, as her plots sometimes tend to be rather thin or else convoluted, but it is too self-deprecating – Gaskell could indeed "manage politics" in the broad sense.

Despite her assertiveness and self-confidence as a writer, Gaskell remained deeply ambivalent about the extent to which women ought to seek self-fulfillment and independence judging from her private letters and from her public work. In an 1850 letter to her friend Eliza "Tottie" Fox, an artist, she tried to work out her feelings on the problems of balancing duty with self-development:

> One thing is pretty clear, *Women,* must give up living an artist's life, if home duties are to be paramount. . . . I am sure it is healthy for them to have the refuge of the hidden world of Art to shelter themselves in when too much pressed upon by daily small Lilliputian arrows of peddling [*sic*] cares . . . the difficulty is where and when to make one set of duties subserve and give place to the other.

After thinking about this question for a few days, Gaskell returned to the letter and wrote a postscript:

> If Self is to be the end of exertions, those exertions are unholy, there is no doubt of *that* – and that is part of the danger of cultivating the Individual Life; but I do believe that we have all some appointed work to do, wh. no one else can do so well; Wh. is *our* work; what *we* have to do in advancing the Kingdom of God; and that first we must find out what we are sent into the world to do, and define it and make it clear to ourselves, (that's *the* hard part) and then forget ourselves in our work, and our work in the End we ought to strive to bring about.

This postscript shows that Gaskell preferred to view her writing as a duty rather than as a selfish refuge from her domestic duties, but the earlier part of the letter reveals that she believed the attraction for women of producing art lay at least partly in its possibilities as a shelter from the trivialities that take up so much of their time. Writing, she implies in the postscript, is her "appointed work," and therefore it would actually be morally wrong for her to stop writing. Although she is certainly sincere here, this point of view did have the decided advantage of allowing Gaskell to devote large amounts of her time to writing without being overwhelmed with guilt for neglecting her home duties.

In an 1862 letter Gaskell tells a female correspondent who is an aspiring writer that she should not pursue a career as a writer at the expense of her domestic responsibilities: "The exercise of a talent or power *is* always a great pleasure; but one should weigh well whether this pleasure may not be obtained by the sacrifice of some duty. When I had *little* children, I do not think I could have written stories, because I should have become too much absorbed in my *fictitious* people to attend to my *real* ones." Writing this letter when her children were between sixteen and twenty-eight, perhaps Gaskell had forgotten her early years as a writer. Contrary to her claims here, she actually wrote two short stories for *Howitt's Journal* when Julia was less than a year old and her other children were ages five, ten, and thirteen. Gaskell also began *Mary Barton,* published when Julia was two, during this time. Indeed, Gaskell's most productive years as a writer coincided precisely with her busiest years as a mother. The disjunction between what Gaskell asserts in this letter and what she in fact did in her life corresponds to the gap she explores in her fiction between mythical ideals of femininity and women's actual lives. In Victorian ideology mothering and writing were opposing activities, but in Gaskell's life they were intimately interconnected.

Reconciling the requirements of duty as defined for women by society with the felt need for self-fulfillment and autonomy presented a puzzle that few women of Gaskell's time were able to solve satisfactorily. The conflict between duties to others and the needs of self forms a recurring theme in her short stories as it does in her novels; one can see its relevance to her own life as well. Whereas Gaskell minimized this conflict in her life by regarding her writing as a moral duty, which partly accounts for the religious purpose of so many of her works, her female characters often experience a more complicated struggle. Several of her short stories treat this struggle as it might be manifested in the life of a woman who is not an artist. Susan Dixon of "Half a Life-Time Ago" (*Household Words,* October 1855) and Maggie Browne of *The Moorland Cottage* (1850), for example, face choices not between two different types of duties but between clearly defined duties on the one hand and self-needs that could not be described as duties on the other hand. The works that deal with these conflicts in female characters' lives are often marred by poor artistic choices, as when *The Moorland Cottage* suddenly shifts from a realistic presentation of a woman's dilemma to a romantic fantasy in which all conflicts are resolved by incredible outside intervention, including acts of God. One problem is that the tension in these women's lives results from forced choices between romantic love and familial responsibility, not from choices between chosen work and mandated duty. Perhaps Gaskell's awareness of the audience for which she was writing her short fiction steered her away from examining more closely the possible role of pleasurable work in women's lives.

One stumbling block for Gaskell was the limited number of options open to middle-class women of her time who did not marry. Despite the deep thought that she gave to the concerns of the female artist, none of her stories has an artist as its heroine, which is also true of most other women writers of the period, including Brontë and Eliot. In fact, few of Gaskell's heroines have meaningful work of any sort, with the absence of such work sometimes an important theme. In a reflection of real social conditions, Gaskell's working-class female characters do perform work for pay, about which Gaskell is ambivalent.

Although all of Gaskell's novels are well within the tradition of realism, many of her short stories are not. The reason is not just that the fluid boundaries of the nineteenth-century short story could more easily accommodate experimentation than could the more defined form of the novel, but also that Gaskell evidently felt freer to let her imagination roam where it would when writing pieces that demanded less time than did the novels. The time commitment demanded by a novel likely kept Gaskell acutely aware of her duty as a writer – and especially as a woman writer – to improve the moral temper of her times. She seems to have enjoyed writing short fiction more than she enjoyed writing novels, perhaps because she did take the short works less seriously. Whereas her letters abound in references to difficulties with writing her novels and the Brontë biography, few such remarks concern her short fiction. Several of the stories have an exuberance seldom evident in Gaskell's novels. "Curious if True," for instance, the first piece Gaskell published in the *Cornhill Magazine* (February 1860), is a witty, almost farcical fantasy in which a dull narrator gets caught up in an adventure with fairy-tale characters that he fails to recognize but that the reader instantly identifies. The stories may have seemed more ephemeral to her than the novels: published in periodicals, they were quickly last

week's news. Gaskell occasionally wrote short fiction to fund a particular project, such as an excursion to Europe with one of her children. The short fiction also had the advantage of double sales, once to the periodical and then again to a publisher as part of a volume, with five collections of stories appearing from 1855 to 1865. In a household chronically short of funds, as was the case with the Gaskells, this must have been a great benefit.

Gaskell's central themes – duty versus self-fulfillment, female sexuality and the dangers of both repression and expression, women's roles in the family, work for women – are touched upon even in the simple stories she wrote for the youthful audience of the *Sunday School Penny Magazine,* such as "Bessy's Troubles at Home" (January 1852), which have a clear moral purpose and an explicitly stated Christian message. They are also present in the straightforwardly realistic pieces written for the working-class audience of *Howitt's Journal,* such as "Libbie Marsh's Three Eras" (June 1847) and the more complex but still realistic stories aimed at the middle-class readership of the *Cornhill Magazine,* such as "Six Weeks at Heppenheim" (May 1862). These themes occur also in the romances, such as "The Heart of John Middleton" (*Household Words,* December 1850) and "Cousin Phillis" and, most interestingly, in the Gothic tales at which Gaskell excelled, such as "The Old Nurse's Story" (1852) and "The Grey Woman." The Gothic stories are most important because they gave her a means of dealing with the tension between her life as a woman and the central myths of womanhood she found in her culture, a task for which realism, and to a lesser extent romance, were inadequate.

The Gothic stories played a pivotal role in Gaskell's development through the freedom this mode allowed her to take her insights to extremes. Gaskell's Gothic stories explore domestic terrors, exposing the hidden aspects of the same world that she describes in her novels of domestic realism. Some Gothic elements make their way into the novels as well to hint at the potential for abuse of power in any hierarchical relationship, regardless of how calm or ordinary that relationship may seem. The Gothic is the ideal form for examining the social attitudes that are reinforced or taken for granted by realistic fiction, consisting as the Gothic does of everything that is unsayable in realism.

The Gothic stories, and the Gothic elements of basically realistic novels, are not odd features of Gaskell's career but absolutely central contributions to her development. Most critics agree that her purpose in writing novels was often religious, in the broad sense of making readers aware of God's presence in all of life and of showing the necessity of Christian love, yet few have noted the connection between this religious purpose and the Gothic forms with which she experimented. The religious imagination and the Gothic imagination are fundamentally similar, with both originating in awe or dread. Gaskell's social-problem novels, *Mary Barton* and *North and South,* depict the problems of the urban poor as infinitely complicated and resistant to simple solutions, and in them Gaskell struggles to reconcile the demands of Christianity with the basic principles of capitalism, refusing to damn capitalism in the facile way some of her contemporaries did. Whereas the endings of these novels are cautiously optimistic, her Gothic fiction is essentially pessimistic. The realistic fiction stresses reconciliation, but the Gothic stories reveal the extent to which she doubts that true reconciliation is possible and her half-buried recognition (and fear) that only a complete revolution in the social order will bring it into accord with Christian values.

Of all Gaskell's shorter works, only four completed stories are entirely in the Gothic mode: "The Old Nurse's Story," "The Squire's Story" (*Household Words,* December 1853), "The Poor Clare" (*Household Words,* December 1856), and "The Grey Woman." There are also two fragments of ghost stories. Many other stories – among them "Morton Hall" (*Household Words,* November 1853), "The Doom of the Griffiths" (*Harper's New Monthly Magazine,* January 1858), "The Crooked Branch" (first published as "The Ghost in the Garden Room" in *All the Year Round,* December 1859), "Lois the Witch," "A Dark Night's Work," and "Crowley Castle" (*All the Year Round,* December 1863) – incorporate Gothic elements, particularly an atmosphere of enervating terror. All of these works share a preoccupation with the tension between cultural myths of womanhood and women's actual lives. They are also all family horror stories; that is, while some of the stories include supernatural events or apparitions, the real horror of each is contained within the domestic world of husbands and wives, parents and children. In this way the Gothic stories are closely related to the realistic novels for which Gaskell is best known, with the stories exploring the chaotic, frightening underside of the superficially orderly world the novels treat.

"The Old Nurse's Story" is both Gaskell's first Gothic work and her only completed ghost story. Several critics have suggested that this story was one of Henry James's models for *The Turn of the Screw* (1898), which points to a parallel between the two: in each the question of whether the ghosts are real is somewhat beside the point. Whether actual apparition or imaginary, "hysterical" manifestations, the ghosts are important principally for what they convey about the characters' psychological states. Through the writing of this story Gaskell may have realized that her deepest interest lay in the emotional lives of her characters and in the ways that the past lives on in the present and concluded that therefore the ghosts were little more than distractions from these central concerns. This would help to explain why she completed no other ghost stories despite her evident skill at the genre.

The most accessible level of "The Old Nurse's Story" is really a cover story, the tale of how a nurse rescues her small charge from threatening ghosts. Beneath this cover story is a complicated dissection of family relationships that is infinitely more frightening than any ghost story, no matter how well told. When Gaskell wrote "The Old Nurse's Story" she was also at work on the later installments of *Cranford,* which is centrally concerned with relationships among women. Whereas *Cranford* centers on a true community of women established upon and sustained by an ethic of care, "The Old Nurse's Story" describes first a failure of community brought about by the triumph of competition over cooperation, envy over care, and vengeance over forgiveness, and then works through this failure to a revitalized female community.

The framing device of "The Old Nurse's Story" emphasizes continuity, with the old nurse, Hester, telling Rosamond's children about the ghostly events that Rosamond experienced in her youth and that form the main part of the tale. The tale Hester tells takes place when Rosamond is four or five years old and begins just a few days after she has been orphaned. Rosamond's much older cousin, Lord Furnivall, decides that the child and her nurse will move to Furnivall Manor House, which turns out to be exactly the sort of building one expects in a Gothic tale: enormous, isolated, on its way to ruin and abandonment, and inhabited only by two old women (Grace Furnivall and her companion, Mrs. Stark) and a few servants. The first third of the story is devoted to creating an eerie atmosphere. Gaskell skillfully describes the isolated house, buried in a dark, wild-seeming park; a portrait, always turned to the wall, of Grace's mysterious older sister, Maude; cryptic comments to Hester from the servants; organ music that plays on despite the organ being destroyed; a wing of the house that remains closed off, with none of the servants allowed a key; and the onset of a particularly harsh winter.

*Pages from an 8 January 1850 letter in which Gaskell asks Charles Dickens for his help in freeing a sixteen-year-old prostitute from prison so that she can start a new life in Australia. Dickens complied with the request, and the girl's story later served as the basis for Gaskell's novel* Ruth *(Pierpont Morgan Library, MA 1352)*

One evening Rosamond disappears and is found unconscious on a snowy hillside. When she awakens, the child tells of being beckoned outdoors by a little girl who led her to the hill, where a crying woman lulled her to sleep. Hester, however, can find only one set of footprints, Rosamond's, in the snow. A few weeks later Hester sees the little girl in a scene that echoes Lockwood's dream in Emily Brontë's *Wuthering Heights* (1847): the child sobs and beats upon the windowpanes, obviously begging to be let in, yet Hester hears no sound.

After this incident the housekeeper tells Hester the previously suppressed family story behind the organ music and the apparition. It seems that Maude and Grace both fell in love with the same man, a foreign music master their father brought to the house to give organ lessons. Maude secretly

married the man and gave birth to a daughter after being abandoned by her husband. The sisters and their father lived separate lives in the vast house, which emboldened Maude to hide her daughter in the east wing. Grace eventually discovered Maude's secret, and her jealousy led her to inform their father, who turned both Maude and the child out; the child died of exposure, and Maude went mad. It turns out that this terrible tale hides an even worse one, which Hester discovers one night through a ghostly reenactment: the father beat the child while driving her and Maude out, as Grace looked on "stony, and deadly serene." Grace suffers a stroke after witnessing this crime of her youth.

Even a greatly abbreviated summary of "The Old Nurse's Story" indicates some of its themes. Grace and Maude are destroyed by their failure to trust themselves or each other and by their reliance on and allegiance to men. In contrast, Hester saves herself through her faith in her own powers of interpretation and her belief in the efficacy of individual action, in this case an act of self-preservation that enables her then to protect Rosamond. Unlike conventional Gothic tales, in which the heroine is rescued by a man after being threatened by another man, this story includes an empowering conclusion that is based on maternal love and alliances among women. Like many female Gothics, this story is a domestic drama that conveys a severe critique of traditional family structure. The mothers are absent, dead, or powerless, while the fathers exert absolute control over their families. The source of the old lord's power over his daughters is not his money but his maleness, which is also the source of his economic power via primogeniture. The emptiness and corruption of patriarchal power are reflected in Hester's discovery that the ghostly organ, although it looks quite grand, is broken and destroyed inside. The absolute power of the father corrupts his daughters, prompting them to behave deviously. Both Grace and Maude accept dominant values instead of acting in accord with the implied values – especially love and preservation – that inform the story.

The issues of power and authority are inflected by both gender and class in "The Old Nurse's Story," as the narrator is both a woman and a servant. Hester's voice is one seldom heard in Victorian fiction – including Gaskell's, despite her abiding interest in class issues and her concern for the plight of the working class, especially working-class women. Even though she prominently features working-class characters in many of her novels and short stories, the text is usually controlled by a recognizably middle-class narrator, as in *Mary Barton* and "The Poor Clare." Among her personal narrators only two others are female – Mary of *Cranford* and Bridget of "Morton Hall" – while the rest are male, with "Cousin Phillis," "Mr. Harrison's Confessions," "Six Weeks at Heppenheim," "The Heart of John Middleton," and "The Poor Clare" – all stories about women – narrated by men. In Gaskell's work, then, the narrative sometimes undercuts the theme, since stories about the working class are mediated by middle-class narrators and stories about women are controlled by male voices. In choosing a working-class female narrator for "The Old Nurse's Story" Gaskell radically departed from her usual practice.

The major themes of "The Old Nurse's Story" recur in Gaskell's other Gothic stories, such as "The Poor Clare," and in some of her realistic fiction as well. "Lizzie Leigh," an early realistic story, includes two families structured along the same lines as the one presented in "The Old Nurse's Story." Like the Gothic tale, "Lizzie Leigh" also focuses on sexual sin and familial destruction. Even well-meaning fathers – such as Dr. Gibson and Squire Hamley, both of *Wives and Daughters* – can unwittingly blight their children's lives through misuse of their power. By the time she wrote "The Grey Woman" nine years later Gaskell had dispensed with the ghosts she so artfully raised in "The Old Nurse's Story" and shifted her attention from relationships between parents and children to the married couple. Again, though, the later story operates on several levels, with feminist themes hidden behind a Gothic thriller of a cover story.

In "The Grey Woman" the narrative structure reinforces the story's themes of women's enclosure in patriarchal marriage and their need to discover or to create alternative ways to live. Arthur Pollard and several other commentators complain about the story's leisurely introduction in which the narrator, an Englishwoman, visits a German mill with a friend and eventually is given a yellowed manuscript. This introduction, however, compresses the main themes of the actual story: this is a woman's story, written by one woman (Anna, the title's "grey woman"), addressed to a second woman (Ursula, Anna's adult daughter), and translated and introduced by two other women. The transfer of the papers to the English visitor takes place in a woman's private room, where the hostess knits as she talks with her women visitors. This community of women is invaded by a man with an important role to play, an event paralleled by the end of Anna's story. In the introduction the man is the miller, who enters, interrupts, and then dominates the conversation and eventually gives the narrator the papers, which he has hidden in a drawer. The miller's wife's paralysis symbolizes the position of women in traditional marriage, which is what Anna's letter concerns as well. The ordinariness, the normalcy, of the mill and the miller, emphasized in the story's opening paragraph, may seem a striking contrast to what the reader later learns about Anna's husband and his prison/manor, but Gaskell emphasizes their similarity. The miller and Anna's husband are variations of a single type, as are their homes; the suggestion is that Anna's husband and his manor are extreme but representative. The many details Gaskell includes in the introduction – important dates, for instance, and a sketch of the miller as kindly but obtuse – give resonance to the story that follows.

Anna's letter is a cautionary tale in which she warns her daughter against marriage by describing her own experience. The dashingly handsome man she married turned out to be the leader of a ruthless band of robbers and murderers, whom Anna escaped with the aid of her servant, Amante. Dressed as a man, an itinerant tailor, Amante rescued the pregnant Anna by having her masquerade as the tailor's wife. The two lived happily together in a parody of a conventional marriage, with Amante staying in her male disguise and working to support Anna and the daughter to whom she gave birth. Eventually, however, Amante is murdered by Anna's husband. Anna ended up marrying the young doctor who heard the women's story from Amante as she lay dying. The ending of "The Grey Woman" is extremely pessimistic, as it suggests that women cannot hope to escape the limited places assigned them by society.

Given the devastating critique of marriage and society in this story, it is surprising that critics ever described Gaskell's works as "charming" and "feminine." "The Grey Woman" offers no simple solutions to women's predicament; each option for living that Gaskell presents carries its own hardships, deprivations, and dangers. In this story she parallels the oppression of women of all classes with the oppression of the working classes through the use of such devices as historically significant dates, implying that all of society requires peaceful and orderly restructuring if it is to avoid the devastation of revolution. Several earlier Gaskell works focus on similar issues but in a far less complex and powerful way. *Mary Barton,* for instance, also emphasizes similarities between gender and class oppression but ends in a flight from the industrial world in which these issues are central to a land of pastoral innocence, where they are barely relevant – an unsatisfying conclusion that suggests Gaskell could not yet imagine an open ending in which her characters must go on struggling.

Like "The Grey Woman," "Cousin Phillis," also a later story, shows her strengths coming together. "Cousin Phillis" is perhaps Gaskell's most complex, subtle, and finely crafted treatment of her characteristic themes. Several critics have noted that Phillis represents the pastoral ideal; however, this is only part of the story. "Cousin Phillis" is about change, both personal and social. The pastoral world of Hope Farm is doomed, Gaskell shows: the railroad is being built near it, and the railroad's representative, Holdsworth, intrudes into the farm and ends Phillis's peaceful, protracted childhood by awakening her sexually. Every element of this story

carries multiple associations: the farm is the old rural England, the past, innocence, country, childhood, and family, while the railroad (and Holdsworth) are the new, industrial England, the future, experience, city, adulthood, and rootlessness. Phillis cannot remain the child of Hope Farm once Holdsworth enters her life, nor can she return to her peaceful past, however much she may desire it. Phillis's position is also representative of all women, as her parents' attempts to keep her childlike parallel society's expectations of women. Gaskell's telling of this story wonderfully embodies the process of change she depicts within it: it proceeds slowly, with changes almost imperceptible until they are irreversible. There can be no return to the past, for Phillis or for England; the only question is how one will manage to live in the changed world. The choice of narrator here is brilliant: Paul is Everyman, bewildered by the changes he witnesses, caught between the past and the present (he loves Hope Farm but works for the railroad), unsure of his own position, and often stumbling as he attempts to understand what is happening to his world. In choosing a male narrator to tell a woman's story Gaskell also underscores the psychological distance she perceives between men and women. The only other work in which she is so confident is *Wives and Daughters,* which is also about change and a woman's response to that change, and which was written at the same time as "Cousin Phillis."

The connection between "Cousin Phillis" and *Wives and Daughters* is closer than that of any other shorter works and novels by Gaskell. "Cousin Phillis" shows her working out a complex theme that becomes more diffuse in the novel. Generally, the connection between Gaskell's novels and her short stories is less direct – except perhaps in the case of "Mr. Harrison's Confessions" and *Cranford,* where the shorter piece seems to be a rehearsal for the infinitely better novel. Themes that are either minor or covert in the novels are often central and overt in the short fiction. Perhaps dealing more directly with taboo subjects such as female sexuality in the shorter works, particularly in her Gothic tales, helped Gaskell to clarify her ideas and enabled her then to work out these themes in a fashion more suitable to the realistic novel. This process sometimes worked in the opposite way as well, with a theme in a novel suggesting a topic for a short story, which may have been the case with *North and South* and "Half a Life-Time Ago" in terms of the issue of women's obligations to their families of origin. Similarly, the theme of the fallen woman is at

10. Mrs. Gaskell by Richmond, 1851

*Gaskell in 1851; portrait by George Richmond (National Portrait Gallery, London)*

the center of "Lizzie Leigh," written soon after the success of *Mary Barton*. It is as if Gaskell decided to give the novel's prostitute, Esther, her own story in "Lizzie Leigh," with a somewhat happier ending. The father's rage, the death of the child, and the psychological damage done to Grace by her secret guilt in "The Old Nurse's Story" find muted parallels in *Ruth: A Novel* (1853), written at about the same time, in the form of the congregation's fury at the deception practiced upon them, Ruth's eventual death, and the guilt the minister suffers for his lie. "A Dark Night's Work" is linked with *Sylvia's Lovers* (1863) through the themes of men's and women's unequal capacities for feeling and the effects of crime upon those who conceal it, but in the story these themes are more explicitly addressed than they are in the novel.

While not yet finished with *Wives and Daughters,* Gaskell died suddenly on 12 November 1865 during a visit to the house she was secretly purchasing in Hampshire as a retirement retreat for herself and her husband. She was buried in the Unitarian cemetery in Knutsford.

On some level all of Gaskell's writing is about power and powerlessness and addresses two cen-

tral questions: what effect does powerlessness have, and what does power mean to those who are denied it? Her female and some working-class male characters respond in a variety of ways to their lack of power in the world. Some try to gain power by exploiting their own powerlessness instead of making any attempt to overcome it. Others ally themselves with the powerful, gaining at least the illusion of power by abandoning personal authenticity. Many withdraw and attempt to establish limited control over their own lives by living apart from the wider society. A few openly rebel and are crushed. The most dangerous repress their rage until it finally explodes, out of control and potentially life-destroying. The best of Gaskell's stories expose the implications of one or more possible attitudes toward power and powerlessness, both for the women themselves and for the patriarchal society that encloses them.

Reading the short stories gives one a renewed appreciation for Gaskell's remarkable gifts as a storyteller and of her sophisticated understanding of psychology. The parallel she perceived and wrote about between the working classes and women of all classes is a profound insight into the social structure. Her greatest artistic achievement lies not in her sensitive treatment of rural themes, as many of her admirers conclude, but in her increasing skill in exploring the many complex issues of female development and the interrelationships of women's position in society and persistent social problems. Gaskell was ahead of most of her contemporaries in seeing women as a class, in the sense of a definable group with certain shared experiences that differ from those of the dominant group. Her stories have much to teach readers about human nature in general and about the varieties of response possible to a lack of power in particular, a concern that remains today.

Several recent critical works — the best being Patsy Stoneman's *Elizabeth Gaskell* (1987) — focus on Gaskell as a woman writer, examining her work in the context of a tradition of women's writing. This interest may seem to take her critical fortunes full circle, but there are crucial distinctions between early attention to Gaskell's gender and contemporary perspectives. Most important, feminist critics do not treat Gaskell's gender or her interest in women's lives as limitations on her artistry. Recent feminist interest, following three decades of renewed attention to Gaskell's work signaled by the publication of her letters and of several biographies and critical analyses, may finally lead to a reassessment of Gaskell's rightful place in literary history.

**Letters:**

*The Letters of Mrs. Gaskell and Charles Eliot Norton: 1855–1865,* edited by Jane Revere Whitehill (London: Humphrey Milford, Oxford University Press, 1932);

*The Letters of Mrs. Gaskell,* edited by J. A. V. Chapple and Arthur Pollard (Manchester: Manchester University Press, 1966);

*Elizabeth Gaskell: A Portrait in Letters,* edited by Chapple (Manchester: Manchester University Press, 1980).

**Bibliographies:**

R. L. Selig, *Elizabeth Gaskell: A Reference Guide* (Boston: G. K. Hall, 1977);

Jeffrey Welch, *Elizabeth Gaskell: An Annotated Bibliography, 1929–75* (New York: Garland, 1977).

**Biographies:**

Mrs. Ellis H. Chadwick, *Mrs. Gaskell: Haunts, Homes and Stories* (London: Pitman, 1910);

Elizabeth Haldane, *Mrs. Gaskell and Her Friends* (London: Hodder & Stoughton, 1931);

Annette Brown Hopkins, *Elizabeth Gaskell: Her Life and Work* (London: Lehmann, 1952; New York: Octagon, 1971);

Arthur Pollard, *Mrs. Gaskell: Novelist and Biographer* (Manchester: Manchester University Press, 1966);

Winifred Gérin, *Elizabeth Gaskell: A Biography* (Oxford: Clarendon Press, 1976);

Jenny Uglow, *Elizabeth Gaskell: A Habit of Stories* (London: Faber & Faber, 1993).

**References:**

Tessa Brodetsky, *Elizabeth Gaskell* (Oxford: Oxford University Press, 1986);

Lord David Cecil, *Early Victorian Novelists* (London: Constable, 1934);

W. A. Craik, *Elizabeth Gaskell and the English Provincial Novel* (London: Methuen, 1975);

Enid L. Duthie, *The Themes of Elizabeth Gaskell* (London: Macmillan, 1980);

Angus Easson, *Elizabeth Gaskell* (London: Routledge & Kegan Paul, 1979);

Margaret Ganz, *Elizabeth Gaskell: The Artist in Conflict* (New York: Twayne, 1969);

Margaret Homans, *Bearing the Word: Language and Female Experience in Nineteenth-Century Women's Writing* (Chicago: University of Chicago Press, 1986);

Coral Lansbury, *Elizabeth Gaskell: The Novel of Social Crisis* (London: Elek, 1975; New York: Barnes & Noble, 1975);

John Geoffrey Sharps, *Mrs. Gaskell's Observation and Invention: A Study of the Non-Biographic Works* (London: Linden Press, 1970);

Jane Spencer, *Elizabeth Gaskell* (New York: St. Martin's Press, 1993);

Patsy Stoneman, *Elizabeth Gaskell* (Bloomington: Indiana University Press, 1987);

Edgar Wright, *Mrs. Gaskell: The Basis for Reassessment* (London: Oxford University Press, 1965).

**Papers:**

The Brotherton Collection at Leeds University Library is a major repository of Elizabeth Cleghorn Gaskell's documents and letters. Other important collections are in Manchester, U.K., at the Manchester University Library, the Central Library, and the John Rylands Library. Harvard University and Princeton University also hold Gaskell materials.

# Gerald Griffin

## (12 December 1803 – 12 June 1840)

### Richard D. McGhee
*Arkansas State University*

BOOKS: *"Holland-Tide": or, Munster Popular Tales,* anonymous (London: Simpkin & Marshall, 1827);

*Tales of the Munster Festivals,* anonymous (3 volumes, London: Saunders & Otley, 1827; 4 volumes, New York: Sadlier, 1868);

*The Collegians: A Tale of Garryowen,* anonymous (3 volumes, London: Saunders & Otley, 1829; 2 volumes, New York: Harper, 1829); republished as *The Collegians: A Novel* (Philadelphia: Gihon, 1854?); republished as *The Collegians; or, The Colleen Bawn: A Tale of Garryowen,* by Gerald Griffin (London: Routledge, Warne & Routledge, 1861; New York: Century, 1906); republished as *The Colleen Bawn; or, The Collegian's Wife: A Tale of Garryowen* (London: G. Vickers, 1861); republished as *The Colleen Bawn: A Tale of Garryowen* (New York: Beadle & Adams, 1881); republished as *The Colleen Bawn; or, The Collegians: A Tale of Garryowen* (New York: Munro, 1881);

*The Rivals; Tracy's Ambition,* anonymous (3 volumes, London: Saunders & Otley, 1829; 2 volumes, New York: Harper, 1830);

*The Christian Physiologist: Tales Illustrative of the Five Senses,* anonymous (London: Bull, 1830); republished as *The Offering of Friendship; or, Tales of the Five Senses,* as Griffin (Dublin: Duffy, 1854); republished as *The Christian Physiologist* (New York: Sadlier, 1885);

*The Invasion,* anonymous (4 volumes, London: Saunders & Otley, 1832; 1 volume, New York: Sadlier, 183?);

*Tales of My Neighbourhood,* anonymous (3 volumes, London: Saunders & Otley, 1835; 2 volumes, Philadelphia: Carey, Lea & Blanchard, 1836);

*The Duke of Monmouth* (3 volumes, London: Bentley, 1836; 2 volumes, Philadelphia: Carey & Hart, 1837); republished as *The Duke of Monmouth: An Historical Romance,* 3 volumes (London: Bentley, 1841);

*Talis Qualis; or, Tales of the Jury Room* (3 volumes, London: Maxwell, 1842; 1 volume, New York: Sadlier, 1885);

*Gisippus: A Play in Five Acts, as Performed at Drury Lane* (London: Maxwell, 1842); republished as *Gisippus; or, The Forgotten Friend: A Play in Five Acts, as Performed at Drury Lane* (London: Maxwell, 1842); republished as *Gisippus; or, The Forgotten Friend: A Play in Five Acts* (New York: Douglas, 1848);

*Adventures of an Irish Giant* (Boston: Donahoe, 1854?);

*Poems* (Dublin: O'Connell Press, 1886).

**Editions:** *The Life and Works of Gerald Griffin* (8 volumes, London: Maxwell, 1842–1843; 10 volumes, New York: Sadlier, 1857);

*Poetical Works* (London: Simpkin & Marshall, 1843);

*The Poetical Works of Gerald Griffin* (London: Simms & M'Intyre, 1851);

*The Poetical and Dramatic Works of Gerald Griffin* (Dublin: Duffy, 1857);

*The Complete Works of Gerald Griffin,* 10 volumes (New York: Sadlier, 1868).

Gerald Griffin was one of modern Ireland's most popular authors of the early nineteenth century. Having sought and failed to find fame in London as a dramatist, he recognized in his friend John Banim's success the potential for stories and novels about life in Ireland. Indeed, Griffin may have emulated John and Michael Banim in many respects, such as in his initial interest in drama. But Griffin's work was never imitative nor derivative, however much the Banims' example stirred him to write. The greatest examples of success, for most writers of the era, were Walter Scott and, in Ireland, Maria Edgeworth. For regional writers examining the lives and characters of Irish peasants as well as those of higher society, however, the growing reputation of William Carleton provided encouragement and inspiration. Griffin held his own with all these, and sometimes his work was superior.

*Gerald Griffin in 1830; portrait by F. W. Wilkin (Christian
Brothers monastery, Dublin)*

Although his first two collections of short fiction were financially and critically successful, Griffin's contemporary fame was determined by the wildly popular reception of his novel *The Collegians* in 1829. This romance of sexual passion and violence was the basis for dramatic and operatic productions, and it derived from a newspaper account of a sensational crime that had occurred in Griffin's own Munster. With the exception of *The Collegians,* however, the work of Griffin has failed to hold the attention of twentieth-century critics and readers. Instead, Griffin's enduring fame has come from his short fiction, works of power and entertainment.

He could describe well the landscape he knew along the estuary of the Shannon, from bog lands to mountains, and he could capture the speech rhythms of his native Munster neighbors. His stories could provide psychoanalytical analysis of character or they could relate exciting and sometimes violent actions of mobs and armies. As an artist he experimented with narrative structure, point of view, and mixed tones, and he wrote in various genres. When he failed, especially in his later writing, he was likely to have deliberately subordinated his art to his message. Few stories, however, have more appeal than Griffin's "Suil Dhuv the Coiner" (1827)

or "Tracy's Ambition" (1829), two of his many during a short life and shorter writing career.

Griffin was born in Limerick on 12 December 1803, the last of nine sons and six daughters of Patrick Griffin, the son of a Limerick country gentleman, who managed a brewery at the time of Griffin's birth, and Ellen Geary Griffin, the sister of a leading Limerick physician. In 1810 the family moved to Fairy Lawn, a house on the Shannon estuary, and in 1820 the eldest son persuaded some of the family, including the parents, to immigrate to Pennsylvania. Griffin remained behind with two brothers, William and Daniel, and three sisters, Ellen, Lucy, and Anne. The six moved from Fairy Lawn to a house in the village of Adare, near Limerick. In a letter to his mother in 1822 Griffin expressed his desire to be with his American family: "I am so weary of the dull, unprofitable, good-for-nothing sort of life I have been leading for some time back, that I should feel great pleasure were I at this very instant scrambling out of one of the small boats upon Market street wharf, in the city of quakers."

In spite of such feelings, Griffin was an enthusiastic reader of newspaper reviews written under the signature of "A Traveller," and he met their writer, John Banim, while participating in a Limerick theatrical society. Griffin persuaded the editor of the Limerick *Advertiser* to accept some of his own writing, and soon he was regularly published, especially after he had pleased readers with his sketch of Richard Colley, Marquess of Wellesley, then lord lieutenant of Ireland. After Griffin read favorable reviews of Banim's play *Damon and Pythias,* which was produced in London in May 1821, in 1822 he tried his skill at writing a drama, which he called "Aguire." The manuscript has not survived, but both William Griffin and John Banim were favorably impressed with this first effort.

William agreed to support Gerald's trip to London in 1823 to find a producer for his plays. But "Aguire" was rejected without comment, and Griffin needed to earn a living. He sought employment as a court reporter, but he still had no work in February 1824. Banim urged him to begin another play, and Griffin did, calling it *Gisippus* (eventually published in 1842). Soon he met Valentine Llanos, a Spaniard who had married John Keats's sister and who gave him some work as a translator. He finished *Gisippus,* but even with Banim's help Griffin did not find a producer. Desperate for income, he wrote pieces for various magazines, including the *Literary Gazette* and the *News of Literature and Fashion.*

Writing from London to his parents to explain a long silence in 1825, Gerald described his disappointments and desperation. He laughed at himself for wanting to revolutionize "the dramatic taste of the time by writing for the stage," but by failing to place his drama, he suffered despair and self-contempt. "I before imagined I could do any thing; now I thought I could do nothing. One supposition was just as foolish as the other. . . . I now lost heart for every thing." Feeling guilty and ashamed that he had failed himself and his family, Griffin withdrew from all social contact. "The fact was," he confessed, "from pure anxiety alone I was more than half dead." Griffin asked his mother to write him a long letter and expressed his continuing hope of joining them someday in America, "as soon as the despotism of circumstances will allow it."

John Banim sought him out and helped him find employment, and Gerald thus eked out a living from 1823 to 1826 – working at the job he had originally sought, reporting proceedings of the House of Commons. It was also during these years that he began writing the prose fiction which would become *"Holland-Tide": or, Munster Popular Tales.* He flirted with opera, but increasingly turned his writing talent to prose narratives, which he was again encouraged to do by the example of John Banim. John and

Michael Banim's "O'Hara Tales" (collected as *Tales by the O'Hara Family,* 1825–1827) were published during the last years of Griffin's first London residence, and he found the English audience enjoyed reading stories of Ireland in prose.

In June 1825 Griffin wrote his brother William in praise of Banim's "O'Hara Tales," which he called "vigorous and original things; overflowing with the very spirit of poetry, passion, and painting." In his friend's tales Griffin particularly admired "the power of creating an intense interest without stepping out of real life." William Griffin arrived to visit his brother in London in early September 1826, and he found his young brother in bad health, thin and weak. Nevertheless, Gerald was able to pursue his work of reporting and reviewing with some energy and regularity, and while William was still in London, Gerald completed his own collection of stories for *"Holland-Tide": or, Munster Popular Tales.* He succeeded in finding a publisher, to whom he sold the copyright of them just before leaving London to return home to Ireland with his brother at the end of January 1827.

*"Holland-Tide"* is a series of seven stories told on All Hallows' Eve at a harvesttime party in Munster. Some are Halloween tales with ghosts and goblins, such as "Saint Martin's Day," "The Brown Man," "The Unburied Legs," and "Persecutions of Jack Edy." Two stories, however, bear the distinctive marks of Griffin's narrative style and interests. "The Hand and Word" tells the story of Charlie Moran and Ellen Sparling, lovers who are separated when he is forced into military duty and then murdered by evil Yamon Dhuv. Similarly, "The Aylmers of Bally-Aylmer" is about young lovers confronting a violent and mysterious fate on the dreary bog lands of Dingle Bay in County Kerry. Young Aylmer's return to his home from Dublin provides the narrative frame for delving into the past, which looms threateningly in his life. Smuggling and murder are found, and suspicion rises that Aylmer's own guardian has been the killer of his father. A closing trial scene provides sensational clarifications and a melodramatic denouement, when Aylmer's father returns and clears the name of young Aylmer's guardian and father of his beloved Katharine. In this, as in all the *"Holland-Tide"* stories, Griffin expressed his personal desolation and tragic dislocation in London. Families divided and sometimes reunited provided Griffin with some emotional relief from his own anguish by writing it out in such tales.

Seeking to reconcile himself with John Banim, who may have inadvertently and innocently offended Griffin through his persistent efforts to help his young and impoverished countryman seeking success in London, Gerald wrote several letters to which Banim did not reply until November 1827. A lively correspondence between the two then followed, during which Gerald reported that he had regained his religious faith after reading works by William Paley and others, and he described his excitement upon hearing political speeches of Banim's friend Richard L. Sheil during the Clare election of 1828. These political events were important in developing the career of Daniel O'Connell and the evolution of Catholic Emancipation. In August 1827 Gerald went again to London to arrange for publication of *Tales of the Munster Festivals* (1827), copies of which he sent to John Banim. Banim wrote in April 1828 to congratulate him "on the talents they [the *Tales*] display, as well as the success they have met with. That you thus at last triumph in a great degree, as I hope, over the neglects and annoyances of your first residence in London, is to me a matter of some triumph."

Reviews of *"Holland-Tide"* were generally favorable, encouraging Griffin to complete the stories for *Tales of the Munster Festivals*. Daniel Griffin says in his *Life of Gerald Griffin* that the title of this second collection "had its origin in the design to include in every tale, a description of some one of those festivals which are celebrated by some traditional ceremony in the south of Ireland." Furthermore, says Daniel, "at this time [Gerald] looked upon works of fiction as a most powerful engine, for giving a healthy tone to public morals, and he spoke with deep sensitiveness of the multitudes of young creatures who are daily sent to ruin in London, by the impassioned feeling, and sickly sentimental garbage placed before them in the shape of novels, by a certain class of publishers. If it was possible to replace these by writings of a healthy tone, he though it would effect an enormous amount of good." One effect of Gerald's reinvigorated religious convictions was that he intended his stories to "be *Catholic* tales," as Daniel reports. "They must represent the Catholic religion as it really exists among the clergy and the people, and not give such caricatures of it, as are too commonly found in most of the writings of the day."

*Tales of the Munster Festivals* contained a preface, an introduction, and three narratives – "Card Drawing," "The Half-Sir," and "Suil Dhuv The Coiner." The introduction creates a fictional setting for discoursing on the aims of fiction, as if Griffin were uneasy about his calling. He puts his narrator into a debate with an old man who claims novels

cannot help the miseries of the real world, but if they must be written they should include the light of life as well as its darkness. The narrator, however, holds that stories should narrate realities – "strong truth," though dark and unflattering to his countrymen.

The realism of these tales is in the details of speech and in the attention to setting, as in the earlier *"Holland-Tide"* stories. However, a realism of character also begins to emerge, as motivations are examined to explain the violence and passion of life in the Irish countryside of Griffin's memory and imagination. Again there is a story of rescue for a man falsely convicted of murder, and again the center of the narrative is that of sexual passion exploding in destructive violence. "Card Drawing" turns upon a superstitious belief that an old woman can predict the future from reading cards drawn by her client. The sailor Duke Dorgan, who fought with Horatio, Viscount Nelson at Trafalgar, returns to his home along the mouth of the Shannon, where he is met by a man who had hoped to profit from Dorgan's absence, one sly and sinister Price Kinchela. This villain has courted Pennie McLoughlen as the prize he would get while Dorgan has been out "to *say*." The narrative recounts how Dorgan and Kinchela had grown up together, gone to the same hedge school, and sought the love of the same girl. She had preferred the open, though wild, Dorgan, but her father had refused to allow their courtship.

Kinchela pretends to welcome Dorgan's return and reconcile their differences. Dorgan hopes his long absence and good fortune will win over Pennie's father, but as he walks toward their cottage he is accosted by the old woman who tells his fortune of death by hanging, and he soon discovers that Pennie's father has been murdered. Just as he is about to be hanged for the deed, Kinchela confesses and Dorgan wins Pennie's love in the end. Although Griffin's narrator denies any correlation between the people of his home region and the perfidious violence of night gangs in other regions of Ireland, Griffin's villain does murder his victim while "disguised" with blackened face like that of a member of such gangs as the Raparees and Whiteboys of the time.

The second story, "The Half-Sir," explores the difficulties of Eugene Hamond, who is sensitive to social slights. At the opening of the narrative Hamond is discovered in his deteriorating mansion, where he has returned after many years in mysterious exile. He is summoned by his servant Remmy O'Lone to respond to the visit of the Wren-boys, celebrating Saint Stephen's Day, one of the Munster Festivals in "Shanagolden, a small village in the south-west of Ireland. [They] were all assembled pursuant to custom on the green before the chapel-door, on a fine frosty morning, being the twenty-sixth of December." Despite Hamond's charitable service to the sick and poor during a recent epidemic, the boys mock him for his uncertain ancestry and precarious social status, and Hamond scorns them in return. The story then presents a flashback to explain Hamond's present spiritual decadence.

Years ago Hamond had courted Emily Bury and hoped to marry her, although he was merely a "half-sir" – a young man whose humble origins a wealthy relative had enhanced by providing him with wealth and an education that had lifted him out of the social class into which he had been born. She had not appreciated his sensitivity to social slights, and when she had insulted him, he had broken off their relationship. Realizing her error Emily had written to apologize but sent her letter by Remmy, who had managed to lose it and thereby turn the romance into a tragedy of missed communication. Hamond had gone into exile; Emily had married another, and years had passed before Hamond's return to Munster. By then Emily's marriage has failed, and Hamond, who has thought her dead, joyfully renews his courtship and eventually marries her. While the story's plot of divided lovers is a familiar one from Griffin, its social analysis and insight into psychological fragility are new and deepening qualities in his fiction.

Griffin's narrator assures his readers that he prefers to dwell on events that provide "the illustration of national character – that being the principal design of these volumes." That Griffin can do best when he writes of his "own Munster," a part of Ireland not yet developed by contemporary writers such as the Banims, those "vigorous hands that penned the O'Hara Tales." In a mechanically awkward conclusion to the romance of his hero and heroine, Griffin puts into Emily's mouth a moral to "advise our neighbors to take warning by our tale." She asserts that "they can be all that true Irish men and women ought to be; that they may retain Irish spirit – Irish worth – and Irish honor, in all their force, without suffering their hearts to be warped and tainted by the vapors of IRISH PRIDE." Earlier, while describing Hamond's sulking departure from Ireland, Griffin has imagined him as "leaving a land, which was, and was not, his home – and where he had filled a nameless place in society, without stamp or station – possessing claims to var-

ious conditions, and properly belonging to none." This also records a truth of the "national character," particularly of Griffin's own, as he realized during the miserable time he spent in London.

But his genius overcomes his moralizing bent, as he lets the tale of "The Half-Sir" be completed by Remmy O'Lone in a dialogue with Emily after her happy marriage to Hamond. Remmy insists, against Emily's moralizing, that Irish "women o' the lower order" are no angels: "'Angels, ershishin?'" said Remmy, with a toss of the head, "'Ay – angels like them that they put upon hearses – all head an wings – with gingerbread gilding – an death under – an sorrow after 'em. That's all the angels I can see in 'em!'" Remmy, unlike Hamond, is not captive to romantic fictions.

In the better-known story "Suil Dhuv the Coiner" Griffin subordinated the romantic fiction of separated lovers to a powerful tale of contempt for law and dark passion in the union of the outlaw Suil Dhuv with Sarah Segur. While this is the longest of the three narratives, it is unified and richly textured. Unity is achieved through compressing the events of "Suil Dhuv the Coiner" into a single day – one of the Munster festivals, the Feast of St. John's Eve (Eha na Shawn) – when the traditional bonfires create an eerie and diabolical background for the exciting climax.

Suil Dhuv is the leader of an outlaw band in the mountains of Munster. He is also Mark Spellacy, who runs an inn with his wife and has also been known as Dinny M'Namara. Before learning more about this man of many names, the reader is introduced to a group of men riding toward the inn, a group led by Isaac Segur, one of the planters brought from Europe to settle Ireland at the opening of the eighteenth century. After several years abroad Segur is returning to his Irish home, where he hopes to find out why his daughter has stopped writing him. In fact his daughter has disappeared with Dinny M'Namara, a boy who once worked for Segur but left when Segur saw Dinny as a threat to his daughter's virtue. For many reasons Dinny M'Namara became an outlaw known as Suil Dhuv, "The Dark-Eyed One."

On the day of the story Suil Dhuv plans to kidnap a woman, rob the guests at his inn, and steal sacred objects from a church. All these plans culminate in two events of great psychological excitement. In the first, Isaac Segur almost recognizes his long-lost daughter in the mad woman at the inn, but he refuses to do so; saying to her instead: "I have looked over all your person, and am satisfied that you are not my daughter – but I'm afraid I'll find it hard to forgive you the shock you caused me. – Go along, you wicked woman, it was a shame for you!" In the second event Suil Dhuv draws down the wrath of God when he steals a holy chalice, and in kidnapping Lilly Byrne he dies after he is shot by Segur. This occurs as the bonfires are lighting up the mountains, and Suil Dhuv, like a devil in hell, cries out, "Look at all the fires breaking through the earth." He does not surrender his diabolical will and yield to a punishing conscience. He dies defiantly, at once satanic outlaw and romantic hero.

Apart from the loss of their sister Ellen, who died at this time, the Griffins enjoyed life at Pallaskenry. Gerald completed his *Munster* tales and began *The Collegians,* and he read the poetry of Scott, Thomas Campbell, and George Gordon, Lord Byron with much enthusiasm, sometimes inspired to compose poems of his own. In London with Daniel to arrange for publication of his first novel, Gerald took the manuscript for one and a half volumes of *The Collegians* and immediately began regular composition on a daily schedule that produced copy for his publishers every day. *The Collegians* was finished at the end of 1828, and its publication earned some £8,000, which Gerald sent to his family in America. This novel made Gerald Griffin famous: Dion Boucicault turned it into a popular drama, *The Colleen Bawn* (1860?), and it provided the basis for an opera called *The Lily of Killarney* (1862). Griffin actually conceived many of the scenes for the novel as if they were dramatic spectacles, and so such stage productions were easily derived from it.

Social status, kidnappings, murder, thwarted romance, flight and pursuit, trial, and confession and punishment – are the concerns of Griffin's fiction, variously used in the stories of his first two published works. He brought all these elements together in his most successful fiction, the long novel *The Collegians.* This is the story of Hardress Cregan's elopement with Eily O'Connor, his courtship of Anne Chute, his betrayal of Eily and his friend Kyrle Daly, and finally his complicity in Eily's murder by the man he had most wronged in the world, sinister humpbacked henchman Danny Mann. The plot was taken from a murder trial in 1820 near Griffin's home; some have said Griffin had reported the trial for a local newspaper, but it is most unlikely. Perhaps the events had been the source for many of Griffin's earlier tales, but he did not need a particular and historical sensation to fuel his imagination. Griffin drew from his own distress sufficient material for his imagination to transmute, although he had not yet suffered the most significant passion that his fiction had portrayed – the

sexual passion of romantic love. This experience soon came, perhaps in part because of his success with *The Collegians.*

He met James and Lydia Fisher in 1829. They knew of his literary fame, and he was attracted to them by their interest in him as well as by Lydia's literary mother. In the course of a few weeks Griffin fell in love with this Quaker wife and mother, to whom he wrote several enthusiastic letters that did nothing to conceal his infatuation, even though he knew James Fisher was also reading them. Soon after their meeting he wrote to her as "my sweet and bright-eyed lady." Quoting from his own character of Gisippus, he called on Lydia to reassure him that she cared for him: "What could I do that would be worth the least of your attention?" he asked, and then he exclaimed, "Would I not sing (if the spirit were in me) until the swan feathers sprouted from my fingers' ends for a single hour of such a day as the Sunday you speak of." Such intense feeling was not unexpected from a young man who hungered for the kind of passionate romance and friendship he missed in life and imagined in fiction. However, it was a relationship doomed by his religious scruples and her marital fidelity.

Despite his literary successes Griffin felt financially insecure about his income from the vocation of fiction writing. He had already discovered this in his ambitious attempt to conquer the London theater. Now, to ensure some security he enrolled as a law student at London University while he was in the city to publish *The Collegians.* As if he were not busy enough, he took up the study of ancient Irish history, which would become the basis for his later novel, *The Invasion,* in 1832. First, however, he had two more short pieces of fiction to publish, "The Rivals" and "Tracy's Ambition," which appeared in 1829, the same year as *The Collegians.* The title of "The Rivals" presents a common theme, that of two men competing for the love of the same woman. It had been central to both "Card Drawing" and *The Collegians,* but it was becoming critical as well in Griffin's own life, as he found himself in love with another man's wife.

Although few have praised "The Rivals," partly because it turns upon such an impossible event as a resurrection from death by the heroine, the story contains a much-admired chapter describing a hedge-school scene at Glendalough in County Wicklow. In this scene boys are made to translate verses from Virgil's *Aeneid* under the direction of the schoolmaster's assistant, who guides them well: "Now, boys, observe the beauty o' the poet. There's great nature in the picture of the boy Ascanius. Just

*The Christian Brothers monastery on North Richmond Street, Dublin, which Griffin entered in 1838*

the same way as we see young Misther Keiley, of the Grove, at the fox chase the other day, batin' the whole of 'em, right an' left, *jamque hos, jamque illos,* and now Misther Cleary, an' now Captain Davis, he outsthripped in his coorse. A beautiful picture, boys, there is in them four lines of a fine high-blooded youth. See; people are always the same; times an' manners change, but the heart o' man is the same now as it was in the days of Augustus." After the heroine's grave is later emptied by the hero, there is a special resonance in the classical allusions employed by a group of medical students visiting the cemetery "on professional business." These are well-executed episodes of comic, insightful vision from a man well aware of classical virtues in romantic fiction and increasingly anxious that he maintain his virtue through his affair with Lydia Fisher.

A clear note is struck in the religious differences that separate the rivals of this story, the Protestant Richard Lacy and the Catholic Francis Riordan. The realities of Griffin's time and place were forcing him to examine prospects for peace after the Catholic Emancipation, toward which O'Connell's victory in Clare was leading. But this story and others do not suggest that Griffin was optimistic, however much he wished to be. The "rivals" are religious ideas more than they are credible characters. Both men pursue Esther Wildermin, of Protestant family but fiercely patriotic, and her resurrection is both a medical miracle and a religious

necessity. As a symbol it is an interesting attempt to merge Griffin's nationalism, religion, and emotional ideals, but there is more faith than reason in this experiment, which may have aimed to challenge William Carleton, whose "Lough Dearg Pilgrim" is alluded to in the story, just as Griffin's earlier stories had been written to challenge the Banims.

More often admired than "The Rivals" is its companion story, "Tracy's Ambition," which is admired for Griffin's experiment with point of view. The tale is told by its main character, who analyzes his ambitions without fully understanding just how ambitious he really is. Putting his story in the words of a Protestant who has married the Catholic Mary Regan, Griffin once again examines Catholic and Protestant perspectives in his country. Abel Tracy had found difficulties of adjustment in his marriage, though they are as much from social as from religious differences he has with his wife's family. Tracy is trapped by his generosity and by his ambition, because he loans money to the Ascendancy magistrate, Dalton, and he then seeks office as compensation for the loan. The power of office seduces Tracy's judgment and makes him the target of peasant anger. Tracy's wife and Dalton's son are murdered by Whiteboys, feuding gangs from Kerry that are led by the Shanahan brothers, whose father was a victim of parricide. The violence and bloodshed are familiar to readers of Griffin, but the self-analysis and ironic detachment are pleasing novelties. Together these features narrate well Griffin's imaginative understanding of the social and religious realities in Ireland. He tries sympathetic imagination as a source of tolerance, but he produces a grimly ironic picture of political failures and personal disasters.

After these stories Griffin spent much of his time traveling, some of it with the Fishers. He accompanied his brother Daniel on an embassy to ask the poet Thomas Moore to stand for election to Parliament from Limerick. Though this political mission failed, Griffin felt elated by the meeting and praised the poet in his correspondence with Lydia. In 1830 he published a collection of moral anecdotes under the title of *The Christian Physiologist*. These tales for children were intended to illustrate moral precepts through analogies with the physiological functions of the five senses. For sight there was "The Kelp Gatherer"; for hearing, "The Day of the Trial"; and for feeling, "The Voluptuary Cured." Smell was illustrated with "The Self-Consumed," and "The Selfish Crotarie" (a crotarie was a harper) illustrated taste. These moral tales depend on strange and sometimes forced analogies that are supposed to be integrated by the power of intellect, illustrated by the allegorical closing tale, titled "A Story of Psyche."

In their didactic design these stories indicate Griffin's growing discontent with his vocation as a writer of fiction. He began increasingly to doubt himself and his direction in life. He told brothers William and Daniel that their work as doctors made him feel useless in what he did: "Here am I spending my whole life in the composition of these trashy tales and novels, that do no good either to myself or anybody else." This self-deprecation was taking its toll on Griffin's art, driving him away from imaginative strength and versatility and toward religious rectitude and moral righteousness. Teaching became more important to him than entertainment, and his stories and novels suffered while his spirit grew calm. *The Christian Physiologist* became an apology for his earlier writings, which he feared may have been damaging to public morals. Thus, the stories of this collection were intended to save his young readers from abandoning their spiritual welfare to the faulty senses of a fallen nature. Characters learn to submit to spiritual law and experience improvements in sensation as their rewards, or, as in "The Voluptuary Cured," they turn from natural pleasure to social duty and its higher spiritual rewards. Some of these stories, including "The Selfish Crotarie," reflect Griffin's interest in the history of Ireland, which provided the setting for his novel *The Invasion*. Yet this interest is more ornamental than substantial, for details of his research into Vik-

ing life are used to render improbable events with scholarly authority. The allegorical tale of Psyche that concludes the collection is virtually a farewell to Imagination, as the soul finds salvation through Christian self-denial.

Nevertheless, Griffin had spent years researching and then writing *The Invasion,* with its story of rivals for love set in the eighth century, when the Vikings invaded Ireland. This novel was to provide his historical explanation for the complicated fabric of contemporary Irish life and culture. He had admired and perhaps envied John Banim's historical romance *The Boyne Water* (1826), and Griffin, though depicting a much earlier time in Irish history, once again worked to compete with his friend by writing in a similar genre. Echoing Griffin's earlier characters and themes, the story pits Elim, the Saxon, against his school friend Kenric, the Celt. While these rivals appear in an ancient time, they have characters and concerns much like those of such figures as Richard Lacy and Francis Riordan, Kyrle Daly and Hardress Cregan, and Price Kinchela and Duke Dorgan from Griffin's previous tales. After a quarrel with his chief, Kenric joins the Vikings and saves Eithne, the girl loved by both Elim and Kenric, from his Viking allies. Kenric dies of illness, his mind greatly disturbed, and leaves Elim free to marry Eithne.

Much of Griffin's own situation is expressed in the story of Kenric, because Griffin was preparing for one of the most important decisions in his life even as he published *The Invasion* in 1832. He wrote to his father early in 1833 to describe this decision long in the making: "I have, however, no longer any doubt that it is my duty to devote myself to religion – to the saving my own soul, and the souls of others. . . . To say that Gerald, the novelwriter, is, by the grace of God, really satisfied to lay aside for ever all hope of that fame for which he was once sacrificing health, repose, and pleasure, and to offer himself as a labourer in the vineyard of Jesus Christ; that literary reputation has become a worthless trifle to him, to whom it once was almost all; and that he feels a happiness in the thought of giving all to God – is such a merciful favour, that all the fame and riches in the world dwindle into nothing at the thought of it." On the threshold of his removal to a life devoted to the church, Griffin was, like Kenric, doing the only thing he knew to save himself from further courtship of Lydia, in competition with her husband, James.

He had more stories to tell and to publish, however, and fourteen were collected under the title *Tales of My Neighbourhood* (1835). These included the comic tales of "Sir Dowling O'Hartigan" and "The Village Ruin," both set in the time of *The Invasion,* and satiric treatments of Irish life in "The Philanthropist," "The Blackbirds and Yellow Hammers," and "Mount Orient." More good humor characterizes the way a naive merchant is tricked and mocked by his social betters at a dinner with Lord Peppercorn in "The Great House." As with *Tracy's Ambition,* the story of "The Great House" works ironically because it is told by the victim himself. But not all these stories are comical good fun – as in "A Night at Sea," which tells how a father pays heavily for poor theories of education, or as in "The Force of Conscience" and "The Sun-Stroke," which narrate the familiar events of violence, murder, and mistaken identity so often found in Griffin's fiction.

For example, one of the more popular of these stories, "The Barber of Bantry," includes the murder of a tax collector, despair, family deterioration, and mistaken accusations of guilt. The story is aesthetically challenging because its point of view changes midway and produces confusion about the relationship of part one with part two. A melodramatic device of sleepwalking is combined with superstition to describe a disturbance of mind in the Barber, whose moral guilt is confused with legal guilt until the denouement. Griffin was determined to communicate the agonies and embarrassments caused by deep social, religious, and political divisions that grew out of long ages of Irish history. The artist in Griffin did not surrender to the moralist so easily as he might have wished, because there is entertainment as well as instruction in several of these tales.

Consciously intended or not, competition with the Banims drove Griffin to write his last piece of fiction, the long historical romance *The Duke of Monmouth* (1836), set in 1685 and based upon a melodramatic plot of sexual betrayal and base passions. An English officer forces the heroine, Aquila Fullerton, into sexual submission and then refuses to complete the bargain he made with her to free her brother. This plot has some historical basis, and both Griffin and John Banim recognized its fictional possibilities. In the historical events Kirke, the Englishman, was even more base than he appears in Griffin's story, because the actual Kirke had executed the brother, a fact not admissible to Griffin's more tender imagination.

After a three-week tour of Scotland with his brother Daniel, Griffin was ready to make his most important decision – to commit himself to his church. He burned his manuscripts and wrote a letter of farewell to Lydia Fisher on 6 September 1838,

the evening before he departed for the Christian Brothers teaching order in Dublin. This order, which Griffin entered in 1838, had been founded in 1808 with an educational mission that attracted Griffin, whose work had become increasingly didactic. While in Dublin he taught in the O'Connell Schools and then in the summer of 1839 transferred to a monastery in Cork. There he taught school until, on 12 June 1840, he died from typhus.

He left in manuscript an unfinished novel, *Adventures of an Irish Giant* (1854?), and an unfinished story, "The Holy Island," set in the period of early Christian settlements in Ireland. Shortly after his death another collection of stories, *Talis Qualis; or, Tales of the Jury Room* was published in 1842, the same year in which William Macready finally produced Griffin's drama *Gisippus.* One of the tales, "Sir Dowling O'Hartigan," had already been published in *Tales of My Neighbourhood,* but the others were new – though there is some doubt that Griffin authored all of them. They were arranged as tales told by members of a jury during a night of discordant deliberations on a verdict in a breach-of-promise case. Twelve tales therefore are presented, with a thirteenth told by a touring Englishman who has wandered into the jury room by mistake. Most have Irish settings, and one, "McEneiry the Covetous," recalls the earliest of Griffin's stories with its fairy-tale subject in the darkling days of Irish history. "The Mistake," like the opening of his unfinished novel *Adventures of an Irish Giant,* is an interesting picture of Irish doctors at work, drawing upon Griffin's long familiarity with the medical careers of his brothers.

His short life and shorter writing career allowed Gerald Griffin time to develop his talent and produce skillful, sometimes powerful, tales and novels. His stories of Irish life and history in Munster have continuing value for many readers. His novel *The Collegians* may not have the readers it once had, but it continues to appeal and sustain interest through its passionate romance, betrayal, and murder. Experimenting with narrative point of view, local dialect, chronological shifts, and multiple plots, Griffin showed himself interested in the art of fiction as well as in the drama of character. He also realized the aesthetic potential of his historical and regional materials from their limited significance, often establishing timeless beauty in such stories as "Suil Dhuv the Coiner" and *Tracy's Ambition.* When Gerald Griffin's personal ethics and religious scruples came into conflict with his artistic sensibility, the consequence was a triumph for religion and a defeat for art. Nevertheless, his art had secured recognition of the value of his sacrifice when Griffin elected to enter the Order of the Christian Brothers in 1838.

## Bibliography:

Michael Sadleir, *XIX Century Fiction,* volume 1 (London: Constable, 1951; New York: Cooper Square, 1969), pp. 155–159.

## Biographies:

Daniel Griffin, *The Life of Gerald Griffin Esq. by His Brother* (London: Simpkin & Marshall, 1843);

Ethel Mannin, *Two Studies in Integrity: Gerald Griffin and the Rev. Francis Mahony ("Father Prout")* (New York: Putnam, 1954);

John Cronin, *Gerald Griffin (1803–1840): A Critical Biography* (Cambridge: Cambridge University Press, 1978).

## References:

Donald Davie, "Gerald Griffin's 'The Collegians,' " *Dublin Magazine,* new series 28 (April–June 1953): 23–31;

Grace Eckley, "Griffin's Irish Tragedy, *The Collegians* and Dreiser's *American Tragedy,*" *Eire,* 19 (3 August 1977): 39–45;

Thomas Flanagan, *The Irish Novelists 1800–1850* (New York: Columbia University Press, 1959), pp. 205–251;

W. S. Gill, *Gerald Griffin: Poet, Novelist, Christian Brother* (Dublin: Gill, 1941);

Benedict Kiely, "The Two Masks of Gerald Griffin," *Studies,* 61 (Autumn 1972): 241–251.

## Papers:

Manuscripts for works by Gerald Griffin are in the Christian Brothers' Dublin house, St. Mary's. Some letters are in the National Library, Dublin.

# Anna Maria Hall
## (6 January 1800 – 30 January 1881)

Jennifer L. Wyatt
*Civic Memorial High School*

BOOKS: *Sketches of Irish Character* (2 volumes, London: Westley & Davis, 1829; 1 volume, New York: Harper, 1829);

*Chronicles of a School-Room* (London: Westley & Davis, 1830; Boston: Cottons & Barnard, 1830);

*Sketches of Irish Character, Second Series* (London: Westley & Davis, 1831);

*The Buccaneer,* anonymous (3 volumes, London: Bentley, 1832); as Mrs. S. C. Hall (1 volume, Philadelphia: Carey, Lea & Blanchard, 1833); revised edition, as Mrs. S. C. Hall (1 volume, London: Bentley, 1840);

*The Outlaw,* as the Author of "The Buccaneer" (3 volumes, London: Bentley, 1835; 2 volumes, New York: Harper, 1835);

*Tales of Woman's Trials* (London: Chapman & Hall, 1835; New York: Wallis & Newell, 1835);

*Harry O'Reardon; or, Illustrations of Irish Pride* (Philadelphia: Carey & Hart, 1836);

*Mabel's Curse: A Musical Drama in Two Acts* (London: Duncombe, 1837);

*Uncle Horace,* anonymous (3 volumes, London: Colburn, 1837); as Mrs. S. C. Hall (2 volumes, Philadelphia: Carey & Hart, 1838);

*St. Pierre, the Refugee: A Burletta in Two Acts* (London, 1837);

*The Groves of Blarney: A Drama in Three Acts* (London: Chapman & Hall, 1838);

*Lights and Shadows of Irish Life* (3 volumes, London: Colburn, 1838; 2 volumes, Philadelphia: Carey, Lea & Blanchard, 1838);

*The Book of Royalty: Characteristics of British Palaces* (London: Ackermann, 1839);

*Marian; or, A Young Maid's Fortunes* (3 volumes, London: Colburn, 1840; 2 volumes, New York: Harper, 1840);

*Stories of the Irish Peasantry* (Edinburgh: Chambers, 1840);

*The Hartopp Jubilee; or, Profit from Play* (London, 1840);

*Anna Maria Hall (Hulton Deutsch Collection)*

*Ireland: Its Scenery, Character, &c.,* 3 volumes, by Anna Maria Hall and S. C. Hall (London: How & Parsons, 1841–1843);

*A Week at Killarney,* by Hall and S. C. Hall (London: How, 1843);

*Characteristic Sketches of Ireland and the Irish,* by Hall, William Carleton, and Samuel Lover (Dublin: Hardy, 1845);

*The Whiteboy: A Story of Ireland in 1822,* 2 volumes (London: Chapman & Hall, 1845); republished as *The White Boy: A Story of Ireland, in 1822* (New York: Harper, 1845);

*Stories and Studies from the Chronicles and History of England,* by Hall and Judith Foster (2 volumes,

London: Darton, 1847; 1 volume, New York: Riker, 1852; enlarged edition, Edinburgh: Gall & Inglis, 1880);

*Midsummer Eve: A Fairy Tale of Love* (London: Longman, Brown, Green, & Longmans, 1848; New York: Francis, 1848);

*Uncle Sam's Money-Box* (Edinburgh: Chambers, 1848);

*Grandmamma's Pockets* (Edinburgh: Chambers, 1849);

*Pilgrimages to English Shrines* (London: Hall, Virtue, 1850); republished with *Pilgrimages to English Shrines, Second Series* as *Pilgrimages to English Shrines* (New York: Appleton, 1854);

*The Whisperer* (Edinburgh: Chambers, 1850; New York: Francis, 1851);

*The Swan's Egg* (Edinburgh: Chambers, 1851);

*Stories of the Governess* (London: Nisbet, 1852);

*Pilgrimages to English Shrines, Second Series* (London: Hall, Virtue, 1853);

*Tales of Domestic Life* (New York: Francis, 1853);

*The Worn Thimble: A Story of Woman's Duty and Woman's Influence* (London, 1853);

*Hand Books for Ireland,* 4 volumes, by Hall and S. C. Hall (London, 1853);

*Homes and Haunts of the Wise and Good; or, Visits to Remarkable Places in English History and Literature* (Philadelphia: Hazard, 1854);

*The Drunkard's Bible* (London, 1854);

*Popular Tales and Sketches* (London, 1856);

*The Two Friends: A Sketch* (London, 1856);

*A Woman's Story,* 3 volumes (London: Hurst & Blackett, 1857);

*The Lucky Penny, and Other Tales* (London: Routledge, 1857);

*All Is Not Gold That Glitters* (London: Chambers, 1858);

*The Boy's Birthday Book* (London: Houlston & Wright, 1859);

*Daddy Dacre's School* (London, 1859 [i.e., 1858]);

*The Book of the Thames,* by Hall and S. C. Hall (London: Hall, Virtue, 1859);

*Tenby: Its History, Antiquities, Traditions and Customs,* by Hall and S. C. Hall (Tenby, U.K., 1860; revised, 1873);

*The Book of South Wales, the Wye, and the Coast,* by Hall and S. C. Hall (London: Virtue, 1861);

*Can Wrong Be Right?,* 2 volumes (London, 1862; Boston: Burnham, 1862);

*The Village Garland: Tales and Sketches* (London & New York, 1863);

*Nelly Nowland and Other Stories* (London, 1863);

*The Way of the World, and Other Stories* (London: Nelson, 1866; London & New York: Nelson, 1867);

*The Playfellow, and Other Stories* (London: Nelson, 1867);

*The Prince of the Fair Family: A Fairy Tale* (London: Chapman & Hall, 1867);

*Alice Stanley and Other Stories* (London & Edinburgh, 1868);

*Animal Sagacity* (London: Partridge, 1868);

*Wearing of the Green; or, Sketches of Irish Character* (Philadelphia: Flint, 1868);

*The Fight of Faith,* 2 volumes (London: Chapman & Hall, 1869);

*Digging a Grave with a Wine Glass* (London: Partridge, 1871; Boston: Bradley & Woodruff, 1871);

*Chronicles of Cozy Nook: A Book for the Young* (London: Ward, 1875);

*Boons and Blessings: Stories and Sketches to Illustrate the Advantages of Temperance* (London: Virtue, Spalding, 1875);

*Annie Leslie and Other Stories* (London, 1877).

PLAY PRODUCTIONS: *The French Refugee,* London, St. James's Theatre, 1836;

*Mabel's Curse,* London, St. James's Theatre, 1837;

*The Groves of Blarney,* London, Adelphi Theatre, 16 April 1838.

OTHER: *The Juvenile Forget Me Not,* 9 volumes, edited by Hall (London, 1829–1837);

John O'Neill, *Handerahan, the Irish Fairyman; and Legends of Carrick,* introduction by Hall (London: Tweedie, 1854);

*The Adventures and Experiences of Biddy Dorking. To Which Is Added the Story of the Yellow Frog,* edited by Hall (London: Griffith & Farran, 1858);

William Finden, *Finden's Gallery of Modern Art,* 2 volumes, includes tales by Hall (London, 1859, 1860);

*The Juvenile Forget-Me-Not,* edited by Hall (London, 1862);

National Temperance League, *Woman's Work in the Temperance Reformation: Being Papers Prepared for a Ladies' Conference Held in London, May 16, 1868,* introduction by Hall (London: Tweedie, 1868);

Gertrude P. Dyer, *Stories of the Flowers,* introduction by Hall (London, 1877).

Although not as well known an author as her friend and inspiration Maria Edgeworth, Anna Maria Hall must certainly be recognized as one of

*Hall's husband, Samuel Carter Hall*

the most prolific of the early-Victorian Anglo-Irish writers. With the occasional help of her husband, Samuel Carter Hall, she wrote and edited dozens of books, including sketches, children's books, novels, and plays. Most of these were about the foibles of her Irish compatriots. While she was never cruelly satiric in her portrayal of the Irish peasant class, her short, fictitious portraits did not stray far from didacticism, and it was in this vein that she was best known.

An only child, Anna Maria Fielding was born in Dublin on 6 January 1800. Her mother's family was descended from the Huguenots, who immigrated to Ireland to escape religious persecution in France. There is no record of her father, who apparently died before she was born. When she was six weeks old she and her mother, Sarah Elizabeth Fielding, moved to the Graige near Bannow in County Wexford to live with her grandmother and stepgrandfather, who later adopted her. This childhood home, which must have provided a secure and

memorable beginning for her life, became the setting for her short fiction. However, by the time she was fourteen her grandfather's estate had dwindled, and he was forced to move the family to London. There she met Samuel Carter Hall, who had also been born in 1800 in Ireland to a military family, and they married when she was twenty-four. The Halls did not have any children. He died in East Mousley on 20 January 1881.

When the Halls met, Samuel Carter Hall was already a familiar figure in the London literary scene. While he was better known as an editor than as an author at the time, he was highly respected. He published her first short story in his journal, *The Amulet,* in 1829. Her tales were successful, and the *New Monthly Magazine* commissioned a series of eight stories it called "Sketches on Irish Highways," which included her well-known "The Irish Jaunting Car." The series ran from November 1834 through August 1835, and most of these stories appeared in Hall's later anthologies. She also contributed to the

*Dublin University Magazine* with "Terence Ryley's Adventures" in October 1835, "Redderbrae: An Irish Story" in November 1838, and "The Fate of the O'Leary's" in January 1841. The January–February 1844 issue of *Ainsworth's Magazine* contained Hall's "The Long Hours." Encouraged by her husband, she published her first book of short stories only five years after their wedding. Her first volume, *Sketches of Irish Character* (1829), is dedicated to Mary Russell Mitford, a writer of similar personal accounts.

Mitford wrote to support her family, and though no such pressures influenced Hall, there is a pervasive theme of women as saviors of the household in this first volume. Coventry Patmore's theory of woman as "the angel in the house" had not been introduced yet, and this role for Victorian women (albeit Irish women) seems much more viable. Hall's intent to instruct her predominantly female audience focused on the ability of a strong female character to provide aid for the suffering rather than simply to care for an already robust family.

In the first story, "Lilly O'Brien," the widow Mrs. Cassidy not only cares for her young son, Edward, but also has adopted and educated her orphaned niece, Lilly. Mrs. Cassidy exemplifies the highest level of the middle-to-lower-class societies Hall represents in her stories. While there are a few stories of the gentry in her writings, they tend to stand out from the norm. Mrs. Cassidy is a loving but stern disciplinarian who rules her household with an iron fist. In this story the reader gets a first-hand view of Hall's value system – cleanliness, temperance, and hard work. Edward is unable to cope with his mother's stringent standards and runs off to sea, but eventually he returns with an unsuitable English Protestant wife. She soon passes away, leaving an infant to be cared for by the women of the household. After some further interference by well-meaning society women, Lilly and Edward are united.

Wealthy women generally play a benevolent role in Hall's stories. They could easily be labeled meddlesome, but they could also be called, especially in Hall's era, protective, even saving. One of the best stories in *Sketches of Irish Character* is not her usual portrait of needy Irish life but an exciting tale of fortune lost and recovered called "Hospitality." Gertrude Raymond is the orphaned and befriended ward of Mrs. Dorrington, a wealthy English landowner. Her holdings are all in Ireland, and this responsibility prevents her from introducing young Gertrude to society. Hall never missed an opportunity to emphasize the importance of resident landlords in Ireland. She deplored the common practice of using Irish overseers and blamed much of Ireland's poverty and misery on this tendency. However, she would never think to suggest in her stories that a character such as Gertrude could find a non-English husband. Whenever any of her characters married a "foreigner," it was a disaster. Therefore, Mrs. Dorrington and Gertrude vacation in England, become temporarily separated, and Mrs. Dorrington – after earlier implying that Gertrude is her heir – dies intestate, leaving her young ward penniless. Undaunted, Gertrude leaves society – none of her old acquaintances offers to help her anyway – and obtains employment in London. There she is sought out by a faithful Irish retainer, who also informs an old suitor of Gertrude's whereabouts. Hall never fails to point out in any of her stories the value of being kind to the Irish tenantry, as they tend (at least in fiction) to repay threefold.

Gertrude's young suitor, Wortley, seeks her out, only to be rebuffed until she can regain her social status. At this point the story deviates from predictability. Not only does Gertrude waste little time in obtaining gainful employment, she professes to be content with her position. Wortley fears a refusal of his marriage proposal because her "high feelings would prevent her from being dependent (as she would call it) even on a husband." Gertrude is contrasted in this story to the bluestocking Miss Spinner, who despite her faults is the mechanism through which Gertrude's inheritance is recovered. Although the plot twist here is contrived, Hall's use of the only other intellectually inclined woman in the story as savior is significant. All the other female contemporaries of Gertrude are good-hearted but fatuous examples of typical Victorian women.

In 1831 Hall published a second series of *Sketches of Irish Character*. Her next book of short stories, *Lights and Shadows of Irish Life* (1838), followed a visit to Ireland in 1834. In contrast to her previous stories, these convey a sense of being overwhelmed by the disillusion Hall must have felt on her return to the country of her childhood, which was not the Ireland she had left, nor had it improved with time. Instead, she found it a country ravaged by the loss of its staple crop, the potato. The Great Famine, following hard on the heels of British industrialization that had economically devastated Ireland's agricultural economy, decimated the Irish population through death and immigration. Hall was reunited not with the genteel poor of her girlhood but with broken people who crowded her traveling carriage begging for pennies.

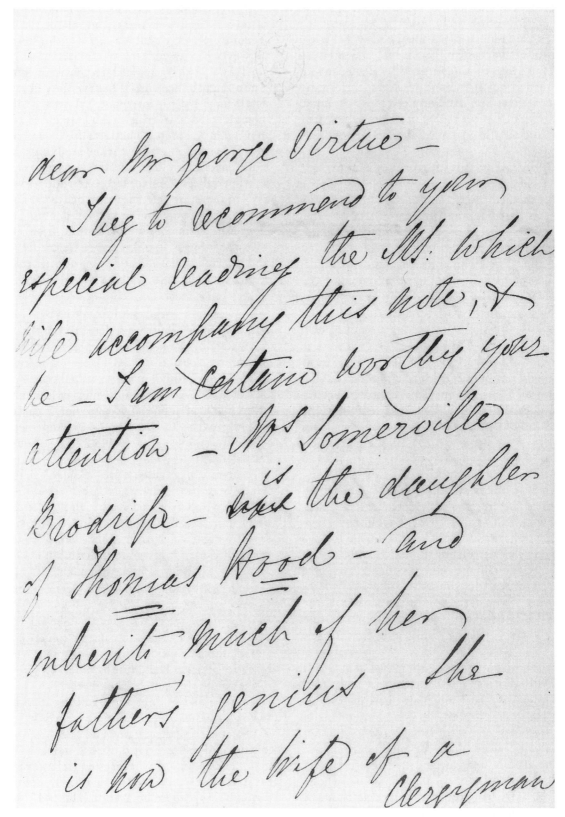

Letter from Anna Maria Hall to the publisher George Virtue, recommending a manuscript by a friend (courtesy of Lilly Library, Indiana University)

In her fiction Hall painted several grim portraits of her beloved Irish, doubly cursed by poverty and mismanaged property. In the second volume of the three-volume collection she includes a group of stories titled "Ruin." One of these, "Florence O'Donnell," describes the last few days of a young girl's life in her native Ireland. Her grandfather, once a wealthy and powerful landowner, is dying with no one to tend to him except two servants and his granddaughter, and he is ignorant of the fact that his "property had been eaten up by mortgages, and bad management, and settlements (as they were called) which ended fruitlessly; and law retainers, and poor relations, too proud to work, but not too proud to beg." In this single statement Hall sums up decades of British interference in Ireland's economy. The O'Donnell estate, described as "green and fertile," could probably have withstood the onslaught of dissolute family members, but it could not endure the added brutalization of famine and legal fees.

Although Florence O'Donnell is not a typical poor Irish tenant, she is one of the many newly poor Irish gentry – like Hall herself – who could not maintain the ancestral standards of living in post–Industrial Revolution Ireland. Many of these people simply did as Hall's family did, leaving Ireland for greener pastures. Florence O'Donnell emigrates, also: after her grandfather's death Florence leaves to join her aunt in a convent in Portugal. Here she takes the veil but dies shortly thereafter. Perhaps in the death of a saintly young woman Hall is trying to show the demise of Ireland's best and brightest and the transformation of the country into a "ruined home" like O'Donnell's. In *Lights and Shadows of Irish Life* there are twice as many stories collectively titled "Ruin" as there are titled "Luck."

The unlucky pattern of absentee landlords and their evil devices in Hall's stories is obvious in the dedication in her last volume of character sketches, *Stories of the Irish Peasantry* (1840), to the "landlords and tenants of Ireland" whose "interests . . . are mutual and inseparable." Perhaps she was eager to blame the hardships of the Irish on these landlords and their often dishonest overseers because her family had fled Ireland after bleeding its tenantry dry. There is no indication that she felt in any way responsible for this situation; there is only the overwhelming amount of repeated blame against the English for many of the problems of Ireland in her stories. In tale after tale, where there are Ireland-based landlords there are industrious, God-fearing, clean Irish tenants. In contrast, when the tenants are allowed self-rule or overseen by a hired hand, they are vindictive, lazy drunkards.

Hall's contemporaries did not criticize her for this depiction of the dark side of Irish life but rather for the lighter characters she created from memory and experience. When she was included in the June 1836 *Fraser's Magazine of Town and Country* "Gallery of Literary Characters," the editors looked upon her descriptions of the Irish poor as "an inexhaustible mine of pathos, as well as fun" and assumed that she was trying to create a satire of Irish life in a sort of macabre Swiftian vein. The August 1840 *Dublin University Magazine* concluded that her stories of abject Irish poverty were created and included in her work "against her will" and preferred her happier sketches.

However, Hall's contemporaries excoriated these happier stories. William Carleton considered her – perhaps because of her gender – unfit to write about the people of her native country, while her friend Edgeworth criticized her for creating a tale instead of writing from life. Yet Hall was not afraid to see the "value of imagination in literature" and continued to write her descriptions with the wild abandon of Irish Romanticism. Some of these descriptions were dimly viewed by more patriotic Irish writers, notably William Butler Yeats, who accused Hall of creating the stereotypical "stage Irishman" later beloved in the public theater.

Hall's intent was to improve the lot of the Irish not only through her own philanthropy but also by making her readers aware of the continuing miserable conditions in Ireland. Although Hall is a writer without political bias, she does note that Ireland's economic problems exacerbate its political ones. In the same way, she tends to blame social problems on a lack of widespread affluence. A typical Hall character will explain a spouse's alcoholism on a lack of steady employment and point out that, while employed, the spouse was honest, sober, and hard-working. It is usually only after a brief stint away from Ireland (either at sea, in England, or in the colonies) that Hall's ruined characters are able to redeem themselves. Ireland, it seems, is only for the strong-willed.

This overview of the problems of Ireland is as evident in Hall's final sketches as in her first. If she mentions Thomas Robert Malthus, the unpopular British economist who proposed limiting population to accommodate available food supplies, in an early sketch, it may be correctly assumed that she will point out starving children in her last. Eventually such social commentary began to wear on Hall and on her readers. After publishing hundreds of short stories and a final novel, Hall turned to collaborating with her husband on travelogues and religious writings. By the mid 1850s her writing had become almost as familiar to the British public as that of Charles Dickens.

Even if Hall's descriptions of Irish scenery could be discounted as overimaginative, her condemnation of alcoholism as overzealous, her evaluation of the economic situation as oversimplified, and her depiction of Irish people as overdone, there is no way to overlook the enormous popularity of her books. This could be due in part to the wholesome blandness of her works. In addition to eschewing negative political statements — she never took a side, only pointing out historical precedents — Hall also declined to become involved in Irish religious issues. If "Father Mike" was the hero and savior to a family in one tale, the minister's daughters rescued a starving mother and children in the next. Rather than writing about the problems of a Catholic-Protestant marriage, there are several successful unions blessed by representatives of both denominations at the ceremony. If any of Hall's marriages fail, it is because of human error (alcoholism, lack of serious intent, poor health) rather than religious differences.

Despite Hall's popularity in her time, she is largely ignored by modern critics. If she is briefly included in an encyclopedia or index it is either because of her better-known husband or because she was one of only a few early Victorian women writers. Many modern scholars contemptuously dismiss her work as repetitive, overly didactic, or sanctimonious. Many of her stories are (there is an apocryphal anecdote of a time when Hall read one of her own stories and, forgetting that she had written it, pronounced it delightful), but she attempted to touch and cure many ills through her many, loving stories of the Irish.

**Biographies:**

William Maginn, "Gallery of Literary Characters no. 73: Mrs. S. C. Hall," *Fraser's Magazine of Town and Country,* 13 (June 1836): 718;

"Our Portrait Gallery no. 10: Mrs. S. C. Hall," *Dublin University Magazine,* 16 (August 1840): 146–149.

Samuel Carter Hall, *Retrospect of a Long Life* (New York: Appleton, 1883);

Isabella Fyvie Mayo, "A Recollection of Two Old Friends: Mr. and Mrs. S. C. Hall," *Leisure Hour,* 38 (1889): 303–307.

# James Hogg

*(November? 1770 – 21 November 1835)*

Gillian H. Hughes

See also the Hogg entries in *DLB 93: British Romantic Poets, 1789–1832, First Series* and *DLB 116: British Romantic Novelists, 1789–1832.*

BOOKS: *Scottish Pastorals, Poems, Songs, etc., Mostly Written in the Dialect of the South* (Edinburgh: Printed by John Taylor, 1801);

*The Mountain Bard: Consisting of Ballads and Songs, Founded on Facts and Legendary Tales* (Edinburgh: Printed by J. Ballantyne for Archibald Constable, and John Murray, London, 1807; enlarged edition, Edinburgh: Oliver & Boyd, and also sold by G. & W. B. Whittaker, London, and William Turnbull, Glasgow, 1821);

*The Shepherd's Guide: Being a Practical Treatise on the Diseases of Sheep* (Edinburgh: Printed by J. Ballantyne for Archibald Constable, and John Murray, London, 1807);

*The Forest Minstrel; a Selection of Songs, Adapted to the Most Favourite Scottish Airs,* by Hogg and others (Edinburgh: Printed for the editor & sold by Archibald Constable, and by Constable, Hunter, Park & Hunter, London, 1810; Philadelphia: M. Carey, 1816);

*The Spy* (nos. 1–52, Edinburgh, 1 September 1810–24 August 1811; 1 volume, Edinburgh: Sold by Constable, 1811);

*The Queen's Wake: A Legendary Poem* (Edinburgh: Printed by Andrew Balfour for George Goldie, and for Longman, Hurst, Rees, Orme & Brown, London, 1813; Baltimore: Coale & Maxwell, 1815);

*The Hunting of Badlewe: A Dramatic Tale,* as J. H. Craig, of Douglas, Esq. (London: Printed for Henry Colburn & George Goldie, Edinburgh, 1814);

*The Pilgrims of the Sun* (Edinburgh: Printed for William Blackwood, and sold by John Murray, London, 1815; Philadelphia: Published by Moses Thomas, printed by J. Maxwell, 1815);

*The Ettricke Garland; Being Two Excellent New Songs on The Lifting of the Banner of the House of Buccleuch, at the Great Foot-ball Match on Carterhaugh, Dec. 4, 1815,* by Hogg and Walter Scott (Edinburgh: Printed by James Ballantyne, 1815);

*A Selection of German Hebrew Melodies,* lyrics by Hogg (London: Printed & sold by C. Christmas, 1815);

*Mador of the Moor: A Poem* (Edinburgh: Printed for William Blackwood, and John Murray, London, 1816; Philadelphia: Published by Moses Thomas, printed by J. Maxwell, 1816);

*The Poetic Mirror; or, The Living Bards of Britain* (London: Printed for Longman, Hurst, Rees, Orme & Brown and John Ballantyne, Edinburgh, 1816; Philadelphia: Published by M. Carey, 1817);

*Dramatic Tales,* 2 volumes (Edinburgh: Printed by James Ballantyne for Longman, Hurst, Rees,

Orme & Brown, London, and John Ballantyne, Edinburgh, 1817);

*The Long Pack* (Newcastle: Printed for John Bell, 1817);

*The Brownie of Bodsbeck; and Other Tales* (2 volumes, Edinburgh: Printed for William Blackwood and John Murray, London, 1818; 1 volume, New York: Charles Wiley, 1818);

*A Border Garland: Containing Nine New Songs,* lyrics by Hogg, music by Hogg and others (Edinburgh: Printed for the editor by Walker & Anderson and sold by Nathaniel Gow & Son, 1819); enlarged as *A Border Garland, Containing Twelve New Songs* (Edinburgh: Printed & sold by R. Purdie, n.d.);

*Winter Evening Tales, Collected among the Cottagers in the South of Scotland,* 2 volumes (Edinburgh: Printed for Oliver & Boyd and G. & W. B. Whitaker, London, 1820; New York: Published by Kirk & Mercein, Wiley & Halsted, W. B. Gilley, and Haley & Thomas, printed by C. S. Van Winkle, 1820);

*The Poetical Works of James Hogg* (4 volumes, Edinburgh: Printed for Archibald Constable, and Hurst, Robinson, London, 1822; 2 volumes, New York: D. Mallory, 1825);

*The Royal Jubilee. A Scottish Mask* (Edinburgh: Blackwood / London: Cadell, 1822);

*The Three Perils of Man; or, War, Women, and Witchcraft. A Border Romance,* 3 volumes (London: Longman, Hurst, Rees, Orme & Brown, 1822);

*The Three Perils of Woman; or, Love, Leasing, and Jealousy: A Series of Domestic Scottish Tales* (3 volumes, London: Printed for Longman, Hurst, Rees, Orme, Brown & Green, 1823; 2 volumes, New York: Ed. Duyckinck, 1823);

*The Private Memoirs and Confessions of a Justified Sinner, Written by Himself: With a Detail of Curious Traditional Facts, and Other Evidence, by the Editor* (London: Printed for Longman, Hurst, Rees, Orme, Brown & Green, 1824; republished as *The Suicide's Grave,* Edinburgh: Clarke, 1828);

*Queen Hynde: A Poem* (London: Printed for Longman, Hurst, Rees, Orme, Brown & Green, and William Blackwood, Edinburgh, 1825);

*Select and Rare Scotish* [sic] *Melodies,* lyrics by Hogg, music by Henry R. Bishop (London: Published by Goulding & D'Almaine, 1829);

*The Shepherd's Calendar,* 2 volumes (Edinburgh: William Blackwood and T. Cadell, London, 1829; New York: Goodrich, 1829);

*Songs, by the Ettrick Shepherd: Now First Collected* (Edinburgh: Blackwood & Cadell, London, 1831; New York: Stodart, 1832);

*Altrive Tales: Collected among the Peasantry of Scotland, and from Foreign Adventurers,* volume 1, with illustrations by George Cruikshank (London: Cochrane, 1832) – no more published;

*A Queer Book* (Edinburgh: Blackwood & Cadell, London, 1832);

*Familiar Anecdotes of Sir Walter Scott,* with "Sketch of the Life of the Shepherd," by S. De Witt Bloodgood (New York: Harper, 1834); unauthorized, altered edition published as *The Domestic Manners and Private Life of Sir Walter Scott* (Glasgow: John Reid / Edinburgh: Oliver & Boyd / London: Black, Young & Young, 1834);

*A Series of Lay Sermons on Good Principles and Good Breeding* (London: Fraser, 1834);

*Tales of the Wars of Montrose* (3 volumes, London: James Cochrane, 1835; 2 volumes, Philadelphia: E. L. Carey & Hart, 1836);

*Tales and Sketches by the Ettrick Shepherd,* 6 volumes (Glasgow, Edinburgh & London: Blackie & Son, 1837);

*A Tour of the Highlands in 1803* (Paisley: Alexander Gardner, 1888; enlarged with additions as *Highland Tours . . . 1802, 1803 and 1804,* edited by William F. Laughlan (Hawick: Byway Books, 1981).

**Editions and Collections:** *Noctes Ambrosianae,* 5 volumes, by Hogg, John Wilson, William Maginn, John Gibson Lockhart, and others, edited by R. Shelton Mackenzie (New York: Redfield, 1854);

*The Works of the Ettrick Shepherd,* 2 volumes, edited by Thomas Thomson (London, Glasgow & Edinburgh: Blackie, 1865);

*The Brownie of Bodsbeck,* edited, with spelling revised to agree with Ettrick pronunciation, by George Lewis (Selkirk: James Lewis, 1903);

*The Private Memoirs and Confessions of a Justified Sinner,* edited by André Gide (London: Cresset Press, 1947);

*The Private Memoirs and Confessions of a Justified Sinner,* edited by John Carey (Oxford: Oxford University Press, 1969);

*Selected Poems,* edited by Douglas S. Mack (Oxford: Clarendon Press, 1970);

*The Ettricke Garland; Being Two Excellent New Songs on The Lifting of the Banner of the House of Buccleuch, at the Great Foot-ball Match on Carterhaugh, Dec. 4, 1815,* by Hogg and Walter Scott, edited by Mack (Greenock: Gian-Aig Press, 1971);

*Memoir of the Author's Life; Familiar Anecdotes of Sir Walter Scott,* edited by Mack (Edinburgh: Scottish Academic Press, 1972);

*The Three Perils of Man or, War, Women and Witchcraft,* edited, with an introduction, by Douglas Gifford (Edinburgh & London: Scottish Academic Press, 1972);

*The Works of the Ettrick Shepherd,* 2 volumes, facsimile (New York: AMS Press, 1973);

*The Brownie of Bodsbeck, and Other Tales,* edited by Mack (Edinburgh: Scottish Academic Press, 1976);

*The Private Memoirs and Confessions of a Justified Sinner,* edited by Gifford (London: Folio Society, 1978);

*Selected Stories and Sketches,* edited by Mack (Edinburgh: Scottish Academic Press, 1982; New York: Harper & Row, 1982);

*Anecdotes of Sir W. Scott,* edited by Mack (Edinburgh: Scottish Academic Press, 1983);

*The Private Memoirs and Confessions of a Justified Sinner,* edited by John Wain (Harmondsworth: Penguin, 1983);

*A Shepherd's Delight: A James Hogg Anthology,* edited by Judy Steel (Edinburgh: Canongate, 1985);

*Tales of Love and Mystery,* edited by David Groves (Edinburgh: Canongate, 1985);

*Selected Poems and Songs,* edited by Groves (Edinburgh: Canongate, 1986);

*Scottish Pastorals, Poems, Songs, Etc.,* edited by Elaine Petrie (Stirling: Stirling University Press, 1988);

*The Poetic Mirror,* enlarged with additions as *Poetic Mirrors,* edited by Groves (Frankfurt am Main: Peter Lang, 1990);

*The Private Memoirs and Confessions of a Justified Sinner,* edited by Groves (Edinburgh: Canongate, 1991);

*The Shepherd's Calendar,* edited by Mack (Edinburgh: Edinburgh University Press, 1995);

*The Three Perils of Woman; or, Love, Leasing, and Jealousy,* edited by Antony J. Hasler, Groves, and Mack (Edinburgh: Edinburgh University Press, 1995);

*A Queer Book,* edited by Peter Garside (Edinburgh: Edinburgh University Press, 1995).

OTHER: *The Jacobite Relics of Scotland; being the Songs, Airs, and Legends, of the Adherents to the House of Stuart,* collected by Hogg (Edinburgh: Printed for William Blackwood, and for T. Cadell & W. Davies, London, 1819; second series, 1821).

*The Works of Robert Burns,* 5 volumes, edited by Hogg and William Motherwell (Glasgow: Fullarton, 1834–1836).

During the 1820s and 1830s James Hogg, or "The Ettrick Shepherd," as he was called from his frequent signature of his magazine articles, was almost as well known a Scottish author as Sir Walter Scott. The works his contemporaries valued most highly were his long narrative poems, led by *The Queen's Wake* (1813), and his many comic, sentimental, and patriotic songs, but perhaps he was even more famous as a fictional character than as an author. From 1822 until his death in 1835 Hogg was featured in the "Noctes Ambrosianae" series of *Blackwood's Edinburgh Magazine* as Hogg or the Shepherd, both a "boozing buffoon" (in the apt phrase of J. G. Lockhart, one of the authors of the series) and a rustic genius: a peasant poet of deplorable appearance and manners, social ineptness, ignorance, and vanity as well as poetic eloquence, a virtuoso command of the Scots language, shrewdness, ready wit, good humor, and deft intelligence.

Until recently Hogg's prose fiction has probably been read more than it has been admired, though George Gordon, Lord Byron, described his short tales as "rough but *racy* – and welcome," and the ones he contributed to *Blackwood's* were surely appreciated by both Edgar Allan Poe and the young Brontë children. Hogg's stories have always been read in his native district of Ettrick Forest and by those with a liking for Scottish folktales of the supernatural, but it is only since World War II that he has been more generally appreciated as a prose writer.

Hogg is chiefly known as a fiction writer for his novel *The Private Memoirs and Confessions of a Justified Sinner* (1824). Reprinted in 1947 with an influential introduction by André Gide, the novel has been the major inspiration for an opera by Thomas Wilson and for several recent novels, including Emma Tennant's *The Bad Sister* (1978). The novel is frequently referred to in passing by literary reviewers who wish to demonstrate their familiarity with the interests and canon of the postmodernist novel. It is worth emphasizing that this reevaluation of *The Private Memoirs and Confessions of a Justified Sinner* followed hard upon the publication of a readily available and unbowdlerized edition of the work: Hogg's fiction is attracting more attention as it becomes available in something like the form in which he wrote it.

Modern scholarly editions of several other Hogg novels followed this resurgence of interest in the *Confessions of a Justified Sinner:* his *The Three Perils of Man* (1822) was republished in 1972, with a paperback reprint coming out in 1989, and *The Brownie of Bodsbeck* (1818) was republished in 1976. As critics and readers have come to understand that Hogg is not a one-book novelist, his shorter fiction has also met with increased respect. Douglas Mack's influential anthology of 1982, *Selected Stories and Sketches,* has been followed by two more anthologies that reprint (with other material) some of his short fiction, *Tales of Love and Mystery* (1985), edited by David Groves, and *A Shepherd's Delight* (1985), edited by Judy Steel. Hunter Steele's novel *Chasing the Gilded Shadow* (1986) was inspired not by the *Confessions of a Justified Sinner* but by "The Bridal of Polmood," which first appeared in Hogg's short-tale collection *Winter Evening Tales* (1820).

In 1995 Hogg's major tale collection, *The Shepherd's Calendar* (1829), was reedited and published as one of the three initial volumes of the new Stirling / South Carolina Research Edition of the Collected Works of James Hogg. This marks a more serious resurgence of interest in Hogg's short fiction: as Hogg's tale collections and magazine contributions appear in the successive volumes of the new edition his reputation as a writer of short fiction will undoubtedly continue to rise.

Hogg was born in the parish of Ettrick, Selkirkshire, in the Scottish Borders: his baptism is recorded in the parish register for 9 December 1770, and as his parents lived near the church it seems likely that he was baptized not long after birth. Hogg himself gave his birthday as 25 January, but this seems easily explained as an act of homage to Robert Burns, his early literary idol, who was born on that day. He was the second son of a struggling tenant sheep farmer, Robert Hogg, and Margaret Laidlaw Hogg, and his formal education consisted entirely of a few months at the parish school, ended by his father's bankruptcy when he was six years old. The boy had then to go into service at various local farms.

Hogg's life was often one of privation and hardship; he recalled that "from some of my masters I received very hard usage; in particular, while with one shepherd, I was often nearly exhausted with hunger and fatigue." As Mack remarks, however, Hogg's lack of bitterness and self-pity is a notable and attractive feature of his account of his childhood: he recalled his habit of running races against himself, his embarrassment at his scanty clothing, and attempts to teach himself to play the violin (and later to read and write) with self-mockery and great good humor. He claimed to have fallen in love at the age of eight with a fellow servant, and his fantasies about her, with his other childhood experiences, clearly inform some of his later fiction: "I wished my master, who was a handsome young man, would fall in love with her and marry her, wondering how he could be so blind and stupid as not to do it. But I thought if I were he, I would know well what to do."

Hogg's imagination was also fed by a wealth of stories related by members of his own family. His father claimed to be descended from the Hoggs of Fauldshope, followers of the Scotts of Harden with a notorious witch among their ancestors, and repeated to his children many local legends and histories. On the maternal side Hogg was proud to be the grandson of a notable local character, Will Laidlaw of Phaup, famous for his athletic prowess and his contacts with the fairies. Even though Laidlaw died when Hogg was no more than four years old, he remembered him well and became familiar with his stories and ballads through their recital by his mother and his uncle, William Laidlaw.

Hogg was also well educated informally in the religious beliefs and traditions of Presbyterianism: his father was an elder of the Church of Scotland and a reader of the Bible, especially of the prophetic books, while his mother seems to have repeated verses from the Psalms to her children so often that Hogg knew several of them by heart in early childhood. This informal education was the foundation of most of his work as a creative writer and supplied him with the basis of his short fiction. From 1790 to 1800 Hogg served as a shepherd to a distant cousin, Mr. Laidlaw of Black House, who lent him books and whose kindness he described as "much more like that of a father than a master," while in Laidlaw's son William (later the amanuensis of Scott and steward of Abbotsford), he made a lifelong friend.

Hogg began to write songs for the local lasses to sing, delighted in their calling him "Jamie the Poeter," and he made a resolution to be a poet and to follow in the footsteps of Robert Burns. With his elder brother, William, and some other young shepherds he formed a literary society that met periodically at the houses of one or other of its members and read and discussed essays previously prepared: in a 22 June 1830 letter quoted in Norah Parr's *James Hogg at Home* (1980) Hogg remarked, "sociality is so completely interwoven in my nature that I have no power to resist indulging in it." He always relished being a member of a literary coterie and one among a band of contributors to a magazine. To the October 1794 *Scots Magazine* Hogg contributed the poem "The Mistakes of a Night," and in 1801 his first collection, *Scottish Pastorals, Poems, Songs, etc., Mostly Written in the Dialect of the South,* appeared. By the age of thirty he had achieved a reputation that was almost exclusively confined to his local district: what allowed him to progress toward a national (and later an international) reputation was his first meeting with Scott in July 1802.

In his account of the meeting published in the 1905 *Transactions of the Hawick Archaeological Society,* William Laidlaw stresses that both men were "born and bred story-tellers," though adding that Hogg's "subjects were too local, and perhaps likewise of too low a caste." Scott's *Minstrelsy of the Scottish Border* (1802–1803) demonstrated to Hogg how the legends and stories of his native district could be presented successfully to a national and literary audience: his first major publication, *The Mountain Bard: Consisting of Ballads and Songs, Founded on Facts and Legendary Tales* (1807), was a collection of ballad imitations inspired by Scott's third volume.

Hogg's detailed notes to his poems demonstrate his fine ear for familiar dialogue, his interest in characterization, and his remarkable ability to handle the supernatural, adding greatly to the pleasures of his book. In the case of "Thirlestane. A Fragment," Elaine E. Petrie has pointed out that the introductory note tells the story in full, ably and succinctly, whereas the poem is merely a dreamlike illustration of one part of it.

From the profits of this volume and those of his book on sheep farming, *The Shepherd's Guide: Being a Practical Treatise on the Diseases of Sheep* (1807), Hogg gained nearly £300, which he subsequently lost in various farming ventures in Dumfriesshire. The financial losses of this period, however, were balanced by the acquisition of many Dumfriesshire legends of the supernatural and of the persecuted Covenanters of the seventeenth century. Toward the end of 1809 he was obliged to return to Ettrick and look for work as a hired shepherd again. Not only was he unable to find employment, but he also discovered that many of his old friends were inclined to blame and shun him: his parents were clearly not the only ones to suspect, as his brother, William, to a friend recorded in a 12 December 1813 letter, that "reading too much would induce a neglect of business." In his *Memoir of the Author's Life* (1972) Hogg writes that in desperation he departed for Edinburgh, "determined, since no better could be, to push my fortune as a literary man."

The time was hardly ripe for a man like Hogg to become a professional author in Edinburgh, however, and had it not been for the kindness of John Grieve and other friends who had faith in his talents he might well have starved. He did not have the formal education to write for journals like the *Edinburgh Review,* which paid its contributors, and the magazines and newspapers of the day still worked on genteel and amateur principles. In *Memoir of the Author's Life* Hogg relates, "any of these were willing enough to accept of my lucubrations, and give them

publicity, but then there was no money going – not a farthing; and this suited me very ill." He published *The Forest Minstrel; a Selection of Songs, Adapted to the Most Favourite Scottish Airs* (1810), then decided that the only way to earn an income by writing for the periodicals was to begin his own literary weekly paper.

*The Spy* was published in fifty-two weekly numbers, from 1 September 1810 to 24 August 1811, and was modeled on earlier successful essay periodicals such as *The Spectator, The Rambler, The Mirror,* and *The Lounger.* Almost half of it was written by Hogg, and it included a substantial number of his earliest short prose tales, most of which were later revised and expanded in his first volume collections. In a variant on the distinction between Addison's urbane Spectator and his country friend Sir Roger de Coverley, Hogg created the genteel and distanced personality of the Spy, whom he contrasted with John Miller, the son of a poor country schoolmaster, educated but speaking in the broad dialect of Nithsdale.

Miller supplies the Spy and his town readers with accounts of typical country customs and events, some chilling tales of the supernatural, and chapbook-style stories of humble virtue rewarded and missing heirs discovered. He visits the Edinburgh theater, and his shrewd and amusing comments on plays reinforce the judgments of the Spy. The Spy relates city ways as an outsider, telling tales of social misfits that are partly picaresque despite the moralistic context of the essay-type periodical. Such tales, particularly one titled "On Instability in One's Calling," in which the narrator seduces his housekeeper and flees to America, affronted Hogg's subscribers, and despite a promising beginning, *The Spy* was a financial failure. In *The Spy,* however, Hogg served his apprenticeship as a professional writer and prefigured many of the stories, themes, and techniques of his later fiction. His education was also continued during this period by his involvement with a debating society called the Forum.

Fame came at last with the publication of his long narrative poem *The Queen's Wake: A Legendary Poem* in 1813, and Hogg immediately tried to interest the publisher Constable in a four-volume collection of his prose fiction titled "The Rural and Traditionary Tales of Scotland," but without success. Until Scott's triumph with *Waverley* (1814) Scottish publishers appear to have been extremely wary of Scottish fiction: John Galt at about the same time was unsuccessfully trying to interest Constable in his *Annals of the Parish,* which was not published until 1820.

The actual publication date of 1818 for Hogg's first volumes of prose fiction postdates by several years his interest in publishing fiction. Hogg's well-known later analysis of his career in *Familiar Anecdotes of Sir Walter Scott* (1834), however, misleadingly asserts that his writing of fiction was caused by Scott's successful novels, which destroyed the market for poetry. Ignoring his early prowess as a storyteller, his notes to *The Mountain Bard,* his tales in *The Spy,* and his attempt to publish a tale collection in 1813, Hogg dated his interest in prose fiction to a period subsequent to the success of Scott's first historical fictions: "the instant that he gave over writing poetry there was neither man nor woman ever read it more! All turned to tales and novels which I among others was reluctantly obliged to do. Yes I was obliged from the tide the irresistible current that followed him to forego the talent which God had given me at my birth and enter into a new sphere with which I had no acquaintance." Only superficially does the shape of Hogg's career support this contention.

In the years after 1813 Hogg published two long poems, *The Pilgrims of the Sun* (1815) and *Mador of the Moor* (1816); two volumes of verse, *Dramatic Tales* (1817); and his brilliant set of parodies of the popular poets of the day, *The Poetic Mirror, or, The Living Bards of Britain* (1816). His success brought him the acquaintance or correspondence of poets such as William Wordsworth and Lord Byron and opened doors in Edinburgh society. Less decorously he also joined a society called the Right and Wrong Club, which was based upon the principle that a friend could do no wrong but must be supported by his friends in every doubtful assertion or undertaking: Hogg became seriously ill as a result of the club's daily convivialities. In 1815 the duke of Buccleuch gave Hogg the farm of Altrive Lake in Yarrow rent-free for life, thus providing him with a base in his native district and a measure of economic security. Because of the pressure of literary tourists and other uninvited visitors on his time and substance, however, Hogg for several years continued to spend the greater part of his time in Edinburgh.

Not until 1818 did Hogg publish *The Brownie of Bodsbeck; and Other Tales* in two volumes, although it probably dates back in some form to his 1813 project of "The Rural and Traditionary Tales of Scotland": Scott's commercial triumphs with Scottish historical fiction clearly favored the publication of Hogg's novel dealing with the Covenanters in his native district, which was immediately seen as a riposte to Scott's *Old Mortality* (1816). With it were published "The Wool-Gatherer" and "The Hunt of Eildon."

"The Wool-Gatherer," extensively revised from a tale in *The Spy,* is in effect an imaginative reworking of Hogg's childhood fantasies about his fellow servant Betty. A ragged but shrewd and intelligent servant lad, Barnaby, succors the young female wool gatherer of the title and in the process communicates to her and the reader his beliefs in the supernatural and some fascinating tales based upon them. She turns out to be of a higher social class and eventually marries Barnaby's master but demonstrates her gratitude to him by advancing his fortunes. Through Barnaby, Hogg is able to explain the way in which superstition unites with religion: "We dinna believe in a' the gomral fantastic bogles an' spirits that fley light-headed fock up an' down the country, but we believe in a' the apparitions that warn o' death, that save life, an' that discover guilt." Hogg's acute observation and imaginative exuberance are evident in many of the details of the story, such as the charming vignette of the collie puppy, or the description of "gumping" (catching fish in one's hands while standing in the middle of a stream).

"The Hunt of Eildon" is a contrasting tale of witchcraft set in the Stuart past: the shepherd Croudy and the king of Scotland live in a disturbing world of supernatural agency, where witches are rife and the devil talks in person with the king and his nobles; and two mysterious sisters, who are alternately deerhounds and lovely maidens, sometimes act benevolently and sometimes with great cruelty. The king's life is saved from a conspiracy to poison him, but Croudy, confused by his temporary transformation into a boar, accuses an innocent girl of witchcraft, and she and her lover escape only by being changed into birds by the uncanny sisters. Croudy's thoughts are "like a hive of bees when the queen is taken from their head," and the reader too is constantly lured into attempting to make moral and narrative sense of a fragmented, ambiguous, and dreamlike world.

*Winter Evening Tales, Collected among the Cottagers in the South of Scotland,* like *The Brownie of Bodsbeck,* is related to his 1813 project "The Rural and Traditionary Tales of Scotland" and includes eleven tales revised from *The Spy,* even though it was not published until 1820. One of its tales, "The Long Pack," an exciting account of a mysterious peddler's foiled attempt to burgle a house by smuggling his associate onto the premises in his pack, had been published as a chapbook in 1817 and reprinted several times. Another of the tales, "Duncan Campbell," which suggests some of Hogg's childhood experiences in relating the wanderings of a ragged boy and his faithful dog among the peasants of Hogg's

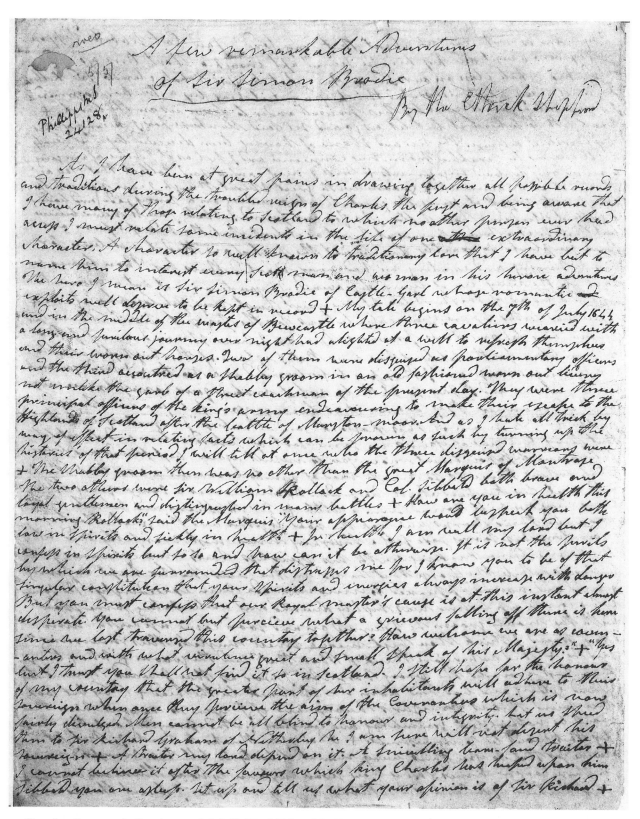

*Pages from the manuscript for a short story included in Hogg's* Tales of the Wars of Montrose *(HM 12410, Henry E. Huntington Library and Art Gallery)*

(p 169)

"My mind is not made up about that my lord" said Col Tibbald "Suppose we pay him a visit and try him he seemed apt enough a short time ago and raised his whole clan on our side + And what did his whole clan do" said Rollock "run all away like traitors And think you not it was by a traitor's command? I am well aware it was by his private order to leave us in the lurch + I am loth to believe it but let us go and see" said Montrose "for I weary of this hypocritical disguise. The sin and shame of having been deceived by that party will never be scrubbed from my conscience and I feel as if I were again going to renew my deplored engagements + Well I must confess" said Rollock "that you act the part of a covenanter's groom with great spirit though I can never help laughing to myself at seeing the great Montrose riding on a sorry jade and leading a gallant steed in a hair halter. As for our friend Tibbald I will never believe but that he is a true reformer at heart or at least that the seeds of reform are there implanted so exactly does he act the part of one. Had it not been for his whining and canting we had never reached thus far. Three times we were on the very eve of being discovered. If you turn not out a covenanter ay and a leader of the herd too let me never trust my philosophy again + You had better spare your calculations for the present Sir William" said Tibbald "and let our deeds prove us. Because I have strained every fold of dissimulation for the safety of those lives that I esteem of the highest value to our sovereign's cause am I therefore to be branded as a traitor + I said you would turn out one and I say so still aye what makes your complexion rise in that manner. By heaven it is because you feel you are charged justly + "No more of this Rollock" said Montrose "I expect you to keep that fiery temper of yours in some sort of subordination and do not let fatigue and disappointment move you to insult your best friends and breed strife where there is so much need of amity. come let us on to Netherby and visit Sir Richard at all hazards. And there comes a squire going the same way we will sound him a little + Sir William and Tibbald then mounted their horses and took the road together and the great Montrose mounting his sorry jade fell a thrashing him most manfully and at the same time kicking with his spurless heels in a manner quite ludicrous while the horse that he led in the hair halter kept capering round and round appeared to incommode him exceedingly. The squire who came up behind was highly diverted and anticipating some sport with the stately groom he spurred on and soon came up with him "Hey friend I think thou hast made a small mistake this morning" said he + "And wherefore think'st thou that" said the groom + "Why because thou hast mounted the wrong horse. An I were as thee I would mount the grand gelding and had that done I could back be the head + Hey but look thee friend this is master's horse and if I were to mount him there would be nothing but grumbling and basting + And pray who is thy master that would be so unreasonable + Oho! thou thinks to smoke I. But let me alone for that. Do you think every man at liberty to tell his master's name in these coward times. Why now for instance who is thine own master + Sir Richard Graham of Netherby is my master. I dcount thinks any

native district and his eventual recognition as the heir to a Highland estate, was subsequently reprinted several times in chapbook form.

Hogg's *Winter Evening Tales,* as the title suggests, is in part an attempt to re-create for a middle-class audience the experience of being a listener around a cottage hearth during the long winter evenings. One group of stories discusses the nature and value of dreams as prophecies, warnings, and agents of revelation: in "The Wife of Lochmaben" a doubting Calvinist is confirmed in her beliefs by the ghost of her former religious associate, who tells her that she did not commit suicide but was murdered by her profligate husband; in the humorous "John Gray o' Middleholm" an idle weaver is instructed in a dream to go to a distant town to discover the hiding place of a hoard of money, which turns out to be in his own garden and to be largely augmented by his own unintended industry as a gardener in digging for it.

Other tales are more ambiguous than these relatively straightforward narratives: in "Cousin Mattie," for example, the fulfillment of the prophetic dream is at least partly brought about by actions designed to evade it. "Singular Dream, from a Correspondent" is a comic variation on the theme, and perhaps suggested Lockwood's dream at the house in Emily Brontë's *Wuthering Heights* (1847). After listening to an acquaintance denounce every person and action in Edinburgh as evil, a simple-minded man dreams that he is in a country church listening to his friend deliver a sermon denouncing his congregation of beautiful women. The friend changes to a devil and is attacked by the dreamer, who wakens to find that he has indeed assaulted his friend. He concludes that "a traducer and backbiter is actually a limb or agent of the devil" and that perhaps his guardian angel sent him the dream as a warning.

Hogg's collection also includes two longer tales that utilize the devices of the picaresque tale to explore the fortunes in life of an alienated personality. The hero of "Love Adventures of Mr. George Cochrane," like many of Daniel Defoe's protagonists, apparently sets himself up as a warning: he deplores the fact that he has never married while amusing the reader with the history of his successive amours. Hogg's narrative is unusual for its portraits of a series of strong-minded women, who in differing ways show their awareness of the narrator's weak character, which he attempts to conceal under a front of chauvinist bravado. Clifford in "Basil Lee," an early portrait of the fallen woman as heroine, is a similarly strong foil to the indecisive male narrator, as Douglas Gifford has pointed out.

Another story, "The Bridal of Polmood," charts the jealous degeneration and eventual destruction of a noble old country laird as a consequence of his marriage to an inexperienced and thoughtless young court lady. Overall, *Winter Evening Tales* is a splendid collection of tales: its few failures, such as "A Peasant's Funeral," occur when Hogg attempts to record peasant customs as a protosociologist. The collection was generally well received in Hogg's own day (though some reviewers commented adversely on Hogg's extended treatment of the Inverness prostitute Clifford in "Basil Lee"), and it sold better than any of his other prose works.

In 1817 Edinburgh became an improved market for Hogg's tales with the advent of *Blackwood's Edinburgh Magazine,* for William Blackwood was willing to pay ten guineas per sheet of sixteen pages for such contributions. In the following years Hogg contributed many songs, poems, and tales to this flourishing periodical and was able to earn a reasonable income in doing so. In his *Memoir of the Author's Life* he claims to have been its founder, and clearly he looked upon himself as one of a band of literary brethren pledged to support it: he was the originator of the "Chaldee Manuscript," an article in pseudobiblical language giving a satiric account of the founding of the magazine and of the publishers and literary men involved that created a scandal in the city and led to recriminations and indeed lawsuits for libel.

As a kind of literary club of contributors, the magazine appealed to Hogg's sociable instincts, while its nationalist and Tory ethos was favorable to his image as the Ettrick Shepherd, an original genius and peasant poet in succession to Robert Burns. The magazine sought to contrast itself to the Whiggish (and, it was implied, unpatriotic and infidel) *Edinburgh Review*. The Ettrick Shepherd, with his Scots tales of a peasant society governed by Providence, had a unique authority on the subject of traditional society, beliefs, and customs and was a key personality in this opposition.

*Blackwood's Edinburgh Magazine* exerted a considerable influence upon Hogg's shorter fiction. Sometimes his work was a direct response to other articles in the magazine: his "Further Anecdotes of the Shepherd's Dog," for instance, was a response to and continuation of articles by Scott and Laidlaw on the same subject. On other occasions Hogg utilized topical subjects of interest in the service of his own fiction: for example, "A Singular Letter from Southern Africa" (which Gifford calls "the earliest version of the *Tarzan* story") draws information about the little-known continent of Africa from factual articles in the magazine and creates a vivid fantasy from them. Hogg's contemporaries found the tale so compellingly mythic and factually plausible that he apparently received several letters inquiring if the events related had actually taken place.

The magazine's avowed championship of religious devotion also made it a fitting context for tales such as "Sound Morality" and "A Tale of the Martyrs," half realistic and half allegorical, that attempt respectively to distinguish the truly charitable man in a fictitious community and to discover the means to salvation. However, tales were also subject to censorship on religious grounds. Blackwood refused to publish "On the Separate Existence of the Soul" because it would shock orthodox Presbyterians with its assumption that the soul could exist separately from the body without at once having its eternal state finally decided. Even though the magazine assumed a mainly masculine readership, censorship of tales on grounds of sexual delicacy was not unknown either: "The Marvellous Doctor," which is about the misuse of a love elixir, was considerably shortened and bowdlerized before publication.

It seems likely, too, that the more fantastic side of Hogg's work was not so welcome in *Blackwood's,* since most of the tales he wrote for it were in keeping with his role as a personality in the magazine, tales of rural Scottish communities and their beliefs. Even those tales that have city settings, such as "Some Passages in the Life of Colonel Cloud" and "Trials of Temper," tend by implication to contrast the town with the secure world of the country. Although Hogg's magazine image enabled and encouraged him to produce excellent work as a teller of country tales, it almost certainly restricted the production of other kinds of fiction.

By 1820 Hogg had his modest farm of Altrive Lake, a series of important publications to his credit (including the 1819 volume *Jacobite Relics of Scotland*), and the prospect of being able to earn some kind of income also from periodical contributions. At the somewhat advanced age of forty-nine he was ready and able to settle in life, and on 28 April 1820 he married Margaret Phillips, the middle-class daughter of an apparently prosperous Dumfriesshire farmer and almost twenty years younger than himself. Hogg had the vigor and high spirits of a much younger man, and by all accounts it was an exceptionally happy marriage, Hogg himself remarking in *Memoir of the Author's Life* that "so uniformly smooth and happy has my married life been, that on a retrospect I cannot distinguish one part from another, save by some remarkably good days of fishing, shooting, and curling on the ice." His son, James Robert Hogg, was born within a year of the mar-

riage, and during the next ten years the births of four daughters followed. After his marriage Hogg spent most of his time at home in Yarrow, with occasional stays in Edinburgh to consult with his publishers and see friends.

These years of emotional stability, however, did not bring the financial stability they might and should have. Instead of being content with Altrive for a home and his earnings from literature to support his living expenses, Hogg seems to have entertained the mistaken ambition of being a farmer on a large scale. His wife was due to inherit a legacy of a thousand pounds by her father's will, and on a promise of this money being made available to him as a dowry Hogg took a nine-year lease of the large farm of Mount Benger in Yarrow that had ruined two well-qualified farmers in the preceding six years. Hogg's father-in-law became bankrupt, and far from being able to pay a dowry, he was obliged to look to Hogg for his own and his wife's support, so that the new farm was never adequately stocked and thus became a financial liability rather than an additional source of income.

Desperate for money, Hogg in the years immediately following his marriage produced a succession of longer prose fictions: *The Three Perils of Man; or, War, Women, and Witchcraft. A Border Romance* (1822); *The Three Perils of Woman; or, Love, Leasing, and Jealousy: A Series of Domestic Scottish Tales* (1823); and *The Private Memoirs and Confessions of a Justified Sinner, Written by Himself: With a Detail of Curious Traditional Facts, and Other Evidence, by the Editor* (1824). These were followed by a long narrative poem, *Queen Hynde* (1825), with which he surely hoped to reproduce the immediate success of his earlier *The Queen's Wake.*

By the mid 1820s Hogg was discovering a less satisfactory aspect to his association with *Blackwood's Edinburgh Magazine,* as his persona of the Ettrick Shepherd seemed partly at least to be passing out of his own control and into that of the writers of the "Noctes Ambrosianae" series. There is some truth in the view that Hogg's position became that of the magazine's buffoon and victim: he was presented from the viewpoint of the gentleman who fastidiously notices all the uncouthness of the peasant, and this presentation significantly placed him as boor outside the code of mutual respect between gentlemen. Hogg himself was probably resigned most of the time to accepting the disadvantages of his position along with the publicity, for he dedicated his later poetry collection *A Queer Book* (1832) to Christopher North and Timothy Tickler, the other magazine personalities of the "Noctes Ambrosianae," but his wife bitterly resented the fact that her husband was held up to public ridicule month after month.

While continuing to look to *Blackwood's* as a major outlet for his short fiction, Hogg as the 1820s moved on was increasingly on the alert for other markets for it. Nevertheless, his work for *Blackwood's* was the backbone of *The Shepherd's Calendar,* one of his finest collections of stories and a worthy successor to *Winter Evening Tales,* even though the published volumes do not fully represent Hogg's own intentions for his work. As a self-confessed uneducated peasant, Hogg was particularly liable to censorship from editors and publishers, and his financial position was such that he was obliged to prefer publication of bowdlerized tales to no publication at all. Blackwood, who must have felt that tales that were acceptable in a masculine magazine would not be suitable for a lady's drawing-room book, employed Hogg's educated nephew Robert to expurgate the stories that were to be included in *The Shepherd's Calendar.* It seems probable that Hogg was not even consulted about these changes but was asked for his approval of his nephew's work only after copies of the printed volumes had already been dispatched to London for publication there.

Until recently Hogg's magazine contributions have more nearly represented his true output than any published version of *The Shepherd's Calendar.* The collection contains a great variety of narratives, going far beyond the title's implications of mere description of the habits of a rural community or analysis of its basic conservatism. Making good use of personal recollection, of hearsay, and of his authority as the Ettrick Shepherd, Hogg includes tales on subjects of particular interest to shepherds, such as dogs and the lasses, and examples of the favorite tales of such men. In his tales of the supernatural, as Jill Rubenstein has indicated, he employs many different kinds of explanation, weaving in eyewitness accounts to present his material forcefully and yet evade charges of easy credulity, and occupying himself with questions of narrative authority; he disturbs rather than satisfies the reader.

Some of Hogg's best-known tales are included in this collection. "The Brownie of the Black Haggs," with its curious bond of attraction and hatred between the wicked Lady of Wheelhope and her demonic servant Merodach, is often compared to the *Confessions of a Justified Sinner.* In "George Dobson's Expedition to Hell" a hackney coachman drives a client both literally and metaphorically straight to the devil, and returns there himself after recounting his experience to his wife and a doctor. In "Mr. Adamson of Laverhope," too, the devil claims his own: after turning

*James Hogg*

out the widow and children of a debtor and ill-treating an orphan, Adamson is challenged by a papist beggar, or the devil in his likeness, and in an evil and deadly storm loses first his sheep and then his own life. The neighboring shepherds interpret this as God's judgment on Adamson for his cruelty to the helpless, a theme taken up again in "Rob Dodds." In explaining the downfall of the Linton family an old shepherd gives an account of the discovery of how Tam Linton's ill-treatment of the lad who assisted him led to the boy's death (the exhaustion and underfeeding of the boy are perhaps based on Hogg's own childhood experiences).

Other tales, such as "Mary Burnet," "The Laird of Cassway," and "The Witches of Traquair," are set in the remote past and have a more overtly magical atmosphere. *The Shepherd's Calendar* is full of good things, not all of which were appreciated at the time of publication. Contemporary reviews were generally extremely favorable chiefly because it was felt that the Ettrick Shepherd was writing on subjects where he possessed the authority of personal experience. The work was praised as a real and factual account of the pastoral life of a shepherd, with quotation most frequently made from "Sheep," "Odd Characters," "Snow-Storms," and "The Shepherd's Dog." The praise of supernatural tales, as in the 14 March 1829 *Edinburgh Literary Journal,* tended to be as "stories, illustrative of the superstitions prevalent among that class which he is describing," though there were occasional acknowledgments of their emotional power over the reader.

A new and lucrative outlet for Hogg's stories started to appear in the early 1820s in the form of the annuals, prettily bound gift books illustrated by the new steel engravings of the day and containing a selection of contemporary verse and prose – the ideal Christmas present for the ladies of a middle-class family. Young and little-known writers, including Alfred Tennyson, gained early if unpaid publication in the annuals; editors lured the literary giants of the day to contribute a few scraps by enormous fees; and well-known and established writers such as Hogg could place their work at rates of pay often twice or even three times that of magazines such as *Blackwood's*. Small wonder then that Hogg was a frequent contributor to the annuals, even though they were a restrictive medium for his tales. A contribution to an annual needed to be short and comply with narrow standards of inoffensiveness in sexual matters because it would be read aloud to ladies and be on display in their drawing rooms to chance visitors: if it had a religious point to make, that would be in its favor. In addition, those annuals designed more specifically for children tended to be downright didactic, eschewing the marvelous and supernatural tales at which Hogg excelled.

Hogg's contributions to the annuals between 1826 and his death are accordingly of varying quality, from the improbably pious and stilted nursery dialogue of "What is Sin?" to the artistic wizardry of "The Cameronian Preacher's Tale." Farley, the preacher of the title, recounts to his flock in his old age how through his agency Providence righted a great wrong and restored a forlorn widow and her children to affluence. Hogg's narrator, who possesses strong traditional values, yet is educated and commands great respect, rationalizes the supernatural on one level in order to reinforce it more deeply on another.

Other tales appear to look back to Hogg's earlier career. "A Tale of Pentland" reworks material previously used in a key scene in *The Brownie of Bodsbeck:* a Covenanter peering into a house at night apparently sees his fellow Presbyterians cutting the throat of a wounded Cavalier; in reality the Cavalier's wounds are being stitched, his life saved by those he has injured, and he is later able to save their lives in his turn. "The Border Chronicler" looks back technically, to the meeting in *The Spy* between an urban narrator and his country visitor to Edinburgh: just as John Miller told supernatural tales to the Spy and his readership, so Charlie Dinmont now relates them to the narrator and to the

readers of the *Literary Souvenir*. This introduction to the fine inset tales of "Gillanbye's Ghost" and "The White Lady of Glen-Tress" seems a fairly clumsy device by comparison with Hogg's creation of the Cameronian preacher.

Hogg occasionally challenges the genteel assumptions of his readership in his contributions to the annuals. Superficially, little Benjy of "The Poachers" recalls the young villain of Scott's *Redgauntlet* (1824). His wickedness, however, is eventually proved to be entirely the result of his deplorable circumstances. He eagerly embraces a decent life when one is offered to him, evolving from a nefarious criminal and poacher into a respectable minister with an allowable fondness for sport.

From 1828 to 1831 Hogg was also contributing to the *Edinburgh Literary Journal,* a weekly literary paper run by one of his young friends who could not afford to pay its contributors at all. This seems surprising in view of Hogg's financial plight, but of course the paper fulfilled other needs, most obviously Hogg's desire for sociability. Hogg naturally took his place among the paper's contributors as the famous senior to a band of aspiring Scots poets: it reported his literary projects and social engagements, praised his work, and treated him with affection and respect. On several occasions Hogg printed in this paper stories which had previously been rejected by *Blackwood's,* and he also demonstrated his independence of the magazine by trying to create his own versions of the "Noctes Ambrosianae," titling one effort "Noctes Bengerianae" after his leased farm and the other "Dr. David Dale's Account of a Grand Aerial Voyage," relating the zany songs, sayings, and doings of the Ettrick Shepherd during an involuntary hot-air-balloon trip.

Hogg probably saw his involvement with the *Edinburgh Literary Journal* as an opportunity to reestablish control of his own public image, but it also gave him the chance of publishing material not easily placed elsewhere, stories dealing with the eccentric, the grotesque, and the magical. "Wat the Prophet" is a delicate character study of a noted local eccentric, a visionary who believed that he conversed with the first Christian martyr, Stephen, and that he had been divinely gifted with the spirit of prophecy. Similarly, "Some Remarks on the Life of Sandy Elshinder," ostensibly a book review, is really an appreciation of the autobiographer's bizarre character. Both "A Story of the Black Art" and "Grizel Graham" offer frank enjoyment of a timeless world of magic and grotesque comedy, and are lightweight but spirited fantasies.

By 1830 Hogg's financial affairs had reached a crisis. At the beginning of the year he applied for a renewal of his lease on the Mount Benger farm, and the refusal of the duke of Buccleuch's agent made it obvious to the world as well as to Hogg himself how much he had lost in unprofitable farming there. By April he was mournfully contemplating a forthcoming sale of his effects, lamenting in a 28 April 1830 letter published in Parr's *James Hogg at Home* that "it is rather hard to have to begin the world anew at 60 years of age." He still had the smaller Altrive Lake farm rent-free for life, however, and gallantly set about attempting to earn what he could for his present support. He must also have contemplated the alarming prospect of the future of his wife and young family after his death.

An income could most obviously be secured by writing for the periodicals, but *Blackwood's* was becoming a more decorous periodical by 1830 and accepting fewer of his stories than it had previously. Hogg must therefore have welcomed the new London-based *Fraser's Magazine,* which imitated many features of the Edinburgh periodical and was willing to accept and pay for his articles in verse and prose. The new magazine permitted Hogg more freedom in religious matters than *Blackwood's* and more freedom in sexual matters than the annuals, and it gradually became the most important outlet for Hogg's fiction in the final years of his life.

Hogg's tales in *Fraser's Magazine* include "Strange Letter of a Lunatic," which has often been compared to the *Confessions of a Justified Sinner* for its deliberately maintained ambiguity between insanity and demonic possession in its explanation of the protagonist's conduct, and "On the Separate Existence of the Soul," which features a jesting exchange of bodies between a conservative old shepherd and his young improving master. Gifford describes "The Barber of Duncow," first published in *Fraser's,* as "one of Hogg's finest extended pieces of Scots," while "The Unearthly Witness" has a haunting atmosphere of brooding uncertainty and watchfulness. In "Extraordinary History of a Border Beauty" Hogg tackles in a picaresque tone material normally treated sentimentally, as a middle-aged woman frankly and humorously recounts the vanities and sexual dangers of her youth, indirectly criticizing the way in which girls like herself are brought up to be empty-headed beauties.

In these last years Hogg also wrote several short stories for *Chambers's Edinburgh Journal,* where his vigorous imagination and earthy humor were somewhat at odds with the instructive tone of a cheap weekly paper aiming at the improvement of the new voters created by the 1832 Reform Act. His "Letter from Canada to the Ettrick Shepherd," for example, is a piece of playful grotesquerie that mocks the paper's fondness for details of emigrant life in Canada. In "The Watchmaker," under the guise of painting the evil consequences of intemperance for the workingman, Hogg gives a comical account of the tricks and stratagems the watchmaker employs to obtain his alcoholic drink.

Hogg's earnings from his periodical contributions might have formed a sufficient income for his family while he lived, but he faced the added responsibility of providing for their future maintenance. Given his relatively advanced age at marriage, the probability was that at his death his son would be some years away from being able to earn any kind of professional income. He doubtless remembered being sent out to service himself at six years of age and the education that had passed him by. Following the example of Scott, who was paying off a portion of his enormous debts by means of the "magnum opus" edition of the Waverley novels, Hogg decided to produce a collected edition of his tales that would at once gather up and preserve his scattered periodical contributions and form a source of income for his widow and young children.

A serious quarrel with Blackwood at the end of 1831 put an end to Hogg's lingering hopes that his Edinburgh publisher would bring out his collected tales, and he then set off for London to secure a publisher there. His first and only visit to the English capital began on 31 December 1831 and lasted for almost three months. He thoroughly enjoyed himself as the lion of the season, dining with literary men and aristocrats and attending clubs and evening parties. There was even a rumor abroad that he might be offered a knighthood.

About a month after his return the first volume of a proposed twelve-volume series of his *Altrive Tales: Collected among the Peasantry of Scotland, and from Foreign Adventurers* was published in London by James Cochrane, priced at six shillings, illustrated by George Cruikshank, and printed uniformly with the Waverley Novels. Almost half of this volume was occupied with a revised and updated memoir of Hogg's life; it also contained three tales, two of which are revisions of work previously published: "Marion's Jock" had formed part of Hogg's novel *The Three Perils of Man,* and "The Pongos" was his *Blackwood's* African tale under another title.

The new tale, "The Adventures of Captain John Lochy," concerns the adventures of a foundling, persecuted by unknown and powerful enemies and aided by his mysterious attendant, Finlayson. He serves the duke of Marlborough and the king of Sweden as a soldier, and then on his return to Scotland unwittingly involves himself in a Jacobite plot. The story is a picaresque account of what it is like to be outside the usual social bonds, "an isolated and lonely being, who seemed thrown upon the world to be a football in it." Unfortunately for Hogg, the publication of the first volume of *Altrive Tales* was quickly followed by the bankruptcy of its publisher, and no more were published despite Hogg's persistent efforts to find another publisher either in England or Scotland to continue the series.

By February 1833, however, Hogg was negotiating with Blackie and Son of Glasgow to bring out a similar collected tales under the title of his most popular earlier collection, *Winter Evening Tales,* but the project was delayed by the firm's unwillingness to pay what Hogg considered to be his fair share of the profits. It seems that an agreement was reached by the end of the year and that Hogg had begun to revise some of his tales for the new collected edition, but he also gave the publishers permission to change the material he sent them just as they pleased. The eventual publication, *Tales and Sketches by the Ettrick Shepherd,* was not brought out by Blackie and Son until 1837, after Hogg's death, and it is not known to what extent the texts it contains embody Hogg's own revisions or the publisher's bowdlerizations and misunderstandings of them. The modern consensus of opinion is that the 1837 edition is unreliable and textually corrupt in comparison with versions in magazines and earlier collections. The 1837 edition, however, also published two new pastoral dramas and two new tales. "The Surpassing Adventures of Allan Gordon." is an imaginative fantasy based on the contemporary love of accounts of polar exploration. Its hero is stranded on the polar ice with a devoted female polar bear for his sole companion, until he discovers the surviving primitive Norwegian colonists of the region. "Gordon the Gipsy" is a more pedestrian tale turning on a question of identity.

The last collection of Hogg's tales published in his lifetime was *Tales of the Wars of Montrose* (1835), which combined new versions of earlier unpublished tales with others created especially for the work. It is a much more unified work than Hogg's earlier collections, since all the tales are set in the 1640s and as a group examine the breakdown of Scottish society. Written in different narrative moods, the stories relate the experiences of Highlander and Lowlander, peasant, aristocrat, and burgess. Each tale, however, has its separate pleasures. The self-revelatory and self-condemning account of Baillie Archibald Sydeserf, "Some Passages in the Life of an Edinburgh Baillie," has been singled out for praise in recent years because of its similarities to the *Confessions of a Justified Sinner.* "Wat Pringle o' the Yair," on the other hand, has been seen in the context of Hogg's other accounts of his native district and its customs.

The poor sales of *Tales of the Wars of Montrose* were undoubtedly the fault of its publisher, Cochrane, back in business, who had insisted on a three-volume format with barely enough material to support it and then overpriced it at a guinea and a half. Contemporary reviews are balanced between praise and blame, although clearly Hogg's "mixture of reality and romance," as described in the 18 April 1835 *Athenaeum,* was felt to be unpleasant in some quarters. The reviewer in the *New Monthly Magazine* summarized the reaction of many of his fellows to Hogg's short fiction generally in describing how during his progress through a Hogg work he was annoyed and teased by coarseness, abruptness, and lack of style "and yet we cannot lay down the book; though we may throw it from us, we are sure to take it up and go on even to the end." During the summer of 1835 Hogg became gradually more debilitated and seemed to realize, on excursions past Blackhouse and his birthplace in Ettrick, that he was seeing them for the last time. By October he was confined to the house, and then to his bed, and he died on 21 November, his illness being diagnosed as "black jaundice." Hogg is buried among his kin in Ettrick churchyard, only a few hundred yards from the place where he was born.

Scholars are only at the beginning of a process of critical revaluation of Hogg's short fiction: as the constraints imposed upon him by the literary marketplace – publishers, periodicals, and social mores – begin to be examined and understood, so the process of his development as a writer is more accurately seen. Unlike his literary exemplar Scott, Hogg was far from being in control of the publication process, and many of his tales were distorted from their natural shape before appearing in book form. The appearance of new texts based wherever possible on Hogg's manuscripts and on the early magazine appearances of his tales is a necessary first stage in the process of revaluation. Nevertheless, Hogg is certainly regarded as one of the most important of Scottish Romantic writers.

**Bibliographies:**
Edith C. Batho, "Bibliography," in her *The Ettrick Shepherd* (Cambridge: Cambridge University Press, 1927), pp. 183–221;

Batho, "Notes on the Bibliography of James Hogg, The Ettrick Shepherd," *Library*, fourth series 16 (December 1935): 309–326;

Douglas S. Mack, *Hogg's Prose, An Annotated Listing* (Stirling: James Hogg Society, 1985);

Gillian H. Hughes, *Hogg's Verse and Drama: A Chronological Listing* (Stirling: James Hogg Society, 1990);

Patrick Scott, *A Checklist of James Hogg Scholarship Since 1960* (Columbia: South Carolina Working Papers in Scottish Bibliography, 1992).

**Biographies:**

George Douglas, *James Hogg* (Edinburgh & London: Oliphant, Anderson & Ferrier, 1899);

Henry Thew Stephenson, *The Ettrick Shepherd: A Biography*, Indiana University Series, no. 34 (Bloomington: Indiana University Press, 1922);

Edith C. Batho, *The Ettrick Shepherd* (Cambridge: Cambridge University Press, 1927);

Alan Lang Strout, *The Life and Letters of James Hogg, the Ettrick Shepherd* (Lubbock: Texas Tech Press, 1946).

**References:**

Barbara Bloede, "The Witchcraft Tradition in Hogg's Tales and Verse," *Studies in Hogg and His World*, 1 (1990): 91–102;

Thomas Crawford, "James Hogg: the Play of Region and Nation," in *A History of Scottish Literature*, volume 3: *The Nineteenth Century*, edited by Douglas Gifford (Aberdeen: Aberdeen University Press, 1988), pp. 94–108;

Peter Garside, "Three Perils in Publishing: Hogg and the Popular Novel," *Studies in Hogg and His World*, 2 (1991): 45–63;

Douglas Gifford, *James Hogg* (Edinburgh: Ramsay Head Press, 1976);

R. P. Gillies, "Some Recollections of James Hogg," *Fraser's Magazine*, 20 (October 1839): 414–430;

David Groves, "The *Confessions* and *The Adventures of Captain John Lochy*," *Newsletter of the James Hogg Society*, 6 (May 1987): 11–13;

Groves, *James Hogg, The Growth of a Writer* (Edinburgh: Scottish Academic Press, 1988);

Groves, "Other Prose Writings of James Hogg in Relation to *A Justified Sinner*," *Studies in Scottish Literature*, 20 (1985): 262–266;

Antony J. Hasler, "Reading the Land: James Hogg and the Highlands," *Studies in Hogg and His World*, 4 (1993): 57–82;

Gillian H. Hughes, "The Evolution of *Tales of the Wars of Montrose*," *Studies in Hogg and His World*, 2 (1991): 1–13;

Hughes, "Reading and Inspiration: Some Sources for 'The Surpassing Adventures of Allan Gordon,'" *Scottish Literary Journal*, 16 (May 1989): 21–34;

Hughes, "*The Spy* and Literary Edinburgh," *Scottish Literary Journal*, 10 (May 1983): 42–53;

Douglas S. Mack, "Hogg, Blackwood, and *The Shepherd's Calendar*," in *Papers Given at the Second James Hogg Society Conference*, edited by Hughes (Aberdeen: Association for Scottish Literary Studies, 1988), pp. 24–31;

Mack and Wilma Mack, "Three Sketches by Hogg," *Studies in Hogg and His World*, 2 (1991): 103–109;

Susan Manning, *The Puritan-Provincial Vision: Scottish and American Literature in the Nineteenth Century* (Cambridge: Cambridge University Press, 1990);

Silvia Mergenthal, *James Hogg: Selbstbild und Bild*, Publications of the Scottish Studies Centre of the Johannes Gutenberg Universität Mainz, no. 9 (Frankfurt am Main: Peter Lang, 1990);

Norah Parr, *James Hogg at Home* (Dollar: D. S. Mack, 1980);

Elaine E. Petrie, "James Hogg: A Study in the Transition from Folk Tradition to Literature," dissertation, University of Stirling, 1980;

Jill Rubenstein, "Varieties of Explanation in *The Shepherd's Calendar*," *Studies in Hogg and His World*, 4 (1993): 1–11;

Louis Simpson, *James Hogg: A Critical Study* (Edinburgh: Oliver & Boyd, 1962; New York: St. Martin's Press, 1962);

Nelson C. Smith, *James Hogg* (Boston: Twayne, 1980).

**Papers:**

The major collection of James Hogg's letters and manuscripts is in the National Library of Scotland, Edinburgh. Additional items are in the Pierpont Morgan Library, New York; the Huntington Library, San Marino, California; the Walpole Collection, The King's School, Canterbury; the Bodleian Library, Oxford; the British Library; the Alexander Turnbull Library, Wellington, New Zealand; and the libraries at Yale, Princeton, the University of South Carolina, and Stirling University.

# Douglas Jerrold

### (3 January 1803 – 8 June 1857)

### Richard D. Fulton
*Clark College*

See also the Jerrold entry in *DLB 158: British Reform Writers, 1789–1832.*

BOOKS: *More Frightened Than Hurt: A Farce, in Two Acts* (London: Duncombe, 1821);

*The Gipsey of Derncleugh; A Melo-Drama in Three Acts* (London: Duncombe, 1821?);

*Dolly and the Rat; or, The Brisket Family* (London: Duncombe, 1823);

*The Smoked Miser; or, The Benefit of Hanging* (London: Duncombe, 1823?);

*The Arts of Cheating, Swindling and Murder,* by Jerrold, Edward Bulwer-Lytton, and Thomas De Quincey (New York: Arnold, 1825);

*Ambrose Gwinett; or, A Sea-Side Story* (London: Cumberland, 1828; London: Richardson, 1828; Philadelphia: Turner, 1833);

*Fifteen Years of a Drunkard's Life* (London: Duncombe, 1828); republished as *The Drunkard's Fate* (New York: Clayton, 1830);

*John Overy, the Miser of Southwark Ferry* (London: Davidson, 1828?);

*The Statue Lover; or, Music in Marble* (London: Duncombe, 1828);

*Wives by Advertisement; or, Courting in the Newspapers* (London: Duncombe, 1828);

*Bampflyde Moore Carew; or, The Gypsey of the Glen* (London: Duncombe, 1829);

*Vidocq, the French Police Spy* (London: Duncombe, 1829; New York: French, 1877);

*Black-Eyed Susan; or, "All in the Downs"* (London: Duncombe, 1829; New York: Elton, 1830); republished as *Black Ey'd Susan* (London: Richardson, 1829);

*The Flying Dutchman; or, The Spectral Ship* (London: Richardson, 1829);

*Law and Lions* (London: Duncombe, 1829?);

*Sally in Our Alley: A Drama, in Two Acts* (London: Dicks, 1829?);

*Thomas à Becket* (London: Richardson, 1829);

*Descart, the French Buccaneer* (London: Duncombe, 1830?);

*Douglas Jerrold; engraving by F. A. Prier (courtesy of Lilly Library, Indiana University)*

*The Mutiny at the Nore; or, British Sailors in 1797* (London: Davidson, 1830);

*The Devil's Ducat; or, The Gift of Mammon* (London: Cumberland, 1831; New York: French, 1876?);

*Martha Willis, the Servant Maid* (London: Lacy, 1831?);

*The Bride of Ludgate* (London: Cumberland, 1832);

*The Golden Calf* (London: Cumberland, 1832?; London: Dicks, 1832?);

*The Rent Day* (London: Chapple, 1832; New York: Clayton / Philadelphia: Neal, 1832);

*The Housekeeper; or, The White Rose* (London: Miller, 1833);

*Nell Gwynne; or, The Prologue* (London: Miller, 1833);

*Beau Nash, the King of Bath* (London: Miller, 1834; London: Wilkes, 1834);

*The Wedding Gown* (London: Miller, 1834);

*Doves in a Cage* (London: Duncombe, 1835?; New York: French, n.d.);

*The Hazard of the Die* (London: Miller, 1835; New York: French, n.d.);

*The Schoolfellows* (London: Duncombe, 1835; New York: French, n.d.);

*The Man for the Ladies* (London: Dicks, 1836);

*The Painter of Ghent* (London: Duncombe, 1836);

*The Perils of Pippins; or, The Man Who 'Couldn't Help It'* (London: Duncombe, 1836);

*Men of Character,* 3 volumes (London: Colburn, 1838); excerpts republished as *Men of Character* (New York: Bunce, 1838);

*Adam Buff, and Other Men of Character,* 2 volumes (Philadelphia: Lea, 1839);

*The Handbook of Swindling,* as Captain Barabbas Whitefeather (London: Chapman & Hall, 1839);

*Heads of the People,* illustrations by Kenny Meadows, text by Jerrold, Laman Blanchard, R. H. Horne, Leigh Hunt, W. M. Thackeray, and others (London: Tyas, 1840; Philadelphia: Carey & Hart, 1841);

*The White Milliner* (London: Duncombe, 1841);

*Bubbles of the Day* (London: How & Parsons, 1842);

*Cakes and Ale,* 2 volumes (London: How & Parsons, 1842);

*Gertrude's Cherries; or, Waterloo in 1835* (London: Berger, 1842);

*The Prisoner of War* (London: How & Parsons, 1842);

*Punch's Letters to His Son* (London: Orr, 1843);

*The Natural History of Courtship,* attributed to Jerrold (Philadelphia: Carey & Hart, 1844);

*The Physiology of the London Medical Student, and Curiosities of Medical Experience,* as Punch, attributed to Jerrold (Philadelphia: Carey & Hart, 1844);

*Punch's Complete Letter Writer* (Philadelphia: Carey & Hart, 1844; London: Punch Office, 1845);

*The Story of a Feather* (London: Punch Office, 1844; Philadelphia: Carey & Hart, 1845);

*The History of St. Giles and St. James* (New York: Burgess, Stringer, 1845; Boston: Redding, 1847); republished as *St. Giles and St. James* (London: Bradbury & Evans, 1851);

*Mrs. Caudle's Curtain Lectures* (New York: Winchester, 1845; London: Punch Office, 1846);

*Time Works Wonders* (London: Punch Office, 1845; Boston: Saxon & Kelt, 1845; New York: Taylor, 1845);

*The Chronicles of Clovernook; With Some Account of the Hermit of Bellyfulle* (London: Punch Office, 1846; New York: Harper, 1846);

*The Dreamer and the Worker* (New York: Burgess, Stringer, 1847);

*A Man Made of Money* (London: Punch Office, 1848–1849; New York: Lockwood, 1849);

*The Catspaw* (London: Punch Office, 1850; New York: Taylor, n.d.);

*Isaac Cheek: The "Man of Wax"* (New York: Bunce, 1851);

*Retired from Business* (London: Punch Office, 1851);

*Blondelle: A Story of the Day* (London: Bentley, 1852);

*St. Cupid; or, Dorothy's Fortune* (London: Bradbury & Evans, 1853; New York: Taylor, 1854);

*A Heart of Gold* (London: Bradbury & Evans, 1854);

*The Brownrigg Papers* (London: Hotten, 1860);

*Paul Pry, A Comedy in Two Acts* (London: Lacy, 1860; New York: French, 1875?);

*Fireside Saints, Mr. Caudle's Breakfast Talk, and Other Papers* (Boston: Lee & Shepherd / New York: Lee, Shepherd & Dillingham, 1873);

*"The Barber's Chair" and "The Hedgehog Letters"* (London: Chatto & Windus, 1874);

*Two Eyes between Two* (London: Dicks, 1888);

*Paul Preudergast; or, The Comic Schoolmaster,* attributed to Jerrold (London: Ward & Locke, n.d.);

*The Tower of Lochlain; or, The Idiot Son* (London & New York: French, n.d.).

**Editions:** *The Writings of Douglas Jerrold,* 8 volumes (London: Bradbury & Evans, 1851–1858);

*The Works of Douglas Jerrold,* 4 volumes, introductory memoir by W. Blanchard Jerrold (London: Bradbury & Evans, 1863–1864; Philadelphia: Lippincott, 1863?); enlarged as *The Works of Douglas Jerrold,* with life by W. Blanchard Jerrold, 5 volumes (London: Bradbury, Agnew, 1869);

*Other Times, Being Liberal Leaders Contributed to "Lloyd's Weekly Newspaper" by Douglas and Blanchard Jerrold* (London, 1868);

*The Essays of Douglas Jerrold,* edited by Walter Jerrold (London: Dent, 1903; New York: Dutton, 1903);

*The Best of Mr. Punch: The Humorous Writings of Douglas Jerrold,* edited by Richard M. Kelly (Knoxville: University of Tennessee Press, 1970).

## SELECTED PLAY PRODUCTIONS:

*More Frightened Than Hurt: A Farce, in Two Acts,* London, Sadler's Wells Theatre, 4 April 1821;

*Mr. Paul Pry; or, I Hope I Don't Intrude,* London, Coburg Theatre, 10 April 1826;

*Ambrose Gwinett; or, A Sea-Side Story,* London, Coburg Theatre, 6 October 1828;

*Fifteen Years of a Drunkard's Life,* London, Coburg Theatre, 24 November 1828;

*Black-Eyed Susan; or, All in the Downs,* London, Surrey Theatre, 8 June 1829;

*Thomas à Becket,* London, Surrey Theatre, 30 November 1829;

*The Mutiny at the Nore; or, British Sailors in 1797,* London, Royal Pavilion Theatre, 7 June 1830;

*The Bride of Ludgate,* London, Drury Lane Theatre, 8 December 1831;

*The Rent Day,* London, Drury Lane Theatre, 25 January 1832;

*The Golden Calf,* London, Strand Theatre, 30 June 1832;

*The Factory Girl,* London, Drury Lane Theatre, 6 October 1832;

*Nell Gwynne; or, The Prologue,* London, Covent Garden Theatre, 9 January 1833;

*Beau Nash, the King of Bath,* London, Theatre Royal, Haymarket, 16 July 1834;

*The Schoolfellows,* London, Queen's Theatre, 16 February 1835;

*Doves in a Cage,* London, Adelphi Theatre, 18 December 1835;

*Bubbles of the Day,* London, Covent Garden Theatre, 25 February 1842;

*The Prisoner of War,* London, Drury Lane Theatre, 1 March 1842;

*Time Works Wonders,* London, Theatre Royal, Haymarket, 26 April 1845;

*The Catspaw,* London, Theatre Royal, Haymarket, 9 May 1850;

*Retired from Business,* London, Theatre Royal, Haymarket, 3 May 1851;

*St. Cupid; or, Dorothy's Fortune,* London, Princess's Theatre, 22 January 1853;

*A Heart of Gold,* London, Princess's Theatre, 9 October 1854.

## SELECTED PERIODICAL PUBLICATIONS –

UNCOLLECTED: "Nothing but Rags," *Athenaeum,* no. 245 (7 July 1832): 441;

"Butcher! Baker!," *Athenaeum,* no. 252 (25 August 1832): 551;

"Time's Laconics," *Athenaeum,* no. 322 (28 December 1833): 897;

"Silas Fleshpots; a 'Respectable Man,' " *Blackwood's Edinburgh Magazine,* 37 (April 1835): 595–604;

"Michael Lynx; 'the Man Who Knew Himself,' " *Blackwood's Edinburgh Magazine,* 37 (May 1835): 730–738;

"An Old House in the City," *Blackwood's Edinburgh Magazine,* 37 (June 1835): 860–874;

"The Science of Swindling," *Blackwood's Edinburgh Magazine,* 38 (September 1835): 304–312;

"Ephraim Rue; the 'Victim of Society,' " *New Monthly Magazine,* new series 62 (June 1841): 212–227;

"Bajazet Gag; the Manager in Search of a 'Star,' " *New Monthly Magazine,* new series 62 (July 1841): 369–390; (August 1841): 522–541; 63 (September 1841): 82–99; (November 1841): 337–356; (December 1841): 489–502; 64 (February 1842): 177–192;

"Mr. Makepeace, the Duellist," *Bentley's Miscellany,* 40 (1842): 461–466.

Playwright, critic, editor, journalist, wit, novelist, and writer of hundreds of essays, short stories, poems, and character sketches, Douglas William Jerrold was one of the most important and influential men of letters of his day. It is safe to say that he knew personally every writer of influence in England at midcentury; certainly every writer, with or without influence, knew him.

In his own lifetime Jerrold was best known — much to his dismay — as a writer of light, entertaining plays and as a journalist. He wanted to establish a reputation as a serious novelist; toward the end of his life he deprecated his plays and his best-known nondramatic work, *Mrs. Caudle's Curtain Lectures* (1845), as mere amusements. Even some contemporary critics recognized his deficiencies as a dramatist and felt that his most important work might well be in fiction. Writing in the *Atlantic Monthly* in November 1857, James Hannay said that "though he had some of the most important qualities of a dramatist, very few of his dramas seem likely to live . . . the 'Man Made of Money' will outlast his best play."

The short story was just beginning to be established as a genre in the early nineteenth century, and Jerrold, wittingly or not, was one of its earliest and most polished practitioners. In fact, although Jerrold is remembered more as a name than as a literary icon, as a personality in literary or journalistic histories rather than as a serious writer, his best short stories are well crafted and bear further study. His contemporaries found them lacking in taste, mainly because too often the satiric nature of the stories leaves them devoid of admirable characters.

Since modern readers are no longer bound by Victorian precepts of taste in criticism, it would be worthwhile to go back and study some of his exemplary stories, many of which were collected under the titles *Men of Character* (1838) and *Cakes and Ale* (1842). Others, particularly those that appeared in *Blackwood's Edinburgh Magazine* in 1835, are also especially good examples of his craft.

Douglas William Jerrold was born on 3 January 1803 in London. His father, Samuel, was an actor and manager of an itinerant theater company. The family mythology had it that Douglas Jerrold's grandfather had been a wealthy horse trader in Hackney and that the family was descended of landed gentry. The family mythology did not explain how Samuel Jerrold found himself reduced to producing plays in the Kentish countryside for pennies a night. Samuel Jerrold's first wife died in the 1780s, and he remarried in 1794. His second wife, a Miss Reid, was young enough to be his daughter. Nevertheless, the marriage was a happy one and produced three children: two daughters and Douglas.

Jerrold's family moved almost immediately after his birth to the county of Kent, first to Wilsby, then, in 1807, to Sheerness. In 1809 an actor named Wilkinson was engaged to double as tutor for the six-year-old Douglas. After a year Wilkinson quit the company, and Douglas was sent to Mr. Herbert's school in Sheerness, where he remained for five years. Like many rural grammar schools, the one run by Mr. Herbert did not aspire to teach much beyond a rudimentary education. Jerrold himself said that he learned little more than reading, writing, and some arithmetic, with no attempt at algebra, Greek, or Latin. Still, Jerrold read a great deal; his grandmother felt he was safest locked in his room, and there, he remembered, he had read Salomon Gessner's *The Death of Abel* (1758), Tobias Smollett's *Roderick Random* (1748), and many other books. He also watched the harbor, which was busy with the naval traffic committed to the Napoleonic Wars. He watched the streets crowded with sailors and occasionally watched the sailors get bilked of their pay by the hangers-on around the docks. At the age of ten he went to sea as a midshipman aboard the guard ship *Namur*, anchored off the Nore. His commander was Capt. Charles Austen, the brother of Jane Austen.

Life aboard the guard ship was routine and fairly dull. Jerrold widened his reading and played around with amateur theatricals. After a year and a half, on 24 April 1815, he was transferred to the brig *Ernest*, a transport convoy vessel working between England and the Belgian coast. What he ob-

served aboard the *Namur*, and, more vividly, aboard the *Ernest*, eventually worked its way into many of his stories. On several trips the *Ernest* was used to transport wounded soldiers, and Jerrold's son Blanchard noted that later in life his father still described the horrors of those trips. While he never became a pacifist as such, Jerrold could never be fooled by descriptions of the glories of war after seeing the agony of the detritus of battle. He also observed the flogging of one Michael Ryan, who received six lashes with the cat-o'-nine-tails for theft. His disgust came out in several later comments and essays, including a vehement attack on Parliament in 1846 after a soldier had been flogged to death.

Jerrold was discharged at the end of the war, on 21 October 1815. His elderly father incurred increasing debts at Sheerness – it was said that peace was bad for theater in the navy port – and finally moved the family to London in January 1816, to the slum of Broad Court, Bow Street. Given his father's physical frailties, the family depended to a great extent on the money Jerrold earned as a printer's apprentice in Northumberland Street, Strand.

At Sidney's printing shop Jerrold began to write drama and poetry. He published a few verses in *Arliss's Magazine* and submitted a play that he wrote in 1818, at the age of 15, to the English Opera House. In 1819 Sidney went bankrupt, and Jerrold moved to Bigg's print shop in Lombard Street, which printed, among other items, the *Monitor* newspaper. Jerrold's first paid piece of writing was an anonymous review of Weber's *Die Freischutz* that he submitted to the *Sunday Monitor* in 1819.

The play that he wrote in 1818 was never produced by the English Opera House. Jerrold retrieved it in 1820, tinkered with it, and gave it to his old tutor, Wilkinson, to read. By this time Wilkinson had become fairly successful as a London actor. Daniel Egerton, the new manager of Sadler's Wells Theatre, wanted Wilkinson for a short run to promote the new theater. Wilkinson agreed, but only if Egerton would buy Jerrold's "The Duelists." Egerton assented but did not care for the title, which Wilkinson subsequently changed. Published as *More Frightened that Hurt: A Farce, in Two Acts* (1821) the play, first performed on 4 April 1821, had a successful run at Sadler's Wells and, although it did not make Jerrold's fortune, was good enough to be stolen and translated into French, then translated back into English by James Kenney under the title *Fighting by Proxy* and performed at the Olympic Theatre on 9 December 1833.

Jerrold continued to work as a printer at Bigg's, although he also regularly wrote anonymous reviews. He also continued to write plays. He became close friends with Laman Blanchard in 1823, and the two seriously considered joining up with George Gordon, Lord Byron, in Greece to battle the Turks. Instead, Jerrold, who knew what combat was and thus was not beguiled by Byron's descriptions of honorable death in such poems as "On This Day I Complete My Thirty-Sixth Year" (1824), married Mary Swann of Yorkshire in 1824. The two moved in with Jerrold's family, which still consisted of mother, father, and two sisters. More than ever, Jerrold needed money; he began writing for the *Weekly Times* and *The Ballot,* sometimes under his own name (or initials), sometimes under the pseudonym Henry Brownrigg. In 1825 he contracted to write pieces for the Coburg Theater. Also in 1825 his first child was born.

Over the next four years Jerrold wrote at least ten plays for George Bowell Davidge, the notoriously cheap manager of the Coburg. He also sold at least one play, *The Statue Lover; or, Music in Marble* (1828), to the Vauxhall. In 1829 Jerrold demanded more money from Davidge; when Davidge refused, Jerrold resigned in a fury and took his talent to Robert W. Elliston, the actor-manager of the Surrey Theatre. He earned five pounds a week and began by writing a series of rather ordinary pieces such as *John Overy, the Miser of Southwark Ferry* (1828?) and *Vidocq, the French Police Spy* (1829). After five such undistinguished efforts, he finally hit the jackpot with *Black-Eyed Susan; or, "All in the Downs"* (1829). In its first year *Black-Eyed Susan* ran for more than four hundred nights at six theaters. It was the sensation of the year, the most successful play in a decade. It netted Elliston thousands of pounds, but Jerrold made exactly sixty pounds, including ten pounds for sale of the copyright. It did, however, give him a reputation, which he converted to writing for one of the legitimate theaters, Drury Lane, by the end of 1829.

Jerrold's early biographers refer to him as a sturdy little fellow. He was barely five feet tall and slight of build, but he was not particularly sturdy. In the 1830s he began suffering from periodic attacks of rheumatism that made writing a painful chore. Still, he continued to turn out plays for a variety of theaters. After 1836 he turned his attention to other writing, and his dramatic output dropped precipitously. In 1835, bedridden from an attack of rheumatism, he met Charles Dickens, then a reporter for the *Morning Chronicle.* The two began a lifelong, if sometimes stormy, friendship.

Journalism in the 1830s and 1840s was a crowded field, with dozens of periodicals starting and dying monthly. Some, such as *Blackwood's Edinburgh Magazine,* the *Spectator,* and the *Athenaeum,* maintained a certain independence and a degree of respectability. Many more were founded to abuse political figures or to advance fringe causes. The Reform Bill of 1832, the agitation against the Corn Laws, and the Chartist movement all spawned a wide spectrum of periodicals. Humorous periodicals, too, abounded, but most were considered by respectable society to be either in bad taste or borderline pornography. Thus, the field for *Punch,* a magazine that would be somewhat radical in its politics but always in good taste, was wide-open. *Punch* would be, according to historian Richard G. G. Price, "a paper that was warm-hearted rather than hot-tempered, happy instead of venomous, and clean enough for the Family, a paper that took the radical line from generosity and not from spite."

Jerrold was a natural for the *Punch* circle. By the 1830s he had become a confirmed, well-known radical in his politics. He mistrusted authority, whether in Britain or abroad, and always identified himself with the masses of common people against the powerful. His politics occasionally broke out in his writing; *The Mutiny at the Nore; or, British Sailors in 1797* (1830) was as much a radical political protest as an attack on the brutality and genuinely evil conditions still existing in the British navy. It was rumored that in 1831 or 1832 he had written a Reform pamphlet so violent that it had been legally repressed. A little later he worked as a subeditor on the radical *Examiner* under Albany Fonblanque. Still later, he wrote as drama critic for the *Constitutional and Public Ledger,* a less radical, and certainly less successful, newspaper than the *Examiner;* the *Constitutional* lasted about a year.

In the early 1830s Jerrold began sending pieces regularly to the *New Monthly Magazine* and published some of his best short fiction there, including "The Tutor Fiend and his Three Pupils" (1831–1832). He published at least short pieces in the *Athenaeum,* including essays and short stories, between 1831 and 1833. He also found himself in continuing financial difficulty because of his propensity for loaning money to his friends or joining in ill-conceived publishing ventures. In 1836 he joined with his brother-in-law, W. J. Hammond, to manage the Strand Theatre, a minor disaster that contributed significantly to his insolvency. In 1835, living in Paris as much for his financial as for his physical health, he wrote a series of character sketches/short stories for *Blackwood's* that are among his best pieces of fiction. The relationship with *Blackwood's* lasted only about a year, ending when Samuel Warren, another *Blackwood's* contributor, persuaded the publishers that Jerrold impaired the tone of the magazine and disgusted its readers. Through the 1830s he also wrote extensively for *The Freemason's Quarterly Review* and several annuals.

In 1832, among the mass of other writing in which he was engaged, Jerrold started *Punch in London;* it ran for seventeen weeks, although Jerrold wrote only for the first two or three numbers. In 1835 Jerrold, Thackeray, and Henry Mayhew began discussions, at Jerrold's apartments in Paris, for an English version of the satiric French journal *Charivari.* Initial attempts were aborted by Thackeray's groundless fear that if the journal went under, each of the principals would be liable for his fellow's private debts. Discussions continued, however, and the circle grew from these three to include Percival Leigh, Orrin Smith, Kenny Meadows, John Leech, Jerrold's old friend Laman Blanchard, and several others. Jerrold, however, was the key. At this point in his life he had become one of the most widely known writers of his time and had more journalistic experience than any of the other collaborators. Besides, he knew personally most of the important journalists and other writers of the day – he had connections.

Because of its concentration on short, lively pieces, bon mots, puns, and brief essays, *Punch* became the perfect vehicle for Jerrold's talent. And because *Punch* was irreverent in its commentary on government, it suited Jerrold's political turn of mind as well. When it became widely known that Jerrold was associated with *Punch* (these were the days of anonymous journalism), he became more popular than any other writer of his time, and no less an author than Thackeray said that he feared a rivalry with Jerrold more than with any of his other contemporaries.

During the mid 1840s Jerrold contributed more material to *Punch* than any of the other writers except Gilbert à Beckett. In 1844 he wrote to George Hodder to complain that he was carrying the magazine on his back; in some issues he wrote more than half of the material and even suggested the cartoons. Meanwhile, he continued his other writing and journalism. He edited the *Illuminated Magazine* from the spring of 1843 to the fall of 1844. He wrote at least five plays between 1842 and 1845, including one of his most successful, *Bubbles of the Day* (1842). He founded and edited *Douglas Jerrold's Shilling Magazine* in January 1845 and continued it through June 1848. In July 1846 he began *Douglas Jerrold's Weekly Newspaper* as an organ for radical political and social philosophy. The newspaper was to

last until January 1848. He even spent a few months as a subeditor of the *Daily News* in 1846. During the decade he published some of his most popular long fiction. *The Chronicles of Clovernook* (1846) appeared in the *Illuminated Magazine. The History of St. Giles and St. James* (1845) appeared in *Douglas Jerrold's Shilling Magazine;* and several pieces, including *Punch's Letters to His Son* (1843), *Mrs. Caudle's Curtain Lectures,* and *The Story of a Feather* (1844), appeared in *Punch.*

Jerrold's short fiction almost invariably was written to serve a social purpose; he used it as one more weapon to advance his radical social and political agendas. For example, in the short story "Nothing but Rags," which appeared in the 7 July 1832 *Athenaeum,* he told a cautionary tale of a Chinese man who was given a genie to work for him and make him rich. The man finds that he must pay the spirit in "nothing but rags," and, because he does so, he becomes "the richest mandarin in China." Jerrold concludes: "Has not the Chinese mandarin left many descendants?" – leaving the reader to ponder those in England who have grown rich while paying their laborers in "nothing but rags."

Jerrold's admirable protagonists – when he included admirable protagonists – are almost invariably of the working class, and those people who serve as symbols of corruption are generally the rich or the politically powerful. His rich are almost always misers. A reader of Jerrold unfamiliar with Victorian England might be led to believe that any working-class person who made lots of money inevitably became obsessed with riches and lived out his life as a solitary miser, hoarding his gold, cheating the rich and the poor alike, and coming to a bleak end. Jerrold's social statement in these stories is that those who pile up money simply for the sake of money have forgotten the old cliché that they cannot take it with them.

Like Henry Fielding's characters, Jerrold's heroes endure many trials before they find reasonable success, a comfortable life, and a philanthropic old age. What sets them apart from Fielding's Tom Jones is that they do not succeed as a result of an unlooked-for inheritance from an unknown, wealthy benefactor or because of unknown family connections; they succeed because of their own good characters, hard work, and often, and most important, because of sheer luck. The world of Jerrold's fiction is a world of chance, and he used chance as a part of the world of irony that he created for both the miser and the man of good fortune.

Jerrold's debt to those eighteenth-century novels he read so avidly in his boyhood is obvious. Several of his stories are picaresques in the Fielding manner. Also, his rambling style shows the influence of another of his favorite authors, Lawrence Sterne. In the middle of a description or a piece of action Jerrold, like Stern, often pauses to discuss a universal truth. Furthermore, the stories included in *Men of Character* are variations on the eighteenth-century character sketch. Since Jerrold was more interested in the greater social commentary concerning his characters than he was in the character type he presented, he often was intrigued by the fiction he created to develop his character type; thus, the character sketches became, in fact, short stories.

His experience in the theater manifested itself in the construction of many of his short stories. Often he constructed his stories as five-act plays, introducing the main characters and the conflict in chapter (act) 1, working through several conflicts to a crisis, building from there to the climax, then adding a chapter of denouement. The dialogue occasionally resembles that found in his comedies and is apparently included more for the comic effect than to develop his characters or advance the plot.

A few of Jerrold's stories are farces, entertainments for comedy's sake. In these, as often happened in his comic drama, he became focused on dialogue and bits of action, and any logical structure or plot design went out the window. Passages from Jerrold's farces read like excerpts from works by P. G. Wodehouse, but the full stories lack Wodehouse's control of farcical structure: the careful development of episodes so that each scene plays an equal part in moving the action toward its satisfying, if manic, conclusion.

Like many of his contemporaries, Jerrold was fascinated by the Gothic, and he wrote several ghost stories. In addition, many of his stories use Gothic elements to add a little psychological thrill to what might be a rather ordinary passage, and occasionally he used Gothic scenes to get himself out of a dead end in his plot. Jerrold's Gothic elements, though, are generally ornaments to his social criticism. Except for the occasional farce, it is the rare Jerrold short story that does not contain a radical theme criticizing prevailing social attitudes toward the poor and the weak, a fact that did not pass unnoted by Jerrold's contemporaries.

"Matthew Clear: The Man Who Saw His Way" shows Jerrold at his most typical. The story criticizes selfish, undeserving, socially blind folk who inherit wealth and do not use it for the public good (one of comedy's stock targets since Roman drama). None of his characters is particularly admirable, and all come to a bad end. His ironies are played out both verbally and through the mischances of life. The dramatic structure, as so often happens in the short stories, falls apart toward the conclusion. Also, Matthew's life is nothing if not picaresque.

The story was originally published in the October 1835 *Blackwood's* and republished in *Men of Character*. It is an unusually short piece, running about seven thousand words. The narrator establishes a certain distance from the story, framing it by including the reader as one of the characters. "Did you, sir, ever descend into a coal-mine, a tin-mine, or, for you have the look of a traveller, into a salt-mine at Cracow?" At the very beginning Jerrold plucks his reader's sleeve and flatters him or her a little while advancing his story. He positions the reader alongside the author, ready to pass judgment on the not particularly sympathetic characters.

Jerrold typically uses one of two openings for his stories: either he begins in medias res, with a quote from a character that plunges the reader theaterlike into the action, or he commences with a short essay on a universal truth. The opening of "Matthew Clear" is a hybrid: the first line is "With such an excellent property, too! ah, sir!" – the kind of line a butler might deliver as the curtain goes up. Jerrold then supplies the reader with a bit of context:

> And, as the speaker touched upon property, his voice trembled, and into either eye there stole one large tear, a diamond of the first water.
> "Ah sir! If Mr. Clear had only seen into himself; for with such a property!" –

It is at this point that Jerrold switches to his second opening tactic and criticizes Matthew: "The truth is, Matthew, though the dimmest owl, had, in his own conceit, the vision of the eagle." This comment also serves to echo the subtitle of the piece and lets the reader know that the piece will be satiric (or at the very least, ironic) and that Matthew will be something of a boob. The narrator then takes the reader into his confidence with an overlong essay on sinking into the earth. At its beginning he warns his audience that few people wish to make such a descent, either into themselves or into the earth, and at its end he leaves the plumber of the depths groping "in darkness, in substantial night."

When Jerrold returns to the story, he introduces Matthew, a young man of twenty-eight who had inherited cash but not sagacity. Matthew suddenly becomes a target for "two mature spinsters and three experienced widows." Obviously using their apparent wealth as a guide to sort through his choices, he finally settles on "a timid, sallow daughter of Eve" who "looked emphatically thirty-four, [though] sure we are she was but thirty-three." Miss Julia Lac hooked Matthew by showing him "her" diamond necklace, which soon turns out not to be hers at all. Nevertheless, by the end of chapter 1, Matthew and Julia are married, because, as Matthew tells his many friends, "he had – seen his way."

As the curtain rises on chapter 2, Matthew and his new bride are seen at breakfast, discussing a parrot. The parrot device is a favorite of Jerrold's, for when dialogue is properly constructed the unwitting bird can speak wisdom. In "The Preacher Parrot" in *Cades and Ale,* for example, the parrot delivers an auctioneer's lines at inopportune times. Mrs. Clear's parrot, Nabob, taught to speak by a sailor, laughs maniacally and shrieks "Ha! ha! ha! Hooked him by ____!" It becomes clear as the story continues that Nabob will deliver his one, devastating line whenever Mrs. Clear comes near to revealing her true self, the aging angler after a rich husband. Love has nothing to do with the Clears' marriage.

At any rate Matthew's attempts to rid his home of the parrot are thwarted by Julia's new-found obstinance. She had promised to turn out the bird, but the narrator reminds readers that this assurance had been given before the marriage. At any rate any further conversation on the subject is blocked by Julia, who, instead of furthering the conversation on the parrot, turns to feed the bird sugar cubes that she holds in her lips.

Chapter 2 also provides two further pieces of information to build the plot: Matthew is informed that one of the unsuccessful spinsters is suing him for breach of promise, and a bill arrives for the diamond necklace, intimating to Matthew that perhaps he has not been completely successful in "seeing his way." The parrot, of course, contributes to this dawning knowledge with his short, half-accusing, half-triumphant "Ha! ha! ha! Hooked him, by ____!"

Chapter 3 brings the plot to its crisis. It begins with an obviously theatrical scene with Matthew and Downey, his lawyer; the dialogue comes right from the music hall:

> "Well Mat . . . I've made the best of bad. I – where's your wife?"
> "Gone to Dorking."
> "Dorking again!"

Then the scene moves on to a carefully staged bit of byplay. When Matthew considers the possibility of siring a son, "Downy turned his grey eye on Matthew; then, looking upward, stared at the portrait of Mrs. Clear. Matthew felt the look to be ingeniously murderous; for it slew the unbegotten. From that hour, Matthew never had the hardihood to enjoy even a possible child."

Matthew learns from Downy that two of his early pursuers have come into considerable fortunes and that Matthew might settle the breach of promise suit for £500. Matthew privately turns the breach of promise case over to Downy's clerk, Felix, who assures Matthew that the wronged Miss Brown "hadn't a leg to stand on." The case winds up costing Matthew £1,500 and nearly bankrupts him. To complicate his life further, Julia returns from Dorking with a small Indian "orphan" named Tippoo, the evil parrot, and the news that all her supposed Indian properties have been lost in a tragic earthquake, leaving her penniless.

In chapter 4 Matthew loses the rest of his money when he tries to cheat a friend who has given him a hot investment tip. He receives the bad news in a theatrical scene with friend Simpson:

> "Indeed," added Simpson, after a brief pause, "'twas very lucky that we didn't purchase" –
> "Lucky!" cried Matthew, and his jaw worked like the jaw of a corpse galvanised; – "lucky!"
> "Very lucky; for you must know," – and here Simpson lowered his voice, took out his box, and impartially showering the snuff up either nostril, continued with a syllabic distinctness – "you must know, that the bonds we were to buy together, have to-day gone down to nothing." So saying, Simpson vanished from the room, leaving Matthew fixed in a chair, an exanimate pauper.

The chapter ends with Matthew attempting to escape to America aboard the *Good Intent*. Unfortunately Julia had earlier also decided to escape to America, by ironic coincidence aboard the same ship, and as Matthew boards in the dead of night and disguised, Julia recognizes him, calls out his name, and begs forgiveness. Her shrieks alert a pair of bailiffs, who carry Matthew off to jail. As the rowboat pulls away, the parrot in the rigging mocks Matthew one last time.

Jerrold could have ended his story here – indeed, he should have ended it here. But he must drive home his radical theme. Matthew sinks further until he contemplates suicide. Unfortunately, the druggist from whom he attempts to buy the arsenic is none other than his foster son, Tippoo; in shame, Matthew leaves with medical salts. He works as a clerk for a miser; when the miser dies,

Matthew inherits nothing but a lawsuit on behalf of the miser that results in his spending an hour in the stocks and two years in prison. In the final scene as he is being led to prison, he is smacked in the face by a handful of "mire."

> "if – if – I – could – see – my – way!" said Matthew with his eyes full of mire.
> "Look straight forward," said a fellow prisoner.
> "Ha!" groaned Matthew, and he thought, "if I had always looked straightforward, how very differently should I have seen my way!"

Until this rather weak concluding chapter, Jerrold had given his readers a well-crafted piece of short, comic fiction, with a protagonist who had long lived in popular British culture.

In another representative short work, *Isaac Cheek: The "Man of Wax"* (1851), Jerrold seems to have begun with the intention of writing a farce and concluded in a more serious vein. The story originally appeared in July and September 1836 in *Blackwood's;* the July portion was clearly intended to be comic, with a minimum of social satire. Perhaps one of *Blackwood's* guardians of public virtue forced a change in the direction of the story; perhaps one of Jerrold's friends convinced him that *Blackwood's* readers needed more than mere comedy. At any rate, in the second half of the story characters become more sympathetic, and a theme emerges. Jerrold's tone also shifts from brittle, Petronian wit to a more Dickensian, sentimental comedy. The story recounts the adventures of what appears at first to be a thoroughly disreputable lot: Isaac Cheek, the Man of Wax; Cox, his employer; Michael Angelo Pups, a dwarf who sculpts murderers for a wax museum; and a host of minor characters. Jerrold concocts a series of perfectly outrageous situations and sets his characters loose to stumble their way through them.

*Isaac Cheek*, like "Matthew Clear," starts as if a curtain were rising. Isaac appears at the door of a fashionable residence; his shabby clothing is described in detail. Sarah, the maid, recoils from him, and the house's owner, Mr. Cox, wrinkles his nose. Isaac presents Mr. Cox a letter that advises him to "Employ [Isaac] in any way," for "he is a man of wax." Like good drama the story engages the reader immediately. Who can trust a man of wax, or indeed, someone who would employ a man of wax? As in the opening of "Matthew Clear," readers are fairly certain that the story will have no sympathetic characters.

No sympathetic characters appear in the first half of the story, but this Victorian defect does not weaken *Isaac Cheek;* on the contrary, the characters are quite amusing. Isaac's first task for Cox is to deliver an elixir to a wealthy client. When he arrives at the house, he does not contradict the assumption that he is a doctor's assistant. Since he has no idea what Cox's profession is, or what is in the elixir except that "it's a matter of life or death," Isaac might, for all he knows, actually be a doctor's assistant. He is rushed to the bedroom of a squalling six-year-old girl, and he administers the entire bottle. As he prepares to leave, another messenger arrives with an elixir from a doctor. As the confusion slowly unravels, it turns out that Isaac's delivery was a bottle of hair dye for the governess, who had matrimonial designs on the master of the house, who might love her but could not love her red hair. Isaac returns to Cox and, unrepentant (and ungrateful), attempts to extort £100 from his master. Cox, instead, persuades Isaac to venture £100 in a sure-fire business, prophetically (and symbolically) a wax museum.

Through the first half of the story, Jerrold carefully develops his plot and judiciously introduces comic characters, including Michael Angelo and a "Persian prince" who speaks pure cockney. His dialogue is carefully crafted and intended to move the story along, reveal the nature of the speakers, and make his readers laugh:

> "There's my hand."
> "And between men of honor, quite enough," said Cox.
> "I don't care much for parchment," observed Cheek, "Yet it is a necessary evil."
> "True, but I can see we want no deed – we shall agree like brothers."
> "And with brothers, says the Italian," and Cheek spoke with the air of a schoolmaster – "two witnesses and a notary."

But in the second half of the story the structure breaks down. Isaac becomes little more than a minor character; Michael Angelo, whose dwarfish qualities have almost disappeared, becomes central; and the unified focus on characters, situation, and theme that is essential to a short work of fiction is lost. Jerrold carries off the story with an awkwardly introduced, almost mawkishly sentimental scene between Michael and his wrongly accused orphan foster child, Eleanor. He concludes with a contrived set of marriages between Eleanor and a hastily introduced farmer and between Isaac and the actress Miss Boss. In a summary chapter of a single paragraph, Jerrold explains that Michael took over as sole proprietor of the wax museum and became "the man of wax." Cox as comic villain seems to have

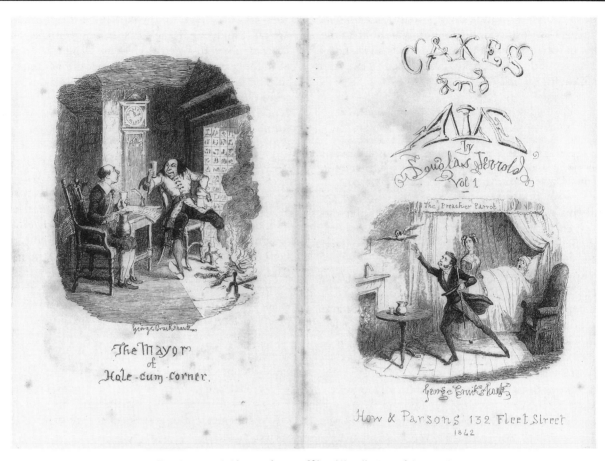

*Frontispiece and title page for one of Jerrold's collections of short stories*

been forgotten, and the cockney Persian somehow mutates into a stock Jew. *Isaac Cheek* has moments of brilliance – short, comic scenes in both the first and second halves are still funny – but it shows how Jerrold's reliance on artificial dramatic structure often damages his achievement in the short-fiction form.

Jerrold experimented with Gothicism in such short stories as "The Black Bank Notes," "The Wine Cellar," and "The Mayor of Hole-Cum-Corner." In "The Black Bank Notes" a Jewish pawnbroker greedily cheats a sailor out of a diamond of inestimable value. He then sells the diamond and all his other jewels to another Jewish pawn broker, who pays in magic banknotes that turn black when exposed to the sun. The satisfying conclusion is, of course, that greed inevitably causes ruination. The only sympathetic character in the story is the cheated sailor, who becomes an agent of the corrupt pawn broker's destruction. The honest, sympathetic sailor is typical of Jerrold, hearkening back to his own days at sea.

The title character of "The Mayor of Hole-Cum-Corner" is basically a good man who, in the pride of his office, convicts an innocent man. The situation of the conviction is typical Jerrold: the innocent Gaffer Nemmington is poor and had twice before been convicted of petty offenses. In the climactic court scene, Mayor Tobias has Gaffer admit that he has been whipped twice previously, works little because he is lame, and has slept in a haystack for the previous three nights:

> "I never saw a clearer case," crowed forth the Mayor of Hole-Cum-Corner. "If, my man, appearances are worth anything, it is plain that you have stolen Dock's gander."
>
> "Your worship wouldn't whip a man upon appearance?" humbly questioned Gaffer.
>
> The impertinence of the query was too much for Tobias; and the Mayor of Hole-Cum-Corner, slapping his hand upon a volume of the statutes, cried with an oath, that "with the greatest pleasure in life, he would!"

A series of disasters is then visited upon Tobias, and each dreadful occurrence is accompanied by a stranger, obviously satanic, who offers Tobias wealth, respect, power, and all the rest of the Mephistophelian bargain, which, to his credit,

Tobias refuses. At the conclusion Tobias is a changed man – literally changed, since he has been executed and reconstituted into another body – and the truth is revealed to him: Gaffer Nemmington sold his soul first to get revenge on Tobias, who had judged him on appearances.

"The Wine Cellar" is yet another tale about greed, Gothic in the same sense that Edgar Allan Poe's "The Cask of Amontillado" (1846) is Gothic. Curlew the goldsmith, described in the story's first sentence as "thrifty" but later described as yet another in a long line of Jerroldian misers, is visited by a strange man who asks for a curious seal ring depicting Death and Bacchus. After Curlew fashions the ring, the stranger produces wine for a toast. Teetotaler Curlew (Jerrold's misers never drink; Jerrold considered wine one of the sweet pleasures of the flesh) is overcome by the wine, and when he awakes he finds the stranger has left a bottle. Curlew hides the bottle in his cellar, and in an attempt to keep the wine safe from imagined thieves, unaccountably nails himself in the cellar with it, where his remains are found 175 years later, an object lesson in greed.

"Mr. Peppercorn at Home" combines all of Jerrold's tendencies into one well-crafted short story. Although written in eight chapters, "Mr. Peppercorn" follows a five-act dramatic structure: chapters 4 and 5 may be read as two scenes of a fourth act, and chapters 6 and 7 serve as two scenes of a fifth. Chapter 8 becomes a brief epilogue, since the resolution – Peppercorn's apparent death – appeared at the end of act 5 and a denouement was necessary.

"Mr. Peppercorn at Home" also contains all the trappings of a Gothic short story. The setting is a row of abandoned houses, reputed to be haunted by the ghosts of people who committed terrible sins in them. From the third chapter forward, the threat of violence hangs heavily in the air. The characters are all grotesques who make a living as exhibits or operatives in freak shows. And finally, balance is offered by young Hyacinth, Mr. Peppercorn's nephew, whose mother had died because of Mr. Peppercorn's greed and who had sworn revenge on the old miser.

Jerrold's social satire is evident in the freak-show characters who inhabit the row of abandoned houses, in Peppercorn, and in the story's theme. The freak-show characters have all, for one reason or another, been forced to live on the fringes of society and indeed make their livings by taking advantage of the greater society's greed and vanity. Mr. Peppercorn's greed knows no bounds; he has

lived a life devoid of both love and trust. By reforming Mr. Peppercorn at the conclusion of the story, Jerrold adds a rather Dickensian uplift to his theme: while greed and a loveless life lead only to destruction, a positive life may yet be built from the ruins.

Jerrold opens the story by describing Isaac Peppercorn through the device of describing Providence Hall, his ironically named home in Lincolnshire. The mansion is nearly ruined: windows that had blown in have never been replaced; the chimneys are all leveled; indeed, "the very penetralia of the building were now open to sun and rain." Like Ebenezer Scrooge, Peppercorn even begrudges the few coals it might take to warm his home: "In the last frost," Jerrold tells the reader, "a cat had been found frozen to death at the fireside." The building stands as a symbol for Peppercorn's soul, empty and seemingly deserted.

The description of the house, the letter that called Peppercorn to London to "attend to his interest" in the matter of some rental houses, the leave-taking, and Peppercorn's first night's stay in a modest inn in the north of London, serve as prologue. The curtain rises with Peppercorn anguishing over the shilling he was billed for a night's lodging, plus nine pence for breakfast, plus four pence for oats. Peppercorn challenges every penny of the bill, revealing Jerrold's familiar characterization of a miser. When the waiter remarks on Peppercorn's not taking supper, he responds, "Do you think I'm from the Diamond Mines or the Gold Coast? Supper! and bed a shilling!"

In the course of this scene, Peppercorn is informed that his horse has died:

"Did you give him a feed?" asked Peppercorn anxiously.
"I tried – I tried," answered the benevolent ostler, "But la! sir, he didn't seem to know what oats was made for."
"Then he didn't eat?" continued Peppercorn, with growing concern.
"Eat!" said the ostler, with emotion – "he looked at the corn for all the world as a christian looks at a bad shilling."
Again Peppercorn cast his eye upon the bill. " 'Oats four-pence.' Take four from two-and-a-penny, and there will remain one-and-ninepence."

This scene not only makes Peppercorn the stock miser figure but also something of a comic figure. He is evil but petty evil, everyday evil, the evil that grinds people down but that can also be laughed at. In the final scene of this first act Peppercorn's lawyer describes the ruined tenements that constitute the interest Peppercorn was called to London to attend to. The tenements were uninhabited and virtually uninhabitable. To bring some kind of closure to the estate would take a month, during which time Peppercorn would have to stay in London. Peppercorn groans about the expense of a month in London. The reader knows from the description of Providence Hall where Isaac will stay.

Chapter 2 takes place in the street outside the tenements. Hyacinth is seen knocking loudly on one of the doors. A stranger asks him his business and in the course of conversation reveals to Hyacinth that all the houses are haunted. Hyacinth's skepticism causes the stranger to retire in a huff. Another stranger then discusses the hauntings in greater detail. Hyacinth's skepticism causes this stranger, too, to retire. When Peppercorn arrives, neither he nor Hyacinth recognizes the other. The dialogue that follows is a stock, comic conversation of misunderstanding: Peppercorn voices his horror at the condition of the houses, and Hyacinth thinks the horror is a result of Peppercorn having just seen a ghost (such dialogues of misunderstanding were one of Jerrold's stock comic devices; "Matthew Clear" depends on them for comic interest as the structure falls to pieces in the second half of the story). At the end of the scene Peppercorn asserts that he is an old friend of the landlord, "a very honest, liberal, excellent kind of man; his name is Peppercorn."

Hyacinth, of course, denounces Peppercorn and curses the houses: "May they become the haunt of wretches as vile and worthless as the wretch who owns them – may they become the miser's curse – his torment – his remorse!" The irony of that curse will become apparent in the next act. Chapter 2, however, ends with Peppercorn carefully pushing open a squeaking door, as heads seem to move about in windows of several adjacent houses.

At the beginning of chapter 3 Jerrold inserts a brief essay on the human condition into his narrative. An appreciation of vagabonds, the essay serves as a critique of a society whose general "respectability" whites over the color around its edges. It satirizes society by making positive those elements that have been marginalized; in the process, it probably crosses over into questionable taste for many readers:

> We love vagabonds – we confess it, we have a kindly yearning towards the knavish faculty – the antic cunning – the adroit wisdom, that lives on the outskirts of life, – and, having altogether shirked what legislators call the social compact, – having from the cradle protested against the impression of a tacit consent to the dull forms of sober men, "clothe the back and fill the maw" from the weakness, the credulity, or the vanity of those who think and dub themselves the grave wise el-

ders! Your real, quick-blooded, genial vagabond is the arabesque of life.

The essay also serves to introduce chapter 3 and the kinds of characters whom the reader will meet there.

As Peppercorn attempts to make himself at home in the ruined house, a series of grotesque vagabonds drifts into the room. Fortunately for Peppercorn they mistake him for one of their number. He senses that it might be bad policy to reveal himself, so he asks about the houses and their homeless tenants indirectly. The threats of horrible violence against the landlord and his lawyer convince him that he is in mortal danger. At the end of this chapter one of the vagabonds announces: "The General will be here and we shall have such a supper!"

Chapter 4 opens on the supper. Jerrold provides a brief description of the personages at the table and some of the background, couched in social satire. The General spoken of at the end of chapter 3 is General Pompey, a dwarf who had once been the main attraction at a number of sideshows. Although he does not draw attention to his parallels, Jerrold describes him in reverse political terms:

> General Pompey, in consequence of his extreme littleness, [had] in his time been patronized by all the courts of Europe. Unfortunately, in two or three instances, when he was in the full blaze of fortune, smaller men supplanted him; and he was compelled from time to time to 'take a more removed ground,' until fortune deposited him in the box of a showman, whence he had emerged to preside on the present occasion.

The General is joined by a stone-eater, whose act is to swallow and then vomit up "pebbles, pins, nails, and other small ware." It is to Jerrold a wonderful paradox that "the honest people perceiving he could swallow stones, never failed to press upon him money to buy bread." Another of the guests is a "posture-master," whose crowning achievement is his ability to impersonate a snake. Again, Jerrold makes his point carefully: "We once knew a minister to throw him a guinea from the window of his drawing room, in pure admiration of this peculiar motion." Other characters are a schoolmaster discharged for not beating his students; a failed philanthropist currently selling snake oil; a great navigator who now plays a psychic; the inventor of gilded gingerbread; and a former hermit who, after renouncing sex and all pleasures of the body, ended up marrying the bearded lady. Hyacinth is there too, because he had just saved the General from a kidnapper who was taking him home as a toy for his children.

This short scene ends with a derisive toast to the landlord, which is ruined by Hyacinth's refusal to drink. When pressed, he admits that he knows the landlord. In the midst of the general consternation that follows this announcement comes a loud knocking on the door, and "every man sprang to his feet, and stared for information in the face of his neighbor."

Chapter 5 introduces the potentially fatal conflict between the vagabonds and the miser and makes the conflict immediate. Flittermouse, who operates a magic lantern show, appears and announces that the landlord's bedding has been delivered and he will soon be among them. Hyacinth explains the evil nature of the landlord and his own knowledge of him, neglecting, however, to tell the company that he is Peppercorn's nephew. Hyacinth has by now figured out that the ancient stranger in their midst must be Peppercorn, and he baits him unmercifully. Meanwhile, the vagabonds curse the landlord and threaten his life in several creative ways. They also resolve to finish stripping the houses of anything of value. Throughout the scene Peppercorn is alternately in fear for his life and in terror that his property will be stolen from him.

The scene ends with the question of what to do with Peppercorn should he appear. Peppercorn's neighbor growls

> "Cut his throat."
> "Ugh! ugh!" cried Peppercorn.
> "What do you say?" said the stone-eater turning to Isaac.
> "The gentleman says nothing," remarked Muzzleby; "but you can see that he's of my opinion. Every feature in his face cries – 'Cut his throat!'"

In chapter 6 Peppercorn comes close to revealing himself to Hyacinth, when a portrait of Hyacinth's mother is found and Hyacinth reveals himself instead. The vagabonds swear to support Hyacinth in whatever revenge he wishes to take on Peppercorn (although Muzzleby continues to campaign for throat cutting). Peppercorn's fear has risen to monstrous proportions.

As chapter 6 opens, the vagabonds drop hints that they might know Peppercorn's real identity, but they continue to leave him in doubt. Peppercorn's fear is allowed to build until the middle of the night, when a light distracts him, then grows, and eventually becomes the specter of his dead sister. Jerrold describes the action in his best Gothic prose:

> The specter, with its fixed eyes, approached the bed, – the lips of the old man moved but his tongue was jellied in his mouth; – as the shade came nearer, the miser drew his frozen legs upwards, and clutching the blanket, he tore it in his hands as he rose – such strength did terror give his years – as it had been woven of the finest thread. Still the specter came nearer, when the terrified wretch, his back fairly creeping up the wall, stood upon his feet to confront it. He stood in the bed, his face white and wet as reeking chalk, and his mouth open as with the death-gasp. In a moment, all was dark; and the miser, with a thrilling shriek, fell huddled in a heap upon the bed!

At this point the parallel drama breaks down. Jerrold twists the old theme that had proved useful in so many of his earlier stories – that those who live as misers live a hollow life and die an empty death. So died such misers as Marvedi in "The Preacher Parrot," Curlew in "The Wine Cellar," and Matthew Clear's miser master. But Peppercorn does not die. In a Dickens-like change of heart, Jerrold lets Peppercorn reform, learn from the specter, and become miraculously transformed into a philanthropist and benefactor to his nephew, Hyacinth. The epilogue, chapter 8, explains that the specter was a product of Flittermouse's magic lantern and the portrait of Hyacinth's mother. Thus, Jerrold changes his theme from the inexorable evil end of the miser to the potential for transformation through the intervention of good-hearted people: the vagabonds and Hyacinth.

Perhaps the reason that Jerrold's short fiction is no longer studied (or even read) is that it is less literature than an artifact of Victorian popular culture. Jerrold anticipated his fate in an essay in the 28 December 1833 *Athenaeum* titled "Time's Laconics." He decried the process that allowed the extensive thoughts and writings of a Sir Philip Sidney or a Thomas Browne to turn to mere epigrams, quotes, and digested volumes: "A time is coming, when men will be recollected by sentences, and not by the number of their pages. Folios will shrink into short chapters, and octavos fall into mere lines." The fertile Jerrold seems to have described his own fate; his output was incredible. In Albert C. Baugh's *A Literary History of England* (1967), however, Jerrold rates three sentences, one for his plays and two for his fiction. Other literary historians and critics have been similarly unkind. Yet even as an artifact of his culture he rates a second look, and modern readers who enjoy Dickens and Thackeray should also enjoy the comedy of Douglas Jerrold.

**Biographies:**

W. Blanchard Jerrold, *The Life and Remains of Douglas Jerrold* (London: Kent, 1859; Boston: Ticknor & Fields, 1859);

Walter Jerrold, *Douglas Jerrold, Dramatist and Wit,* 2 volumes (London: Hodder & Stoughton, 1914).

**References:**

Albert C. Baugh, *A Literary History of England,* 4 volumes (New York: Appleton, 1967);

Charles Dickens, *The Letters of Charles Dickens,* 3 volumes, edited by Walter Dexter (London: Nonesuch, 1938);

Walter E. Doyle, "Through the Domestic Drama Darkly: Douglas Jerrold and Early Nineteenth Century Minor Drama," *Victorian Institute Journal,* 9 (1980–1981): 83–98;

Monica Fryckstedt, "Geraldine Jewsbury and *Douglas Jerrold's Shilling Magazine,*" *English Studies,* 66, no. 4 (1985): 326–337;

John Fyvie, "A Forgotten Jester," *Macmillan's,* 87 (March 1903): 382–389;

"Genius and Writings of Douglas Jerrold," *Eclectic,* 32 (June 1854): 166–175;

James Hannay, "Douglas Jerrold," *Atlantic Monthly,* 1 (November 1857): 1–12;

Walter Jerrold, *Douglas Jerrold and "Punch"* (London: Macmillan, 1910);

Richard M. Kelly, "The Birth of a Snob: Douglas Jerrold and William Makepeace Thackeray and the 'Jenkins Papers,' " *Satire Newsletter,* 8 (1970): 10–15;

Kelly, "Chesterfield's Letters to His Son: The Victorian Judgment," *Tennessee Studies in Literature,* 15 (1970): 109–123;

Kelly, *Douglas Jerrold* (New York: Twayne, 1972);

Kelly, "Mrs. Caudle, a Victorian Curtain Lecturer," *University of Toronto Quarterly,* 38 (April 1969): 295–309;

Kelly, "Punch's Letters to His Son," *Satire Newsletter,* 4 (1967): 58–62;

Christopher Kent, "The Whittington Club: A Bohemian Experiment in Middle Class Social Reform," *Victorian Studies,* 18 (September 1974): 31–55;

William Charles Macready, *The Diaries of William Charles Macready,* 2 volumes, edited by William Toynbee (London: Chapman & Hall, 1912);

Sir Nathaniel, "Notes on Noteworthies," *New Monthly Magazine,* new series 110 (August 1857): 404–417;

Allardyce Nicoll, *Early Nineteenth Century Drama, 1800–1850* (Cambridge: Cambridge University Press, 1955);

Margaret Oliphant, *William Blackwood and His Sons,* 3 volumes (Edinburgh: Blackwood, 1897);

Thomas Powell, *The Living Authors of England* (New York: Appleton, 1849);

Richard G. G. Price, *A History of Punch* (London: Collins, 1957);

Gordon N. Ray, *Thackeray: The Uses of Adversity, 1811–1846* (New York: McGraw-Hill, 1955);

Michael Slater, "Carlyle and Jerrold into Dickens: A Study of *The Chimes,*" *Nineteenth Century Fiction,* 24 (1969): 506–526;

Marion H. Spielmann, *The History of Punch* (New York: Cassell, 1895);

James Hutchinson Stirling, *Jerold, Tennyson, and Macaulay* (Edinburgh: Edmonston & Douglas, 1868);

Richard Stoddard, ed., *Personal Reminiscences by Barham, Harness, and Hodder* (New York: Scribner, 1875);

Henry Viztelly, *Glances back through Seventy Years,* 2 volumes (London: Kegan Paul, 1893);

Bruce A. White, "Douglas Jerrold's 'Q' Papers in *Punch,*" *Victorian Periodicals Review,* 15 (Winter 1982): 131–137.

# Patrick Kennedy

## (1801 – 29 March 1873)

### Betsy Gordon
*McKendree College*

BOOKS: *Legends of Mount Leinster,* as Harry Whitney (Dublin: P. Kennedy, 1855);
*The Banks of the Boro: A Chronicle of the County of Wexford* (Dublin: McGlashan & Gill, 1867);
*Evenings in the Duffrey* (Dublin: McGlashan & Gill, 1869).

OTHER: *Fictions of Our Forefathers,* collected by Kennedy (Dublin: McGlashan & Gill, 1859);
*Legendary Fictions of the Irish Celts,* collected by Kennedy (London: Macmillan, 1866; Detroit: Singing Tree Press, 1968);
*The Fireside Stories of Ireland,* collected by Kennedy (Dublin: McGlashan & Gill, 1870);
*The Bardic Stories of Ireland,* collected by Kennedy (Dublin: McGlashan & Gill, 1871);
*The Book of Modern Irish Anecdotes, Humour, Wit and Wisdom,* collected by Kennedy (London: Routledge, 1872).

Patrick Kennedy is mainly known for recording the legends, folklore, and folklife of Ireland. Although he wrote many scholarly articles and reviews, he was a modest literary critic who often submitted articles anonymously. His known works consist of personal recollections and re-created folktales, legends, and customs. The Irish peasants of his childhood come alive in his descriptions of school, weddings, harvest homes, priests, parsons, jokes, and songs. His more durable works are collections of Irish stories, legends, and fairy tales that he gathered from the area where he was raised. One of the unique elements of his work is that he recorded in English stories that had been told in Irish for centuries. He is widely credited with preserving Irish idioms in the turn of a phrase, sentence structure, Irish words, love of description, and moralizing commentary. He was widely read during his lifetime. In his notes he mentioned being influenced by early oral literature collectors such as the Brothers Grimm in Germany and Peter Christen Asbjørnsen in Norway. He was also familiar with *Popular Tales of the West Highlands* (1860, 1862), the translation of Scottish-Gaelic tales by John Campbell of Islay, a Scottish folklorist and Gaelic scholar who not only collected tales but also taught folklore fieldwork techniques to others.

Kennedy was born in Kilmyshal, County Wexford, Ireland, in 1801. Little is recorded of his early life, and his parents' names and his father's occupation are unknown. His writings indicate that his family was of peasant stock; but it must have been financially comfortable, since he stayed in school until he was seventeen or eighteen. He went to local schools, finishing at Cloughbawn, which took Roman Catholics and Protestants, boys and girls, rich and poor, providing Kennedy with an eclectic exposure to local life. The school at Cloughbawn was established and maintained by the Carew family, who lived in Castleboro Castle. According to Kennedy's *The Banks of the Boro: A Chronicle of the County of Wexford* (1867), the family arrived in the area in 1668, and their tenure was marked by continued concern for the welfare of the people. Robert Carew, the owner during Kennedy's boyhood, was one of the first in Ireland to provide the elementary education that was denied by the state at that time.

Another influence also had a lasting impact on Kennedy. The parish priest, Father Murphy, called on him to clerk, tend his mare, be godfather for christenings, and witness at weddings. These experiences also became a part of Kennedy's portrait of Irish life.

After Kennedy completed his schooling in 1818 or 1819 he worked as an elementary teacher and a principal. In 1820 or 1821 he went to Dublin for a teacher-training course at the Society for the Promotion of Education of the Poor of Ireland. He made such a strong impression that the school, usually referred to as Kildare Place Society, hired him in 1822 or 1823. He married a woman named Maria (her surname may have been Kelly), and they had daughters named Elizabeth, Monica, and Margaret and sons named John, Charles, and James. It is not clear when he left teaching, but he was registered as a bookseller and librarian in the Dublin directory of 1840. His bookstore on Anglesea Street was frequented by book lovers and folklorists. Because of his humble nature, much of his writing resulted from the prodding of friends and colleagues.

Kennedy began his writing career with scholarly articles on English and French literature, folklore, and legends and reviews of contemporary books. His exposure to folklorists seems to have led him to write down the tales and legends he had heard while growing up. To this work he added stories he remembered from boyhood. His early literary outlets for articles were the *Wexford Independent, Duffrey's Fireside Magazine,* and other periodicals.

Though colleagues recognized Kennedy as a prolific contributor of magazine and newspaper articles, his periodical writings are difficult, if not impossible, to locate. Among the anonymous pieces he is known to have contributed are "Reviews of the First Four Volumes of the Ossianic Society's Publications," "Reviews of the Productions of the Living Writers of France," and several reviews and literary articles. Much of his work appeared in the *Dublin University Magazine,* including "European and Asiatic Folklore," "A Tale of Dublin Thirty Years Ago," "Dublin Newspapers of the Last Century," general reviews, and articles on Celtic archaeology.

Encouraged by friends and editors, Kennedy eventually collected his magazines into books. The first, *Legends of Mount Leinster,* was published pseudonymously in 1855. The stories are presented as the recollections of a group of relatives and friends who gather in the evening around the fire of Mrs. K. One of the characters is a local faggot cutter, described in Kennedy's later book *Legendary Fictions of the Irish Celts* (1866) as a local storyteller who knows what story elements are pleasing and interesting and who can invent if necessary. *Legendary Fictions of the Irish Celts* also furnishes additional information about the hostess introduced in *Legends of Mount Leinster.* Kennedy explains that Mrs. K. learned about the legendary history of Ireland from a wandering peddler and poet. Such storytellers entertained people on their rounds, drawing crowds whenever they found lodging in a neighborhood.

*Legends of Mount Leinster* opens with a description of the area and describes the gathering and the meal before beginning the stories told by the fire. The stories are simple folktales, but Kennedy incorporates literary elements, such as historical background, that expand these simple tales into much longer accounts. In the process he incorporates details of manners and customs of the times. Some local or regional elements occur in these tales, such

*Frontispiece by W. Small for Patrick Kennedy's* Legendary Fictions of the Irish Celts

as interactions between the people in the neighboring counties of Carlow and Wexford. The group of tales ranges in subject matter from monsters and battles of old to matchmaking and wedding tales that cover local traditions. The collection ends with personal biographical information about Kennedy's teaching and bookshop.

In the preface to *The Banks of the Boro* Kennedy says that his goal is to preserve a sense of the life and customs that he saw dying out: "The tale is somewhat clogged by various phrases and incidents of ordinary country life, but the writer was more anxious to preserve the faithful memory of these things than to produce a well-constructed story." The collection includes conversations, games, ballads, and similar pieces.

After these two books Kennedy turned from local customs and traditions to more-universal Irish folktales and legends. In his later collections Kennedy avoids local stories. Kennedy's early works reproduce the style of his informants or storytellers: the stories do not begin with the standard "Once upon a time . . . " and go on to deal with royalty in distant fantasy lands and magical happenings. Except for stories about fairies, the early tales are about ordinary people and commonplace events rather than supernatural elements. Even the more-universal tale opens with a commentary on the state of the Irish peasant, such as the often-repeated opening "Once there was a poor widow. . . . " Intrusive social comment is widespread in the tales Kennedy collected. He retains the errors of the original tellers also.

"Jack and His Comrades," included in *Legendary Fictions of the Irish Celts,* includes many of the Irish peasant folktale characteristics typical of the stories Kennedy collected. Jack, the hardworking son of a poor widow who values his mother's blessing over material goods or even food, experiences adventures in which he helps an ass, a dog, and a cock with no thought of reward. His honest, caring nature is repaid when the animals provide Jack with information that impresses the Lord of Dunlavin and his pretty daughter. But Jack does not instantly become a nobleman and live happily ever after: the story ends with him happily settled with a good job, his mother living nearby. The narrator ends the story by saying that he hopes that, if Jack and the lord's daughter married, that Jack "spent two or three years getting the education of a gentleman. I don't think that a country boy would feel comfortable, striving to find discourse for a well-bred young lady." Knowing one's place and maintaining success through hard work are common closing themes when poor people do well in Irish folktales.

Kennedy's first folk collection, *Fictions of Our Forefathers* (1859), assembles Irish tales with commentaries that criticize, explain the historical background, or clarify information about the characters. It includes a glossary of Gaelic terms. His most comprehensive collection, *Legendary Fictions of the Irish Celts,* is divided into sections: "Legends of the Good People," "Witchcraft and Sorcery," "Ghosts and Fetches," "Ossianic and Other Early Legends," and "Legends of the Celtic Saints." "The Origin of Aileach" is typical of the bardic tales in the volume. A provincial king and queen visit the palace of the king of Ireland. The visitor discovers his wife "receiving addresses" from the king's son and kills him. The king recognizes the betrayed husband's right to protect the sanctity of his marriage but cannot condone his committing a crime within the castle walls. He decrees that rather than be executed for homicide the man must pay the penalty of carrying the corpse on his back until he finds a suitable tombstone. When he finally finds a stone he bur-

ies the corpse, then dies of fatigue and sorrow. The fatal spot becomes a fortress and is "called from the circumstance related, the 'Stone Fort of Groans' (Aileach). It was the greatest stronghold of the Clann Conaill for centuries."

Kennedy's literary and critical background is evident in the explanatory notes scattered throughout his collections of Irish legends. Some set forth grammatical explanations, as in *Legendary Fictions of the Irish Celts:* "We must beg rigid grammarians to excuse some solecisms, without which the peasant idiom could not be truly given." Others give lengthy literary explanations of a name or phrase, such as a footnote in the same collection to explain "Damer's estate": "A rich Dublin money-lender, contemporary with Dr. Jonathan Swift, and commemorated by him in an appropriate lament. Damer is to the Irish peasant what Croesus was to the old Greeks." Some notes correct peasant misspellings or mispronunciations: after the title "Adventures of Gilla Na Chreck An Gour" Kennedy notes, "Correctly, 'Giolla na Chroicean Gobhar.' " Kennedy spends half a page tracing the possible evolution of the word *Fairy* as used by the Irish Celts. He draws parallels between the Druids and ancient Irish heroes and the Greek gods and goddesses. The introduction to *Fictions of Our Forefathers* includes a twelve-page discussion contrasting Homer's Greek heroes to Irish ones and claiming that the Greeks were unfeeling and savage compared to the Celtic warriors.

Kennedy died on 29 March 1873 after a bout of bronchitis that lasted several months. His obituary in the *Dublin University Magazine* reports that his illness had "baffled all the skill of his medical advisors." He was attended by his family, none of whom are named in the obituary.

During his time, Kennedy's early works were popular for their capacity to remind readers of their own experiences. The Irish folktales appealed to nostalgia for the simple life. For modern readers he provides scholarly yet highly descriptive accounts of the common people of the early half of the 1800s, using humor and a keen eye to make his subjects seem real. Though his critical sense survives in his footnotes and explanations, on the whole he captured the stories and legends, and the method of their transmission, as he intended, rendering them still vivid.

## References:

James Delaney, "Patrick Kennedy," *The Past,* 7, (1964): 8–87;

"Patrick Kennedy," *Dublin University Magazine,* 81 (January–June 1873): 581–582.

# Joseph Sheridan Le Fanu

*(28 August 1814 – 7 February 1873)*

Kathryn West
*Bellarmine College*

See also the Le Fanu entries in *DLB 21: Victorian Novelists Before 1885* and *DLB 70: British Mystery Writers, 1860–1919.*

BOOKS: *The Cock and Anchor: Being a Chronicle of Old Dublin City,* anonymous (3 volumes, Dublin: William Curry / London: Longmans / Edinburgh: Fraser, 1845; 1 volume, New York: Colyer, 1848); revised as *Morley Court* (London: Chapman & Hall, 1873); republished as *The Cock and the Anchor* (London: Downey, 1895);

*The Fortunes of Colonel Torlogh O'Brien: A Tale of the Wars of King James,* anonymous (Dublin: James McGlashan / London: William S. Orr, 1847; New York: Colyer, 1847);

*Ghost Stories and Tales of Mystery,* anonymous (Dublin: James McGlashan / London: William S. Orr, 1851);

*The House by the Churchyard* (3 volumes, London: Tinsley, 1863; 1 volume, New York: Carleton, 1866);

*Wylder's Hand* (3 volumes, London: Bentley, 1864; 1 volume, New York: Carleton, 1865);

*Uncle Silas: A Tale of Bartram-Haugh* (3 volumes, London: Bentley, 1864; 1 volume, New York: Munro, 1878);

*The Prelude, Being a Contribution Towards a History of the Election for the University,* as John Figwood, Esq., Barrister at Law (Dublin: G. Herbert, 1865);

*Guy Deverell* (3 volumes, London: Bentley, 1865; 1 volume, New York: Harper, 1866);

*All in the Dark* (2 volumes, London: Bentley, 1866; 1 volume, New York: Harper, 1866);

*The Tenants of Malory: A Novel* (3 volumes, London: Tinsley, 1867; 1 volume, New York: Harper, 1867);

*A Lost Name,* 3 volumes (London: Bentley, 1868);

*Haunted Lives,* 3 volumes (London: Tinsley, 1868);

*The Wyvern Mystery,* 3 volumes (London: Tinsley, 1869);

*Joseph Sheridan Le Fanu*

*Checkmate* (3 volumes, London: Hurst & Blackett, 1871; 1 volume, Philadelphia: Evans, Stoddart, 1871);

*The Rose and the Key,* 3 volumes (London: Chapman & Hall, 1871);

*The Chronicles of Golden Friars,* 3 volumes (London: Bentley, 1871);

*In a Glass Darkly,* 3 volumes (London: Bentley, 1872; 1 volume, New York: Oxford University Press, 1993);

*Willing to Die,* 3 volumes (London: Hurst & Blackett, 1873);

*The Purcell Papers,* 3 volumes (London: Bentley, 1880; New York: AMS Press, 1975);

*The Watcher and Other Weird Stories* (London: Downey, 1894);

*The Evil Guest* (London: Downey, 1895);

*The Poems of Joseph Sheridan Le Fanu,* edited by Alfred Perceval Graves (London: Downey, 1896; New York: AMS Press, 1975);

*Madam Crowl's Ghost and Other Tales of Mystery,* edited by M. R. James (London: Bell, 1923; New York: Books for Libraries Press, 1971);

*A Strange Adventure in the Life of Miss Laura Mildmay: A Tale from Chronicles of Golden Friars,* introduction by Herbert Van Thal (London: Home & Van Thal, 1947);

*Best Ghost Stories of J. S. Le Fanu,* edited by E. F. Bleiler (New York: Dover, 1964);

*Ghost Stories and Mysteries,* edited by Bleiler (New York: Dover, 1975);

*Borrhomeo the Astrologer: A Monkish Tale* (Edinburgh: Tragara Press, 1985);

*The Illustrated J. S. Le Fanu: Ghost Stories and Mysteries by a Master Victorian Storyteller,* edited and collected by Michael Cox (Wellingborough: Equation / New York: Sterling, 1988);

*Green Tea and Other Ghost Stories* (New York: Dover, 1993).

**Collection:** *The Collected Words of Joseph Sheridan Le Fanu,* 52 volumes, edited by Sir Devendra P. Varma (New York: Arno, 1977).

Joseph Sheridan Le Fanu wrote fifteen novels, ranging from historical romances to mysteries, as well as essays, poetry, patriotic ballads, sentimental lyrics, and journalistic pieces. Yet it is largely for his more than forty short stories — often stories of the supernatural — that he is known today. The novels *The House by the Churchyard* (1863), *Uncle Silas: A Tale of Bartram-Haugh* (1864), *Wylder's Hand* (1864), and *The Wyvern Mystery* (1869) still receive some critical attention; *Uncle Silas* was filmed in 1988 by the BBC with Peter O'Toole as Silas Ruthyn. Yet the frequently anthologized "Carmilla," "Green Tea," "Schalken the Painter," and "The Familiar," as well as the collection *In a Glass Darkly* (1872), are the works most likely to maintain Le Fanu's name among modern readers.

A contemporary of Edgar Allan Poe (although he outlived his American counterpart by twenty-four years), Le Fanu shared Poe's fascination with the workings of the imagination, the nature of reality, and the intrusion of the inexplicable into people's lives. The two differ significantly in style, however. While Poe advocated and practiced a

"unity of effect" and a certain brevity, Le Fanu was by temperament a storyteller. As Wendell V. Harris notes, Le Fanu achieves "a kind of richness of character, situation, or narrative style possible only in more leisurely storytelling." His stories are often framed by two or more narrative voices. He contributed stories to at least eight periodicals (there may be many that remain unidentified), later republishing them in a variety of combinations and often adding to the later versions. Indeed, the length of many pieces makes it difficult to decide whether to classify them as short stories or novellas. Most of all, however, it is Le Fanu's habit of reworking and retelling stories — making sometimes small, sometimes significant changes in plot, adding or altering a character, transplanting the action to a different setting — that complicates any discussion of his short fiction.

For instance, in "Passage in the Secret History of an Irish Countess," published in November 1838 in the *Dublin University Magazine,* Le Fanu introduces a young heroine sent to live with an uncle whose reputation has been compromised by an unsolved murder that occurred in his home. When the uncle's plot to gain her property by marrying her to his son fails, he and the son attempt to kill her, accidentally murdering her faithful cousin instead. A second version of this story, differing only slightly, appeared as "The Murdered Cousin" in *Ghost Stories and Tales of Mystery* (1851). Finally, *Uncle Silas* has an expanded version of this plot, giving a greater role to the sinister French governess, Madame de la Rougierre, and allowing her to be accidentally killed by her accomplices, the wicked uncle and his son, in the place of the heroine. To complicate the picture further, an earlier version of the character of Madame de la Rougierre appears as Mademoiselle de Barras in "The Evil Guest," also published in *Ghost Stories and Tales of Mystery.* E. F. Bleiler has described Le Fanu as combining "the gentle weaknesses and terrible dreams of the visionary with the strengths of the very competent businessman." Certainly this reworking of material served Le Fanu well in terms of profit. More important, Le Fanu was fascinated with the idea of revisiting places, people, and themes to change an element or two and discover what vision might then result.

Ann Radcliffe, Charles Robert Maturin, Sir Walter Scott, Charlotte and Emily Brontë, and contemporaries such as Charles Lever, William Carleton, and Charles Dickens are generally cited as literary influences on Le Fanu. Le Fanu's works, however, show even more the inspiration of Irish folklore, Irish politics, and the tussles he witnessed among various religious factions; his fascination with the supernatural; and the philosophy of Emanuel Swedenborg.

Much less detailed biographical information is available for Le Fanu than for many Victorian writers. He left behind no autobiography, diary, or journal. Most of his letters to his contemporaries, such as Dickens and Lever, have not come to light. His biographers, particularly S. M. Ellis and W. J. McCormack, have pieced together some information, particularly from memoirs of other Le Fanu family members, such as his brother William's *Seventy Years of Irish Life* (1893) and his son Thomas Phillip Le Fanu's *Memoir of the Le Fanu Family* (1924), but in many respects Le Fanu seems fated to remain as shadowy a figure as some of the apparitions he created.

Le Fanu was born in Dublin on 28 August 1814 to Thomas Philip and Emma Dobbin Le Fanu. The Le Fanu family, descendants of Huguenots, had lived in Dublin since the 1730s. Through marriage they were linked to the Sheridan family, of which Richard Brinsley Sheridan, the playwright and great-uncle of Le Fanu, is the best-known member. Joseph Sheridan Le Fanu was the middle child, with an older sister, Catherine, and a brother, William, who was two years younger. With William he was educated at home by his parents and various tutors. In his memoir William reports that "my father's library was a large and good one; there my brother spent much of his time in poring over many a quaint and curious volume."

Le Fanu's father was the resident chaplain of the Royal Hibernian Military School in Phoenix Park, Dublin. The brothers often watched the soldiers of the Royal Irish Artillery drilling in the park, an experience that probably influenced Le Fanu's later work. In 1826 the family moved to Abington, a few miles east of Limerick in the southwest of Ireland, where Le Fanu's father served as rector and dean of Emly.

Abington was an area of extreme poverty. As Protestants in a Catholic area, the family was especially resented when the Tithe Wars began in 1831; the brothers barely escaped being stoned on at least one occasion. The Irish Catholics refused payments to the dean, causing the family income to drop by half. While the Le Fanus may have felt some sympathy with the Irish rebels, they believed that British rule was best for the Irish people. These experiences formed the basis for the conservativism Le Fanu would demonstrate both at Trinity College, Dublin, where he would strongly oppose the Reform Bill of 1832, and later in his journalistic work.

Also, the brutality he witnessed or about which he heard firsthand accounts during the Tithe Wars probably provided the germ of some of the violent scenes of his later fiction.

In the fall of 1832 Le Fanu entered Trinity College, where he studied classics and was noted for his gift for oratory. He finished his education in 1837 and was called to the Irish bar in 1839, but he never practiced law. In January 1838 he had seen the publication of his first story in the *Dublin University Magazine*, edited by Isaac Butt. "The Ghost and the Bone-Setter" is notable for its introduction in the preface of Father Francis Purcell, the character who provides the link connecting the stories collected posthumously in *The Purcell Papers* (1880). A comic tale, "The Ghost and the Bone-Setter" is characteristic of many of Le Fanu's comic and supernatural works in the way it draws on folk material. The story is based on an Irish Catholic folk belief that the last person buried in a cemetery must carry water to those thirsting in purgatory, and its comic twist comes at the end when it is revealed that the visit of a ghost complaining of pains in his leg because of carrying so much water was in fact the dream of a drunken bonesetter who has pulled the leg off a nearby chair.

Between 1838 and 1840 Le Fanu published twelve stories in the *Dublin University Magazine*, including three more comic stories, historical fictions, and several stories that involve the supernatural — all framed by the Father Purcell figure. Le Fanu claimed that he based Purcell on an eighteenth-century parish priest who, as described in the first pages of "The Ghost and the Bone-Setter," "for nearly fifty years discharged [his] arduous duties . . . in the south of Ireland. . . . [He was] of the old school, a race now nearly extinct — whose habits were from many causes more refined, and whose tastes more literary than those of the alumni of Maynooth." Purcell's interest in literature leads him to collect tales from the peasants in the area. Some of the tales he narrates himself; others are told to him in the dialect of the Irish peasantry.

Le Fanu's next two published efforts — "The Fortunes of Sir Robert Ardagh, Being a Second Extract from the Papers of the Late Father Purcell," published in the March 1838 *Dublin University Magazine*, and "The Last Heir of Castle Connor," published in the June 1838 issue — feature a tone quite different from that of "The Ghost and the Bone-Setter." In both is a concern that occupied Le Fanu throughout his career: the demise of the last member of an old family.

Purcell tells two versions of Ardagh's story. First he relates a tale that he says has become a popular legend about Ardagh, basically a Faustian tale in which the protagonist, after being seen in the company of a strange-looking man, prospers until an appointed time and then suffers a violent death. Purcell says that this legend is false and proceeds to relate the version he has heard from more-reliable sources. In the second telling the "strange-looking man" is Ardagh's foreign valet, nicknamed Jacque the Devil by his fellow servants and generally despised for the delight he takes in any misfortune that befalls his master. Ardagh, however, is much attached to the man and insists that "his commands are mine." Ardagh displays inexplicable wealth but, instead of waging a fierce battle for his life as in the first version, merely announces the time and date of his death and calls on relatives to join his wife at the appointed time. Thus in both versions of Ardagh's death, the popular oral version and the supposedly more reliable historical one, there is the possibility that supernatural forces somehow manipulate his destiny, but the second version lacks the retribution usually earned for making a pact with the devil. Le Fanu would rework this tale as "The Haunted Baronet," first published in 1870 in *Belgravia,* and place it as the second of *The Chronicles of Golden Friars* (1871) and then again as "Sir Dominick's Bargain: A Legend of Dunoran" in the 6 July 1872 issue of *All the Year Round.*

"The Last Heir of Castle Connor" is a realistic narrative Father Purcell relates as an eyewitness, having participated in its events in his youth. It again addresses the situation of an old and respected family on the verge of dying out. O'Connor, the last heir of an aristocratic line, returns from three years abroad only to offend Fitzgerald, a professional duelist. Purcell tries to convince the men not to fight, but O'Connor grows immediately fatalistic, insisting that his death is inevitable and even vowing to fire wide so as not be guilty of spilling the other man's blood. After several delays the brilliantly described duel takes place, and O'Connor is indeed mortally wounded. He rouses for a moment to state that he believes he will survive. When the doctor tells him his wound is too serious, he despairs and appears "to collapse and shrink together as a plant might, under the influence of a withering spell." Purcell reveals that his remorse at not being able to stop this tragedy greatly influenced his decision to become a priest.

Two other Le Fanu stories appeared in the *Dublin University Magazine* in 1838: "The Drunkard's Dream" (August), another tale in which supernatural forces – in this case through an alcohol-induced dream – predict a man's death, and "Passage in the

Secret History of an Irish Countess." Notable in "The Drunkard's Dream" is Le Fanu's tribute to William Beckford and his Gothic novel *Vathek* (1786) in a description of the underworld cavern seen by the dreamer, emphasized by Father Purcell's remark that "this was long before Vathek and the hall of Eblis had delighted the world."

In 1839 Le Fanu published "The Bridal of Carrigvarah" (April), "A Strange Event in the Life of Schalken the Painter" (May), "Scraps of Hibernian Ballads" (June), "Jim Sulivan's Adventures in the Great Snow" (July), and "A Chapter in the History of a Tyrone Family" (October). He followed these in 1840 with "An Adventure of Hardress Fitzgerald, a Royalist Captain" and "The Quare Gander" in February and October respectively; all appeared in the *Dublin University Magazine.* "The Bridal of Carrigvarah" is another tale of the decline of a once-prosperous and influential family, this time turning on an ill-fated marriage between the young heir of the manor and the daughter of a local farmer. "Jim Sulivan's Adventures in the Great Snow" and "The Quare Gander" are examples of Le Fanu's comic use of dialect and folk anecdote. "An Adventure of Hardress Fitzgerald, a Royalist Captain" illustrates his experimentation with historical fiction in the vein of Scott. Filled with scenes of narrow escapes against overwhelming odds, the story features a particularly violent and bloody death. It became part of Le Fanu's second novel, *The Fortunes of Colonel Torlogh O'Brien: A Tale of the Wars of King James* (1847).

"A Chapter in the History of a Tyrone Family" opens with an example of Le Fanu's penchant for weaving stories into stories. The opening frame, in the voice of Father Purcell, says that he is relating the words of a valued friend as accurately as possible, lamenting only that he cannot also bring before the reader "her animated gesture, her expressive countenance, the solemn and thrilling air and accent with which she related the dark passages in her strange story." The countess first tells of a time when an apparitional coach drove up to the old family home accompanied by sounds of a cracking whip and the barking of the family's dogs. A sister was expected to be arriving then, but the family finds "the courtyard . . . perfectly empty." The next day they hear that the woman died at the same time they heard the approach of the coach. At this point Le Fanu adds a long footnote, reporting that he has been charged with "dealing too largely in the marvelous; and it has been half insinuated that such is his love for *diablerie,* that he is content to wander a mile out of his way, in order to meet a fiend or a

*Le Fanu around 1843; artist unknown (Collection of Mrs. Susan Digby-Firth)*

goblin, and thus to sacrifice all regard for truth and accuracy to the idle hope of affrighting the imagination, and thus pandering to the bad taste of his reader." He pleads his innocence, stating that he has "never *pandered to his bad taste,* nor went one inch out of his way to introduce witch, fairy, devil, ghost, or any other of the grim fraternity." He goes on to emphasize that these tales were "*written down*" by Father Purcell and that, if anything, as editor of Purcell's papers he has acted not to exaggerate any supernatural events but indeed to soften or even account for them. Le Fanu's simultaneous emphasis on both the oral provenance and the historical recording – on the supernatural character and the factual basis – of these tales suggests an attempt to appeal to a cross section of audiences.

The bulk of the story goes on to tell of the narrator's marriage to Lord Glenfallen and his odd request that she not explore the back rooms of his castle. She soon meets a blind woman wandering the castle, Flora Van Kemp, who claims to be Glenfallen's first wife. After attempting to kill the new wife, Flora is brought to trial and executed, in-

sisting all the while that Glenfallen had been the instigator of her actions. Shortly thereafter he shows signs of madness, reporting conversations with the dead Flora. He is found in a locked room with his throat slashed; it is implied, although not confirmed, that he committed suicide. "A Chapter in the History of a Tyrone Family" has been suggested as a precursor to Charlotte Brontë's *Jane Eyre* (1847). Le Fanu later expanded the story into *The Wyvern Mystery.*

The most enduring of the stories that were to make up *The Purcell Papers* is "A Strange Event in the Life of Schalken the Painter," still reprinted in anthologies of horror fiction. Jack Sullivan has summarized it as the abduction, rape, and final seduction of a young woman by a living corpse, all from the point of view of the girl's befuddled uncle and horrified fiancé. Le Fanu reportedly much admired the Dutch painter's work, particularly his use of light and shadows. Father Purcell claims to have heard this story from the owner of a Godfrey Schalken painting that depicts "a chamber in some antique religious building; . . . its foreground . . . occupied by a female figure, in a species of white robe, part of which is arranged so as to form a veil. . . . In her hand the figure bears a lamp, by which alone her figure and face are illuminated; and her features wear such an arch smile . . . in the background . . . in total shadow, stands the figure of a man, . . . his hand being placed upon the hilt of his sword, which he appears to be in the act of drawing." Purcell notes that this is one of those pictures that impresses the onlooker as representing "not the mere ideal shapes and combinations which have floated through the imagination of the artist, but scenes, faces, and situations which have actually existed."

Schalken loves Rose Velderkaust, the niece of his mentor, Gerard Douw. Not knowing of his protégé's feelings, Douw agrees to a marriage for Rose with the wealthy Minheer Vanderhausen, a stranger who appears suddenly in their lives. Douw and Schalken experience a strange sense of dread in Vanderhausen's presence, but Rose notes only his ugliness. She does remark that "when I saw him standing at the door, I could not get it out of my head that I saw the old painted wooden figure that used to frighten me so much in the Church of St. Laurence at Rotterdam." Nevertheless, Rose and Vanderhausen marry. They are not heard from for several months, at which time Douw goes to Rotterdam to search for them, only to find that no one there has ever heard of Vanderhausen. Rose appears a few months later, distraught and exhausted. She begs her father to send for a minister, declaring that only "he can deliver me: the dead and the living can never be one: God has forbidden it." She begs not to be left alone, but when the candles mysteriously go out her uncle leaves the room for more. The door slams shut, and Rose's shrieks are heard; when the door is finally forced open, there is no trace of her, although there are signs that she may have jumped from a window into a canal below. Years later Schalken visits a church in Rotterdam, where he has a vision of Rose beckoning to him and disclosing a bed that contains the demonic form of Vanderhausen. Schalken faints but later immortalizes the scene in his painting. Thus this telling of a tale of a demon lover suggests that both uncle and bride are oddly complicit in her fate, while her true love can only stand by to observe and record.

By the early 1840s Le Fanu was a part-time owner of the *Warder,* a Tory newspaper, and held part ownership in other Dublin newspapers, including the *Statesman,* the *Dublin Evening Packet,* and the *Evening Mail.* These publications advocated conservative views on politics and church policies. As an editor and newspaper proprietor, Le Fanu exercised a great deal of influence in the significant public debates of his time, generally advocating the views of the Irish Protestant ascendancy. Harold Orel suggests, however, that events of the 1840s challenged some of Le Fanu's conservative political views. For instance, the Tory refusal to take positive action during the famine of 1845 to 1847 may have spurred Le Fanu to contribute anonymously to *The Nation,* the paper of the Young Ireland movement.

During this period Le Fanu wrote "Shamus O'Brien," a sentimental ballad about a young man who, at his execution for participation in the Rising of '98, delivers a rousing nationalist speech and then escapes at a meeting of the last moment. An instant success, the poem was first read in 1840 at a meeting of the College Historical Society, of which Le Fanu was an active member and, for a time, president. It was not published until July 1850, appearing in the *Dublin University Magazine.* Until the end of the 1840s Le Fanu would turn his attention to other matters and away from the production of shorter fiction.

From 1842 to 1852 Le Fanu held a position as tipstaff of the Court of Common Pleas, for which he earned a small salary. There he met Susanna Bennett, the daughter of a barrister. They married in 1843 and proceeded to lead an active social life in Dublin. In a March 1844 letter to his mother Le Fanu reported that they were "uncommonly snug & happy together." Their first child, Eleanor Frances, was born on 10 February 1845; a second girl,

Emma Lucretia, was born on 21 May 1846; and their first son, Thomas Philip, was born on 3 September 1847.

During the early years of the marriage the Le Fanus were often financially unstable. His first published novel, *The Cock and Anchor: Being a Chronicle of Old Dublin City* (1845), was only marginally successful. That same year the *Warder* was sued for libel. The owners lost the case and were fined £500 plus costs. Another suit arose in 1849, further straining the Le Fanu budget. Meanwhile, a second novel — another Irish historical romance, *The Fortunes of Colonel Torlogh O'Brien* — appeared in 1847 but was not much more successful than the first. He did not attempt to publish a novel again for fourteen years. In 1851 the family moved into a large Georgian house belonging to Le Fanu's father-in-law, George Bennett, at 18 Merrion Square in Dublin. Le Fanu would live there until his death. On 1 August 1854 a second son and final child, George Brinsley, was born there.

Le Fanu did not return to the short story until 1848. From April of that year to December 1853 he had several pieces published in the *Dublin University Magazine.* "Some Account of the Latter Days of the Hon. Richard Marston of Dunoran" appeared from April to June 1848. A story of unhappy marriage, an arrogant servant, adultery, murder, blackmail, bigamy, and suicide, it is Le Fanu's first use of a plot he would rework in "The Evil Guest" and again in the novel *A Lost Name* (1868).

In "The Mysterious Lodger" (January–February 1850) Le Fanu explores a common Victorian theme, crisis in religious faith. An atheist and his religious wife have, despite his disbelief, agreed to raise their two children as Christians. The woman is tested by the arguments of a sinister lodger who wears goggles and a respirator, while her husband is challenged by a man who had first appeared in his wife's dreams and periodically comes into their lives with "a grace, a purity, a compassion, and a grandeur of intellect in his countenance, in his language, in his mien, that was beautiful and kinglike." The latter figure argues that salvation comes through suffering; his position seemingly wins out, as the couple find themselves reconciled to life only after losing first their baby and then their elder daughter.

Le Fanu returned to the comic tale with "Billy Malowney's Taste of Love and Glory" (June 1850). This story would be included with Le Fanu's earliest twelve to form *The Purcell Papers.* Perhaps most notable is the narrator's praise of Irish dialect, which he proclaims the "glorious brogue, that . . . will leave a burden of mirth or of sorrow with nearly equal propriety, tickling the diaphragm as easily as it plays with the heartstrings, and is in itself a national music."

January 1851 brought the publication of "Ghost Stories of Chapelizod," consisting of "The Village Bully," "The Sexton's Adventure," and "The Spectre Lovers." All are set in a Dublin suburb that would also serve as the location of *The House by the Churchyard*. The first two are fairly straightforward ghost stories involving people being visited by long-dead spirits; the latter has a more complicated plot in which a man has visions of his village as it appeared years earlier. Ghosts of a young captain and the lady he seduced and ruined, the "spectre lovers," eventually lead the man to his death with their promise of a treasure waiting to be found, as he falls in the old house they entice him to search.

*Ghost Stories and Tales of Mystery* also appeared in 1851. This volume collected the previously published "A Strange Event in the Life of Schalken the Painter" along with a slightly revised version of "Passage in the Secret History of an Irish Countess," retitled "The Murdered Cousin"; a revised version, transplanted to England, of "Richard Marston," retitled "The Evil Guest"; and "The Watcher." Nelson Browne notes that "The Evil Guest" is probably the bloodiest of Le Fanu's stories. It was expanded into the novel *A Lost Name* and was republished as a single volume in 1895. "The Watcher" was reprinted in 1872 in *In a Glass Darkly* as "The Familiar"; when anthologized since, it has usually been under this title.

"The Watcher" takes place "somewhere about the year 1794." Sir James Barton, a frigate commander during the Revolutionary War, lives "an orderly and moral life" and claims to have no belief in the supernatural. To the surprise of his friends and acquaintants, he proposes to a Miss Montague but immediately thereafter has an experience shared by many of Le Fanu's protagonists: he finds himself haunted by a ghost from his past. Barton cannot be sure that the ghost is of a former member of his crew, severely punished by the captain for mistreating his own daughter, but the ghost certainly does represent a guilt Barton carries with him. As he finds himself more and more frequently being followed by this "watcher," Barton's faith in the laws of cause and effect and his disbelief in the supernatural waver. On the first evening he finds himself in the presence of the ghost, "in spite of all his skepticism, he felt something like a superstitious fear stealing fast upon him." Eventually a member of the House of Commons sees the demon with Barton; it is not a hallucination. Barton eventually vis-

its a Doctor Macklin, saying that although he is an unbeliever he now feels "that there does exist beyond this a spiritual world." In a particularly striking scene General Montague, the father of Barton's fiancée, chases the demon through the streets and returns to Barton with the comment, "But where is the good or the harm of seeing him?" Barton dies in the presence of a sinister bird that takes the place of the watcher. The story not only criticizes the doctrine that all things can be explained rationally but also seems to point out people's lack of ability to do anything about the presence of the supernatural whether they believe in it or not. Orel suggests that it also implicitly critiques arranged marriages in which no real affection exists.

"An Account of Some Strange Disturbances in Aungier Street" (December 1853) is usually read as a study in subjectivism versus objectivism; it investigates a haunted house inhabited by two students. Some of the apparitions and events they see and experience have rational explanations; others do not. After this story Le Fanu published no more short fiction or novels until 1861.

On 26 April 1858 Le Fanu's wife fell ill; she died two days later at age thirty-four. Within an hour of his wife's death Le Fanu wrote to his mother, "The greatest misfortune of my life has overtaken me. My darling wife is gone. The most affectionate the truest I think . . . She was the light of my life . . . . Oh, look through her letters to you & copy any words in which she said I loved her & was kind to her. I adored her." Her death seems to have shaken his faith in medicine and science and led him to become something of a recluse during the last years of his own life.

In 1861 Le Fanu purchased the *Dublin University Magazine* for £850. The publisher of almost all of Le Fanu's earlier fiction, it was the foremost periodical in Ireland; conservative and opposed to the nationalist cause, it had been started by a group of Tory students at Trinity College in 1833. In the same year Le Fanu bought the magazine he resumed writing novels, beginning with *The House by the Churchyard,* which appeared there serially between October 1861 and February 1863. Eight of Le Fanu's novels were serialized in the *Dublin University Magazine* between 1861 and November 1869, including *Wylder's Hand, Uncle Silas, Guy Deverell* (1865), and *The Wyvern Mystery,* all widely considered to be among his best novels. Several Le Fanu ballads also appeared during the 1860s. It is unlikely, however, that all the shorter, unsigned pieces Le Fanu produced for the *Dublin University Magazine* during this period will ever be identified as his.

Le Fanu resumed his production of shorter fiction with "Ultor de Lacy: A Legend of Cappercullen," which appeared in the *Dublin University Magazine* in December 1861. He reports that it was told to him by "Old Miss Croker, of Ross House, who was near seventy in the year 1821, when she related this story to me." She had known a nun who claimed to be the last surviving member of an old Irish family destroyed by a curse originating as a result of an ancestor's cruelty to a rebel prisoner in 1601. Le Fanu followed "Ultor de Lacy" with "Borrhomeo the Astrologer: A Monkish Tale," published anonymously in the *Dublin University Magazine* in January 1862.

Le Fanu's "Authentic Narrative of a Haunted House" (October 1862) opens with a note from the editor – that is, Le Fanu – attesting to the veracity of this story about a couple's experiences with three ghosts in a house near the shore that they rent while the husband recuperates from a nervous illness. Le Fanu also claims to realize that the narrative is "valueless" as a "mere story," being solely of interest because of "its absolute truth." Ivan Melada suggests that Le Fanu used the story to make the point that "a too scientifically objective approach to supernatural phenomena inhibits the attitude of wonder that makes the appreciation of the supernatural possible." Bleiler argues that Le Fanu was being truthful in describing it as an incident he heard from those involved, in which case it would be more accurately categorized as an essay.

Le Fanu stayed busy with *Wylder's Hand* and *Uncle Silas* in 1863 and early 1864 but returned to the short form with "My Aunt Margaret's Adventure" and "Wicked Captain Walshawe of Wauling," which appeared in the *Dublin University Magazine* in March and April 1864, respectively. The former is a realistic tale in which the odd presence of a corpse has a perfectly rational explanation; it is notable for its affectionate portrait of Aunt Margaret and for its description of the trials of traveling by road and coach. "Wicked Captain Walshawe of Wauling," on the other hand, is a story of retribution thoroughly imbued with the supernatural. Captain Walshawe, who has led a scandalous and disreputable life and bankrupted himself, marries a young heiress in order to be able to continue his lifestyle. After she dies he is furious when he discovers that she has been prepared for a Roman Catholic funeral. The old women in attendance are horrified at his behavior, and one, the woman's nurse and companion, prays that the captain's soul will be trapped in the wick of the candle he has snatched from the coffin. Years later, long after the captain's

death, a guest at the house, the narrator's uncle, finds the candle and lights it. In a minutely detailed scene the captain appears first as a tiny manikin who grows until he reaches normal size, then begins to age until nothing is left but "little wriggling knots of sparks such as we see running over the residuum of a burnt sheet of paper."

In January 1868 "Squire Toby's Will" appeared in *Temple Bar*. It treats themes seen in many of Le Fanu's earlier works: guilt, a dispute over a will, and the decline of a family. It was later reprinted in *Madam Crowl's Ghost and Other Tales of Mystery* (1923), edited and collected by M. R. James. "The Bird of Passage" (April–July 1870), about a country squire who falls in love with a Gypsy woman only to discover that to "possess" this "specimen of Nature" would be to change her very nature, also appeared in *Temple Bar*, as did "Hyacinth O'Toole," a comic tale submitted in 1884, after Le Fanu's death, by his son George.

In 1869 Le Fanu sold the *Dublin University Magazine* at a considerable profit and continued to write at the prolific pace he had set earlier in the decade. During this period he came to be known as the "Invisible Prince" of Dublin, seldom venturing out into society except for late-night excursions to booksellers in search of works on the occult and other subjects of interest to him. Brinsley Le Fanu described his father's work habits in his final years to Ellis:

> He wrote mostly in bed at night, using two copy-books for his manuscript. He always had two candles by his side on a small table; one of these dimly glimmering tapers would be left burning while he took a brief sleep. Then, when he awoke about 2 a.m. amid the darkling shadows of the heavy furnishings and hangings of his old-fashioned room, he would brew himself some strong tea – which he drank copiously and frequently throughout the day – and write for a couple of hours in that eerie period of the night when human vitality is at its lowest ebb and the Powers of Darkness rampant and terrifying. What wonder then, that, with his brain ever peopled by day and by night with mysterious and terrible beings, he became afflicted by horrible dreams.... Le Fanu always breakfasted in bed, and at midday went down to the dining-room at the back of the house, where he would resume work, writing at a little table which had been a favourite possession of his granduncle, Richard Brinsley Sheridan.

The 23 October and 13 November 1869 issues of Dickens's *All the Year Round* published one of Le Fanu's masterpieces, "Green Tea." Like several of his later stories, it is presented as one of the cases of Dr. Hesselius, a German physician who is in many ways a precursor to the modern psychotherapist.

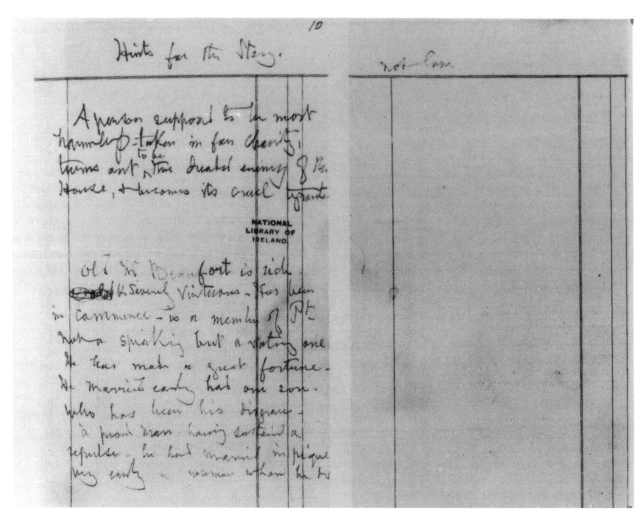

*Pages from one of Le Fanu's notebooks (National Library of Ireland)*

An updated, scientifically inclined Father Purcell, Hesselius claims an interest in the occult and in the philosophy of Swedenborg, noting that he is not in sympathy with purely rational explanations. Dr. Hesselius's Swedenborgianism – and Le Fanu's – is summed up by a passage from "Green Tea":

> I believe the entire natural world is but the ultimate expression of that spiritual world from which, and in which alone, it has its life. I believe that the essential man is a spirit, that the spirit is an organized substance, but as different in point of material from what we ordinarily understand by matter, as light or electricity is; that the material body is, in the most literal sense, a gesture, and death consequently no interruption of the living man's existence, but simply his extrication from the natural body – a process which commences at the moment of what we term death, and the completion of which, at furtherest a few days later, is the resurrection "in power."

The Hesselius cases – "Green Tea," "The Familiar," "Mr. Justice Harbottle," "The Room in the Dragon Volant," and "Carmilla" – are gathered in *In a Glass Darkly*. These stories include some scientific and medical vocabulary to add to their credibility as "medical files." They are considered by many critics and readers to be Le Fanu's best work.

The opening voice of "Green Tea" is that of Dr. Hesselius's medical secretary, who says that the doctor writes in two distinct characters: "he describes what he saw and heard as an intelligent layman might . . . and returns upon the narrative, and in terms of his art and with all the force and originality of genius, proceeds to the work of analysis, diagnosis and illustration." Then Hesselius's own narrative opens with a description of meeting the Reverend Mr. Jennings in a somewhat humorous dinner-party scene, where they discuss the doctor's

"Essays on Metaphysical Medicine." This discussion prompts Jennings to tell Hesselius of his dilemma: he sees a black monkey following him everywhere. This has resulted in his leaving his pulpit in the middle of a sermon and often following something with his eyes no one else can see. After persecuting Jennings continuously for a while, the monkey is not seen for a month, allowing Jennings to regain his equilibrium. It then reappears to follow a pattern of appearing and disappearing for arbitrary amounts of time, so that Jennings experiences as much anxiety when it is not present as when it is, worrying over how soon it will reappear. He finds that when it is present, even closing his eyes gives him no relief: "I know it is not to be accounted for physically," he says, "but I do actually see it though my eyes are closed." Eventually the apparition begins speaking to him, although Jennings reports that "it is not by my ears it reaches me – it comes like a singing through my head." Although the reader never hears what the monkey says to him, Jennings suggests that it utters "dreadful blasphemies" designed to prevent him from praying. After three years of harassment the monkey persuades Jennings to cut his own throat. Jennings's servant brings the news to Hesselius.

Unlike many of Le Fanu's haunted protagonists, Jennings appears to have no guilty secret in his past. The apparition seems to be the result of his drinking strong green tea in order to stay up late and read the sacred writings of other cultures. Some critics have suggested that the monkey is the product of neurosis, a representative of original sin, or a manifestation of intellectual pride and loss of faith. Although he has been researching the non-Christian beliefs of ancient peoples, however, there is no evidence that Jennings has lost his faith. Indeed, he continues to try to pray in spite of the continual interference of the monkey. Sullivan suggests that the fundamental irony of the tale lies in its title: all Jennings has done is drink great quantities of green tea while working late at night. Thus, there appears to be an inexplicable gap between cause and effect, crime and punishment. Hesselius suggests a particularly dark version of Swedenborgian philosophy: "If evil spirits could perceive that they were associated with man, and yet that they were spirits separate from him, and if they could flow in into the things of his body, they would attempt by a thousand means to destroy him; for they hate man with a deadly hatred." In the end Hesselius claims that the Jennings case is not really his failure, for he had not been able to start treating the man. He believes that he could have sealed the "inner eye" that had been opened by the green tea, yet he finally attributes Jennings's situation to a "hereditary suicidal mania."

In "Mr. Justice Harbottle" the central figure's guilt and the reason for his haunting are made quite clear. The story first appeared as "The Haunted House in Westminster" in the January 1872 *Belgravia*. It tells of a mid-eighteenth-century judge with the "reputation of being about the wickedest man in England," as suggested by his "big carbuncled nose, fierce eyes, and grim and brutal mouth." He suffers from gout, suggesting a habit of overindulgence. He has hanged the husband of the woman he has made his mistress. Harbottle receives a letter from an "Officer of the Crown Solicitor in the Kingdom of Life and Death" ordering him to appear and answer for his crimes. After attending a play one night Harbottle finds himself waylaid and taken to a courtroom presided over by "Chief Justice Twofold," "an image of Mr. Justice Harbottle, at least double his size, and with all his fierce colouring, and his ferocity of eye and visage, enhanced awfully." Harbottle is pronounced guilty of wrongly hanging the other man and is told he will be executed on the tenth of the following month. Two iron bands are placed around his ankles. He awakes, complaining of an attack of gout.

As in "The Watcher," other characters witness the apparition haunting the protagonist: Harbottle's mistress and the child of his housekeeper see a vision of the hanged man, while a maid sees "a monstrous figure, over a furnace, beating with a mighty hammer the rings and rivets of a chain." The next morning, the tenth of the month, Harbottle is found dead, having been hanged by the neck from his own banister.

"The Room in the Dragon Volant," which appeared in *London Society* in 1872 as well as in *In a Glass Darkly,* has no elements of the supernatural but instead focuses on the effect of a drug, "Mortis Imago," which renders its victims immobile but conscious. Michael H. Begnal has interpreted this as "the death of illusion," perhaps an apt characterization of the experience of many Le Fanu protagonists. Richard Beckett, a naive young Englishman, narrates his story. He is the victim of the Countess de St. Alyre and her gang. The countess leads him to believe that she cares for him romantically, all to the purpose of using him in her scheme to sell her fake diamonds for £30,000. She has woven an ingenious plot that has already successfully entrapped two other victims; Beckett only escapes the fate of his predecessors by chance at the last minute. In a particularly striking scene near the end of the story,

Beckett lies immobile in a coffin and must listen to the greedy scheming of the countess and her cohorts.

"Carmilla" first appeared in 1871–1872 in *The Dark Blue*. A vampire story, it evokes all the complexities of the myth, especially the tension between the victim's simultaneous attraction for and repulsion to the vampiric seducer. Le Fanu picks up elements from John Polidori's *The Vampyre* (1819), such as the vampire's association with mist, moonlight, and storms and its ability to change shape and form, and adds a picturesque old castle. Le Fanu also greatly heightens the erotic aspects of the vampiric encounter. "Carmilla" is widely considered one of the most important influences on Bram Stoker's *Dracula* (1897). Perhaps the most anthologized of Le Fanu's stories, it has been filmed several times. Many readers and critics consider it his most brilliant effort.

The striking colors of the story — predominated by black, white, and scarlet — create a sensuous yet frightening atmosphere. Mircalla, the Countess of Karnstein, who anagrams her name into Carmilla and Millarca at various times, seduces and eventually saps the life from young girls. The reader learns in particular the experience of Laura, a young girl living in Styria with her English father. Carmilla gains herself a place in Laura's home through a staged coach accident. She grows increasingly close to Laura, both emotionally and physically, even causing Laura to wonder if her guest is a boy disguised as a girl in order to be close to his love. Laura finds herself growing more and more languorous and pale, especially in the daytime. She is saved because a General Spilsdorf, who has lost his own daughter to Carmilla's vampirism, has figured out the vampire's identity and arrives to warn Laura and her father. In a stunning scene Mircalla/Carmilla/Millarca is found floating in seven inches of blood in her coffin and is staked through the heart. The conclusion notes that under certain circumstances a suicide becomes a vampire.

Laura's voice — the voice of an older woman looking back on an earlier traumatic experience and simultaneously the voice of the young girl going through that experience — is one of Le Fanu's most brilliant creations. Naive and yet full of sexual yearning, Laura rings eerily true. Although Carmilla has been destroyed, the power of the vampire to seduce — and the power of the attraction between the two women — remains, for in the last words of the story Laura says that "to this hour the image of Carmilla returns to memory with ambiguous alternations — sometimes the playful, languid, beautiful girl; sometimes the writhing fiend I saw in the ruined church; and often from a reverie I have started, fancying I heard the light step of Carmilla at the drawing-room door." The simultaneous notes of fear and yearning are unmistakable.

Le Fanu had several stories published in *All the Year Round* in 1870. "The Child That Went with the Fairies" (Febrary) and "The White Cat of Drumgunnoil" (April) are both in Irish idiom; the former is a version of a common Celtic fairy tale in which a child is taken by the fairies. Le Fanu refuses to include the traditional rescue, however: "So little Billy was dead to mother, brother, and sisters; but no grave received him." "The White Cat of Drumgunnoil" is similarly about loss and death. More a report than a tale, it records the history of the Donovan family, each member of which was visited by a white cat just before dying. "The Vision of Tom Chuff" (October) is a more elaborately detailed, although not necessarily better, rewriting of the early "The Drunkard's Dream," moved from Limerick to Cumberland.

"Stories of Lough Guir" (April) comprises five tales told to Le Fanu by Anne Baily of Lough Guir in Limerick when he was twelve or thirteen years old. He notes that Lough Guir "is a kind of centre of the operations of the Munster fairies." He speaks of Anne Baily with obvious affection and respect, noting of her and her sister that "never were old ladies more hospitable, lively, and kind, especially to young people." In particular, Anne Baily "told her stories with the sympathy, the colour, and the mysterious air which contribute so powerfully to effect, and never wearied of answering questions about the old castle, and amusing her young audience with fascinating little glimpses of old adventure and bygone days." The five tales include ghosts, an apparitional earl who reappears periodically complete with castle and retinue, and a banshee. McCormack suggests that the "implication is that evil is death and the fear of death." One can, however, also note in these stories Le Fanu's fascination with the undeniable, if undocumentable, presence of the supernatural in some people's lives.

"Madam Crowl's Ghost" (December) was later incorporated into "A Strange Adventure in the Life of Miss Laura Mildmay" in the *Chronicles of Golden Friars*. Madam Crowl is reminiscent of the flamboyant and evil Madame de la Rougierre of *Uncle Silas*. A ghost leads Madam Crowl's grandson to a sealed compartment, where he discovers the bones of a small child, the stepson Madam Crowl had murdered so that her own son would inherit an estate.

Also in 1870 "The Haunted Baronet" appeared in the July–November *Belgravia;* it was reprinted in *Chronicles of Golden Friars.* In length it is closer to a novella than a short story, but in theme it is closer to Le Fanu's short fictions than his novels, since it is filled with symbolic patterns and supernatural incidents, including unexplained voices, omens, and apparitions. A much-expanded reworking of "The Fortunes of Sir Robert Ardagh," it leads one to expect a Faustian tale, yet Sir Bale Mardyke prospers and lives a long life. After his death his enemy's family inherits his property, but by this point it is difficult to imagine this as a story of retribution. "The Haunted Baronet" has frequently been praised for its evocation of place; Melada notes that "a mixture of a Byronic feeling of solitude and a Burkean sense of the sublime is evident in Le Fanu's description of the mountains surrounding the village."

Le Fanu contributed "The Dead Sexton" to the 1871 Christmas number of *Once a Week.* Toby Crooke returns to the village of his wild youth in the guise of a prodigal son. He is found dead, having been hit on the head by a bell he was trying to steal along with the church silver and other valuables. That same night a mysterious stranger on a black horse arrives, frightening the townspeople with his coarse humor over the circumstances of the sexton's death. He is seen carrying off the corpse later that night; the devil has come for his own. While not as complicated as some of Le Fanu's stories, "The Dead Sexton" is notable for its evocation of the lives and characters of the villagers and for its depiction of their fortitude and fright in the face of the diabolical.

"Sir Dominick's Bargain," which appeared in *All the Year Round* in 1872, is a reworking of the material in "The Fortunes of Sir Robert Ardagh" and "The Haunted Baronet." It is framed by two narrators, a reasonable and even-tempered traveler and the old man he meets in the south of Ireland. The old man, a former servant of Sir Dominick Sarsefield, relates the bulk of the story in dialect. This version turns on the extra day created by a leap year: Sir Dominick thought he had escaped payment when 28 February ends, as he had been told he would be called to account by the first of March. When his evil benefactor returns on 29 February, Sir Dominick descends his staircase as if going to his death; when he reaches the bottom, the bargainer seizes him and "dashes his brains out against the wall of the staircase."

"Laura Silver Bell," the story of an orphan seduced by a tall, dark man with strange powers, ap-

*Joseph Sheridan Le Fanu*

peared in the annual issue of *Belgravia* in 1872. As Melada points out, some of the illusions in this tale are more symbolic than supernatural; they throw into relief Laura's lack of connection to the world around her because of her identity as an orphan and her need to be loved, to be part of a community, and thus to see a handsome gentleman in velvet in the place of a dirty scarecrow.

The last story published in Le Fanu's lifetime was "Dickon the Devil," which appeared in the 1872 Christmas number of *London Society.* The ghost of Squire Barwyke, who had been a kind man during his lifetime, takes offense at the disposition of his property and begins causing trouble for the two ladies who have inherited it. He eventually carries off Dickon, a young man who had come to help them, returning him as an idiot.

Le Fanu died early in the morning of 7 February 1873 (10 February, according to some sources) of complications from bronchitis. Reportedly, he had told his doctor of a recurring dream in which a large house threatened to fall on him. When the doctor pronounced him dead, legend has it that he said, "So the house has fallen at last." Le Fanu's daughter Emmie wrote in a letter, however, "His face looks so happy with a beautiful smile on it. It comforts me to think he is in Heaven, for no one could have been better than he was. He lived only for us, and his life was a most troubled one."

Le Fanu was a best-selling writer from the 1860s through the 1880s. His reputation has since waxed and waned periodically but never reached the levels of attention given to better-known authors. In "The Liar" (1888) Henry James noted "the customary novel of Mr. Le Fanu for the bed-table; the ideal reading in a country house for the hours after midnight." Since the 1923 publication of *Madam Crowl's Ghost and Other Tales of Mystery,* Le Fanu's followers have been loyal and often enthusiastic but never legion. Today he is read primarily as a writer of supernatural and sensational fiction, a fate predicted by M. R. James in his preface: "He stands absolutely in the first rank as a writer of ghost stories. . . . Nobody sets the scene better than he, nobody touches in the effective detail more deftly." Yet, as Gregory A. Schirmer notes, Le Fanu probably deserves more broadly based praise: "The best stories of Le Fanu also anticipate not only the formal purity of the modern short story, but also, in their exploration of psychological reality, many of the concerns of twentieth-century fiction. . . . [His] examination of the dark side of human nature runs against the grain of Victorian optimism, and anticipates the post-Freudian psychological despair of so much twentieth-century literature." Michael Begnal notes that generally Le Fanu's protagonist "can make no sense out of the absurd universe which is revolving around him" – certainly a characteristic many later writers share. Le Fanu's characters often face a crisis of religious faith. Even the tales based firmly in Irish folklore frequently pay close attention to the psychological states of their characters. Wayne Hall notes the prevalence of "lost causes and heroic defeats, the decay of the social landscape, the inability of spiritually shaken characters to reunite the fragments of their society" – all important thematic concerns in fiction written even a hundred years after Le Fanu's work.

Standing in the way of a widespread contemporary enthusiasm for Le Fanu's short stories is the fact that they are longer than the typical modern short story. Yet a strong basis for his continuing influence lies in the inherent interest of his explorations of issues such as guilt, the causes for suicide, the appropriate line of inheritance, the tension between oral traditions and written records, and the boundary between the natural and the supernatural. Finally, it is in his treatment of the supernatural that he is most distinctively interesting. Seeing supernat-

ural manifestations is not usually a sign of internal madness in Le Fanu's protagonists, although the presence of guilt or conflict over sexual expression seems to increase the likelihood of supernatural manifestations considerably. He saw the natural and supernatural as points on a continuum; his investigations of the tensions intrinsic to various places on that continuum provide some of the most philosophically sophisticated supernatural fiction extant.

## Biographies:

William Richard Le Fanu, *Seventy Years of Irish Life* (London: Macmillan, 1893);

Thomas Phillip Le Fanu, *Memoir of the Le Fanu Family* (Manchester: Sherrat & Hughes, 1924);

W. J. McCormack, *Sheridan Le Fanu and Victorian England* (Oxford: Clarendon Press, 1980).

## References:

Michael H. Begnal, *Joseph Sheridan Le Fanu* (Lewisburg, Pa.: Bucknell University Press, 1971);

E. F. Benson, "Sheridan Le Fanu," *Spectator,* 21 February 1931, pp. 263–264;

Elizabeth Bowen, Introduction to Le Fanu's *The House by the Churchyard* (London: Blond, 1968);

Nelson Browne, *Sheridan Le Fanu* (London: Morrison & Gibb, 1951);

S. M. Ellis, *Wilkie Collins, Le Fanu and Others* (London: Constable, 1931), pp. 140–191;

Barbara T. Gates, "Blue Devils and Green Tea: Sheridan Le Fanu's Haunted Suicides," *Studies in Short Fiction,* 24 (Winter 1987): 15–23;

Wayne Hall, "Le Fanu's House by the Marketplace," *Eire: A Journal of Irish Studies,* 21 (Spring 1986): 55–72;

Wendell V. Harris, *British Short Fiction in the Nineteenth Century* (Detroit: Wayne State University Press, 1979);

Jean Lozes, "Joseph Sheridan Le Fanu: The Prince of the Invisible," in *The Irish Short Story,* edited by Patrick Rafroidi and Terence Brown (Lille: University of Lille, 1979), pp. 91–101;

Ivan Melada, *Sheridan Le Fanu* (Boston: Twayne, 1987);

Alison Milbank, *Daughters of the House: Modes of the Gothic in Victorian Fiction* (New York: St. Martin's Press, 1992);

Harold Orel, "'Rigid Adherence to Facts': Le Fanu's *In a Glass Darkly* (1872)," *Eire: A Journal of Irish Studies,* 20 (Winter 1985): 65–88;

Audrey Petersen, *Victorian Masters of Mystery: From Wilkie Collins to Conan Doyle* (New York: Ungar, 1984);

Kel Roop, "Making Light in the Shadow Box: The Artistry of Le Fanu," *Papers on Language and Literature,* 21 (Fall 1985): 359–369;

Gregory A. Schirmer, "Tales from Big House and Cabin: The Nineteenth Century," in *The Irish Short Story: A Critical History,* edited by James F. Kilroy (New York: Twayne, 1984), pp. 21–44;

Helen Stoddart, "'The Precautions of Nervous People Are Infectious': Sheridan Le Fanu's Symptomatic Gothic," *Modern Language Review,* 86 (January 1991): 19–34;

Jack Sullivan, "'Green Tea': The Archetypal Ghost Story," in his *Elegant Nightmares: The English Ghost Story from Le Fanu to Blackwood* (Athens: Ohio University Press, 1978), pp. 11–31;

St. John Sweeney, "Sheridan Le Fanu, the Irish Poe," *Journal of Irish Literature,* 15 (January 1986): 3–32.

**Papers:**

A large collection of Le Fanu family papers is available in microfilm through the National Library of Ireland (N. 2973–2988; P. 2594–2609). The diaries (1846–1894) of William Richard Le Fanu are in the library of Trinity College, Dublin. The family papers of Le Fanu's in-laws, the Bennetts, are in the Brotherton Library, University of Leeds. The Dufferin and Ava papers (which include letters from Le Fanu to Helen, Lady Dufferin) are in the Public Record Office of Northern Ireland. The papers of the publishing firm of Bentley are in the library of the University of Illinois.

# Samuel Lover

*(24 February 1797 – 6 July 1868)*

## Leslie Haynsworth

BOOKS: *Legends and Stories of Ireland* (Dublin: Wakeman, 1831; London: Baldwin, 1834; Philadelphia: Carey & Hart, 1835);

*Rory O'More: A National Romance* (3 volumes, London: Bentley, 1837; 2 volumes, Philadelphia: Carey, Blanchard & Lea, 1837; revised and corrected edition, 1 volume, London: Bentley, 1853);

*Rory O'More* (London: Dicks' Standard Plays, 1837);

*The White Horse of the Peppers: A Comic Drama in Two Acts* (London: Acting National Drama, 1838; New York: Berford, 1847);

*The Hall Porter: A Comic Drama in Two Acts* (London: Acting National Drama, 1839);

*The Happy Man: An Extravaganza in One Act* (London: Acting National Drama, 1839);

*Songs and Ballads* (London: Chapman & Hall, 1839; enlarged, 1844; Philadelphia: Lea & Blanchard, 1847; enlarged and corrected edition, New York: Wiley & Putnam, 1847);

*The Greek Boy: A Musical Drama in Two Acts* (London: Acting National Drama, 1840);

*Il Paddy Whack in Italia: An Operetta in One Act* (London: Duncombe, 1841);

*Handy Andy: A Tale of Irish Life* (London: F. Lover, 1842; Philadelphia: Coates, 1842);

*Mr. Lover's Irish Evenings: The Irish Brigade* (London: Johnson, 1844);

*Treasure Trove: The First of a Series of Accounts of Irish Heirs, Being a Romantic Irish Tale of the Last Century* (London: F. Lover, 1844; New York & Philadelphia: Appleton, 1844); republished as *He Would Be a Gentleman; or, Treasure Trove* (London: Chapman & Hall, 1866; New York: Sadlier, 1872);

*Characteristic Sketches of Ireland and the Irish* (Dublin: Hardy, 1845);

*Songs of America* (New York: Firth, Hall & Pond, 1847);

*Barney the Baron: A Farce in One Act* (London: Dicks' Standard Plays, 1850);

*The Lyrics of Ireland* (London: Houlston & Wright, 1858);

*Rival Rhymes, in Honour of Burns,* as Ben Trovato (London & New York: Routledge, Warnes & Routledge, 1859);

*Metrical Tales and Other Poems* (London: Houlston & Wright, 1860);

*Mac Carthy More; or, Possession Nine Points of the Law: A Comic Drama in Two Acts* (London: Lacy, 1861);

*Original Songs for the Rifle Volunteers,* by Lover, Charles Mackay, and Thomas Miller (London: Clarke, 1861);

*Further Stories of Ireland,* edited by D. J. O'Donoghue (London: Constable, 1899).

**Collections:** *The Poetical Works of Samuel Lover* (London: Routledge, 1868; New York: Sadlier / Boston: Brady, 1872);

*The Novels and Tales of Samuel Lover,* 4 volumes (New York: Sadlier, 1880–1884);

*Works,* 6 volumes, edited by D. J. O'Donoghue (New York: Brentano's, 1900);

*Works,* 6 volumes (New York: Atheneum Society, 1901);

*Collected Writings,* 10 volumes (Boston: Little, Brown, 1901–1903);

*The Works of Samuel Lover,* 6 volumes (Boston: Little, Brown, 1902).

PLAY PRODUCTIONS: *The Happy Man,* London, Theatre Royal, 20 May 1839;

*The Hall Porter,* London, Theatre Royal, 25 July 1839;

*The Greek Boy,* London, Covent Garden, 26 September 1840;

*Il Paddy Whack in Italia,* London, Theatre Royal, April 1841;

*Mac Carthy More; or, Possession Nine Points of the Law,* London, Royal Lyceum Theatre, 1 April 1861.

OTHER: *Popular Tales and Legends of the Irish Peasantry,* edited by Lover (Dublin: Wakeman, 1834);

*The Lyrics of Ireland,* edited by Lover (London: Houlston & Wright, 1858); republished as *Poems of Ireland* (London & New York: Ward, Lock, 1884).

Taking as their main subjects both contemporary Irish life and Irish myths and legends, Samuel Lover's stories are noteworthy precursors to the Celtic revival movement centered around figures such as William Butler Yeats and John Millington Synge, which began shortly after Lover's death. Lover's contributions to this national renaissance have largely gone unrecognized, but he was truly a renaissance man: painter, novelist, dramatist, poet, musician, composer, and performer. He was best known in his own time as a miniaturist whose works were exhibited to considerable acclaim both at the Dublin Academy and the Royal Academy in London. But his popular 1842 novel, *Handy Andy: A Tale of Irish Life,* also brought him wide renown as a writer, and his self-illustrated *Legends and Stories of Ireland* (1831) was an immediate success. Peopled by rogues and buffoons of a sort that an English audience might recognize as being stereotypically Irish in their indolence and ignorance, Lover's comic stories nevertheless encourage the reader to share the author's own sense of the spirited joie de vivre of Irish life. In making available to the reading public, both English and Irish, legends and tales that had long been part of an exclusively oral tradition, these stories also serve to codify the defining myths of Irish national identity. Any student of the works of Yeats, Synge, James Joyce, Samuel Beckett, or Flann O'Brien will recognize at once both the characters and the settings for Lover's stories. While all of these later writers are better known, *Legends and Stories of Ireland* merits attention as well. The themes of Lover's comic tales may not be as profound as those of his famous compatriots, but these tales are nevertheless distinguished both by their interest in fostering harmony and mutual understanding between the long-antagonistic Irish and English and by their uniquely detailed and beautiful descriptions of Irish landscape, marvelously rendered through Lover's painter's eye.

The eldest son of Irish Protestant parents, Lover was born in Dublin on 24 February 1797. His father was a prosperous and respected stockbroker, and Lover was raised in a comfortable middle-class home. But the political situation in Ireland at the turn of the century was far from stable; as biographer Bayle Bernard puts it, "Rarely indeed has a humourist made his appearance in the world under less congenial circumstances." There was a major Irish rebellion against English rule in 1797 and another in 1803, and as a child Lover frequently witnessed the beating, hanging, and imprisonment of his compatriots by English soldiers. His desire to promote the interests of the Irish people was thus formulated almost from his infancy, as he explains:

> What a scene was this for a delicate child to witness, one who was more than usually susceptible of terrifying impressions. Here was an English soldier outraging an Irish Protestant home. What other feelings could it awaken than those of aversion to a red-coat? In such a mental soil as mine, is it any wonder that the seeds of patriotism took root and sprang up quickly? Every word I heard after that of English oppression and Irish wrong I eagerly caught at and well remembered, till my sixteenth year I had become as staunch an assertor of national rights as ever trod my native soil.

With their richly textured portraits of Irish life and their frequently explicit reminders of the ways in which Irish culture is and ought to remain distinct from that of the English, Lover's novels and stories represent his most direct expression of this patriotism. But, given his clearly stated aversion to the "English oppressors," what is remarkable about the *Legends and Stories of Ireland* is their evenhanded tone, their insistence that the English and the Irish alike ought to learn to tolerate and appreciate the differences in their respective cultures. Rather than using his popular tales as a vehicle for inciting Irish hatred of the English, Lover instead offers them, to an audience clearly envisioned as being both Irish and English, as educational pieces that will foster a better understanding of the positive values of Irish culture and traditions. Despite the fiery rhetoric with which he describes the genesis of his patriotic sentiments, then, Lover's stories demonstrate a belief that the Irish are better served by a diffusion of Anglo-Irish antagonism through mutual sympathy and understanding than they are by perpetuating hostility and rebellion. In "Lough Corrib," for example, the narrator's highest praise is extended to the English wife of an Irish gentleman who, "instead of sneering at the deficiencies which a poorer country than her own laboured under, was willing to be amused by observing the difference which exists in the national character of the two people, in noticing the prevalence of certain customs, superstitions, &c. &c.; while the popular tales of the neighborhood had for her a charm, which enlivened a sojourn in a remote district, that must otherwise have proved lonely." To follow this woman's example is what Lover's stories as a whole encourage every reader to do.

Lover was educated privately in Dublin, first at a dame school and then at a boys' academy. When he was twelve his health broke down to the extent that he was given a rest from his studies and sent to the country to recover his strength. During this visit he first developed the appreciations for both Irish landscape and Irish peasant life manifest in so many of his stories.

His health fully restored, Lover returned to Dublin at age thirteen to complete his education. He was a gifted student and was recommended by his teachers for preparation for a place at Dublin's prestigious Trinity College, but the city at this time was in the throes of an economic depression; worried about his son's future, Lover's father determined that Samuel would be better served by a career in business. Lover's formal education thus came to an end in 1812, and he began training as a stockbroker.

For two years Lover worked in his father's office, but he quickly discovered that he had neither the talent nor the inclination for a career in finance. Instead, he found himself increasingly drawn to the arts; when his day's work in the office was done, he would engage in painting, writing, and musical composition, and he began to see painting as his true vocation. This preference for the arts over business

created conflict between Lover and his father, and in 1814, at age seventeen, Lover left his job, broke relations with his father, and determined that he would make his living as a painter. He began as a marine landscape artist but achieved greatest success and renown as a miniaturist. By 1828 he was acknowledged as one of Ireland's greatest miniaturists and was elected to the Royal Hibernian Academy, to which he was named secretary in 1830. His talent and his wit also soon earned him a leading place in Irish social and artistic circles, and in 1827 he married a Miss Berrel, daughter of a prominent Dublin architect.

During this time Lover was also engaged in writing stories and sketches of Irish life and legends for publication in Dublin literary magazines, and these were first collected and published together in *Legends and Stories of Ireland*. The volume sold well but did not change the course of Lover's career. For several subsequent years he continued to earn his living and his reputation primarily as an artist. In the same year, for instance, he supplied all the illustrations for the *Irish Horn Book*, a broadly satiric collection of sketches reported to have had the largest sales of any book published in Ireland up to that time, and in 1832 he produced his best-known portrait when he was commissioned to paint a miniature of the celebrated violinist Niccolò Paganini. This picture was exhibited to considerable acclaim in both Dublin and London, gaining Lover a reputation in England to complement the one he had already established in Ireland.

Taking advantage of the name he had made for himself in England and seeking to remove to a climate more beneficial to his wife's delicate health, Lover moved to London in 1835. By this time he had begun to take more of an interest in literary matters. In 1833 he was one of the cofounders of the *Dublin University Magazine*, to which he also contributed several stories. Also in London, while he continued to enjoy a successful career as a miniaturist, he began to move in literary circles as well. His first novel, *Rory O'More: A National Romance*, was published in 1837, the same year in which, along with Charles Dickens, Harrison Ainsworth, and others, Lover was a founder of the popular British magazine *Bentley's Miscellany*. While in London Lover also wrote several plays and a burlesque opera, *Il Paddy Whack in Italia* (1841). He never achieved wide renown as a playwright, but his literary career took off with the publication of *Handy Andy*, which is reminiscent of the works of Maria Edgeworth and Henry Fielding in its comic and haplessly innocent protagonist.

Lover's literary success was fortunate, because by 1844 failing eyesight compelled him to abandon his painting career. To augment his income, which had long been earned primarily through painting, he developed a sort of one-man show, titled "Irish Evenings," in which he performed his own songs and stories. These performances were so successful in England that from 1846 to 1848 he went on an extended tour of the United States and Canada, where he was also well received. During this trip he composed several "American Sketches," which employ a comic tone to explore from a foreigner's point of view those habits and customs unique to the New World.

In 1848, while Lover was still in America, his wife died. He returned to London, where he continued his live performances and his musical compositions. (In the course of his life he wrote more than three hundred songs and ballads.) In 1852 he married Mary Wandby, the daughter of a Cambridgeshire squire, and from then until 1864, when his health began to fail, he devoted most of his energies to songwriting. After suffering a hemorrhage of the lungs in 1864 Lover was told by his doctor to move to a warmer climate; for the last four years of his life he lived in Jersey as an invalid. He died on 6 July 1868 at his home in St. Heliers and was buried at Kensal Green. A tributary plaque was also erected in his honor at St. Patrick's Cathedral in Dublin.

Lover's stories comprise only a small part of a large and varied opus. But these stories share a purpose with the ballads that make up a major component of his overall output. As he explains in his sketch "Ballads and Ballad Singers," ballads are the art form that "may, in the strictest sense, be termed 'our national literature,' and which . . . moves and influences the people . . . more than any other species of writing whatever." Ballads are, as Lover sees it, the most effective forms of nationalist propaganda, and the fact that he composed so many of them, all of them rooted in Irish folklore and traditions, demonstrates his commitment to the cause of preserving and promoting a distinctly Irish cultural identity. But this same function of celebrating and, when need be, defending, the myths, customs, and characteristics that make Ireland and the Irish unique is also performed by Lover's stories. Almost invariably lighthearted in tone, the *Legends and Stories of Ireland* nevertheless make frequent allusions to the grim subject of Anglo-Irish political strife. Yet despite Lover's frequent reminders to his readers about the countless injustices the Irish have suffered at the hands of the English, the comic tone of these stories is finally the most appropriate, for, as Lover

would have it, the ability to laugh in the face of adversity is one of the greatest strengths of the Irish character, a strength that can actually be turned into a weapon with which to combat oppression. In "The White Horse of the Peppers," for example, an Irish servant goes head-to-head with an English soldier who is trying to usurp his master's lands. While playing the part of the ignorant buffoon that accords with the Englishman's notion of the typical Irish peasant, the servant deceives and waylays the soldier at every step of his journey until the soldier is finally tricked into trading the estate back to its rightful owner for a horse. Of one episode in which the servant "set[s] all his wits to work how he could make the rest of the road as tiresome as possible to the stranger," Lover comments that "the scene would have been an amusing one to a third person; it was an encounter between phlegm and wit – a trial between English reserve and Irish ingenuity" and goes on in an uncharacteristically sober tone to note, "The oppressed and the pursued have only stratagem to encounter force, or escape destruction. The fox and other animals of the chase are proverbial for their cunning, and every conquered people have been reduced to the expedient of finesse, as their last resource."

But if Lover suggests that Irish wit is a survival tactic in the struggle against English oppression, he is also careful to avoid antagonizing the English members of his audience. In "The Burial of the Tithe," for example, he gives a careful disclaimer:

> [I]n stating what the Irish peasant's feelings are respecting tithe, I have not the most distant notion of putting forward any opinions of my own on the subject. In the pursuit of my own quiet art, I am happily removed from the fierce encounter of politics, and in my little volume I do not wish to offend against the feelings or opinions of any one; and I trust, therefore, that I may be permitted to give a sketch of a characteristic incident, as it came to my knowledge, without being mistaken for a partisan.

This disclaimer is necessary if Lover's purpose is not to seem stridently political, for this tale teaches the tremendous extent to which the Irish, particularly among the lower classes, suffered from the tithe system, under which they were required to pay heavy taxes to the English. Despite Lover's purported disinterestedness, this is one instance in which his display of Irish wit cannot conquer his bitterness about English greed and violence. The characters in the story, a group of Irish peasants, are celebrating the rumored repeal of the tithe with typical Irish humor and glee by symbolically burying it when a madman appears. Lover recounts his history: "In the rebellion of '98 his cabin had been burned over his head by the yeomanry, after every violation that could disgrace his hearth had been committed. He and his son, then little more than a boy, had attempted to defend their hut, but they were both left for dead. His wife and his daughter, a girl of sixteen, were murdered. The wretched father, unfortunately, recovered his life, but his reason was gone for ever." This madman brings to the "grave" a "bag full o' stones to throw a top o' the tithes to keep them down," and the story ends on an eerie and ominous note as he cries, "'These stones are from that desolate place and the curse of God that follows oppression is on them. – And let them be cast into the grave, and they will lie with the weight of a mountain on the monster that is buried forever.' So saying, he lifted stone after stone, and flung them fiercely into the pit; then, after a moment's pause upon its verge, he suddenly strode away with the same noiseless step with which he had approached, and left the scene in silence."

Few of Lover's stories, however, ever sound such somber tones. For the most part the glimpses they provide of Irish life are cheerful and uplifting and are clearly meant to instill in his compatriots a sense of pride in their uniquely Irish habits, talents, and traditions. "King O'Toole and St. Kevin," for instance, is a rollicking yarn about how the saint receives large amounts of land from the king for the church by saving the life of a goose to which the king is sentimentally attached to a ridiculous degree. King O'Toole's foolish affection and his gullibility reveal foibles in the "typical" Irish character, but the king also earns the reader's admiration for treating Saint Kevin, who appears to him as a peasant stranger, with great courtesy and respect. Lover thus uses his folkloric account of a genial king to advance the notion that the Irish have always been inherently democratic in their dealings with one another. The king serves as an example of the fact that political hierarchies need not translate into systems of social snobbery as they have traditionally done in England.

This and other positive features of Irish culture make it important that the Irish not assimilate to English customs, as Lover points out in "The Battle of the Berrins" when he acerbically remarks:

An attempt has been made by those who fancy it genteel, to graft the English accent upon the Broguish stem – and a very bad fruit it has produced. The truth is, the accents of the two countries could never be happily blended; and far from making a pleasing amalgamation, it conveys the idea that the speaker is endeavouring to *escape* from his own accent for what he considers a superior one.

In other words, the Irish will always remain a stronger, more proud people through the preservation of their own distinctive traits, mannerisms, and even accents. To prove this point Lover's stories frequently demonstrate that even the supposed weaknesses of the Irish character can often be turned to advantage.

That Lover wishes his English readers to share his own appreciation of Irish culture as well is apparent through his careful presentation of his subject matter as though he is aware that it will be alien to much of his audience. In several of the stories, for instance, he presents himself as a narrator who is also something of an anthropologist, traveling his native land seeking out legends and tales that will help him better understand his own national heritage. Also, particularly in the earlier stories in the volume, he makes frequent use of footnotes that explain particular Irish turns of phrase or episodes in Irish history. This practice reveals that these tales are meant to educate as much as they are meant to amuse.

Moreover, while Lover allows several of his Irish characters to win laughs at the expense of the English, he also frequently makes jokes at the expense of the Irish themselves. In so doing he is only being typically Irish, as he explains in "The Burial of the Tithe": "A sense of the ridiculous is so closely interwoven in an Irishman's nature, that he will even jest upon his *own* misfortunes; and while he indulges in a joke, (one of the few indulgences he can command) the person that excites it may as frequently be the object of his openheartedness as his mirth." In Lover's best-known story, "The Gridiron," an Irish servant traveling to America gets lost at sea and turns up in France, where he fancies himself capable of communicating with the natives because he speaks the one "French" phrase "Parly voo frongsay," which he regards merely as a special greeting unique to France. After introducing himself to a Frenchman with these words, Paddy expects to be able to converse with him in English, and he becomes increasingly enraged when the Frenchman refuses to respond to his request for the loan of a gridiron (or grill) upon which to cook his meat. The Frenchman of course does not understand a word of this request, while the Irishman remains completely unaware that the French actually speak an entirely different language and finally concludes that this particular Frenchman is one of the most singularly rude people he has ever encountered. The Irish, then, are portrayed as just as capable of being insular fools as the English are, and Lover's ability to poke fun at his own countrymen softens the blow of his critiques of English practices in Ireland, while at the same time making the point that, whether one is English or Irish, the inability to understand or appreciate the customs of others can make anyone look like a fool.

Lover's desire to foster his readers' appreciation of all things Irish also appears in his lush descriptions of Irish landscape. In "Lough Mask," for example, the protagonist finds himself atop a mountain:

> On one side, the Atlantic lay beneath him, brightly reflecting the glories of an autumnal setting sun, and expanding into a horizon of dazzling light; on the other lay the untrodden wilds before him, stretching amidst the depths of mountain valleys, whence the sun-beam had long since departed, and mists were already wreathing round the overhanging heights, and veiling the distance in vapoury indistinctness: as though you looked into some wizard's glass, and saw the uncertain conjuration of his wand. On the one side all was glory, light, and life — on the other, all was awful, still, and almost dark. It was one of Nature's sublimest moments; — such as are seldom witnessed and never forgotten.

Lover's Ireland is a land rich in majestic scenery peopled by a citizenry rich in wit, imagination, and spirit. Thus, while he asserts that ballads serve as the most effective means of galvanizing nationalist sentiment, his *Legends and Stories of Ireland* demonstrate that fiction too can foster patriotism at the same time that its less aggressively nationalistic tone can also encourage appreciation of Irish culture even among an audience that, like the English, might ordinarily be inclined to be scornful.

In the lineage of Irish writers Lover rests between the celebrated novelists Maria Edgeworth and Lady Morgan and more overtly nationalistic writers such as Yeats and Synge. His stories share the wit of the former and the politics of the latter, but the tremendous popularity of Edgeworth and Morgan and the militancy of the Celtic revivalists have largely eclipsed Lover's reputation. Nevertheless, his stories represent a significant contribution to the history of Irish literature. While Edgeworth and Morgan are primarily interested in the aristocracy, Lover was one of the first to explore, with sympathy and insight, the lives of rural Irish peasants. In so doing he is better able to portray a truly Irish culture, one less permeated by English customs and mannerisms. Also, although the more urgently nationalistic tones of the Celtic revivalists may do more to awaken sympathy for the plight of the Irish under English rule, Lover's tales, with their stress on tolerance and their plea for mutual understanding between the English and the Irish, can certainly be seen as preparing the ground for the harder political line of the writers who followed him by asking the English to become more receptive to all things Irish.

**Biographies:**

Bayle Bernard, *The Life of Samuel Lover, R. H. A., Artistic, Literary, and Musical* (London: King, 1874);

Andrew James Symington, *Samuel Lover: A Biographical Sketch* (London: Blackie, 1880; New York: Harper, 1880).

# William Maginn

*(10 July 1794 – 21 August 1842)*

David E. Latané Jr.
*Virginia Commonwealth University*

See also the Maginn entry in *DLB 110: British Romantic Prose Writers, 1789–1832, Second Series.*

BOOKS: *Whitehall: or, The Days of George IV,* by Maginn and J. G. Lockhart (London: Marsh, 1827);

*Magazine Miscellanies* (London: Mortimer, 1841);

*John Manesty, The Liverpool Merchant,* 2 volumes, completed by Charles Ollier (London: Mortimer, 1844);

*Maxims of Sir Morgan O'Doherty, Bart.* (Edinburgh & London: Blackwood, 1849);

*Shakespeare Papers: Pictures Grave and Gay* (London: Bentley, 1859; enlarged, 1860);

*A Gallery of Illustrious Literary Characters (1830–1838) Drawn by the Late Daniel Maclise, R.A., and Accompanied by Notices Chiefly by the Late William Maginn,* edited by William Bates (London: Chatto & Windus, 1873).

**Collections:** *Miscellaneous Writings of the Late Dr. Maginn,* 5 volumes, edited by Robert Shelton Mackenzie (New York: Redfield, 1855–1857);

*Miscellanies: Prose and Verse,* 2 volumes, edited by R. W. Montagu (London: Sampson Low, Marston, Searle & Rivington, 1885);

*Ten Tales* (London: Partridge, 1933).

OTHER: John Wilson, *The Noctes Ambrosianæ of "Blackwood,"* 4 volumes, includes contributions by Maginn (Philadelphia: Carey & Hart, 1843);

*Homeric Ballads,* translated by Maginn (London: Parker, 1850).

*William Maginn*

William Maginn, along with John Wilson, was one of the supreme magazinists of the first half of the nineteenth century, though his once-brilliant reputation has fallen into the decay usually associated with writers of miscellany and of literary journalism. Robert Shelton Mackenzie dedicated his posthumous edition of Maginn's *Miscellaneous Writings* (1855–1857) to a friend of the author, noting that without his assistance, "I should have been unable . . . to affiliate many of the articles, so pertinaciously did [Maginn] maintain the anonymous, and so Protean were his changes of style and subject." But even in the 1850s and with the aid of friends, Mackenzie made errors of attribution that modern scholars are still trying to sort out. Maginn's reputation, earned mostly through anonymous contributions to *Blackwood's Edinburgh Magazine, Fraser's Town and Country Magazine,* and *Bentley's Magazine,* has greatly suffered because of his greatest strengths. His variety of genres, his pungent particular satiric vent, and his great learning turned to comic ends make him difficult for the general readers of today. It is doubtful if a complete, accurate bibliography of his anonymous and pseudonymous writings, including his short fiction, will ever be compiled. Maginn also did not turn his attention, at any one time, exclusively to any single genre. His tales are intermixed in the vast body of his periodical work, and it was not until 1933 that the first selection of them was presented in book form and found by a reviewer in the 23 October *Times Literary Supplement* to be "a revelation in their skill, charm, and high spirits." In an expanded definition of fiction, it could also be argued that his gift for tale-telling can be found in the perplexing farragoes that he composed using a variety of masks.

William Maginn was born on 10 July 1794 in Cork, Ireland, to John Maginn, a Protestant schoolmaster, and Anne Eccles Maginn, who was from an old Scottish family. John Maginn noted his son's early proclivity for learning, especially ancient languages, and gave him the intense preparation characteristic of a prodigy; in completing his entrance examination for Trinity College, Dublin, at age twelve, he was placed among the top ten of more than a hundred applicants, many of them more than twice his age. By the time he left Ireland in 1824, Maginn had some acquaintance with at least fifteen languages, ancient and modern, and was accomplished in many.

After receiving his A.B. in 1811, Maginn returned to Cork to teach at his father's school. Two years later John Maginn died after having become embroiled in a civil suit against a powerful local politician, instituted after the elder Maginn was nearly run over by the alderman's gig while insisting on his right of way as a pedestrian; he had then been severely thrashed by the alderman's coachman. The nineteen-year-old William Maginn took over the stewardship of the school, supporting his mother and siblings, and moved into the set of men who formed the Cork Philosophical and Literary Society, one of two such bodies in the town. In 1819 Maginn received an LL.D. from Trinity College, earning the sobriquet "The Doctor," by which he was to be known to his friends and to periodical readers. He also developed at this time his unique talent for learned, multilingual foolishness, as well as libelous satire, though E. V. Kenealy reports that

none of his early squibs from the privately distributed *Freeholder* "will bear transcription. They are as ephemeral as the boobies who provoked them."

It was in 1819 that Maginn began contributing to national periodicals by sending articles, letters, poems, and squibs to William Jerdan's *Literary Gazette* under various assumed names; in November 1819 the two-year-old *Blackwood's Edinburgh Magazine* – generally known as *Maga* – welcomed its first contribution from "our Cork correspondent." For *Maga* he wrote initially as R. T. Scott, and he kept his real identity secret from all, including the publisher, until 1821, when he turned up at Blackwood's offices in Edinburgh and asked to speak with the proprietor. Pretending to be an irate resident of Cork, he demanded to know who the Irish correspondent for *Maga* was – something that Blackwood truthfully could not answer. After the discovery of the joke Maginn spent several weeks as a guest of Blackwood and became acquainted with the other contributors to the magazine, notably Wilson, John Gibson Lockhart, and R. P. Gillies.

Magazine miscellanies usurped much of Maginn's energies, and after his marriage on 31 January 1824 he turned over management of the school in Cork to a brother and moved to London to make a career in literature and journalism. His wife, Ellen Cullen Maginn, was the daughter of a clergyman of the Church of Ireland; the union produced three children. The Tory Party connections of *Blackwood's* enabled Maginn to secure introductions in London, including that of the leading publisher, John Murray, who, despite Maginn's probable hand in several magazine spoofs of the poetry and scandalous life of George Gordon, Lord Byron, entrusted Byron's papers to Maginn so that he might prepare an authorized biography of the poet. Some of Byron's friends, however, convinced Murray that the biographical commission should be in more circumspect hands than Maginn's, and the papers were returned to Murray. Byron's memoirs were burned in Murray's office fireplace, and the biography was written by the Irish poet Thomas Moore – another figure frequently satirized by Maginn, chiefly through his parodic "Moore-ish Melodies."

In 1825 Murray sent Maginn to Paris to be foreign correspondent for a new Tory daily, *The Representative,* at the handsome salary of £500 per annum, plus allowances. The newspaper, instigated by the young Benjamin Disraeli, was quickly in financial trouble, and Murray recalled Maginn to London to help with the editing. After the paper folded, Maginn was given the coeditorship of another Tory organ, *The Standard,* in conjunction with

Stanley Lees Giffard. While Giffard steadily handled the day-to-day tasks, Maginn supplied the wit that made *The Standard* a success, and he continued his association with the paper for nine years, during which time it was his main source of income.

Maginn's contributions to *Blackwood's* remained steady until 1828, and under the guise of the "Ensign and Adjutant, Sir Morgan Odoherty" he helped to instigate the magazine's best-known feature, the "Noctes Ambrosianæ," which later became a vehicle mainly for "Christopher North" (Wilson). The first "Noctes" featured an easy, liquid conversation between the Ensign and North in which Odoherty relates the latest gossip from London; gives the purported verse original of a prose letter of Byron to his publisher, Murray; sings a song in Italian satirizing Leigh Hunt; discusses Byron's recently published plays; and concludes with a song about a "Lady of Leith" who falls in love with a "tearing, swearing, thumping, bumping, ramping, roaring I-rish-man."

In his first decade of authorship Maginn frequently wrote under the pseudonym "Ensign Odoherty," one of a group of pseudo-authors created by the *Blackwood's* group. The names they wrote under were varying pseudonyms under which they published aspects of their work that seemed to be most appropriate for the particular pseudo-authors' personae. It is in such an ephemeral form that Maginn spent his talents at this time, both in literary criticism and in poetry and fiction. Maginn's early criticism of contemporary literature is never straightforward analysis; he usually inaugurates or collaborates in a fictional frame that allows the discussion to veer off toward burlesque or parody, as in his slashing review (December 1821) of Percy Bysshe Shelley's "Adonais" which ends with the receipt of a new poem by Shelley, "Elegy on My Tomcat": "Weep for my Tomcat! all ye Tabbies weep, / For he is gone at last!"

His sketches for *Blackwood's* outside the "Noctes" in the 1820s tend to contain as much personal and political allusion as narrative, as in "A Traveler's Week" (September 1823), and some of his contributions were rejected because of their wild content; the publisher admonished Maginn at one point in a letter, saying "it really will not do to run a-muck in this kind of way." A *Blackwood's* burlesque rejected by the publisher for fear of giving offense to Sir Walter Scott became Maginn's first book publication, *Whitehall: or, The Days of George IV* (1827), which was written in collaboration with J. G. Lockhart, Scott's son-in-law. The book, which purports to be a historical novel written in 2227, is a

roman à clef that mocks the chief characters of 1827 and parodies the style of Horace Smith, author of the historical novel *Brambletye House* (1826). Neither Maginn nor Lockhart seems to have been satisfied with it, nor were they willing to own up to authorship. In January 1828 Lockhart even reviewed the work in the Tory *Quarterly Review,* of which he was the editor, as a "laudable joke spoiled by wire-drawing it to 330 pages," and he went on to criticize its "malice" and "coarseness."

Maginn's tales are scattered through several periodicals during a twenty-year period. While relatively few in number, they exhibit a variety that has convinced some critics that he had a large unfulfilled potential. George Saintsbury, writing near the end of the nineteenth century, observed that "A gift which Maginn must have had in extraordinary measures, but which . . . he seems to have left for the most part uncultivated, was his talent for prose fiction in little." Maginn's stories remain of concern to historians of the genre but are little read or anthologized today. All of the best are self-contained tales that do not strain toward fuller development but are witty and exact in their structure. His longer narratives, on the other hand — *Whitehall* and the posthumously published *John Manesty, The Liverpool Merchant* (1844) — have never led anyone to wish that Maginn had turned exclusively to the novel. His best stories appeared in *Blackwood's*; in *The Literary Souvenir,* one of the "gift books" popular in the 1820s and 1830s; and in *Bentley's Miscellany,* a journal associated with Charles Dickens.

The earliest, "The Man in the Bell" (1821), reminds the reader today of a work by Edgar Allan Poe. It is a first-person narrative by a bell-ringer caught in the belfry, lying on a floor "principally composed of crazy laths" when the bells begin to ring. The interest lies in the psychological effect: "The roaring of the bell confused my intellect, and my fancy began to teem with all sorts of strange and terrifying ideas. The bell pealing above, and opening its jaws with a hideous clamour, seemed to me at one time a hideous monster." Driven temporarily mad by the ringing, the narrator can no longer tolerate the bells, and envies the Muslims for "the sonorous voice of the Muezzin." Another story, "Jochonan in the City of Demons," has a more overtly gothic tinge. Maginn apparently planned a series based on the legends of the rabbis, and this one, beginning with the opening "In days of yore," explores the supernatural world of a wise but miserly rabbi of Cairo tempted sorely by the *mazokin* (demons), to whose city he has been transported in order to administer rites to a dying Jewish infant.

He escapes by following the mother's injunction neither to eat, nor sleep, nor accept any fee. Despite being tempted with "amethysts, topazes, rubies, beryls, and all other precious stones," the rabbi resists and is rewarded with "a paltry bunch of rusty iron" – the keys to his own home. Maginn handles the narrative with a light touch and pulls the story into the English present at the end by revealing a narrative frame.

A third Gothic story, "A Night of Terror," published in *Bentley's Miscellany* in January 1838, explodes the conventions of the genre altogether. The narrator begins by announcing that "You will recollect that, three years ago, we had a dreadful winter throughout Europe." He proceeds to tell a harrowing tale of a trip from Lithuania to Bohemia by carriage in the midst of this winter as he and his sister attempt to return to their father's deathbed. They are set upon by wolves and forced into a hunting lodge; their horses are killed and their ammunition is exhausted. "The shaggy wolves, howling incessantly, glared down upon us from the top, waiting the moment to spring. Below stood Henrich and I, illumined in the blaze of the faggots, our reversed fowling-pieces in our hands ready to strike, Louise lay at our feet prostrate." It is a situation from which there is seemingly no escape. Maginn then pulls back to the frame: the author is characterized as a dilettante who has just given his unfinished manuscript to "cousin Lucy," who insists that he write the rescue – but he is engaged to go shooting, and Lucy (and the reader) must imagine the ending for themselves if they wish to "get rid of the story." Maginn's tales almost always bring the reader into an imagined frame; the convivial act of storytelling is as important as the obviously fictional characters and events told.

Maginn's retellings of Irish legend have been much praised; they were written, while Maginn was still living in Cork, in collaboration with his friend Thomas Crofton Croker, the first man to collect southern Irish folktales by following the methods of the Grimm brothers, and were published in *Fairy Legends and Traditions in the South of Ireland* (1825). They include "The Legend of Bottle Hill," in which Mick Purcell sells a cow to a little person for a magical bottle; "The Legend of Knocksheogowna," in which the queen of the fairies in Tipperary defends her hill against the musical cowherd, Larry Hoolahan; and "The Legend of Knockgrafton," in which the humpback Lusmore loses his hump after charming the fairies with song. In the genre of the collected folktale, Maginn's stand out for the ease and wit of the prose.

Maginn's great triumph may be "Bob Burke's Duel with Ensign Brady of the 48th," which appeared in *Blackwood's* in May 1834. Bob Burke narrates the story of his first love from a distance of "sixteen or seventeen years." The object of his affections was "Miss Theodosia Macnamara," a "fine grown girl, full of flesh and blood," who "rose five foot nine at least when shod." Her mother had brought her to the spa at Mallow because of her "delicate" health, but all of Burke's attempts to characterize "Dosy" as a fragile, cupid's-bow-mouthed *"Keepsake"* beauty reveal her as a large, loud hoyden – which is what he finds attractive, though his terms of description are better suited for fillies than for girls. Bob's rival, Ensign Brady, was a pretentious and mendacious officer – he compared potato cake to *gateau aux truffes* and recounted his experiences in the company of the duke of Devonshire. After two hours of the ensign's blarney, as well as a consultation with the Macnamaras' attorney, "old Six-and-Eightpence" Barney Pulvertaft, Burke discovered that he was in love. He rhapsodizes: "What I had just heard had kindled my passion for the divine Theodosia into a quenchless blaze. Yes, I exclaimed out loud, I *do* love her. Such an angel does not exist on earth. What charms! What innocence! What horsewomanship! Five hundred a year certain! Ten thousand pounds in perspective!" The story of the duel is told with great drollery, as the seconds maneuver two scared young men into position and through a first round of shots; as both are being forced unwillingly into a second round, a cousin of Bob's informs him that Theodosia's eighty-four-year-old uncle, from whom her fortune was to proceed, has just married a pregnant housemaid of eighteen. Bob relinquishes Theodosia to the ensign, and the company assembled to hear the tale begin to think of dinner.

A related story had appeared in *Blackwood's* in April 1834. "A Story without a Tail" includes Bob Burke as one of six men at a dinner party in the Temple in London who eat and drink themselves into oblivion. At 11:00 P.M. one of them, Humpy Harlow, who has hitherto been silent, tells a story beginning "Humphries told me." The next day the others find themselves unable to recollect more than these words, and two of them arrange to meet Harlow again. By the time he repeats his story, they are once again too far gone in drink to remember more the next day than "Humphries told me." The third night, as the less inebriated group prompts Harlow to tell it again, he "flares up" and refuses to continue. The narrator concludes that the purpose of the "Story without a Tail" is to "impress upon the minds of my readers the perishable nature of mundane affairs." The tone is alternately mock-heroic (an epic list of victuals is read), mock-scientific (a diagram is drawn showing the geometry of the angles of the slice made out of the round of cheese), and solemnly legal ("Chairs being made to be sat upon, it is sufficient to say that they answer their purposes; and whether they had backs or not – whether they were cane-bottomed, or hair-bottomed, or rush-bottomed, is nothing to the present inquiry"). Saintsbury claimed to have read the story "literally scores of times and never without fresh enjoyment," and it does perfectly capture the mood of a group of legal students and hangers-on enjoying a potluck feast.

By 1829 Maginn had established himself as a power in the world of London and Edinburgh publishing and journalism. His criticism, essays, political leaders, spoofs, poems, and tales were welcomed in many newspapers, magazines, and annuals, from the respectable *Literary Souvenir* to the scurrilous *Age*. Having broken with *Blackwood's* for reasons that remain unclear, Maginn decided to found a London magazine that would rival the Edinburgh periodical and that could be shaped to his rambunctious style. He joined with Hugh Fraser, a literary man-about-town with some capital to spare, and they selected James Fraser as the publisher – reportedly after walking by his shop and being struck by the coincidence of the identical surnames. The result of this resolve was *Fraser's Magazine for Town and Country,* the first issue of which appeared in February 1830. (It would last until 1882.)

*Fraser's* is Maginn's greatest achievement, in part because it published works by such now-canonical writers as Thomas Babington Carlyle (*Sartor Resartus* was serialized in 1833–1834) and William Makepeace Thackeray, but also because it catches the mood of the times. While the magazine was ostensibly conservative in politics, Maginn's oppositional nature provided for a Tory radicalism, and the nation was receptive. Alexis de Tocqueville visited England in 1833 and noted that "a spirit of discontent with the present and hatred of the past shows itself everywhere. . . . [this spirit] only looks for what is wrong around it, and is much more bent on correcting what is wrong than in preserving what is good." The new magazine, while modeled after the format of *Blackwood's,* took its tone not from the Regency but from the new era; nothing was sacred, not even the foibles of its own contributors – one of the few pieces by Maginn still in print (in an appendix to the 1987 Oxford World Classics edition of *Sartor Resartus*) is a parody published in

*Fraser's* of Carlyle's Germanic prose style. The magazine was an almost instant success; the circulation topped eight thousand within a year, which put Maginn's progeny on a par with *Blackwood's,* the *Quarterly Review,* and the *Edinburgh Review.*

Maginn's motto for the magazine was "Naught to do but be jocose, or with a pin impale our pygmy foes," and from the farcical opening numbers, in which an election for the editorship is described (Samuel Taylor Coleridge makes a drunken speech from the hustings), *Fraser's* went after its enemies with éclat. Following Maginn's example, the "Fraserians" set about ridiculing what they considered bad writing – especially novelists of the "silver-fork" school, Byronic poets, and writers of sentimental verse. Edward Bulwer-Lytton was a particular target, singled out for his novel of life among the dandies, *Pelham* (1828); his editorship of the rival *New Monthly Magazine*; and his Whig politics. They also continuously attacked the poet Robert "Satan" Montgomery, who combined religion and Byronism in a series of long poems. The magazine followed a peculiar line in politics; while loudly proclaiming its Toryism, *Fraser's* in the early 1830s published a series of articles that exposed corruption in the courts and argued for legal reform (an issue usually left to the utilitarian radicals), and also attacked abuses in the apprentice system and child labor in the factories. In an antiaristocratic era, Maginn's Toryism did not blindly uphold tradition; as he would say at the time of the Grantley Berkeley affair, "Tory as I am, and habitually respecting rank and station, I do not imagine that birth, dignity, or office command of themselves respect." For its first six years *Fraser's* was the British magazine most in vogue – despite Carlyle's calling it a "dog's meat-tart of a periodical" – and Maginn was its guiding spirit.

A turning point in Maginn's relationship with *Fraser's* occurred with the celebrated affair of *Berkeley Castle* (1836). Grantley Berkeley's historical novel about his family was the subject of a hastily written review by Maginn, which appeared unvetted in the August 1836 number of *Fraser's.* In addition to savaging the construction and style of the novel, Maginn pointed out certain lacunae in Berkeley's tale of his forebears, derived from the journals of the House of Lords: for example, that "Mr. Grantley Berkeley's mother lived with Mr. Grantley Berkeley's father as his mistress, and that she had at least one child before she could induce the old and very stupid lord to marry her." Berkeley's response was to appear at the publisher's shop with his brother Craven, where they beat a defenseless Hugh Fraser nearly to death with a loaded riding crop. He suffered permanent injuries, and when Maginn acknowledged his authorship of the review he and Berkeley fought a duel in which three shots were exchanged, though none struck home. Maginn was reportedly indifferent to his own safety, while Berkeley – a sporting gentleman with a reputation as a crack shot – afterward complained about the quality of the pistols and spread rumors about Maginn's relationship with the poet Letitia Landon ("L.E.L."), whom he had met through her sponsor, Jerdan, when he had first arrived in London. While there is no firm evidence of an affair, the rumors disrupted Maginn's marriage for a time. Years after Maginn's death, Berkeley was still pursuing Maginn in his *My Life and Recollections* (1865–1866), giving partial and somewhat improbable versions of the affair.

Maginn had fallen hopelessly into debt, which may account for his recklessness at this time, both with the pen and the pistol; he was forced to live in hiding, chiefly in the slums, and to absent himself from the offices both of *Fraser's* and *The Standard,* a newspaper that provided much of his income. By October 1836 he was no longer effectively the editor of *Fraser's*. Paradoxically, despite his debt, marital problems caused by the "L.E.L." rumors, and his guilt over the injury to Fraser resulting from the Berkeley affair, Maginn produced his most sustained scholarly productions, chiefly on Homer and on William Shakespeare. His series "Shakespeare Papers" appeared in *Bentley's Miscellany* in 1837 and contained several novel interpretations – notably of Lady Macbeth as a "sorely urged and broken-hearted" woman. In examining Homer, he argued forcefully and learnedly for the unity of the *Iliad* and hence against the theory that the poem was composed by several persons over a span of time. His translations of Homer into English hexameters and ballad meters were judged by Matthew Arnold to be "vigorous and genuine poems" but also "not at all Homeric" because of the movement of the verse. Maginn's friend E. V. Kenealy describes him at this time as a "glorious ruin," a man who "will write you one of his ablest articles while standing in his shirt or sipping brandy."

Maginn's last book was *Magazine Miscellanies* (1841), which republished some of his earlier work; the volume was hastily put together with the hope of raising enough money to satisfy his creditors. The scheme failed, and the publisher sued Maginn, who was incarcerated in the Fleet prison in early 1842 for failure to pay his debts. There he shared quarters with the Chartist leader Richard Oastler, who wrote his weekly *Fleet Papers* at the same table

at which Maginn produced leaders for *The Age;* Oastler records the still-amusing Maginn's ability to sketch out "embryo 'tales' " at the drop of a hat. Maginn's friends and family petitioned for his release on grounds of ill health, and after a few months their request was granted. When he emerged he retired with his wife and children to Walton-on-Thames, where he died of consumption on 21 August 1842. The family was left in extreme financial need, despite the donation of £100 to Maginn on his deathbed by Sir Robert Peel. Five days after Maginn's death Francis Mahoney, who had written under the pseudonym "Father Prout," applied for relief on the Maginns' behalf to the Royal Literary Fund, and his widow was voted £50. On the application form in the blank marked "Cause of distress," Mahoney inscribed, "The casualties of a life wholly dependent on literature." Maginn's friend, the publisher Charles Ollier, subsequently completed a novel Maginn had begun while living in Liverpool in 1839; it was published for the benefit of the family as *John Manesty, The Liverpool Merchant* (1844). Despite the illustrations by the popular George Cruikshank, it produced little pecuniary reward.

After his death Maginn's contemporaries were not quite sure what to make of him. Some of his enemies, such as the writer and editor S. C. Hall, a fellow native of Cork, were also active leaders of the strengthening temperance movement, and they found it easy to discredit "Maginn and Water" as a disreputable hangover from the looser morals of the Regency era. His association with *Fraser's Magazine* hurt his reputation, as the high spirits of its early contributors were judged by the later Victorians as highly improper; Harriet Martineau remarks in her autobiography (1877) about one of the hoaxes in *Fraser's* that "plotter and publisher deserved to be whipped from one end of London to the other." The more sympathetic Jerdan says in his autobiography (1852–1853), "Of Maginn, the precocious, the prolific, the humourous, the eccentric, the erratic, the versatile, the learned, the wonderfully endowed, the Irish, – how shall I attempt to convey any idea?" While the universal impression of Maginn's genius lingered on, his reputation slipped away with the demise of the generation of men and women who knew him personally. His stories were buried in somewhat carelessly edited posthumous collections or reprinted in omnibus *Tales from Blackwood's*. He came to stand in for a type of literary man, feckless, improvident, careless of his art, and willing to write on both sides of an issue. This last charge is grounded in one of his own satires,

"The Tobias Correspondence," published in *Blackwood's* in July and August 1840, which was read as an autobiographical confession, as well as by the understanding that the disreputable Captain Shandy in Thackeray's novel of the Grub Street of the 1830s, *The History of Pendennis* (1848–1850), is an accurate portrait of Maginn rather than a conflation of several men the novelist had known in his days as a magazine writer and editor.

As a writer of tales Maginn might have made a name as a folklorist, but England and Grub Street beckoned; he likewise failed to develop a substantial body of Gothic or suspense tales, though he wrote a few fine ones – founding *Fraser's* was evidently of more interest. And, what is most to be regretted, his droll stories of Bob Burke and friends were not continued. He turned, despite financial distress, back to his love of learning and scholarship in the last few years of his life, even while the public was clamoring for Dickens's *Pickwick Papers* (1836–1837) and Thackeray's works by "Michael Angelo Titmarsh." Nevertheless, his stories remain a key part of a career that, in its very mishaps, pranks, satiric spoofs, and tragedies, perhaps best represents the spirit of British literature in the 1820s and 1830s.

## References:

J. H. Alexander, ed., *The Tavern Sages: Selections from the Noctes Ambrosianae* (Aberdeen: Association for Scottish Literary Studies, 1992);

Matthew Arnold, *On Translating Homer* (New York: Chelsea House, 1983);

Grantley Berkeley, *My Life and Recollections,* 4 volumes (London: Hurst & Blackett, 1865–1866);

Alexis de Tocqueville, *Journeys to England and Ireland,* edited by J. P. Mayer (New Haven: Yale University Press, 1958);

J. Lyle Donaghy, "William Maginn," *Dublin Magazine,* new series 13 (July–September, 1938): 43–51;

Malcolm Elwin, *Victorian Wallflowers* (London: Cape, 1934; Port Washington, N.Y.: Kennikat, 1966);

John Gross, *The Rise and Fall of the Men of Letters* (New York: Macmillan, 1969);

Samuel Carter Hall, *Retrospect of a Long Life, From 1815 to 1883* (London: Bentley, 1883);

Harold Herd, *Seven Editors* (London: Allen, 1955);

William Jerdan, *The Autobiography of William Jerdan, With His Literary, Political and Social Reminiscences and Correspondence During the Last Fifty Years,* 4 volumes (London: Hall, Virtue, 1852–1853);

E. V. Kenealy, "William Maginn, LL.D.," *Dublin University Magazine,* 23 (January 1844): 72–101;

Patrick Leary, "*Fraser's Magazine* and the Literary Life, 1830–1847," *Victorian Periodicals Review,* 27, no. 2 (1994): 105–126;

John Gibson Lockhart, "The Doctor," *Fraser's,* 2 (January 1831): 716;

Harriet Martineau, *Harriet Martineau's Autobiography, with Memorials by Maria Weston Chapman* (3 volumes, London: Smith, Elder, 1877; 2 volumes, Boston: Osgood, 1877);

Michael Monahan, "Doctor Maginn," in his *Nova Hibernia: Irish Poets and Dramatists of Yesterday and Today* (New York: Kennerley, 1914), pp. 203–235;

Peter T. Murphy, "Impersonation and Authorship in Romantic Britain," *ELH,* 59 (Fall 1992): 625–649;

George Saintsbury, "Three Humourists: Hook, Barham, Maginn," in his *Essays in English Literature, 1780–1860,* second series (New York: Scribners, 1895), pp. 270–302;

P. A. Sillard, "Doctor Maginn," *Gentleman's Magazine,* 296 (March 1904): 286–295;

Miriam M. H. Thrall, *Rebellious Fraser's: Nol Yorke's Magazine in the Days of Maginn, Thackeray, and Carlyle* (New York: Columbia University Press, 1934);

Ralph M. Wardle, "Outwitting Hazlitt," *Modern Language Notes,* 57 (June 1942): 459–462;

Wardle, "Who Was Morgan Odoherty?" *PMLA,* 58 (September 1943): 716–727.

# Harriet Martineau
*(12 June 1802 – 27 June 1876)*

## Deborah A. Logan
*University of North Carolina at Chapel Hill*

See also the Martineau entries in *DLB 21: Victorian Novelists Before 1885* and *DLB 55: Victorian Prose Writers After 1867.*

SELECTED BOOKS: *Devotional Exercises for the Use of Young Persons* (London: Hunter, 1823; Boston: Bowles, 1833);

*Addresses with Prayers and Original Hymns for the Use of Families and Schools* (London: Hunter, 1826);

*Principle and Practice; or, The Orphan Family* (Wellington: Houlston, 1827; New York: Printed for W. B. Gilley, 1828);

*The Rioters; or, A Tale of Bad Times* (London: Houlston, 1827);

*Mary Campbell; or, The Affectionate Granddaughter* (Wellington: Houlston, 1828);

*The Turn Out; or, Patience the Best Policy* (London: Houlston, 1829);

*Traditions of Palestine* (London: Longman, Rees, Orme, Brown & Green, 1830); republished as *The Times of the Saviour* (Boston: Bowles, 1831);

*The Essential Faith of the Universal Church Deduced from the Sacred Records* (London: Printed for the Unitarian Association, 1831; Boston: Bowles, 1833);

*Five Years of Youth; or, Sense and Sentiment* (London: Harney & Darton, 1831; Boston: Bowles & Greene, 1832);

*Sequel to Principle and Practice; or, The Orphan Family* (London: Printed for Houlston, 1831);

*Illustrations of Political Economy* (25 monthly parts, London: Fox, 1832–1834; 8 volumes, Boston: Bowles, 1832–1835);

*The Faith as Unfolded by Many Prophets: An Essay Addressed to the Disciples of Mohammed* (London: Printed for the Unitarian Association, 1832; Boston: Bowles, 1833);

*Prize Essays* (London: British & Foreign Unitarian Association, 1832);

*Providence as Manifested Through Israel* (London: Printed for the Unitarian Association, 1832; Boston: Bowles, 1833);

*Harriet Martineau in 1849; portrait by George Richmond (National Portrait Gallery, London)*

*Poor Laws and Paupers Illustrated* (4 volumes, London: Fox, 1833–1834; 1 volume, Boston: Bowles, 1833);

*Christmas-Day; or, The Friends* (London: Printed for Houlston, 1834);

*Illustrations of Taxation,* 5 volumes (London: Fox, 1834);

*The Children Who Lived by the Jordan: A Story* (Salem, Mass.: Landmark, 1835; London: Green, 1842);

*The Hamlets* (Boston: Munroe, 1836);

*Miscellanies,* 2 volumes (Boston: Hilliard, Gray, 1836);

*Society in America,* 3 volumes (London: Saunders & Otley, 1837);

*Deerbrook: A Novel* (3 volumes, London: Moxon, 1838; New York: Harper, 1839);

*The Guide to Service,* 3 volumes (London: Knight, 1838–1839);

*How to Observe Morals and Manners* (London: Knight, 1838; New York: Harper, 1838);

*My Servant Rachel: A Tale* (London: Houlston, 1838);

*A Retrospect of Western Travel* (3 volumes, London: Saunders & Otley, 1838; 2 volumes, New York: Lohman, 1838);

*The Martyr Age of the United States* (Boston: Weeks, Jordan/Otis/Broaders / New York: Taylor, 1839; Newcastle upon Tyne: Printed for the Emancipation and Aborigines Protection Society, 1840);

*The Hour and the Man: A Historical Romance* (3 volumes, London: Moxon, 1841; 2 volumes, New York: Harper, 1841);

*The Playfellow: A Series of Tales* (4 volumes, London: Knight, 1841–1843; 1 volume, London & New York: Routledge, 1883);

*Life in the Sick-Room: Essays, By an Invalid* (London: Moxon, 1844; Boston: Bowles & Crosby, 1844);

*Dawn Island: A Tale* (Manchester: Gadsby, 1845);

*Letters on Mesmerism* (London: Moxon, 1845); republished as *Miss Martineau's Letters on Mesmerism* (New York: Harper, 1845);

*Forest and Game-Law Tales,* 3 volumes (London: Moxon, 1845–1846);

*The Billow and the Rock* (London: Knight, 1846);

*The Land We Live In,* by Martineau and Charles Knight, 4 volumes (London: Knight, 1847);

*Eastern Life, Present and Past* (3 volumes, London: Moxon, 1848; 1 volume, Philadelphia: Lea & Blanchard, 1848);

*Household Education* (London: Moxon, 1849; Philadelphia: Lea & Blanchard, 1849);

*History of England during the Thirty Years' Peace 1816–1846* (2 volumes, London: Knight, 1849–1850; 4 volumes, Philadelphia: Porter & Coates, 1864);

*Two Letters on Cow-Keeping, by Harriet Martineau, Addressed to the Governor of the Guiltcross Union Workhouse* (London: Charles Gilpin / Edinburgh: Black / Dublin: J. B. Gilpin, 1850);

*Half a Century of the British Empire: A History of the Kingdom and the People from 1800 to 1850,* Part I (London, 1851);

*Introduction to the History of the Peace from 1800 to 1815* (London: Knight, 1851);

*Letters on the Laws of Man's Nature and Development,* by Martineau and Henry George Atkinson (London: Chapman, 1851; Boston: Mendum, 1851);

*Merdhen, The Manor and The Eyrie, Old Landmarks and Old Laws* (London: Routledge, 1852);

*Letters from Ireland* (London: Chapman, 1852);

*Guide to Windermere, with Tours to the Neighbouring Lakes and Other Interesting Places* (Windermere: Garnett / London: Whittaker, 1854);

*A Complete Guide to the English Lakes* (Windermere: Garnett / London: Whittaker, 1855);

*The Factory Controversy: A Warning Against Meddling Legislation* (Manchester: Printed by A. Ireland for the National Association of Factory Occupiers, 1855);

*A History of the American Compromises* (London: Chapman, 1856);

*Sketches from Life* (London: Whittaker / Windermere: Garnett, 1856);

*British Rule in India: A Historical Sketch* (London: Smith, Elder, 1857);

*Corporate Tradition and National Rights: Local Dues on Shipping* (London: Routledge / Manchester: Dinham, 1857);

*Guide to Keswick and Its Environs* (Windermere: Garnett / London: Whittaker, 1857);

*The "Manifest Destiny" of the American Union* (New York: American Anti-Slavery Society, 1857);

*Suggestions towards the Future Government of India* (London: Smith, Elder, 1858);

*Endowed Schools of Ireland* (London: Smith, Elder, 1859);

*England and Her Soldiers* (London: Smith, Elder, 1859);

*Health, Husbandry and Handicraft* (London: Bradbury & Evans, 1861); republished in part as *Our Farm of Two Acres* (New York: Bunce & Huntingdon, 1865);

*Biographical Sketches* (London: Macmillan, 1869; New York: Leypoldt & Holt, 1869);

*Harriet Martineau's Autobiography, with Memorials by Maria Weston Chapman* (3 volumes, London: Smith, Elder, 1877; 2 volumes, Boston: Osgood, 1877);

*The Hampdens: An Historiette* (London: Routledge, 1880).

OTHER: *The Positive Philosophy of Auguste Comte Freely Translated and Condensed,* 2 volumes (London: John Chapman, 1853; New York: Appleton, 1854).

SELECTED PERIODICAL PUBLICATION –
UNCOLLECTED: "Letter to the Deaf," *Tait's Edinburgh Magazine,* new series 1 (April 1834):
174–179.

Harriet Martineau exhibited remarkable intellectual precocity, discovering John Milton's *Paradise Lost* (1667) at age seven. Beginning with her study of Malthusian political economy at age fourteen and culminating in her editorializing against the Contagious Diseases Acts in her seventies, Martineau's lively participation in the issues and controversies of her time marks her as a true representative of the Victorian age. She was learned, articulate, opinionated, and, detractors claimed, intellectually inflexible. Martineau's life and work reveal a consistent determination never to lapse into what she regarded as middle-class complacency or superficial gentility. There was much work to be done in the world, and there was, as she put it in her autobiography (1877), "more or less evidence" that she was the one to do it.

Born on 12 June 1802 in Norwich, England, Martineau was the sixth of eight children of Elizabeth Martineau, née Rankin, and Thomas Martineau, a bombazine manufacturer. Martineau's account of her early childhood in her three-volume autobiography – despite its subjectivity, still regarded as the definitive account of her life – reveals the effects of the "taking-down" system of child rearing typical of the era on this sensitive, gifted child. The clarity of her childhood memories is impressive – for example, she dates her interest in politics from age four, when she grieved for Lord Nelson's death – as is the integrity exhibited by her reluctance fully to blame others for her early unhappiness.

Malnutrition suffered during infancy left Martineau with chronic digestive and nervous system ailments that plagued her throughout her life. She admits that a plain, sickly child haunted by vague fears does not invite nurturance: "I have no doubt I was an insufferable child for gloom, obstinacy and crossness." But she also notes that "a little more of the cheerful tenderness which was in those days thought bad for children, would have saved me from my worst faults, and from a world of suffering."

For years following the onset of her deafness at age twelve, Martineau's family rejected her impairment as an adolescent's attempt to call attention to herself. Martineau later regarded her disability as "the best thing that ever happened to me; – the best, in a selfish view, as the grandest impulse to self-mastery; and the best in a higher view, as my

most peculiar opportunity of helping others." The loneliness of her early years suggested by her family's response to a progressive and irreversible debility is captured in the poignancy of her statement that "the first person I was ever not afraid of was Aunt Kentish, who won my heart and my confidence when I was sixteen."

Compassion and nurturance may have been lacking in the Martineau household, but opportunities for intellectual growth abounded. In addition to being a self-styled "walking concordance of Milton and Shakespeare," Martineau became as well versed in Latin poetry as she was in the economic and social theories of her day. She read newspapers, journals, and periodicals and, in that age of avid public interest in literature and literary criticism, followed the lively and often volatile critical debates.

Despite the extreme lack of self-esteem that marked her early years – "I was always in a state of shame about something or other" – Martineau was grateful for the sacrifices her parents made to educate both sons and daughters. Unlike her college-bound brothers, however, Martineau studied academics along with her more important domestic tasks; yet she regards herself doubly blessed in that she was thus prepared to "get my bread by my needle . . . before I won a better place and occupation with my pen." Throughout her life she was proud of the dual economic self-sufficiency provided by both her domestic skills and literary ability.

Martineau's first article, "Female Writers on Practical Divinity," was published in the Unitarian journal *Monthly Repository* in 1820. The subsequent period of literary apprenticeship included nonfiction articles and moral fables, culminating in Martineau's characteristically didactic style of fiction writing. Throughout her lifelong career, and regardless of the genre in which she wrote or the topic she addressed, Martineau never lost sight of her intended audience: the common reader. Her ability to popularize social issues did not always produce great literature, but it did fulfill her aim of educating those who would most benefit by understanding the complexities of social and economic principles. For Martineau, culturewide social change grows out of individual self-sufficiency, which is in turn fostered by access to information.

Martineau's single status afforded her a measure of freedom and mobility unavailable to most Victorian women. Her physical plainness, the deafness that necessitated her using an ungainly and awkward ear trumpet, and her highly developed intellect, which was considered unfeminine, minimized her marriageability. When in 1825 Martineau became engaged to John Worthington, she pragmatically accepted his premature illness and death as her exemption from the domestic role: "I am, in truth, very thankful for not having married at all." At the age of twenty-three Martineau became a confirmed spinster.

When her family lost its fortune in 1829 and with it any claim to middle-class respectability, Martineau responded with characteristic pragmatism: "I rather enjoyed it . . . for there was scope for action." The necessity for economic self-sufficiency led Martineau to a life full of "work, friends, and independence" as well as to opportunities to travel the world. Distinct from most languishing Victorian ladies, Martineau "truly lived instead of vegetated."

Martineau's youthful habit of studying early and late so as to fulfill her domestic duties during the day became her adult habit of writing early and late while supporting herself by needlework. Between 1827 and 1830 Martineau published articles in the *Monthly Repository* and other journals, won first prize in three categories of a Unitarian essay contest, and published *Traditions of Palestine* (1830), a study of the Bible in its historical context.

Among the short fiction she wrote during this period is *Five Years of Youth; or, Sense and Sentiment* (1831), a children's tale for and about "motherless daughters." Since the death of their mother, young Anna and Mary Byerley, although well trained academically by their politician father, grew haphazardly in matters of appearance and social decorum. As the girls mature, their comparative strengths and weaknesses are characterized by Mary's "sense" or practicality and Anna's "sentiment" or self-indulgent emotionalism. Thinking their lives too sheltered, Mr. Byerley takes the girls abroad, where they are exposed to wider cultural perspectives.

As the stronger character, Mary thrives on challenge, while Anna deteriorates into a helpless bundle of nerves. Self-absorbed and morbid, she thinks suicide a grand romantic gesture and suffers from the tragedy of her universally misunderstood sensibility. When problems arise Mary is the emotional mainstay of the family, while Anna cannot rise above her self-pity. The tale concludes with Mr. Byerley's realization that Mary has learned to integrate both sense and sensitivity; but Anna retreats into her narrow perspective, creating a rift that divides the formerly harmonious family. Thematically similar to Jane Austen's *Sense and Sensibility,* which Martineau claims not to have read, "Sense and Sentiment" emphasizes the importance of a comprehensive education for young girls, one that incorporates sensitivity and knowledge with moral

and religious training and is well grounded in healthy human relationships. The consequence of an emotional sensibility like Anna's untempered by realism is a perpetual childhood; the result of healthy assimilation like Mary's is a strong character prepared to assume adult responsibilities.

With the publication of the first volumes of her short-fiction series *Illustrations of Political Economy* in 1832, Martineau experienced the professional acceptance and public fame that was to characterize the remainder of her long writing career. Her earliest articles were published under the pseudonym "V"; but unlike many Victorian women writers, Martineau soon ceased all attempts to conceal her identity, her intelligence, or her gender, preferring to brave public opinion solely on the basis of professional integrity.

A significant factor of Martineau's writing method is her refusal to rewrite or edit, which she regarded as an "immense" waste of time. Believing that later alterations inevitably detract from the "distinctness and precision" of the original utterance, Martineau's practice was to visualize her topic and then write quickly, without hesitance. The naturalness and spontaneity of Martineau's writing led to the impressive range of her literary production. Aesthetically, she was averse to the "Confusion of thought, and cloudiness or affectation in style" produced by repetitive revisions. As a result, her writing can never be called *mannerist,* her derogatory term for stylized, consciously polished writing.

Martineau's aesthetics are important because, despite a highly respected, worldwide popularity during her lifetime, today this writer is all but unknown except to literary scholars. Critics argue that Martineau's forte was journalistic writing such as periodical articles, newspaper leaders, travelogues and how-to manuals on subjects ranging from animal husbandry to the health hazards of crinolines and hoop skirts. Because such writing is timely, the endurance of its popularity is more limited than that of much fiction and poetry. Further, Martineau's emphasis on moral and ethical concerns in her fiction produced literature that is too didactic for modern tastes.

The successful and popular *Illustrations of Political Economy* (1832–1834) demonstrates Martineau's potential as a fiction writer. This twenty-five-part series consists of tales illustrating principles of political economy, with each tale followed by a "Summary of Principles Illustrated in This Volume." Such summaries suggest Martineau's doubt as to the efficacy of fiction alone to convey more "serious" messages.

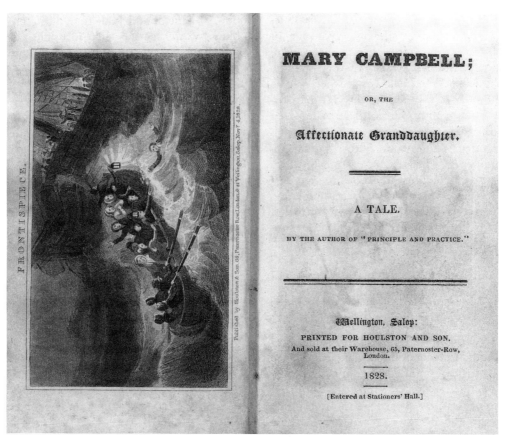

*Frontispiece and title page for an early novel by Martineau (courtesy of Lilly Library, Indiana University)*

Martineau's method of composition was first to write down her personal opinions on the issues raised by a particular topic, then to familiarize herself with the standard reference works for that topic, and finally, to allow the story's setting to suggest itself according to whichever culture or society could most effectively illustrate the problems and solutions. She sought to "embody each leading principle in a character: and the mutual operation of these embodied principles supplied the action of the story." Martineau's tales rely less on action and literary "accessories" than on a series of lengthy expository conversations between characters who debate the principles each represents. While such conversations are informative, they weaken Martineau's effectiveness as a fiction writer in that ordinary people would not address each other in the rhetoric of political economy, nor would they conduct conversations in so stilted and artificial a manner.

One of the tales in *Illustrations of Political Economy,* "Ella of Garveloch," was reputed to be Princess Victoria's favorite. It explores the relationships between laborers, capitalists, and landowners, and ex-

plains the concept of paying rent as a "symptom, not a cause, of prosperity." Garveloch is located off the coast of Scotland; its geographical isolation is reflected in its scanty population and in the difficulties of the islanders' daily lives.

The tale begins with a rare visit from the "laird" of Garveloch, an absentee landlord whose arrival coincides with the funeral of Ella's father. The death of the family patriarch leaves twenty-five-year-old Ella in charge of her three brothers, the youngest of whom, Archie, is mentally impaired and requires almost constant supervision. The laird's arrival is particularly timely, since the father's death nullifies the lease, leaving Ella and her brothers homeless and without resources for income.

Ella, whose hard life has made her strong and direct — as the laird observes, "masculine" — negotiates with the landlord for use of a shabby cottage and a small plot of land. Ella's determination impresses the laird, prompting him to agree to her request. Ella and her brothers proceed to conduct their affairs with honesty, thrift, and hard work, emphasizing their inherent integrity. Although family responsibilities, particularly her duty to Archie, have made Ella prematurely careworn, her stern demeanor is transformed by the reappearance of Angus, her avowed lover, whose long absence implies desertion. Once it is clear that Angus has returned to claim his bride, Ella resigns her role as head of the family to him and eagerly anticipates wearing the bonnet that marks her as a married woman.

The chapter "Understand Before You Complain" exemplifies Martineau's use of an expository conversation to convey the tale's economic underpinnings. After much hard work and economizing, Ella pays the overseer their year's rent. But when he learns that her brother cleared a piece of land not part of the original agreement, he raises the rent on the justification that the former wasteland is now capable of yielding profit. Ella is not able to pay, and the long-anticipated wedding is postponed.

The subsequent expository conversation between Angus and the overseer is for the benefit of Ella and her outraged brothers and for readers who suspect the family is being unfairly victimized. Once Ella and her brothers understand the economic principles, the much-maligned overseer is appeased as well as impressed by Angus's superior intelligence, although not enough to rescind the rent increase. Consistent with their inherent dignity and their receptivity to logic, Ella and her brothers submit to the need to economize further and work harder than before. "Ella of Garveloch" concludes abruptly with Archie's tragic death, Ella's marriage, and a scholarly cataloguing of economic principles.

The next story in the series, "Weal and Woe in Garveloch," begins ten years after Ella's marriage. Since the laird of Garveloch transferred his property interests to a large fishing company, the once sparsely populated, self-sufficient community of individual fishing families is now a thriving commercial economy controlled by a conglomerate of professional "outsiders." Hardworking, thrifty native inhabitants like Ella and Angus, while not rich, have benefited from the general economic prosperity; with their brood of ten children and their large, rambling house, they live in comparative comfort. This is because of their respect for the value of industry and thrift; unlike their more imprudent neighbors, Ella and her family live frugally and save against potential hard times.

This tale opens at the end of a "Peculiarly" abundant fishing harvest that has left Garveloch's inhabitants well fed and prosperous. But trouble brews in the midst of prosperity, and Fergus, Ella's brother, discovers that his fishing nets, the source of

his livelihood, were destroyed by a jealous neighbor. The incident reveals that, although honest and hardworking, Fergus lacks foresight, for he has not saved against the possibility of economic reversals and now has no way to provide for his wife and five children.

An expository conversation between Angus and the magistrate links sudden economic prosperity, profligate spending, and the abandonment of a frugal lifestyle to a growing spirit of greed and discontent. Formerly united by the simplicity of their spare lifestyle, the residents of Garveloch increasingly abandon traditional values in favor of material wealth. The most problematic symptom of abundance is a continued increase in population that is not equaled by an adequate increase in food production. When the large families of Garveloch face starvation hard on the heels of prosperity, they learn, too late, the hard lessons of Malthusian economics. The woe that follows weal dramatically poses fluctuating food resources against the insistent hunger of children.

Martineau's commitment to population control is evident in the magistrate's questioning the viability of the nuclear family structure: "What inducement has a man to marry, when he must either expose his children, or see them die at home, or take his chance of a gratuitous dole of food for them?" Also under scrutiny are the assumptions that marriage implies unbridled rather than controlled production of children, that only the rich can adequately sustain the economic burden of large families, and that the only solution for poor families is "the dole" or celibacy.

Martineau explores this last option through the example of the young widow Katie Cuthbert, who struggles to raise and provide for three children by making fishing nets. Ella's brother Ronald loved Katie from afar for many years, striving to earn enough to marry her. But when faced with culturewide economic dearth, Ronald heroically relinquishes his suit, arguing that the decision to not bring any more children into an already overburdened economy is a social commitment of far greater import than the personal gratification of marriage. While Martineau questions the necessity for such drastic selflessness, she presents Ronald's decision as exemplary and noble, while Katie must struggle on as best she can.

A series of events beginning with an average (as opposed to "peculiarly" abundant) crop yield leads to a lengthy expository conversation between Ella and Katie. As the women watch while fever wastes their children, they consider the possibility that disease is nature's way of diminishing a population too abundant for its resources. Katie suggests it is God's way, as well: "Since Providence had not made food increase as men increase . . . it is plain that Providence wills restraint here as in the case of other passions." The euphemistic *restraint* implies birth control is both a religious and a social responsibility. When Ella agrees, Katie asks pointedly why she did not consider this before bearing ten children! Following the death of their youngest child, Ella and Angus lose their eldest son to the British units scouring the countryside for hungry recruits. Thinking to lessen the burden on his family, Kenneth enlists, confirming Ella's observation that war and disease are a standard solution to famine and overpopulation.

According to Martineau's "Summary of Principles in this Volume," "The increase in population is necessarily limited by the means of subsistence" while "ultimate checks" to excessive procreation take the form of "vice and misery." This is symbolized by the destruction of Fergus's nets, the death of Ella's child, Kenneth's enlistment and its association with war, Katie's premature widowhood, and Ronald's bachelorhood. Such "ultimate checks" can be avoided by the "timely use of the mild preventive check" of bringing "no more children into the world than there is a subsistence provided for." For it is only when productivity and procreativity are brought into balance that society can attain the utilitarian ideal of "the greatest happiness for the greatest number."

"Sowers not Reapers" examines the effects of the Corn Laws, which forbade the importation of foreign grain, on the working classes, the landowners, and the social fabric of community. Martineau wrote "Sowers not Reapers" in haunting, graceful prose worthy of Emily Brontë and with a psychological insight that anticipates Charlotte Brontë; further, she addresses the delicate subject of female alcoholism with the courage of Elizabeth Gaskell's "woman question" fiction. "Sowers not Reapers" shows the superior level of fiction writing Martineau was capable of when not churning out tales at the rate of newspaper leaders.

This tale begins on the Yorkshire moors late at night, where Mrs. Kay and her sister-in-law, Mary Kay, hold a vigil in the hope for a trickle of water from the dried-up river bed. The landscape is eerie and silent; they wait by the motionless mill wheel that symbolizes the drought, the lack of harvest, and the hopelessness of their night mission. The women hide from one of the many bands of night-wandering marauders, people drawn out to the dark, like them, by desperate circumstances. Their conversation is a more credible version of Martineau's earlier expository exchanges and presents an effective picture of rising food prices, insufficient money, scarcity of crops, and famine and drought. Weakened by her vigil, Mrs. Kay returns home to her children faint and empty-handed.

Rain does come at last, although too late to save the harvest, and falls in such a violent deluge that any remaining crops are destroyed or washed away. Designed to force a no longer agrarian society to be entirely self-sufficient and to ensure that English farmers would not be undersold by foreign grain growers, the Corn Laws were enacted to strengthen English economy. Unfortunately, those unable to afford English prices could not obtain grain elsewhere and either paid or starved. Worse, the Corn Laws failed to account for the possibility of drought or other natural causes diminishing crop yield. The situation in the story deteriorates as starving masses roam the countryside destroying silent mills and empty storehouses; landowners lose money yet still have food to eat, while laborers like Mrs. Kay's husband cannot earn enough to feed their families with food prices as inflated as they are.

But a more insidious effect of this economic sequence concerns Mrs. Kay, whose depression and faintness suggest malnutrition or some wasting illness such as consumption. Like her husband, her family, and her community, readers are encouraged to excuse her behavior as anything but the alcoholism it in fact is; significantly, the shock of Mrs. Kay's confession is mitigated by the purity of her motives. As a chronically ill child, Mrs. Kay was regularly dosed with alcoholic medicines, which early established her habit. As an adult faced with feeding her family on insufficient means, she gave her share of food to husband and children, secretly assuaging her hunger with gin. Notoriously cheap and available where nutritious food was not, gin lead to widespread alcoholism among the lower classes. Upon learning that his wife's habit stems more from selflessness than from character weakness, Kay vows to help her quit. Mrs. Kay never breaks their pact, but the malnutrition is too far advanced. She dies sober for the sake of her husband and children, as she had lived drunk so that they could eat.

"Sowers not Reapers" concludes with the lifting of the Corn Laws, the importation of grain, and the alleviation of hunger, but only after years of unnecessary suffering. Many lives, from the premature death of Mrs. Kay to the bankruptcy of the local gentry, have been shattered by forces beyond their control. "Sowers not Reapers" emphasizes the tragedy of a society whose inability to feed itself is reflected in its propensity to foster alcoholism. Despite her rejection of political affiliations, Martineau makes a powerful political statement by demonstrating the vulnerability of the family to economic conditions.

"Ireland," the ninth tale in *Illustrations of Political Economy,* addresses several controversial topics that continue to complicate Anglo-Irish relations today. Among the more volatile issues raised by Ireland's Catholicism is overpopulation and its effect on chronic economic dearth. Taking an apolitical stance that focuses on economics and education rather than on national or religious prohibitions, Martineau in her preface states that her purpose is to write a tale that will best serve the interests of the Irish poor and give a more unbiased voice to their daily suffering than that available in the sensationalistic popular press. Martineau believed that correcting England's continued "misgovernance" of Ireland would remove the causes of civil rebellion, a stand she insists is not treasonous but rather patriotic.

Dora Sullivan, the heroine, is an exemplary young woman who attends school, is docile and obedient, and waits patiently for her parents' approval to marry Dan, her childhood sweetheart. But the combination of Dora's minimal education and her blind filial obedience proves to be her downfall more than once. When her father orders Dora to sign the new lease and refuses to heed her warning that its wording seems duplicitous, he initiates what proves to be the financial ruin of his family.

This tale considers the complex problems created by absentee landlords: overseers who as middlemen often cheat the peasants as well as the landlord and peasants who, ignorant of even the most rudimentary of farming principles such as the need for crop rotation, deplete the land. Religious issues are conveyed through expository conversations between the Catholic priest and the Protestant clergyman, while the class-based underpinnings of landlord/tenant relationships and the proposed poor laws are debated by the upper-class Alexander and his friend Henry.

Just when the Sullivans realize that they have signed away their home and possessions and are penniless as well, Dan appears to claim his bride and provide for her parents. Dan's character defies the "lazy Irish" stereotype with his unflagging "spirit of enterprise." He works day and night forg-

ing a new life for them all, even building a large addition to their rented cottage at his own expense.

But disaster strikes anew when the overseer capriciously refuses to renew the lease. All improvements to cottage and property will benefit someone else, while Dora and her family again find themselves destitute. Martineau effectively portrays how an enterprising man like Dan is transformed from a loving husband and energetic provider into a thief, rebel, and murderer by repeated and unnecessary misfortunes against which he has no legal recourse. One result of such arbitrary destruction of local families is an escalation of social, economic, and religious tensions into a small-scale civil war.

In a frenzy Dan destroys his unharvested crops, sinks all their possessions in a bog, and burns the cottage; after leaving Dora and her mother hidden in a shack, Mr. Sullivan joins an illegal distillery ring while Dan becomes an outlaw. On a rare visit to his wife, Dan discovers her transformed from his darling bride into an automaton half-crazed by grief. Hidden for months with no outside contact, Dora's resulting emotional paralysis is compounded by the birth of her child and the death of her mother.

In a striking parallel to Dora's earlier signing of the lease, Dan instructs Dora to write a letter which threatens the lives of Major Greaves and the English soldiers who oppose the rebel outlaws. Once again, the educated woman is the pawn of the man to whom she is legally bound; once again, she will share in the misfortunes yielded by her obedience. But this time, Dora pays for her knowledge and for her passive acquiescence to husband and father in ways not anticipated by anyone.

It is not long before Dora is arrested and jailed for perjury. Neither husband nor father comes to her aid, and the priest visits only to take the child for adoption. Despite her psychic numbness, Dora realizes the hopelessness of her impending trial: "In her mind it was evident that the whole matter was settled from the beginning," which is subsequently borne out when she is condemned to transportation for life. A neighbor notes with irony that "If she had never been taught to write . . . this murtherous letter could never have been brought against her," to which Dora replies with a stirring speech as she is led from the courtroom. Even if all writing implements were destroyed and all education obliterated from Ireland, she proclaims, rebellion against unjust tyranny and inept government would continue to flourish in the minds of those victimized by "The Irish Question."

The tale ends with the assertion that Dan, "who was once the pride[,] is now the scourge of the Glen of the Echoes," suggesting that social deviants, criminals and victims alike, are often products of arbitrary sociocultural circumstances. The powerful simplicity of Ireland's tragedy is reinforced in the "Summary of Principles Illustrated in This Volume." In particular, Martineau notes the unfair and illogical tax and fine system and the complex social and economic difficulties of Ireland's religious conflicts.

Martineau's immediate solution to Ireland's many problems is a more balanced proportion between food availability and population; the former concerns government reforms, while the latter, she delicately suggests, requires "educating the people till they shall have become qualified for the guardianship of their own interests." Martineau is careful not to overtly criticize the Catholic Church's stand on birth control; however, her allusion to excessive procreation under restrictive economic circumstances places some of the burden for change on the Irish themselves. A thorough Malthusian, Martineau reduces complex social problems to simple equations with logical, direct solutions.

Despite her careful handling of the issue of population control, critics were outraged at Martineau's audacity in addressing this taboo subject. A case in point is John Wilson Croker of the *The Quarterly Review,* a literary critic notorious for his character assassinations in print. Croker's 1833 review of *Illustrations of Political Economy* effectively captures the sort of literary criticism typically reserved for women writers. Croker railed against this "female Malthusian" whose "unfeminine" social doctrine regards "child-bearing a crime against society! An unmarried woman who declares against marriage!" Characteristically turning adversity into a learning experience, however, Martineau viewed the incident as character-strengthening rather than damaging.

It is a tribute to Martineau's popularity that she was approached early in her career by Lord Henry Peter Brougham and the Society for the Diffusion of Useful Knowledge, who requested she write a poor law series patterned after the successful political economy series. After studying government documents (Blue Books) about existing poor laws and proposed reforms, Martineau produced a four-volume series, *Poor Laws and Paupers Illustrated* (1833–1834). Termed "dreary tales" by biographer Valerie Pichanick, the stories exposed a system that fostered indiscriminate charity at the expense of those who strove for economic self-sufficiency.

Such tales as "The Parish," "The Hamlets," and "Cousin Marshall" address public dissatisfaction with the dole or workhouse. Designed to ensure that those in economic difficulty would always have food and shelter, the system worked only too well: once on the dole, the poor were better provided for than they could provide for themselves and were not expected to work in return. The workhouse being a more lucrative situation than employment was symptomatic of the need for poor law reform. Martineau's method was to pose the undeserving poor, who were tempted by a system that made it all too easy to leave behind a life of lack and deprivation, against the deserving poor, who suffered many trials but never gave in to the temptation to simply "go on the dole." Of inferior literary quality, *Poor Laws and Paupers Illustrated* sold primarily on the strength of the success of her first series; written in great haste, they are not regarded as exemplary among Martineau's works.

Martineau's next short-fiction series, *Illustrations of Taxation* (1834), consists of five tales about the inequities of the English tax system. Here, Martineau eliminates the concluding summary of principles, which increases the difficulties for modern readers in understanding the subtle complexities of nineteenth-century British tax laws. Her purpose, however, is clear from her preface:

> . . . our methods of Taxation . . . are unjust, odious and unprofitable, to a degree which could never be experienced under a system of simple, direct taxation.

Aimed at "stimulating the public mind" to demand reform, the series exposes this inequitable tax system through a variety of perspectives.

"The Park and The Paddock" begins with the return of the Cranston children to their long-abandoned ancestral home. Following the death of their father, the family prepares to resume its place at the head of a community of peasant-farmers so poor they are often forced to resort to poaching to keep their families from starving. Of course, the unexpected return of the Cranstons brings a halt to years of unhindered poaching on the empty estate.

Martineau's criticism of tax-system inequities focuses on undeserved upper-class privilege. James Cranston, a clergyman who is anything but spiritually inclined, is an avid hunter – for sport, as opposed to subsistence – who flirts with peasant girls for whom he has no serious regard. When James seems to have fallen in love with Sarah, a farmer's daughter, and consults her about plans for his new house, the entire community believes their match is

*Martineau circa 1835*

inevitable. But James makes no declaration; and, hurt and betrayed, Sarah agrees to an arranged marriage with a local farmer while her reputation is still intact. Absurdly, James performs the ceremony, which he cuts short in order to join the hunt, again emphasizing his lack of scruples.

James schedules weddings, christenings, and other official duties at the convenience of his hunting forays. When a young boy is killed in a poaching accident, James negotiates with the grieving father over the time of the funeral, which interferes with his hunting plans. The juxtaposition of the boy's death with James's insatiable urge to hunt suggests that a lower-class life – male or female – is as dispensable as those of game animals. One might certainly argue, therefore, that "The Park and the Paddock" is more a comment on class stratification than on the inequities of British tax laws.

For the uneducated working class, lack of knowledge about tax laws often ruined families economically, frequently resulting in imprisonment, heavy fines, or transportation of tax offenders who were unaware of the existence of the laws they were accused of breaking. Such working-class naiveté is

portrayed by the LeBocqs, the subjects of "The Jerseymen Meeting" and its sequel, "The Jerseymen Parting." A self-sufficient family of peasant farmers living on the Channel Island of Jersey, the LeBocqs take in a "blind" beggar, Stephen, who repays their hospitality by telling tales of life on the mainland, where taxes are practically nonexistent. Stephen's duplicitous pretense of blindness is exposed the next morning when the family discovers he has gone and taken every stitch of the family's linens and clothes, a serious material loss. His second lie, the false account of mainland prosperity, is exposed soon after.

When the LeBocqs inherit a pottery business on the mainland, their subsequent introduction to the realities of the British tax system is tragic. Initially, the LeBocqs are drawn to Durrell, an excise man and a fellow Jerseyman, but this is altered by his relentless harassment of the pottery business. At the conclusion of "The Jerseymen Meeting" Aaron LeBocq joins a gang of smugglers after being falsely accused of producing untaxed glass – he is, in fact, "caught in the act" of experimenting with new methods of production – and his father is imprisoned for a series of tax "evasions" of which he was not aware.

Martineau's presentation of the degradation of debtors' prison in "Jerseymen Parting" anticipates Charles Dickens's indictment of the Marshalsea in *Little Dorrit* (1855–1857). Heavily in debt, publicly disgraced, with no income and his family split apart, LeBocq wastes away in prison; when his daughter Anne visits, they write a letter to the king emphasizing their naive trust in the system that later proves to be the catalyst that saves them.

But the cycle of injustice has not yet run its course. Like most Jersey farm girls, Anne is well schooled in domestic thrift. Appalled by the exorbitant price of tea, she mixes it with cheaper leaves, a secret she shares with her neighbors. For this, of course, she is arrested and brought to trial for tax evasion, which does not surprise the authorities at all, given her family's "criminal" background. But when the situation seems most hopeless, the judge reads her letter to the king and realizes how completely victimized the LeBocqs have been by the system that purports to protect the interests of ordinary people like them.

Released and reunited, the LeBocqs return to their native Jersey where the tax system is not such a mystery, although Aaron vows to remain a smuggler as long as British tax laws continue to be inequitable. There is some hope for positive change, Martineau suggests, so long as trusting people write letters of grievance and those in authority have the capacity to respond. Nevertheless, the LeBocqs' pardons are less indicative of structural change than of an isolated response to injustice. Aaron's vow implies that this "unjust, odious, and unprofitable" system breeds criminal activity because it is itself criminal.

Martineau apologizes in her preface for the speed with which she wrote the taxation tales, a circumstance resulting in their inferior literary quality. At the time, she states, she felt it was imperative to make these issues available to the reading public as quickly as possible. A prolific writer by any standard, Martineau wrote and published three series of tales — *Illustrations of Political Economy, Poor Laws and Paupers Illustrated,* and *Illustrations of Taxation* — between 1832 and 1834, totaling an astonishing thirty-seven volumes. Her apology both attests to her remarkable productivity and acknowledges her literary limitations.

During Martineau's American sojourn (1834–1836) she met and associated with the most prominent political, social, and literary figures of the day and traveled the country with little regard for inconvenience. From an abolitionist meeting in Boston to a session of Congress in Washington to slave quarters in the South, Martineau regarded new experiences as preventive medicine for middle-class complacency and welcomed every challenge as both character building and food for literary thought. Although undaunted by Indians, alligators, or strange customs, several threats against her life by some antiabolitionists who reacted violently to a foreigner "meddling" in American issues concerned her enough to alter her itinerary at one point. A passionate abolitionist, Martineau had broken her vow not to become involved in American politics by speaking out, insisting that human affairs transcend geopolitical boundaries.

Back in England Martineau published *Society in America* (1837), followed by her first novel, *Deerbrook* (1838), and *A Retrospect of Western Travel* (1838). After traveling in England, Scotland, and Europe, she developed an illness (possibly a uterine tumor) that was to keep her an invalid for nearly seven years. As productive as ever despite her poor health, Martineau in 1841 published a second novel, *The Hour and The Man: A Historical Romance,* and a short-fiction series, *The Playfellow: A Series of Tales* (1841–1843).

The four tales in *The Playfellow,* intended for younger readers, were immensely popular. Written in light, easy prose, although not without the inevitable moral message, these tales evidence Mar-

tineau's understanding of children's perspectives. "Settlers at Home" describes the Linacres, a family of Dutch immigrants who settle in a region of England that had formerly been underwater but is now drained and cultivated. This region is a pawn between two opposing political factions, one favoring the Dutch settlement and the other urging a return to the original swampland. The Linacres are thrifty, hardworking, conscientious people who are harassed by the Redfurns, a family of drifters.

The Redfurns are singularly lacking in moral principles. Like a gang of modern-day hoodlums, they periodically descend on the Linacre farm, trampling crops, killing livestock, stealing, and destroying randomly. Young Oliver and Mildred Linacre are terrified of Roger Redfurn, who enjoys torturing small animals and children. When political dissidents destroy the structure that keeps the region above water, the entire area is flooded, destroying homes, farms, livestock, and human lives. In the three-day deluge that follows, Oliver, Mildred and baby George fight for survival, a key to which involves the dreaded Roger Redfurn.

Despite their youth, the children reveal depth of character when forced to be self-reliant in the absence of adult supervision. Confronted with Mildred's fear, George's incessant crying, and Roger's cruelty, timid Oliver rises to the occasion by acquiring food and shelter for the survivors. Roger subverts his efforts and repays Oliver's help by physical violence and theft. He rejects Oliver's and Mildred's overtures and continues untouched by human connection until baby George, who is dying, elicits an emotional response from him.

Roger's short life is marked by brutality, hunger, and deprivation; cruelty to creatures weaker than he is his only source of power — until the death of the one person who had ever expressed affection for him. In contrast, Oliver's and Mildred's brave conviction that George has gone to live with God and, perhaps, Mother and Father, emphasizes what is for Martineau the desirability of a morally strengthening upbringing that allows one to prevail over adverse circumstances.

The most popular volume in this series is "The Crofton Boys," another tale of character formation through difficult experiences. Although middle-class Hugh Proctor's most serious concern is being "one of the boys" at the Crofton School, subsequent events test and shape his character in ways few could endure. Hugh's dream is realized when he is granted early admission to the school his older brother attends; but his illusions are quickly shattered by the hazing practices typical of such institutions, by his homesickness, and by his brother's avoidance of him.

Hugh manages to endure the often cruel peer pressures at school; he learns that "fitting in" includes friendships with the "right" people. Holt, an Anglo-Indian and therefore socially marginalized, repeatedly offers Hugh his friendship and is just as repeatedly rejected by him. When Hugh is harassed by schoolmates while on a snow-covered wall, he falls and his foot is crushed by a stone; what follows is a harsh lesson in the nature of authentic human relationships.

The thus-far leisurely tale now moves rapidly from accident and injury to diagnosis and immediate amputation. As the doctor removes Hugh's foot without benefit of anesthesia, the boy's thoughts range from the now impossible dream of traveling the world to his mother's appeal that he trust in God and rise above present suffering. Hugh endures the ordeal with barely a whimper and refuses to reveal the names of those responsible for his calamity. As a result, those who had earlier hazed him mercilessly hold a constant, weeping vigil outside his sickroom door. Ironically, little Hugh Proctor is now the school hero.

Hugh eventually adjusts to his disability and returns to his studies at Crofton. His priorities, of course, have changed, and he realizes that his rejection of Holt is as unfair as the hazing he himself endured. Significantly, once Hugh accepts Holt's friendship, he is rewarded by a career opportunity. Holt's father, a diplomatic official in India, offers Hugh a position upon completion of his studies, one that satisfies his desire to travel the world and experience foreign cultures. Martineau implies that authentic human relationships, particularly those that transcend physical disabilities or racial differences, may lead one down a more complex path than that traveled by social conformists, but it is a divinely inspired one.

Lionized by London's literary establishment and both celebrated and threatened in America, Martineau seemed unable to avoid notoriety. In 1843 she was criticized for refusing to accept a government pension because she believed its political associations would compromise her professional integrity. In *Letters on Mesmerism* (1845) she attributed the cure of her long-endured illness to hypnosis, which did compromise her integrity in public opinion. In response, Martineau's physician brother-in-law, stung by the humiliation of having his medical credibility challenged by such "quackery," published the full gynecological details of Martineau's case, which no proper Victorian woman would

want publicized. The resulting family breach endured for many years.

In 1845 and 1846 Martineau wrote her last short-fiction series, *Forest and Game-Law Tales,* based on her survey of game laws from the Middle Ages through the nineteenth century. Although the class issues of game laws were alluded to in "The Park and the Paddock" and problems of Corn Law legislation in times of famine addressed in "Sowers not Reapers," the game law series aimed for a more direct link between famine, food supplies, free trade, and class privilege or marginalization. While the series was not critically acclaimed, Martineau argued that if even a few readers were influenced by its content, then it was successful.

The series' last tale, "Gentle and Simple," is the story of an old woman who sets fire to her tumbledown shack when her grandson is thrice jailed for poaching one hare. She vows to live in the middle of the lane until such time as having enough to eat is considered a right of all humans, not the privilege of a few. That otherwise law-abiding people are driven to such extremes in a land of prosperity and plenty raises serious questions about the disparity between hunting for sport and poaching for survival.

In 1845 Martineau also published a single-volume tale, *Dawn Island,* set in an exotic tropical island in the Pacific. Despite her antipathy to middle-class complacency, Martineau's portrayal of the primitive natives of Dawn Island is typically colonialist. Far from idealizing the islanders as noble savages, Martineau portrays them as superstitious, brutal, and barbarous. Such images bolster her argument that what such cultures need is the civilizing Christian influence of English society to which the islanders would be exposed in a free-trade agreement.

In the tale old wise man Miava broods over the ancient prophecy that "The forest-tree shall grow; the coral shall spread and branch out; but man shall cease." He senses that his race is doomed to extinction but cannot connect his tribe's time-honored ritual slayings of infants, virgins, and warriors to the systematic diminution of his culture. Disturbed by the prophecy, Miava begins to question this god, who is clearly a god of death.

Miava's faith is further tested when it is time for him to surrender his beloved ward, Idya, to a husband whose cruelty and abuse of women and children is tribally sanctioned. When Idya grieves over her husband's ritual murder of their first child (an act he threatens to repeat again and, perhaps, again if she cannot contain her "blasphemous" attitude), Miava's doubt grows. It is at this time of spiritual conflict that a party of English sailors lands on the island, and the lives of the Dawn Islanders change dramatically.

After the usual reciprocal superstitious fears, communication of sorts is established and the natives trade food and water for items of Western technology. Nearsighted Miava is amazed by the magical eyeglasses that clarify his vision; Idya sees her reflection for the first time in a mirror. The white men are amused that the natives seem to regard them as semidivine and consider it their Christian duty to civilize the islanders for the sake of their endangered souls rather than for material gain. The sailors' moral integrity provides a compelling argument in favor of free trade.

Difficulties in England caused by the Corn Laws were obvious enough to its citizens; Martineau's innovation in approaching the free-trade issue from the islander's perspective utilizes the Victorian emphasis on Christian values, moral duty, and responsibility to those "less fortunate." "Don't you see," asks the English captain, "the best kindness I can do . . . is to teach them to trade, – and honestly?" Along with the tin cups, mirrors, and combs the savages would be exposed to civilizing ideas: women should not be beaten and starved, nor should children be ritually sacrificed.

But these are difficult concepts to convey across cultural and linguistic barriers, and it is not until the captain opens fire on the island that the natives realize this man is clearly more potent than the island gods. Miava relates the ancient prophecy to the captain, who explains that the tribe will necessarily cease so long as it continues killing its most precious resources: child-bearing women, newborn children, and young men. Rather than bow to an inevitable fate, the people themselves can choose whether or not to continue on their path to extinction.

The islanders are left with the captain's decrees that taboos be lifted, ritual sacrifices cease, and trade always be an honest exchange. The captain asserts, "it warmed my heart and filled my head to see how these children of nature were clearly destined to be carried on some way towards becoming men and Christians by my bringing Commerce to their shores." Thus, "Dawn Island" appeals to readers on several levels: the sentimentality associated with women and children; the civilizing superiority of the English, embodied in the captain's character; and religious justification that aligns material choice – or rescinding the Corn Laws in favor of free trade – with spiritual duty.

As a fiction writer, Martineau's particular gift for conveying cultural perspectives different from her own, whether it be Jersey farmers or Scots fishermen, alcoholic women or dying children, ship's captains or Pacific island natives, remains her most effective rhetorical tool. However, following *Dawn Island* most of Martineau's writing for the remainder of her life was nonfiction. Her later preference for autobiographies, histories, and philosophical treatises replaces her earlier efforts at writing novels, while the energy formerly reserved for short fiction and novellas is subsequently channeled into journal articles, notably from 1850 in Dickens's *Household Words* and from 1852 in columns in the *Daily News* of London.

After moving into The Knoll, her new home in the Lake District in 1846, Martineau went to Egypt where she visited harems and pyramids, often traveling by camel. Her account of these travels, *Eastern Life, Present and Past* (1848), was followed by her English history, *History of England during the Thirty Years' Peace 1816–1846* (1849–1850). After publishing *The Positive Philosophy of Auguste Comte Freely Translated and Condensed* (1853), Martineau again became seriously ill; believing death imminent, she wrote her three-volume autobiography. This lively account of the first fifty-two years of her life is a storehouse of anecdotes of contemporary figures, literary trivia, and name-dropping. Humorous, gossipy, irreverent, the autobiography is hardly the work of a dying woman; as it turns out, twenty-four years would pass before its posthumous publication.

During this period Martineau continued writing and publishing on behalf of social reform until 1869, when illness and age forced her to put aside her pen. Characteristically, although this influential writer was unable to continue her protest against the 1869 Contagious Diseases Acts in print, Martineau traded pen for needle and stitched items to be sold for the benefit of the repeal campaign. One way or another, this avowedly apolitical writer was a political activist until the end of her long life.

If the dramatic conclusion of *Harriet Martineau's Autobiography* – "The world as it is is growing somewhat dim before my eyes" – was premature, it is nevertheless consistent with another of Martineau's "self-assessments," her obituary. After characterizing her intellect as earnest though not brilliant and acute though not inventive, Martineau summarizes her life's work as her contribution to the advancement of humanity. Pragmatic to the end, she regarded death as the logical conclusion of life and therefore not a cause for reluctance, fear, or anxiety. Martineau continued as active as declining health permitted through even the last months of her life. In June 1876 she contracted bronchitis and died soon after; she was buried among her family in Birmingham.

Martineau was eulogized eloquently by her many friends and professional associates. Essayist W. R. Greg wrote, "The executive efficiency of her intelligence was absolutely unrivalled, her style was always . . . clear, lucid, vigorous and simple, without a trace of effort." George Eliot, herself one of the century's most respected women writers, called Martineau "a perfect trump . . . the only English woman that possesses thoroughly the art of writing." And even her old literary nemesis, *The Times,* acknowledged in its 29 June 1876 issue, "If any lady of the 19th century . . . may be allowed to put in a claim for the credit of not having lived in vain, that woman, we honestly believe, was Harriet Martineau." Martineau's primary concern was the common reader, the class that stood to gain most by being informed. It is this audience to which her short fiction is addressed, and it is to this audience that she owes her greatest success.

## Letters:

Elisabeth Sanders Arbuckle, ed., *Harriet Martineau's Letters to Fanny Wedgwood* (Stanford, Cal.: Stanford University Press, 1983).

## Bibliography:

Joseph B. Rivlin, *Harriet Martineau: A Bibliography of Her Separately Printed Books* (New York: New York Public Library, 1947).

## Biographies:

Vera Wheatley, *The Life and Work of Harriet Martineau* (London: Secker & Warburg, 1957);

R. K. Webb, *Harriet Martineau: A Radical Victorian* (London: Heinemann, 1960);

Valerie Kossew Pichanick, *Harriet Martineau: The Woman and Her Work, 1802–1876* (Ann Arbor: University of Michigan Press, 1980).

## References:

Deirdre David, *Intellectual Women and Victorian Patriarchy: Harriet Martineau, Elizabeth Barrett Browning, George Eliot* (Ithaca, N.Y.: Cornell University Press, 1987);

Maria H. Frawley, "Harriet Martineau in America: Gender and the Discourse of Sociology," *Victorian Newsletter,* 81 (Spring 1992): 13–20;

Patricia Marks, "Harriet Martineau: Fraser's 'Maid of (Dis)Honour,' " *Victorian Periodicals Review,* 19 (Spring 1986): 28–34;

Linda H. Peterson, "Harriet Martineau: Masculine Discourse, Female Sage," in *Victorian Sages and Cultural Discourse: Renegotiating Gender and Power,* edited by E. Thais Morgan (New Brunswick, N.J.: Rutgers University Press, 1990);

Peterson, "Harriet Martineau's Household Education: Revising the Feminine Tradition," *Bucknell Review,* 34, no. 2 (1990): 183–194;

Diana Postlethwait, "Mothering and Mesmerism in the Life of Harriet Martineau," *Signs: Journal of Women in Culture and Society,* 14 (Spring 1989): 583–609;

Valerie Sanders, *Reason Over Passion: Harriet Martineau and The Victorian Novel* (New York: St. Martin's Press, 1986);

Gillian Thomas, *Harriet Martineau* (Boston: G. K. Hall, 1985);

Gayle Graham Yates, ed., *Harriet Martineau on Women* (New Brunswick, N.J.: Rutgers University Press, 1985).

# George Meredith

## (12 February 1828 – 18 May 1909)

### Natalie Bell Cole
### *Oakland University*

See also the Meredith entries in *DLB 18: Victorian Novelists After 1885, DLB 35: Victorian Poets After 1850,* and *DLB 57: Victorian Prose Writers After 1867.*

BOOKS: *Poems* (London: Parker, 1851; New York: Scribners, 1898);

*The Shaving of Shagpat: An Arabian Entertainment* (London: Chapman & Hall, 1856; Boston: Roberts, 1887);

*Farina: A Legend of Cologne* (London: Smith, Elder, 1857);

*The Ordeal of Richard Feverel: A History of Father and Son* (3 volumes, London: Chapman & Hall, 1859; 1 volume, Boston: Roberts, 1887);

*Evan Harrington; or, He Would Be a Gentleman* (New York: Harper, 1860; 3 volumes, London: Bradbury & Evans, 1861);

*Modern Love, and Poems of the English Roadside, with Poems and Ballads* (London: Chapman & Hall, 1862); republished, edited by E. Cavazza (Portland, Maine: Mosher, 1891);

*Emilia in England,* 3 volumes (London: Chapman & Hall, 1864); republished as *Sandra Belloni* (London: Chapman & Hall, 1886; Boston: Roberts, 1887);

*Rhoda Fleming: A Story* (3 volumes, London: Tinsley, 1865; 1 volume, Boston: Roberts, 1886);

*Vittoria,* 3 volumes (London: Chapman & Hall, 1866; Boston: Roberts, 1888);

*The Adventures of Harry Richmond* (3 volumes, London: Smith, Elder, 1871; 1 volume, Boston: Roberts, 1887);

*Beauchamp's Career* (3 volumes, London: Chapman & Hall, 1876; 1 volume, Boston: Roberts, 1887);

*The House on the Beach: A Realistic Tale* (New York: Harper, 1877);

*The Egoist: A Comedy in Narrative,* 3 volumes (London: Kegan Paul, 1879; New York: Harper, 1879);

*The Tragic Comedians: A Study in a Well-Known Story* (2 volumes, London: Chapman & Hall, 1880; 1 volume, New York: Munro, 1881);

*George Meredith (photograph by Thomson, circa 1888)*

*Poems and Lyrics of the Joy of Earth* (London: Macmillan, 1883; Boston: Roberts, 1883);

*Diana of the Crossways* (3 volumes, London: Chapman & Hall, 1885; 1 volume, New York: Munro, 1885);

*Ballads and Poems of Tragic Life* (London: Macmillan, 1887; Boston: Roberts, 1887);

*A Reading of Earth* (London: Macmillan, 1888; Boston: Roberts, 1888);

*Jump-to-Glory Jane* (London: Privately printed, 1889; London: Sonnenschein, 1892);

225

The Case of General Ople and Lady Camper (New York: Lovell, 1890);

The Tale of Chloe: An Episode in the History of Beau Beamish (New York: Lovell, 1890);

One of Our Conquerors (3 volumes, London: Chapman & Hall, 1891; 1 volume, Boston: Roberts, 1891);

Poems: The Empty Purse, with Odes to the Comic Spirit, to Youth in Memory and Verses (London: Macmillan, 1892; Boston: Roberts, 1892);

The Tale of Chloe; The House on the Beach; The Case of General Ople and Lady Camper (London: Ward, Lock & Bowden, 1894);

Lord Ormont and His Aminta: A Novel (3 volumes, London: Chapman & Hall, 1894; 1 volume, New York: Scribners, 1894);

The Amazing Marriage, 2 volumes (London: Constable, 1895; New York: Scribners, 1895);

An Essay on Comedy and the Uses of the Comic Spirit (London: Constable, 1897; New York: Scribners, 1897);

Selected Poems (London: Constable, 1897; New York: Scribners, 1897);

The Nature Poems (London: Constable, 1898);

Ode in Contribution to the Song of French History (London: Constable, 1898; New York: Scribners, 1898);

The Story of Bhanavar the Beautiful (London: Constable, 1900);

A Reading of Life, with Other Poems (London: Constable, 1901; New York: Scribners, 1901);

Last Poems (London: Constable, 1909; New York: Scribners, 1909);

Chillianwallah (New York: Marion Press, 1909);

Love in the Valley, and Two Songs: Spring and Autumn (Chicago: Seymour, 1909);

Poems Written in Early Youth, Poems from "Modern Love," and Scattered Poems (London: Constable, 1909; New York: Scribners, 1909);

Celt and Saxon (London: Constable, 1910; New York: Scribners, 1910);

Up to Midnight (Boston: Luce, 1913).

**Editions and Collections:** The Works of George Meredith, De Luxe Edition, 39 volumes (London: Constable, 1896-1912);

The Works of George Meredith, Library Edition, 18 volumes (London: Constable, 1897-1910);

The Works of George Meredith, Boxhill Edition, 17 volumes (New York: Scribners, 1897-1919);

The Works of George Meredith, Memorial Edition, 27 volumes (London: Constable, 1909-1911; New York: Scribners, 1909-1911);

"George Meredith's Publications in the New Quarterly Magazine, a Critical Edition of 'The House on the Beach,' 'On the Idea of Comedy,' 'The Case of General Ople and Lady Camper,' and 'The Tale of Chloe,' " 2 volumes, edited by Maura Carey Ives, dissertation, University of Virginia, 1990.

SELECTED PERIODICAL PUBLICATIONS – UNCOLLECTED: "A Story Telling Party," Once a Week, 1 (24 December 1859): 535-542;

"The Parish Clerk's Story," Once a Week, 4 (23 February 1861): 246-249;

"The Friend of the Engaged Couple: An Unpublished Short Story by George Meredith," edited by Lewis Sawin, Victorians Institute Journal, 14 (1986): 135-145.

George Meredith is known chiefly as a Victorian novelist and poet; his shorter fiction appeared toward the beginning of his career, in the late 1850s and early 1860s, and reached its fullest development in three stories published in the 1870s in the New Quarterly Magazine. Most of these stories explore themes that are also keynotes of Meredith's novels: the danger that egotism poses to the self and others; exhortation to celebrate nature and avoid sentimentality and prudery; the curative powers of laughter; the slipperiness of self-definition in a rapidly altering society; and the moral integrity, intelligence, and independence of women.

Meredith's fiction has presented difficulties to Victorian as well as twentieth-century readers. Henry James decried the "tortuosities" of Meredith's prose; E. M. Forster compared a Meredith plot to "a series of kiosks most artfully placed among wooded slopes, which his people reach by their own impetus"; V. S. Pritchett agreed: "His stories do not progress; they are waltzed with violence from line to line, and chapter to chapter." Meredith's short fiction tends to be more tightly plotted and less given to extended metaphor than his novels, but it still can be seen as characteristically "Meredithian" in style and theme. Meredith's work continues to attract critical attention because of its rich psychological portraits and its ambitious and complex strategies of narrative voice; his interest in presenting the flux of human consciousness places him in the company of such diverse writers as James, George Eliot, D. H. Lawrence, James Joyce, and Virginia Woolf. The short stories, as well as the novels, hold an important position in the changing of the guard from Victorian to modernist moral and aesthetic values, most prominently in their narrative technique, development of female characters, and treatment of diverse psychological perspectives.

Born in Portsmouth on 12 February 1828, Meredith was the son and grandson of tailors, a biographical fact that appears in his fiction in a preoccupation with characters' struggles to hide or raise their social status. In 1838, five years after Meredith's mother, Jane Macnamara Meredith, died, his father, Augustus Meredith, went bankrupt, moved with his son to London, and married his housekeeper. Little is known about Meredith's childhood except what Lionel Stevenson says in his biography of the writer (1953): as the only child of a father with pretensions to gentility, Meredith seldom mingled with the neighborhood boys, earning himself the nickname "Gentleman Georgy." He was educated at St. Paul's at Southsea and from 1843 to 1844 at the Moravian Brothers school in Neuweid on the Rhine. In 1846 he was articled to a London solicitor, Richard Charnock, to study law, but he quickly became interested in a literary career. Indeed, Meredith's proposal to the Court of Chancery to study law with Charnock seems to have been simply a way to free some of his inheritance from his aunt. Instead of studying the law, between 1846 and 1849, Meredith participated actively in an informal literary and intellectual group led by Charnock, wrote poetry, and met his future wife.

On 9 August 1849 he married Mary Ellen Nicolls, a beautiful young widow who was the daughter of the writer Thomas Love Peacock. They had one child, Arthur Gryffydh, in 1853. The financial hardship the young couple experienced as Meredith struggled to gain recognition as a writer contributed to the breakdown of the marriage, as did the highly intelligent, sensitive, critical, and keen-tongued personalities of both wife and husband. In 1857 Mary Meredith left England with the painter Henry Wallis, later bearing his child. Many of Meredith's short stories feature themes of incompatibility in marriage, as well as a generous appreciation of the woman's position in such situations. Although Meredith refused to see Mary after her return to England or to attend her funeral after her death of renal dropsy on 22 October 1861, his fiction often identifies male egotism as the most destructive force in unhappy romances and marriages.

Meredith's long short story or novella *Farina: A Legend of Cologne* (1857) lacks the narrative realism and the interest in mental processes that are so evident in his later fiction. Although less fantastic than his Arabian allegory *The Shaving of Shagpat: An Arabian Entertainment* (1856), *Farina* also employs a remote, exotic setting: in this case, medieval Germany. Stevenson characterizes Meredith's story as "grotesque" or "comic-gruesome," a mode in which Meredith's father-in-law, Peacock, and his contemporaries Robert Browning and William Makepeace Thackeray had also written. The 28 November 1857 *Athenaeum* called *Farina* "a full-blooded specimen of the nonsense of Genius"; the 29 August 1857 *Saturday Review* praised "a neatness and finish in the turns of language" but concluded that the "whole seems to us flat and dull"; it admitted, however, that "the dulness is that of a clever man."

*Farina* is a tale rather than a short story, a genre that emerged most distinctively in the 1890s. Wendell Harris's comment that much short fiction of this time took the form of "miniatures of either the Gothic romances or the novel" is true of *Farina*. Its characters have a fairy-tale quality: the evil robber baron Werner's men are "big and black as bears; wolf-eyed, fox-nosed," and the heroine, Margarita, is "as bright as the sunset gardens of the Golden Apples." The battle of Monk Gregory and the devil and the intervention of the "Lady of the Water" to save Margarita from the baron are supernatural elements derived from Gothic romances such as Matthew Gregory Lewis's *The Monk* (1796). Another obvious Gothic element is the oft-threatened chastity of women and the division of men into either ravishers or protectors of female honor.

Despite the story's obvious generic traits, it exhibits themes that are more fully developed in Meredith's later fiction. First, there is the independence, wit, and courage shown by Margarita, whose father praises her by saying, "she's worthy to be a man" – words echoed by an Italian patriot who praises Emilia in *Emilia in England* (1864). Margarita is both a hero worshiper like later Meredith heroines, most notably Aminta of *Lord Ormont and His Aminta: A Novel* (1894), and ready to bear arms herself. Second, the poor but noble-hearted Farina wins Margarita through courageous action and skill in chemistry – he invents eau de cologne to rid the city of the devil's stench and becomes a national hero; this theme of the social underdog receives its fullest treatment in *Evan Harrington; or, He Would Be a Gentleman* (1860) but is also prominently featured in Meredith's short fiction of the 1870s. Third, in the character of Monk Gregory, who cannot resist the temptation to tell others of his miraculous defeat of the devil, Meredith sounds the theme of egotism as a destructive force. Gregory says: "Vanity has wrecked me, in this world and the next. I am the victim of self-incense." "Self-incense," or ego, poses a danger not only to Gregory's soul but also to the city of Cologne and the German nation. Meredith

something for people to laugh over and tell again, if they please. I think the stories rather amusing: but I have not worked them up, and purposely not. *Don't put my name.*" Meredith's refusal to be identified as the author makes sense: the piece, in which a group of men tell stories around a punchbowl on a cold night, is loosely constructed, and its language is not recognizable as Meredith's; C. L. Cline notes that Meredith "pilfered the stories from his friend Francis Burnand." The stories depend heavily on physical comedy: a man must fight a dog for bedcovers; a robber gets revenge on a squire by holding a gun to his head in bed; strangers take a seat in the compartment of a man who is trying to change his trousers on a train.

The second piece in *Once a Week,* "The Parish Clerk's Story" (23 February 1861), tells of a genteel ne'er-do-well whose father denies him permission to marry his sweetheart, the daughter of one of the father's tenants. Set in a village called Bentholme, "just between two market towns and . . . not such a distance from a tolerable city," the story takes place in the early decades of the nineteenth century, at a time when "London was ten times as far away from us as it is now," and when village gossips rather than electric telegraphs spread the latest news. The son leaves home and reappears anonymously as "the Borrower," a gentleman robber who has the uncanny ability to demand the exact amount of cash his victims are carrying. When the father discovers his son's identity he relents and allows the marriage. A working-class cousin of the bride "confesses" to being "the Borrower" in a generous act that frees the groom from his past sin. The story borrows from Charles Dickens's *A Tale of Two Cities* (1859) its theme of the gentleman highwayman and one man's sacrificial adoption of another's identity, but it also forecasts Meredith's abiding interest in lower-class women who become romantically involved with their male "superiors," a subject that finds its fullest expression in *Rhoda Fleming: A Story* (1865).

Meredith's next venture into short fiction was probably "The Friend of the Engaged Couple," a piece apparently intended for *Once a Week* but for some reason never published there. Lewis Sawin, who edited the manuscript for the *Victorians Institute Journal* (1986), dates the work between 1860 and 1862. This story is much more skillfully told than the previous ones; it is richly comic and ironic, employing a female first-person narrator whose self-deception spurs the plot. The unnamed narrator's friend Laura Manners is engaged to the worthy but dull Reginald Mostyn, whom she does not love.

*"Our first novelist": caricature of Meredith by Max Beerbohm (Vanity Fair, 24 September 1896)*

would continue to emphasize the destructiveness of egotism, repeating the metaphor of the poisonous odor in *Beauchamp's Career* (1876), in which Doctor Shrapnel rails against the "stench of the trail of Ego" in England.

After *Farina* Meredith, still struggling to find a distinctive narrative approach, wrote two incidental pieces for the Bradbury and Evans periodical *Once a Week,* edited by Samuel Lucas. "A Story Telling Party" (24 December 1859) is a variant of the usual Christmas story. Meredith wrote to Lucas on 6 December 1859: "The stories are (intended to be) all fun. There is no ghost-walking, and picturing of the season, as we are accustomed to see, but there is

Laura is "the malicious naughty child that played pranks, and had to be forgiven," and Mostyn "never knew his own mind two minutes together." The narrator, disapproving of an engagement with affection only on one side, involves herself in the relationship, exercising her considerable powers as a spy: "Mr. Mostyn's life, as he told me, depended upon accurate information of her [Laura's] doings, and sayings, and thinkings. I transcribed them, according to my impressions. I could not, in my loving analysis of her character, proclaim her an angel." In the process of mediating between the couple the narrator falls in love with Mostyn, but she does not realize that she has done so. Laura, meanwhile, falls in love with a Captain Herbert but uses the narrator as a decoy to deceive her fiancé, who believes that Laura is making a match between the captain and the narrator. All four characters believe that their deaths are imminent when a fire breaks out on a train on which they are passengers; Laura reveals her love for Captain Herbert by embracing and kissing him in front of Mostyn, and the narrator reveals her feelings by clutching Mostyn's arm. The fire turns out to be a small one, ignited by Mr. and Mrs. Day, newlyweds who are burning letters from previous lovers. The narrator never admits that she loves Mostyn, but she watches him for a year in the belief that her care will rescue him from a duel with Captain Herbert. She is finally told that Mostyn has gotten married to "escape [her] persecution." The story's theme of egotistical moral posturing that obscures self-understanding looks forward to Meredith's *The Egoist: A Comedy in Narrative* (1879). "The Friend of the Engaged Couple" also features plot elements that appear in Meredith's later fiction: the misguided attempt to force affection for the sake of respectability in *Rhoda Fleming,* the use of a fire to compel a declaration of love in *The Adventures of Harry Richmond* (1871), a woman mediating between lovers in *The Tale of Chloe: An Episode in the History of Beau Beamish* (1890), and the broken engagements of *The Egoist.*

Meredith's novel *The Ordeal of Richard Feverel: A History of Father and Son* (1859) promised success when Mudie's Circulating Library ordered three hundred copies, but Mudie's sudden refusal to circulate it because of its treatment of adultery killed sales and consigned the novel to commercial oblivion. For the rest of his career Meredith felt himself at odds with popular and critical taste, and he developed technical, aesthetic, and moral standards for fiction that were different from those of many of his contemporaries. Meredith became a reader for the publishing firm of Chapman and Hall in 1862; in

this position, which he retained until 1894, he encouraged and influenced such writers as Robert Louis Stevenson, George Gissing, Thomas Hardy, and Olive Shreiner. On 20 September 1864 Meredith married Marie Vulliamy after persuading her father that he could support her by his writing and that he was not to blame for his past marital difficulties. Meredith's vulnerability during his negotiations with his future father-in-law may be another reason for his persistent sympathy for characters whose past errors are exposed. Meredith found happiness with the sensible and calm Marie Vulliamy, as he predicted he would in a 6 June 1864 letter to his friend Augustus Jessopp: "I know that I can work in an altogether different fashion, and that with a wife and such a wife by my side, I shall taste some of the holiness of this mortal world and be new-risen in it. Already the spur is acting, and health comes, energy comes." In 1868 the Merediths settled at Flint Cottage, at the foot of scenic Box Hill in Surrey. Later Meredith had a two-room chalet built near the cottage as a study and retreat.

In December 1872 and January 1873 Meredith's five-part series of short dialogues of a hybrid essay/narrative genre, *Up to Midnight,* was published in *The Graphic,* a weekly illustrated journal (the series was published as a book in 1913). Seven characters, of various temperaments and political philosophies, form "the Parliament of the Lesser House" and discuss such topics as India, foxhunting, women's rights, polar exploration, laborer-tenant-landlord relations, and Napoleon III. Lionel Stevenson likens the dialogues to the "ideological puppets" of Peacock's *Crotchet Castle* (1831). The *Graphic* series provided a more appropriate outlet for Meredith's discursive, philosophical vein than the constraints of short fiction allowed. In its attacks on middle-class complacency the series anticipates Meredith's later short fiction, and his diagnosis of the danger of the English "habit of sucking phrases like sweetmeats" while ignoring actual events and conditions prepares the way for "The Case of General Ople and Lady Camper" (1890), one of his most successful short stories.

Between 1877 and 1879 three of Meredith's short stories were published in the *New Quarterly Magazine.* The magazine's founder and editor, Oswald Crawfurd, announced that his quarterly would include "Tales of considerable length by Eminent Writers. *The Tales will invariably be completed in the numbers in which they appear.*" This publishing innovation eliminated the waiting to which readers of serialized fiction were accustomed and may have encouraged the production of good short fiction.

Maura Carey Ives, editor of a critical edition of Meredith's stories in the *New Quarterly Magazine,* comments that "Meredith became a contributor to the *NQM* at a time when his reputation was rising; and his contributions set a new standard for the magazine, which to that point had attracted fiction more notable for its sentimentality and sensationalism than its literary merit."

The three stories are exceptional examples of nineteenth-century short fiction. Harris aligns Meredith with James as a practitioner of "the sophisticated tale and the true short story," in contrast to the short-story modes most frequently employed at the time: "the humorous anecdote, the fantastic legend, or the out-and-out thriller." In his *New Quarterly Magazine* stories particularly, Harris claims, Meredith trusted "the expression of strongly held values and personal points of view to shorter fiction" and "took a step seldom ventured upon except in stories whose total reason for existence was moralistic."

Meredith's first publication in the *New Quarterly Magazine* was "The House on the Beach," which appeared in January 1877; the story was published in book form the same year by the Harper firm of New York. *The House on the Beach: A Realistic Tale* deals with upward mobility, snobbery, shameful personal exposure, and women as pawns in contests between men. Martin Tinman, the son of a shopkeeper, prospers enough to sell the shop and aspire to gentility as bailiff and gentleman of the Cinque Port of Crikswich. He is visited by an old friend, the former Philip Ribstone, who has inherited a fortune from a transported convict in Australia and has taken the convict's name, Van Diemen Smith. Smith finds Tinman a changed man – stingy, snobbish, and ridiculously vain, renting a cheval glass in front of which he parades in court costume as he practices an address he hopes to make to the queen. Smith's daughter, Annette, has a suitor, the gentleman journalist Herbert Fellingham; but when Tinman threatens to expose her father's desertion from the army twenty years before, Annette agrees to marry him in exchange for his silence. Tinman's abominably cheap wine contributes to the frequent altercations between him and Smith. A flood exposes Tinman's vanity and small-mindedness to the whole community, and Smith finds out that his past offense is no longer legally actionable. The story ends with Annette's laughter as Tinman is rescued from the flood, ludicrous in the suit in which he had planned to appear at court.

Meredith's imaginative use of symbols distinguishes this work from the commonplace short story of the period. Tinman's name suggests that his character lacks the true metal of honor and gentlemanliness. The name Van Diemen Smith, beyond its reference to Van Diemen's Land, the Australian island settled by British convicts in the early nineteenth century and later renamed Tasmania, is suggestive: *Diemen* sounds both like *diamond,* symbolizing the worth of Smith's loyalty to his friend, and *demon,* indicating the haunting of Smith by his past. Tinman's cheval glass is defective, "causing an incongruous and absurd reflection" that symbolizes his fatal misreading of self. Smith shatters the cheval glass, just as Tinman's snobbish pretensions to society are shattered. Tinman's bad wine circulates through the community, symbolizing the poisoning effect of a mercantile mentality that tries to buy and sell human affection. Finally, the image of the house on the beach is a metaphor for the human being living at risk in a society that is being redefined and that is urging new self-definition as well. Although Tinman is exposed by the flood, he is not alone in his vulnerability: Meredith emphatically declares Tinman to be a typical "Englishman who is bursting merely to do like the rest of his countrymen, and rise above them to shake them class by class as the dust from his heels." The sentimental Van Diemen Smith fears exposure in graphic images, feeling himself "flat as a pancake, and transparent as a pane of glass." Herbert Fellingham may ridicule Tinman's wine and pronunciation, but his arrogance delays his understanding of Annette's true value and almost causes him to lose her. Annette, who declares, "I belong to my father," even when that means he will trade her to maintain a public perception of respectability, is most vulnerable of all. It is appropriate that the sea floods this community of typically English, "artificially-reared people" so that natural affections can be expressed and the true natures of the characters can be revealed to themselves and to others.

The story shares themes with Meredith's novels, looking forward to the destructive egotism of Willoughby Patterne in *The Egoist* and Victor Radnor in *One of Our Conquerors* (1891). Tinman foreshadows Willoughby's gigantic ego and eventual social exposure; like Tinman, he is eventually "unroofed," "naked and blown upon." Meredith combines Tinman and Smith in the complex character of Radnor, a man of wealth, generosity, and sentimentality like Smith, who, like Tinman, fatally misunderstands his own ambition. The sale of women to satisfy cultural notions of respectability was explored earlier in *Rhoda Fleming.* Meredith's reminder that author and readers now live in "the days we see through Mr. Darwin's glasses" looks backward to *Emilia in England,* in which social climbing is depicted in evolutionary images, and forward to *The Egoist,* in which Meredith employs his most extensive evolutionary imagery and metaphor. Annette's liberating laughter, which clears her mind by its "beneficent exercise," connects the story to the concept of comedy as "full of healing, the wit of good breeding, the wit of wisdom" that Meredith describes in "The Idea of Comedy and the Uses of the Comic Spirit," a lecture delivered at the London Institution on 1 February 1877 and published in the *New Quarterly Magazine* in April of the same year and in book form in 1897 as *An Essay on Comedy and the Uses of the Comic Spirit.*

The curative power of laughter that trims the unwieldy ego appears also in "The Case of General Ople and Lady Camper," published in the *New Quarterly Magazine* in July 1877 and in book form in New York in 1890. General Ople, retired on half-pay at age fifty-five, purchases a "gentlemanly residence" outside of London, where his nearest neighbor is the formidable widow Lady Camper. "The inflammable officer" is both fascinated by and afraid of the "clever" Lady Camper, and he becomes so caught up in his image of himself as "a lord and conqueror of the [female] sex" that he is blind to the budding romance of his daughter, Elizabeth, and Lady Camper's nephew Roland. When Lady Camper strives to enlighten the general about the young people's relationship, he misinterprets her conversation as romantic interest in himself and proposes to her. Amazed at his obtuseness, she tells him that she is seventy years old – she is actually in her forties – and enjoys his discomfiture at the news. Finding that the patent falsehood does not help to turn the general's attention away from himself and toward his daughter, Lady Camper goes abroad and mails a barrage of caricatures to the general, depicting his isolated egotism and his neglect of his daughter. General Ople learns to know himself after seeing his identity visually ridiculed by the all-seeing eye of Lady Camper.

Meredith's use of military metaphors contributes to the humor of the story: Ople sights "the fair enemy's flag," employs his weapon of "masculine passion to gain this fortress," is "ready for battle," and feels the "anticipation of victory." While the general belongs with other egotistical conquerors, such as the royal pretender Richmond Roy in *The Adventures of Harry Richmond,* Radnor of *One of Our Conquerors,* or even Tinman, all of whom hunger to be recognized as social and cultural leaders, he is more of an everyman: "modest, retiring, humbly contented; a gentlemanly residence appeased his

ambition. . . . He was one of us; no worse, and not strikingly nor perilously better." General Ople's recognition of his limitations does not make him as self-aware as he needs to be, primarily because of "a lamentable susceptibility to ladies' charms." Lady Camper is not the typically submissive woman the general has wooed in the past: she is well educated, combining a ladylike drawing talent with the ability to use a pair of pistols. She is particular about language as the medium of personal and social values, and her correction of the general's vulgar speech is an attempt to shake him loose from the clichéd thinking to which he is prone. She has contempt for his inactivity, telling him: "I could follow my husband still on a campaign, if he were a warrior instead of a pensioner." She realizes that he requires a wife who will be "a commanding officer" to him, and she assumes this role indirectly by firing a volley of caricatures at him.

As Donald R. Swanson has noted, much of the story's power derives from the multiple narrative angles Meredith employs. The reader initially understands events from the general's point of view, but gradually the narrator begins to report the general's behavior through the perspectives of other characters. This technique reaches a climax in the description of the caricatures of the general, wherein Lady Camper's reading of him is contrasted with his understanding of his own behavior. After he justifies his retirement by saying that he wants only limited responsibilities, Lady Camper draws a caricature showing him in the isolation and confinement of a sentry box, oblivious to the despairing young lovers beneath him, irresponsible as a father and as a citizen of a community beyond the self. She depicts Ople's "gentlemanly residence" as a series of soap bubbles, indicating his retreat from life and his self-deluded existence. This refracted vision of himself unravels Ople, who starts to stutter, lose weight, and literally "forget himself." Lady Camper's seeming omniscience leads Swanson to see her as a magical, fairy-tale figure, but other readers might see her as a therapist who offers Ople a counterinterpretation of his behavior. Meredith again emphasizes the vulnerable position of one who is mentally and physically exposed: "The senses of General Ople were struck by the aspect of a lurid Goddess, who penetrated him, read him through, and had both power and will to expose and make him ridiculous forever." Despite feeling "bare," "defenceless," and "haunted," Ople shows the caricatures to everyone in the community, indicating that he accepts the justice of Lady Camper's reading of him.

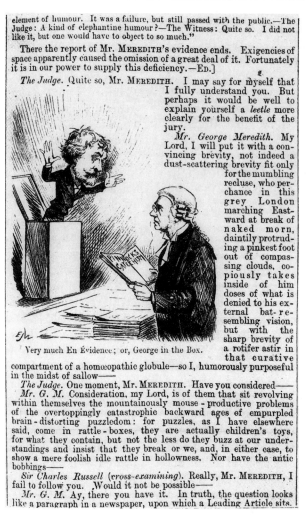

element of humour. It was a failure, but still passed with the public.—The Judge: A kind of elephantine humour?—The Witness: Quite so. I did not like it, but one would have to object to so much."

There the report of Mr. MEREDITH's evidence ends. Exigencies of space apparently caused the omission of a great deal of it. Fortunately it is in our power to supply this deficiency.—ED.]

*The Judge.* Quite so, Mr. MEREDITH. I may say for myself that I fully understand you. But perhaps it would be well to explain yourself a *leetle* more clearly for the benefit of the jury.

*Mr. George Meredith.* My Lord, I will put it with a convincing brevity, not indeed a dust-scattering brevity fit only for the mumbling recluse, who perchance in this grey London marching Eastward at break of naked morn, daintily protruding a pinkest foot out of compassing clouds, copiously takes inside of him doses of what is denied to his external bat-resembling vision, but with the sharp brevity of a rotifer astir in that curative compartment of a homœopathic globule—so I, humorously purposeful in the midst of sallow——

*The Judge.* One moment, Mr. MEREDITH. Have you considered——

*Mr. G. M.* Consideration, my Lord, is of them that sit revolving within themselves the mountainously mouse-productive problems of the overtoppingly catastrophic backward ages of empurpled brain-distorting puzzledom: for puzzles, as I have elsewhere said, come in rattle-boxes, they are actually children's toys, for what they contain, but not the less do they buzz at our understandings and insist that they break or we, and, in either case, to show a mere foolish idle rattle in hollowness. Nor have the antic bobbings——

*Sir Charles Russell (cross-examining).* Really, Mr. MEREDITH, I fail to follow you. Would it not be possible——

*Mr. G. M.* Ay, there you have it. In truth, the question looks like a paragraph in a newspaper, upon which a Leading Article sits.

Page from a Punch article about an 1891 libel suit against the publishing firm of Chapman and Hall, for which Meredith was a reader. The caricature depicts Meredith in the witness box, testifying for the defense.

"The Tale of Chloe: An Episode in the History of Beau Beamish" appeared in the *New Quarterly Magazine* in July 1879 and was published in book form in New York in 1890. Percy Lubbock, reviewing Meredith's collected works in the *Quarterly Review* (April 1910), calls the story "that fine picture of tragic passion in a setting of the most fantastic rococo." Although Meredith had long been concerned in his novels with the potential tragedy of characters who are self-deluded or are victims of the self-delusion of others, his previous short stories of the 1870s emphasize the comic aspects of such figures. Nowhere in his fiction is the tragic tone more pervasive than in *The Tale of Chloe.*

Meredith modeled the character Chloe on Fanny Braddock, who took her own life in Bath in 1731 after heavy gambling losses and whose story was told in the *Gentleman's Magazine* (September 1731); by John Wood in his *Essay Towards a Description of Bath* (1749); and in an embellished account by Oliver Goldsmith in *The Life of Richard Nash* (1762). Lionel Stevenson suggests that the character of Duchess Susan derives from the 1791 marriage of Henry Cecil, the Earl of Exeter, to Sarah Hoggins, a farm girl, and links Meredith's story to an alleged incident in which Maria Rossetti prevented her sister Christina's elopement with an unworthy suitor by obstructing the doorway of their house every night for a week. (Meredith had shared a house in Cheyne Walk, Chelsea, with Maria and Christina's brother Dante Gabriel Rossetti and Algernon Charles Swinburne in 1861–1862.)

In the story a duke has wed his dairy maid Susan only to discover after three years that his passion for his much younger bride has waned. He does not want to be her "playfellow," but neither does he want to imprison her in the "narrow" world of their home. He has promised her a month of entertainment at Bath; but he cannot with dignity accompany her there, and he fears that she is unprepared by her birth, education, and innocent youth to comport herself at such a place with credit to himself and without danger to her virtue. Beau Beamish, a leader of society in Bath, undertakes to protect the duchess by attaching her to a virtuous young woman named Chloe. Seven years ago Chloe gave away her fortune to save Count Caseldy, the man she loved, from financial ruin; as a result, she was disowned by her family. Abandoned by Caseldy, she now resides quietly in Bath. After Duchess Susan, using an assumed name to protect her husband's identity, arrives in Bath, Caseldy appears, and the intrigue begins. Beamish is duped into believing that other suitors pose a greater threat to the duchess than does Caseldy; Chloe tries to deceive herself about the growing passion between Duchess Susan and Caseldy, who pretends that he has come at last to claim Chloe's hand; and Susan believes that Chloe and Beamish love each other and that her elopement with Caseldy will not hurt Chloe, of whom she has grown fond. Chloe becomes aware of Caseldy's treachery and begins weaving a silken skein, tying a knot in it each time she perceives his deceit. Finally she hangs herself with the skein, preventing the duchess from eloping by obstructing the door with her corpse. Caseldy is reformed, and the duchess returns to the duke with her virtue intact, saying "No more of love!"

Meredith turns a critical eye on the cross-purposes and ambivalences of the duke regarding his lowborn wife, but he is sympathetic to the plight of the duchess, who has been schooled in the physical graces expected in aristocratic society but with little attention given to her moral or intellectual education. She can walk in a hoop skirt but says, "I haven't got fine language yet. I shall. It seems to come last." Bath does not prove to be a good place to "refine" the duchess; her presence destabilizes the artificially civilized world of the town and unleashes an unruly passion in the men, turning them into "hounds" and "madmen" in a way that alarms Beau Beamish, the "monarchical" and "princely father of our domestic civilization." Here Meredith examines English civilization in a way that prepares for his criticism of England's despiritualized merchant identity in *One of Our Conquerors:* Beamish's remark, "Society, my dear Chloe, is a recommence-

ment upon an upper level of the savage system; we must have our sacrifices," reveals the barbarity of accepted social customs. This criticism is at the core of Chloe's heroism: her selfless devotion to a faithless man has resulted, according to unwritten social law, in her loss of family connections and even of her name – she was born Catherine Martinsward but was rechristened Chloe after her "disgrace." Beamish's tactics for maintaining decorum among visitors to Bath can be brutal: he tells a lady contemplating adultery that she is on her way to join the "ancient" company of prostitutes, and he strips false lace from the duchess's dress in front of an assembly of gentlemen and ladies. He "tamed the bumpkin squire and his brood, but at the cost of their animal spirits and their gift of speech," an operation Meredith compares to a "tracheotomy" in which "an artificial windpipe" is inserted.

*The Tale of Chloe* has much to say about the position of women. Chloe's suicide is seen by herself and by the other characters as a final act of wisdom: "Everything assured her that she saw more clearly than others; she saw too when it was good to cease to live." Ives offers a more complex analysis of her motives, suggesting that Chloe, who has been defined by men such as Beamish and Caseldy, is attempting an eloquent rebuttal through the crafting of her own death. She plaits the skein of silk she will use as a noose as "a way of patterning, weaving, and reconciling the conflicts she faces." Further, Chloe's corpse blocking the door represents her final assertion of her natural, material self, a self long eclipsed by the spiritualized, ghostly self she developed through her suffering; thus, through her death Chloe links her passionate physical self with that of Duchess Susan in a way that can be seen both as Susan's salvation and as a rival's revenge on her.

Harris says that "the short story is the natural vehicle for the presentation of the outsider," citing Gissing and Arthur Morrison as late-Victorian fiction writers who employed this vehicle. While Meredith nowhere attempts an examination of the urban poor, as Gissing and Morrison do, he does depict women on the margins of Victorian society. His interest in the rural or formally untutored beauty who rises socially and finds herself confused by social rules and customs that "ladies" take for granted appears not only in Duchess Susan but also in Lucy Desborough of *The Ordeal of Richard Feverel,* Dahlia in *Rhoda Fleming,* Emilia in *Emilia in England,* Judith Marsett in *One of Our Conquerors,* and Carinthia Jane Kirby in *The Amazing Marriage* (1895). The men who are sexually drawn to these lower-class women refuse the responsibility of educating them for society and, when married to them, fail to acknowledge their wives publicly. Duchess Susan is objectified in ways familiar to readers of nineteenth-century literature, but Meredith moves inside her mind at the end of the story to explore her choice to elope, thus granting her a fuller identity than do the other characters, who characterize her as a "child," a "toy," "a treasure-laden Spanish galleon," and a woman "with the odour of the shepherdess about her." Like Dahlia Fleming, who, bereft of her true love, feels herself "buried alive," Susan sees her life with the duke as "an old, a worn, an end-of-autumn life, chill, without aim, like a something that was hungry and toothless." Unable to face this prospect, "she burned to fly" with Caseldy, who has made her "a creature inflamed." Meredith acknowledges the importance of sexual passion, but the duchess's passion must be tempered with moral responsibility and intellectual understanding. Appropriately, it is the other female "outsider," Chloe, who administers this lesson to Duchess Susan.

Meredith achieved popular success at last with *Diana of the Crossways* (1885), a novel based on the life of the writer Caroline Norton that demonstrates his continuing interest in independent and intelligent female heroines. That same year he lost his wife to cancer and began to be affected by the spinal malady that would cripple him. Between 1885 and 1909 he garnered increasing critical and popular attention not only in England and America but also in France, Germany, and Italy. Although criticism of his difficult style continued, he was lionized as an important man of letters, and his opinions on domestic and international issues were sought after. He succeeded Alfred Tennyson as president of the Society of Authors in 1892 and was made vice president of the London Library in 1902. He received the Order of Merit in 1905.

Sometime during these years Meredith began a work of which only a fragment was completed. "The Gentleman of Fifty and the Damsel of Nineteen" is included in volume twenty-two of the Memorial Edition of his works (1909–1911), where it occupies forty-six pages; it is not known whether Meredith intended the piece as a long short story or as a novel. Gilbert Pollingray (the final syllable of whose name indicates his age) finds himself attracted to his lively goddaughter, Alice Amble. Feeling "undeveloped" and looking for ways to enrich his life, he invites Alice to visit him so that he can "study" her. Alice is both fascinated and resentful about being studied, although she is obviously studying her host as well. Meredith splits the narra-

tive into alternating chapters titled "He" and "She," in which he explores two minds that readers might suppose to be radically divided by age and gender. Meredith skillfully suggests a potential for erotic and intellectual harmony between the two, but the fragment ends before the problem of the age discrepancy is resolved. Possibly Meredith was remembering his infatuation with Janet Duff Gordon around the period of his composition of *Evan Harrington,* which Duff Gordon called "*my* novel"; she was then seventeen and Meredith was in his early thirties. Meredith's title is an ironic one, for neither Pollingray nor Alice can be fixed exclusively by their ages; each is a constellation of thoughts and sensations that changes dynamically as they react to each other. Thus, "The Gentleman of Fifty and the Damsel of Nineteen" might be seen as an anticipation of the works of D. H. Lawrence and Virginia Woolf, who destabilized traditional ideas of "character" and experimented with narrative voice.

Meredith's contribution to the short-story genre reached its height in the 1870s, immediately preceding the publication of one of his most enduring critical and popular successes. It might be suggested that the more compact form of the short story compelled Meredith to distill his narrative energies into tighter structures and that *The Egoist* benefits from this discipline.

Meredith died at Flint Cottage on 18 May 1909 and, according to his wishes, was buried at Dorking Cemetery. His well-known agnosticism prohibited his burial in Westminster Abbey, and Meredith himself was reputed to have said at Browning's funeral, "better the green grass turf than Abbey pavements"; a memorial service was, however, held at the abbey. Lubbock's review of Meredith's collected works characterizes not only the novels but also the short fiction: "Meredith's art, indeed, as we follow it from book to book, reflects one long conflict with stubborn and recalcitrant material. It is as though he could never be content until he should make language do a little more than it ever will. . . . He never lost sight of the sane relations of man and woman to each other."

**Letters:**

*The Letters of George Meredith,* 3 volumes, edited by C. L. Cline (Oxford: Clarendon Press, 1970).

**Bibliographies:**

Maurice Buxton Forman, *A Bibliography of the Writings in Prose and Verse of George Meredith* (Edinburgh: Bibliographical Society, 1922);

Forman, *Meredithiana, Being a Supplement to the Bibliography of Meredith* (Edinburgh: Bibliographical Society, 1924);

H. Lewis Swain, "George Meredith: A Bibliography of Meredithiana, 1920–1953," *Bulletin of Bibliography,* 21 (September–December 1955): 186–191, 215, 216;

Michael Collie, *George Meredith: A Bibliography* (Toronto: University of Toronto Press, 1974);

John C. Olmstead, *George Meredith: An Annotated Bibliography of Criticism 1925–1975* (New York: Garland, 1978).

**Biographies:**

Lionel Stevenson, *The Ordeal of George Meredith: A Biography* (New York: Scribners, 1953);

Jack Lindsay, *George Meredith: His Life and Work* (London: Bodley Head, 1956).

**References:**

James M. Barrie, "The Lost Works of George Meredith," *Scots Observer,* 24 November 1888, pp. 12–13;

E. M. Forster, *Aspects of the Novel* (San Diego, New York & London: Harcourt Brace Jovanovich, 1927), p. 90;

Wendell Harris, *British Short Fiction in the Nineteenth Century: A Literary and Bibliographic Guide* (Detroit: Wayne State University Press, 1979), pp. 83–85;

Henry James, Letter to Edmund Gosse, 22 August 1894, *Meredith: the Critical Heritage,* edited by Ioan Williams (New York: Barnes & Noble, 1971), pp. 406–407;

Carl H. Ketchum, "Meredith at Work: 'The Tale of Chloe,' " *Nineteenth Century Literature,* 21 (December 1966): 235–247;

Maurice McCullen and Lewis Sawin, *A Dictionary of Characters in George Meredith's Fiction* (New York & London: Garland, 1977);

V. S. Pritchett, *Books in General* (New York: Harcourt, 1953), p. 206;

Donald R. Swanson, *Three Conquerors: Character and Method in the Mature Works of George Meredith* (Paris: Mouton, 1969);

Ioan Williams, *Meredith: The Critical Heritage* (London: Routledge & Kegan Paul, 1971; New York: Barnes & Noble, 1971);

Walter Wright, *Art and Substance in George Meredith: A Study in Narrative* (Lincoln: University of Nebraska Press, 1953).

**Papers:**

George Meredith's papers are in the Altschul Collection of the Beinecke Rare Book and Manuscript Library, Yale University; the Berg Collection of the New York Public Library; and the Huntington Library, San Marino, California. The manuscript for *The Tale of Chloe: An Episode in the History of Beau Beamish* is in the Widener Collection, Harvard University.

# William Mudford

*(8 January 1782 – 10 March 1848)*

Thomas L. Cooksey
*Armstrong State College*

BOOKS: *A Critical Enquiry into the Moral Writings of Dr. Samuel Johnson. In Which the Tendency of Certain Passages in the Rambler, and Other Publications of that Celebrated Writer, is Impartially Considered. To Which is Added an Appendix. Containing a Dialogue Between Boswell and Johnson in the Shades,* as Attalus (London: Printed for C. Connall, 1802); revised as *A Critical Enquiry into the Writings of Dr. Samuel Johnson, in which it is shown that the Pictures of Life contained in the Rambler and Other Publications of that Celebrated Writer, have a Dangerous Tendency, to which is added an Appendix, containing a Facetious Dialogue between Boz and Poz in the Shades,* (London: Printed for M. Jones, 1803);

*Augustus and Mary; or, the Maid of Buttermere. A Domestic Tale* (London: M. Jones, 1803);

*Nubilia in Search of a Husband: including Sketches of Modern Society, and Interspersed with Moral and Literary Disquisitions* (Philadelphia: Bradford & Inskeep / New York: Inskeep & Bradford / Boston: William M'Ilhenney Jr. / Baltimore: Coale & Thomas, 1809; enlarged edition, London: Printed for J. Ridgway; Sherwood, Neely & Jones; and J. Booth, 1809);

*Justice and Generosity Against Malice, Ignorance, and Poverty; or, An Attempt to Shew the Equity of the New Prices at the Theatre Royal, Covent Garden,* as Attalus (London: Printed for Sherwood, Neely & Jones, 1809);

*The Contemplatist: A Series of Essays Upon Morals and Literature* (London: Sherwood, Neely, & Jones, 1810);

*The Life and Adventures of Paul Plaintive, Esq., an Author. Comp. from Original Documents, and Interspersed with Specimens of his Genius, in Prose and Poetry,* as Martin Gribaldus Swammerdam, 2 volumes (London: Printed by W. Flint for Sherwood, Neely & Jones, 1811);

*A Critical Examination of the Writings of Richard Cumberland, with an Occasional Inquiry into the Age in which he Lived, and the Contemporaries with whom*

William Mudford; engraving after a photograph by Ad. Braun and Company, Paris (Hulton Deutsch Collection)

*he Flourished,* 2 volumes (London: Sherwood, Neely & Jones, 1812);

*An Historical Account of the Campaign in the Netherlands in 1815, under His Grace the Duke of Wellington, and Marshal Prince Blücher, comprising the battles of Ligny, Quatre Bras, and Waterloo; with a Detailed Narrative of the Political Events connected with those Memorable Conflicts, down to the Surrender of Paris, and the Departure of Bonaparte for St. Helena* (London: H. Colburn, 1817);

*The Five Nights of St. Albans. A Romance of the Sixteenth Century* (Edinburgh: William Blackwood, 1829; Philadelphia & Baltimore: E. L. Carey & A. Hart, 1833);

*The Premier,* 3 volumes (London: H. Colburn & R. Bentley, 1831);

*Church Establishment and Church Rates, in Reference to the Speech of the Rev. E. Totteham, M.A., delivered at the Assembly Rooms, Bath, Feb. 14, 1837,* as Geoffrey Oldcastle (London: Ridgway, 1837);

*The Iron Shroud; or, Italian Revenge* (Glasgow: Orr & Sons, 1839);

*Stephen Dugard. A Novel,* 3 volumes (London: R. Bentley, 1840);

*Tales and Trifles, from Blackwood's and Other Popular Magazines,* 2 volumes (London: William Tegg, 1849);

*Arthur Wilson: A Study,* 3 volumes (London: Tinsley Brothers, 1872).

TRANSLATIONS: Sylvain Meinrad Xavier de Golbéry, *Travels in Africa* (London: M. Jones, 1803);

Claude Adrien Helvétius, *De l'Esprit; or Essays on the Mind,* with a life of the author by Mudford (London: M. Jones, 1807);

Huguet de Grafigny, *The Letters of a Peruvian Princess,* 2 volumes (London: M. Jones, 1809);

Cardinal Louis François de Bausset, *The Life of Fénelon, Archbishop of Cambrai,* 2 volumes (London: Printed for Sherwood, Neely & Jones, 1810);

Eugène Francis, Prince of Savoy, *Memoirs of Prince Eugène, of Savoy* (London: Sherwood, Neely & Jones, 1811; New York: Printed for Ezra Sargeant, 1811).

OTHER: Oliver Goldsmith, *Essays on Men and Manners, With a Life and Critique on the Writings and Genius of the Author by W. Mudford,* edited by Mudford (London: M. Jones, 1804);

James Beattie, *Beauties Selected from the Writings of James Beattie,* edited, with a life, by Mudford (London: Longman, 1809);

*The British Novelists; Comprising Every Work of Acknowledged Merit Which is Usually Classed Under the Denomination of Novels,* edited, with notes, by Mudford, 5 volumes (London: W. Clarke, Goddard, 1810–1817);

"First and Last Dinner," in *Stories from "Blackwood"* (New York: Appleton, 1852), pp. 9–20.

SELECTED PERIODICAL PUBLICATIONS – UNCOLLECTED: "First and Last Crime – James Morley," *Blackwood's Edinburgh Magazine,* 25 (March 1829): 303–310;

"The First and Last Appearance – Mr. Henry Augustus Constantine Stubbs," *Blackwood's Edinburgh Magazine,* 25 (April 1829);

"The First and Last Kiss," *Blackwood's Edinburgh Magazine,* 25 (May 1829): 581–592;

"First and Last Love," *Blackwood's Edinburgh Magazine,* 26 (August 1829): 189–200;

"The First and Last Sacrifice," *Blackwood's Edinburgh Magazine,* 26 (September 1829): 444–452;

"Malavolti: a Neapolitan Story," *Blackwood's Edinburgh Magazine,* 26 (November 1829): 716–728;

"The First and Last Birthday," *Blackwood's Edinburgh Magazine,* 28 (November 1830): 751–770;

"Felix Binocular, a Legal Sketch," *Fraser's Magazine,* 3 (May 1831): 472–477;

"Cemeteries and Churchyards: A Visit to Kensal Green," *Bentley's Miscellany,* 9 (January 1841): 92–97;

"Ghost Gossips at Blakesley House: The Old Chest, The Screaming Woman," *Bentley's Miscellany,* 9 (May 1841): 462–473;

"Ghost Gossips at Blakesley House: Cromwell, Richard Warbeck," *Bentley's Miscellany,* 9 (June 1841): 622–634;

"Nicolas Dunks; or Fried Mackerel for Dinner," *Blackwood's Edinburgh Magazine,* 50 (September 1841): 363–373;

"Seven Years," *Bentley's Miscellany,* 10 (September 1841): 623–619;

"The Funeral," *Bentley's Miscellany,* 10 (December 1841): 623, 624;

"Ghost Gossips at Blakesley House: The Banquet-Hall of Death," *Bentley's Miscellany,* 11 (March 1842): 309–314.

William Hazlitt had vivid memories of William Mudford, his old journalist colleague and rival at the *Morning Chronicle.* In his essay in *Table-Talk* (1821), "Coffee-House Politicians," he recalled how his friend, Roger Kirkpatrick, would impersonate Mudford. "Oh! it was a rich treat to see him describe M – df – rd, him of the Courier, the Contemplative Man, who wrote an answer to Coelebs, coming into a room, folding up his great coat, taking out a little pocket volume, laying it down to think, rubbing the calf of his leg with grave self-complacency, and starting out of his reverie when spoken to with an inimitable vapid exclamation of 'Eh!'" Summarizing, Hazlitt declared, "M – df – rd is like a man made of fleecy hosiery . . . fat, pert, and dull as it was possible to be."

For Hazlitt, Mudford embodied the sort of hack journalist and government tool that Hazlitt despised, and he rarely missed an opportunity to ridicule Mudford. Mudford's name also inspired the young Charles Dickens to create the town of Mudfog as a parody of Chatham for his *Mudfog Sketches,* first appearing in *Bentley's Miscellany* (1837–1839). A staunch advocate of Tory principles and eventually a warm supporter of foreign minister George Canning, Mudford also had his admirers. His consummate abilities as the editor of the *Courier,* "during a most trying period of our history," were acknowledged in an obituary appearing in the June 1848 *Gentleman's Magazine.* Samuel Taylor Coleridge found Mudford a loyal supporter and confidant in his time of need.

While Mudford was known chiefly as a journalist, he was also regarded as a busy and prolific man of letters, producing translations, critical and philosophical essays, reviews, and novels at a prodigious rate. His novel *The Five Nights of St. Albans: A Romance of the Sixteenth Century* (1829) even achieved the rare distinction of a favorable review by John Gibson Lockhart, "The Scorpion." Today, however, Mudford is primarily remembered for his short fiction, the tales and sketches that he published in such periodicals as *Blackwood's Edinburgh Magazine, Fraser's Magazine,* and *Bentley's Miscellany.* Indeed his story "The Iron Shroud," which appeared in the August 1830 *Blackwood's* before being published separately as a chapbook in 1839, influenced Edgar Allan Poe's "The Pit and the Pendulum" and is still found in print. Writing with easy vigor, Mudford was a master at creating atmosphere. If his stories lack the subtle plot or the psychological depth of those of a Poe, they nevertheless exemplify the so-called *Blackwood's* tale and can still amuse and entertain.

William Mudford was born on 8 January 1782 in London, where his father was a small shopkeeper in Piccadilly. Little information is available on his early life, other than that he was given a conventional education, receiving, like the heroine of his novel *Nubilia in Search of a Husband* (1809), "the necessary accomplishments of a rational being and a Christian." Early on, Mudford demonstrated an aptitude for literature, though his tastes were orthodox, looking to John Milton, Joseph Addison, Samuel Johnson, William Cowper, William Collins, Mark Akenside, Thomas Gray, and Oliver Goldsmith as models.

Like many young men of the middle class of this time who aspired to be gentlemen, the young Mudford combined his literary talents with his strong ambitions, courting the powerful and famous. At the age of seventeen Mudford approached John Kemble, the producer of the Covent Garden Theatre, with the proposal of dedicating a pamphlet to him. (Several years later, he again approached the exasperated Kemble, this time with the manuscript of a play. Nothing came of the project, and the play itself is now lost.) The eighteen-year-old Mudford finally became the

assistant secretary to the duke of Kent, accompanying him to Gibraltar in 1802.

Mudford also published his first book in 1802, a small work with the ambitious title *A Critical Enquiry into the Moral Writings of Dr. Samuel Johnson.* With this success to his name he returned to London the following year to produce a second edition and to publish his first novel, *Augustus and Mary; or, the Maid of Buttermere: A Domestic Tale* (1803). Over the next decade Mudford supported himself with literary hackwork, producing translations and editing Goldsmith's *Essays on Men and Manners* (1804), *Beauties Selected from the Writings of James Beattie* (1809), and a series known as *The British Novelists* (1810–1817). He also published works intended to build his reputation, such as his second novel, *Nubilia in Search of a Husband,* a deliberate attempt to capitalize on the success of Hannah More's popular *Coelebs in Search of a Wife* (1808).

During this period Mudford also attended lectures at the University of Edinburgh, pursuing an interest in political philosophy. Here he became friends with John Black, a fellow student also supporting himself with hackwork. The two collaborated on an exchange of letters, which Mudford eventually contrived to get published in William Cobbett's *Political Register.* In the exchange they debated the merits of a classical education, Black taking the affirmative, Mudford the negative.

In London Mudford continued his literary pursuits, writing and editing a short-lived periodical, *The Contemplatist,* the title Hazlitt recalled with some irony. The essays of *The Contemplatist,* a series of disquisitions on matters of literature and morality in the spirit of the *Spectator* or Johnson's *Rambler,* were collected and published in 1810. Like much of Mudford's critical writing, the essays of the *Contemplatist* looked back to the style and ideas of the previous century and attracted little contemporary interest.

He eventually joined the staff of James Perry's *Morning Chronicle* as a parliamentary reporter, seemingly an essential part of the literary apprenticeship of English writers from Johnson to Dickens. With some twelve volumes to his credit by this time, Mudford soon became the drama critic of the *Chronicle.* In 1812 he published *A Critical Examination of the Writings of Richard Cumberland,* the prolific playwright and diplomat (1732–1811) whom Richard Brinsley Sheridan had caricatured as Sir Fretful Plagiary in *The Critic* (1781).

Hazlitt joined the staff of the *Chronicle* in 1813 as a parliamentary reporter. Five years Mudford's senior, resentful of Mudford's intellectual and political pretensions, and envious of his position as the drama critic of a major paper, Hazlitt took an instant dislike to him, a view that Mudford seems to have reciprocated, despite the warnings of their mutual friend Black, who had also joined the *Chronicle* staff. In the 17 September 1813 issue Mudford published an article bemoaning the decline of comedy in the contemporary theater. It was a weak effort, "a patchwork of random reflections, slack hypotheses, and untested theories," according to Stanley Jones.

Seeing his opportunity, Hazlitt shot off a long letter in the 25 September issue of the *Chronicle,* attacking Mudford's piece with devastating effect. Compelled to respond, Mudford replied weakly on 4 October, trying to retreat from his original position. On 15 October Hazlitt launched a powerful counterattack. James Perry, recognizing Hazlitt's abilities, decided to divide the duties of the drama critic between both men. By 1814, however, Mudford left the *Chronicle,* becoming the assistant editor of the *Courier.* Writing twenty years later in *The Canterbury Magazine* of September 1834, he still recalled Hazlitt with bitterness: "I knew the man well, and, besides having the greatest contempt for his turgid nothings and bombastic paradoxes (which passed for fine writing with some) I thoroughly disliked his cold artificial character, and his malignant disposition."

In its heyday the *Courier,* an evening paper, rivaled the *Times* in circulation and influence. It had begun in 1792 in the political and journalistic ferment around the French Revolution with distinct Jacobin sympathies. Daniel Stuart took control of the paper in 1796, shifting its political sympathies to the Tories. Supporting the policies of George Canning during his first turn as foreign minister (1807–1809) and his conduct of the war against Napoleon, the *Courier* became known as "Canning's *Courier.*" In 1809 Stuart turned control of the paper over to T. G. Street. Because of a split in the Tory Party, Canning had lost favor with the Ultra-Tory Street, who thereafter used the *Courier* to dog Canning.

Mudford, an old-school Tory in the spirit of Edmund Burke, continued Street's policy of attacking Canning when he became the editor of the paper in 1817. Matters reached a crisis in the winter of 1822 and 1823. The foreign office refused to provide any official information to the *Courier* on government policy. Mudford increased his attacks on Canning, who declared his belief that Mudford was in the pay of the French government. (Ironically, the French ambassador had dismissed Mudford in an 1817 report to Paris: "Mr. Mudford, the present editor, has none of Street's force, character or tal-

ent.") James Stuart, who still retained an interest in the paper, finally intervened, prevailing upon Mudford to relent in his criticism. With Mudford and Canning reconciled, the *Courier* again became a warm supporter during Canning's second stint as foreign minister (1823–1827).

During his tenure as the editor of the *Courier* Mudford enjoyed a period of personal success. He married and was known as a generous and convivial host with a wide circle of friends. He helped to found a glee club called The Melodist, which held its first meetings at his home. He also made the acquaintance of Coleridge, who had long held a professional relationship with Daniel Stuart, contributing articles and poems to the paper. When Stuart retired from the *Courier,* Mudford took over the liaison between the paper and the poet, soon becoming a friend and confidant. An exchange of letters between the two deals with Coleridge's course of philosophical lectures in 1818 and 1819 and his anxieties over matters of advertising, reviews, and attendance. Mudford also advised Coleridge on political matters, helping the poet with his 1818 pamphlet supporting Sir Robert Peel's bills opposing the Corn Laws and child labor. Mudford eventually published his correspondence with Coleridge in the September 1834 issue of *The Canterbury Magazine.*

Ever anxious to capitalize on opportunity, Mudford approached Arthur Wellesley, Duke of Wellington, with the proposal of writing a history of the campaign in the Netherlands and the battle of Waterloo. Wellington, who did not desire a history of the battle, rebuffed Mudford's offer with some irritation, much as he had earlier rebuffed John Wilson Croker's offer. Undeterred, Mudford persevered with the project, publishing *An Historical Account of the Campaign in the Netherlands in 1815, under His Grace the Duke of Wellington, and Marshal Prince Blücher* (1817) with illustrations by George Cruikshank. The book received little notice, though it gave Hazlitt yet another opportunity to direct a barb at both Mudford and Wellington. "Julius Caesar and Xenophon recorded their own acts with equal clearness of style and modesty of temper. The Duke of Wellington (worse off than Cromwell) is obliged to get Mr. Mudford to write the History of his life."

With the ascension of Wellington to prime minister in 1828, the Ultra-Tories sought to make the *Courier* the official instrument of the government. Arthur Aspinall notes that the Ultra-Tories judged Mudford to be "a very indifferent editor" and they prevailed upon the proprietors of the paper to replace him with Street on 30 January 1828. The following morning, Mudford responded with a letter published in the *Morning Chronicle,* accusing the government of pressuring the proprietors against him because of his support for the late Canning. "Something like a feeling of pride kindles in my bosom," declared Mudford, "at the reflection of my having become personally obnoxious, in any quarter, from the cause I have stated, while no one dared to hope I would render myself *acceptable,* by assailing him, dead, whom, living, I honoured."

Unemployed at the age of forty-six, a problem compounded by serious losses because of bad stock speculations, Mudford was forced to return to hackwork to support his now large family. In quick succession he wrote and published two more novels, *The Five Nights of St. Albans* and *The Premier* (1831). Inspired by some of the romances of Richard Cumberland, *The Five Nights of St. Albans,* a "Gothic grotesquerie" set in Elizabethan England, is probably Mudford's best novel, and it received favorable notice by John Gibson Lockhart in the October 1829 issue of *Blackwood's:* "we pronounce the writer of the Five Nights of St. Albans to be master of a vividly original and picturesque imagination, and of a truly masculine and energetic English style." Free of the "Cockney" enthusiasms that Lockhart despised in most contemporary fiction, the novel borders on satire. At about this time, Mudford was also invited by the conservative party of East Kent to edit the *Kentish Observer,* a provincial paper. Accepting the offer, he and his family moved to Canterbury, where he subsequently became proprietor of the paper. He also founded another periodical, *The Canterbury Magazine,* writing under the pseudonym Geoffrey Oldcastle.

At this time Mudford also began to publish short fiction in *Blackwood's.* The first was a series of seven "first and last" sketches. The tales in *Blackwood's,* as Wendell V. Harris observes, tend to fall into one of three types: the humorous story, the legend, or the narrative of some curious or exotic event in some foreign location. The plots are predictable, often formulaic, but move forward with smooth vigor to their inevitable conclusions. Tracing the development from the first time something happened to the last time it happened, Mudford's contributions exemplify the well-made *Blackwood's* tales.

The first sketch, "First and Last Dinner," originally appeared in the magazine in February 1829 and was published in *Stories from "Blackwood"* (1852). The story traces the annual progress of a group of twelve young men who vow to meet for an annual dinner until only one is left. The group dwindles over the years until the last survivor dies at what then becomes the last dinner. "With a feeble and re-

luctant grasp he took the 'frail memorial' of a youthful vow; and for a moment memory was faithful to her office. She threw open the long vista of buried years; and his heart travelled through them all: Their lusty and blithesome spring, – their bright and fervid summer, – their ripe and temperate autumn, – their chill, but not too frozen winter." Playing with this formula, Mudford generated six more such stories for *Blackwood's:* "First and Last Crime – James Morley" (March 1829), "The First and Last Appearance – Mr. Henry Augustus Constantine Stubbs" (April 1829), "The First and Last Kiss" (May 1829), "First and Last Love" (August 1829), "The First and Last Sacrifice" (September 1829), and "The First and Last Birthday" (November 1830). In all of these sketches Mudford was less interested in constructing a complex plot than in following the logic of the opening premises to their inevitable conclusions.

With the success of the "first and last" series, Mudford turned to short Gothic tales in the successful manner of *The Five Nights of St. Albans.* "Malavolti; a Neapolitan Story" appeared in the November 1829 issue of *Blackwood's* and was followed by "The Iron Shroud" in August of the next year. The latter is Mudford's most famous tale, if not necessarily his best, in part because of its influence on Poe. Vivenzio, the hero, finds himself imprisoned in an iron cell which daily shrinks in size. Where Poe was interested in exploring the psychology of the prisoner, eventually rescuing him from his fate, Mudford was more concerned with describing the ingeniousness of the cell and creating an unrelieved atmosphere of horror. "As he lay gathered up in lessened bulk," the story concludes, "the bell beat loud and frequent – crash succeeded crash – and on, and on, and on came the mysterious engine of death, till Vivenzio's smothered groans were heard no more! He was horribly crushed by the ponderous roof and collapsing sides – and the flattened bier was his *Iron Shroud.*"

Mudford also provided *Blackwood's* with reviews and political commentary written under the name "the silent member." Perhaps recalling his earlier dealings with Wellington and the Ultra-Tories, Mudford inaugurated the series in April 1830 with an evaluation of the duke's ministry, suggesting that much of his fame and success depended on the circumstances of history. "Had there been no French Revolution, Napoleon Bonaparte would have lived and died, probably, an officer of engineers. Had Napoleon never been Emperor of France, the Honourable Arthur Wellesley would now be only a general, with the colonelcy of a regiment." Venting his wrath, "the silent member" finally declares, "beyond all comparison the greatest military commander of this, or perhaps of any other age, he is equally beneath all comparison – as a statesman."

Some of Mudford's sketches, such as "Felix Binocular, A Legal Sketch" in the May 1831 *Fraser's* and "Nicolas Dunks; or Fried Mackerel for Dinner" in the September 1841 *Blackwood's* also took on the tone of political or social satire. Felix Binocular, for instance, is a lawyer who sees both sides of an issue and can move from one side to the other without the slightest sense of contradiction.

In the 1830s Mudford labored as the editor of both the *Kentish Observer* and *The Canterbury Magazine*. He continued to write essays, reviews, and tales for *Blackwood's* and occasionally published one of each in a single issue. In 1840 he published *Stephen Dugard*, his last novel. When Theodore Hook retired as the editor of the newspaper *John Bull* in 1841, Mudford was invited to succeed him and returned to London to take up the editorship, though he continued his association with the *Kentish Observer*.

At the time of his return to London Mudford published his final series of short tales that were probably inspired by the popular *Arabian Nights Entertainments*. In the "Ghost Gossips at Blakesley House" series of tales, which appeared in *Bentley's Miscellany*, a Christmas gathering provides the narrative frame for recounting ghost stories. Each installment of "Ghost Gossips" is linked by the repeated promise and deferral of the hostess to tell the story of the "Black Riband." Instead, each installment features ghost stories told by other members of the party. The first installment includes a pair of stories, "The Old Chest" and "The Screaming Woman" (May 1841), and features visitations by two ghosts, one benevolent and the other malevolent. The second pair, "Cromwell" and "Richard Warbeck" (June 1841), are stories of selling one's soul to the devil. The last tale, "The Banquet-Hall of Death" (March 1842), is an elaborate Gothic hoax, revolving around a dream.

It is not clear whether Mudford intended to end his Ghost Gossips series with "The Banquet-Hall of Death," or whether his new duties at the *John Bull* prevented him from continuing. One way or the other, he produced no more tales, and never revealed the mystery of the "Black Riband." The Ghost Gossips are in many ways Mudford's most satisfying tales, combining his mastery for creating atmosphere to produce an effective ghost story, with the comic juxtaposition of the narrative frame.

The last years of Mudford's life were marked by continuous labor in support of various conservative causes. His busy schedule and long years of effort, however, began to take their toll. Working late on an article that appeared in the 5 March 1848 issue of *John Bull*, attacking the new revolution in France, Mudford's health broke. Five days later, 10 March 1848, he died at the age of sixty-six, leaving a widow and eight children. Adding to the family's grief, the youngest child died of convulsions the following day.

William Mudford's achievement as a journalist was both direct and indirect. Not only was he known in his day as the able and hardworking editor of several periodicals, but his second son, William Heseltine Mudford, became a prominent journalist himself, editing the *Standard* for many years. Unfortunately, Mudford's success as a man of letters has largely become a footnote to William Hazlitt's career. It is in his achievement in short fiction, especially as the consummate master of the *Blackwood's* tale, that Mudford emerges from Hazlitt's caricature of the fat man made of "fleecy hosiery."

**References:**

Michael Allen, *Poe and the British Magazine Tradition* (New York: Oxford University Press, 1969);

Arthur Aspinall, *Politics and the Press, c. 1780–1850* (London: Home & Van Thal, 1949);

H. R. Fox Bourne, *English Newspapers: Chapters in the History of Journalism* (London: Chatto & Windus, 1887);

David Lee Clark, "The Sources of Poe's *The Pit and the Pendulum*," *Modern Language Notes*, 44 (June 1929): 349–356;

Wendell V. Harris, *British Short Fiction in the Nineteenth Century: A Literary and Bibliographic Guide* (Detroit: Wayne State University Press, 1979);

*The History of the Times: "The Thunderer" in the Making, 1785–1841* (New York: Macmillan, 1935);

Stanley Jones, *Hazlitt: A Life from Winterslow to Firth Street* (Oxford: Clarendon Press, 1989);

Stephen Koss, *The Rise and Fall of the Political Press in Britain* (Chapel Hill: University of North Carolina Press, 1981);

John Gibson Lockhart, "The Five Nights of St. Albans," *Blackwood's Edinburgh Magazine*, 26 (October 1829): 561–566;

William Maginn, *The Odoherty Papers*, 2 volumes, edited by Shelton Mackenzie (New York: Redfield, 1855);

"William Mudford," *Gentleman's Magazine*, 29 (June 1848): 665, 666.

# Caroline Norton

*(22 March 1808 – 15 June 1877)*

Kathryn Ledbetter
*Oklahoma Baptist University*

See also the Norton entry in *DLB 21: Victorian Novelists Before 1885.*

BOOKS: *The Sorrows of Rosalie: A Tale with Other Poems,* anonymous (London: Ebers, 1829; Boston: C. S. Francis, 1854);

*The Undying One and Other Poems* (London: Colburn & Bentley, 1830; Boston: Crosby, Nichols, 1854);

*Mrs. Norton's Story Book* (London: J. Harris, 1830);

*Poems* (Boston: Allen & Ticknor, 1833);

*The Coquette, and Other Tales and Sketches, in Prose and Verse,* 2 volumes (London: E. Churton, 1834); republished as *Kate Bouverie and Other Tales and Sketches in Prose and Verse* (Philadelphia: Carey & Hart, 1835);

*The Wife and Woman's Reward,* anonymous (3 volumes, London: Saunders & Otley, 1835; 1 volume, New York: Harper, 1835);

*A Voice from the Factories* (London: John Murray, 1836; Boston: Putnam, 1847);

*The Separation of Mother and Child by the Laws of "Custody of Infants" Considered,* anonymous (London: Roake & Varty, 1837);

*The Natural Claim of a Mother to the Custody of Her Child* (London: Privately printed, 1837);

*A Plain Letter to the Lord Chancellor on the Infant Custody Bill,* as Pearce Stevenson, Esq. (London: Ridgway, 1839; New York: Rogers, 1922);

*Lines (On the Young Queen Victoria)* (London: Saunders & Otley, 1840; Philadelphia: Carey & Hart, 1840);

*The Dream, and Other Poems* (London: Colburn, 1840; Philadelphia: Carey & Hart, 1841);

*The Child of the Islands: A Poem* (London: Chapman & Hall, 1845; New York: Francis, 1846);

*Aunt Carry's Ballads for Children: Adventures of a Wood Sprite; The Story of Blanche and Brutikin* (London: Cundall, 1847);

*Letters to the Mob,* as Libertas (London: Bosworth, 1848);

*Tales and Sketches, in Prose and Verse* (London: E. Churton, 1850);

*Caroline Norton*

*Stuart of Dunleath: A Story of Modern Times,* 3 volumes (London: Colburn, 1851; New York: Harper, 1851);

*English Laws for Women in the Nineteenth Century* (London: Privately printed, 1854);

*A Letter to the Queen on Lord Chancellor Cranworth's Marriage and Divorce Bill* (London: Longman, Brown, Green & Longmans, 1855);

*The Lady of La Garaye* (Cambridge & London: Macmillan, 1862; New York: Bradburn, 1864);

*Lost and Saved,* 3 volumes (London: Hurst & Blackett, 1863; Philadelphia: Lippincott, 1863);

*Old Sir Douglas,* 3 volumes (London: Hurst & Blackett, 1867; Philadelphia: Lippincott, 1867);

*Bingen on the Rhine* (Philadelphia: Porter & Coates, 1883; London: Walker, 1888).

PLAY PRODUCTION: *The Gypsy Father,* London, Covent Garden, May 1831.

OTHER: "Walter Errick," *Gem for 1830* (London: W. Marshall, 1829), pp. 29–44;

"Jane," *Gem for 1832* (London: W. Marshall, 1831), pp. 74–106;

"The Orphan, a Country Tale," in *Friendship's Offering for 1832* (London: Smith, Elder, 1831), pp. 150–175;

"Lawrence Bayley's Temptation," in *The Keepsake for 1834,* edited by Frederic Mansel Reynolds (London: Longman, Rees, Orme, Brown, Green & Longman, 1833), pp. 142–161;

"Count Rodolph's Heir," in *The Keepsake for 1836,* edited by Norton (London: Longman, Rees, Orme, Brown, Green & Longman, 1835), pp. 97–129;

"The Artist's Love," in *The Keepsake for 1836,* edited by Norton (London: Longman, Rees, Orme, Brown, Green & Longman, 1835), pp. 299–324;

"The Invalid: A Sketch," in *The Keepsake for 1840,* edited by Lady E. Stuart Wortley (London: Longman, Orme, Brown, Green, & Longmans, 1839), pp. 148–164;

Elizabeth Melville, *A Residence at Sierra Leone: Described from a Journal Kept on the Spot, and from Letters Written to Friends at Home,* edited by Norton (London: John Murray, 1849).

SELECTED PERIODICAL PUBLICATIONS – UNCOLLECTED: "Campbell of Spernie's Three Wives," *New Monthly Magazine,* 31 (January 1831): 33–41;

"Lucy Franklin," *New Monthly Magazine,* 31 (May 1831): 455–466;

"The Coffin-Maker," *New Monthly Magazine,* 34 (March 1832): 257–272.

Caroline Norton is often cited by feminist scholars for her role in the battle for women's rights in the nineteenth century. On her separation from her husband, George Norton, in 1836, she faced the shocking reality of a woman's powerlessness when she was denied the right to see her three children. She also lost her inheritance; copyright earnings from years of publication; her clothing, jewelry, letters, and other personal possessions; and her reputation. George Norton's suit against the prime min-

ister, William Lamb, Viscount Melbourne, for adultery was the biggest event in London for 1836 – the trial inspired Charles Dickens's "Bardell v. Pickwick" in *The Pickwick Papers* (1837), and Norton later became the model for the title character in George Meredith's *Diana of the Crossways* (1885) because of her involvement in political intrigue. She channeled her frustration and anger into tireless political lobbying, which resulted in the first feminist legislation to pass Parliament, the Infants' Custody Bill in 1839. Passed largely because of the prose pamphlets she published and circulated herself through influential friends, the bill granted child-custody rights to women, recognizing their legal existence for the first time. Norton also influenced the passage of the Marriage and Divorce Act of 1857, which protected a wife's earnings against the demands of her husband; a woman could finally support herself without fear that her husband would claim her money. Norton's role in these victories for women is well documented, but her prolific contribution as a writer of stories, poems, novels, and essays is often ignored. A complete reference guide to her work does not exist, and none of the existing bibliographies lists the many tales and stories she wrote for magazines and literary annuals.

The granddaughter of the playwright and politician Richard Brinsley Sheridan and his first wife, the singer Elizabeth Linley, Caroline Elizabeth Sarah Sheridan inherited beauty, wit, and talent from her celebrated family. Born on 22 March 1808, she was one of seven children of Thomas Sheridan and Caroline Henrietta Callandar Sheridan of Craigforth, Scotland; her mother was the anonymous author of *Carwell* (1832), *Aims and Ends* (1832), and other novels well known in her day. Like many of the Sheridans, Thomas suffered from poor health most of his life, and, searching for good weather for his breathing disorder, he took a post as colonial secretary at the Cape of Good Hope in 1813. The family was split by the move; her mother and older sister, Helen, went to the Cape, while she and her younger sister, Georgina, and brothers, Brinsley and Thomas, went to the homes of two unmarried aunts in Ardkinglass, Scotland.

Her father died on 12 September 1817, and her mother returned to Britain with Helen and two more children, Frank and Charles. Her mother's earnings from her novels were their major source of income, but Frederick, Duke of York, gave the family a private apartment at Hampton Court, where Caroline was raised in privileged splendor with children of the lesser aristocracy. Her uncle, Charles Sheridan, encouraged her to write; she and Helen often wrote poetry together and tried to publish a collection of their work. The Sheridan children were talented, talkative, and often in trouble; Caroline in particular was considered to be uncontrollable. At age fifteen she was sent away to boarding school at Shalford in Surrey, where the chief neighboring landowner was Fletcher Norton, Third Lord Grantley, of Wonersh Park. The pupils were invited to the home of Lord Grantley with their governess, and there Caroline met her future husband, George Chapple Norton, Lord Grantley's brother, when she was sixteen. His sister Augusta Norton, who wore bloomers and sported an Eton haircut, encouraged Caroline in her poetry and music. George Norton proposed marriage after speaking to Caroline only three times, even though his family was not pleased at his attraction to a woman with no dowry. Her mother, however, refused to consider the marriage until her daughter was older, and moved to temporary quarters at Great George Street, Westminster, so that her daughters could be introduced to London society.

Although Caroline had many admirers in London – including the poet Thomas Moore, who wrote that she was the prettiest of all the girls at the dances at Almack's in 1826 and later dedicated his poem "Summer Fete" to her – she was unsuccessful in finding a husband and feared being an old maid. Further influenced by her sister Helen's happy marriage to Capt. Price Blackwood of the Royal Navy, she consented to marry George Norton. The wedding took place on 30 July 1827 at St. George's, Hanover Square; she was nineteen years old, he was twenty-six. Their first home was his bachelor quarters at Garden Court in the Middle Temple; then finally a house at Storey's Gate, overlooking Birdcage Walk at St. James's Place. Her first book of poetry, *The Sorrows of Rosalie: A Tale with Other Poems* (1829), attracted the attention of such notable figures as Edward Bulwer-Lytton, Samuel Rogers, Benjamin Disraeli, Lord Melbourne, and the poet and actress Fanny Kemble, who described Norton in her *Records of a Girlhood* (1879) as looking "as if she were made of precious stones, diamonds, emeralds, rubies, sapphires; she is radiant with beauty." Many Victorian personalities thought it noteworthy to mention in their memoirs and letters that they had seen the stunning Mrs. Norton at parties in London. She and her sisters became known as the "Three Graces" of London society.

George Norton was a good-looking but slow-witted man. He had been elected to Parliament for Guildford as a Tory in 1826, but lost his seat in 1830. Caroline approached Lord Melbourne in an effort to acquire a position for her husband, who received a judgeship in the Lambeth division of the Metropolitan Police Courts at a salary of one thousand pounds a year – a job he would keep for the rest of his life. Her acquaintance with Melbourne grew into a friendship that would soon become the scandal of the decade.

George Norton began to resent his wife's beauty and talent; she resented his drinking, intellectual dullness, bad taste, and uncouth manners. Her relatives were terrified by his brutal temper, which was often aggravated by her quick tongue. Once he poured fuel over the writing materials on her desk and set them on fire to teach her not to oppose him. Although pregnancies were always difficult because of the violence she endured, she had three sons: Fletcher Spencer Conyers, born in 1829; Thomas Brinsley, born in 1831; and William Charles Chapple, born in 1833. In spite of her troubles she never lost her sense of humor, and the painful events in her life provided the background for most of her poetry and fiction.

The stormy relationship between Norton and her husband would last for the rest of their lives. After she left him in May 1836, the two fought over the management of their children; financial arrangements; and, before the Women's Property Act, which would allow her to keep the earnings from her writings, the copyrights of her books. In June 1836 he filed a ten-thousand-pound suit against Lord Melbourne for adulterous intentions; the sensational trial, in which Norton lost his suit, was seen by many as a Tory political ploy to unseat the prime minister. Meanwhile, Caroline Norton endured embarrassment, and later, attacks on her character by journalists who fabricated stories about her exploits with men.

George Norton took their children to Scotland, persisting with his temperamental power plays by keeping Caroline away from the sons she adored; she heard that they were flogged for attempting to answer her letters and that Brinsley was tied naked to a bedpost and whipped with a riding whip by his aunt Grace Menzies for defending his mother. In July 1842 William fell from a pony and received a scratch on his arm; because of the neglect of his caretakers he contracted blood poisoning, and he died in September. She was not notified of his illness until the family realized that his condition was worsening; by the time she arrived to see him he was dead. After this event George Norton allowed her to see the boys whenever she wished.

After the separation Norton lived with her brother Charles at Grosvenor Square, her uncle in Mayfair, and her mother at Hampton Court until she took a house in July 1845 on Chesterfield Street, where she lived alone for thirty years. From 1836 to 1842 she wrote pamphlets and lobbied passionately for the passage of legislation for women's rights. There was always much gossip about her; a woman living alone in London was unheard of unless she was up to something immoral, which everyone believed was true since she was always entertained by scores of men. She had many good male friends (gossip linked her with Sidney Herbert, the secretary of state at war during the Crimean War in the 1840s), but she was seldom romantically involved with them. In spite of the loss of her reputation, Norton continued an active social life, cultivating friendships – including one with Mary Wollstonecraft Shelley, who had first approached her for advice on how to get a pension for her father, William Godwin.

Norton was able to spend her remaining years in relative happiness since she could communicate with her surviving sons and enjoy her grandchildren. Fletcher went to Eton, then into diplomatic service at Lisbon in 1847. He had inherited the disease that had killed his grandfather and had to return to England in 1848, but he later became an attaché at Paris. In 1859 he was appointed secretary of legation at Athens, but he died in Paris on 13 October before he could assume his new duties. Thomas Brinsley, who was the author of an anonymous volume of verse published in 1856 and also wrote for the literary annuals, became the fourth Lord Grantley and married an Italian woman, Maria Chiara, against Norton's wishes. They had two children, Richard in 1855 and Carlotta in 1856.

Norton wrote tirelessly to support herself throughout her career – she once confessed to earning fourteen hundred pounds a year for her contributions to literary annuals. Both signed and anonymous essays, poetry, stories, and literary criticism appeared in ladies' magazines, contemporary periodicals, and annuals from 1830 to 1875. She edited *La Belle Assemblee and Court Magazine* from 1832 to 1834, *The English Annual* in 1834–1835, *The Keepsake* of 1836, and *Fisher's Drawing Room Scrap-Book* from 1846 to 1849. She frequently contributed poetry and stories to literary annuals during their heyday, including *Friendship's Offering* (1830, 1831, 1834), *The Keepsake* (1834, 1836, 1840), *The Literary Souvenir* (1830), *The Amulet* (1830), *The Gem* (1830, 1832), and *The Mignonette* (1856). In these annuals she is often confused with the Hon. Mrs. Erskine Norton of Rio de Janeiro, whose novel, *Altamont; or, The Charity Sister* (1852), is often incorrectly ascribed to her. Norton also wrote for *Fraser's,*

*New Monthly Magazine,* and *Macmillan's.* She wrote popular songs, many of which were republished several times in England and the United States; her biographer Jane Gray Perkins mentions fifty-five original song publications.

Critics often praised Norton's poetry. Reviewing her *The Dream, and Other Poems* (1840) in the September 1840 *Quarterly Review,* Hartley Coleridge called her the "Byron of our modern poetesses" and said that her sonnets were "worthy to be laid up in cedar with the best in our language." R. G. Horne compared her with Elizabeth Barrett Browning, writing that "there are few poems which would be more acceptable to the majority of lovers of poetry than Mrs. Norton's 'Dream.' " Her powerful political pamphlets appeared frequently, arguing for attention to social concerns such as child labor and women's issues. Although she never considered herself a feminist, Norton's pamphlets involving her concerns for women's rights were highly influential in parliamentary reform for women. Norton also wrote four novels, heavily autobiographical in nature, reflecting her tragic experiences with love and marriage. The novels contain many of the same themes that appear in her poetry as well as in her tales and stories. All of Norton's novels were well reviewed, and *Stuart of Dunleath: A Story of Modern Times* (1851), probably her most popular novel, went through at least five printings in London.

Norton's short fiction is difficult to catalogue because many of her stories were published anonymously, especially later in her life. They can often be identified, however, by their female heroes, who are rejected lovers, abandoned mothers, disillusioned wives, or innocent virgins embarking on their ruin by trusting foolish lovers. Men are crude, impatient, restless, unfaithful, manipulative, and fickle. For the woman, the future holds only the promise of more pain and an early death, sometimes from a broken heart. Acquisitive nineteenth-century society forces men and women into loveless unions that produce much heartache, and parental interference contributes to the chaos and confusion. Norton's stories rarely end happily because they are always about loves and marriages that hold, as in Norton's own marriage, no hope of contentment. Most of her fiction is to some degree autobiographical; many of the stories are overly didactic and melodramatic, but just as many are fascinating for their rich characterization and for Norton's bleak perspective, which makes her work seem to stand outside the ordinary line of domestic fiction, in which the predictable mating of middle to upper class is successful, and the reader's taste for a happy ending is satisfied.

Norton published two collections of stories, *The Coquette, and Other Tales and Sketches, in Prose and Verse* (1834) and *Tales and Sketches, in Prose and Verse* (1850). Both collections include much of the same material, works published in the *Court Magazine* from 1832 to 1834. The remainder of her short fiction was published in the literary annuals and *New Monthly Magazine.* The 1830s were the most prolific years of her writing career, even though during this time Norton was living with her abusive husband. From 1831 to 1836 she published eighteen stories, two collections of tales and poems, a novel, and a play and edited the *Court Magazine* and the *English Annual.*

One of her first short stories, "Campbell of Spernie's Three Wives," published in *New Monthly Magazine* in January 1831, is an epistolary warning to Campbell's cousin, who is about to be married. Campbell wants to give his cousin some friendly advice about marriage by recording his experiences with his wives. "Matrimony is little better than a snare; a spring-trap laid in our paths to disable us from liberty and enjoyment," he says, "and when you quoted my having changed my condition three several times, as an encouragement, it wrung my heart to think my reserve on the subject should so fearfully have misled you!" Campbell sets out to demonstrate how his wife's vanity, parental interference, and her love of London society kept her from being satisfied with his Scottish Highland ways at Spernie Castle.

After his first wife dies from a fever caught "attending a fancy ball," Campbell decides that his problem with Lady Charlotte was that she was too high in rank and station. He marries a barefoot Highland girl, Beenie: "I calculated that to *her,* at least, I must seem a superior being; that from *her* I should undergo no haughtiness, – be stung by no real or affected coldness." Unfortunately, Campbell is ashamed of Beenie's crude country ways. He marries his third wife to get a manager and housekeeper, but he is unhappy with the way she conducts their affairs. Campbell advises his cousin to "fly while it is yet in your power; do not, I beseech you, be so mistaken as to imagine that wit, wealth, beauty, sweetness of disposition, or mutual attachment, can promise a security of happiness . . . live, love, and die – a bachelor." The story parallels Norton's own Scottish relatives and is meant to be ironic and humorous, similar to Maria Edgeworth's *Castle Rackrent: An Hibernian Tale* (1800) in its self-effacing narrator. The story is alive with vivid and comic characterizations of Scottish lairds and shows Norton's talent with Scottish dialect. The narrator is humorous in his complaints about wives in this early story, but few of Norton's later tales joke about the misery of being married.

In "Kate Bouverie," first published in *Court Magazine* in 1832 and reprinted in *The Coquette,* Norton anticipates Charlotte Brontë's idea in *Jane Eyre* (1847) of the woman who chooses to be single rather than marry a man who wants to change her into something she is not. Kate is a free, natural soul who likes to race her spirited Arabian horse, Selim, across the countryside while her friends – the languishing Pamela, the conceited Annette, and the contemptuous Gertrude – watch jealously from inside the social circle. Harry, Kate's betrothed for a marriage arranged by her parents, is ashamed of her wildness, although she is graceful, honest, and beautiful. He marries a duke's daughter, who turns out to be spoiled and egotistical. Kate opts to be single the rest of her life, not wanting to be a "slave to the opinions of others"; yet she goes mad, becomes ill, and finally dies from a fall that kills both her and her magnificent horse. Harry comes to regret his foolishness in marrying a spoiled society girl and sees the genuine love he rejected from Kate, asking, "was it for such a heart, I scorned you?"

Norton's message to lovers in "Kate Bouverie" is to accept one another's special beauty, because trying to change another person is not only impossible, it sometimes has tragic consequences. She protests against parental interference and arranged marriages and attacks the middle class for its unreasonable concern for appearances. Kate becomes a model for the woman of the future: educated in more than painting and music, courageous, openly honest, and independent. However, Norton fails to reach too far into the future, for Kate's inability to live out her independence without collapsing into madness, sickness, and death indicates that the woman of Norton's world is yet doomed to be victimized by her fate of singleness.

Part of Norton's unique contributions as a writer are the observations she makes about London society; many of her stories are an education in ballroom customs. She knew firsthand how to use her beauty and wit to make influential friends at parties and balls. In "The Coquette," first published in *Court Magazine* in 1832 and reprinted in *The Coquette,* she takes this knowledge a step further to show the damage that can be done by flirting. Bessie Ashton, who has just announced her engagement to Lord Glenallan, enjoys the feeling of triumph she gets by encouraging men to believe she is interested in them. She is enchanted by the "spirit of coquetry," which, according to her scolding cousin, is to "traffic for compliments – to barter looks for words, and words for feelings," making everyone miserable for the gratification of her vanity.

Indeed, this becomes the "curse" of her existence, as her cousin George prophesies. For Bessie flirtation is an "envious thirst for power over the hearts of men." She wreaks havoc in innocent lives because of her meddling, but Norton's attack is not only on Bessie. Rather, Bessie is victimized by a society that empowers flirtation as one of the few sources of gratification for women whose beauty opens the door to success with men. She looks for men who can supply her with "diamonds and an Opera-box" and plans to continue her ways after her marriage, for it "would be so exceedingly ridiculous to fall in love with one's husband; it would look as if nobody else thought it worth his while to pay her any attention." Bessie learns her lesson the hard way, and the Victorian "angel of the house" takes her proper place at the end of the story, but Norton's attack remains as an echo of Mary Wollstonecraft's assertion in *A Vindication of the Rights of Woman* (1792) that women who use their femininity for a source of power are weak.

Not all of Norton's stories are about broken-hearted women and ill-fated love. First published in 1833 in *Court Magazine* and reprinted in *The Coquette*, "The Lost Election" is a political satire on elections, exposing the hypocrisy involved in campaigning for office. The story is a timely piece published during the controversy over the Reform Bill of 1832. The characters are comical and ironic, again much like those in Edgeworth's *Castle Rackrent*. As the candidates, some of whom Norton describes as "strongly resembling a family of large puppies with black and tan muzzles," shake hands, kiss babies, and patronize through the county, few of the residents know for whom or what they are voting, and relations with individual merchants go awry when the candidates cannot keep their promises straight.

In "Curious Customs in the County of Middlesex" the narrator, Mr. Charlton, observes the customs of Middlesex in three separate sketches, which were published in separate issues of *Court Magazine* in 1833. "Public Prints and Private Characters" attacks the powerful and potentially evil press. Norton had yet to realize the extent of this potential in 1833, but her sketch shows journalists to be vindictive and greedy for gossip. "Great Ladies and Little Ladies" shows how monetary value wins over moral worth, and "The Invisibility of London Husbands" returns to

*Drawing of Norton by Sir Edwin Landseer (from* The Dream, and Other Poems, *1840)*

Norton's familiar complaint against the institution of marriage and the emotional damage wrought when economics is used as a motivation for marriage. Her humorous experiment with satire is regrettable only because she so rarely wrote in this mode. The greater part of her fiction is sad and sometimes maudlin.

"The Coffin-Maker," published in *New Monthly Magazine* in March 1832, is a gloomy tale told by Tom Collins, a youth whose family comes upon hard times after their father dies and who is forced to accept employment as a coffin maker. The boy hates his work, but he continues because he wants to support his mother. As the hammer descends on the wood of the coffin he says, "I recalled some scene of sorrow and agony that I had witnessed in the day; and as the echo of some shriek or stifled moan struck in fancy on my ear, I would pause to wipe the dew from my brow and curse the trade of a coffin-maker." He begins to feel as if he is cursed and separated from society by imaginary evils as he watches the burials of loved ones whose coffins he has built. When he encloses a young woman who has been mistaken for dead in a coffin, she moans, but he opens the coffin too late; he takes the blame for her death. Predictably, there is no hope for a happy ending; Tom's wife dies from the excitement over the woman's mistaken death, and he continues to be a coffin maker, for, as he says, "what was death, or the pomp of death, to me afterwards?"

The story presents grotesque, bloody images that echo the fascination with death in horror literature. It also offers obvious opportunities for Freudian interpretations with Collins's relationship with his mother, who lives, while his wife and unborn child die. Death is common in Norton's fiction; it becomes the ultimate fate of most of her heroines, who often die from a broken heart (more frequently called "brain fever"). In "Lucy Franklin," published in *New Monthly Magazine* in May 1831 the narrator is Lucy's lover, Frederick, telling the tragic story of their ill-fated love from her grave, where he stands. He remembers how happy they were during their first year of marriage, but financial worry and weak character caused him to gamble and flirt while Lucy bore the burden of an irresponsible, uncaring husband, who eventually ran off to Paris with a married woman, scorning his "portionless village beauty."

Regrets come heavily, if not quickly, for Frederick, but Lucy dies on the morning of his return. Norton shows Frederick's egotism even in his hope of their reconciliation: "I pictured to myself Lucy reviving under my care and consolations; I vowed eternal constancy and devotedness to her; I figured her weeping on my bosom, and looking up, in the midst of tears, to bless my return." Although she dies from a broken heart, Lucy finally escapes the pain and degradation of life with such a man; death is a viable alternative to living hell.

First published in *Court Magazine* in 1832 and reprinted in *The Coquette,* "The Young Heir's Death Bed" is a short tale about the death of a young boy who was to inherit great wealth. Of the many people standing around the boy at his deathbed, only his mother grieves. The father, Lord Rothseaton, thinks of his hatred for the cousin who is the next heir; the physicians discuss the day's news; and the nurse worries about losing her job. Norton explains, "Sorrow has one thing in common with prosperity – it makes us selfish." But Lord Rothseaton goes beyond selfishness when he blames his wife for their son's death: "If you had taken more care of yourself," he says, "before your infant was born, instead of romping like a child, he might not have been dying now." The cruelty of a man toward his wife again becomes the dominant theme for Norton, but the patriarchal system must be regenerated, and the last line of the story comes from a guest in the house who reacts to the boy's death with " 'Indeed! pray who does the property go to!' " The sorrow of motherhood was something with which Norton was familiar.

"The Forsaken Child," published in *Court Magazine* in 1833 and reprinted in *The Coquette,* is a fictional account of a woman who betrays her motherhood and leaves her husband and son to marry another man. Lady Madeline Wentworth is an early representation of the "fallen woman," and the devastating price of her decision to leave a brutal husband for the hope of happiness is the death of her son and the loss of what Norton saw as woman's most sacred role, motherhood. Madeline's lover, Henry Marchmont, persuades her to run away with him by saying, "you would relinquish my love, and drag on a life of wretchedness for a vain shadow – the hope of devoted affection, from that little being whose first few years are all that ever can be yours." Norton might have been playing out the alternatives that were bothering her own conscience at the time.

As would happen to Norton, Madeline Wentworth finds no relief from the remorse she feels as she watches her son grow up through accounts in the newspapers. One story tells of a nurse dropping her child onto the pavement at a horse show – almost a premonition of Norton's son William's fall from his pony. Madeline's Frank has a stepmother; Norton's children would be under the control of an abusive aunt and George Norton's live-in lover. Madeline has two other children by her new husband, although they are spoiled and grow up to be ashamed of her past. The example of Madeline Wentworth explores Norton's worst fears about abandoning her children; she knew that the law would not allow visitation, and she knew her husband would try to deny her rights as a mother if she left.

One of Norton's best short works was published in *The Keepsake* in 1835. In "Count Rodolph's Heir" Leona, the Italian mistress of a landowner, is displaced when her lover, Count Rodolph, is pressured by his uncle into marrying a wealthy heiress. Rather than return to Italy to live with her mother, who has been shamed by her daughter's living arrangements, Leona moves into a ruined castle on Rodolph's property, haunts his wedding by giving the bride a bouquet of poisonous plants, and curses Rodolph's future heir as her enemy – and indeed, both of the couple's children die. Leona goes mad and cries for the return of her lost love from the depths of the eerie castle, and the count realizes too late that losing the woman he loved was a grave error. Rodolph's submission to parental demands that he protect his family name and reputation by marrying a moneyed woman has kept both Leona and Rodolph from having the ideal, loving relationship meant for man and woman. Parental interference has drastic results, and the lack of financial independence for women often causes them to retreat to despair in a sanctuary of madness. The tense Gothic melodrama in "Count Rodolph's Heir" is reminiscent of Ann Radcliffe's exciting novels from earlier in the century, and Norton's madwoman predates the familiar image found in later novels such as *Jane Eyre*.

Norton's work has been criticized for being oversentimental. One reviewer wrote in *Temple Bar* (1878), "The chief fault of these works is the melancholy tone which pervades them, which is apt to depress the readers, and make them rise more wearied and dismal than when they opened the book, which is obviously a mistake, as the essential object of fiction should be not exactly mere amusement, but an interesting relaxation of the mind." Yet readers enjoyed Norton's melancholy tone enough to make her a professional writer highly in demand by many Victorian periodicals and literary annuals for most of her life. She was a career woman before women had careers, and the sheer volume of her output indicates that she was driven by more than mere financial need: much of her income was stolen by her husband, and many women would prefer not to write rather than have a man they despised take the rewards of their labor. Norton's creative energy was as unstoppable as her desire to enjoy life in spite of her troubles.

There is much to learn about love and marriage, London society, and women's rights in the Victorian period from Norton's fiction and poetry. Her status among the writers of the nineteenth century may never be more than minor, but she deserves critical recognition because of her artful portrayal of women in love and because her readers, in their demand for her "melancholy tone," themselves identified with her pain as an oppressed woman.

Norton found a few months of happiness as a wife when, after George Norton's death in 1875, she was able to marry a friend, the scholar Sir William Stirling-Maxwell of Kier. The wedding took place in her drawing room at Chesterfield Street on 1 March 1877, when she was sixty-eight. She records her happiness in a letter dated 4 March: "It is now *twentynine* years since my husband and I were first knit in friendship – and no Bride of blooming years – marrying for enamoured love – ever signed her new name with more satisfied trust in the goodness and affection of the man who bestows it,

than I do." She died on 15 June, followed by her remaining son, Brinsley, on 24 July and by Stirling-Maxwell, from a fever he contracted in Venice, in January 1878.

**Letters:**

A. I. Macnaghten, "Some Unrecorded Letters," *Notes and Queries,* 194 (8 January 1949): 6–12; (22 January 1949): 32–35; (5 February 1949): 51–55; (5 March 1949): 99–103;

"Some Unrecorded Letters," *Notes and Queries,* 17 (September 1970): 335–339;

*The Letters of Caroline Norton to Lord Melbourne,* edited by James O. Hoge and Clarke Olney (Columbus: Ohio State University Press, 1974).

**Biographies:**

Percy Fitzgerald, *The Lives of the Sheridans,* 2 volumes (London: Bentley, 1886);

Jane Gray Perkins, *The Life of the Honourable Mrs. Norton* (New York: Holt, 1909);

Alice Ackland, *Caroline Norton* (London: Constable, 1948).

**References:**

Margaret Forster, *Significant Sisters: The Grassroots of Active Feminism 1839–1939* (London: Secker & Warburg, 1984);

R. G. Horne, *A New Spirit of the Age,* 2 volumes (London: Smith, Elder, 1844);

Clarke Olney, "Caroline Norton to Lord Melbourne," *Victorian Studies,* 8 (March 1965): 255–262;

Sylvia Bailey Shurbutt, "The Popular Fiction of Caroline Sheridan Norton: The Woman Question and the Theme of Manipulation," *Studies in Popular Culture,* 9, no. 2 (1986): 24–40;

Dorothy E. Zaborsky, " 'Domestic Anarchy and the Destruction of the Family': Caroline Norton and the Custody of Infants Bill," *International Journal of Women's Studies,* 7 (November–December 1984): 397–411.

**Papers:**

Many of Caroline Norton's letters, private papers, and manuscripts can be found in the Altschul Collection at Yale University and at Harvard University; the British Library; the Pierpont Morgan Library, New York; and the Huntington Library, San Marino, California.

# Margaret Oliphant

## (4 April 1828 – 25 June 1897)

### Mary Lou Fisk
*University of New Mexico*

See also the Oliphant entry in *DLB 18: Victorian Novelists After 1885.*

BOOKS: *Passages in the Life of Mrs. Margaret Maitland, of Sunnyside, Written by Herself* (3 volumes, London: Colburn, 1849; 1 volume, New York: Appleton, 1851);

*Merkland: A Story of Scottish Life,* 3 volumes (London: Colburn, 1851 [i.e., 1850]); republished as *Merkland, or Self-Sacrifice,* 1 volume (New York: Stringer & Townsend, 1854);

*Caleb Field: A Tale of the Puritans* (London: Colburn, 1851; New York: Harper, 1851);

*Memoirs and Resolutions of Adam Graeme of Mossgray* (3 volumes, London: Colburn, 1852; 1 volume, New York: Munro, 1885);

*Katie Stewart* (New York: Harper, 1852; Edinburgh & London: Blackwood, 1853);

*Harry Muir: A Story of Scottish Life* (3 volumes, London: Hurst & Blackett, 1853; 1 volume, New York: Appleton, 1853);

*The Quiet Heart: A Story* (Edinburgh & London: Blackwood, 1854; New York: Harper, 1854);

*Magdelen Hepburn: A Story of the Scottish Reformation* (3 volumes, London: Hurst & Blackett, 1854; 1 volume, New York: Riker, Thorne, 1854);

*Lilliesleaf, Being a Concluding Series of Passages in the Life of Mrs. Margaret Maitland, of Sunnyside. Written by Herself,* anonymous (3 volumes, London: Hurst & Blackett, 1855; 1 volume, Boston: Burnham, 1862);

*Zaidee, A Romance* (3 volumes, Edinburgh & London: Blackwood, 1856; 1 volume, Boston: Jewett, 1856);

*The Athelings; or, The Three Gifts* (3 volumes, Edinburgh & London: Blackwood, 1857; 1 volume, New York: Harper, 1857);

*The Days of My Life: An Autobiography* (3 volumes, London: Hurst & Blackett, 1857; 1 volume, New York: Harper, 1857);

*Sundays* (London: Nisbett, 1858);

*Margaret Oliphant (photograph by H. L. Mendelssohn)*

*The Laird of Norlaw: A Scottish Story,* anonymous (3 volumes, London: Hurst & Blackett, 1858; 1 volume, New York: Harper, 1859);

*Orphans: A Chapter in Life* (London: Hurst & Blackett, 1858; New York: Munro, 1880);

*Agnes Hopetoun's Schools and Holidays* (London: Macmillan, 1859; Boston: Gould & Lincoln, 1859);

*Lucy Crofton,* anonymous (London: Hurst & Blackett, 1860 [i.e., 1859]; New York: Harper, 1860);

*The House on the Moor,* anonymous (3 volumes, London: Hurst & Blackett, 1861; 1 volume, New York: Harper, 1861);

*The Last of the Mortimers: A Story in Two Voices,* anonymous (3 volumes, London: Hurst & Blackett, 1862; 1 volume, New York: Harper, 1862);

*The Life of Edward Irving, Minister of the National Scotch Church, London* (2 volumes, London: Hurst & Blackett, 1862; 1 volume, New York: Harper, 1862);

*The Chronicles of Carlingford* (Boston: Littell, 1862?) — comprises "The Rector," "The Executor," and "The Doctor's Family"; republished, without "The Executor," as *The Rector; and The Doctor's Family,* anonymous, 3 volumes (Edinburgh & London: Blackwood, 1863);

*Heart and Cross* (London: Hurst & Blackett, 1863; New York: Gregory, 1863);

*Salem Chapel,* anonymous (2 volumes, Edinburgh & London: Blackwood, 1863);

*The Perpetual Curate,* anonymous (3 volumes, Edinburgh & London: Blackwood, 1864; 1 volume, New York: Harper, 1865);

*Agnes* (3 volumes, London: Hurst & Blackett, 1866 [i.e., 1865]; 1 volume, New York: Harper, 1866);

*A Son of the Soil* (New York: Harper, 1865; 2 volumes, London: Macmillan, 1866);

*Miss Marjoribanks,* anonymous (3 volumes, Edinburgh & London: Blackwood, 1866; 1 volume, Boston: Littell & Gay, 1866);

*Madonna Mary* (New York: Harper, 1866; 3 volumes, London: Hurst & Blackett, 1867);

*The Brownlows* (3 volumes, Edinburgh & London: Blackwood, 1868; 1 volume, New York: Harper, 1868);

*Francis of Assisi* (London: Macmillan, 1868; London & New York: Macmillan, 1888);

*Historical Sketches of the Reign of George II* (2 volumes, Edinburgh & London: Blackwood, 1869; 1 volume, Boston: Littell & Gay, 1869);

*The Minister's Wife* (3 volumes, London: Hurst & Blackett, 1869; 1 volume, New York: Harper, 1869);

*John, a Love Story* (2 volumes, Edinburgh & London: Blackwood, 1870; 1 volume, New York: Harper, 1870);

*The Three Brothers* (3 volumes, London: Hurst & Blackett, 1870; 1 volume, New York: Appleton, 1870);

*Squire Arden* (3 volumes, London: Hurst & Blackett, 1871; 1 volume, New York: Harper, 1874);

*At His Gates* (3 volumes, London: Tinsley, 1872; 1 volume, New York: Scribners, Armstrong, 1873);

*Ombra* (3 volumes, London: Hurst & Blackett, 1872; 1 volume, New York: Harper, 1872);

*Memoir of Count de Montalembert: A Chapter of Recent French History,* 2 volumes (Edinburgh & London: Blackwood, 1872);

*May* (3 volumes, London: Hurst & Blackett, 1873; 1 volume, New York: Scribners, Armstrong, 1873);

*Innocent: A Tale of Modern Life* (3 volumes, London: Low, Marston, Low & Searle, 1873; 1 volume, New York: Harper, 1873);

*A Rose in June* (Boston: Osgood, 1874; 2 volumes, London: Hurst & Blackett, 1874);

*For Love and Life* (3 volumes, London: Hurst & Blackett, 1874; 1 volume, New York: Munro, 1879);

*Whiteladies* (3 volumes, London: Tinsley, 1874; 1 volume, New York: Holt, 1875);

*The Story of Valentine and His Brother* (3 volumes, Edinburgh & London: Blackwood, 1875; 1 volume, New York: Harper, 1875);

*The Curate in Charge* (2 volumes, London: Macmillan, 1876; 1 volume, New York: Harper, 1876);

*An Odd Couple* (Philadelphia: Porter & Coates, 1876);

*Phoebe, Junior: A Last Chronicle of Carlingford,* anonymous (3 volumes, London: Hurst & Blackett, 1876; 1 volume, New York: Harper, 1876);

*Dress* (London: Macmillan, 1876; Philadelphia: Porter & Coates, 1879);

*The Makers of Florence: Dante, Giotto, Savonarola; and Their City* (London: Macmillan, 1876; London & New York: Macmillan, 1878);

*Dante* (Edinburgh & London: Blackwood, 1877; Philadelphia: Lippincott, 1877);

*Carità* (3 volumes, London: Smith, Elder, 1877; 1 volume, New York: Harper, 1877);

*Young Musgrave* (3 volumes, London: Macmillan, 1877; 1 volume, New York: Harper, 1878);

*Mrs. Arthur* (3 volumes, London: Hurst & Blackett, 1877; 1 volume, New York: Harper, 1877);

*The Primrose Path: A Chapter Annals of the Kingdom of Fife* (3 volumes, London: Hurst & Blackett, 1878; 1 volume, New York: Harper, 1878);

*Molière,* by Oliphant and F. B. C. Tarver (Edinburgh & London: Blackwood, 1879; Philadelphia: Lippincott, 1879);

*Within the Precincts* (3 volumes, London: Smith, Elder, 1879; 1 volume, New York: Harper, 1879);

*The Greatest Heiress in England* (3 volumes, London: Hurst & Blackett, 1879; 1 volume, New York: Harper, 1880);

*The Fugitives: A Story* (New York: Harper, 1879);

*A Beleaguered City, Being a Narrative of Certain Recent Events in the City of Semur* (New York: Munro, 1879; London: Macmillan, 1880);

*He That Will Not when He May* (3 volumes, London: Macmillan, 1880; 1 volume, New York: Harper, 1880);

*Cervantes* (Edinburgh & London: Blackwood, 1880; Philadelphia: Lippincott, 1881);

*Harry Joscelyn* (3 volumes, London: Hurst & Blackett, 1881; 1 volume, New York: Harper, 1881);

*In Trust: The Story of a Lady and Her Lover* (New York: Munro, 1881; 3 volumes, London: Longmans, Green, 1882);

*The Literary History of England in the End of the Eighteenth and Beginning of the Nineteenth Century* (3 volumes, London: Macmillan, 1882; 1 volume, New York: Macmillan, 1882);

*A Little Pilgrim in the Unseen* (London: Macmillan, 1882; Boston: Roberts, 1882);

*The Duke's Daughter* (New York: Munro, 1882); enlarged as *The Duke's Daughter; and, The Fugitives*, 3 volumes (Edinburgh & London: Blackwood, 1890);

*Sheridan* (London: Macmillan, 1883; New York: Harper, 1883);

*The Ladies Lindores* (3 volumes, Edinburgh & London: Blackwood, 1883; 1 volume, New York: Harper, 1883);

*It Was a Lover and His Lass* (3 volumes, London: Hurst & Blackett, 1883; 1 volume, New York: Harper, 1883);

*Hester: A Story of a Contemporary Life* (3 volumes, London: Macmillan, 1883; 1 volume, New York: Macmillan, 1883);

*Sir Tom* (New York: Harper, 1883; 3 volumes, London: Macmillan, 1884);

*The Lady's Walk: A Tale* (New York: Munro, 1883; London: Methuen, 1897);

*The Wizard's Son* (3 volumes, London: Macmillan, 1884; 1 volume, New York: Lovell, 1884);

*Madam* (New York: Harper, 1884; 3 volumes, London: Longmans, Green, 1885);

*Two Stories of the Seen and the Unseen* (Edinburgh & London: Blackwood, 1885) — comprises "Old Lady Mary," "The Open Door";

*Oliver's Bride: A New Novel* (New York: Munro, 1885); revised and enlarged as *Oliver's Bride: A True Story* (London: Ward & Downey, 1886);

*Two Prodigals and Their Inheritance* (New York: Munro, 1885; 2 volumes, London: Methuen, 1894);

*A Country Gentleman and His Family* (3 volumes, London: Macmillan, 1886; 1 volume, New York: Macmillan, 1886);

*Effie Ogilvie: The Story of a Young Life* (2 volumes, Glasgow: Maclehose, 1886; 1 volume, New York: Harper, 1886);

*A House Divided against Itself* (3 volumes, Edinburgh & London: Blackwood, 1886; 1 volume, New York: Harper, 1886);

*The Son of His Father* (New York: Harper, 1886; 3 volumes, London: Hurst & Blackett, 1887);

*A Poor Gentleman* (New York: Munro, 1886; 3 volumes, London: Hurst & Blackett, 1889);

*The Makers of Venice: Doges, Conquerors, Painters, and Men of Letters* (London & New York: Macmillan, 1887);

*Joyce* (3 volumes, London: Macmillan, 1888; 1 volume, New York: Harper, 1888);

*The Second Son,* by Oliphant and Thomas Bailey Aldrich (3 volumes, London: Macmillan, 1888; 1 volume, Boston & New York: Houghton, Mifflin, 1888);

*Memoir of the Life of John Tulloch* (Edinburgh & London: Blackwood, 1888);

*Cousin Mary* (London: Partridge, 1888);

*The Land of Darkness, along with Some Further Chapters in the Experience of the Little Pilgrim* (London & New York: Macmillan, 1888) — comprises "The Land of Darkness," "On the Dark Mountains," "The Little Pilgrim in the Seen and Unseen";

*Neighbours on the Green: A Collection of Stories,* 3 volumes (London & New York: Macmillan, 1889) — comprises "My Neighbour Nelly," "Lady Denzil," "The Stockbroker at Dinglewood," "The Scientific Gentleman," "Lady Isabella," "An Elderly Romance," "Mrs. Merridew's Fortune," "The Barley Mow," "My Faithful Johnny";

*Lady Car: The Sequel of a Life* (London: Longmans, Green, 1889; New York: Harper, 1889);

*Grove Road, Hampstead* (New York: Munro, 1889); enlarged as *The Two Marys and Grove Road, Hampstead* (London: Methuen, 1896);

*Stories of the Seen and Unseen* (Boston: Roberts, 1889) — comprises "A Little Pilgrim," "The Little Pilgrim: Further Experiences," "Old Lady Mary," "The Open Door," "The Portrait"; (Edinburgh & London: Blackwood, 1902) — comprises "The Open Door," "Old Lady Mary," "The Portrait," "The Library Window";

*Kirsteen: A Story of a Scottish Family Seventy Years Ago* (3 volumes, London: Macmillan, 1890; 1 volume, New York: Harper, 1890);

*Sons and Daughters* (Edinburgh & London: Blackwood, 1890);

*Royal Edinburgh: Her Saints, Kings, Prophets, and Poets* (London: Macmillan, 1890; New York: Mershon, 1890);

*The Mystery of Mrs. Blencarrow* (London: Blackett, 1890; Chicago: Donohue, Henneberry, 1894);

*The Railway Man and His Children* (3 volumes, London: Macmillan, 1891; 1 volume, New York: Lovell, 1891);

*Janet,* 3 volumes (London: Hurst & Blackett, 1891); republished as *The Story of a Governess* (New York: Fenno, 1895);

*Jerusalem: Its History and Hope* (London & New York: Macmillan, 1891);

*Memoir of the Life of Laurence Oliphant and of Alice Oliphant, His Wife,* 2 volumes (Edinburgh & London: Blackwood, 1891; New York: Harper, 1891);

*The Heir Presumptive and the Heir Apparent* (New York: Lovell, 1891; 3 volumes, London: Macmillan, 1892);

*The Marriage of Elinor* (New York: United States Book, 1891; 3 volumes, London: Macmillan, 1892);

*The Cuckoo in the Nest* (3 volumes, London: Hutchinson, 1892; 1 volume, New York & Chicago: United States Book, 1892);

*Diana Trelawney: The History of a Great Mistake,* 2 volumes (Edinburgh & London: Blackwood, 1892); republished as *Diana: The History of a Great Mistake* (New York & Chicago: United States Book, 1892);

*The Victorian Age of English Literature,* by Oliphant and F. R. Oliphant, 2 volumes (London: Percival, 1892; New York: Dodd, Mead, 1892);

*Lady William* (3 volumes, London: Macmillan, 1893; 1 volume, New York: Macmillan, 1893);

*The Sorceress* (3 volumes, London: White, 1893; 1 volume, New York: Taylor, 1893);

*Thomas Chalmers, Preacher, Philosopher, and Statesman* (London: Methuen, 1893; Boston & New York: Houghton, Mifflin, 1893);

*A House in Bloomsbury* (2 volumes, London: Hutchinson, 1894; 1 volume, New York: Dodd, Mead, 1894);

*Historical Characters of the Reign of Queen Anne* (New York: Century, 1894);

*Who Was Lost and Is Found* (Edinburgh & London: Blackwood, 1894; New York: Harper, 1895);

*Two Strangers* (London: Unwin, 1894; New York: Fenno, 1895);

*Sir Robert's Fortune: The Story of a Scotch Moor* (New York: Harper, 1894; London: Methuen, 1895);

*A Child's History of Scotland* (London: Unwin, 1895);

*"Dies Irae": The Story of a Spirit in Prison* (Edinburgh & London: Blackwood, 1895);

*The Makers of Modern Rome* (London & New York: Macmillan, 1895);

*Old Mr. Tredgold: A Story of Two Sisters* (New York: Longmans, 1895); republished as *Old Mr. Tredgold* (London: Longmans, 1896);

*Jeanne d'Arc: Her Life and Death* (London & New York: Putnam, 1896);

*The Unjust Steward; or, the Minister's Debt* (London & Edinburgh: Chambers, 1896; Philadelphia: Lippincott, 1896);

*Annals of a Publishing House: William Blackwood and His Sons, Their Magazine and Friends* (2 volumes, Edinburgh & London: Blackwood, 1897; 3 volumes, New York: Scribners, 1897–1898);

*The Ways of Life, Two Stories* (London: Smith, Elder, 1897; New York & London: Putnam, 1897) — comprises "Mr. Sanford," "The Strange Story of Robert Dalyell";

*A Widow's Tale, and Other Stories,* introduction by J. M. Barrie (Edinburgh & London: Blackwood, 1898; New York: Fenno, 1898) — comprises "A Widow's Tale," "Queen Eleanor and Fair Rosamond," "Mademoiselle," "The Lily and the Thorn," "The Strange Adventures of John Percival," "A Story of a Wedding-Tour," "John," "The Whirl of Youth," "The Heirs of Kellie";

*That Little Cutty. Dr. Barrère. Isabel Dysart* (London & New York: Macmillan, 1898);

*The Autobiography and Letters of Mrs. O. W. Oliphant,* edited by Mrs. Harry Coghill (Edinburgh & London: Blackwood, 1899; New York: Dodd, Mead, 1899);

*Queen Victoria: A Personal Sketch* (London: Cassell, 1901).

**Editions:** *Selected Short Stories of the Supernatural by Margaret Oliphant,* edited by Margaret Gray, Association for Scottish Literary Studies (Edinburgh: Scottish Academic Press, 1985);

*A Beleaguered City and Other Stories,* edited by Merryn Williams (Oxford & New York: Oxford University Press, 1988).

**OTHER:** "John Rintoul," in *Tales from Blackwood,* First Series, volume 11 (Edinburgh & London: Blackwood, 1860);

"The Secret Chamber," in *Tales from Blackwood,* Second Series, volume 1 (Edinburgh & London: Blackwood, 1878);

"A Railway Junction," in *Tales from Blackwood,* Second Series, volume 4 (Edinburgh & London: Blackwood, 1878);

"The Two Mrs. Scudmores," in *Tales from Blackwood,* Second Series, volume 7 (Edinburgh & London: Blackwood, 1879);

"Witcherly Ways: A Christmas Tale," in *Tales from Blackwood,* Second Series, volume 10 (Edinburgh & London: Blackwood, 1879).

SELECTED PERIODICAL PUBLICATIONS –
UNCOLLECTED:
FICTION

"The Executor," *Blackwood's Edinburgh Magazine,* 89 (May 1861): 595–614;

"Earthbound," *Fraser's Magazine,* old series 101, new series 21 (January 1880): 118–144;

"A Visitor and His Opinions," *Blackwood's Edinburgh Magazine,* 153 (April 1893): 481–511;

"The Land of Suspense," *Blackwood's Edinburgh Magazine,* 161 (January 1897): 131–157.

NONFICTION

"The Laws Concerning Women," *Blackwood's Edinburgh Magazine,* 79 (April 1856): 379–387;

"The Condition of Women," *Blackwood's Edinburgh Magazine,* 83 (February 1858): 139–154;

"Sensation Novels," *Blackwood's Edinburgh Magazine,* 91 (May 1862): 564–584;

"The Great Unrepresented," *Blackwood's Edinburgh Magazine,* 100 (September 1866): 367–379;

"The Grievances of Women," *Fraser's Magazine,* old series 101, new series 21 (May 1880): 698–710;

"Fancies of a Believer," *Blackwood's Edinburgh Magazine,* 157 (February 1895): 237–255;

"The Anti-Marriage League," *Blackwood's Edinburgh Magazine,* 159 (January 1896): 135–149.

Even though she was Queen Victoria's favorite novelist, by the end of the nineteenth century Margaret Oliphant had disappeared into the land of the unknown and unread. Her banishment into the critical wilderness was due in part to her prodigious production – at least ninety-eight novels; many travel books, histories, and biographies; more than fifty short stories; and at least four hundred periodical essays – a pace, established as early as 1860, that suggested to her critics, and perhaps to Oliphant herself, that she was, as she reports in her autobiography (1899), "working too fast and producing too much." Her comment in a 6 October 1896

letter to the publisher William Blackwood that "I have worked a hole in my right forefinger – with the pen, I suppose – and can't get it to heal," is often cited as evidence of her unremitting industry. Oliphant did little to alter this perception of her work; her autobiography alternates between justifying its quantity and disparaging its value.

Recently she has had a modest resurgence in popularity, due primarily to her best-known series, the Chronicles of Carlingford. These novels reveal Oliphant at her best, engaging in a finely tuned irony focused on social conventions and on the complex relationships between men and women and between the clergy and the laity. Modern critics also recognize that her uncharacteristic heroines, endowed with strong, if not always lovable, personalities and powerful needs for their own self-fulfillment, seriously question Victorian stereotypes of women.

Oliphant's tendency to pad her stories to fill out a standard Victorian three-volume novel has been a major criticism of her longer works and has resulted in a heightened appreciation of her shorter fiction pieces. As early as 1883 John Skelton noted that the plots of her novels often ran out before the three volumes were filled; therefore, "considered simply as the story-teller, she is at her best, I think, in her shorter tales." Her biographer Merryn Williams observes that "some of her short stories are as good as any in the English language, if only because she did not pad them out." Her more tightly written short-fiction pieces still reveal her characteristic wit and irony and must be considered a significant segment of the Oliphant canon.

In these works Oliphant explores relationships between the individual and the community, between two individuals, between the artist and his or her work, and between the natural and supernatural worlds. In many stories more than one kind of relationship is explored and developed. Scottish or English society provides the warp through which she weaves her stories.

Margaret Oliphant Wilson was born on 4 April 1828 in Wallyford, Scotland. She was the youngest child and the only daughter of the three children of Francis and Margaret Oliphant Wilson who survived infancy. She came from a family of Dissenters who belonged to the Free Church of Scotland, and this background helped her to sympathize with, if not always understand, the dilemma facing Dissenting clergymen, an issue she would often explore in her fiction. The family moved to Glasgow in 1834. When Wilson was ten, her father took a position in the Liverpool customs house. He was a shadowy figure in her life, and her zest for reading and learning probably came from her mother; her autobiography makes no mention of formal education. Her first novel, a juvenile effort written to pass the time while she sat by the bed of her sick mother, was never published; *Passages in the Life of Mrs. Margaret Maitland, of Sunnyside, Written by Herself* (1849), her first published work, appeared when she was twenty-one.

In 1852, with the serial publication of her novel *Katie Stewart,* she began what was to be a life-long association with *Blackwood's Edinburgh Magazine.* Oliphant's contributions to the magazine expanded from serialized novels to travel pieces, historical evaluations, literary reviews, and short fiction.

Wilson married her cousin, Frank Oliphant, on 4 May 1852. They settled in London, where Frank established a studio for his work in stained glass. In London, Margaret Oliphant gave birth to five children, only two of whom, Maggie and Cyril, survived infancy. Frank's tuberculosis necessitated a move to Italy in 1859; but the change of climate did not alter the course of the illness, and he died in Rome in October of the same year. Their last child, Francis ("Cecco"), was born in December. Oliphant was young, alone, in a foreign country, £1,000 in debt, and with three children to support. An attack of writer's block exacerbated her emotional and financial woes. She and her children returned to Britain in 1860, settling in Edinburgh and moving the next year to Ealing in England.

She overcame at least her financial and artistic hurdles in 1861 by launching her successful fiction series, the Chronicles of Carlingford, in *Blackwood's* with three short pieces: "The Executor" in May, "The Rector" in September, and the novella "The Doctor's Family" from October to January 1862. These works established a recurring pattern for Oliphant of using writing to compensate for personal losses and worries; some of her best work appeared at the most sorrowful and hopeless periods of her life.

With the appearance of these stories, Oliphant found her voice; and although the balance of the series was made up of novels, the audience for it was created and captured with the shorter works that introduced it. Williams calls "The Doctor's Family" "one of the best short novels in English." Oliphant's earlier biographers, Vineta and Robert A. Colby, observe that these three works were not the result of "a sudden flash of inspiration" but were "simply the culmination of a gradual development and maturing of her talent." Oliphant was always aware of

her literary reputation, ironically observing in her autobiography that the Chronicles of Carlingford made her "*almost*" but not quite "one of the popularities of literature."

"The Executor" and "The Doctor's Family" are part of the series only because the stories are set in Carlingford. The characters do not appear again in the four novels that comprise the series – *Salem Chapel* (1863), *The Perpetual Curate* (1864), *Miss Marjoribanks* (1866), and *Phoebe, Junior: A Last Chronicle of Carlingford* (1876) – and "The Executor" was rewritten and expanded into the 1868 novel *The Brownlows.* "The Rector" does, however, provide an excellent introduction to the series. A middle-aged rector comes to Carlingford after fifteen years as a fellow of All Souls College, Oxford. Although he is splendidly educated, he begins to doubt his fitness to perform the offices required of a parish priest. His ultimate disillusionment occurs when he finds himself unable to offer either comfort or understanding to a dying parishioner. Branding himself a failure, he returns to the safe, yet sterile, intellectual cocoon of Oxford; but this move does not satisfy him, either: he longs for contact with the community from which he has fled. The conflict between the world of learning and the world of life and the compromises such a conflict demands was one that haunted Oliphant throughout her writing career. She recognized, as she said in her autobiography, that family responsibilities barred her from the "self-restrained life" that "the greater artist imposes upon himself," but it was never a comfortable choice for her.

In 1863 Oliphant, her children, and some of her women friends began a tour of Italy; in January 1864 Oliphant's eleven-year-old daughter, Maggie, died of gastric fever in Rome. Oliphant and her remaining children returned to Britain in 1865, settling in Windsor so that her sons could attend Eton. The next twenty-six years were productive, if financially precarious. Oliphant's reputation as a hack writer was heightened during this period as her need to support an ever-expanding family required an ever-increasing bank account. The business of her eldest brother, Frank, failed in 1868, and his son, also named Frank, joined Oliphant's household. When her brother Frank's wife died in 1870, he and his two daughters also moved in with her. A distant cousin, Annie Walker, orphaned, homeless, and penniless, also moved into the household (as Mrs. Henry Coghill, she was to be the editor of Oliphant's autobiography). Oliphant was also supporting her brother Willie, who was living in Rome; alcoholism had forced him to relinquish his post as

*Portrait of Oliphant by Frederick Sandys, 1881 (National Portrait Gallery, London)*

a Presbyterian minister in 1852. School expenses added to her financial burdens. Wanting the best for her sons, she sent them, and later her nephew Frank, to Eton; after Eton her sons attended Oxford, and Frank went to Cooper Hill Engineering College. A glance at her publication dates during this period indicates the frantic pace at which she wrote, always struggling to keep up with expenses.

Oliphant's brother Frank died in 1875, and her nephew Frank – her "good steady boy" – died in 1879 in India of typhoid fever. Her nephew's death was a terrible blow for Oliphant, since he was the only one of the three boys who was making his own way in the world. While she continued her prolific output of novels, biographies, histories, and travel books, as well as articles and reviews, she also began to write stories of the supernatural, exploring the terrain, as she termed it, between "the seen and unseen." Her stories differ from the typical Victorian thriller because they neither shock nor terrorize the reader but instead explore the world of the unknown and its possible connections to the world of the living. Several of her supernatural stories are noteworthy for their tender portrayal of the spirit realm. That she believed in some kind of af-

terlife is clear from essays such as "Fancies of a Believer" (1895) and passages in her autobiography in which she wonders "if what has been ever dies!" Yet she never demanded that her audience agree with her. Many of her supernatural stories have an open ending, allowing readers to give the events a naturalistic explanation. The stories served as a catharsis for Oliphant, allowing her to exorcise her suffering and to try to understand why God took the lives he did. In addition, the stories enabled Oliphant to reconnect with her loved ones and to believe they were still imbued with a purpose. Hence, her spirits always have a lofty goal. They struggle either to find their way to God or to create in the living a greater awareness of the significance of life. Since early death, usually from disease, was a constant nineteenth-century visitor, these stories found an interested and sympathetic audience searching for comfort and reassurance; they were quite popular during Oliphant's lifetime.

Her first exploration into the supernatural was the novella *A Beleaguered City, Being a Narrative of Certain Recent Events in the City of Semur* (1879). Semur, a French city, is invaded by an enemy whose presence is felt rather than seen. Oliphant explores the ways in which various individuals react to this terrifying situation. Differing interpretations are effectively presented through multiple narrations of the same events. The pure hearts of a few of the citizens enable them to glimpse the spirits and recognize their benevolent purpose: to reawaken a religious consciousness in the inhabitants of Semur. But the realist in Oliphant cannot stay submerged for long, and the ending suggests that the citizens are little altered by the supernatural event. The book was popular with both critics and readers; the editor of the *Spectator* (7 February 1880), for example, praised Oliphant's "wonderful mastery of the borderland of the natural and the supernatural." It is one of her finer, subtler, and more carefully crafted productions; the Colbys call it a "minor classic of our literature."

Oliphant developed two kinds of supernatural stories; those like *A Beleaguered City,* in which spirits return to earth to fulfill some uncompleted mission, and those in which the spirits seek reunion with God. Her better stories unquestionably come from the first group; the latter stories, generally known as the Little Pilgrim series, are – with one exception – cloying and ludicrous, and they are often boring.

In both "Earthbound," published in Fraser's (January 1880), and "The Portrait," published in *Blackwood's Edinburgh Magazine* (January 1885), the successful penetration by female spirits of the border between the natural and the supernatural worlds brings about a positive effect. In "Earthbound" the hero, Edmund, encounters a young woman in white with whom he walks, converses, and eventually falls in love. His efforts to identify her fail, and his fiancée's father suggests that she is a hallucination induced by a subconscious recollection of a century-old portrait of a young woman that is stored in the attic. Later, Edmund falls asleep next to the portrait, and the spirit appears a final time to explain that she is doomed to remain earthbound because when she was alive she "was all for the earth, and nothing more." She must prevent a similar fate for Edmund by making him more conscious of the spiritual aspect of life. Edmund awakens a distraught but presumably changed young man, no longer completely earthbound but aware of a higher order of existence.

"The Portrait" is less effective than "Earthbound" because it does not sustain the ambiguity of interpretation as well. The ghost of his mother, brought into the house when her portrait is hung in the parlor, takes possession of Philip, who narrates the story. When Philip discovers a young woman in mourning waiting to see his father, he suddenly understands that his father's refusal to provide a home for this poor, orphaned young relative of his dead mother is the source of the spirit's agitation. Philip convinces his father that justice and love demand that they take the woman into the household. Philip says of his mother's spirit, "Had we been less earthly we should have seen her – herself, and not merely her image." In her autobiography Oliphant speculates that spirits of the dead surround the living, but the living, so bound up in the activities of the world, are unaware of them except when they experience a fleeting sensation of an unseen presence.

"The Open Door" (January 1882) and "Old Lady Mary" (January 1884), which involve spirits whose interchange with the living is not so successful, are closer to the typical Victorian ghost story. Because "The Open Door" is, as the Colbys term it, "the most Gothic of her supernatural stories," it has appeared frequently in anthologies of ghost fiction even though it is far from terrifying. The narrator, Colonel Mortimer, has moved his family to a country estate near Edinburgh so that his sickly son, Roland, may attend school but still live at home. They have been in the house a short time when Roland begins to hear an eerie voice pleading, "Oh, mother, let me in." Roland's stress over his inability to help the voice makes him ill, and he asks for his father's assistance. Colonel Mortimer brings in a local clergyman, who recognizes the voice as that of a youth

named Willie who deserted his mother and disappeared years ago. The minister believes that Willie's ghost cannot depart the world permanently without making amends to his mother; therefore, he stands outside the no-longer-existent door begging for admittance. The clergyman informs the spirit that his mother is now dead, so he must seek her out in the other world. This knowledge frees the spirit, his pathetic crying ceases, and Roland recovers. Autobiographical details are not hard to spot in this story: Roland's frail health is reminiscent of that of Oliphant's sons, and the ghost has the name of her exiled brother. She sent the story to *Blackwood's Edinburgh Magazine* with a letter in which she noted that "Stories of this description are not like any others. I can produce them only when they come to me."

The title character of "Old Lady Mary" has had a prosperous life and enjoys the companionship of her goddaughter, "little" Mary. She has failed to make a will, in spite of the anxious urgings of those around her; without a will, her estate will pass to her grandson, who is already wealthy, and "little" Mary will be left destitute. One night Old Lady Mary does write a will, but she hides it in a secret drawer of an antique Italian cabinet. She dies unexpectedly, and as a spirit she learns that her refusal to confront the prospect of her own death has ruined her goddaughter's life. Contrite, she returns to earth to tell "little" Mary the location of the will; but though other children and animals can see her, she cannot communicate with the goddaughter she loves. The will is eventually found without help from the spirit world: the desk is sold, and the new owner's young sons discover the secret drawer.

This story reflects Oliphant's concerns at the time she wrote it. She worried constantly about her sons, neither of whom was supporting himself in 1884, and about Frank's two young daughters, who were unmarried and penniless; she knew that if she were to die, she would leave four individuals as destitute as "little" Mary in the story. Oliphant may also have been envious of her title character: the opening passage describes an elderly woman whose declining years are comfortable and who, as a result, finds it "hard to accept the necessity of dying." Oliphant, under constant financial pressure to work in her mid fifties, may have wished for the leisurely retirement of Old Lady Mary.

The death of Oliphant's neighbor at Windsor, Ellen "Nelly" Clifford, in 1882 prompted the first of the Little Pilgrim stories. The tales are dull, unimaginative, and poorly developed, but they were immensely popular with the Victorians. The stories are intensely personal and reflect Oliphant's fond hope of a connection between this life and the next. In "The Little Pilgrim Goes Up Higher," published in *Macmillan's* (September 1882), the Pilgrim encounters a technically skilled but imaginatively limited artist who gains satisfaction by creating backgrounds for a master artist who paints the subjects. Oliphant's husband, Frank, had been an artist with similar limitations, and she regarded herself as a lesser writer than many of her contemporaries. But, significantly, the artist in the story enjoys doing his mundane painting, suggesting that satisfaction in one's work is what truly matters.

One story in the Little Pilgrim series is remarkable for its sense of alienation and futility, which aligns it with modern dystopian fiction. The setting of "The Land of Darkness," published in *Blackwood's Edinburgh Magazine* in January 1887, is never specified; it may be purgatory, or hell, or nineteenth-century industrial England. The narrator moves through a surreal landscape in search of something that is not clearly defined, and as he does so he encounters indifference, callousness, self-centeredness, betrayal, hatred, greed, apathy, and fear. Because "there is no love" in this land, there is no way to redeem it. With extraordinary effort and perseverance, the narrator eventually frees himself from this evil world. Oliphant suggests that most people are willing to endure terror, corruption, indifference, and depravity rather than exert the effort to care for others; the evil, therefore, is within them. The Little Pilgrim stories were collected as *A Little Pilgrim in the Unseen* (1882) and *The Land of Darkness, along with Some Further Chapters in the Experience of the Little Pilgrim* (1888) and were included in *Stories of the Seen and Unseen* (1889).

Oliphant has been accused of being unsympathetic toward women's rights because of some conservative essays she wrote for *Blackwood's* in the late 1850s and early 1860s and because of a frequently quoted passage from a 16 August 1866 letter to John Blackwood in which she referred to John Stuart Mill's "mad notion of the franchise for women." The heroines of her novels, however, rarely conform to the Victorian ideal of the "angel in the house"; many of her female protagonists work outside the home, and some even hold traditionally male jobs. The title character of *Hester: A Story of a Contemporary Life* (1883), for example, is a banker. Oliphant places many of her female characters in the same position as that in which she found herself: a strong woman who holds together a family of weak men.

"Queen Eleanor and Fair Rosamond," published in *The Cornhill Magazine* (January and Febru-

ary 1886), is a reworking of an old fable in which the queen sets off with a bowl of poison in pursuit of her husband's mistress. In Oliphant's adaptation the queen is metamorphosed into a respectable middle-class wife who, during one of her husband's repeated and extended absences from home, decides that he must be ill and goes into London to find him. Eleanor soon discovers that it is not poor health but a bigamous marriage to a much younger woman that is keeping him from home. That she must unhesitatingly banish her husband from her life is never questioned, but the Victorian Eleanor never considers revenge; her major concerns are how she can explain her husband's behavior to her grown children and how she can avoid a scandal. She never allows her emotional devastation to upset her sense of decorum. Her husband reappears briefly later in the story as a broken, disheveled, and pathetic old man. J. M. Barrie, who introduced a posthumous collection of Oliphant's stories (1898), called this story "as terrible and grim a picture of a man tired of fifty years of respectability as was ever written"; a modern reader would tend to empathize with the wife rather than the husband. The story demonstrates how limited the options were for a woman spurned after "fifty years of respectability."

"Mademoiselle," published in the *The Cornhill Magazine* in November and December 1889, is a rare specimen in Oliphant's canon: a love story with a happy ending. Claire is a thirty-five-year-old governess from an impoverished noble French family; her English employers refer to her simply as "Mademoiselle," showing that they have no interest in her as a person. Her employer's rich, handsome brother, Charles, falls in love with her, but she refuses his advances. Although she and Charles are the same age, she is well aware that thirty-five is old for an unmarried woman but young for a single man. The family encourages Claire's love affair until they learn the identity of her suitor; suddenly the match becomes intolerable, and they dismiss Claire and send her back to France. Charles pursues her there, persuades her to marry him, and saves her from a lonely and destitute old age. But, as Williams notes, it is "only a piece of luck" that Claire is saved "from a terribly monotonous life," and the story reminded Victorian readers that most genteel but poor single women would have no romantic suitor to save them.

Oliphant was brutally honest about her writing, admitting in her autobiography that she would never be mentioned "in the same breath with George Eliot" but rationalizing that "to bring up the boys for the service of God was better than to write a fine novel, supposing even that it was in me to do so." By 1888, however, she had begun to question her success as a mother, as well. Neither of her sons was capable of supporting himself, even though Cyril was thirty-two and Cecco was twenty-nine. Oliphant blamed herself for their lack of direction and motivation, fearing that she had been too indulgent with them. In "Mr. Sanford," published in *The Cornhill Magazine* in April and May 1888, she reveals her twin fears of artistic and maternal failure. But, as in so many of her stories, she transforms an intensely personal crisis into a small masterpiece.

For more than thirty years Mr. Sanford kept his family in luxurious circumstances through his work as an artist. Suddenly he ceases to receive commissions; artistic taste has turned away from his contrived, posed historical pieces toward what one of his son's friends calls "the beauty of colour for itself and art for art." His attempt to paint in the new style is a failure. Grim images of his family devastated by financial ruin haunt him. He realizes that his two eldest sons view their occupations as pastimes rather than as work. Sanford's financial worries begin to eclipse his anguish over his lack of creative talent. Because he has life insurance, he realizes that the most benevolent thing he can do for his family is to die; but religious qualms prevent him from committing suicide. Fate steps in: he is fatally injured in a carriage accident. After a brief period of grief, his family regroups and survives quite nicely. His wife moves into smaller quarters; his sons begin to take their work more seriously; and his pictures begin to sell again. But, Oliphant concludes, "it is not everyone that it is given to die at the right moment, as Mr. Sanford had the happiness to do." In both "Mr. Sanford" and "Mademoiselle" Oliphant reminds her readers that these are only stories: in real life thirty-five-year-old governesses do not marry rich, handsome men, nor do faded artists conveniently die at the right moment.

The death of Cyril in 1890 marked the beginning of what Oliphant called her "ebb tide." Between Cyril's death and that of Cecco in 1894 she wrote one important short-fiction piece: "The Widow's Tale," published in *The Cornhill Magazine* from July to September 1893, explores the Victorian attitude toward young widows, who were expected to withdraw suddenly from social activities; if they failed to do so, they were assumed to be sexually available. Nellie Brunton learns that an innocent flirtation can have serious consequences when a selfish, shallow young man places her in a compromising situation. To salvage her reputation, she submits to a loveless second marriage with the man, who not only spends her small inheritance but also refuses to allow her children to live with them. "The Widow's Tale" may explain why Oliphant never considered remarrying.

"The Library Window," published in *Blackwood's Edinburgh Magazine* in January 1896, is another tale of the supernatural. A sensitive young woman is told that a library window sometimes mysteriously appears in the blank brick wall of the building across the street from her aunt's apartment. She intensely examines the facade and is finally able to discern a room furnished with books, writing table, and chair. At length she also sees a scholar who has been dead for many years and who, according to local legend, gave up love to pursue his work. She never sees him idle; he writes endlessly and effortlessly. As always, Oliphant leaves the reader with a rational explanation: the apparition could be the product of the girl's overactive imagination.

Thick Scottish dialect makes "The Heirs of Kellie," published in *Blackwood's Edinburgh Magazine* in March 1896, difficult to read. The aging Sir Walter Oliphant, whose own sons are dead, must decide whether to leave his property to his cousin Peter, a responsible yeoman, or to Lord Oliphant, the head of the clan. Sir Walter's sister, Jean, who is young enough to be his granddaughter, lives with him, but he never considers her as his heir. He finally decides to leave the property to the aristocratic branch of the family. When they take over after his death, they prove to be mean, bloodthirsty, ungrateful boors. Peter and Jean bitterly but wisely conclude that they must not fight for the land because it will cause too many unnecessary deaths. The lords die out ignobly, and the only remaining bearers of the old and honored name are the peasant farmers who succeed Peter and Jean.

Oliphant's letters during the three years between Cecco's death and her own express profound despondency and weariness. She continued to write, although she recognized that her style was no longer popular. Her last large undertaking was a history of the Blackwood publishing house, which she was unable to complete before she died on 25 June 1897. She was buried between her two sons in the Eton Parish Cemetery.

Oliphant's industry ultimately led to her obscurity, but as Williams notes, "The really surprising thing is not that she produced a great deal of hack-work, but that so much is so good." Much of what "is so good" can be found in her short fiction, where page count was not the primary consideration. In these shorter pieces she was able to deal with social problems and to explore the motivations of her characters. Her wit and irony, balanced by compassion and understanding, make her short fiction worthy of attention.

## Bibliography:

John Stock Clarke, *Margaret Oliphant: A Bibliography,* Victorian Fiction Research Guides, 11 (St. Lucia, Australia: University of Queensland Department of English, 1986).

## Biographies:

Vineta and Robert A. Colby, *The Equivocal Virtue: Mrs. Oliphant and the Victorian Market Place* (Hamden, Conn.: Archon, 1966);

Merryn Williams, *Margaret Oliphant: A Critical Biography* (London: Macmillan, 1986).

## References:

Robert A. and Vineta Colby, "A Beleaguered City: A Fable for the Victorian Age," *Nineteenth-Century Fiction,* 16 (March 1962): 283-301;

Valentine Cunningham, *Everywhere Spoken Against: Dissent in the Victorian Novel* (Oxford: Clarendon Press, 1975), pp. 231-248;

Philip Davis, *Memory and Writing from Wordsworth to Lawrence,* Liverpool English Texts and Studies, 21 (Totowa, N.J.: Barnes & Noble, 1983), pp. 283-331;

Joseph O'Mealy, "Scenes of Professional Life: Mrs. Oliphant and The New Victorian Clergyman," *Studies in the Novel,* 23 (Summer 1991): 245-261;

John Skelton, "A Little Chat about Mrs. Oliphant," *Blackwood's Edinburgh Magazine,* 153 (January 1883): 73-91;

R. C. Terry, *Victorian Popular Fiction, 1860-1880* (London: Macmillan, 1983), pp. 68-101.

## Papers:

The largest collection of Margaret Oliphant's papers, including her letters to the Blackwoods, are in the National Library of Scotland, Edinburgh. Letters to the publishers Bentley and Macmillan are in the British Museum. Some letters between Oliphant and the publisher William Isbister are in the Parrish Collection, Princeton University.

# Amelia Opie

*(12 November 1769 – 2 December 1853)*

James R. Simmons Jr.
*University of South Carolina*

See also the Opie entry in *DLB 116: British Romantic Novelists, 1789–1832.*

BOOKS: *Dangers of Coquetry,* 2 volumes (London: Printed for W. Lane, 1790);

*The Father and Daughter, A Tale, in Prose: With an Epistle from the Maid of Corinth to Her Lover, and Other Poetical Pieces* (London: Printed by Davis, Wilks & Taylor and sold by Longman & Rees, 1801; New York: Printed & sold by John Harrison, 1802);

*Poems* (London: Printed for T. N. Longman & O. Rees by Taylor & Wilks, 1802);

*Elegy to the Memory of the Late Duke of Bedford* (London: Longman & Rees, 1802);

*Adeline Mowbray; or, The Mother and Daughter,* 3 volumes (London: Longman, Hurst, Rees & Orme, 1805; Georgetown: Published by J. Milligan, Dinmore & Cooper, printers, 1808);

*Simple Tales* (4 volumes, London: Printed for Longman, Hurst, Rees & Orme, 1806; 2 volumes, Georgetown: Published at J. March's Bookstore, R. C. Weightman, printer, 1807);

*The Warrior's Return and Other Poems* (London: Longman, Hurst, Rees & Orme, 1808; Philadelphia: Bradford & Inskeep, 1808);

*Temper, or, Domestic Scenes* (3 volumes, London: Longman, Hurst, Rees, Orme & Brown, 1812; 2 volumes, Boston: Bradford & Read, 1812);

*Tales of Real Life* (3 volumes, London: Longman, Hurst, Rees, Orme & Brown, 1813; 1 volume, Boston: S. G. Goodrich, 1827);

*Valentine's Eve* (3 volumes, London: Longman, Hurst, Rees, Orme & Brown, 1816; 2 volumes, Boston: Wells & Lilly, 1816);

*New Tales* (4 volumes, London: Longman, Hurst, Rees, Orme & Brown, 1818; 2 volumes, New York: Gilley, 1818);

*Tales of the Heart* (4 volumes, London: Longman, Hurst, Rees, Orme & Brown, 1820; 2 volumes, New York: William B. Gilley, Haly &

*Amelia Opie (portrait by John Opie; National Portrait Gallery, London)*

Thomas, A. T. Goodrich, and Wiley & Halsted, 1820);

*Madeline* (2 volumes, London: Printed for Longman, Hurst, Rees, Orme & Brown, 1822; 1 volume, Boston: S. G. Goodrich, 1827);

*The Negro Boy's Tale* (London: Harvey & Darton, 1824);

*Illustrations of Lying, in All Its Branches* (2 volumes, London: Longman, Hurst, Rees, Orme, Brown & Green, 1825; 1 volume, Boston: Munroe & Francis and nine others, 1826);

*Tales of the Pemberton Family, for the Use of Children* (London: Harvey & Darton, 1825; Boston: Munroe & Francis, 1825);

*The Black Man's Lament; or, How to Make Sugar* (London: Printed for Harvey & Darton, 1826);

*Detraction Displayed* (London: Longman, Rees, Orme, Brown & Green, 1828; New York: Published by Orville A. Roorbach, W. E. Dean, printer, 1828; Philadelphia: Carey, Lea & Carey, sold in New York by G. & C. Carvill, in Boston by Munroe & Francis, 1828);

*Lays for the Dead* (London: Longman, Rees, Orme, Brown, Green & Longman, 1834).

OTHER: *Twelve Hindoo Airs with English Words Adapted to Them,* music adapted by Edward Smith Biggs, words adapted by Opie (London: Printed by Birchall, circa 1800);

*A Second Set of Hindoo Airs with English Words Adapted to Them,* music adapted by Biggs, words adapted by Opie (London: Printed by Birchall, circa 1800);

John Opie, *Lectures on Painting, Delivered at the Royal Academy of Arts,* edited, with a memoir, by Amelia Opie (London: Longman, Hurst, Rees & Orme, 1809);

Margaret Roberts, *Duty,* 3 volumes, edited by Opie (London: Longman, Hurst, Rees & Orme, 1809);

Margaret Roberts, *Duty,* edited by Opie (3 volumes, London: Longman, Hurst, Rees, Orme & Brown, 1814; 2 volumes, New York: Printed & published by I. Riley, 1815).

Among early-nineteenth-century short-fiction writers, perhaps no other author produced as eclectic a body of work as Amelia Opie. From her early tales of domestic fiction to her later stories, which are almost exclusively of a morally didactic nature, Opie's diverse contributions to Romantic short fiction can be seen as representative of a time in which many authors were attempting to come to terms with societal changes and to reflect those changes in their works. While Opie's fiction defies strict categorization, her work, as a reviewer for the *British Critic* noted in September 1818, "is distinguished by a simplicity of language, a fidelity of description, a justness of sentiment, a consistency of character, and a liberality of opinion, which cannot fail to infix on any work, in which they are found the stamp and impress of genuine excellence."

Born in Norwich on 12 November 1769, Amelia Alderson was the only child of Dr. James Alderson, a prominent physician and Dissenter, and Amelia Alderson, née Briggs. Although Amelia was never formally educated, she was exposed to a wide array of literature; in addition, her mother impressed on her the evils of slavery and prejudice — concerns that would manifest themselves in her writings. Her lifelong friendship with the Gurneys, a Quaker family in Norwich, would also have a profound influence on her personal life and her literary output. But the most telling influence of her formative years occurred after the death of her mother when Amelia was fifteen: as hostess in her father's home, Amelia benefited from exposure to such leading intellectuals of the period as William Godwin, Harriet Martineau, Thomas Holcroft, and John Aiken. Amelia began corresponding with Aiken, who encouraged her in her literary endeavors and urged her to have her poetry published.

Some of her poems appeared in *The Cabinet* in the early 1790s. She also wrote several plays — at least one of which, *Adelaide,* was produced at a private theater of one of her father's friends in 1791 — and a novel, *Dangers of Coquetry,* which was published in 1790. These first literary efforts were afforded little critical attention but gained her a reputation that allowed her to increase her circle of prominent acquaintances. She was befriended by Elizabeth Inchbald and Mary Wollstonecraft, as well as the Cornish painter John Opie, whom she married on 8 May 1798. With his encouragement Amelia dedicated herself to writing in earnest and entered the most productive period of her literary career. Her novel *The Father and Daughter* (1801) was a popular and critical success; *Poems* (1802) was followed by the immensely popular novel *Adeline Mowbray; or, The Mother and Daughter* (1805). Her first collection of stories, *Simple Tales* (1806), however, received less-than-favorable reviews.

One of the problems with *Simple Tales* was, according to the *Edinburgh Review* for July 1806, "we see through the whole story from its first opening; and few of her personages can be said to be original." As an example of a story that was "not very natural" the reviewer cited "The Robber," in which Theodore Mortimer believes that his past is forever tainted by a theft he committed against Mr. Sedley. Sedley, however, forgives Mortimer and helps him to find employment and a wife. Mortimer overcomes the stigma of his past and goes on to live a productive life.

In July 1806 the *Edinburgh Review* found "The Fashionable Wife and the Unfashionable Husband" even worse than "The Robber": "though many of the particular scenes are well-drawn," it said, the story was "inadequate and fantastic." Louisa Howard is an upper-class woman who wants to marry a man who treats her as an equal, not an inferior.

Lord H. appears to be that man; but after they are married, Louisa incurs debts through gambling, and Lord H. punishes her by refusing to treat her in the manner in which she is accustomed. When she nearly dies, he forgives her. The deathbed act of forgiveness would become a mainstay of Opie's later stories, although that Louisa does not die is unusual in her fiction.

Opie's husband died in 1807, and she returned to Norwich to live with her father. There she widened her circle of acquaintances to include William Wordsworth, Walter Scott, and Sarah Siddons. Her second collection of stories, *Tales of Real Life* (1813), includes some of Opie's best fiction, and readers expecting to see more of the well-drawn characters found in Opie's novels were not to be disappointed. One of the stories in *Tales of Real Life,* "The Mysterious Stranger," anticipates some of the detective fiction that would proliferate later in the century. Lord Delborough goes on a European tour to try to recover from the recent deaths of his wife and son; he is accompanied by his lifelong friend, Moreton. On a ship Delborough meets the beautiful Rosabel S. Clair Macdonald, also recently widowed, and the two are eventually married. Moreton, however, never trusts her because of inconsistencies in her accounts of her past life and her often mysterious behavior. It turns out that Rosabel's first husband did not die; she left him for his infidelity by faking her suicide. When she discovers that her first husband was not unfaithful after all, and that she has destroyed the lives of two men through her bigamous second marriage, her health gives way under the stress of this knowledge, and she dies.

"Austin and His Wife" is a morality-laden tale that anticipates the didactic stories that Opie would write later in her career. Austin and his wife are raising their son, Edwin, through trust and mutual respect, unlike their neighbor Brograve, who rules his son, Hugh, by beatings and humiliation. Brograve convinces Austin that Edwin is a liar and a thief, and Austin adopts Brograve's disciplinary methods. After years of his father's distrust and insinuations, Edwin does turn to a life of crime. Brograve's son dies in a knife fight, and Edwin, unwittingly robbing his parents' home, stabs his mother in a scuffle and then dies himself, leaving Austin alone to regret his dubious methods of raising the boy.

*Tales of Real Life* was well received. *The British Critic* (December 1814) said that the stories contain useful warnings and that "no person can read these tales without deriving as much benefit from them as

*Medallion of Opie (engraved by P. Lightfoot, after the original by Jacques-Louis David)*

pleasure." Opie's early stories strike a delicate balance between entertainment and morality that her later tales lack.

Another collection of stories, *New Tales,* appeared in 1818. In "Proposals of Marriage" the sixty-four-year-old Tynley Tresgothic, a rich bachelor, is the friend and confidant of the much younger Lady Mary Lovely. Lady Mary's parents have arranged her engagement to Lord Lawless, but she is in love with the penniless Arthur Merital. Through Tresgothic's intermediation – and a sizable financial contribution – Lady Mary is allowed to marry the humble Merital. The banal plot and the obvious symbolism of the names of the characters make this one of Opie's most hackneyed stories.

"The Quaker, and the Young Man of the World" is a better story than "Proposals of Marriage." Frank Warburton, a wealthy young man, meets John Reynolds, an old Quaker. Reynolds learns that Warburton broke off relations with his mother after she married a clerk who once worked for his father, who recently died. Reynolds tells Warburton that he underwent a similar trauma but was reconciled with his mother, who thanked him on her deathbed for his understanding. Reynolds warns Warburton that, should his mother die, he would forever blame himself for their fractured relationship. Warburton reconciles with his mother and finds out that she remarried to provide for her sons, because her deceased husband's fortune had been dissipated.

The reviews for *New Tales* were favorable, though reserved. *The British Critic* (September 1818) found merit in the collection but said that Opie's "stories were beset with improbabilities, and that they occurred so often that an idea of absolute impossibility . . . arises to our senses, and forces us to turn away with all the apathy of indifference and incredulity of disgust from those occurrences."

*Tales of the Heart* (1820) reveals a decline in the quality of Opie's fiction. In "The Two Sir Williams," an obvious variation on the Cinderella story, the poor but beautiful Caroline lives with her conceited aunt and cousins. The cousins and their mother denigrate the sister of Sir William Dormer in his presence, because they believe him to be Sir William Maberly. Caroline defends Dormer's sister, although she, too, is unaware of his real identity. Dormer marries the poor orphan with the heart of gold, much to the chagrin of her cousins and aunt. Opie characterizes "The Opposite Neighbour" as a story about "the evils which it has pleased our creator to mingle with the blessings of existence." Mr. Evelyn is locked into an arranged marriage, but he loves his wife's poor, orphaned cousin, Rosabel. After ten years his wife, Matilda, dies, and a year later Evelyn and Rosabel marry. Eventually Evelyn becomes convinced that Rosabel is having an affair. He disappears, resurfaces in disguise, and spies on his wife. He finds that the person of whom he is jealous is his brother-in-law, whom everyone had believed dead. Rosabel is sheltering him because he was a fugitive, which explains her mysterious comings and goings. The story shows the folly of suspicion and jealousy.

Opie's novel *Madeline* (1822) was to be the last of her fiction unfettered by heavy moralizing. Since 1814 she had been attending Quaker meetings with her old friend Joseph John Gurney, and by the time she formally joined the Society of Friends in 1825 her career as a writer of popular fiction had, for all practical purposes, ended. *Illustrations of Lying, in All Its Branches* (1825) typifies Opie's didactic later work, which appeared almost exclusively in such publications as *The Amulet, or, Christian and Literary Remembrancer* and *The Christian Keepsake and Missionary Annual*. She became active in the Abolitionist cause, writing sentimental pieces decrying the evils of slavery. This later work garnered absolutely no critical attention, and until her death on 2 December 1853 Opie was known as a literary enigma, an artist who had thrown away a promising career to become a writer of religious tracts.

**Biographies:**

Cecilia Lucy Brightwell, *Memorials of the Life of Amelia Opie* (Norwich: Fletcher & Alexander, 1854);

Brightwell, *Memoir of Amelia Opie* (London: Religious Tract Society, 1855);

Jacobine Menzies-Wilson and Helen Lloyd, *Amelia: The Tale of a Plain Friend* (London & New York: Oxford University Press, 1937).

**References:**

Jan Fergus and Janice Farrar Thadeus, "Women, Publishers, and Money, 1790–1820," *Studies in Eighteenth-Century Culture,* 17 (1987): 191–207;

William Dean Howells, "Heroines of Miss Ferrier, Mrs. Opie, and Mrs. Radcliffe," in his *Heroines of Fiction,* 2 volumes (New York & London: Harper, 1901), I: 79–89;

Gary Kelly, "Amelia Opie, Lady Caroline Lamb, and Maria Edgeworth: Official and Unofficial Ideology," *Ariel,* 12 (October 1981): 3–24;

Kelly, "Discharging Debts: The Moral Economy of Amelia Opie's Fiction," *Wordsworth Circle,* 11 (Autumn 1980): 198–203;

Margaret Eliot MacGregor, *Amelia Alderson Opie: Worldling and Friend* (Northampton, Mass.: Smith College, 1933);

Basem Ra'ad, " 'D.D.' Revealed," *Melville Society Extracts,* 86 (September 1991): 10–11;

Anne Thackeray Ritchie, *A Book of Sibyls* (London: Smith, Elder, 1883).

**Papers:**

The major repositories of Amelia Opie's papers are the British Library and the Huntington Library, San Marino, California.

# Jane Porter

*(3 December 1776 – 24 May 1850)*

and

# Anna Maria Porter

*(1780 – 21 June 1832)*

Linda Mills Woolsey
*King College*

See also the Jane Porter and Anna Maria Porter entries in *DLB 116: British Romantic Novelists, 1789–1832.*

BOOKS: *Artless Tales,* by Anna Maria Porter, 2 volumes (London: Printed & sold for the author by L. Wayland, 1795, 1798);

*Walsh Colville; or, A Young Man's First Entrance into Life,* anonymous [by Anna Maria Porter] (London: Lee & Hurst/T. C. Jones, 1797);

*Octavia: A Novel,* by Anna Maria Porter, 3 volumes (London: Lee & Hurst, 1798);

*The Spirit of the Elbe: A Romance,* by Jane Porter, 3 volumes (London: Printed for T. N. Longman & O. Rees, 1799);

*A Defence of the Profession of an Actor,* by Jane Porter (London: Miller, 1800);

*The Two Princes of Persia, Addressed to Youth,* by Jane Porter as I. Porter (London: Printed by J. Cundee for Crosby & Letterman, 1801);

*Thaddeus of Warsaw,* by Jane Porter (4 volumes, London: Printed by A. Strahan for T. N. Longman & O. Rees, 1803; 2 volumes, Boston: L. Blake, 1809);

*The Lake of Killarney: A Novel,* by Anna Maria Porter (3 volumes, London: Printed for T. N. Longman & O. Rees, 1804; 2 volumes, Philadelphia: Printed for Thomas De Silver, 1810);

*Sketch of the Campaign of Count A. Suwarrow Ryminski,* by Jane Porter (London: Longman, Hurst, Rees & Orme, 1804);

*A Sailor's Friendship, and a Soldier's Love,* by Anna Maria Porter (2 volumes, London: Longman, Hurst, Rees & Orme, 1805; 1 volume, Baltimore: Warner & Hanna, 1810);

*Aphorisms of Sir Philip Sidney; with Remarks* selected by Jane Porter (London: Longman, Hurst, Rees, & Orme, 1807);

*The Hungarian Brothers,* by Anna Maria Porter (3 volumes, London: Printed by C. Stower for Longman, Hurst, Rees & Orme, 1807; 2 volumes, Philadelphia: Bradford & Inskeep / New York: Inskeep & Bradford, Printed by Robert Carr, 1809);

*Don Sebastian, or, The House of Braganza: An Historical Romance,* by Anna Maria Porter (4 volumes, London: Printed for Longman, Hurst, Rees & Orme, 1809; 2 volumes, Philadelphia: Printed by A. Small for M. Carey, 1810);

*The Scottish Chiefs: A Romance,* by Jane Porter (5 volumes, London: Longman, Hurst, Rees & Orme, 1810; 2 volumes, New York: Longworth, 1810);

*Ballad Romances, and Other Poems,* by Anna Maria Porter (London: Printed for Longman, Hurst, Rees, Orme & Brown, 1811; Philadelphia: M. Carey / Boston: Wells & Lilly, 1816);

*Tales of Pity on Fishing, Shooting, and Hunting, Intended to Inculcate in the Mind of Youth, Sentiments of Humanity Toward the Brute Creation,* by Anna Maria Porter (London: Printed for J. Harris, 1814);

*The Recluse of Norway,* by Anna Maria Porter (4 volumes, London: Longman, Hurst, Rees, Orme & Brown, 1814; 2 volumes, Philadelphia: A. Small, 1815; New York: Printed for I. Riley, 1815);

*The Pastor's Fire-Side: A Novel,* by Jane Porter (4 volumes, London: Longman, Hurst, Rees, Orme & Brown, 1817; 2 volumes, New York: W. B. Gilley, 1817);

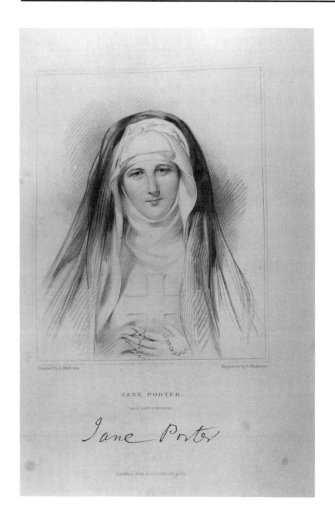

*The Knight of St. John: A Romance,* by Anna Maria Porter (3 volumes, London: Printed for Longman, Hurst, Rees, Orme & Brown, 1817; 2 volumes, Philadelphia: Thomas, 1817; New York: J. Eastburn, 1817);

*The Fast of St. Magdalen: A Romance,* by Anna Maria Porter (3 volumes, London: Longman, Hurst, Rees, Orme & Brown, 1818; 2 volumes, Boston: Wells & Lilly, 1819; New York: W. B. Gilley & C. Wiley, 1819);

*The Village of Mariendorpt: A Tale,* by Anna Maria Porter, 4 volumes (London: Longman, Hurst, Rees, Orme & Brown, 1821);

*Roche-Blanche, or, The Hunters of the Pyrenees: A Romance,* by Anna Maria Porter (3 volumes, London: Longman, Hurst, Rees, Orme & Brown, 1822; 2 volumes, Boston: Wells & Lilly, 1822);

*Duke Christian of Luneberg; or, Tradition from the Hartz,* by Jane Porter, 3 volumes (London: Longman, Hurst, Rees, Orme, Brown & Green, 1824);

*Tales round a Winter Hearth,* by Jane Porter and Anna Maria Porter (London: Longman, Rees, Orme, Brown & Green, 1826);

*Honor O'Hara: A Novel,* by Anna Maria Porter (3 volumes, London: Longman, Rees, Orme, Brown & Green, 1826; 2 volumes, New York: Harper, 1827);

*Coming Out; and The Field of Forty Footsteps,* 3 volumes [volumes 1 and 2: *Coming Out,* by Anna Maria Porter; volume 3: *The Field of Forty Footsteps,* by Jane Porter] (London: Longman, Rees, Orme, Brown & Green, 1828; New York: Printed by J. & J. Harper, for E. Duyckinck, Collins & Hannay, E. Bliss, G. & C. Carvill, O. A.

Roorbach, W. B. Gilley, A. T. Goodrich, and W. B. Burgess, 1828);

*The Barony,* by Anna Maria Porter (3 volumes, London: Longman, Rees, Orme, Brown & Green, 1830; 2 volumes, New York: Harper, 1830);

*Sir Edward Seaward's Narrative of His Shipwreck and Consequent Discovery of Certain Islands in the Caribbean Sea: With a Detail of Many Extraordinary and Highly Interesting Events of His Life, from the Year 1733 to 1749, as Written in His Own Diary, Edited by Miss Jane Porter,* 3 volumes (London: Longman, Rees, Orme, Brown & Green, 1831; New York: Harper, 1831).

PLAY PRODUCTIONS: *The Fair Fugitives,* by Anna Maria Porter, London, Covent Garden Theatre, 16 May 1803;

*Switzerland,* by Jane Porter, London, Theatre Royal, Drury Lane, 5 February 1819;

*Owen, Prince of Powys; or Welsh Feuds,* by Jane Porter, London, Theatre Royal, Drury Lane, 28 January 1822.

OTHER: *Young Hearts: A Novel, by A Recluse,* anonymous, preface by Jane Porter (London: Saunders & Otley, 1834);

"A Scottish Tradition," by Jane Porter, in *The Tale Book: Collection of Ancient and Modern British Novels and Romances,* First Series, volume 57 (Paris: Baudry's European Library, 1834).

Jane Porter and her younger sister, Anna Maria, were well-known popular novelists of the early nineteenth century. The public's response to Jane Porter's moral and patriotic romance *Thaddeus of Warsaw* (1803) was so enthusiastic that Robert Tate Irvine, likening her to the author of *Gone with the Wind* (1936), calls her "the Margaret Mitchell of 1803." Though both sisters enjoyed such popularity, neither has received much critical attention. In both their novels and their shorter tales the Porters drew their stories from contemporary life, from military history, and from legend, yet wrote in an idiom foreign to twentieth-century taste – a language of sentiment, moral certainty, and idealized heroism. Nineteenth-century readers enjoyed the Porters' use of conventional moral example, pure and breathless love, and high adventure. That the Porter sisters took seriously their vocation as writers is suggested by Jane's description of their similar objectives: "[W]hen we began to write for publication, we regarded our works not as a pastime for ourselves, or a mere amusement for others, but as the use to be made of an entrusted talent 'given to

us for a purpose': and for every word we set down in our pages, we believed we must be accountable to Heaven and to our country."

Jane and Anna Maria Porter were born into a relatively poor but respectable family in which education, moral seriousness, and religious faith were central. Their father, William Porter, was an army surgeon, and their mother, Jane Blenkinsop Porter, was a serious Christian from the borderland of Scotland. In 1776 Dr. Porter's regiment was quartered at Durham, England, where Jane was born on 3 December. Her older brothers were John Blenkinsop, born in 1771 or 1772, and William Ogilvy, born in 1773 or 1774. A third brother, Robert Ker, was born in 1777. Two years later their father died, leaving Jane with a strong and persistent sense of loss that was compensated in part by her tendency to idealize fathers and to see the heroes of history and legend as father figures. In her "Retrospective Preface" to *The Scottish Chiefs* (1810), Jane links her childhood sympathy toward the national hero Sir William Wallace with her grief over the loss of her own beloved father. Anna Maria, the youngest of the children, was born in 1780, after their father's death.

From their earliest days the Porter children were nurtured in a home where religious faith was central, and the daughters were expected to conform to high standards of respectability and ladylike behavior. A 1777 letter Dr. Porter wrote to his wife from France reveals that, despite the importance he placed on the education of children, he maintained different expectations for his sons and his daughter. While he wanted Billy to be made a "good scholar" and described Jacky as promising to be "a lad of Genius," he emphasized Jane's appearance and the womanly end of her education: "My Jenny is beautiful; it will be my pride to dress my little Queen handsomely and decently. The rest I leave to your good sense to make up the rest of her education fitting her for a good wife to an Honest Man."

When the death of her husband left Mrs. Porter with five children to raise on a widow's pension, she moved to Edinburgh, where expenses were more moderate. John and William remained at school in Durham, under the care of their grandfather. John later joined the army and was a merchant in the West Indies but seems not to have lived with the family after his father's death. The years in Edinburgh were important in shaping the imaginations of Jane, Robert, and Anna Maria, for they lived surrounded by relics of history in a house with a view of the Firth of Forth. While their mother taught them a strict morality and active piety, they heard from nursemaids and neighbors tales of history and folklore that fed their active imaginations.

The girls studied at a dayschool kept by George Fulton, a compiler of dictionaries, who seems to have encouraged them in their love of language and books. Anna Maria was a quick, apt child who began her schooling at the age of four and was reportedly able to read the works of William Shakespeare by the time she was five. Soon she was moved to the head of the class, surpassing students much older than herself. Though not so precocious, Jane was also a good student, highly motivated and bright. Anna Maria early evidenced what contemporaries saw as a "poetical temperament," painstakingly printing out at the age of seven her first verses in honor of her mother's birthday. While she primarily wrote prose, Anna Maria continued to compose highly conventional religious and sentimental verse. Even as a schoolgirl, Jane was more drawn to the heroic and romantic than Anna Maria was.

Edinburgh life for the Porter sisters was steeped in oral tradition, with nursery maids singing ballads to the girls and servingmen recounting tales of medieval Scottish history to their brother. Anna Maria's nurse took the little girls on rambles through the narrow passageways of High Street and regaled them with accounts of old Jacobite ladies, some of whom still lived in Edinburgh. Jane remembered an elderly neighbor, Luckie Forbes, as her principal teacher of Scots heritage and heroic values. This old woman spent hours feeding Jane tales that mingled themes of valor against tyranny with allusions to biblical heroes and linked Scotland's Wallace with Abraham of the Old Testament. Another Edinburgh friend was a college student named Walter Scott, whose mother was a good friend of Mrs. Porter. Young Scott liked to play with the Porter children and tell them stories of magic and adventure.

The family remembered the Edinburgh years with delight, but these were also years of study, with the children beginning a lifelong habit of keeping notebooks of extracts from their reading. All three children delighted in history, biography, and narrative poetry: they read Scripture; the works of Plutarch, Homer, Shakespeare, and David Hume; and popular verse, particularly ballads. Sometime before 1790 the family moved to the north of England, where the children had access to the Episcopal Library; there Jane rose early in the morning to read Edmund Spenser's *The Faerie Queene* (1590; 1596) and old chronicles and romances. During this period they may have visited the Holy Island of Lindisfarne and heard an aunt's tales of the place, which later formed the basis for incidents in Jane's novel *The Pastor's Fire-Side* (1817).

In 1790 the family moved to London, where they lived in a rather poor section of the city at St. Martin's Lane. There Mrs. Porter opened her house to a widening circle of friends, among them some who were distinguished for their moral, literary, or social excellence. This circle included Benjamin West, Hannah More, Anna Barbauld, John Flaxman, James Northcote, and Martin Archer Shee. The Porter family also entertained veterans of the armed forces who had known their father. Both Jane and Anna Maria declared that these friends were models for their heroes and heroines. Mrs. Porter also welcomed a stream of French and Polish exiles; for Jane, the tales of these exiles echoed those of Scots heroes she had heard in Edinburgh: "Our animated sympathies were soon aroused by narratives so similar to those which had excited the pitying tears of our childhood and it was then I first felt the impulse to preserve some of the affecting accounts I had listened to, by writing them down in the form of a regular story." Thus, one of the central impulses of her work appeared — a desire to create narratives of compassion as well as heroism.

Anna Maria began writing and publishing early, beginning her *Artless Tales* at thirteen and publishing the first volume anonymously in 1795, the second in 1798. Although these juvenile attempts were conventional and overdrawn, they were well received. Anna Maria, however, was conscious of their immaturity. Although Jane would later disclaim any early ambitions as a writer, her memorandum book for 1796 shows that she was already writing short pieces under the pen name of "Classicus" and sending papers on "The Errors of the Heart" and "Youthful Imprudence" to the editor of a popular weekly magazine.

By the time Anna Maria was twenty-one she had joined the ranks of female romance writers who were flooding the London market with noble feelings, idealized heroines, and conventional plots. As early as 1797 Anna Maria had anonymously published *Walsh Colville; or, A Young Man's First Entrance into Life,* a tale of a decent young man who is led astray by his reckless companion, Charles Stanhope, but recovers his respectability in time to gain the hand of the virtuous Lady Francis Surrey. In this tale the evils of drinking, gambling, dueling, and keeping mistresses are handled discreetly but with enough sensation to titillate the contemporary reader. Finally, however, the tale embraces the virtues of safety, parental wisdom, and avoiding wayward company. She followed this work with *Octavia* (1798), a conventional moral romance that owes something to the influence of the contemporary novelist Fanny Burney.

One of Jane's favorite friends was her "Gentle Bard," the Reverend Percival Stockdale, an old poet who had been an acquaintance of Samuel Johnson. Jane was also fiercely devoted to her brother Robert, and her diary and letters record her vicarious enjoyment of his growing fame as a painter. In conjunction with some literary and moralistic friends, Robert, Anna Maria, and Jane were anonymous contributors in 1797–1798 to a short-lived publication called *The Quiz*, which had been established by a fictitious "Society of Gentlemen" (at least two of whom were ladies) to attack vice and defend virtue.

Both Jane and Anna Maria continued to keep their "Extract Books," in which they copied quotations from their reading. Jane's show that she admired the work of Mary Wollstonecraft, particularly her novels, and she described Wollstonecraft as a "Sun-Eyed Genius" and "Immortal Mind." Wollstonecraft may have had some influence on Jane's fictional heroines, who often exhibit exceptional moral (and sometimes physical) courage and intelligence within a framework of highly conventional female virtue. Another important source for Jane was history, which continued to be a ruling passion in the Porter household. With the money from Robert's paintings and Anna Maria's novels, the family had been able to move to the more fashionable neighborhood of Leicester Square. Here Jane was often invited to attend meetings of a society of young artists known as "The Brothers," whose central interest was topographical and historical painting. A. D. Hook suggests that here Jane may have found inspiration to write fiction analogous to the paintings by her brother and his friends.

For the sisters London also included the fascinating world of the theater. In 1800 Jane wrote a pamphlet entitled *A Defence of the Profession of an Actor*, which she dedicated to Mrs. Sarah Siddons; more than a decade later, Jane tried to establish herself as a playwright. An incident of 1801 illustrates some of the tension between propriety and her true feelings that may have plagued Jane throughout her life and found expression in the fallen and rebellious women who occasionally appear in her fiction. In 1801 at Campion Lodge while she was visiting Mary de Crespigny, the respectable bluestocking and author of *The Pavilion* (1796), the company received news of the death of well-known actress Mary "Perdita" Robinson, a woman Jane knew personally. In that respectable household Jane felt compelled to deny her friendship with the actress, but the denial cost her a struggle, as she recorded in her diary: "Oh! how it cut my heart, that I was thus forced to hide a regret which I thought laudable! I one moment despised myself for being ashamed to avow feelings which I could not condemn; and the next excused myself from the conviction that it was only a prudence due to my sister and myself not to publish a conduct, which, however guiltless, would draw on us the disrespect of many of our friends, and most likely the scandal of the world." While actresses were scandalous, lady playwrights were more acceptable, and in 1803 Anna Maria tried her hand at a musical called *The Fair Fugitives,* with a score by Dr. Thomas Busby. The production was a failure, and Anna Maria apparently never ventured into playwrighting after that.

After the successful exhibition of Robert Porter's large canvas of "The Storming of Seringapatam" in 1800, the Porters moved to the still more fashionable Grand Street. There the young women continued to have admirers, with Jane fretting in her diary over the attentions that a young artist named Kearsley was paying to Anna Maria. Jane also confided to her diary that she admired the actor Charles Kemble, a frequent visitor in the Porter household, and she even admitted that she would marry him if he were to ask her.

But Jane's disappointment in love paled beside the growing inspiration she found in the tales of exiles and émigrés. Shutting herself in her brother's study with a blood-stained coat and bullet-torn vest at her side, she began to compose *Thaddeus of Warsaw*. According to Jane, the novel was originally written to entertain her family, but when a friend who was a partner with publishers Longman and Rees read the manuscript, he offered to publish it. *Thaddeus of Warsaw* was an immediate best-seller, as the reading public responded enthusiastically. Jane's success prompted Anna Maria to begin acknowledging her own works, which had been appearing anonymously. Even Thomas Carlyle found the novel interesting despite its deficiencies, but its main appeal was to a reading public hungry for patriotism, nationalism, and Christian heroism in the wake of recent events in France.

In 1802 William Porter received his M.D. at Aberdeen and went to sea as a naval surgeon, while Czar Alexander called Robert to Saint Petersburg to serve as a historical painter. Without the men of the family, Mrs. Porter decided that she and her daughters would fare better if they were removed from the distractions and temptations of London society.

They moved to a cottage nicknamed "Little Arcadia," in Thames Ditton, near Hampton Court. There the sisters continued to write, take long walks, and visit with neighbors. With a generosity that sometimes strained their income, all three women devoted themselves to charity.

While at Thames Ditton, Anna Maria wrote *The Lake of Killarney* (1804), *A Sailor's Friendship, and a Soldier's Love* (1805), and *The Hungarian Brothers* (1807), a story of the French Revolution. The last novel was often admired for its glorious action and patriotic themes, and some nineteenth-century readers considered it the strongest of her works. Jane's *Aphorisms of Sir Philip Sidney; with Remarks* (1807) probably grew out of her extract books, since it consists primarily of quotations grouped by subjects. While one reviewer commended it as a "valuable pocket and travelling companion," it was not popular.

Around 1806 Robert's brilliant career had been interrupted by a romance of the sort his sisters liked to write about. He had fallen in love with a Russian princess whose parents had objected to him, and in the ensuing storm at court he had been forced to leave Russia. He wandered for a while in Sweden and later published an account of his travels. Robert's life and wanderings, and the stories he brought back on his visits home, became important sources of material for his sisters' work.

In 1809 Anna Maria published *Don Sebastian, or, The House of Braganza,* a story of a prince-errant's chivalric adventures in Spain, North Africa, and Persia. While the work was well received, it was soon overshadowed by Jane Porter's most popular novel about Wallace's patriotic struggles, *The Scottish Chiefs.* Yet while *The Scottish Chiefs* was a great success with the public, its success was shadowed by family difficulties. Although by this time William Porter had established a successful medical practice in Bristol, John Porter was a dismal failure; in 1810 he died in a debtors' prison on the Isle of Man leaving behind a child and a wife, who had to sell her bed to buy him a coffin. For Jane and Anna Maria the quiet and productive life at Thames Ditton flowed on, with Anna Maria publishing *Ballad Romances, and Other Poems* in 1811.

In February 1812 Robert, who had proved himself as a soldier, an author, and a painter and had been knighted by the king of Sweden, returned to Russia to marry Princess Marie Sherbatoff. In 1813 he was knighted by the British Prince Regent, and when London celebrated the triumph of King Louis XVIII on 30 April 1814, Robert's wife was among the royalty in attendance. The Porter sisters,

who loved pageantry and idolized national heroes, basked in the splendor of Robert's career and turned it to good stead in their writing of noblemen, star-crossed loves, and adventurous careers. Around this time the Porters renewed their acquaintance with Scott, by then a celebrated poet although yet to be recognized as author of the first of the widely acclaimed Waverley novels that began to appear in 1814.

The sisters continued their own work on novels with historic or exotic settings and chivalric, romantic plots. In 1814 Anna Maria published *The Recluse of Norway* in four volumes as well as a single volume of short narratives in a different mode. Entitled *Tales of Pity on Fishing, Shooting, and Hunting, Intended to Inculcate in the Mind of Youth, Sentiments of Humanity Toward the Brute Creation,* this collection was intended to teach young readers the importance of compassion. Jane, however, was still fascinated by the theater and determined to try her hand at playwriting. In 1816 she submitted "Egmont, or the Eve of St. Alyne" to the Theatre Royal at Drury Lane but, although Edmund Kean praised it, the play was neither performed nor printed. The winter of 1817–1818 found the Theatre Royal again considering a play by Jane Porter, this time a tragedy entitled *Switzerland.* Exasperated by her failure to get a decision about whether or not this play would be produced, Jane eventually withdrew this script. Yet early in 1819 the theater asked to see the play again and produced it on 15 February with Kean in the leading role.

By all accounts his performance was terrible — he may even have been drunk. The audience was disgruntled, and the play closed; Anna Maria accused Kean of deliberately sabotaging the performance. There is no way to judge the play's merits, since it, too, was not printed, and the manuscript has been lost. The failure of the play was a blow to Jane — who fell ill, her theatrical hopes dampened. She did eventually recover from her mortification, trying once more in January 1822, when the Theatre Royal produced her *Owen, Prince of Powys; or Welsh Feuds.* But this play also failed miserably.

Despite such tribulations Jane Porter published four volumes with the misleadingly placid title *The Pastor's Fire-Side* (1817). This work full of violence and intrigue was favorably received, but it was much overshadowed by the great speculation about the identity of the author of the Waverley novels.

During the years Jane was trying unsuccessfully to take Drury Lane by storm, Robert Porter had left his wife behind in Russia to travel in Persia and the Middle East, sketching and writing about his travels, gathering material useful to both Jane and Anna Maria. The latter continued to pour out romantic stories in a familiar vein but with varied settings. In quick succession Anna Maria published *The Knight of St. John* (1817), a fictional account of Jean de La Valette's defense of Malta against the Turks in 1565; *The Fast of St. Magdalen* (1818), set in the years 1509 to 1512 and recounting the expulsion of the Medici from Florence, as well as their eventual victory and return; and *The Village of Mariendorpt* (1821), about the Thirty Years' War, with a hero whom nineteenth-century acquaintances saw as modeled on her brother Robert. *Roche-Blanche, or, The Hunters of the Pyrenees* (1822) was the last of Anna Maria's works written at Thames Ditton.

In 1824 Robert Porter took a diplomatic post in Venezuela, but before he left he helped his mother and sisters move to another house on a higher and drier site at Esher, near the ruins of Esher Place, which had once belonged to Cardinal Thomas Wolsey. There they soon resumed what Jane called their " 'troubadour' employment," reading their morning's work aloud to their mother at the tea table and "often benefit[ing] by her clear-sighted but gentle criticism." In 1824 Jane published *Duke Christian of Luneberg; or, Tradition from the Hartz*, written at the request of King George IV, whose librarian furnished her with materials. This made-to-order novel lacked the energy and conviction of Jane's earlier work and was not popular with a public whose taste had been reshaped by Scott's Waverley novels.

In 1826 Jane and Anna Maria collaborated on *Tales round a Winter Hearth*, their principal contribution to short fiction. Jane's preface anchors these tales in conversation and table talk, making the short tale not so much an original composition as a reworking of oral narrative for a wider reading public: "Stories told in general society, may fairly be considered as public property; or rather as *wefts and strays*, which any one may appropriate, keep unaltered, mar or mend, without dread of prosecution."

The first volume of *Tales round a Winter Hearth* contains three tales by Anna Maria and a brief frame story by Jane that introduces "The Old House of Huntercombe, or Berenice's Pilgrimage." The first of Anna Maria's tales is "Glenrowan," a tale of a woman's courage in Scotland during the 1740s. Colonel Ferguson, a Scots laird loyal to his exiled prince, and Ferguson's devoted but weak and fearful sister, Annie, are visited by a friend, Miss Mackay, who proves herself a woman of honor and

spirit. When Ferguson needs someone to convey gold to messengers from the front, Miss Mackay agrees to do so — setting aside her womanly fears and going alone at night to a secret place in an ancient tower. One night after a messenger has left, the door to the secret chamber blows shut and traps her. In her terror she prays fervently and then faints, waking to find Ferguson — having returned from the front to retrieve an important document — at her side. Ferguson falls at Culloden, and Miss Mackay marries a Highlander impressed by her courage. The timorous Annie remains unmarried but lives a charitable and pious life. In this tale female courage is rewarded by Providence and romantic love, and the romance of the Scots' cause is embodied in the honorable but melancholy Ferguson and his tragic fate.

In "Lord Howth" Anna Maria turned to Roman Catholic Ireland to create a curious tale about loyalty and control of temper. The plot is launched by Lord Howth's rescuing a water rat from one of his friend's terriers. The grateful rat later appears in his chambers and gradually becomes a pet. When Howth is about to go on a journey, he ties a golden thread about the rat's paw so that he will recognize it when he returns. The rat, however, follows him on board the ship without his knowledge. There Howth inadvertently kills the rat in a fit of temper, recognizing it only as he witnesses its "dying look and dying cry." His subsequent mental suffering subdues and improves his character.

On the third anniversary of this disaster, Howth rescues a woman from a shipwreck. They do not speak the same language, but they read each other's looks: Alma, "full of woman's tender gratitude," and Howth fall in love and marry. But after their marriage, Howth is distressed by Alma's insistence on wearing a golden bracelet, which he begins to suspect is a gift from a former lover. Although she warns him that to remove it would cost her life, in a fit of jealousy he removes it while she sleeps. Alma then dies and, at the moment of her death, a rat scuttles away — the bracelet having been worked around the golden thread Howth had tied on his pet. Grief-stricken for a second time, Howth retires to a monastery, where he lives only a few months. While this tale turns from history to fantasy, Anna Maria emphasizes the same values evident in "Glenrowan," focusing on the terrible consequences resulting from a failure of loyalty, trust, and self-control.

The third tale, "Jeannie Haliday," is the ballad-like story of Alan Forsyth's unselfish love for Jeannie Halliday, even after his hope of marrying her is dashed by the appearance of another suitor, the handsome and manly Malcom Cameron. Alan is overwhelmed by Jeannie's "moral value even more than her beauty" and proves this by a love that respects her wishes and seeks to provide for her without recompense. In time, Alan expends his affection on Jeannie's small daughter, Janet. After Malcolm disappears at sea, because of the terms of the will of Alan's father Alan can help Jeannie financially only if he marries her. He proposes a platonic marriage, which Jeannie at first refuses. At last, however, the thought of her children enables her to make the sacrifice. Malcolm comes home to find Jeannie married to a dying Alan, who assures Malcolm that the marriage has never been consummated. The tale consists more of descriptions of emotional states, especially Alan's, than of action. It takes the sentimental ballad story and embroiders it in ways that depict ideals of selflessness, emotional purity, and honor in a world where courtship and family life are central. Much space is devoted to sentimental partings and reunions and to excruciatingly tender feelings.

Jane contributed one long tale, "The Old House of Huntercombe, or Berenice's Pilgrimmage," that occupies the whole of the second volume and reads like a loosely structured novella. In this tale Jane depicts scenes from her brother's Eastern travels, including scenes of Babylon. This was one of her favorite works, because she very much enjoyed taking her heroine to scenes central to her own pious faith, including the Mount of Olives and Jerusalem. For Jane, it was a tale of "woman's heart, pure, . . . kept unspotted from the world; of man's spirit, ennobled, because to serve and protect were the proofs of a gentleman." "Berenice's Pilgrimmage" is initiated on Berenice's sixteenth birthday when the Reverend Mother of the abbey where she is staying recounts Berenice's mother's death and father's disappearance. Berenice then travels to the Holy Land in search of her father's true identity. She finds friends along the way and finally a true love, the Earl of Beaufort. Her own search for identity is interlaced with descriptions of foreign scenes, tales of religious struggle, and discourse on Christian honor and charity.

In 1826 Anna Maria also published the novel *Honor O'Hara*, a three-volume narrative of modern domestic life, before the sisters in 1828 brought out another joint work in three volumes that comprised Anna Maria's *Coming Out* and Jane's *The Field of Forty Footsteps*. *Coming Out* deals with fashionable life in the nineteenth century; *The Field of Forty Footsteps* is based on historical legend.

In the same year Anna Maria Hall, a well-known author of Irish sketches and novels and the wife of popular writer and editor Samuel Carter Hall, visited the Porters and invited them to contribute to *The Amulet,* a well-paying annual produced by the Halls. During this visit Mrs. Hall — whom the Porter sisters had met at Bristol in 1816 — found Jane dwelling more in her imagination than in the real world, having for years "lived more with heroes than with real men and women." Both sisters contributed to *The Amulet* in 1828 and 1829. Anna Maria submitted poems that deal with Christian conscience and devotion. Both "The Lament of the Vaudois Exile" (1828) and "A Christian's Day" (1829) celebrate a life of faithfulness and even suffering that will be repaid in a heaven where "fadeless meads at length bestow / The food we hungered for below."

Jane contributed narratives that purport to be retellings of true events. "Peter the Great and the Shipwreck" (1828) demonstrates once more Jane's fascination with the noble hero seen as a civilizing influence and savior figure, as "ordained by Providence" to shape history. The narrative is constructed as a tale within a tale told by an old sailor at the unveiling of a statue of Peter the Great. In this sailor's tale the young czar literally saves one of his subjects from "a watery grave." The sailor also recounts his working side by side with laborers and "showing them, that, when able, every man, from the highest to the lowest, was expected to do his duty" and curbing the violence of his troops as they threaten to massacre citizens in the siege of Narva. Peter is characterized, finally, as "the father of Russia," another instance of Jane's fascination with literal and metaphoric fathers and of her insistence on the analogy between family and nation.

In 1829 Jane contributed "The South Sea Chief, A Fragment" to *The Amulet.* Again the narrative purports to be a retelling of someone else's firsthand story — the account of Laonce, a Frenchman shipwrecked on a South Sea Island. There he adopts the clothing and the customs of the savages among whom he lives, finally marrying a native king's daughter and using his royal power to discourage cannibalism. His campaign against cannibalism includes a brief but sensational scene in which warriors slay a woman "as they would have done a beast, and . . . [commence] their horrible repast upon her body." He is separated from his native wife, Berea, when he helps a ship in distress, and the Europeans, unable to sympathize with his attachment to his savage life, carry him off. His wanderings take him to Moscow, and Czar Alexander I sends him back to the South

Seas. Although the narrator does not know if he has arrived there, she wants to believe in a divine justice in which "he who shewed mercy, found mercy!" This tale clearly reflects Jane's use of her brother Robert's life and stories, as well as her insistence on the strength of family devotion that is sometimes disrupted by an uncaring world.

By this time failing health had begun to slow Anna Maria's literary production, but she published *The Barony* (1830), a tale set in Cornwall and London during the reign of King James II in which domestic peace is threatened by civil strife. In the following year Jane published *Sir Edward Seaward's Narrative of His Shipwreck and Consequent Discovery of Certain Islands in the Caribbean Sea* (1831), a work of fiction that purports to be a diary. Despite its inaccuracies the tale, which was probably much informed by her brother William, fooled many readers. Reviewers were skeptical of the truth of the story but praised it as true to life. When questioned about her source, Jane stuck to her story that the diary had been its source by saying, "Sir Walter Scott had his great secret: I must be allowed to keep my little one."

Mrs. Porter died in the summer of 1831; her death was a severe blow to Jane and Anna Maria, for their mother had been protectress, confidante, critic, and chief supporter throughout their lives. In the spring of 1832 the sisters moved to Bristol to be near their brother William. Anna Maria contracted typhus and died on 21 June 1832. Jane became a wanderer who lived in London between extended visits to friends.

Those friends urged Jane to seek solace in writing, but without her mother and sister she had lost heart to do so and declared, "I neither felt the power nor the desire to touch a literary pen again. They were gone whose words had kindled my emulations, whose approving smiles had been the most prized reward of my labors." During 1834 Jane did work on a biographical account of Anna Maria, which she apparently never completed, and the manuscript was lost. As the years passed, Jane wrote less and less, although she appeared more in London society.

In 1834 Jane contributed "A Scottish Tradition" to *The Tale Book*, a collection of narratives by well-known writers such as Scott, Washington Irving, and Mary Wollstonecraft Shelley. In the story a man describes having heard the late Scott at a club and recounts Scott's tale of a woman who was protected by Prince Charles when she followed the "royal fugitive over sea." When the hearers guess that the unnamed lady is Flora Macdonald, a stranger says no, for he has met Flora Macdonald as

*Anna Maria Porter (from the New York edition of* The Recluse of Norway, *1815; courtesy of Lilly Library, Indiana University)*

a respectable widow. The stranger reveals the lady's identity by recounting an anecdote about meeting, as a boy, a gentleman in mourning with soft, white hands. The gentleman's declarations of loyalty to the cause were mingled with wild talk of being wounded and sinful. Finally, he declared that "fidelity is not always holy" and gave the stranger a rose as he told him to pray for God to "pardon a breaking heart." When this "gentleman" later died, he "proved" to be a woman – Jeannie Cameron herself – and was buried in Prince Charles's plaid. The tale is thought to be based on Jane's own experience in Edinburgh, and the recasting of the narrator's gender is typical of Jane's identification with a masculine world: she found in the boy and the man powerful contrasts to her own ladylike constraints and to the wild fidelity of women like Cameron.

In the last years of her life Jane Porter became infatuated with a handsome young American journalist and writer, Nathaniel Parker Willis. Although he was only in his twenties and Jane was old enough to be his mother, they began an intimate and intense friendship. Even though Willis eventually married another, younger woman, their friendship continued. With characteristic gallantry, Jane chaperoned him to his wedding and, after he returned to the United States, corresponded with him for the rest of her life.

273

Feeling financial need by 1836, Jane did some writing for S. C. Hall's *New Monthly Magazine* and sought a pension. Her health continued to decline through the latter part of the 1830s, but she still wandered, appeared in London society, and worked on editions of *The Scottish Chiefs* and *Thaddeus of Warsaw*. In her lengthy "retrospective prefaces" to such works she provided a gentle view of her past and a noble vision of her calling as a writer, painting a sentimental picture of her "bird-nest chamber under the thatched eves of our rustic dwelling" and stressing her Christian moral responsibility. In these prefaces she preserves her ladylike enthusiasms and disavows any literary ambitions, yet glories in the popularity of her fiction and claims that Scott praised her work.

In 1841, while Jane was visiting Robert in Saint Petersburg, he died of a stroke. Jane returned to England and settled his estate, then went to Bristol to live with William. Though her writing days had passed, reminders of her popularity still appeared through later editions of *The Scottish Chiefs* and *Thaddeus of Warsaw*. Jane Porter died in Bristol on 24 May 1850.

During their lifetimes Jane and Anna Maria Porter were better known as best-selling novelists than as writers of short fiction. To contemporaries the romantic moralizing in which the the sisters delighted was appealing, but even during the last decades of their lives public taste was changing. While a contemporary might praise them for being "the first to inculcate Christianity in stories of romance," for embracing the evangelical Christian dismantling of a sexual double standard by teaching "that there was and is, the same moral law for man as for woman" and for appealing to youth who "look for pictures of that world in which they are panting to become actors," later readers were finding the same works outdated, overwrought, and unbelievable.

But even in their own day Jane and Anna Maria Porter were not taken seriously by writers and critics who have come to be regarded as the great minds of the nineteenth century, and the sisters received mixed reviews from contemporary women writers. Many in fact simply ignored Jane and Anna Maria, although Lady Morgan and Mary Russell Mitford were positive about their work and Joanna Baillie highly respected Jane's novels. Though most of their works have not stood the test of time, both Jane and Anna Maria delighted many readers throughout the nineteenth century by bringing to fictional narrative the emotion of balladry and by participating in the romantic reconstruction of folk legend and national history. Strongly identi-

fying with the patriarchal heroes they created, both sisters also shared the nineteenth-century fascination with the heroic; but their heroines, despite their conventionality, also exemplified ideals of female courage and loyalty. The Porter sisters placed romance and the romance of history, the manners of nineteenth-century society, and even the power of the uncanny at the service of morality and patriotism, chastity, courage, and integrity. Jane saw this moral impulse as a form of Christian service that made her popular entertainments useful and important, as she wrote: "[L]et us remember that when a nation ceases to recollect the great and the good amongst their own forefathers, they soon cease to be a people of much account at home; and in proportion to that internal decline they sink the estimation of the nations around." As does William Wordsworth's celebration of domestic affections in "Michael" (1800), works such as "Jeannie Halliday" and the "South Sea Chief" validate romantic feelings and human connections. Yet the extravagant sentiment and black-and-white morality of their works causes them to speak a language of idealistic, patriotic, conventional fantasies — and makes them artifacts of a world that is truly, for twentieth-century readers, gone with the wind.

**Biography:**

Robert Tate Irvine, "The Life of Jane Porter," M.A. thesis, University of Virginia, 1942.

**References:**

A. D. Hook, "Jane Porter, Sir Walter Scott, and the Historical Novel," *Clio,* 5 (Winter 1976): 181–192;

Winfield H. Rogers, "The Reaction Against Melodramatic Sentimentality in the English Novel, 1796–1830," *PMLA,* 49 (March 1934): 98–122.

**Papers:**

The Michael Sadlier Collection of Gothic Novels at the University of Virginia contains a manuscript diary and several letters of Jane Porter. Jane Porter's correspondence with Nathaniel Parker Willis is housed in the Joint Free Library of Morristown and Morris Township, New Jersey. Other Porter family papers are held by the British Library; the Bodleian Library, Oxford; the Samuel Carter Hall and Anna Maria (Fielding) Hall Collection in the Knox College Archives; the Houghton Library, Harvard University; the University of Kansas Library; and the Rutgers University Library.

# Sir Walter Scott

*(15 August 1771 – 21 September 1832)*

Richard D. McGhee
*Arkansas State University*

See also the Scott entries in *DLB 93: British Romantic Poets, 1789–1832, First Series; DLB 107: British Romantic Prose Writers, 1789–1832, First Series; DLB 116: British Romantic Novelists, 1789–1832; and DLB 144: Nineteenth-Century British Literary Biographers.*

BOOKS: *The Eve of Saint John. A Border Ballad* (Kelso: Printed by James Ballantyne, 1800);

*The Lay of the Last Minstrel* (London: Printed for Longman, Hurst, Rees & Orme, and A. Constable, Edinburgh, by James Ballantyne, Edinburgh, 1805; Philadelphia: Printed for I. Riley, New York, 1806);

*Ballads and Lyrical Pieces* (Edinburgh: Printed by James Ballantyne for Longman, Hurst, Rees & Orme, London, and Archibald Constable, Edinburgh, 1806; Boston: Published & sold by Etheridge & Bliss and by B. & B. Hopkins, Philadelphia, 1807);

*Marmion: A Tale of Flodden Field* (Edinburgh: Printed by J. Ballantyne for Archibald Constable, Edinburgh, and William Miller & John Murray, London, 1808; Philadelphia: Hopkins & Earle, 1808);

*The Lady of the Lake: A Poem* (Edinburgh: Printed for John Ballantyne, Edinburgh, and Longman, Hurst, Rees & Orme and William Miller, London, by James Ballantyne, 1810; Boston: Published by W. Wells & T. B. Wait, printed by T. B. Wait, 1810; New York: E. Sargeant, 1810; Philadelphia: E. Earle, 1810);

*The Vision of Don Roderick: A Poem* (Edinburgh: Printed by James Ballantyne for John Ballantyne, Edinburgh, and Longman, Hurst, Rees, Orme & Brown, London, 1811; Boston: Published by T. B. Wait, 1811);

*Rokeby: A Poem* (Edinburgh: Printed for John Ballantyne, Edinburgh, and Longman, Hurst, Rees, Orme & Brown, London, by James Ballantyne, Edinburgh, 1813; Baltimore: J. Cushing, 1813);

*Sir Walter Scott (portrait by Sir Henry Raeburn; by permission of the Scottish National Portrait Gallery)*

*The Bridal of Triermain, or The Vale of St John. In Three Cantos* (Edinburgh: Printed by James Ballantyne for John Ballantyne and for Longman, Hurst, Rees, Orme & Brown and Gale, Curtis & Fenner, London, 1813; Philadelphia: Published by M. Thomas, printed by W. Fry, 1813);

*Waverley; or 'Tis Sixty Years Since* (3 volumes, Edinburgh: Printed by James Ballantyne for Archibald Constable, Edinburgh, and Longman, Hurst, Rees, Orme & Brown, London, 1814; 1 volume, Boston: Published by Wells & Lilly and Bradford & Read, 1815; 2 volumes, New York: Van Winkle & Wiley, 1815);

*Guy Mannering; or, The Astrologer. By the Author of "Waverley"* (3 volumes, Edinburgh: Printed by James Ballantyne for Longman, Hurst, Rees, Orme & Brown, London, and Archibald Constable, Edinburgh, 1815; 2 volumes, Boston: Published by West & Richardson and Eastburn, Kirk, New York, printed by T. W. White, 1815);

*The Lord of the Isles: A Poem* (Edinburgh: Printed for Archibald Constable, Edinburgh, and Longman, Hurst, Rees, Orme & Brown, London, by James Ballantyne, 1815; New York: R. Scott, 1815; Philadelphia: Published by Moses Thomas, 1815);

*The Field of Waterloo: A Poem* (Edinburgh: Printed by James Ballantyne for Archibald Constable, Edinburgh, and Longman, Hurst, Rees, Orme & Brown, and John Murray, London, 1815; New York: Van Winkle & Wiley, 1815; Philadelphia: Published by Moses Thomas, printed by Van Winkle & Wiley, 1815);

*The Ettricke Garland; Being Two Excellent New Songs on The Lifting of the Banner of the House of Buccleuch, At the Great Foot-Ball Match on Carterhaugh, Dec. 4, 1815,* by Scott and James Hogg (Edinburgh: Printed by James Ballantyne, 1815);

*Paul's Letters To His Kinsfolk* (Edinburgh: Printed by James Ballantyne for Archibald Constable, Edinburgh, and Longman, Hurst, Rees, Orme & Brown and John Murray, London, 1816; Philadelphia: Republished by M. Thomas, 1816);

*The Antiquary. By the Author of "Waverley" and "Guy Mannering"* (3 volumes, Edinburgh: Printed by James Ballantyne for Archibald Constable, Edinburgh, and Longman, Hurst, Rees, Orme & Brown, London, 1816; 2 volumes, New York: Van Winkle & Wiley, 1816);

*Tales of My Landlord, Collected and Arranged by Jedediah Cleishbotham, Schoolmaster and Parish-Clerk of Gandercleugh* (4 volumes, Edinburgh: Printed for William Blackwood and John Murray, London, 1816; 1 volume, Philadelphia: Published by M. Thomas, 1817) — comprises *The Black Dwarf* and *Old Mortality*;

*Harold the Dauntless: A Poem* (Edinburgh: Printed by James Ballantyne for Longman, Hurst, Rees, Orme & Brown, London, and Archibald Constable, Edinburgh, 1817; New York: Published by James Eastburn, printed by Van Winkle Wiley, 1817);

*Rob Roy; by the Author of "Waverley," "Guy Mannering," and "The Antiquary"* (3 volumes, Edinburgh: Printed by James Ballantyne for Archibald Constable, Edinburgh, and Longman, Hurst,

Rees, Orme & Brown, London, 1818 [i.e., 1817]; 2 volumes, New York: J. Eastburn, 1818; New York: Published by Kirk & Mercein, printed by E. & E. Hosford, Albany, 1818; Philadelphia: Published by M. Thomas, printed by J. Maxwell, 1818);

*Tales of My Landlord: Second Series, Collected and Arranged by Jedediah Cleishbotham, Schoolmaster and Parish-Clerk of Gandercleugh ,* 4 volumes (Edinburgh: Printed for Archibald Constable, 1818; Philadelphia: M. Carey & Son, 1818) — comprises *The Heart of Mid-Lothian*;

*Tales of My Landlord: Third Series, Collected and Arranged by Jedediah Cleishbotham, Schoolmaster and Parish-Clerk of Gandercleugh,* 4 volumes (Edinburgh: Printed for Archibald Constable, Edinburgh, and Longman, Hurst, Rees, Orme & Brown and Hurst, Robinson, London, 1819; New York: Published by Charles Wiley, W. B. Gilley & A. T. Goodrich, printed by Clayton & Kingsland, 1819; Philadelphia: M. Thomas, 1819) — comprises *The Bride of Lammermoor* and *A Legend of Montrose*;

*Provincial Antiquities and Picturesque Scenery of Scotland,* text by Scott with plates by J. M. W. Turner and others (10 parts, Edinburgh: Printed by James Ballantyne, 1819–1826; 2 volumes, London: J. & A. Arch, 1826);

*Miscellaneous Poems* (Edinburgh: Printed for Archibald Constable, Edinburgh, and Hurst, Robinson, London, 1820);

*Ivanhoe: A Romance; By "the Author of Waverley" &c.* (3 volumes, Edinburgh: Printed for Archibald Constable, Edinburgh, and Hurst, Robinson, London, 1820 [i.e., 1819]; 2 volumes, Philadelphia: M. Carey & Son, 1820);

*The Monastery: A Romance; By the Author of "Waverley"* (3 volumes, Edinburgh: Printed for Longman, Hurst, Rees, Orme & Brown, London, and for Archibald Constable and John Ballantyne, Edinburgh, 1820; 1 volume, Philadelphia: Published by M. Carey & Son, 1820);

*The Abbott; By the Author of "Waverley"* (3 volumes, Edinburgh: Printed for Longman, Hurst, Rees, Orme & Brown, London, and for Archibald Constable and John Ballantyne, Edinburgh, 1820; 2 volumes, New York: J. & J. Harper, 1820; 1 volume, Philadelphia: M. Carey & Son, 1820);

*Kenilworth: A Romance. By the Author of "Waverley," "Ivanhoe," &c.* (3 volumes, Edinburgh: Printed for Archibald Constable and John Ballantyne, Edinburgh, and Hurst, Robinson, London,

1821; Hartford: S. G. Goodrich, 1821; Philadelphia: M. Carey & Son, 1821);

*The Pirate; By the Author of "Waverley," "Kenilworth,"* &c. (3 volumes, Edinburgh: Printed for Archibald Constable, and Hurst, Robinson, London, 1822; [i.e., 1821]; 2 volumes, Boston: Wells & Lilly, 1822; 1 volume, Hartford: S. G. Goodrich and Huntington & Hopkins, 1822; 2 volumes, New York: E. Duyckinck, 1822; 1 volume, Philadelphia: Carey & Lea, 1822);

*The Fortunes of Nigel; By the Author of "Waverley," "Kenilworth,"* &c. (3 volumes, Edinburgh: Printed for Archibald Constable, Edinburgh, and Hurst, Robinson, London, 1822; 2 volumes, New York: T. Longworth, 1822; Philadelphia: Carey & Lea, 1822);

*Halidon Hill: A Dramatic Sketch* (Edinburgh: Printed for Archibald Constable, and Hurst, Robinson, London, 1822; New York: S. Campbell, printed by E. B. Clayton, 1822; Philadelphia: Carey & Lea, 1822);

*Peveril of the Peak; By the Author of "Waverley, Kenilworth,"* &c. (4 volumes, Edinburgh: Printed for Archibald Constable, Edinburgh and Hurst, Robinson, London, 1822 [i.e., 1823]; 3 volumes, Philadelphia: Carey & Lea, 1823);

*Quentin Durward; By the Author of "Waverley, Peveril of the Peak,"* &c. (3 volumes, Edinburgh: Printed for Archibald Constable, Edinburgh, and Hurst, Robinson, London, 1823; 1 volume, Philadelphia: Carey & Lea, 1823);

*St. Ronan's Well; By the Author of "Waverley, Quentin Durward,"* &c. (3 volumes, Edinburgh: Printed for Archibald Constable, Edinburgh, and Hurst, Robinson, London, 1824 [i.e., 1823]; Philadelphia: Carey & Lea, 1824);

*Redgauntlet: A Tale of the Eighteenth Century. By the Author of "Waverley"* (3 volumes, Edinburgh: Printed for Archibald Constable, and Hurst, Robinson, London, 1824; 2 volumes, Philadelphia: Carey & Lea, 1824);

*Tales of the Crusaders; By the Author of Waverley* (4 volumes, Edinburgh: Printed for Archibald Constable, Edinburgh, and Hurst, Robinson, London, 1825; New York: Published by E. Duyckinck, Collins & Hannay, Collins, E. Bliss & E. White, and W. B. Gilley, printed by J. & J. Harper, 1825; 2 volumes, Philadelphia: Carey & Lea, 1825) – comprises *The Betrothed* and *The Talisman;*

*Letter to the Editor of the Edinburgh Weekly Journal from Malachi Malagrowther, Esq. on the Proposed Change of Currency and Other Late Alterations, As*
*They Affect, or Are Intended to Affect, the Kingdom of Scotland* (Edinburgh: Printed by James Ballantyne for William Blackwood, 1826);

*A Second Letter to the Editor of the Edinburgh Weekly Journal, from Malachi Malagrowther, Esq.: On the Proposed Change of Currency and Other Later Alterations, As They Affect, or Are Intended to Affect, the Kingdom of Scotland* (Edinburgh: Printed by James Ballantyne for William Blackwood, 1826);

*A Third Letter to the Editor of the Edinburgh Weekly Journal, from Malachi Malagrowther, Esq.: On the Proposed Change of Currency, and Other Late Alterations, As They Affect, or Are Intended to Affect, the Kingdom of Scotland* (Edinburgh: Printed by James Ballantyne for William Blackwood, Edinburgh, and T. Cadell, London, 1826);

*Woodstock; or, the Cavalier; A Tale of the Year Sixteen Hundred and Fifty-One; By the Author of "Waverley, Tales of the Crusader,"* &c. (3 volumes, Edinburgh: Printed for Archibald Constable, Edinburgh, and Longman, Rees, Orme, Brown & Green, London, 1826; 2 volumes, Philadelphia: Carey & Lea, 1826);

*The Life of Napoleon Buonaparte, Emperor of the French: With a Preliminary View of the French Revolution,* 9 volumes (Edinburgh: Printed by Ballantyne, for Longman, Rees, Orme, Brown & Green, London, 1827; Philadelphia: Carey, Lea & Carey, 1827);

*The Miscellaneous Prose Works of Sir Walter Scott, Bart.,* 6 volumes (Edinburgh: Cadell, 1827; Boston: Wells & Lilly, 1829);

*Chronicles of the Canongate; By the Author of "Waverley,"* &c. (2 volumes, Edinburgh: Printed for Cadell, Edinburgh, and Simpkin & Marshall, London, 1827; 1 volume, Philadelphia: Carey, Lea & Carey, 1827) – comprises "The Highland Widow," "The Two Drovers," and "The Surgeon's Daughter";

*Religious Discourses. By a Layman* (London: Henry Colburn, 1828; New York: Printed by J. & J. Harper, sold by Collins & Hannay, 1828);

*Chronicles of the Canongate: Second Series; By the Author of "Waverley"* &c. (3 volumes, Edinburgh: Printed for Cadell, Edinburgh, and Simpkin & Marshall, London, 1828; 1 volume, Philadelphia: Carey, Lea & Carey, 1828) – comprises *The Fair Maid of Perth;*

*Tales of a Grandfather: Being Stories Taken from Scottish History,* first–third series (9 volumes, Edinburgh: Printed for Cadell, 1828–1830 [i.e., 1827–1830]; 8 volumes, Philadelphia: Carey, Lea & Carey, 1828–1830);

*Scott (leaning on cane) in 1825 with Archibald Constable; James Hogg; John Gibson Lockhart; Scott's daughter Anne; his wife, Charlotte; his daughter Sopia Scott Lockhart; Maria Edgeworth; Scott's son Walter and niece, Anne Scott; Harriet Edgeworth; Scott's son Charles; and Robert Shortreed. Painting by William Stewart Watson (from a 1901 edition of John Gibson Lockhart's* Memoirs of the Life of Sir Walter Scott, Bart.)

*Anne of Geierstein; or, The Maiden of the Mist; By the Author of "Waverley," &c.* (3 volumes, Edinburgh: Printed for Cadell, Edinburgh, and Simpkin & Marshall, London, 1829; 2 volumes, Philadelphia: Carey, Lea & Carey, 1829);

*The History of Scotland,* 2 volumes, in *The Cabinet Cyclopaedia, Conducted by Rev. Dionysis Lardner* (London: Printed for Longman, Rees, Orme, Brown & Green and John Taylor, 1830);

*The Doom of Devorgoil: A Melo-drama. Auchindrane; or, the Ayrshire Tragedy* (Edinburgh: Printed for Cadell, Edinburgh, and Simpkin & Marshall, London, 1830; New York: Printed by J. & J. Harper, 1830);

*Letters on Demonology and Witchcraft* (London: J. Murray, 1830; New York: J. & J. Harper, 1830);

*Tales of a Grandfather: Being Stories Taken from the History of France* (3 volumes, Edinburgh: Cadell, 1831; 2 volumes, Philadelphia: Carey & Lea, 1831);

*Tales of My Landlord: Fourth and Last Series, Collected and Arranged by Jedediah Cleishbotham, Schoolmaster and Parish-Clerk of Gandercleugh* (4 volumes, Edinburgh: Printed for Robert Cadell, Edinburgh, and Whitaker, London, 1832; 3 volumes, Philadelphia: Carey & Lea, 1832) — comprises *Count Robert of Paris* and *Castle Dangerous;*

*The Journal of Sir Walter Scott,* 3 volumes, edited by John Guthrie Tait and W. M. Parker (Edinburgh: Oliver & Boyd, 1939–1949).

**Editions:** *Waverley Novels,* Magnum Opus Edition, 48 volumes, with Scott's prefaces and final revisions (Edinburgh: Cadell, 1829–1833);

*Miscellaneous Prose Works,* 30 volumes, edited by John Gibson Lockhart (Edinburgh: Cadell, 1834–1846);

*Miscellaneous Prose Works of Sir Walter Scott,* 30 volumes (Edinburgh: A. & C. Black, 1870–1871);

*The Waverly Novels,* Centenary Edition, 25 volumes (Edinburgh: A. & C. Black, 1870–1871);

*The Waverley Novels,* Dryburgh Edition, 25 volumes (London & Edinburgh: A. & C. Black, 1892–1894);

*The Waverley Novels,* Border Edition, 48 volumes, edited by Andrew Lang (London: J. C. Nimmo, 1892–1894; Boston: Estes & Lauriat, 1893–1894);

*The Poetical Works of Sir Walter Scott, with the Author's Introduction and Notes,* edited by J. Logie Robertson (London: H. Frowde, 1894);

*Lives of the Novelists* (London, New York & Toronto: Oxford University Press, 1906);

*Minstrelsy of the Scottish Border,* edited by Scott, newly edited by Thomas Henderson (London: Harrap, 1931);

*Private Letters of the Seventeenth Century,* edited by Scott, newly edited by Douglas Grant (Oxford: Clarendon Press, 1947);

*The Life of John Dryden,* edited by Scott, newly edited by Bernard Kreissman (Lincoln: University of Nebraska Press, 1963);

*Sir Walter Scott on Novelists and Fiction,* edited by Ioan Williams (New York: Barnes & Noble, 1968);

*The Journal of Sir Walter Scott,* edited by W. E. K. Anderson (Oxford: Clarendon Press, 1972);

*The Prefaces to the Waverley Novels,* edited by Mark A. Weinstein (Lincoln: University of Nebraska Press, 1978);

*The Letters of Malachi Malagrowther,* edited by P. H. Scott (Edinburgh: Blackwood, 1981);

*Scott on Himself: A Collection of the Autobiographical Writings of Sir Walter Scott,* edited by David Hewitt (Edinburgh: Scottish Academic Press, 1981);

*The Edinburgh Edition of the Waverley Novels,* 30 volumes projected, 3 volumes published; Hewitt, editor in chief (Edinburgh: Edinburgh University Press / New York: Columbia University Press, 1993– ).

OTHER: *The Chase, and William and Helen: Two Ballads from the German of Gottfried Augustus Bürger,* translated by Scott (Edinburgh: Printed by Mundell & Son for Manners & Miller and sold by T. Cadell & W. Davies, 1796);

*Goetz von Berlichingen, With the Iron Hand: A Tragedy. Translated from the German of Goethe,* translated by Scott (London: Printed for J. Bell, 1799);

"The Fire King," "Glenfinlas," "The Eve of Saint John," "Frederick and Alice," and "The Wild Huntsmen," in *Tales of Wonder; Written and Collected by M. G. Lewis, Esq., M.P.,* 2 volumes (London: Printed by W. Bulmer for the author & sold by J. Bell, 1801), I: 62–69, 122–136, 137–147, 148–152, 153–163;

*Minstrelsy of the Scottish Border,* 2 volumes, edited by Scott (Kelso: Printed by James Ballantyne for T. Cadell, Jun. & W. Davies, London, and sold by Manners & Miller and A. Constable, Edinburgh, 1802); enlarged edition, 3 volumes (Edinburgh: Printed by James Ballantyne for Longman & Rees, London, and sold by Manners & Miller and A. Constable, Edinburgh, 1803; revised, 1810; Philadelphia: Carey, 1813);

*Sir Tristrem: A Metrical Romance of the Thirteenth Century; by Thomas of Ercildoune,* edited and completed by Scott (Edinburgh: Printed by James Ballantyne for Archibald Constable, Edinburgh, and Longman & Rees, London, 1804);

*Original Memoirs, Written during the Great Civil War: Being the Life of Sir Henry Slingsby, and Memoirs of Capt. Hodgson,* edited by Scott (Edinburgh: Printed by J. Ballantyne for A. Constable, 1806);

*The Works of John Dryden,* 18 volumes, edited, with a biography, by Scott (London: Miller, 1808);

*Joseph Strutt, Queenhoo-Hall: A Romance; and Ancient Times: A Drama,* 4 volumes, edited by Scott (Edinburgh: Printed by J. Ballantyne for J. Murray, London, and A. Constable, Edinburgh, 1808);

*Memoirs of Capt. George Carleton, An English Officer. . . . Written by Himself,* edited by Scott (Edinburgh: Printed by J. Ballantyne for A. Constable and J. Murray, London, 1808);

*Memoirs of Robert Cary, Earl of Monmouth,* edited by Scott (Edinburgh: Constable, 1808);

*The State Papers and Letters of Sir Ralph Sadler, Knight-Banneret,* edited, with an introductory essay, by Scott (Edinburgh: Printed for Archibald Constable and for T. Cadell & W. Davies, William Miller, and John Murray, London, 1809);

*A Collection of Scarce and Valuable Tracts* [The Somers Tracts], second edition, 13 volumes, edited by Scott (London: Printed for T. Cadell & W. Davies, 1809–1815);

*English Minstrelsy: Being a Selection of Fugitive Poetry from the Best English Authors,* 2 volumes, edited by Scott (Edinburgh: J. Ballantyne, 1810);

*The Poetical Works of Anna Seward; with Extracts from Her Literary Correspondence,* 3 volumes, edited by Scott (Edinburgh: J. Ballantyne, 1810);

*Secret History of the Court of James the First,* 2 volumes, edited by Scott (Edinburgh: Printed for J. Ballantyne, 1811);

*The Works of Jonathan Swift,* 19 volumes, edited, with a biography and notes, by Scott (Edinburgh: Constable, 1814);

*The Border Antiquities of England and Scotland,* 2 volumes, includes an introduction by Scott (London: Printed for Longman, Hurst, Rees, Orme & Brown, 1814, 1817);

James, eleventh Baron Somerville, *Memorie of the Somervilles,* 2 volumes, edited by Scott (Edinburgh: Constable, 1815);

*Ballantyne's Novelist's Library,* 10 volumes, edited, with biographical prefaces, by Scott (London: Hurst, Robinson, 1821–1824);

*Memorials of the Haliburtons,* edited by Scott (Edinburgh: Printed by J. Ballantyne, 1824).

Sir Walter Scott was a great novelist, a good scholar, and a successful attorney. When, through no fault of his own, his bookselling partnership with John Ballantyne became involved with the bankruptcy of Archibald Constable's publishing company in 1826, Scott's moral strength was demonstrated by his commitment to repay his own and others' debts. He was a faithful son, husband, and father; a convivial friend of many, in high as well as low places of British society; and an influential voice in the politics of his time. Scott's greatest gift, of course, was his ability to create forceful narratives, whether verse or prose.

Although Scott's achievement as a novelist is well known, few readers have paid close attention to his short stories – possibly because there are so few of them. Unless stories are separated from the multiple plots and framing devices of his long fictions, Scott's short stories can be counted on the fingers of one hand. His experiments in this genre of prose fiction include the story-within-a-story of Wandering Willie's Tale in *Redgauntlet: A Tale of the Eighteenth Century* (1824) and the three powerful stories published together as the first series of *Chronicles of the Canongate* (1827): "The Highland Widow," "The Two Drovers," and "The Surgeon's Daughter."

Scott was born in Edinburgh, Scotland, on 15 August 1771 to Walter Scott and Anne Rutherford Scott. Crippled by infantile paralysis, he was often sent to his grandfather Robert Scott's country home, where it was hoped that his condition would improve. He was sent to high school in Edinburgh in October 1779, and in November 1783 he enrolled in Edinburgh University. He was apprenticed to his father to study law in March 1786, joining the Faculty of Advocates in July 1792. In 1796 the woman he loved, Williamina Belsches, became engaged to another. The next year he joined a voluntary cavalry unit, the Royal Edinburgh Volunteer Light Dragoons, which was made up mostly of middle-

class citizens who cherished the order they saw threatened by the French Revolution. On 27 December 1797 he married Charlotte Carpenter, with whom he had four children: Charlotte Sophia, born in 1799; Walter, born in 1801; Anne, born in 1803; and Charles, born in 1805. In 1799 he became sheriff, or county judge, of Selkirkshire.

While his legal practice and earnings increased steadily, Scott enjoyed an even more successful career as a poet, beginning in 1796 with his translation of *The Chase, and William and Helen: Two Ballads from the German of Gottfried Augustus Bürger* and progressing to his first important original poem *The Lay of the Last Minstrel* in 1805. The poet and attorney was also a scholar who edited literary papers, prepared learned introductions, and composed impressive biographies, including one of John Dryden for his edition of Dryden's works, published in 1808. In the same year he broke his relationship with Francis Jeffrey and the Whig *Edinburgh Review,* later writing instead for the Tory *Quarterly Review,* with which he established a long and productive relationship. Scott continued delighting his public with narrative poems, including *Marmion: A Tale of Flodden Field* (1808) and *The Lady of the Lake* (1810). With profits from his poetry sales he bought a modest farm on the River Tweed that he transformed into a gentleman's estate he called Abbotsford.

Scott had begun writing *Waverley; or, 'Tis Sixty Years Since* as early as 1804. On 7 July 1814 he put the novel before an eager audience of readers, whose appetite for his writing seemed insatiable. Though the work was published anonymously, the name of the author soon became an open secret. *Waverley* is centered on the Jacobite uprising of 1745, exhibiting for the first time in fiction Scott's lifelong interest in the history of his native country, in particular its military and political struggles with England.

After a voyage to survey Scottish lighthouses, Scott wrote *Guy Mannering; or, The Astrologer* (1815), a novel set in the late eighteenth century, as was his next novel, *The Antiquary* (1816). To introduce the two novels of *Tales of My Landlord* (1816) Scott created Jedediah Cleishbotham, a pedantic pseudonymous rival to the anonymous author of *Waverley* (the schoolmaster was also known as "Jedediah Thwackass of Gander's Hollow"). The first novel, *The Black Dwarf,* set in Scotland after the Act of Union in 1707, deals with the supernatural and hidden identities, as many of Scott's stories do. The second novel, *Old Mortality,* is based on an uprising by the Covenantors in 1679. Two of Scott's most popular novels are set during the 1715 Jacobite uprising: *Rob Roy* (1817) and *The Heart of Mid-Lothian,* the latter of which constituted *Tales of My Landlord: Second Series* (1818).

In spite of an attack of gallstones, Scott wrote the novels *A Legend of Montrose* and *The Bride of Lammermoor* for *Tales of My Landlord: Third Series,* which was published in June 1819, then went on to write *Ivanhoe* (1819). Scott established his conservative, even reactionary, political credentials as a defender of the 16 August 1819 "Peterloo Massacre" at Manchester, in which hundreds of demonstrators for parliamentary reform were wounded and eleven were killed. Perhaps to explore the intellectual origins of his ideological orientation, Scott wrote a narrative set in the Reformation of the sixteenth century, *The Monastery* (1820). His next work, *The Abbot,* also published in 1820, is based on the imprisonment of Mary, Queen of Scots. *Kenilworth* (1821) focuses on Mary's rival, Queen Elizabeth I.

Following *The Pirate* (1821), which is set in the Orkney Islands, Scott completed *The Fortunes of Nigel* (1822) and began *Peveril of the Peak* (1823). Scott's sympathy for James I and Charles II in these novels expresses his Tory political orientation, and in both works saving family honor and estates has a special relevance for an author with dreams of a family crest and lordly domains. *St. Ronan's Well* (1823) marks a departure from Scott's historical novels . The social prejudices that limit freedom, especially women's, are given satiric treatment in this tale of illicit passion set in a nineteenth-century health resort.

A more complicated and ambitious study of power, both sexual and political, is presented in Scott's next novel, *Redgauntlet: A Tale of the Eighteenth Century,* set during the futile Jacobite uprising in support of the Stuart Pretender, Charles Edward. This novel brings events of English and Scottish history much closer to Scott's own time, and many of the details evoke Scott's experiences as an attorney. Darsie Latimer is kidnapped, discovers his true identity in learning that his father was a Jacobite martyr during the uprising of 1745, and refuses to compromise his patriotism. One of Scott's successful short stories, and the work that can be considered his first effort in the genre, occurs as an episode of *Redgauntlet.* The characters in this story-within-a-story, told by Wandering Willie, are Steenie Steenson, an ancestor of Willie's, and Sir Robert Redgauntlet, an ancestor of the major characters in the novel, who summons Steenie Steenson into hell.

The novels *The Betrothed* and *The Tailsman* were published as *Tales of the Crusaders* in 1825. In July of that year, Scott visited Dublin, where his son Walter was stationed as a captain of Hussars. Scott was much acclaimed and received an LL.D. from Trinity College. Back home in late August he began work on his biography of Napoleon Bonaparte, and on Sunday, 20 November 1825, he started keeping a journal. In January 1826 his publisher, Constable, went bankrupt, and Scott, caught in the financial chaos, dedicated himself to paying off his debts. Even more painful was the death of his wife in May 1826. In June he resumed work on his life of Napoleon. Scott's concern that he might lose Abbotsford is reflected in Sir Henry Lee's predicament in *Woodstock; or the Cavalier; A Tale of the Year Sixteen Hundred and Fifty-One* (1826).

*The Life of Napoleon Buonaparte, Emperor of the French: With a Preliminary View of the French Revolution* was published in the summer of 1827, and later in the same year appeared *The Miscellaneous Prose Works of Sir Walter Scott, Bart.* and the first series of *Chronicles of the Canongate,* containing three tales of ironic violence: "The Highland Widow," "The Two Drovers," and "The Surgeon's Daughter." Mr. Chrystal Croftangry, a young lawyer, is Scott's imaginary editor of the *Chronicles of the Canongate* who reads the stories aloud to his friends. Scott created this character as a mockery of his earlier attempt to remain anonymous. These shorter narratives were produced to fulfill a commitment to publish a collection of tales for Cadell and Company.

In "The Highland Widow" Elspat MacTavish, the widow of the brutal Hamish MacTavish Mhor, makes her son Hamish Bean an army deserter by drugging him while he is home on leave and then urges him to kill the soldier sent to find him. She curses Michael Tyrie, a clergyman who reports her son's execution, and then roams the Highlands, a fright to all, for years, until her disappearance and presumed death. Hamish Bean is a pathetic hero who disappoints his mother because he is not as savage as his father, a thug who terrorized the people of the Scottish Lowlands. Hamish Bean's career toward shameful execution is launched when he enlists in the army to raise money for his mother's support. His love for her is, though tame by Elspat's standards, the reason he suffers a terrible fate. This frightening story is told to the narrator, Bethune Baliol, who is touring the Highlands as an escape from grief after a family loss, like Elspat. Unlike Elspat, Baliol is not responsible for her loss, and thus the pain of Elspat's tragedy is mitigated by the distance of intermediate narration.

"The Two Drovers" is narrated by Croftangry. Robin Oig M'Combich, a Scottish Highland

*Portrait of Scott by William Nicholson, R.S.A. (Scottish National Portrait Gallery)*

cattle drover, quarrels with the English drover Harry Wakefield over pastureland, murders him in an English tavern, and is executed. The violence is a result of misunderstanding and mutual ignorance of rights to rent. One of the principals, Mr. Fleecebumpkin, who rented pasture to Harry Wakefield, carries a name typically expressive of Scott's humor, but in this story the humor seems misplaced if not determinedly cynical. Dame Heskett, landlady of the English inn, tries to make peace, but her efforts, so contrary to her husband's mean-spirited taunts, are in vain as the story's dark fate will not be denied. This fate had been predicted for Robin Oig by his aunt, Janet of Tomahourich, who has the gift of second sight. Such a tale, depending on unavoidable fate, would be more tolerable if it were presented as an event of history; however, as a product of passion and character, it portrays a view of such pessimism that few of Scott's readers found it attractive. Twentieth-century readers regard the story more highly as a tightly composed narrative with tragic power.

Scott expresses this same pessimistic outlook in "The Surgeon's Daughter," a bleak, sterile narra-

tive of empty lives, blind ambition, and moral stupidity. Told to Croftangry by Kate, the daughter of his lawyer friend Mr. Fairscribe, it is the story of one of their family's unmarried aunts, Marion Gray. Once the virtue of the surgeon, Dr. Gideon Gray, is granted, there is little more to celebrate in this story, since even the heroine is shown to be morally blind as well as pathetically victimized. Dr. Gray is paid well by a mysterious aristocrat to care for a masked woman of Jewish and Portuguese background who bears the aristocrat's child without benefit of marriage. Both mother and father disappear, leaving the child, Richard Middlemas, in the care of Dr. Gray. Meanwhile, the doctor's wife dies giving birth to their only child, Marion (Menie) Gray, who grows up loving her foster brother Richard. When a young apprentice, Adam Hartley, is brought in with Richard to study medicine with Gray, he contends for the affections of Menie. But she is fated to love only Richard, who is well aware of his ambiguous family status. Indeed, he romanticizes his background so much that he convinces himself that he is due not only the name of his father but also the wealth of both mother and father.

Although Menie loves Richard, he loves no one but himself. Adam loves Menie and saves both her and Richard more than once from terrible situations. Eventually all make their way to India during the heyday of the East India Company. Against a background of rampant British colonialism, Richard shocks his mother to death, earns his father's contempt, betrays his country, and tries to sell Menie into slavery. Ever faithful Adam prevents the enslavement of Menie, but he cannot prevent Richard being crushed to death by an elephant on the command of the Indian prince Richard hoped to serve and planned to betray. Scott describes this scene in gruesome detail. Adam dies within two years, and Menie returns home to Scotland with a fortune in money but utterly poor in heart and spirit. This is a strikingly unattractive collection of stories with no illusions about family relations, friendship, or sexual love.

Scott next produced one of his strongest novels, *The Fair Maid of Perth,* which was published as *Chronicles of the Canongate: Second Series* (1828). Like the short tales of this time, *The Fair Maid of Perth* is characterized by macabre violence, senseless carnage, torture, betrayal, and cowardice. Because it is a longer narrative, it subordinates much of its cynical and nihilistic material to a leisurely pace of romantic courtship, but it cannot conceal the emptiness that hovers over the lives of all the characters. Also in 1829 Scott wrote introductions and notes for the collected edition of his *Waverley Novels* (1829–1833) and finished writing *Anne of Geierstein; or, The Maiden of the Mist,* which is set in the fifteenth century during conflicts between the duke of Burgundy and King Louis XI of France. So many of the principals die in this story that the history in the subject is overwhelmed by a nihilistic theme of death and destruction. The public executioner, Stephen Steinernherz, might stand as a symbolic example of Scott's themes of the time: desiring to become an aristocrat, he betrays and executes his lawful lord and then helps himself to other people's property.

After suffering a stroke in 1830 Scott retired from the Court of Session near the end of that year. In 1831 he was drawn into debates over the Reform Bill, which he opposed. Attempting to speak at a public meeting, he was hooted down, and, later, his carriage was stoned by crowds of hostile laborers. The events of his life doubtless seemed to confirm the pessimism of his imagination as expressed in his narratives. His next novels, *Count Robert of Paris* and *Castle Dangerous,* were published as *Tales of My Landlord: Fourth and Last Series* (1832).

While touring with his daughter Anne to Malta in the fall of 1831, he was grief stricken on hearing the news of a beloved grandson's death. Scott returned home by crossing the Alps and sailing down the Rhine River, reaching Abbotsford in July 1832. He lingered in illness and then died on 21 September 1832, leaving an unfinished manuscript for a novel to be called "The Siege of Malta." In the title he captured the essence of a theme long a preoccupation of his fiction. He died after producing many great romantic tales but in later works was unable to sustain the triumph of romance over darkening reality in his life and in his art.

During his life there was not a writer to challenge him for his popularity and fame. Although his reputation declined after his death, his accomplishments could not long be denied. His short fiction is not great in quantity, but it is often powerful. While there is a great distance in tone from the comic and shrewd satire of Wandering Willie's tale in *Redgauntlet,* to the ironic nihilism of "The Surgeon's Daughter," there is no loss of craftsmanship. Scott will be known best for his novels and poems, but he will not be forgotten for his short fiction.

## Letters:

*The Letters of Sir Walter Scott,* 12 volumes, edited by Sir Herbert J. C. Grierson, assisted by David-son Cook, W. M. Parker, and others (London: Constable, 1932–1937).

## Bibliographies:

Greville Worthington, *A Bibliography of the Waverley Novels* (London: Constable, 1931);

William Ruff, *A Bibliography of the Poetical Works of Sir Walter Scott, 1796–1832* (Edinburgh: Edinburgh Bibliographical Society, 1938);

James Clarkson Corson, *A Bibliography of Sir Walter Scott: A Classified and Annotated List of Books and Articles Relating to His Life and Works, 1797–1940* (Edinburgh & London: Oliver & Boyd, 1943);

Jill Rubenstein, *Sir Walter Scott: A Reference Guide* (Boston: G. K. Hall, 1978).

## Biographies:

John Gibson Lockhart, *Memoirs of the Life of Sir Walter Scott, Bart.,* (7 volumes, Edinburgh: Cadell, 1837–1838; revised, 10 volumes, 1839);

Sir Herbert Grierson, *Sir Walter Scott, Bart.: A New Life Supplementary to and Corrective of Lockhart's Biography* (London: Constable, 1938);

Hesketh Pearson, *Sir Walter Scott: His Life and Personality* (New York: Harper, 1955);

Edgar Johnson, *Sir Walter Scott: The Great Unknown,* 2 volumes (New York: Macmillan, 1970).

## References:

James Anderson, "Sir Walter Scott as Historical Novelist: Scott's Opinions on Historical Fiction," *Studies in Scottish Literature,* 4 (July 1966): 29–41; 4 (October 1966): 63–78; 4 (January 1967): 155–178; 5 (July 1967): 14–27; 5 (October 1967): 83–97; 5 (January 1968): 143–166;

David Daiches, "Scott's Achievement as a Novelist," *Nineteenth-Century Fiction,* 6 (September 1951): 80–95; 6 (December 1951): 153–173;

Peter D. Garside, "Scott and the 'Philosophical' Historians," *Journal of the History of Ideas,* 36 (July 1975): 497–512;

Wendell V. Harris, *British Short Fiction in the Nineteenth Century: A Literary and Bibliographic Guide* (Detroit: Wayne State University Press, 1979);

A. Norman Jeffares, ed., *Scott's Mind and Art* (Edinburgh: Oliver & Boyd, 1969);

James Kerr, *Fiction Against History: Scott as Storyteller* (Cambridge: Cambridge University Press, 1989);

John Lauber, *Sir Walter Scott,* revised edition (Boston: Twayne, 1989);

George Lukács, *The Historical Novel,* translated by Hannah Mitchell and Stanley Mitchell (London: Merlin Press, 1962);

Graham McMaster, *Scott and Society* (Cambridge: Cambridge University Press, 1981);

Jane Millgate, *Walter Scott: The Making of the Novelist* (Toronto: University of Toronto Press, 1984);

Susan Morgan, "Old Heroes and a New Heroine in the Waverley Novels," *English Literary History,* 50 (Fall 1983): 559–587;

Harry E. Shaw, *The Forms of Historical Fiction: Sir Walter Scott and His Successors* (Ithaca, N.Y.: Cornell University Press, 1983);

Alexander Welsh, *The Hero of the Waverley Novels* (New Haven: Yale University Press, 1963);

Judith Wilt, *Secret Leaves: The Novels of Sir Walter Scott* (Chicago: University of Chicago Press, 1985).

**Papers:**
Collections of manuscripts, letters, documents, and memorabilia are in the Henry W. and Albert A. Berg Collection and the manuscript division of the New York Public Library; the Boston Public Library; the British Museum; the Folger Shakespeare Library, Washington, D.C.; the Forster Collection in the Victoria and Albert Museum; the Houghton Library and the Harry E. Widener Library of Harvard University; the Huntington Library, San Marino, California; the Pierpont Morgan Library; the National Library of Scotland; the Carl Pforzheimer Collection of the New York Public Library; the library of Princeton University; and the library of the University of Rochester.

# Mary Wollstonecraft Shelley

*(30 August 1797 – 1 February 1851)*

Edward Ball
*University of North Carolina at Asheville*

See also the Shelley entries in *DLB 110: British Romantic Prose Writers, 1789–1832, Second Series* and *DLB 116: British Romantic Novelists, 1789–1832.*

BOOKS: *Mounseer Nongtongpaw; or, The Discoveries of John Bull in a Trip to Paris* (London: Printed for the Proprietors of the Juvenile Library, 1808);

*History of a Six Weeks' Tour through a Part of France, Switzerland, Germany, and Holland, with Letters Descriptive of a Sail round the Lake of Geneva, and of the Glaciers of Chamouni* (London: Published by T. Hookham, jun., and C. & J. Ollier, 1817);

*Frankenstein; or, The Modern Prometheus* (3 volumes, London: Lackington, Hughes, Harding, Mavor & Jones, 1818; revised edition, 1 volume, London: Colburn & Bentley, 1831; 2 volumes, Philadelphia: Carey, Lea & Blanchard, 1833);

*Valperga: or, The Life and Adventures of Castruccio, Prince of Lucca,* 3 volumes (London: Whittaker, 1823);

*The Last Man* (3 volumes, London: Colburn, 1826; 2 volumes, Philadelphia: Carey, Lea & Blanchard, 1833);

*The Fortunes of Perkin Warbeck, A Romance* (3 volumes, London: Colburn & Bentley, 1830; 2 volumes, Philadelphia: Carey, Lea & Blanchard, 1834);

*Lodore* (3 volumes, London: Bentley, 1835; 1 volume, New York: Wallis & Newell, 1835);

*Lives of the Most Eminent Literary and Scientific Men of Italy, Spain, and Portugal,* volumes 86–88 of *The Cabinet of Biography,* in *Lardner's Cabinet Cyclopedia,* edited by Dionysius Lardner (London: Printed for Longman, Orme, Brown, Green & Longman and John Taylor, 1835–1837); republished in part as *Lives of the Most Eminent Literary and Scientific Men of Italy,* 2 volumes (Philadelphia: Lea & Blanchard, 1841);

*Falkner: A Novel* (3 volumes, London: Saunders & Otley, 1837; 1 volume, New York: Harper, 1837);

*Mary Wollstonecraft Shelley; portrait by Richard Rothwell, 1840 (National Portrait Gallery, London)*

*Lives of the Most Eminent Literary and Scientific Men of France,* volumes 102 and 103 of *The Cabinet of Biography* (London: Printed for Longman, Orme, Brown, Green & Longman, 1838, 1839); republished in part as *Lives of the Most Eminent French Writers,* 2 volumes (Philadelphia: Lea & Blanchard, 1840);

*Rambles in Germany and Italy in 1840, 1842, and 1843,* 2 volumes (London: Moxon, 1844);

*The Choice – A Poem on Shelley's Death,* edited by H. Buxton Forman (London: Privately printed, 1876);

*Tales and Stories,* edited by Richard Garnett (London: Paterson, 1891);

*Proserpine & Midas: Two Unpublished Mythological Dramas,* edited by A. Koszul (London: Milford, 1922);

*Mary Shelley's Journal,* edited by Frederick L. Jones (Norman: University of Oklahoma Press, 1947);

*Mathilda,* edited by Elizabeth Nitchie (Chapel Hill: University of North Carolina Press, 1959);

*Collected Tales and Stories,* edited by Charles E. Robinson (Baltimore & London: Johns Hopkins University Press, 1976);

*The Journals of Mary Shelley,* 2 volumes, edited by Paula Feldman and Diana Scott-Kilvert (Oxford: Clarendon Press, 1987).

**Editions and Collections:** *The Last Man,* edited by Hugh J. Luke Jr. (Lincoln: University of Nebraska Press, 1965);

*Frankenstein, or The Modern Prometheus,* edited by M. K. Joseph (Oxford & New York: Oxford University Press, 1969);

*Frankenstein, or The Modern Prometheus* [1818 text], edited by James Rieger (New York: Bobbs-Merrill, 1974);

*The Mary Shelley Reader,* edited by Betty T. Bennett and Charles E. Robinson (New York: Oxford University Press, 1990);

*The Works of Mary Shelley,* 8 volumes, edited by Nora Crook, Betty T. Bennett, Jane Blumberg, Pamela Clemit, Doucet Fisher, Jeanne Moskal, and Fiona Stafford (N.p.: Pickering & Chatto, forthcoming, 1995).

OTHER: *Posthumous Poems of Percy Bysshe Shelley,* edited by Mary Shelley (London: Printed for John & Henry L. Hunt, 1824);

*The Poetical Works of Percy Bysshe Shelley,* 4 volumes, edited by Mary Shelley (London: Moxon, 1839);

Percy Bysshe Shelley, *Essays, Letters from Abroad, Translations and Fragments,* 2 volumes, edited by Mary Shelley (London: Moxon, 1840);

"Roger Dodsworth: The Reanimated Englishman," in Cyrus Redding, *Yesterday and To-day,* volume 2 (London: T. C. Newby, 1863), pp. 150–165.

When Mary Shelley returned to England from the Continent in August 1823 and began writing short fiction in earnest, she was already a well-known figure on the English literary scene. She was the author of a children's book, *Mounseer Nongtongpaw; or, The Discoveries of John Bull in a Trip to Paris* (1808); a travel book, *History of a Six Weeks' Tour through a Part of France, Switzerland, Germany, and* Holland, *with Letters Descriptive of a Sail round the Lake of Geneva, and the Glaciers of Chamouni* (1817); her masterpiece, *Frankenstein; or, The Modern Prometheus* (1818); and a three-volume historical romance, *Valperga: or, The Life and Adventures of Castruccio, Prince of Lucca* (1823). Although she had not received substantial compensation for those works, she had developed a network of influential contacts who could help her in future efforts to supplement her income with the proceeds of her literary efforts. Widowed, and supporting her only surviving child, Percy Florence, she needed as much financial help as she could get.

Shelley returned, as well, to an England that knew her as the mistress and later the wife of an avowed atheist; as the friend of the exiled poet George Gordon, Lord Byron; and as the daughter of the feminist freethinker Mary Wollstonecraft, who had died shortly after Mary's birth on 30 August 1797, and the radical political philosopher William Godwin. Wollstonecraft's *A Vindication of the Rights of Woman* (1792) and Godwin's *An Enquiry Concerning Political Justice* (1793) had established the couple as outspoken advocates of liberal causes at a time when most of England shared the conservatism espoused by Edmund Burke in the aftermath of the French Revolution. Born into a literary, as well as a politically unconventional, home, Mary faced early in her life the contradictions that would influence her writing. She was burdened with the suspicion, however irrational, that she was partly responsible for her mother's death. From her parents' political tracts she developed ideas about female independence and sexual freedom that contradicted the values of the English majority. Although she would be close to poets who defied the prejudices of their contemporaries and wrote primarily for an audience capable of appreciating their innovative work, she would have to deal with a publishing world that took its middle-class audience seriously.

Like most women of her class, Mary received no formal education; but Godwin designed her home schooling on the basis of the progressive ideas of the years following the French Revolution, and she grew up in an environment that encouraged reading and discussion. Along with her half-sister, Fanny Imlay, Wollstonecraft's illegitimate daughter, she explored the open books that littered her father's study and overheard the readings and conversations of his guests, among them William Wordsworth, Samuel Taylor Coleridge, Charles Lamb, and William Hazlitt.

In 1801 Godwin married the widowed Mary Jane Clairmont, and her children, Charles and Jane (later known as Claire), became part of the household. Godwin, who had often been a distant parent, seemed to pull even further away from his daughter. Mary's sense of injustice at her alienation from her father's affections grew, and there was little beyond reluctant toleration in her relations with his wife. As her biographer Anne K. Mellor has argued, what Mary perceived as the loss of domestic bliss during this period would become a major theme in her fiction.

In November 1812 she met Percy Bysshe Shelley and his wife, Harriet Westbrook Shelley, at her father's home. The wealthy and attractive young man, heir to a baronetcy and considerable landholdings, embodied many of Mary's ideals and shared the liberal ideas of her parents. He openly acknowledged his atheism, for which he had been expelled from Oxford; he advocated free love and the independence of women; and he was a poet filled with dreams of human perfectibility and imaginative transcendence. It is easy to imagine the effect this larger-than-life romantic figure had on the fifteen-year-old girl, and his financial assistance to her father could only further elevate him in her eyes. For his part, Shelley was clearly fascinated by the daughter of the union of Godwin and Wollstonecraft.

Mary spent much of the years 1812 to 1814 in an extended visit with the family of her father's acquaintance William Baxter in Dundee, Scotland. When she returned to London she found that while Jane Clairmont had received some education at a boarding school and was given music and singing lessons, Mary's half-sister, Fanny, had assumed the drudgery of housekeeping for the family. Fanny may have represented for Mary what her own future, as the other unloved stepdaughter, might be.

Percy Shelley continued to frequent the Godwin house and pay attention to her, and in May 1814 the sixteen-year-old Mary fell in love. With Jane as her companion and coconspirator and the garden of the Charterhouse School their purported destination, she began to meet secretly with Shelley. Their walks to St. Pancras, where they visited Wollstonecraft's grave, gave them the opportunity to discuss politics, poetry, and the liberal ideas they shared. In June she refused an offer of marriage from Baxter's son Robert. Later that month Shelley was spending even more time at the Godwins' to avoid his creditors, and by the end of June he and Mary had made plans to live together. Despite Shelley's financial assistance to him and Godwin's

avowed liberalism, the enraged father banned Shelley from his home and tried to prevent his daughter from seeing him. In the early hours of 28 July 1814 Mary and Jane joined Shelley in a hired chaise bound for Dover, where they boarded a ship to the Continent. Mary's account of the trip became *History of a Six Weeks' Tour.*

In September she returned to England, three months pregnant. Within six months Percy Shelley became a father twice: in November, Harriet delivered a son and heir, Charles; on 22 February 1815 Mary gave premature birth to a daughter, who died two weeks later, on 6 March. On 24 January 1816 she bore a son, William. She continued to live as Shelley's common-law wife until they married on 20 December 1816, two weeks after they learned of Harriet Shelley's suicide. In the eyes of her father — and of English society — she had become a "fallen woman" and a moral outcast.

Mary, Percy, and William Shelley and Claire Clairmont spent the summer of 1816 on Lake Geneva. During evenings in June at Byron's rented house, the Villa Diodati, she conceived the story of *Frankenstein.* Shortly after the publication of the novel in January 1818 the Shelleys, Claire Clairmont, and Claire's daughter by Byron, Allegra, left England for Italy. The Shelleys' third child, Clara Everina, born in England on 2 September 1817, died just after her first birthday. Between late 1819 and early 1820 Mary wrote *Mathilda,* which was not published until 1959; her mythological dramas *Proserpine* and *Midas,* which were not published until 1922, were written in the spring of 1820. William died in Rome on 7 June 1819; on 12 November Percy Florence, her only child to reach adulthood, was born in Florence. On 16 June 1822 Mary nearly died from a miscarriage. She was still bedridden when her husband and Edward Williams set sail for Leghorn on 1 July in their boat, the *Don Juan.* Returning on 8 July, the two friends drowned in the Gulf of Spezia. Since her husband's death came during a time when she felt emotionally distanced from him, she carried feelings of guilt that she later expressed in her letters and her fiction.

Mary Shelley returned to England in June 1823 and petitioned her father-in-law, Sir Timothy Shelley, for an allowance; he agreed to give her £100 a year. With her husband she had been accustomed to an annual income as great as £1,000; and even with increases in the allowance to £200 in 1824 and £300 in 1829, along with loans against her inheritance, she was forced to earn money by writing. While still in Italy she had submitted two pieces of short fiction to periodicals; Leigh Hunt's

Drawn by J. M. W. Turner                                                    Engraved by Robert Wallis

VIRGINIA WATER

*Engraving by Robert Wallis of J. M. W. Turner's* Virginia Water, *around which Shelley wrote the story "The Mourner" in*
The Keepsake *for 1830*

*Liberal* had published "A Tale of the Passions" in January 1823, and *The Weekly Entertainer; and West of England Miscellany* carried it later that year. "Recollections of Italy" appeared in the January 1824 issue of *London Magazine*.

Although it has a fictional narrator, the romantic Edmund Malville, "Recollections of Italy" is actually a travelogue that praises the beauty and temperate climate of Mary Shelley's beloved Italy, framed by the narrator's disparaging remarks about the filth of Venice and a humorous twist ending at a rainy English picnic. "A Tale of the Passions," however, introduces some of the thematic elements of her subsequent tales and stories: political commentary (in this case, on the Guelphs and Ghibilines), a strong and suffering heroine, an aristocratic milieu, and an antagonist whose character develops at the end of the tale, when he recognizes the evil of his past actions. Like the majority of her works of short fiction, this tale is passionate, contains Gothic elements (dungeons and hearses), and is, at times, awkwardly plotted. Shelley, along with her contemporaries, was more accustomed to longer works of fiction and was adapting to a genre that was still in its infancy.

In many of her stories there are thinly veiled parallels between people, places, and events in Shelley's life and her characters, settings, and plots. Nowhere, perhaps, are such parallels clearer than in her next published story, "The Bride of Modern Italy," which appeared in the April 1824 issue of *London Magazine*. This satiric account of upper-class love and marriage in Italy is based on her husband's platonic infatuation in 1820 with the young Emilia Viviani, to whom he dedicated "Epipsychidion" (1821). In the story Viviani appears as the fickle Clorinda Saviani, secured in a Rome convent as her parents try to arrange an acceptable marriage. Her lover of the moment is Giacomo de' Tolomei, the brother of Clorinda's friend and fellow inmate, Teresa. When Giacomo travels to Siena, he requests the seventeen-year-old English painter, Marcott Alleyn, a character based on Percy Shelley, to visit Clorinda for him. Clorinda falls in love almost immediately with Alleyn and plots to elope with him. He refuses to see her again, and, by the time Giacomo returns to Rome, Clorinda's parents have pushed her into a quickly arranged, acceptable marriage with another man.

In this story, as in most of her others, Shelley treats the issue of marriage, which, for the middle class, was becoming increasingly a matter of love and choice rather than one of class and property. Although she had been jealous during her husband's infatuation with Viviani and hurt by his portrayal of her as "the cold moon" in his poem, she shared his outrage over the arranged marriages of upper-class Italy as well as his scorn for Catholicism. Through the experiences of Lord Byron she had learned that such marriages often involved socially condoned adultery as the frustrated wife, with her husband's approval, took a discrete lover or *cavaliere servente.*

In her next story, "Roger Dodsworth: The Reanimated Englishman," written in 1826, Shelley attempted to capitalize on a hoax of that year involving the supposed revival of an Englishman frozen in an avalanche nearly two centuries earlier. Her speculation about his reaction to the changes in England arouses her sense of humor and allows her to satirize contemporary politics. She submitted the story to the *New Monthly Magazine,* but it was rejected. It appeared posthumously in 1863 in *Yesterday and Today,* the reminiscences of the editor of the *New Monthly Magazine,* Cyrus Redding.

After Shelley's novel *The Last Man,* about the destruction of humanity by a mysterious plague, met unfavorable reviews in 1826, Sir Timothy demanded that she keep the Shelley name out of public view and temporarily suspended her allowance — the major source of her income at the time. During 1827 and 1828 she traveled in England and visited Paris. Her next story, "The Sisters of Albano," appeared in 1828 in *The Keepsake,* an example of a new publishing phenomenon, the gift book or annual. Beginning in 1823 with Rudolph Ackerman's *Forget-Me-Not,* such publications capitalized on the growing appetite of the middle class for reading material. The best known of the publishers of these annuals was Charles Heath, whose *Keepsake* featured engravings from steel plates, a novelty in an age of copper plates and woodcuts; expensive silk or leather covers; gilded pages; and stories and poems by celebrated literary figures such as Wordsworth and Sir Walter Scott, who received as much as £500 for their contributions. Although the annuals were at first similar to earlier ladies' pocket books, they increased to octavo and eventually to folio size, developing into desirable objets d'art as well as literary collections. The typical *Keepsake* included an engraved dedication page with space for an inscription, an ornate title page, and as many as eighteen illustrations of high quality. Contributors often wrote or revised stories around illustrations contracted prior to the stories themselves. Most of Shelley's contributions to *The Keepsake* from 1829 to 1834 and from 1836 to 1839, to *Original Compositions in Prose and Verse* in 1833, and to *Heath's Book of Beauty* in 1834 followed this format and integrated the illustration into the narrative. Many of her stories appeared simultaneously in American annuals, such as *Match-Making and Other Tales* and *Leaflets of Memory,* and it was not unusual for American publishers to reprint the stories years after their initial publication in England. In addition to serving as the most complete collection of the stories, Charles E. Robinson's edition provides an exhaustive chronicle of their publication history.

Shelley compromised to some extent with Sir Timothy's request that she protect the family name by signing nearly all of her stories as "the Author of Frankenstein." Because of the continuing popularity of that novel — a new edition appeared in 1831 — and its stage adaptations, the name helped to attract buyers. There is no evidence that Shelley received the large compensation enjoyed by Scott and Wordsworth, and Emily W. Sunstein estimates that she made no more than fifty pounds a year from her periodical work. Still, she was sufficiently popular and respected to appear along with such writers as Scott, Wordsworth, Coleridge, Robert Southey, and Percy Shelley in *The Keepsake* for 1829. The November 1829 *Athenaeum* review of that edition praised her contributions.

The annuals clearly addressed the demands of a middle-class readership for adventure, romance, melodrama, and happy — or, at least, morally satisfying — endings. Shelley had as many as three stories a year published in annuals; much of her success in this genre stemmed from her acute sensitivity to her audience's tastes, although she never entirely concealed her sober view of human existence. Her stories are usually set in strange and exotic locations such as Italy, medieval France, Albania, and Greece and are populated by aristocrats, brave warriors, bandits, and freedom fighters. Common in them are Gothic elements and the suggestion of supernatural forces. With a few exceptions, such as "The Mortal Immortal" (1834), women are the central figures, or at least the catalysts, in the stories, and they are influential beyond the domestic sphere.

Italy is the most frequent location for the stories in the annuals, which play on English stereotypes about Italians' passionate blood and propensity to violence. Convents, castles, unequal marriages, political turmoil, and hostility between families lend these stories a strangeness that appealed to English readers. "The Sisters of Albano" and "Ferdinand Eboli," both of which appeared in *The Keepsake* for 1829, are set in Italy during the Napoleonic period. In "The Sisters of Albano" the hero, Domenico, is a bandit and a resistance fighter against French occupation; his lover, Anina, enters a convent after the executions of Domenico and her sister, praying for both and looking forward to joining Domenico in heaven. The title character of "Ferdinand Eboli" is a young count whose identity is stolen by his lookalike half-brother, his father's illegitimate son; when the brother confesses, Ferdinand forgives him. The story concludes with the brother's death at the Battle of Moscow and Count Eboli's return to home and love in Naples. Both stories use a plotting technique Shelley introduced in *Frankenstein:* the doppelgänger who serves to suggest a character's psychological complexity.

*The Keepsake* for 1830 included three Shelley stories: "The Mourner," "The Evil Eye," and "The False Rhyme." One of the six stories she set in England, "The Mourner" frames two engravings from J. M. W. Turner's depictions of Virginia Water, the setting of the story, and chronicles the death from grief of Clarice, a mysterious woman living in a rustic cottage in Windsor Forest. Clarice, left motherless early in life, is suicidal, plagued by guilt over the death of her father. The hero, the Percy Shelley-like Horace Neville, consecrates her unmarked grave in the forest. "The Evil Eye" takes place in the rugged mountains of Albania, where the warrior Dmitri goes on a rampage after his home is sacked, his wife murdered, and his infant daughter stolen by a rival tribe. With Dmitri, a self-sufficient Byronic hero tamed by the feminine influence of his daughter, Shelley infuses into her story what Mellor, in discussing *The Last Man,* calls "a critique of male egoism." Characteristically, the evil or misguided dominant male in the stories survives only when he is tempered and humanized by the feminine principle. "The False Rhyme" is an unusually short story about the constancy of women.

One of Shelley's most frequently reprinted stories, "The Transformation," and a tale of political persecution, "The Swiss Peasant," were included in *The Keepsake* for 1831. "The Transformation" features magic and a doppelgänger as the desperate hero, Guido, exchanges bodies with a hideous dwarf, who pays Guido with a casket of gold and gems. When the dwarf fails to return Guido's body, the hero pursues him and nearly loses his life when he stabs his own form, allegorically destroying the evil in his own nature. He survives, marries his

love, and lives happily ever after. As in "The Swiss Peasant," a misguided or dissolute hero is saved by love and marriage, overcoming the excesses of his masculinity.

*The Keepsake* for 1832 included one Shelley story, "The Dream," a romance with Gothic and supernatural aspects. One of its plot elements, the reconciliation of feuding families through a second generation's love, is the focal point of one of her stories in the next year's *Keepsake:* "The Brother and Sister: An Italian Story." "The Invisible Girl," the second story in *The Keepsake* for 1833, is short, awkwardly framed, and self-consciously apologetic. Set in England it includes such familiar elements as the tyrannical father, the orphaned and untitled heroine, and reconciliation and marriage despite seemingly insurmountable obstacles, but it is Shelley's only attempt in her short fiction to give an entirely naturalistic explanation for what seems to be supernatural – in this case, a ghost. A third tale, "The Smuggler and His Family," was published in *Original Compositions* (1833) and signed "Mrs. Shelley"; it chronicles the capture and execution of an outlaw fisherman, whose morally independent wife and law-abiding son overcome poverty and the taint of crime. It is illustrated by a sublimely Romantic drawing by Louis Haghe of the son battling a raging sea toward the shore where his mother and faithful dog wait in fear.

In 1834 *The Keepsake* included "The Mortal Immortal: A Tale," Shelley's most frequently anthologized story, especially in collections of science fiction, and "The Trial of Love." Winzy, the 323-year-old narrator of "The Mortal Immortal," describes the drawbacks of his gift of immortality – he drank Agrippa's elixir by mistake – and, like Victor Frankenstein and Roger Dodsworth before him, he finds that defying nature brings grief. By the end of his narrative, Winzy is bent on self-destruction. In "The Trial of Love" the heroine, Angeline, loses her love, Ippolito, to the shallow Faustina, who only finds disappointment in her marriage. As their passion fades, Ippolito becomes unfaithful and Faustina consoles herself with a *cavaliere servente.* Angeline winds up in a convent, triumphant in virtue, despite the loss of her love.

Shelley had only one story published in *Heath's Book of Beauty,* an annual known for its illustrations of beautiful women. "The Elder Son" presents a thinly veiled attack on the institution of primogeniture and aristocratic ambivalence about illegitimacy. The bastard son, Clinton, succeeds despite his scheming younger brother and marries the orphaned and dowered Ellen. Her moral influence contributes to the transformation of the character of Clinton's profligate, somewhat Byronic father, Sir Richard.

In 1836 Shelley's father died, still in debt; Shelley arranged for him to be buried next to Wollstonecraft. Her story "The Parvenue," in *The Keepsake* for 1836, combines references to her father with an idealized mother/daughter relationship in a narrative addressing middle-class economic fears. The heroine, Fanny, is rescued from a fire in her humble home and suddenly finds herself the object of the affection of her neighbor, Lord Reginald Desborough. They marry, but Fanny is out of place in aristocratic circles, choosing charity over indulgence in luxury. Persistent requests for money by members of her family destroy her marriage. Money corrupts the relations between her parents, leading to their bankruptcy and deaths, and Fanny's fairy-tale rise from peasant to aristocrat leaves her longing for her own death.

Shelley's last *Keepsake* story, "Euphrasia: A Tale of Greece" (1838), is set during the Greek revolution against Turkey. Euphrasia is kidnapped into an Athens harem; like other heroines with similar misfortunes in nineteenth-century prose, she dies – in this case, while escaping after the siege of the harem by her freedom-fighter brother, Constantine. Constantine returns to the hills to battle the Turks, single-mindedly pursuing his own death. Without his sister, Shelley suggests, Constantine is psychologically incomplete.

With Percy Florence's graduation from Cambridge in 1841 and Sir Timothy's death in 1844, Shelley was relieved of the financial pressure that had driven her in earlier years. Her son married in June 1848. Despite her poor health and the emotional stress she experienced as Percy Shelley's reputation and merit were debated, she spent her final years in relative contentment. After her death from a brain tumor on 1 February 1851, her son and daughter-in-law arranged to move the remains of her parents from St. Pancras to St. Peter's Churchyard in Bournemouth, and Shelley was buried beside them in a nonreligious service.

One more story by Shelley appeared posthumously in January 1877 in *Appleton's Journal,* following the manuscript's discovery among Hunt's papers. "The Heir of Mondolfo" returns to the cliffs of the Italian coast to relate the story of a cruel and abusive father, his Byronic son, the peasant girl the son marries, and the ultimate reconciliation of the family. Prince Fernando, like other paternal figures in Shelley's stories, ends his life as a doting father, never again regretting his son's marriage to a

*Miniature of Shelley, painted after her death by Reginald Easton (Bodleian Library, Oxford)*

woman beneath his station in life. First the son and later the father are domesticated by the ideal bourgeois marriage.

In addition to the completed stories attributed to Mary Shelley by her signatures "Author of Frankenstein" and "Mrs. Shelley" or through examination of her letters, there are two fragments: "Valerius: The Reanimated Roman," probably written in 1819, and "An Eighteenth Century Tale," probably composed prior to 1824. Two other unfinished tales were lost: "Hate," written in 1814, and a story begun in 1821 for Hunt's *The Indicator.* Another story, "The Pole," was published in 1832 in *The Court Magazine, and Belle Assemblée* under the "Author of Frankenstein" signature and was included in the collections edited by Richard Garnett (1891) and Charles E. Robinson (1976), despite its striking stylistic difference from the other stories; it was attributed to Claire Clairmont by Bradford Allen Booth in 1938. At least five anonymous stories have also been suggested as Shelley's. Garnett's collection includes one of these, "The Pilgrims," which had originally been published in *The Keepsake* for 1837, and it appears in Robinson's collection with a caveat. Although Sunstein considers "The Pilgrims" and "The Magician of Vicenza," which appeared in *Forget-Me-Not* for 1829, of questionable attribution, her bibliography includes three other anonymous stories: "The Clouds," from the *London Magazine* (November 1823); "Lacy de Vere," from *Forget-Me-Not* for 1827; and "The Ritter von Reichenstein," from *The Bijou* for 1828. Considering the volume of anonymous tales and stories that appeared in periodicals and annuals during the 1820s and 1830s, as well as Shelley's difficulties with her father-in-law, it is quite likely that there are more Shelley stories to be discovered.

The reviews of *Tales and Stories,* the collection edited by Garnett, were mixed, with the *Athenaeum* noting in January 1891 that "There is no introspection in these stories, no searching study of character" and the *Spectator* concluding in that same month that "They are interesting mainly as the work of the author of *Frankenstein.*" Even though most of the stories were well received, especially by the *Athenaeum,* when they were first published, developments in the craft of writing short fiction since Shelley's time make her stories seem technically unsophisticated. As Robinson explains in the introduction to his collection, the intrusive, self-conscious narrator; the failure to complete the narrative framework of some of the stories; and the compression of long periods of time into a passing comment are not as easily accepted by the modern reader as by Shelley's contemporary audience. Modern readers are also accustomed to finding more careful treatment of character psychology in short stories. Moreover, she often imitates the Latinate diction and elaborate compound and complex sentences of earlier male writers.

Whatever her shortcomings in terms of modern narrative and stylistic expectations, Mary Shelley remains an important figure in the history of prose fiction and a central figure in the history of women's writing. She was a member of the group of literary women who influenced the direction of prose fiction in the post–French Revolutionary world, and she refused to be complacent in her fictional representation of that world. Read closely, her stories are ideologically subversive, psychologically insightful, and subtly innovative. And in the last half of the twentieth century her reputation has undergone a radical reassessment. Since her death she had been known as a successful writer, the daughter of Wollstonecraft and Godwin, and a member of the Shelley circle – ironically, her dedication to her husband's work had enhanced his reputation at the expense of hers. Motion pictures, comic books, and television adapted her *Frankenstein* until the popular image of the story had little relationship to the remarkable "hideous progeny" of the young Mary Shelley's imagination. Although Muriel Spark's 1951 biography and Elizabeth Nitchie's edition of her novel *Mathilda* helped to restore her reputation and set the stage for serious readings first of *Frankenstein,* then of her lesser-known novels, it was only in the 1970s and 1980s that she was acknowledged as a subject of serious scholarship. A new edition of *The Last Man* appeared in 1965; Robinson's edition of her tales and stories was published in 1976; and in the 1980s her letters (1980–1988) and journals (1987) received the careful editing they deserved. Criticism and scholarship have proliferated. By the time her bicentennial is celebrated in 1997, new editions of her novels and travel writing will be available.

**Letters:**

*The Letters of Mary W. Shelley,* 2 volumes, edited by Frederick L. Jones (Norman: University of Oklahoma Press, 1944);

*The Letters of Mary Wollstonecraft Shelley,* 3 volumes, edited by Betty T. Bennett (Baltimore & London: Johns Hopkins University Press, 1980–1988).

**Bibliographies:**

Andrew Boyle, *An Index to the Annuals* (Worcester: Boyle, 1967);

W. H. Lyles, *Mary Shelley: An Annotated Bibliography* (New York: Garland, 1975).

**Biographies:**

Jane, Lady Shelley, ed., *Shelley Memorials* (London: Smith, Elder, 1859);

Helen Moore, *Mary Wollstonecraft Shelley* (Philadelphia: Lippincott, 1886);

Florence A. Marshall, *The Life and Letters of Mary Wollstonecraft Shelley,* 2 volumes (London: Bentley, 1889);

Lucy Maddox Rossetti, *Mrs. Shelley* (London: Allen, 1890);

Richard Church, *Mary Shelley* (London: Howe, 1928; New York: Viking, 1928);

Rosalie Glynn Grylls, *Mary Shelley* (London & New York: Oxford University Press, 1938);

Muriel Spark, *A Child of Light – A Reassessment of Mary Wollstonecraft Shelley* (Hadleigh, Essex: Tower Bridge Publications, 1951); revised as *Mary Shelley – A Biography* (New York: Dutton, 1987);

Eileen Bigland, *Mary Shelley* (London: Cassell, 1959; New York: Appleton-Century-Crofts, 1959);

Noel B. Gerson, *Daughter of Earth and Water: A Biography of Mary Wollstonecraft Shelley* (New York: Morrow, 1973);

James Dunn, *Moon in Eclipse – A Life of Mary Wollstonecraft Shelley* (London: Weidenfeld & Nicolson, 1978);

Anne K. Mellor, *Mary Shelley: Her Life, Her Fiction, Her Monsters* (New York: Methuen, 1988);

Emily W. Sunstein, *Mary Shelley: Romance and Reality* (Boston, Toronto & London: Little, Brown, 1989).

**References:**

Betty T. Bennett, "The Political Philosophy of Mary Shelley's Historical Novels: *Valperga* and *Perkin Warbeck*," in *The Evidence of the Imagination: Studies of the Interactions between Life and Art in English Romantic Literature,* edited by Donald H. Reiman and others (New York: New York University Press, 1978), pp. 354–371;

Harold Bloom, ed., *Mary Shelley: Modern Critical Views* (New York: Chelsea House, 1985);

Bradford Allen Booth, "'The Pole': A Story by Claire Clairmont," *Journal of English Literary History,* 5 (March 1938): 67–70;

Audrey A. Fish, Anne K. Mellor, and Esther H. Schor, eds., *The Other Mary Shelley: Beyond Frankenstein* (New York: Oxford University Press, 1993);

Nick O'Donohoe, "'The Mortal Immortal' and 'The Man Who Never Grew Young,'" in *Death and the Serpent: Immortality in Science Fiction and Fantasy,* edited by Donald M. Hassler (Westport, Conn.: Greenwood Press, 1985), pp. 83–90;

Burton R. Pollin, "Mary Shelley as the Parvenue," *Review of English Literature,* 8 (July 1967): 9–21;

Mary Poovey, *The Proper Lady and the Woman Writer: Ideology as Style in the Works of Mary Wollstonecraft, Mary Shelley, and Jane Austen* (Chicago & London: University of Chicago Press, 1984);

Charles R. Robinson, "Mary Shelley and the Roger Dodsworth Hoax," *Keats-Shelley Journal,* 24 (1975): 20–28.

**Papers:**

Mary Wollstonecraft Shelley's journals, workbooks, unpublished papers, and much of her correspondence are in the Abinger Collection at the Bodleian Library, Oxford. Other significant collections of letters are in the Carl H. Pforzheimer Library, New York Public Library; the Huntington Library, San Marino, California; and the British Library.

# William Henry Smith

## (January 1808 – 28 March 1872)

### Richard D. McGhee
#### Arkansas State University

BOOKS: *Guidone: A Dramatic Poem* (London: Saunders & Otley, 1834);

*Solitude: A Poem* (London: Saunders & Otley, 1834);

*Ernesto: A Philosophical Romance,* volume 15 of *The Library of Romance,* edited by Leitch Ritchie (London: Smith, Elder, 1835);

*A Discourse on Ethics of the School of Paley* (London: William Pickering, 1839);

*Remarks on Law Reform; Addressed More Particularly to the General Reader* (London: Privately printed, 1840);

*Athelwold, a Tragedy in Five Acts* (Edinburgh: Blackwood, 1842);

*I. Sir William Crichton. II. Athelwold. III. Guidone. Dramas* (London: William Pickering, 1846);

*Thorndale; or, The Conflict of Opinions* (Edinburgh & London: Blackwood, 1857; Boston: Ticknor & Fields, 1859);

*Gravenhurst; or, Thoughts on Good and Evil* (Edinburgh: Blackwood, 1862);

*Knowing and Feeling: A Contribution to Psychology,* with a memoir of the author by Lucy Caroline Smith (Edinburgh: Printed by T. & A. Constable for private circulation, 1874).

PLAY PRODUCTION: *Athelwold,* London, Drury Lane, Spring 1843.

SELECTED PERIODICAL PUBLICATIONS –
UNCOLLECTED: "On Martyrs," as Wool-gatherer, *Athenaeum,* no. 44 (27 August 1828): 699–700;

"On Mysticism," as Wool-gatherer, *Athenaeum,* no. 47 (17 September 1828): 745–746;

"A Popular and Practical Introduction to Law Studies," *Quarterly Review,* 56 (July 1836): 521–530;

"Wild Oats – A New Species," *Blackwood's Edinburgh Magazine,* 47 (June 1840): 753–762;

"Wordsworth," *Blackwood's Edinburgh Magazine,* 49 (March 1841): 359–370;

"Gabrielle De Belle Isle," *Blackwood's Edinburgh Magazine,* 51 (May 1842): 609–618;

"Angelo: A Tale," *Blackwood's Edinburgh Magazine,* 51 (June 1842): 799–812;

"Leap-Year: A Tale," *Blackwood's Edinburgh Magazine,* 53 (May 1843): 603–614;

"The Diligence: A Leaf from a Journal," *Blackwood's Edinburgh Magazine,* 55 (June 1844): 692–697;

"The Superfluities of Life," *Blackwood's Edinburgh Magazine,* 57 (February 1845): 194–203;

"The Novel and the Drama," *Blackwood's Edinburgh Magazine,* 57 (June 1845): 679–687;

"Manner and Matter," *Blackwood's Edinburgh Magazine,* 58 (October 1845): 431–438;

"Hakem The Slave: A Tale Extracted from the History of Poland," *Blackwood's Edinburgh Magazine,* 58 (November 1845): 560–570;

"The Mountain and the Cloud (A Reminiscence of Switzerland)," *Blackwood's Edinburgh Magazine,* 58 (December 1845): 704–710;

"Mildred: A Tale," *Blackwood's Edinburgh Magazine,* 60 (December 1846): 709–721; 61 (January 1847): 18–35; (February 1847): 213–229;

"Giacomo Da Valencia: or, The Student of Bologna," *Blackwood's Edinburgh Magazine,* 62 (September 1847): 359–370;

"Emerson," *Blackwood's Edinburgh Magazine,* 63 (June 1848): 701–712;

"Goldsmith," *Blackwood's Edinburgh Magazine,* 67 (February 1850): 137–153; (March 1850): 296–308;

"Voltaire in the Crystal Palace," *Blackwood's Edinburgh Magazine,* 70 (August 1851): 142–153;

"The Papal Government," *Blackwood's Edinburgh Magazine,* 88 (October 1860): 396–407;

"Scraps of Verse from a Tourist's Journal," *Blackwood's Edinburgh Magazine,* 99 (May 1866): 645–646; 100 (November 1866): 601–604;

"The Coming Race," *Blackwood's Edinburgh Magazine,* 110 (July 1871): 46–61;

"Mr. W. R. Greg's Political Essays," *Contemporary Review,* 20 (July 1872): 211–237.

Few today recognize the achievements of William Henry Smith, who wrote many anonymous ar-

*William Henry Smith*

ticles for the periodical press from 1828 to 1872, when his last piece appeared in the *Contemporary Review*. Although in his own time his name was before the public as the author of poetry, drama, and philosophical romances, it has, ironically, been his work for journals and magazines that has preserved his name for some slight attention from posterity. All published anonymously, Smith's short tales are marked by direct address to readers, interrupting the narrative to make ethical and religious points. The pleasures of reading Smith's fiction come from his experiments in narration, his mixing of dialogue with descriptive analysis, and his tonal shifts from world-weary sorrow to indignant outrage.

Despite his old-fashioned style Smith wrote some tales with the power to hold the modern reader's interest in character development and plot structures and at times made effective use of point of view. The use of a limited point of view, however, is an unusual fictional technique for Smith. More commonly he tightly controls the reader's view of his characters, employing a narrator who has large themes to share and profound truths to bear. Smith's writing is marked by both a discontent with the abstraction of philosophy and an impatience with fiction's limits. Restlessly, Smith pursued in his life and writing an imaginative form that

would be adequate to his intellectual need for answers: he found few forms and fewer answers.

Smith was born at North End, Hammersmith, London, in January 1808. His father, Richard, was a barrister, and one of his elder brothers, Theyre Townsend Smith, was to become a famous preacher. The law and religion would be strong influences on Smith's career. He began his formal education as a private student of a clergyman and from 1818 to 1821 attended the Radley School, a Dissenting institution near Abingdon. There he discovered the poetry of George Gordon, Lord Byron. In 1821 he became a student at Glasgow University, where he lodged with his brother Theyre and met the writer John Sterling.

When his father died in January 1823, Smith returned home from Glasgow. From 1823 to 1828 he was articled with Sharon Turner, an attorney. Smith disliked law and did not go into practice, preferring to enjoy the financial independence provided by a small inheritance. Influenced by friendships with such men of letters as John Stuart Mill, Frederick Denison Maurice, and Sterling, Smith turned to writing books and review essays.

Among his earliest essays, published in the *Athenaeum* in 1828, were "On Martyrs," arguing for freedom of speech, and "On Mysticism." The themes of these two essays anticipate the concerns Smith develops in *Ernesto: A Philosophical Romance* (1835). This first venture into long fictional prose is a loose narrative of a young man's education in the ideas and ways of the world. Though set in six-teenth-century Rome, the story is pointedly in-tended for nineteenth-century English audiences eager for easy answers to religious doubts. With some of the self-conscious style of Walter Pater's *Marius the Epicurean* (1885), the tale moves slowly as Ernesto experiments in love and meets a variety of people with views that attract his interest but fail to alter his convictions.

While the Italian plot echoes Gothic romances of an earlier era, the quotation from Percy Bysshe Shelley's drama *The Cenci* (1819) that appears in book 1 gives a better indication of Smith's intent to explore human psychology for the origin of evil:

It is a trick of this same family
To analyse their own and other minds.
Such self-anatomy shall teach the will
Dangerous secrets; for it tempts our powers,
Knowing what must be thought, and may be done,
Into the depth of darkest purposes.

Using the foil of an idiot companion, the natu-ral man without a soul, the narrative puts Ernesto through trials of tolerance, faith, skepticism, and po-litical intrigue that conclude with the hero finding his true love at last. In a thematic pattern that be-came familiar in Smith's writings, the story devel-ops an attitude of theistic affirmation out of an amoral quest for pleasure. It echoes such works as Thomas Carlyle's *Sartor Resartus,* first published in *Fraser's Magazine* (1833–1834), which recorded he-roic rejections of Byronic sorrow to assert Words-worthian optimism.

Smith published reviews in the *Quarterly Review* in 1836, including "A Popular and Practical Intro-duction to Law Studies," drawing on his training in the law but also indicating his desire to synthesize the many, sometimes conflicting, intellectual inter-ests of his era. One of Smith's earliest sustained pieces of intellectual analysis was *A Discourse on Eth-ics of the School of Paley* (1839), in which he discusses the origin of ethical principles, whether natural or derived from culture and training, as a basis for reli-gious life and the theory of conscience. Clearly in-fluenced by the writings of Mill, this work sought to find some clear direction for spiritual confidence without compromising reason and experience. Also in 1839 Smith began his long association with *Blackwood's Edinburgh Magazine,* for which he contin-ued as reviewer for thirty years.

Smith's first experiment in short fiction was "Wild Oats – A New Species," published in the June 1840 *Blackwood's.* The narrator prepares the reader for meeting its hero by analyzing the idea of "wild oats," applying it to intellectual adventures as well as to the more common life of action. The tur-moil of spirit that the hero reaps is similar to those of Byron's Manfred or Carlyle's Diogenes Teu-felsdrockh in *Sartor Resartus.* Unlike either of these, however, Smith's hero, called Howard, has a mun-dane sense of humor that drives him to bury his po-etry (of which not a single copy was sold) and assert his blindness to love through a plodding career in the law. He is introduced "droning away" in perfor-mance of his profession. Howard confesses his wasted life to the narrator, whose visit arouses such an energy of reminiscence that the reader realizes how much energy has been left untapped even as Howard claims that he has no creative powers left. Like Ernesto, Howard went from poetry to philoso-phy, but he, less happily than Ernesto, missed the love that might have been his in a happy marriage.

Like many writers during the Victorian era, including Carlyle and Mill, Smith had been shaped by Byron's poetry as a youth and by William Wordsworth's poetry as a man. In March 1841 Smith published an important essay, "Words-worth," in *Blackwood's.* In the essay Smith praises the philosophical powers of Wordsworth's poetry, which he considers superior to the works of Shelley.

"Leap-Year: A Tale," published in *Blackwood's* in May 1843, has considerable charm in its econ-omy of narration that turns on an ironic mispercep-tion by the hero, Reginald Darcy, who nearly loses his love because he underestimates her powers of perception. The story is a slighter version of Jane Austen's *Pride and Prejudice* (1813), even borrowing characters' names from that novel, and shows some of Austen's spark without any of her genius for ren-dering rich social textures. Darcy admits his love for Emily Sherwood, but he cannot court her be-cause of his poverty and her wealth. Instead he sac-rifices himself so that she can pursue a wealthy bar-onet, but in the end he discovers how foolish he has been, because Emily refuses Darcy's sacrifice and asks him to marry her, bringing the story to an ironic but happy conclusion. The reversal of con-ventional courtship is appropriate, the title allows, because Emily's proposal is made during leap year. Smith's method of telling this tale is to arrange dia-logues between the two lovers and their most inti-mate friends, who engage the reader in their confi-dences and develop the dramatic ironies of the story.

In the autumn of 1843 Smith went to France, attending lectures at the Sorbonne in Paris. In the summer of 1845 he toured Switzerland, which provided the basis for his experimental piece called "The Mountain and the Cloud (A Reminiscence of Switzerland)," published in *Blackwood's* in December 1845. This prose monologue plays upon an analogy between cloud/mountain and motion/sea. Filaments of thought are drawn together from associations, including references to Lake Leman and Mont Blanc, made along the lines of this analogy. In the center is a romantic discovery that a "woman's heart" lies in the waters of the lake and a man's strength in the heights of the mountain. The tone of the prose is so affected, at times so cloyingly "poetic," that readers will divide responses between laughter at its absurdity and boredom with its banality. One hopes Smith was being satiric but cannot be certain.

"Manner and Matter," published in the October 1845 issue of *Blackwood's,* is one of Smith's better stories, about a good man who deserves better but suffers deprivation and shame to the end of his life. Because he would not compromise his conscience by endorsing a lie about an unpaid debt, the old mathematics tutor Mr. Simpson dies in the poorhouse after Mrs. Vincent, who inherits an estate kept intact by Mr. Simpson's honesty, refuses to continue the old tutor's annuity. Neither Charles Dickens nor Thomas Hardy could have created a more ironic tale of virtue unrewarded. Smith plays with point of view, limiting the perspective to the naive perceptions of Mr. Simpson himself. The reader cannot sympathize entirely with the poor tutor, who seems to have learned little during his long life.

"Hakem The Slave: A Tale Extracted from the History of Poland," published a month later in the same magazine, is a much less deft piece of writing. There is little more than pulp romance in this tale of the loyal, sacrificing servant and the morally blind objects of his love. Political intrigue, assassination, and sentimental attachments abound in this story of a faithful Muslim and treacherous Christians. At best the story points toward a moral theme of religious tolerance, although it requires bloody violence and blind egotism to make its plot move forward and produce a happy marriage between Maria Laski and Augustus Glinsky, the son of Maria's father's deadly enemy. To make this happen, Hakem the slave must kill Maria's father and then kill himself. One hopes the concluding words are meant to be read with some irony: "The generous object of the slave was fully accomplished. His death procured the long happiness of Maria."

In the winter of 1845–1846 Smith stayed with his oldest brother, Frederick, in Brussels, where he wrote *Sir William Crichton,* a play based on incidents during the reign of James II of Scotland. In 1846 he published it along with two earlier works, *Athelwold, a Tragedy in Five Acts* (1842) and *Guidone: A Dramatic Poem* (1834). He visited Italy in the same year and on the return home became ill and stayed again with Frederick until he was well. His travels provided the basis for his ambitious "Mildred: A Tale." Appearing in three issues of *Blackwood's* from December 1846 to February 1847, it is one of Smith's longest narratives for the magazine.

Although the story begins with Mildred Willoughby's limited and provincial point of view, Smith soon switches to an omniscient narrator. The story follows the heroine from Dorsetshire in England to Brussels and finally to Italy, where she is courted by a mysterious stranger with strong feelings but little fortune. Just when Mildred believes she can freely encourage the romantic attentions of Alfred Winston, he kills himself because he has wasted his opportunity for true love by proposing marriage to another woman for her wealth.

In one episode the narrator, directly addressing his English readers, expresses outrage at Roman Catholic superstition:

> Most candid of men! and most liberal of Protestants!... Just step across the water – we do not ask you to travel into Italy or Spain, where the symptoms are ten times more violent – just walk into some of these churches in Belgium, *and use your own eyes.* It is but a journey of four-and-twenty hours; and if you are one of those who wish to bring into our own church the more frequent use of form and ceremony and visible symbol, it will be the most salutary journey you ever undertook.

This is such a shocking interruption to the otherwise unremarkable movement of the story that one cannot help but believe that Smith put much of his own feeling into the exclamation of outrage. It is not, however, inconsistent with his devotion to principles of tolerance, because it involves his astonishment at the power of thoughtless superstition to overwhelm reason.

Smith's Alfred and Mildred – who turns out to be far more stupid in moral matters than anyone might have guessed from her intellectual and aesthetic interests – fall victim to their own refined sensibilities, celebrating the pleasures of art and discourse while blindly driving past the possibility of love for one another. This situation would often be treated masterfully by Henry James, but Smith deserves credit for his ironic perspective on futile passion.

In 1848 or 1849 Smith made his first sojourn in the English Lake District, where he would soon take up residence, living chiefly at Keswick. In 1851 he was offered the position of professor of moral philosophy at Edinburgh on a temporary basis, but he declined the offer to continue his work on the philosophical romance *Thorndale; or, The Conflict of Opinions* (1857).

In *Thorndale* Smith reprises his attempt, first made in *Ernesto,* to analyze and synthesize the many religious ideas of his day. In a secluded grotto overlooking the Bay of Naples, the narrator finds the diary of his friend Charles Thorndale, who had died there some time before and who had left unpublished his thoughts on religion. Thorndale records dialogues between several characters undergoing tests of their beliefs: Cyril is the skeptic becoming a Roman Catholic, Luxmore the poet without a creed, Clarence the painter and progressive enthusiast, and Seckendorf the German-English physician who sneers at idealists and celebrates pragmatism.

Although well received by its readers, *Thorndale* is a conventional spiritual autobiography, in which the search for meaning is unresolved. Its imagined voices are those of European prejudices as an Englishman might hear them. Smith's characters are bloodless mouthpieces, not the creatures of deeply felt and considered human experience.

On 5 Mary 1861 Smith married Lucy Caroline Cumming. The following year he published *Gravenhurst; or, Thoughts on Good and Evil,* a book less noticed than other works by Smith, although it is similar in subject matter and dialogue form to the well-regarded *Thorndale.* Margaret Oliphant, in her October 1872 obituary of Smith in *Blackwood's,* may have identified the reason *Gravenhurst* had a poor reception, calling it "a somewhat elaborate attempt to prove that evil is a necessity in the world." Smith's health began to decline in 1869, and he died at Brighton on 28 March 1872.

In 1874 his widow published his *Knowing and Feeling: A Contribution to Psychology* with a memoir of her husband.

William Henry Smith was an important contributor to *Blackwood's Edinburgh Magazine* and deserved the tribute Oliphant paid him, in her obituary. His writings from some thirty years contributed to the one "big voice," as she called it, of the magazine. Where he speaks in his own name, as in *Thorndale* and *Gravenhurst,* Smith shows intellectual tolerance and sympathetic imagination. His writings were not sufficient, however, to earn Smith lasting fame as thinker or stylist; too many others of the era – including Dickens, Carlyle, Mill, John Ruskin, Matthew Arnold, and George Eliot – demonstrated virtues of mind and art more powerful than he could command. Smith's talent, however, was sufficient to the needs of *Blackwood's,* and that is enough to make him worthy of some continuing admiration.

**Letters:**

"Letters of William Henry Smith to the Blackwoods, 1836–1862," edited by Kenneth Waldron Davis, dissertation, Vanderbilt University, 1963.

**Biographies:**

Margaret Oliphant, "William Smith," *Blackwood's Edinburgh Magazine,* 112 (October 1872): 429–438;

George S. Merriam, *The Story of William and Lucy Smith* (Boston & New York: Houghton, Mifflin / Cambridge: Riverside, 1890).

**References:**

David E. Latané Jr., "William Henry Smith and the Poetics of the 1830s," *Wordsworth Circle,* 20 (Winter 1989): 159–165;

John Tulloch, "The Author of 'Thorndale' and Modern Scepticism," in his *Modern Theories in Philosophy and Religion* (Edinburgh & London: Blackwood, 1884), pp. 89–122.

# William Makepeace Thackeray

*(18 July 1811 – 24 December 1863)*

Tony Giffone

*State University of New York at Farmingdale*

See also the Thackeray entries in *DLB 21: Victorian Novelists Before 1885* and *DLB 55: Victorian Prose Writers Before 1867.*

BOOKS: *Flore et Zéphyr: Ballet Mythologique par Théophile Wagstaffe* (London: Mitchell, 1836);

*The Yellowplush Correspondence,* as Charles J. Yellowplush (Philadelphia: Carey & Hart, 1838);

*Reminiscences of Major Gahagan,* as Goliah O'Grady Gahagan (Philadelphia: Carey & Hart, 1939);

*An Essay on the Genius of George Cruikshank* (London: Hooper, 1840);

*The Paris Sketch Book, by Mr. Titmarsh,* 2 volumes (London: Macrone, 1840; New York: Appleton, 1852);

*Comic Tales and Sketches, Edited and Illustrated by Mr. Michael Angelo Titmarsh,* 2 volumes (London: Cunningham, 1841);

*The Second Funeral of Napoleon, in Three Letters to Miss Smith of London; and The Chronicle of the Drum, by Mr. M. A. Titmarsh* (London: Cunningham, 1841); republished as *The Second Funeral of Napoleon, by M. A. Titmarsh and Critical Reviews* (New York: Lovell, 1883);

*The Irish Sketch Book, by Mr. M. A. Titmarsh* (2 volumes, London: Chapman & Hall, 1843; 1 volume, New York: Winchester, 1843);

*Jeames's Diary* (New York: Taylor, 1846);

*Notes of a Journey from Cornhill to Grand Cairo, by Way of Lisbon, Athens, Constantinople, and Jerusalem, Performed in the Steamers of the Peninsular and Oriental Company, by Mr. M. A. Titmarsh* (London: Chapman & Hall, 1846; New York: Wiley & Putnam, 1846);

*Mrs. Perkins's Ball, by Mr. M. A. Titmarsh* (London: Chapman & Hall, 1847);

*Vanity Fair: A Novel without a Hero* (19 monthly parts, London: Bradbury & Evans, 1847–1848; 2 volumes, New York: Harper, 1848);

*The Book of Snobs* (London: Punch Office, 1848; New York: Appleton, 1852);

*William Makepeace Thackeray; portrait by Samuel Laurence (from Charles and Frances Brookfield,* Mrs. Brookfield and Her Circle, *1905)*

*Our Street, by Mr. M. A. Titmarsh* (London: Chapman & Hall, 1848);

*The Great Hoggarty Diamond* (New York: Harper, 1848); republished as *The History of Samuel Titmarsh and the Great Hoggarty Diamond* (London: Bradbury & Evans, 1849);

*The History of Pendennis: His Fortunes and Misfortunes, His Friends and His Greatest Enemy* (23 monthly parts, London: Bradbury & Evans, 1848–1850; 2 volumes, New York: Harper, 1850);

*Doctor Birch and His Young Friends, by Mr. M. A. Titmarsh* (London: Chapman & Hall, 1849; New York: Appleton, 1853);

*Miscellanies: Prose and Verse*, 8 volumes (Leipzig: Tauchnitz, 1849–1857);

*The Kickleburys on the Rhine*, by Mr. M. A. Titmarsh (London: Smith, Elder, 1850; New York: Stringer & Townsend, 1851);

*Stubbs's Calendar; or, The Fatal Boots* (New York: Stringer & Townsend, 1850);

*Rebecca and Rowena: A Romance upon Romance*, by Mr. M. A. Titmarsh (London: Chapman & Hall, 1850; New York: Appleton, 1853);

*The History of Henry Esmond, Esq., a Colonel in the Service of Her Majesty Q. Anne, Written by Himself* (3 volumes, London: Smith, Elder, 1852; 1 volume, New York: Harper, 1852);

*The Confessions of Fitz-Boodle; and Some Passages in the Life of Major Gahagan* (New York: Appleton, 1852);

*A Shabby Genteel Story and Other Tales* (New York: Appleton, 1852);

*Men's Wives* (New York: Appleton, 1852);

*The Luck of Barry Lyndon: A Romance of the Last Century*, 2 volumes (New York: Appleton, 1852–1853);

*Jeames's Diary, A Legend of the Rhine, and Rebecca and Rowena* (New York: Appleton, 1853);

*Mr. Brown's Letters to a Young Man about Town; with the Proser and Other Papers* (New York: Appleton, 1853);

*Punch's Prize Novelists, The Fat Contributor, and Travels in London* (New York: Appleton, 1853);

*The English Humourists of the Eighteenth Century: A Series of Lectures Delivered in England, Scotland, and the United States of America* (London: Smith, Elder, 1853; New York: Harper, 1853);

*The Newcomes: Memoirs of a Most Respectable Family, Edited by Arthur Pendennis Esqre* (23 monthly parts, London: Bradbury & Evans, 1853–1855; 2 volumes, New York: Harper, 1855);

*The Rose and the Ring; or, The History of Prince Giglio and Prince Bulbo: A Fireside Pantomime for Great and Small Children* (London: Smith, Elder, 1855; New York: Harper, 1855);

*Miscellanies: Prose and Verse*, 4 volumes (London: Bradbury & Evans, 1855–1857);

*Ballads* (Boston: Ticknor & Fields, 1856);

*Christmas Books* (London: Chapman & Hall, 1857; Philadelphia: Lippincott, 1872);

*The Virginians: A Tale of the Last Century* (24 monthly parts, London: Bradbury & Evans, 1857–1859; 1 volume, New York: Harper, 1859);

*The Four Georges; Sketches of Manners, Morals, Court and Town Life* (New York: Harper, 1860; London: Smith, Elder, 1861);

*Lovel the Widower* (New York: Harper, 1860; London: Smith, Elder, 1861);

*The Adventures of Philip on His Way through the World; Shewing Who Robbed Him, Who Helped Him, and Who Passed Him By* (3 volumes, London: Smith, Elder, 1862; 1 volume, New York: Harper, 1862);

*Roundabout Papers* (London: Smith, Elder, 1863; New York: Harper, 1863);

*Denis Duval* (New York: Harper, 1864; London: Smith, Elder, 1867);

*Early and Late Papers Hitherto Uncollected*, edited by James T. Fields (Boston: Ticknor & Fields, 1867);

*Miscellanies, Volume IV* (Boston: Osgood, 1870);

*The Orphan of Pimlico; and Other Sketches, Fragments, and Drawings*, with notes by A. I. Thackeray (London: Smith, Elder, 1876);

*Sultan Stork and Other Stories and Sketches (1829–1844), Now First Collected*, edited by R. H. Sheppard (London: Redway, 1887);

*Loose Sketches, An Eastern Adventure, Etc.* (London: Sabin, 1894);

*The Hitherto Unidentified Contributions of W. M. Thackeray to Punch, with a Complete Authoritative Bibliography from 1845 to 1848*, edited by M. H. Spielmann (London & New York: Harper, 1899);

*Mr. Thackeray's Writings in the "National Standard" and the "Constitutional,"* edited by W. T. Spencer (London: Spencer, 1899);

*Stray Papers: Being Stories, Reviews, Verses, and Sketches 1821–47*, edited by Lewis S. Benjamin as Lewis Melville (London: Hutchinson, 1901; Philadelphia: Jacobs, 1901);

*The New Sketch Book: Being Essays Now First Collected from the "Foreign Quarterly Review,"* edited by R. S. Garnett (London: Rivers, 1906);

*Thackeray's Contributions to the "Morning Chronicle,"* edited by Gordon N. Ray (Urbana: University of Illinois Press, 1955).

**Collections:** *The Works of William Makepeace Thackeray*, Library Edition, 22 volumes (London: Smith, Elder, 1867–1869);

*The Works of William Makepeace Thackeray*, Biographical Edition, 13 volumes (London: Smith, Elder, 1898–1899);

*The Works of William Makepeace Thackeray*, 20 volumes, edited by Lewis S. Benjamin as Lewis Melville (London: Macmillan, 1901–1907);

*The Oxford Thackeray*, 17 volumes (London: Oxford University Press, 1908);

*The Works of William Makepeace Thackeray*, Centenary Biographical Edition, 26 volumes (London: Smith, Elder, 1910–1911);

*The Works of William Makepeace Thackeray*, Critical Edition, 4 volumes published, edited by Edgar

F. Harden and Peter F. Shillingsburg (New York: Garland, 1989– ).

William Makepeace Thackeray was, after Charles Dickens, the most celebrated British novelist of the nineteenth century. Today his reputation rests mostly on *Vanity Fair* (1847–1848) and has been eclipsed by that of George Eliot; even Anthony Trollope, who considered himself a "lesser Thackeray," has more novels still in print and a more loyal following. In his own day, however, many intellectuals preferred Thackeray to Dickens. Trollope ranked Thackeray first among the English novelists of the nineteenth century; Charlotte Brontë, who dedicated the second edition (1848) of *Jane Eyre* (1847) to Thackeray, found in him a "profound and unique intellect"; Leslie Stephen compared him to Honoré de Balzac.

As a novelist Thackeray constantly fought for literary realism, and this quest led him into parodying and burlesquing literary forms, genres, and conventions. If the eighteenth century was the age of satire and the nineteenth century was the age of sincerity or earnestness, Thackeray can be seen as an eighteenth-century satirist born a century late. His championing of literary realism led not only to the debunking of literary conventions but also to a debunking of the heroic/Romantic view of human nature. *Vanity Fair* is subtitled *A Novel without a Hero,* and there are virtually no heroes anywhere in Thackeray's fiction, long or short. Instead, Thackeray loved to satirize the pretenses of individuals to heroism. Two types tend to populate his fiction: the rogue who attempts to camouflage his roguishness and the commoner who adopts aristocratic airs. Both kinds of protagonist pretend to be what they are not. The mock-heroic is Thackeray's most natural mode.

Thackeray's realism – his refusal to believe in heroic action, or in marriage as a "happily-ever-after" conclusion to a narrative – is often seen as cynicism. His realism extends to endings in which individuals accept their diminished expectations. *Vanity Fair* concludes, "Which of us has his desire? or, having it, is satisfied?" Yet the tone of Thackeray's work is not bleak or tragic; it is convivial and witty. His omniscient narrators are all great conversationalists, people one would be enchanted to meet in a pub or at a literary club. Even though Thackeray's short fiction does not measure up to his achievement as a novelist, it is often in the shorter works that his gifts for satire, irony, wit, and burlesque are most in evidence.

Most of Thackeray's short fiction was written early in his career and can be considered a literary apprenticeship for his longer works. He had no special affinity for the developing genre of the short story; his interest in the short-fiction form was mostly confined to using it as a vehicle for parody and satire. Like Henry Fielding, who was in many ways his literary mentor, Thackeray began as a parodist who grew into a first-rate creative writer. If one accepts the definition of a short story as a literary work with essentially one event and one mood that can be read in one sitting, then much of Thackeray's short fiction would be better classified as novellas. Burlesques of popular genres, these tales could have been developed into complete novels had Thackeray had any interest in them beyond using them for literary satire; in that sense, Thackeray's works of short fiction are aborted novels.

Thackeray was born on 18 July 1811 in Calcutta, where his father, Richmond Thackeray, was stationed with the East India Company. His mother, Anne Becher Thackeray, became ill shortly after Thackeray's birth and could have no more children, leaving Thackeray an only child. His father died on 13 September 1815; his mother married an old love, Capt. Henry William Carmichael-Smyth, on 13 March 1817. Thackeray was sent back to England to live alternately with his maternal grandmother and his father's sister, Mrs. John Ritchie, until his mother and stepfather returned to England on 5 July 1820. Thackeray began his six years at Charterhouse Public School on 15 January 1822; he spent 1829 and 1830 at Trinity College, Cambridge, where he contributed to *The Snob,* a literary weekly, and to its successor, *The Gownsman.* After leaving Cambridge he traveled in France and Germany, spending six months in Weimar. In 1831 he returned to London to study law at the Middle Temple of the Inns of Court and to lead the life of a dandy, frequenting the brothels and gambling dens. In 1833 he went to Paris to study art; the eye for realistic detail he cultivated in his art studies would serve him well in his realistic fiction. In 1835 he met Isabella Shawe in Paris; they were married on 20 August 1836 and had three daughters: Anne Isabella, Jane, and Harriet Marian. The marriage seems to have been relatively happy until his wife's mental breakdown, an event that colors much of his writing. In 1842, after bouts with melancholy, depression, and an attempt at suicide, she was committed to an asylum, where she remained for the rest of her life.

Throughout these early years Thackeray made his living by writing for periodicals; it was in this period that most of his short fiction was produced. He became an editor at *The National Standard of Literature, Science, Music, Theatricals, and the Fine Arts* in 1833 and contributed anonymous pieces nearly every week. The journal shortened its cumbersome name to *The National Standard and Literary Representative* in 1834 but ceased publication with the 1 February issue that year. Among the works in the periodical that can be clearly identified as Thackeray's is "The Devil's Wager," a ghost story that appeared in the 10 and 24 August 1833 issues. While clearly a youthful work, it is filled with the pleasures of the ghost-story genre, including a repetition of events to build suspense and a surprise ending that violates the expectations set up by that repetition. In the tale the devil makes a wager with the deceased evil knight Sir Roger de Rollo that neither Sir Roger's brother, his nephew, nor his niece will say a prayer to release Roger from purgatory. The niece is too busy receiving songs from her lover to pray for him; the nephew fails for lack of a prayer book; and the devil has made a pact with the brother, a priest, never to pray again. The "trick" of the tale is how Roger gets his brother to break his pact with the devil and pray again.

Stories probably written by Thackeray for *The National Standard* include "A Tale of Wonder" (12 October 1833), about an old woman who witnesses a murder and is compelled to reveal the identities of the killers when the victim's head appears to her; "The History of Krakatuk" (30 November and 7 December 1833), a loose translation of a tale by the German writer E. T. A. Hoffmann; "King Odo's Wedding" (4 January 1834), in which a king who marries a woman as she is about to become a nun is visited on his wedding night by the ghosts of other nuns who have come for their "sister" and who leave the king dead; and "The Minstral's Curse," published in the final issue of the journal, a prose translation of a German ballad with fairy-tale motifs. In these efficiently told early works Thackeray reveals himself to be a master at creating atmosphere.

From 1832 to 1846 Thackeray contributed a prolific amount of fiction and essays to *Fraser's Magazine,* founded by William Maginn as a rival to *Blackwood's Edinburgh Magazine;* more of Thackeray's early work appeared in *Fraser's* than in any other periodical. Maginn shaped Thackeray's critical sensibility, which remained essentially unchanged for the rest of his life. The earliest work in *Fraser's* that has been attributed to Thackeray is "Elizabeth Brownrigge," a parody of Edward Bulwer-Lytton's *Eugene Aram* (1832) that appeared in the August and September 1832 issues. Critics are undecided whether the tale was written by Thackeray, by Douglas Jerrold, or by Maginn himself.

Thackeray's "The Professor" was published in the September 1837 issue of *Bentley's Miscellany*

under the pseudonym Major Goliah O'Grady Gahagan. The title character is a ne'er-do-well disguised as a professor of gymnastics and dancing at a seminary for young ladies. Nineteen-year-old Adeliza Grampus falls in love with her teacher; she is the daughter of a shellfish monger, "which induced the young lady to describe herself as a daughter of the Ocean." Thackeray's ability to cut pretensions down to size is already evident in this early work. The professor ingratiates himself with the girl's family by pretending to mistake her mother for her sister, showing Thackeray's view of humans as essentially vain. The story ends with a typical Victorian moral exemplum: "My tale is told. If it may have deterred one soul from vice . . . the writer seeks for no other reward," but Thackeray adds a postscript saying that he is instructed not to part with the manuscript until the proceeds from its sale are in the mail. This ending suggests that Victorian sentimentality and earnestness are cant and that writing is merely a way to make a living.

Major Goliah O'Grady Gahagan reappeared the following year, narrating his life story in the *New Monthly Magazine* from February 1838 to February 1839, though there is little similarity between "The Professor" and this bragging mock-memoir. Gahagan chronicles his adventures in India, boasting of his victories in love, war, and drink. Gahagan's bragging has been seen as a burlesque of Irish gab, of military yarns, of the adventure narratives popularized by Frederick Marryat, and even of British imperialism.

While Gahagan's memoirs were appearing in the *New Monthly Magazine,* Thackeray was writing the memoirs of another persona, the footman Charles J. Yellowplush, for *Fraser's.* The humor in *The Yellowplush Correspondence,* which ran from November 1837 to August 1838, comes not so much from Yellowplush's picaresque adventures as from Thackeray's approximation of Cockney speech. There are several distinct adventures among the memoirs, each of which forms a separate story; each ends with Yellowplush leaving his employer and seeking a new position. "Miss Shum's Husband" concerns a woman who learns that her husband is really a crossing-sweeper; Thackeray uses the tale to expose social pretensions, including those of Yellowplush himself. In "The Amours of Mr. Deuceace," the longest part of the memoir, Yellowplush follows his master, "the youngest and fifth son of the Earl of Crabs" and a thorough rogue, to Paris; here Thackeray draws on his knowledge of the gambling dens of the French capital. Much of Yellowplush's memoir is tedious, but it is also witty

*Self-portrait of Thackeray, 1835 (Henry E. Huntington Library and Art Gallery, San Marino, California)*

in its social observations, as in Yellowplush's insistence that British servants "like being insulted by noblemen, – it shows that they're familiar with us." There is a clear influence of Dickens's *Pickwick Papers* (1836–1837): Yellowplush shares certain traits with Sam Weller and at one point refers to Dickens's work explicitly when he begs off describing a prison because he could not equal the description in *The Pickwick Papers*. Thackeray's humor, however, is much crueler than Dickens's; Yellowplush's pretensions to intellectual elitism meet with satiric disdain, not the humorous pathos that marks Dickens's treatment of the Pickwick Club.

Yellowplush's narration of his adventures alternates with book reviews that are Thackeray's satire on such reviews; many of Yellowplush's reviews are of books that Thackeray had reviewed elsewhere. In these fictional reviews Thackeray is imitating a Cockney failing in his attempts to imitate a

pretentious intellectual. For instance, in "Skimmings from the Dairy of George IV" Yellowplush thinks he is reviewing the *dairy* rather than the *diary* of the recent king; when he comments that the "cream of the Dairy" has already been given away in extracts from the book, he thinks that he is being witty but is, in fact, only revealing his ignorance. In the final episode of his correspondence, "Mr. Yellowplush's Ajew," Yellowplush bids adieu to *Fraser's* because he has come to the realization that he is "trampling upon the first princepills of English grammar." He plans to write a novel, he says, after he learns to spell. Yellowplush proved popular enough for Thackeray to revive the character in *Fraser's* from January to August 1840 in a series titled "Epistles to the Literati."

In the meantime Thackeray embarked on a novella for *Fraser's* under the pseudonym Ikey Solomons Esq. Junior. While Solomons is the least interesting of the various personae that Thackeray created, the novella, "Catherine," which ran from May 1839 to February 1840, is significant as an early attempt on Thackeray's part to burlesque literary genres of which he disapproved. Thackeray uses the true story of Catherine Hayes, who was burned at the stake in 1726 for the murder of her husband, to reject the romanticizing of the criminal in such Newgate novels as Bulwer-Lytton's *Paul Clifford* (1830) and *Eugene Aram* and Harrison Ainsworth's *Rookwood* (1834) and *Jack Sheppard* (1839). Thackeray's aim is to retire the tradition by writing realism, not romance. Implicit in Thackeray's rejection of the Newgate novel is the early-Victorian fear of the corrupting influence of novels on the masses.

In 1839 Thackeray also contributed "Stubbs's Calendar, or the Fatal Boots" to *George Cruikshank's Comic Almanac*. The tale is in twelve parts, one for each month of the year, with each part accompanied by an illustration by Cruikshank. It takes the form of a bildungsroman as the narrator, Bob Stubbs, relates his picaresque adventures. His rise and fall correspond to the seasons, so that the springtime of Stubbs's life corresponds to the spring months and his autumn years accompany the passages for the fall months; the heading of the December episode, in which Stubbs must adjust to diminished expectations, is "Winter of Our Discontent." Stubbs's adventures involve the military, duels, courtship, exile, family squabbles, and deceiving and being deceived. The following year Thackeray contributed another twelve-part tale, again accompanied by Cruikshank illustrations, to the *Comic Almanac*. In "Barber Cox, and the Cutting of His Comb," – or "Cox's Diary," as it is more commonly called –

Thackeray lampoons aristocratic social rituals and middle-class aspirations toward them in the story of a barber and his family who inherit property and learn to love fox hunting, billiards, opera, ballet, education, charity events, jousting, and vacations abroad. Like Yellowplush, Barber Cox, the narrator, frequently employs misspellings — *bally* for *ballet*, for instance. There are playful references: on learning of their inheritance, Cox says, the family "formed a splendid tableaux such as the great Cruikshank might have depicted." Thackeray's admiration for the illustrator is expressed in his "George Cruikshank's Works," published in the *London and Westminster Review* in June 1840 and in book form later in the year as *Essay on the Genius of George Cruikshank*. Thackeray writes from the perspective of a fellow illustrator, praising Cruikshank for never having "in all the exuberance of his frolicsome humour caused a single painful or guilty blush." The essence of Thackeray's own theory of humor can be found in this remark.

Thackeray's story "The Bedford-Row Conspiracy," about the young lovers John Perkins and Lucy Gorgon, was published in *The New Monthly Magazine* from January to April 1840; it is an adaptation of a French novel, Charles de Bernard's *Le Pied d'Argile*. It was followed from June to October by "A Shabby Genteel Story" in *Fraser's*. The story is the best that Thackeray had written up to that time. Caroline Gamm is a Cinderella figure whose mother and stepsisters have pretensions to gentility. Caroline is young, romantic, inexperienced, and without proper guidance; the closest thing in her world to a fairy godmother is the kitchen maid, Becky. Nor is there a Prince Charming; there are only the residents at her mother's boardinghouse: Andrea Fitch, a sham artist in search of a new mistress, and George Brandon, a rake pretending to be royalty. Caroline runs off with Brandon, who deceives her into thinking that they are married by arranging a fake ceremony. Fitch is based on John Brine, a Scottish artist Thackeray knew in Paris, and Brandon is modeled on Harry Matthews, a fellow dandy from Thackeray's youth. His wife's breakdown forced Thackeray to rush the ending of the story, and he left it incomplete; the final line — "God Bless, thee, poor Caroline! Thou art happy now for some short space at least" — begs for a sequel, which Thackeray would not produce until he wrote the novel *The Adventures of Philip* (1862).

Thackeray had visited Paris regularly since 1829, frequenting the theaters, museums, brothels, and gambling dens, and in 1840 he collected many of his writings about the city into *The Paris Sketch Book*, a volume "edited" by Michael Angelo Titmarsh. Thackeray would employ this persona more frequently than any other in the years to follow; Titmarsh would be the "editor" of most of Thackeray's travel writings and children's books and would surface throughout the 1840s as a contributor to literary periodicals, including *Fraser's*, particularly in the guise of an art and food critic. About half of the contents of *The Paris Sketch Book* had already appeared in periodical form. Most of the nineteen pieces are essays on French history or art, but several qualify as short stories. "A Caution to Travellers" is the story of Sam Pogson, Titmarsh's young friend who comes to Paris for romantic escapades and is "had" by swindlers and cheats. Pogson always travels with a copy of George Gordon, Lord Byron's *Don Juan* (1819–1824), and Thackeray's tale serves as an antidote to the Byronic vision. Again, Thackeray reveals himself as a literary realist, but in striving for realism he helps to perpetuate English stereotypes about the French. In "A Gambler's Death" Titmarsh meets another old friend, John Attwood, who has become a gambler. The work is moralistic, with Attwood committing suicide rather than face a life of poverty; the only mourners at his funeral are Titmarsh and two other drunken friends. Gordon N. Ray, in *William Makepeace Thackeray: The Uses of Adversity* (1955), found the tale "interesting for its anticipation of the bleakest naturalism" and as a "capital autobiographical document" revealing Thackeray's growing disillusionment with his life as a dandy. The title character and narrator of "Beatrice Merger" is a servant in the boardinghouse where Titmarsh resides in Paris. She says in the opening sentence that she is not a traditional heroine of romance since she is not a countess; again, Thackeray substitutes realism for romance as she leaves her widowed mother, her aunt, and her younger brothers in a farm village to find employment in the city. The story is one of the rare instances where Thackeray uses a female narrator.

"The Story of Mary Ancel," which had appeared in *The New Monthly Magazine* in October 1838, is a loose translation of a piece by Charles Nodier in the *Revue de Paris;* it is set during the French Revolution. Mary and her cousin, Pierre, are in love. Pierre is studying in Strasbourg with a Benedictine monk named Schneider, to whom he sings Mary's praises. When Mary's father is accused of being an enemy of the Republic and a friend of the old aristocracy, Schneider, the "Administer of Justice of the Republic," agrees not to turn Ancel in if he can have Mary's hand in marriage. The tale has a happy ending in which Schneider is brought to justice and Pierre and Mary are wed. "Little Poinsinet," a slight tale set in 1760 that appeared in *Fraser's* in October 1839, is also a translation. The naive Poinsinet is convinced by a Portuguese magician that he is invisible. In "The Painter's Bargain," which appeared in *Fraser's* in December 1838, the devil agrees to grant the penniless painter Simon Gambouge's wishes for seven years, at the end of which he will claim Simon's soul. This variation on the Faust legend descends into a mere misogynist joke as Simon saves his soul by coming up with a wish that the devil cannot fulfill: that he live with Simon's shrewish wife for six months. In the end Simon wakes up; it was all a dream. Also included in the volume is "The Devil's Wager," which has nothing to do with Paris but is the best tale in the collection.

In 1841 Thackeray gathered much of his magazine work into the volume *Comic Tales and Sketches* in the hope that book publication would focus greater literary attention on him. In addition to the "memoirs" of Gahagan and Yellowplush, the volume included "The Professor," "The Bedford-Row Conspiracy," and "Stubbs's Calendar, or the Fatal Boots." Although the Gahagan and Yellowplush pieces had already been published in book form in America, this was their first appearance in that form in England. "Catherine" was undoubtedly left out because it did not fit the rubric of "comic tale"; likewise "A Shabby Genteel Story" was not strictly comic and was incomplete; but there is no discernible reason "Cox's Diary" should not have been included. The volume was "edited" by Michael Angelo Titmarsh; the frontispiece shows Yellowplush, Titmarsh, and Gahagan arm-in-arm, with Titmarsh leading the way.

Michael Angelo Titmarsh's cousin, Samuel Titmarsh, is the narrator of *The History of Samuel Titmarsh and the Great Hoggarty Diamond,* a rambling series of picaresque adventures that appeared in *Fraser's* from September to December 1841 (it was published in book form in New York in 1848 as *The Great Hoggarty Diamond* and in London in 1849 under its original title). Samuel is a naive and honest clerk whose Irish Aunt Hoggarty owns the diamond broach of the title. The diamond allows Samuel to enter high society, though his true love, whom he finally marries, is his country sweetheart. The last chapter is sentimentally titled "In Which It Is Shown That a Good Wife Is the Best Diamond a Man Can Wear in His Bosom." The wife is clearly modeled on Isabella. Thackeray was forced to shorten the story, one of the few instances in which he came into conflict with the editors of *Fraser's*.

Thackeray contributed three sketches – two under his own name – to the two volumes of *Heads of the People* (1840–1841), a collection of "portraits of the English by distinguished writers" illustrated by Kenny Meadows. In these stories, plot is suppressed in favor of characterization. In "Captain Rook and Mr. Pigeon," which originally appeared in *The Corsair* on 28 September 1839, Thackeray proclaims that he has "travelled much" and discovered that "There is no cheat like an English cheat. Our society produces them in the greatest number as well as the greatest excellence. We supply all Europe with them." The innocent dupe Frederick Pigeon is taken in by the rogue Captain Rook; the moral of the tale is "Be not a Pigeon in thy dealings with the world, but it is better to be a Pigeon than a Rook." The title character of "The Fashionable Authoress" is Lady Fanny Flummery, who has "published forty-five novels, edited twenty-seven new magazines, and . . . many annuals, besides publishing poems, plays, desultory thoughts, memoirs, recollections of travel and pamphlets without number" in the last fifteen years. Thackeray may be satirizing his own prolific output during this period. The sketch reveals Thackeray's sense of the literary marketplace. In "The Artists," written under the Michael Angelo Titmarsh pseudonym, Thackeray attempts to do for the artists in Soho what "The Fashionable Authoress" does for writers; but the satire is not as biting. Thackeray could write about the art world with detached satire, whereas his sketch of the literary establishment, of which he was still on the fringes, is laced with a barely concealed disdain.

In October 1841 Thackeray contributed to *George Cruikshank's Omnibus,* under Titmarsh's name, the story "Little Spitz." Lorenzo, a student at a German university, and Rebecca, the Jewish daughter of a banker, are in love. In the opening paragraph Rebecca says that she could eat a sausage; since Rebecca is Jewish and cannot eat pork, Lorenzo sends his dog, Little Spitz, who runs all his errands, to the butcher with a basket and a note requesting "the best sausage meat, NOT pork." The butcher's wife, an anti-Semite who also has a vendetta against the dog, cuts off Little Spitz's tail and sends it as a sausage. The tale is of some interest today because of its treatment of anti-Semitism, but it was not popular in its own day and was only collected posthumously.

"Sultan Stork," which appeared in *Ainsworth's Magazine* from February to May 1842, is allegedly translated from the Persian by Major Gahagan and purports to be the tale that Scheherazade told her husband, the Sultan Stork, on the one thousand and second night. The sultan provides a running commentary on the tale, which he thinks is the most "monstrous" that Scheherazade has yet told him. Before the tale is over, the sultan falls asleep, and Scheherazade defers the rest of the story for another occasion.

George Savage Fitz-Boodle, Thackeray's fourth major persona after Gahagan, Yellowplush, and Titmarsh, made his first appearance in *Fraser's* in 1842. Fitz-Boodle is the least tedious of the personae who tell their own histories (Titmarsh does not). Fitz-Boodle is refreshingly honest and willing to be the butt of his own joke, whereas Gahagan and Yellowplush are too obtuse to know when the joke is on them. There is also more of Thackeray in Fitz-Boodle than in Yellowplush and Gahagan: Fitz-Boodle was educated at Slaughterhouse School, based on Charterhouse; he is a bachelor, as Thackeray was, for all practical purposes, after Isabella's breakdown; like Thackeray, he is unsuccessful in love (all of the women for whom Fitz-Boodle falls are modeled on women Thackeray had met on an early trip to Germany). "Fitz-Boodle's Confessions," which ran in *Fraser's* from June 1842 to February 1843 (and was published in book form in 1852 in *The Confessions of Fitz-Boodle; and Some Passages in the Life of Major Gahagan*), consists mostly of a series of adventures and misadventures with women. An early romance comes to naught because the woman is tricked into believing that Fitz-Boodle loves tobacco better than any woman in the world; Thackeray's vision of female dominance often revolves around a woman not permitting a man to smoke in her company. Fitz-Boodle's flirtation with Fräulein Dorothea ends when he falls on a slippery floor while dancing with her. He decides that Ottilia Schlippenschlopp, who eats five meals a day, is not the right woman for him when she devours nine rotten oysters. Thackeray's misogyny is barely concealed in these stories. In "Miss Lowe" – the second installment of *Fitz-Boodle's Confessions,* which was deleted from the book edition – Thackeray reveals a strain of anti-Semitism, as well. Fitz-Boodle becomes enraptured by Minna Lowe, the daughter of a Jewish banker imprisoned for forgery, and nearly becomes a victim of her family's schemes to ensnare his wealth.

The month after his own confessions ended, Fitz-Boodle began in *Fraser's* a series of four short stories, collectively titled *Men's Wives,* exposing the romantic unhappiness of his friends. "The Ravenswing" is the longest of the stories. The coquettish Morgiana Crump, whose parents own a tavern in Mayfair, is called the Ravenswing because of her

long, beautiful black hair. She is an actress, as was her mother, and she has several suitors, including Eglantine, a hairdresser who is favored by her mother; Woolsey, a tailor who is favored by her father; and Howard Walker, a sea captain with whom she elopes. If the first half of the story is a comic romance, the second half is a penetrating analysis of the difficulties of early married life that is undoubtedly rooted in Thackeray's biography. The story reveals a sensitivity, especially toward the female character, that is rarely associated with Thackeray. The first part of "Mr. and Mrs. Frank Berry" describes a fight between two students, Biggs and Berry, at Slaughterhouse; in the second part Berry is a henpecked husband whose wife treats him in much the same manner as she does her poodle. Berry's rebellious spirit – his manhood – has been crushed by marriage. "Dennis Haggarty's Wife" presents another henpecked husband, a victim not only of his wife and overbearing mother-in-law but also of his need for submission. Fitz-Boodle intends the story as a warning for "bachelors who are about to change their condition." In its day the story's pessimistic view of marriage drew admiration from August Strindberg and George Saintsbury and was praised for its realism. The Gothic "The _____'s Wife," set in a castle in Germany, is the most negligible and least realistic of the four tales. Ernst, the earnest suitor, dies of a broken heart when he is rejected by the bewitching and vixenish Angelica because he is poor; Max, Ernst's older brother, avenges his death by tricking Angelica into marrying an executioner. *Men's Wives* was published in book form in 1852. "The _____'s Wife" was omitted from the book version and subsequently published in *Stray Papers* (1901).

"Bluebeard's Ghost," which appeared in *Fraser's* under Titmarsh's name in October 1843 as *Men's Wives* was nearing its completion, could be considered a sort of fifth story in that series. Bluebeard is killed by his wife's brother; the widow becomes the object of the passion of the young, lovesick Frederic Sly, who twice tries to kill himself because his love is unrequited; the widow is delighted at his devotion but considers Frederic too ugly to marry. The tale presents an image of women as sirens and hussies; the widow is a creature of intense but repressed sexuality. The widow almost marries Sly when the ghost of her husband tells her to do so, but she learns that the ghost is a trick devised by Sly to win her. She decides instead to marry a Captain Blackbeard.

DECEMBER—"THE WINTER OF OUR DISCONTENT."

*Illustration by George Cruikshank for Thackeray's "Stubbs's Calendar, or the Fatal Boots," which appeared in* George Cruikshank's Comic Almanac *in 1839*

*The Irish Sketch Book* (1843), written under the Michael Angelo Titmarsh pseudonym, is a travel book based on a trip to Ireland Thackeray had taken with his wife in 1841. Though it includes no original short fiction, Thackeray retells stories that he heard or read in Galway. These "Irish and Hibernian" tales include "The Black Thief," which Thackeray likens to a story from "The Arabian Nights' Entertainments"; "Donald and His Neighbours"; and "The Spaeman." In 1844 he made a journey to the East; though there are no embedded tales in *Notes of a Journey from Cornhill to Grand Cairo* (1846), many of Thackeray's stories from the 1840s contain oriental motifs.

Thackeray's misogyny is again in evidence in *The Luck of Barry Lyndon,* the novel that appeared in *Fraser's* under Fitz-Boodle's name throughout 1844 (it was published in book form in 1852–1853): "Since the days of Adam, there has hardly been a mischief done in the world but a woman has been at the bottom of it." While *The Luck of Barry Lyndon* was appearing in *Fraser's,* Thackeray also wrote for *The New Monthly Magazine* under a new persona, that of Lancelot Wagstaff, Esq. Wagstaff is a typical middle-class family man who feigns interest in his wife and daughter but is, in reality, completely

self-absorbed. In "The Partie Fine" (May 1844) Wagstaff accepts a dinner invitation while his wife, Arabella, is away; he finds himself in the company of three hysterical French women and is stuck with the bill. The following month, in "Arabella, or the Moral of the Partie Fine," Thackeray uses one of his personae to comment on a story written by one of the others: Titmarsh, in a moment of uncharacteristic sentimentality, suggests that the moral element in Wagstaff's story is its depiction of Arabella, the long-suffering wife.

Two other stories by Wagstaff appeared the next year in *The New Monthly Magazine.* In "The Chest of Cigars" (July) Wagstaff is at a dinner party where he encounters a general who, chagrined to find that Wagstaff does not smoke cigars (out of deference to his wife's sensibilities), embarks on a long-winded tale of a colonel who was reconciled with his estranged father-in-law because of expensive cigars. At the end the reader learns that the general is Goliah O'Grady Gahagan, who has been promoted from major. "Bob Robinson's First Love" (August) is a sentimental, romantic tale of Robinson's infatuation with Eliza Griggs, a clergyman's daughter who is betrothed to another clergyman. A bittersweet, melancholy mood pervades the piece;

this time Thackeray does not poke fun at the follies of his characters.

In 1843 Thackeray joined the staff of a new magazine, *Punch,* founded in 1841 by Mark Lemon, Henry Mayhew, Douglas Jerrold, and Gilbert à Beckett. Each issue was discussed by the entire staff and contributors, originally in pubs and later around a large table in the *Punch* office. Thackeray, who may have written for the magazine as early as 1841, said of it later that "There never were before published in this world, so many volumes that contained so much cause for laughing, so little for blushing." It is not clear whether he was the author of "The Legend of Jawbrahm-Heraudee," published anonymously in the 18 June 1841 issue. King Poof-Alle-Shaw of Armenia has the ability to recite a poem after hearing it only once; a courtesan in his court can do the same after hearing a poem twice, and a eunuch can do so after three hearings. The king devises a plan to enrich the kingdom: he invites foreign poets to recite their works before his court, promising them large amounts of money; if a poem is found out to be unoriginal, however, the poet must pay a fine. In each case the king, the courtesan, and the eunuch repeat the poems, making it appear that they are well known and, therefore unoriginal; the poets are fined and tortured. One poet outwits the king by reciting a poem so long and boring that everyone falls asleep and no one can repeat it. Much of the humor in the story comes from the use of English names, slightly orientalized: for instance, the eunuch's favorite poet is Woordswoorth-el-Muddee (*el-Muddee* means "of the Lake").

Thackeray translated Alexandre Dumas's story "Othon l'Archer" (1845) as "A Legend of the Rhine" for *George Cruikshank's Table Book* (June–December 1845). That same year he revived Charles J. Yellowplush for *Punch* with "A Lucky Speculator," a brief notice in the 2 August 1845 issue in which he announced that C. Jeames De La Plush – as Yellowplush now called himself – had won a fortune speculating in railroads. Two weeks later "Jeames" wrote a letter to the editor complaining about the attention given to him; this was the first of many letters from Jeames, whose wealth from his railroad speculations leads him to romantic and political success, even though he remains virtually illiterate. Most critics concur that *Jeames's Diary,* which appeared in *Punch* from 8 November 1845 to 7 February 1846 and in book form in 1846, is an advance over Yellowplush's earlier appearances in that Thackeray is better able to sustain the satire.

Thackeray invented a new persona, "the Fat Contributor," for his travel writings for *Punch,* while simultaneously writing about many of the same places for *Fraser's* as Titmarsh. The travel writings of the Fat Contributor tend to be more superficial and frivolous than those of Titmarsh. The most significant appearance of the Fat Contributor is not in one of his travel writings but in a story Thackeray contributed to *Punch's Pocket Book* (1847), "An Eastern Adventure of the Fat Contributor," in which the Fat Contributor is willing to "become a Turk" – the Victorian term for "going native" – for the love of a woman; the whole affair turns out to be a practical joke played on him by some friends.

"Punch's Prize Novelists," Thackeray's series of parodies of some of the most popular writers of the day, ran in *Punch* from 3 April to 9 October 1847. Thackeray's interest in literary parody went back to "Catherine" and to Yellowplush's early book reviews, but these were parodies of genres rather than of individual authors. Thackeray's seven satires are not really short stories but read like excerpts from unwritten novels. Among the authors parodied are Bulwer-Lytton in "George DeBarnwell" (3–17 April), Benjamin Disraeli in "Codlingsby" (15–29 May), Catherine Gore in "Lords and Liveries" (12–26 June), G. P. R. James in "Barbazure" (10–24 July), Charles Lever in "Phil Fogarty" (7–21 August), and James Fenimore Cooper in "Stars and Stripes" (25 September–9 October). Thackeray's planned parody of Dickens was vetoed by the *Punch* staff; nevertheless, Dickens was among the writers who took exception to the project, feeling, along with Ainsworth and John Forster, that it was bad practice for authors to mock each other. "Lords and Liveries," which Thackeray introduces as being by the author of "Dukes and Dejeuners," "Hearts and Diamonds," and "Marchionesses and Milliners," chronicles the adventures of a dandy whose ennui is cured by his pursuit of a much-sought-after heiress; the footman who plays an instrumental role in the plot turns out to be Jeames, who writes a subsequent installment of the series, "Crinoline," which is Thackeray's parody of his own writing.

Thackeray's "The Snobs of England. By One of Themselves" had appeared anonymously in *Punch* from 28 February 1846 to 27 February 1847; when the book edition appeared in 1848 under the title *The Book of Snobs* the chapters of political and literary satire were deleted, but Thackeray's name was prominently displayed. From 27 May to 29 July 1848 *Punch* published Thackeray's story "A Little Dinner at Timmins's," which can be seen as an extension of *The Book of Snobs.* Mr. and Mrs. Fitzroy Timmins gave a dinner party; among the guests are Sir Thomas and Lady Kicklebury, who would resurface two years later in Thackeray's Christmas book *The Kickleburys on the Rhine.* The party is beyond the Timminses' means, and they go into debt; but they will have to give further dinner parties so as not to offend those who were not invited to this one. George Orwell called "A Little Dinner at Timmins's" "one of the best comic short stories ever written."

The publication in 1847–1848 of *Vanity Fair,* one of the great novels of the nineteenth century, made Thackeray famous; his literary apprenticeship was over. One of his main outlets for short fiction in the years during and immediately following the publication of *Vanity Fair* was a series of annual Christmas books that he wrote under the name of Titmarsh: *Mrs. Perkins's Ball* (1847), *Our Street* (1848), *Dr. Birch and His Young Friends* (1849), *Rebecca and Rowena* (1850), and *The Kickleburys on the Rhine* (1850). From 1844 to 1847 Thackeray had reviewed Christmas literature for *Fraser's* and *The Morning Chronicle;* these reviews reveal Thackeray's evolving ideas about such works.

Thackeray had begun writing *Mrs. Perkins's Ball* in 1844, when he was quarantined after returning from his Eastern travels. Titmarsh, who is "giving lessons in drawing, French, and the German flute" to the Perkins family, is invited to a dinner party and dance that they are giving. This event provides an occasion for Thackeray to lampoon snobs and social climbers. *Our Street,* a satire on gentrification, sketches the inhabitants of Titmarsh's street, Pocklington Gardens, in the newly renamed and newly fashionable Pocklington Quarters. One of the residents is Clarence Bulbul, the self-pronounced "lion of the street," who "has written an Eastern book of considerable merit." Titmarsh, whose *Notes of a Journey from Cornhill to Grand Cairo* had been published two years previously, asks, "Has not everybody written an Eastern book?" In *Dr. Birch and His Young Friends* Titmarsh is no longer a private tutor but "assistant manager and professor of English and French languages, flower painting, and the German flute in Doctor Birch's Academy." The story is another satire of Charterhouse. By the end of the book Titmarsh has resigned and is seeking employment as a private tutor.

For his next work Thackeray took a decidedly new tack. *Rebecca and Rowena* is a continuation of Sir Walter Scott's medieval romance *Ivanhoe* (1819) prompted by Thackeray's belief that Ivanhoe should have married Rebecca instead of Rowena. Thackeray portrays Rowena as an anti-Semite – she calls Jews "misbelieving wretches" – and is inclined

to give herself airs by, for example, comparing herself to Maid Marian. Ivanhoe is eager to leave Rowena and join King Richard in Normandy, and Rowena is not sorry to see him go. When Ivanhoe meets Richard, the king greets him as "Wilfred of Templestone, Wilfred the Married Man, Wilfred the henpecked!" The tale is filled with the misogyny that mars so much of Thackeray's work, but it serves as an antidote to the sentimental vision of courtship and marriage that pervaded Victorian ideology. Richard is depicted as susceptible to flattery and prone to violence. Thackeray does not narrate the battles; instead, he editorializes against battle scenes in which "everything passes off agreeably – the people are slain, but without any unpleasant sensations to the reader." If Victorian propriety will not permit Thackeray to depict battles in all their bloody reality, then he will not depict them at all. Believing false reports that Ivanhoe has been killed, Rowena remarries; Thackeray's irony is at its most controlled when he says, "She was a lady of such fine principles that she did not allow grief to overmaster her." Rowena dies, and her final wish – that Ivanhoe not marry a Jewess – is moot because Rebecca has converted to Christianity. Still, Thackeray undercuts the happy ending by concluding: "I think these were a solemn pair and died very early."

*The Kickleburys on the Rhine* is similar to the Christmas books that preceded *Rebecca and Rowena.* The setting – a cruise on the Rhine – allows for another series of satiric character sketches; it also permits Thackeray to indulge his fondness for travel writing. On the cruise Titmarsh meets the Kickleburys, who say that they admire all of Titmarsh's books "except the last," in which he ridiculed Scott. *The Kickleburys on the Rhine* was negatively received in the *Times* (3 January 1851), prompting Thackeray to forsake Christmas books for the next five years.

"Yesterday; A Tale of the Polish Ball" appeared in the 10 June 1848 issue of *Punch.* Sir Lionel de Boots promises to dance with Frederica de Toffy at the Polish ball but is called away to put down a Chartist uprising. He dies of a fever he catches in the uprising, she pines away for love of him, and they are buried together. The moral is: "How much agony might have been spared if the odious Chartists would but have stayed at home." The tale reveals something of Thackeray's conservatism in politics, but the tone is too light and frivolous for the seriousness of the events depicted.

"The Story of Koompanee Jehan," in the 17 March 1849 issue of *Punch,* is set in India. Prince Koompanee Jehan seizes control of the kingdom of

THE RIVALS.

*Illustrations by Thackeray for his Christmas book* The Rose and the Ring; *clockwise from top left: Princess Angelica, the queen, and King Valoroso XXIV at breakfast; the governess, Gruffanuff; Princess Angelica and Prince Giglio; Princess Angelica, Prince Giglio, and Prince Bulbo*

Ingleez by outwitting the former ruler, who was, "like many other valiant sovereigns, the slave of a woman" – in this case his mother, to whom he could not say no. If Victorian sentimentality had it that behind every great ruler there was a woman, Thackeray reversed the dictum: behind every weak ruler there was a woman. In "Hobson's Choice," which ran in *Punch* from 12 January to 26 June 1850, Hobson tells how it is impossible to keep female help in his home because of his interfering mother-in-law; the first male servant who is hired is spoiled by the mother-in-law until she catches him mimicking her, at which point he, too, is fired.

"The Lion Huntress of Belgravia," in the 24 August to 21 September 1850 issues of *Punch,* consists of Lady Nimrod's "journal of the past season." She is a "lion huntress," that is, one who seeks to have certain guests at her dinner parties and soirees. The story continues the themes of *The Book of Snobs,* "A Little Dinner at Timmins's," and *Vanity Fair,* but this time Thackeray addresses the subject of social snobbery in the snob's own words. It is to Thackeray's dissection of snobbery what *The Luck of Barry Lyndon* was to his dissection of rogues: both Lyndon and Lady Nimrod reveal more about themselves and their values than they intend to.

"Mr. Brown's Letters to a Young Man about Town," in the 24 March to 18 August 1849 issues of *Punch,* is an etiquette manual in which Brown advises his nephew on how to get along in London, where the nephew is about to begin his law studies. Mr. Brown's letters are essays on such topics as tailoring, women, friendship, balls, dinners, and clubs. The moral of the essay is sometimes illustrated by an anecdotal tale, but the essay on friendship qualifies as a piece of short fiction. In 1810 Mr. Brown was a bachelor at the Inns of Court, where he boarded next to a Mr. Bludyer, who once borrowed Brown's rooms for a party. A rich female relative of Brown's paid a surprise visit and was insulted by Bludyer, who did not know who she was, and Brown was cut out of the family fortune. The lesson for the nephew is to be careful whom he chooses for friends.

Thackeray's story "An Interesting Event" appeared in *The Keepsake* for 1849. It is a slight tale that Titmarsh overhears at his club. Mr. Smith tells Mr. Jones that he gave up an invitation to a dinner at the residence of the Topham Sawyers (who were characters in "A Little Dinner at Timmins's") to attend a dinner given by his old schoolmate Budgeon, but he was cheated out of his meal because Budgeon was preoccupied with the birth of his child; to add insult to injury, Smith had promised to buy Bud-

geon a dinner at a future date. *The Keepsake* for 1851 included "Voltigeur," which presents a more penetrating portrait of a marriage than do Thackeray's earlier tales. Although he has promised his wife that he will no longer wager on horse races, Lord Raihes bets on the horse Voltigeur and wins. Though her own brother tells her that the money her husband won was given to him to help pay off old debts, a former suitor convinces Lady Raihes that her brother is in league with her husband and that Lord Raihes used his winnings to buy a necklace for another woman. Far from a feminist tale – the woman is depicted as hysterical and jealous – "Voltigeur" is not just another misogynistic joke: the reader becomes convinced that the wife might be right in her jealousy; as the seeds of doubt are sown in her mind, they are sown in the reader's mind, as well. Like *Vanity Fair,* the story ends with a rhetorical question: "But who hasn't had his best actions misinterpreted by calumny: And what innocence or good-will can disarm jealousy?"

In 1852–1853 Thackeray delivered a lecture series at Oxford, Cambridge, Liverpool, Manchester, Glasgow, Edinburgh, and the United States on English humorists of the eighteenth century, including Fielding, Jonathan Swift, William Congreve, Joseph Addison, Richard Steele, Matthew Prior, John Gay, Alexander Pope, William Hogarth, Tobias Smollett, Laurence Sterne, and Oliver Goldsmith; the lectures were published in 1853. From October 1855 to the spring of 1857 Thackeray made a similar tour, lecturing on the reigns of George I, II, III, and IV. Those lectures were published in 1860 as *The Four Georges; Sketches of Manners, Morals, Court and Town Life.*

In 1855 Thackeray brought out *The Rose and the Ring; or, The History of Prince Giglio and Prince Bulbo,* his only Christmas book written for children. The tale begins with the royal family of the kingdom of Paflagonia assembled for breakfast, but the idyllic domestic scene is punctured as Thackeray relates the family history. The ironically named king, Valoroso XXIV, is anything but valorous: on the death of his brother he stole the crown from the rightful heir, Valoroso's nephew Giglio. Valoroso's daughter, the "accomplished" Princess Angelica, lacks any accomplishments at all, as her lessons and tasks are done by her handmaiden, the street urchin Beatrice. Thackeray incorporates Shakespearean overtones into the tale: Valoroso's theft of the crown echoes *Hamlet* (circa 1600–1601), and Valoroso quotes "Uneasy lies the head that wears a crown" from *Henry IV,* part 2 (circa 1596–1597). The most important Shakespearean echoes come, however, from *A Midsummer Night's Dream* (circa 1595–1596), as Princess Angelica is adored by everyone only as long as she is in possession of a magic ring; when her gruesome governess, Gruffanuff, puts on the ring, the princess's suitors – her cousin Giglio and Prince Bulbo of a neighboring kingdom – transfer their affections to the governess. Giglio lost his kingdom because the fairy Blackstick, who was not invited to his christening, put a curse on him. Blackstick also cast a spell on Princess Rosalba of the neighboring kingdom of Crim Tarta, even though she *was* invited to Rosalba's christening; as a result, Rosalba lost her fortune and has to live the life of a servant. Blackstick's wish of "a little misfortune" does Giglio and Rosalba good because it prevents them from being idle and vain; in contrast, Angelica and Bulbo need magical rings to solidify their love.

The four-volume *Miscellanies: Prose and Verse* (1855–1857) collected much of Thackeray's early work at *Fraser's* and *Punch,* including the memoirs of Gahagan, Yellowplush, and Fitz-Boodle, as well as many of the burlesques and short stories. In July 1857 he ran for Parliament from Oxford as an Independent, losing by only sixty-five votes.

In October 1859 Thackeray became one of the most powerful literary figures in England when he was made editor of the new *Cornhill Magazine.* Among the writers Thackeray's name drew to the magazine were Trollope, whose *Framley Parsonage* opened the first number, for January 1860, Alfred Tennyson, Harriet Beecher Stowe, Elizabeth Cleghorn Gaskell, Matthew Arnold, and Elizabeth Barrett Browning. Thackeray's own contributions to *The Cornhill Magazine* included the long story *Lovel the Widower,* which appeared from January to June 1860. It is a prose version of Thackeray's two-act play *Wolves and the Lamb,* which had been written in 1854 but never performed. The "lamb" is Horace Milliken, a City merchant who was thoroughly henpecked while his wife was alive and now, as a widower, is dominated by the "wolves": his mother-in-law, Mrs. Kicklebury (from *The Kickleburys on the Rhine*), and his own mother, Mrs. Bonnington, who often quarrel about which of them is more meddlesome and which spoils the children more. Milliken marries Julia Prior, his children's governess, and the play ends with the suggestion that his new mother-in-law might be as meddlesome and domineering as Mrs. Kicklebury and Mrs. Bonnington. In *Lovel the Widower* Milliken becomes Mr. Lovel, Mrs. Kicklebury becomes Lady Baker, and the governess is Elizabeth – not Julia – Prior. The governess's secret – that she was once a dancer – is re-

*Thackeray in his library*

vealed at the end of the first chapter instead of saved for a later surprise. Batchelor, the narrator, is an acquaintance of Fitz-Boodle's and one of Thackeray's most autobiographical personae. Jilted once before, he falls in love with Elizabeth Prior; it is he who introduces her to the Lovel household, an act that results in his losing out on love again.

From the beginning of his tenure at *The Cornhill Magazine* Thackeray contributed a series of essays under the persona Mr. Roundabout; he completed more than two dozen of them. The only "Roundabout Paper" that remotely qualifies as short fiction is "The Notch on the Axe – A Story a la Mode," which appeared in the April, May, and June 1862 issues. In the story, which is a satire of the sensationalist novels that were the rage in the 1860s, Roundabout encounters a mysterious old man, Mr. Pinto, who seems to have lived through many historic epochs.

Thackeray resigned as editor of *The Cornhill Magazine* in the spring of 1862 because of ill health; the last of the Roundabout essays was published in November 1863. He died on Christmas Eve of that year and was buried in Kensal Green Cemetery. From March to June 1864 *The Cornhill Magazine* posthumously published his unfinished novel, *Denis Duval.* Unlike the unfinished works left by Gaskell and Dickens – *Wives and Daughters* (1866) and *The*

*Mystery of Edwin Drood* (1870), respectively – this novel is hardly begun; the eight chapters are closer to a novella than a novel. Duval, born in 1763, is writing his memoirs in 1820; the fragment suggests that the work would have included an examination of antipapal sentiments during the reign of George III.

Shortly after his death a bust of Thackeray was placed in Westminster Abbey, a sign of his stature among the Victorians; the twentieth century, however, has tended to see Thackeray mainly as a satirist. Attitudes toward the short fiction are exemplified by two extreme views. John Carey, echoing Orwell, argues that "Because the Victorians preferred his later and staider works, they have come to be regarded as the major achievements" but that it was the earlier, shorter works where Thackeray was most creative. On the other hand, Wendell Harris argues that Thackeray's short stories "do not stand out nor contribute anything" to the genre and that "no amount of juggling with the help of theories of reliable and unreliable narrators, personae, or ironies within ironies will offset the general sense of snobbery and scorn one finds running through the shorter works." For Harris, Thackeray's primary failure "is to not take the shorter form of fiction seriously." Most critics would agree with neither extreme, seeing most of Thackeray's short fiction as the work of a young man; the stories are to the novels, these critics would say, as a sketch is to a painting. They are the training ground for a satirist who reached genius with *Vanity Fair* and whose style and sensibility was better suited for the longer forms of fiction.

**Letters:**

*The Letters and Private Papers of William Makepeace Thackeray,* 4 volumes, edited by Gordon N. Ray (London: Oxford University Press, 1945–1946);

*The Letters and Private Papers of William Makepeace Thackeray: A Supplement to Gordon Ray,* 2 volumes, edited by Edgar F. Harden (New York: Garland, 1994).

**Bibliographies:**

Gordon N. Ray, "Thackeray and 'Punch': 44 Newly Identified Contributions," *Times Literary Supplement,* 1 January 1949;

Henry S. Van Duzer, *A Thackeray Library* (Port Washington, N.Y.: Kennikat Press, 1965);

Edward M. White, "Thackeray's Contributions to *Fraser's Magazine,*" *Studies in Bibliography,* 19 (1966): 67–84;

Dudley Flamm, *Thackeray's Critics: An Annotated Bibliography of British and American Criticism 1836–1901* (Chapel Hill: University of North Carolina Press, 1967);

John Olmstead, *Thackeray and His Twentieth-Century Critics: An Annotated Bibliography, 1900–1975* (New York & London: Garland, 1977);

Sheldon Goldfarb, *William Makepeace Thackeray: An Annotated Bibliography 1976–1987* (New York: Garland, 1989).

**Biographies:**

Lionel Stevenson, *The Showman of Vanity Fair: The Life of William Makepeace Thackeray* (New York: Scribners, 1947);

Gordon N. Ray, *William Makepeace Thackeray: The Uses of Adversity* (New York: McGraw-Hill, 1955);

Ray, *William Makepeace Thackeray: The Age of Wisdom* (New York: McGraw-Hill, 1958);

Ann Monsarrat, *An Uneasy Victorian: Thackeray the Man, 1811–1863* (New York: Dodd, Mead, 1980).

**References:**

Patrick Brantlinger, "Thackeray's India," in his *Rules of Darkness* (Ithaca, N.Y.: Cornell University Press, 1980), pp. 73–107;

Charles and Frances Brookfield, *Mrs. Brookfield and Her Circle,* 2 volumes (London: Pitman, 1905; revised, 1906);

John Carey, *Thackeray: Prodigal Genius* (London: Faber & Faber, 1977);

Robert A. Colby, *Thackeray's Canvass of Humanity: An Author and His Public* (Columbus: Ohio State University Press, 1979);

Colby, "William Makepeace Thackeray," in *Victorian Fiction: A Second Guide to Research,* edited by George H. Ford (New York: Modern Language Association of America, 1978), pp. 114–142;

*Costerus,* special Thackeray issue, new series 2 (1974);

John W. Dodds, *Thackeray: A Critical Portrait* (New York: Oxford University Press, 1941);

Spencer L. Eddy Jr., *The Founding of "The Cornhill Magazine"* (Muncie, Ind.: Ball State University Press, 1970);

Lambert Ennis, *Thackeray: The Sentimental Cynic* (Evanston, Ill.: Northwestern University Press, 1979);

Ina Ferris, "Breakdown of Thackeray's Narrator: Lovel the Widower," *Nineteenth Century Fiction,* 32 (June 1977): 36–53;

Harold Strong Gulliver, *Thackeray's Literary Apprenticeship* (Valdosta, Ga.: Southern Stationery & Printing, 1934);

Edgar F. Harden, *Thackeray's English Humorists and Four Georges* (Newark: University of Delaware Press, 1985);

Barbara Hardy, *The Exposure of Luxury: Radical Themes in Thackeray* (London: Owen, 1972);

Wendell Harris, *British Short Fiction in the Nineteenth Century* (Detroit: Wayne State University Press, 1979);

John Harvey, "'A Voice Concurrent or Prophetical': The Illustrated Novels of W. M. Thackeray," in his *Victorian Novelists and their Illustrators* (London: Sidgwick & Jackson, 1970), pp. 76–102;

Keith Hollingsworth, *The Newgate Novel* (Detroit: Wayne State University Press, 1963);

Adolphus A. Jack, *Thackeray: A Study* (London: Macmillan, 1895; Port Washington, N.Y.: Kennikat Press, 1970);

David L. James, "Story and Substance in *Lovel the Widower*," *Journal of Narrative Technique*, 7 (Winter 1977): 70–79;

Charles Plumptre Johnson, *The Early Writings of William Makepeace Thackeray* (London: Stock, 1888; Folcroft, Pa.: Folcroft Library Editions, 1970);

George Levine, *The Boundaries of Fiction* (Princeton: Princeton University Press, 1968);

John Loofbourow, *Thackeray and the Form of Fiction* (Princeton: Princeton University Press, 1964);

Juliet McMaster, "*The Rose and the Ring:* Quintessential Thackeray," *Mosaic*, 9 (1976): 157–165;

Isadore G. Mudge and M. Earl Sears, *A Thackeray Dictionary* (New York: Dutton, 1910);

Selma Ann Muresianu, *The History of the Victorian Christmas Book* (New York: Garland, 1987);

George Orwell, "Oysters and Brown Stout," in *The Collected Essays, Journalism, and Letters of George Orwell,* 4 volumes, edited by Sonia Orwell and Ian Angus (New York: Harcourt, Brace & World, 1968), III: 299–302;

Catherine Peters, *Thackeray's Universe* (London: Faber & Faber, 1987);

S. S. Prawer, *Israel at Vanity Fair: Jews and Judaism in the Writings of William Makepeace Thackeray* (New York: Brill, 1992);

Mario Praz, *The Hero in Eclipse in Victorian Fiction* (Oxford: Oxford University Press, 1950);

R. G. G. Price, *A History of Punch* (London: Collins, 1957);

Stephen Prickett, *Victorian Fantasy* (Bloomington: Indiana University Press, 1979);

Jack P. Rawlins, *Thackeray's Novels: A Fiction That Is True* (Berkeley, Los Angeles & London: University of California Press, 1974);

Gordon N. Ray, *The Buried Life: A Study of the Relation between Thackeray's Fiction and His Personal History* (London: Oxford University Press, 1952);

Matthew Rosa, *The Silver Fork School* (New York: Columbia University Press, 1936);

George Saintsbury, *A Consideration of Thackeray* (London: Oxford University Press, 1931);

Peter Shillingsburg, *Pegasus in Harness: Victorian Publishing and W. M. Thackeray* (Charlottesville: University Press of Virginia, 1992);

M. H. Spielmann, *The History of* Punch (London: Cassell, 1895);

Lionel Stevenson, "William Makepeace Thackeray," in *Victorian Fiction: A Guide to Research,* edited by Stevenson (Cambridge, Mass.: Harvard University Press, 1964), pp. 154–187;

John Sutherland, "*Cornhill's* Sales and Payments: The First Decade," *Victorian Periodicals Review,* 19 (Fall 1986): 106–108;

Miriam Thrall, *Rebellious Fraser's* (New York: Columbia University Press, 1934);

Geoffrey Tillotson and Donald Hawes, eds., *Thackeray: The Critical Heritage* (London: Routledge & Kegan Paul, 1968);

Anthony Trollope, *An Autobiography* (2 volumes, Edinburgh & London: Blackwood, 1883; 1 volume, New York: Harper, 1883);

Trollope, *Thackeray* (London: Macmillan, 1879; New York: Harper, 1879);

Alexander Welsh, ed., *Thackeray: A Collection of Critical Essays* (Englewood Cliffs, N.J.: Prentice-Hall, 1968);

James H. Wheatley, *Patterns in Thackeray's Fiction* (Cambridge, Mass. & London: M.I.T. Press, 1969);

Ioan M. Williams, *Thackeray* (London: Evans, 1968).

**Papers:**

Manuscripts, correspondence, page proofs, and other papers of William Makepeace Thackeray are in the British Library; Trinity College, Cambridge; the National Library of Scotland, Edinburgh; the Berg Collection and the Arents Collection of the New York Public Library; the Fales Collection of New York University; the Houghton Library, Harvard University; the Beinecke Library, Yale University; the Taylor Collection and the Parrish Collection at Princeton University; the Huntington Library, San Marino, California; the Pierpont Morgan Library, New York; and the Harry Ransom Humanities Research Center, University of Texas at Austin. Many of the original manuscripts are missing.

# Anthony Trollope

## (24 April 1815 – 6 December 1882)

### Thomas L. Cooksey
*Armstrong State College*

See also the Trollope entries in *DLB 21: Victorian Novelists Before 1885* and *DLB 57: Victorian Prose Writers After 1867.*

BOOKS: *The Macdermots of Ballycloran* (3 volumes, London: Newby, 1847; 1 volume, Philadelphia: Peterson, 1871);

*The Kellys and the O'Kellys; or, Landlords and Tenants: A Tale of Irish Life* (3 volumes, London: Colburn, 1848; 1 volume, New York: Munro, 1882);

*La Vendée: An Historical Romance,* 3 volumes (London: Colburn, 1850);

*The Warden* (London: Longman, Brown, Green & Longmans, 1855; New York: Dick & Fitzgerald, 1862);

*Barchester Towers* (3 volumes, London: Longman, Brown, Green & Longmans, 1857; 1 volume, New York: Dick & Fitzgerald, 1860);

*The Three Clerks: A Novel* (3 volumes, London: Bentley, 1858; 1 volume, New York: Harper, 1860);

*Doctor Thorne: A Novel* (3 volumes, London: Chapman & Hall, 1858; 1 volume, New York: Harper, 1858);

*The Bertrams: A Novel* (3 volumes, London: Chapman & Hall, 1859; 1 volume, New York: Harper, 1859);

*The West Indies and the Spanish Main* (London: Chapman & Hall, 1859; New York: Harper, 1860);

*Castle Richmond: A Novel* (3 volumes, London: Chapman & Hall, 1860; 1 volume, New York: Harper, 1860);

*Framley Parsonage* (3 volumes, London: Smith, Elder, 1861; 1 volume, New York: Harper, 1861);

*Tales of All Countries* (London: Chapman & Hall, 1861);

*Orley Farm* (20 monthly parts, London: Chapman & Hall, 1861–1862; 1 volume, New York: Harper, 1862);

*The Struggles of Brown, Jones, and Robinson, by One of the Firm* (New York: Harper, 1862; London: Smith, Elder, 1870);

*Anthony Trollope*

*North America* (2 volumes, London: Chapman & Hall, 1862; pirated edition, 1 volume, New York: Harper, 1862; authorized edition, 2 volumes, New York: Lippincott, 1862);

*Tales of All Countries, Second Series* (London: Chapman & Hall, 1863);

*Rachel Ray: A Novel* (2 volumes, London: Chapman & Hall, 1863; 1 volume, New York: Harper, 1863);

*The Small House at Allington* (2 volumes, London: Smith, Elder, 1864; 1 volume, New York: Harper, 1864);

*Can You Forgive Her?* (20 monthly parts, London: Chapman & Hall, 1864–1865; 1 volume, New York: Harper, 1865);

*Hunting Sketches* (London: Chapman & Hall, 1865; Hartford, Conn.: Mitchell, 1929);

*Miss Mackenzie* (2 volumes, London: Chapman & Hall, 1865; 1 volume, New York: Harper, 1865);

*The Belton Estate* (3 volumes, London: Chapman & Hall, 1866; pirated edition, 1 volume, New York: Harper, 1866; authorized edition, 1 volume, New York: Lippincott, 1866);

*Travelling Sketches* (London: Chapman & Hall, 1866);

*Clergymen of the Church of England* (London: Chapman & Hall, 1866);

*The Claverings* (New York: Harper, 1867; 2 volumes, London: Smith, Elder, 1867);

*Nina Balatka: The Story of a Maiden of Prague,* 2 volumes (Edinburgh & London: Blackwood, 1867; London & New York: Oxford University Press, 1951);

*The Last Chronicle of Barset* (32 weekly parts, London: Smith, Elder, 1867; 1 volume, New York: Harper, 1867);

*Lotta Schmidt and Other Stories* (London: Strahan, 1867; London & New York: Ward & Lock, 1883);

*Linda Tressel* (2 volumes, Edinburgh & London: Blackwood, 1868; 1 volume, Boston: Littell & Gay, 1868);

*He Knew He Was Right* (32 weekly parts, London: Virtue, 1868-1869; 1 volume, New York: Harper, 1870);

*Phineas Finn: The Irish Member* (2 volumes, London: Virtue, 1869; 1 volume, New York: Harper, 1869);

*Did He Steal It? A Comedy in Three Acts* (London: Privately printed by Virtue, 1869);

*The Vicar of Bullhampton* (11 monthly parts, London: Bradbury & Evans, 1869-1870); pirated edition, 1 volume, New York: Harper, 1870; authorized edition, 1 volume, New York: Lippincott, 1870);

*An Editor's Tales* (London: Strahan, 1870);

*The Commentaries of Caesar* (Edinburgh & London: Blackwood, 1870; Philadelphia: Lippincott, 1870);

*Ralph the Heir* (19 monthly parts, London: Hurst & Blackett, 1870-1871; 1 volume, New York: Harper, 1871);

*Sir Harry Hotspur of Humblethwaite* (London: Hurst & Blackett, 1871; New York: Harper, 1871);

*The Golden Lion of Granpère* (London: Tinsley, 1872; New York: Harper, 1872);

*The Eustace Diamonds* (New York: Harper, 1872; 3 volumes, London: Chapman & Hall, 1873);

*Australia and New Zealand,* 2 volumes (London: Chapman & Hall, 1873);

*Lady Anna* (2 volumes, London: Chapman & Hall, 1874; 1 volume, New York: Harper, 1874);

*Phineas Redux* (2 volumes, London: Chapman & Hall, 1874; 1 volume, New York: Harper, 1874);

*Harry Heathcote of Gangoil: A Tale of Australian Bush Life* (London: Low, Marston, Low & Searle, 1874; New York: Harper, 1874);

*The Way We Live Now* (20 monthly parts, London: Chapman & Hall, 1874-1875; 1 volume, New York: Harper, 1875);

*The Prime Minister* (8 monthly parts, London: Chapman & Hall, 1875-1876; 1 volume, New York: Harper, 1876);

*The American Senator* (3 volumes, London: Chapman & Hall, 1877; 1 volume, New York: Harper, 1877);

*Christman at Thompson Hall* (New York: Harper, 1877; London: Low, 1885);

*The Lady of Launay* (New York: Harper, 1877);

*Is He Popenjoy? A Novel* (3 volumes, London: Chapman & Hall, 1878; 1 volume, New York: Harper, 1878);

*South Africa,* 2 volumes (London: Chapman & Hall, 1878);

*How the "Mastiffs" Went to Iceland* (London: Virtue, 1878);

*An Eye for an Eye* (2 volumes, London: Chapman & Hall, 1879; 1 volume, New York: Harper, 1879);

*John Caldigate* (3 volumes, London: Chapman & Hall, 1879; 1 volume, New York: Harper, 1879);

*Cousin Henry: A Novel* (2 volumes, London: Chapman & Hall, 1879; 1 volume, New York: Munro, 1879);

*Thackeray* (London: Macmillan, 1879; New York: Harper, 1879);

*The Duke's Children: A Novel* (3 volumes, London: Chapman & Hall, 1880; 1 volume, New York: Munro, 1880);

*The Life of Cicero,* 2 volumes (London: Chapman & Hall, 1880; New York: Harper, 1880);

*Dr. Wortle's School: A Novel* (New York: Harper, 1880; 2 volumes, London: Chapman & Hall, 1881);

*Ayala's Angel* (3 volumes, London: Chapman & Hall, 1881; 1 volume, New York: Harper, 1881);

*Why Frau Frohmann Raised Her Prices, and Other Stories* (London: Isbister, 1882; New York: Harper, 1882);

*The Fixed Period: A Novel* (2 volumes, Edinburgh & London: Blackwood, 1882; 1 volume, New York: Harper, 1882);

*Lord Palmerston* (London: Isbister, 1882);

*Marion Fay: A Novel* (3 volumes, London: Chapman & Hall, 1882; 1 volume, New York: Harper, 1882);

*Kept in the Dark: A Novel* (2 volumes, London: Chatto & Windus, 1882; 1 volume, New York: Harper, 1882);

*The Two Heroines of Plumplington* (New York: Munro, 1882; London: Deutsch, 1953);

*Not If I Know It* (New York: Munro, 1883);

*Mr. Scarborough's Family* (3 volumes, London: Chatto & Windus, 1883; 1 volume, New York: Harper, 1883);

*The Landleaguers* (3 volumes, London: Chatto & Windus, 1883; 1 volume, New York: Munro, 1883);

*An Autobiography,* edited by Henry M. Trollope (2 volumes, Edinburgh & London: Blackwood, 1883; 1 volume, New York: Harper, 1883);

*Alice Dugdale and Other Stories* (Leipzig: Tauchnitz, 1883);

*La Mère Bauche and Other Stories* (Leipzig: Tauchnitz, 1883; New York: Munro, 1884);

*The Mistletoe Bough and Other Stories* (Leipzig: Tauchnitz, 1883);

*An Old Man's Love* (1 volume, New York: Lovell, 1883; 2 volumes, Edinburgh & London: Blackwood, 1884);

*The Noble Jilt: A Comedy,* edited by Michael Sadleir (London: Constable, 1923);

*London Tradesmen,* edited by Sadleir (London: Mathews & Marrot, 1927; New York: Scribners, 1927);

*Four Lectures,* edited by M. L. Parrish (London: Constable, 1938);

*The Tireless Traveller: Twenty Letters to the "Liverpool Mercury" 1875,* edited by Bradford Allen Booth (Berkeley: University of California Press, 1941);

*Novels and Tales,* edited by J. Hampden (London: Pilot Press, 1946);

*The Parson's Daughter and Other Stories,* edited by Hampden (London: Folio Society, 1949);

*The Spotted Dog and Other Stories* (London: Pan, 1950);

*Mary Gresley and Other Stories,* edited by Hampden (London: Folio Society, 1951);

*The New Zealander,* edited by N. John Hall (London: Oxford University Press, 1972);

*Miscellaneous Essays and Reviews* (New York: Arno, 1981);

*Writings for Saint Paul's Magazine* (New York: Arno, 1981).

**Collections:** *The Oxford Illustrated Trollope,* 15 volumes, edited by Michael Sadleir and F. Page (Oxford: Oxford University Press, 1948–1954);

*Selected Works of Anthony Trollope,* 62 volumes, edited by N. John Hall (New York: Arno, 1980);

*Anthony Trollope: The Complete Shorter Fiction,* edited by Julian Thompson (New York: Carroll & Graf, 1992).

OTHER: *British Sports and Pastimes,* edited, with contributions, by Trollope (London & New York: Virtue, 1868).

SELECTED PERIODICAL PUBLICATION – UNCOLLECTED: "Never, Never, – Never, Never," *Sheets for the Cradle,* 1 (6 December–11 December 1875).

For the Victorian audience, the Christmas tale represented one of the most popular and widespread types of short fiction. Acting under the ubiquitous influence of Charles Dickens, various periodicals and annuals regularly commissioned Christmas stories from the popular authors of the day. While Anthony Trollope produced his share of these stories over the years, he never cared for the practice, finding it artificial and distasteful. Comparing the calling of literature to the call to upholsterers and undertakers to supply funerals, he complained in his autobiography that his Christmas stories "have had no real savour of Christmas about them." It was a task to be endured, not enjoyed. It is not surprising, then, that he found himself making excuses to the publisher Edmund Routledge. In a 23 April 1870 letter he apologized for the brevity of his annual contribution, explaining, "There is no probability that I shall write another Christmas story as I have very much work on hand, – and stories do not come as thick as blackberries." Referring to the enclosed story, he added, "but I fear mine for you will not exceed 20 pages, as your pages are long and I have always found that a short story does not require about 18 to 20 pages to tell itself."

Trollope's comments to Routledge suggest a good deal about his practice and production of short fiction. First, although Trollope protests that he cannot produce stories like blackberries, both he and his publisher knew that when the topic suited his taste the harvest could be abundant. In addition to publishing forty-eight novels, four substantial travel books, three biographies, an autobiography,

miniature nor an episode abstracted from a larger work, but a unified whole with a size and structure appropriate to its topic. While much of his short fiction lacks the unity, focus, concision, and textual density of such modern masters as James Joyce, Ernest Hemingway, or Jorge Luis Borges, among others, most still interest and entertain. They are, as Julian Thompson argues in his introduction to *Anthony Trollope: The Complete Shorter Fiction* (1992), "lucid, sinewy exercises in their chosen form." Perhaps the key to Trollope's aesthetics and his enduring appeal is best summarized in a review of *Lotta Schmidt and Other Stories* (1867), appearing in the 21 September 1867 *Saturday Review:* "Commonplace in subject, but neither vulgar nor mean, pure in tone, but not in the least noble or enthusiastic, it is essentially the literature of the moral and respectable middle-class mind – of people too realistic to be bothered by sentiment, too moral to countenance the sensationalism of crime, and too little spiritual to accept preachments or rhapsody for their daily use."

Anthony Trollope was born to writing. His mother, Frances Trollope, was a popular novelist, producing forty-one novels and travel books. His older brother, Thomas Augustus, wrote some sixty books and was commemorated after his death with the inscription *Scriptor copiosissimus.* Trollope's father, Thomas Anthony Trollope, devoted the later years of his life to an abortive multivolume *Encyclopaedia Ecclesiastica.* In each case writing served both as a means for combating terrible poverty and as a therapy against frustration and disappointment. Both motivations inform Trollope's own literary efforts.

Anthony Trollope was born on 24 April 1815 in Keppel Street, Russell Square, London, the fifth in a line of seven children. While his mother came from a good family and his father was a Chancery barrister, Trollope's early years were marked by poverty and humiliation. As the child of a genteel family, he was expected to observe standards of dress and decorum that the family's lack of means prevented him from meeting, thus opening him to constant ridicule from both his status-conscious peers and his masters. "My boyhood," he wrote in his posthumously published *Autobiography* (1883), "was as unhappy as that of a young gentleman could be, my misfortunes arising from a mixture of poverty and gentle standing on the part of my father, and from an utter want on my own part of that juvenile manhood which enables some boys to hold up their heads even among the distresses which such a position is sure to produce." His father's expectations far exceeded their realization. The senior Trollope failed at every enterprise he entered, and

*Trollope circa 1855*

and several volumes of sketches, reviews, and criticism, Trollope also managed to produce and publish forty-two to forty-five works of short fiction (depending on how his novellas are counted). One reviewer humorously wondered if Trollope could remember the content or even the titles of his vast output. Second, the conception of the short story as a page count is reminiscent of Trollope's famous description of his working habits with regard to novels, methodically producing 250 words every fifteen minutes for a fixed number of hours each day. The short story, like the novel, became a sort of blank form to be filled with an appropriate number of words on an appropriate number of pages, and, like the novels, a commodity to be produced and sold according to the demands of the marketplace. For Trollope, then, the process and discipline of producing short fiction was not significantly different from that of producing novels. But at the same time Trollope conceived an organic relationship between the story and its dimensions. The short story was neither a novel in

like the Reverend Mr. Crawley in *The Last Chronicle of Barset* (1867), he suffered debilitating bouts of depression.

Trollope was sent to Harrow as a day student, where he showed little aptitude as a scholar and received almost continual abuse and humiliation. Later as a boarder at Winchester he was frequently beaten, often by his brother Tom, and returned to Harrow. Throughout his life Trollope sustained a longing for companionship, coupled with the need to be liked. At the same time his early circumstances left him isolated and scorned. Forced to turn inward upon his own resources, he developed the habit of daydreaming. "Thus it came to pass that I was always going about with some castle in the air firmly built within my mind." Such an intellectual and imaginative discipline, he thought, allowed him eventually to construct his novels. "I learned in this way to maintain an interest in a fictitious story, to dwell on a work created by my own imagination, and to live in a world altogether outside the world of my own material life."

Meanwhile, family circumstances worsened. Frances Trollope traveled to the United States and set up a store in Cincinnati. She was soon joined by her husband, leaving Anthony at Winchester with an inadequate supply of money, further adding to his humiliations. The Cincinnati bazaar failed, and the family returned to England. As the senior Trollope's depression deepened and his health declined, Frances Trollope turned her experiences of the United States into her first book, *The Domestic Manners of the Americans* (1832). Although it proved a great success and prompted her to take up the pen as a means of supporting the family, Mr. and Mrs. Trollope still found it necessary to flee England to avoid their debtors. Setting up a household near Bruges in Belgium, Frances continued writing while caring for her sick husband and nursing a dying son and daughter. By 1836 husband, son, and daughter were dead. Of her seven children, only Thomas, Anthony, and a daughter, Cecilia, were still alive. Reflecting in later years on his mother's plight Trollope noted, "I have written many novels under many circumstances; but I doubt much whether I could write one when my whole heart was by the bedside of a dying son."

Leaving Harrow to join his family in Belgium at the age of nineteen, Trollope served briefly as an usher at a school in Brussels but soon returned to London, obtaining an appointment as a clerk in the general post office on 4 November 1834. Given his limited academic acquirements and lack of self-discipline, his first seven years in the civil service were "neither creditable to myself nor useful to the public service." He describes his experiences from this period of his life in *The Three Clerks: A Novel* (1858), the most explicitly autobiographical of his novels. He was also at this time pursued by a woman who thought that he should marry her, an experience that he incorporated in *Ralph the Heir* (1870–1871) and his short story "Alice Dugdale" (1878). Not surprising, it was with a deep sense of relief and good riddance that Trollope's superiors approved his appointment as an assistant to a post office surveyor in the west of Ireland in 1841.

Ireland marked the turning point in Trollope's fortunes. Separated from his past experiences and reputation, he began to mature as an efficient civil servant, discovering a vast capacity for both work and play. It was during this period that Trollope developed his love of hunting and riding the hounds, a passion he vigorously pursued the rest of his life. He also began courting Rose Heseltine, the daughter of an English banker, whom he married on 11 June 1844. While Rose often disappeared in the shadows of the ever-boisterous Trollope, their marriage seems to have been happy. As Victoria Glendinning suggests in her 1992 biography of Trollope, "Rose was bone of his bone, flesh of his flesh, a phrase he used repeatedly when describing strong marriages." His wife was invariably the first reader of all of Trollope's works, frequently making clean copies of manuscripts. In addition he trusted and accepted many of her editorial judgments. Their marriage produced two children: Henry Merivale, born 13 March 1846, and Frederic James, born 27 September 1847. Because of the difficulties of living in Ireland at this time as well as the dangers associated with childbirth, the Trollopes chose to have no more children.

In the dark days as a clerk before he went to Ireland, Trollope had, like his father, thought of writing as a sort of therapy, a way of giving structure to his life. Soon after his marriage, anticipating the need for more income to support a family, Trollope turned with purpose to the family vocation, producing his first novel, *The Macdermots of Ballycloran* (1847). It was published under the unpromising arrangement of half profits after expenses by Thomas Newby, who brought out Emily Brontë's *Wuthering Heights* the same year under even worse conditions. Four hundred copies were printed, and Trollope received a grand total of £48 for his efforts. Switching publishers but receiving similar arrangements, he published his second novel, *The Kellys and the O'Kellys; or, Landlords and Tenants: A Tale of Irish Life* (1848), which brought

£123 and the advice that "Irish" novels were not currently popular. He then produced a historical romance set in France during the time of the French Revolution, *La Vendée* (1850), for which he earned a grand total of £20.

In 1851 Trollope's literary efforts were interrupted by his duties as a civil servant. Recalled to England to participate in an extended reorganization of the rural postal network, he spent the next two years surveying and charting routes over Devonshire, the part of England that would serve as the model for Barsetshire, the imaginary setting of six novels. After a trip to Florence in 1853 to visit his mother and brother, Trollope and Rose returned to Ireland. With a new posting in Belfast he began work on his next novel. After being promoted to surveyor in the post office the following year, he sent the completed manuscript of *The Warden,* the first of the Barsetshire novels, to William Longman, who published it in January 1855. While *The Warden* initially proved only a moderate success, Trollope had nevertheless finally discovered his voice and idiom and followed it with *Barchester Towers* in 1857. These novels together earned their author £727. After stumbling again with *The Three Clerks* he returned to Barsetshire with *Doctor Thorne: A Novel* (1858), a work that represented his critical and popular breakthrough. A reviewer from *The Leader* declared that Trollope had joined the "circulating firmament" when *Doctor Thorne* entered the lists of Mudie's Circulating Library.

Professional duties called again in 1859, and Trollope was first sent on a mission to Egypt, which included a side trip to the Holy Lands, and subsequently to the West Indies, Cuba, and Panama to negotiate postal treaties. The success of these missions resulted in Trollope's promotion to the post of surveyor to the Eastern District of England, allowing him to move back to England. His experiences in the Middle East provided a rich source of material, most immediately for his next novel, *The Bertrams: A Novel* (1859), and subsequently a quartet of short stories. The mission to the West Indies and Central America led to five stories and his best travel book, *The West Indies and the Spanish Main* (1859).

Returning to England via the United States after his mission across Panama, Trollope was approached by the American publisher Fletcher Harper to contribute a short story to *Harper's New Monthly Magazine.* Harper proposed to publish stories by "the most brilliant Novelist of the day," commissioned expressly for an American audience. Interested in an additional source of revenue, as well

as a new literary venue, Trollope sent Harper "La Mère Bauche," a tragic story based on an incident he had heard about during a vacation in the Pyrenees, and "Relics of General Chassé," a farce about the chastening of English tourists in Belgium. In a 1 September 1859 letter to Harper, Trollope wrote, "I think of writing a series of tales, of which the two which I have sent you will be the two first — to be called when completed, 'Tales of All Countries.' Each would refer to some different nation or people; and in each case to some country which I have visited." Indicating a desire to maximize his profits, he added, "my intention would be to republish them in two series, as they should be finished, certainly here in England, and I should hope in the States, with your assistance." As it turned out, *Harper's* only published a handful of Trollope's stories, preferring a serialization of *Orley Farm* (1861–1862).

Undeterred, Trollope wrote in October 1859 to William Makepeace Thackeray, then editor of the newly forming *Cornhill Magazine.* Trollope had long admired Thackeray's work and considered *Henry Esmond* (1852) one of the great novels of the age. Echoing the proposal he had given Harper, Trollope suggested a series of five short stories. Thackeray's publisher, George Smith, answered with the offer of £20 per story but indicated his preference for a serialized novel instead, for which he offered Trollope £1,000. Too good an offer to refuse, Trollope prepared the first installment of *Framley Parsonage* – the fourth of the Barsetshire series – which appeared in the first issue of the *Cornhill* just after Christmas 1859. Both the novel and the magazine were successful, selling some 120,000 copies. The experience introduced Trollope to the practice of serializing novels, a technique, along with part-publication, that he would use to good effect with many of his later great novels.

With the growing success of his novels, especially *Framley Parsonage* (1861), Trollope soon found a ready outlet for his short stories in various "family" magazines such as *Good Words, Cassell's Illustrated Family Paper,* and *Argosy,* as well as newer periodicals such as *London Review* and *Public Opinion.* He was also soon approached to contribute Christmas stories to the annuals. Receiving about £20 apiece for the early stories, he would regularly command £100 for a story at the height of his fame. In a 30 September 1878 letter to A. F. A. Woodford, editor of the *Masonic Magazine,* Trollope wrote, "it does not suit me to write any story for less than £100. . . . The labour," he explained, "is in arranging a plot, rather than in writing the tale. . . . I would write a story equal to 10,000 words for £100; – but, as I have explained, I should be unwilling to write any story of any length for a less sum." Trollope was also able to convince the publishers Chapman and Hall to bring out the first installment of *Tales of All Countries*. The first series appeared in 1861 and contained eight stories. With the exception of "La Mère Bauche," each had first appeared in either *Harper's* or *Cassell's*.

*Tales of All Countries* received mixed notices. A reviewer for the *Saturday Review* offered the doubtful compliment that "Mr. Trollope is alone in his power of telling a story about absolutely nothing" (28 February 1863). Henry James gave a more sympathetic shading of the same theme when, in the context of a 1865 review of Harriet Prescott Spofford's *Azarian* (1864) in *North American Review,* he suggested that Trollope had "a delicate perception of the actual which makes every whit as firm ground to work upon." In *The Trollopes: The Chronicle of a Writing Family* (1945) Lucy and Richard Poate Stebbins dismiss the stories as "not even second-rate" and of little value aside from the psychological insights they offer into Trollope. Such an evaluation seems excessively harsh.

Most of the stories of the first series fall into one of two categories. The first group, involving the comic misadventures of English travelers in foreign places, includes "The O'Connors of Castle Conor," "John Bull on the Guadalquivir," "Relics of General Chassé," and "An Unprotected Female at the Pyramids." The second group includes more-serious courtship stories set in foreign locales: "La Mère Bauche," "Miss Sarah Jack of Spanish Town, Jamaica," "The Courtship of Susan Bell," and "The Chateau of Prince Polignac." The last story, featuring the doubts and deliberations of a widowed English lady who is courted by a Frenchman who turns out to be a highly successful tailor, borders on both categories. The distinction drawn is one of degree, not kind, for with the exception of "La Mère" the tone of all of the stories of the second group is relatively light, and with the exception of "Relics of General Chassé," all of the stories of the first group also involve a courtship of some sort.

In general these early stories are based on one or two comic situations that Trollope overworks. "The O'Connors of Castle Conor" introduces the narrator Archibald Green, a Trollopean persona who also appears in two later stories, "Father Giles of Ballymoy" and "Miss Ophelia Gledd." Invited to a ball after a fox hunt by the local Irish gentry and discovering that his fishing boots have been packed

instead of his dancing pumps, Green tries to borrow a pair of shoes from a servant, with disastrous results. In "John Bull on the Guadalquivir," a boorish young Englishman makes a fool of himself in front of a Spanish grandee he has mistaken for a bullfighter, accidentally tearing a gold button off the gentleman's costume. Both stories were based on actual events, and each offers a satiric self-portrait of Trollope as the headstrong Englishman. "Relics of General Chassé" is probably the weakest contribution to the collection. Michael Sadleir, in *Trollope: A Commentary,* complains that it is reminiscent of the strained humor of Mrs. Trollope, though contemporary reviewers were more sympathetic. Visiting a museum in Antwerp, the young Rev. Augustus Horne decides impulsively to try on a pair of leather riding breeches that belonged to the Napoleonic hero. Another group of souvenir hunters comes along and cuts large pieces out of Horne's abandoned trousers, supposing them to be a relic of General Chassé. By contrast "An Unprotected Female at the Pyramids" and "Miss Sarah Jack of Spanish Town, Jamaica" show greater control and merit.

"Miss Sarah Jack" offers the portrait of an independent and highly sensual young woman, Marion Leslie, courted by Maurice Cummings, an impoverished young sugar planter. Their courtship is almost destroyed over a misunderstanding, arising from Marion's insistence on dancing all night at a ball. As in Jean Rhys's *Wide Sargasso Sea* (1966), Trollope's Jamaica is an erotic space marked by powerful passions, as much a state of mind as an actual place, and the story is remarkable for his treatment of the theme of female sexuality. "An Unprotected Female," ostensibly a satire on feminism, is characteristic of Trollope's antiromanticism. A group of English tourists visit the Great Pyramids but are plagued by a combination of trivial difficulties that dwarf the ancient monument. Here Trollope explores the figure of the independent female tourist traveling without companions. While Miss Dawkins proclaimed her independence, insisting that "she had no idea of being prevented from seeing anything she wished to see because she had neither father, nor husband, nor brother available for the purpose," it is soon evident that she will attach herself to any party that will supply her needs. In the essay "The Unprotected Female," appearing in *Travelling Sketches* (1866), Trollope expressed his admiration for such women. The problem with Miss Dawkins is not that she is liberated but that she only claims to be.

"La Mère Bauche" and "The Courtship of Susan Bell" provide a study in contrasts, each treating the same theme but with different variations and different results. In "La Mère Bauche" Madame Bauche's son, Adolphe, a spineless fop, courts the orphaned Marie, a servant girl brought up by Madame. The strong-willed Madame Bauche, the proprietor of a successful resort hotel, prefers that her son marry someone of a higher class and so convinces Adolphe to break his pledge to Marie, who, brokenhearted, commits suicide. Like Mrs. Proudie in *Barchester Towers* and *The Last Chronicle of Barset*, Madame Bauche is among a long list of Trollope's strong-willed female characters who unintentionally cause harm by their obstinacy. The lighter "Courtship of Susan Bell" is set in New England, where Mrs. Bell runs a boardinghouse. Aaron Dunn, a young engineer building bridges for the railroad, takes a room with the Bells and soon begins courting Mrs. Bell's younger daughter. The uncertainty of his future raises many doubts in the older woman's mind, but where Madame Bauche was a tyrant, Mrs. Bell is timid. Thus, after an assortment of fits and starts, propriety gives way to love; Susan Bell marries her engineer; and both presumably live happily ever after.

Trollope's plots are often claimed to lack inventiveness and originality, but this criticism misses the point. Together "La Mère Bauche" and "The Courtship of Susan Bell" illustrate Trollope's use of the short story as a convenient narrative device for examining a series of variations on a single basic theme, like a series of oil sketches produced by a painter to test various combinations of tone and texture. The short story, as Donald D. Stone suggests in "Trollope as a Short Story Writer" (1976), provided the author with a compact form for exploring the "innumerable possibilities for each given set of imagined facts."

Trollope's secure position with the post office and his taking up residence in London in 1859 provided the necessary stability and stimulation for the busiest and most productive decade of his life. Aside from his professional duties with the post office, which he pursued until his retirement in 1867, he served on various boards and committees; traveled the lecture circuit; published essays and sketches; became an active clubman, joining, among others, the Garrick, the Cosmopolitan, the Arts, the Athenaeum, and the Turf; dabbled in founding and editing periodicals; and pursued his passion for hunting. During this decade he also produced thirteen novels, including some of his best work: *The Small House at Allington* (1864), *Can You Forgive Her?*

(1864–1865), *The Last Chronicle of Barset, He Knew He Was Right* (1868–1869), and *Phineas Finn: The Irish Member* (1869). This decade also saw changes at home as well. As Trollope's sons completed their education their futures became a matter of active concern. The older son, Harry, found a place as a partner in the offices of the publishers Chapman and Hall in 1869 after drifting through various professions with his father's backing. Fred decided to take up sheep ranching and sailed to Australia in 1865.

In 1860 Trollope again visited his mother and brother in Florence for several months, where he made the acquaintance of Kate Field, a pretty twenty-two-year-old American woman who was studying singing and writing articles for the *Boston Courier*. She was also "collecting" literary lions, including both Robert and Elizabeth Barrett Browning; a deeply smitten, albeit elderly, Walter Savage Landor; and Frances Trollope and her two famous sons. Trollope soon became infatuated with Kate, initiating an intense, though probably platonic, relationship that lasted the rest of his life. In his *Autobiography* he candidly confesses that "there is an American woman, of whom not to speak in a work purporting to be a memoir of my own life would be to omit all allusion to one of the chief pleasures which has graced my later years." He goes into few details beyond saying "in the last fifteen years she has been, out of my family, my most chosen friend" (1875).

Trollope's short stories are perhaps more revealing. "Miss Ophelia Gledd," which was first published in 1863 in the feminist magazine *A Welcome*, retells the story of an 1862 sleigh ride and accident Trollope and Kate Field experienced when he visited Boston and features Trollope's persona, Archibald Green. At the end of the story the narrator wonders if Miss Gledd would be accepted in London society. One of Trollope's best stories, "Mary Gresley," first published in *Saint Paul's Magazine* in November 1869, is also suggestive. It features a relationship between the narrator, a rather pretentious middle-aged editor, and a young woman who wants to contribute to his magazine. At first the narrator insists, "In love with Mary Gresley, after the common sense of the word, we never were, nor would it have become us to be so." He soon confesses, however, "we loved her, in short, as we should not have loved her, but that she was young and gentle, and could smile." Like the editor, Trollope helped Field in her attempts at poetry and fiction, writing her long letters of advice.

While in Florence, Trollope also frequented the local emigré circles, which provided material for

*Trollope (right) with his older brother, Tom, in the early 1860s*

his story "Mrs. General Talboys." Translating Florentine literary-artistic society to Rome, the tale describes the wife of an English general wintering in Rome. Trollope portrays himself and Rose in the guise of Mr. and Mrs. Mackinnon, minor figures in the story. To make a name for herself in the bohemian artistic circles Mrs. General Talboys is free with unconventional opinions on free love. An impressionable young Irish sculptor named O'Brien takes her at her word and offers to run off with her. As with Miss Dawkins in "An Unprotected Female," Mrs. General Talboys is not sincere in her bohemianism and angrily rebuffs the perplexed O'Brien. Trollope sent the story, followed by "Ride Across Palestine" (originally titled "Banks of the Jordan"), a story that conveys religious skepticism, off to the publisher George Smith, hoping to publish both in the *Cornhill.*

"I have completed Mrs. Talboys," he wrote 10 November 1860. He added, providentially, "my wife, criticizing it, says that it is ill-natured." Thackeray quickly responded, rejecting both stories as inappropriate and indecent because of references to O'Brien's bastard children and Mrs. Talboy's behavior. Trollope shot back an angry reply dated 15 November 1860. "I will not allow that I am indecent, and profess that squeamishness – in so far as it is squeamishness and not delicacy – should be disregarded by a writer." He then pointed to a series of examples of illegitimate children and questionable

women in the contemporary literature, including works by Sir Walter Scott, George Eliot, and Thackeray himself. He also mentioned Charlotte Brontë's *Jane Eyre* (1847) and Dickens's *Oliver Twist* (1837–1838). "I have mentioned our five greatest names & feel that I do not approach them in naughtiness any more than I do in genius." He asked Thackeray rhetorically, "you speak of the squeamishness of 'our people.' Are you not magnanimous enough to feel that you write *urbi et orbi;* – for the best & wisest of English readers; and not mainly for the weakest?"

Despite this appeal Thackeray persisted in his rejection, so Trollope submitted both stories along with "The Parson's Daughter of Oxney Colne" to the *London Review,* which published all three in 1861. As it turned out the two stories proved too strong for the magazine's readership, resulting in letters to the editor. In February 1861 an embarrassed Laurence Oliphant, proprietor of the *London Review,* forwarded an extract of the complaints to Trollope. One reader declared, "for my own part I shall immediately destroy the supplements containing the two tales that have as yet come out and if they are continued I shall be compelled to give up the paper." Another complained, "you must make your election whether you will adapt your paper to the taste of men of intelligence & high moral feelings *or* to that of persons of morbid imagination & *a low tone of morals.*" Oliphant explained with an apology that he had not read the tales before their publication, adding, "I felt such perfect confidence that anything from your pen would have defied any such criticism as the above. . . . I still believe that tales of a high moral tendency and possessing the literary merit which I know it is in your power to impart to them would have exercised a most beneficial influence not only on the circulation but on the character of the paper." In filing this letter Trollope noted "From Laurence Oliphant/ A wonderful letter" and never again published in the *London Review*.

After his misadventures with the *London Review* Trollope in 1861 and 1862 sold a series of five stories to the magazine *Public Opinion*. With encouragement from Kate Field and George Eliot, Trollope also contributed the story "The Journey to Panama" in 1861 to *The Victoria Regia* for no pay. This was unusual not only because he provided the story gratis but because *The Victoria Regia*, like *A Welcome*, where he would later publish "Miss Ophelia Gledd," was edited by Adelaide Ann Procter for Emily Faithfull, a feminist lecturer and publisher. Called "that female Caxton of the age" by Trollope biographer Glendinning, Faithfull founded Victoria Press, a printing firm that employed only women, even down to the compositors. Both *The Victoria Regia* and *A Welcome* featured contributions by the leading authors of the day, including Alfred Tennyson, Matthew Arnold, Thackeray, and Harriet Martineau.

"The Journey to Panama," Trollope explained in a November 1867 letter, was based on his own experience of meeting on shipboard a woman who was traveling to Panama to be married. On receiving news that her fiancé had died she asked that her trunk be brought to her. "In the course of an hour I found her packing & unpacking the trunk, putting the new wedding clothing at the bottom & bringing the old things, now suitable for her use, to the top. And so she employed herself during the entire day." Trollope developed the incident to explore the psychology of a woman forced by economic circumstances to marry a husband she hardly knows and does not love. Having imagined and recorded her dilemma, Trollope let his character off the hook by disposing of the intended husband and providing the lady with a suitable inheritance.

Taking a leave of absence from the post office soon after his return to England from Italy, Trollope sailed in March for the United States with a commission to write a book on America and especially the "War of Secession." The journey also gave Trollope an opportunity to see Field again. Visiting various battlefields as well as retracing his mother's old stomping grounds, Trollope gathered material for his book on America and various short stories. *North America*, in which Trollope looked on the conflict with despair, appeared in 1862, becoming his most successful book to date, aside from *Orley Farm*.

In 1863 Trollope collected nine stories in *Tales of All Countries, Second Series:* the three stories published in *The London Review* – "Mrs. General Talboys," "A Ride Across Palestine," and "The Parson's Daughter of Oxney Colne"; the Christmas tale "The Mistletoe Bough," which first appeared in the *Illustrated London News* in 1861; and the stories that were published in *Public Opinion* – "Aaron Trow," "George Walker at Suez," "Returning Home," "The House of Heine Brothers in Munich," and "The Man Who Kept His Money in a Box." The stories of the second series generally echo the pattern and format of the first in featuring comic tales about tourists and courtships in foreign lands. A reviewer for the 28 February 1863 *Saturday Review* remarked on Trollope's skill at sketching his characters, especially the young women. "He alone can describe young ladies – and especially young ladies in a state of flirtation or love – as they really are," adding, "He can sketch their characters, and paint their ways, and reveal their thoughts, and make them natural, pleasant, and easy. . . ."

"The Parson's Daughter of Oxney Colne" revises the themes of "La Mère Bauche." A prototype of Captain Aylmer in *The Belton Estate* (1866), Captain Broughton falls in love with Patience Woolsworthy but eventually breaks off their engagement when he realizes that she is poor, preferring a well-connected heiress. In this variation of the theme, however, Trollope chooses to save the jilted heroine, having her befriended by a wealthy spinster. Thus, Patience ends her days "a confirmed old maid," rehearsing in miniature the story of Lily Dale, the heroine of *The Small House at Allington* and *The Last Chronicle of Barset* in the final installments of the Barsetshire series. Like Lily, Patience accepts her fate and finds her life fulfilling despite the title "old maid."

"Aaron Trow" and "Returning Home" are of a different order from the other stories of the second series. Both hearken back to Trollope's experiences around the Caribbean, the first set in Bermuda, the second in Costa Rica. "Returning Home," based on a combination of Trollope's own trip through the jungles of Panama and an actual incident he had heard about, begins like a comic tourist tale. After many years of exile in Costa Rica the Awkrights, an English couple, decide to hazard the journey through the jungle in order to visit England and show off their new child. The hardships through the jungle shift from the comical to the increasingly unbearable, culminating in an overturned canoe that leaves mother and child drowned. Heartbroken, Mr. Awkright abandons his journey and returns home. In "Aaron Trow" Anastasia Bergen is courted by Caleb Morton, a Presbyterian minister. One evening Aaron Trow, an escaped convict from a penal colony, breaks into Anastasia's isolated cottage. Driven by hunger and desperation, he demands food and money. When Anastasia is unable to provide the money Trow attacks her. Driven by her own passions and will to survive, Anastasia puts up a violent defense, eventually driving Trow away. "But now the foam came to her mouth, and fire sprang from her eyes, and the muscles of her body worked as though she had been trained to deeds of violence." Morton soon arrives with help and then pursues Trow, eventually cornering him in a sea cave and killing him in the ensuing underwater struggle. The story presents a psychologically complex study of violence and passion, showing that even the most seemingly mild-mannered when driven to extremes is capable of explosive acts of violence. In "Aaron Trow" and later in "Malachi's Cove" and "The Spotted Dog" Trollope explores beyond the conventional limits of Victorian fiction and anticipates later writers such as D. H. Lawrence.

In 1867 Trollope brought out a third collection of nine stories in the mode of *Tales of All Countries,* which he titled *Lotta Schmidt and Other Stories.* Deeply influenced by his visit to the United States and his experience of the American Civil War, Trollope's stories are unified by the themes of difference and reconciliation. The title story, first published in *Argosy* in July 1866, is set in Vienna, which Trollope visited on a tour of central Europe in 1867, a trip that also provided material and inspiration for his novels *Nina Balatka: The Story of a Maiden of Prague* (1867) and *Linda Tressel* (1868). The new collection was generally well received, though one reviewer criticized the authenticity of the foreign heroines. Lotta Schmidt, he suggested in the 21 September 1867 *Saturday Review,* was really Lotty Smith dressed "à la Viennoise," and Ophelia Gledd was really Lucy Robarts of *Framley Parsonage* "with a Yankee twang."

Lotta Schmidt is a shop girl, admired and courted by two suitors, Herr Crippel, an elderly musician, and Fritz Planken, a handsome young man. When Crippel conducts an orchestra, Planken ridicules his appearance and musicianship. To fur-

ther spite Lotta, Planken ignores her, dancing repeatedly with a rival, reversing the plot of "Miss Sarah Jack." The angry Lotta, seeing Planken's pettiness, agrees to marry Herr Crippel, reconciling youth with age, the dancer with the "cripple." In a similar fashion "Father Giles of Ballymoy," "The Adventures of Fred Pickering," and "Malachi's Cave" are all stories in which differences are reconciled.

"Father Giles" reprises the character Archibald Green, who is visiting an isolated Irish village on business. Finding what he takes to be an intruder in the night, the impetuous Green throws the stranger down the stairs only to discover to his horror and chagrin that it is the local Catholic priest in whose room Green is staying. Only Father Giles's generosity and charity save the Protestant Green from the anger of the locals. "The Adventures of Fred Pickering," originally published in *Argosy* in September 1866 as "The Misfortunes of Fred Pickering," rehearses a comic version of the plot Trollope later uses in "The Spotted Dog." A young attorney aspiring to be a poet, Fred marries against his father's wishes and moves to London to pursue a career in letters. Failing at this he finally reconciles with his father and returns to Manchester with his wife and baby to practice law. "Malachi's Cove," first published in *Good Words* in December 1864, explores passion and violence, much like "Aaron Trow." The wild young Cornish woman Mahala Tringlos is crushed into a near animal existence, gathering seaweed for fertilizer. When Barty Gunliffe steals some of her supply of seaweed, she explodes with violent passion and hopes that he will be killed. But when Barty falls into a whirlpool, Mahala risks her life to save him and discovers that her passionate anger has become passionate love. As in "Aaron Trow" Trollope is interested in exploring variations on the theme of passion, here reversing the situation. Thus, where passion reduced the gentle Anastasia and Caleb to animal violence, it transforms the bestial Mahala into a gentle and loving young woman.

The stories "The Two Generals" and "The Widow's Mite" were both first published in *Good Words.* In 1863 the magazine's editor, Dr. Norman Macleod, a well-known Presbyterian minister based in Glasgow, invited Trollope to submit a novel. Recalling his unhappy experiences with the *London Review,* Trollope hesitated, offering the two stories instead. Macleod published these but persisted in his desire for a novel. Trollope obliged by writing *Rachel Ray: A Novel* (1863) in three months, but Macleod found its realism inappropriately provocative for a Christian magazine and turned it down with some embarrassment, paying Trollope a kill fee of £500. Trollope pocketed the fee philosophically and thereafter limited his contributions to edifying parables.

The idea for "The Two Generals" came from Sen. John Crittenden, whose two sons fought as opposing generals in the American Civil War. Trollope's tale is about Tom and Frank Reckenthorpe of Frankfort, Kentucky. Rivals for the hand of Ada Forster, the brothers are further alienated by the secession of the Southern states. "Fathers were divided from sons, and mothers from daughters. Terrible tales were told of threats uttered by one member of a family against another. Old ties of friendship were broken up. Society had so divided itself, that one side could hold no terms of courtesy with the other." Frank joins the Union Army and becomes a general, while Tom joins the Confederate forces, also becoming a general. After a terrible battle Tom is wounded, losing a leg, and taken prisoner. Despite their differences the brothers achieve a sort of courtesy, and Frank, who commands the Union forces in the region, arranges to have his brother returned to Frankfort so that he can marry Ada. Trollope closes his story by paraphrasing President Abraham Lincoln: "The carnage of their battles, and the hatreds of their civil contests, are terrible to us when we think of them; but may it not be that the beneficent power of Heaven, which they acknowledge as we do, is thus cleansing their land from that stain of slavery, to abolish which no human power seemed to be sufficient?" "The Widow's Mite," originally published as a Christmas tale, looked at the Civil War from the other side of the Atlantic. Engaged to a wealthy American, Nora Field, a young Englishwoman, is distressed by the plight of the weavers who were suffering from a famine caused by the war's disruption of the cotton trade. As a gesture of sympathy she donates the money that was to go to her trousseau for the relief of the weavers.

"The Last Austrian Who Left Venice," also first published in *Good Words,* translates the plot of "The Two Generals" to an Italian setting, specifically the Italian struggle for unity and independence from Austria, and refocuses attention on the heroine. Nina Pepé loves Captain Von Vincke, but her brother, a follower of Italian patriot Giuseppe Garibaldi, makes her promise that she will not marry until Venice is liberated from the Austrians. When Venice is finally returned to the Italians, Nina goes in search of her love, eventually finding him wounded in a Verona hospital. Because Austria has

reconciled with Italy, and Venice is free, Nina is also free to marry Captain Von Vincke. What had begun in division and sadness ended in reconciliation and happiness.

Between 1853 and 1861 the various taxes had been abolished in England, including newspaper duties and advertisement taxes. The result was a great bubble of enthusiasm for publishing magazines, newspapers, and other sorts of periodicals. Many writers of the day took up editing or even founded periodicals as a way of securing a convenient vehicle for publication. Noteworthy examples include Thackeray's editorship of *Cornhill Magazine* and Dickens's proprietorship of *Master Humphrey's Clock* (1840), *Household Words* (1850), and *All the Year Round* (1859). In 1863 George Smith, the publisher of the *Cornhill,* started the *Pall Mall Gazette* and enticed Trollope to join the editorial board. In the ensuing years he contributed criticism for the *Pall Mall Gazette* as well as an assortment of humorous pieces which were subsequently collected and republished as *Hunting Sketches* (1865), *Travelling Sketches, Clergymen of the Church of England* (1866), and *London Tradesmen* (1927).

Caught up in the enthusiasm for periodicals and feeling sufficiently flush, Trollope joined with the publisher Frederic Chapman and others to found the *Fortnightly Review* in 1865. George Henry Lewes, the longtime companion of George Eliot, became the editor. Trollope provided material regularly, including the first installment of *The Belton Estate* for the inaugural issue on 15 May 1865. The project soon proved too ambitious, even for the everindustrious Trollope, with the result that the *Fortnightly Review* came out monthly. "Of all the serial publications of the day, it is probably the most serious, the most earnest, the least devoted to amusement, the least flippant, the least jocose," Trollope recalled. "And yet it has the face to show itself month after month to the world, with so absurd a misnomer!" When Lewes retired from the project for reasons of health in 1866, Trollope also withdrew from active participation. Under the subsequent editorship of John Morley, the *Fortnightly Review* became the leading forum for liberals and freethinkers. Still caught up in the enthusiasm and now retired from the post office, Trollope founded *Saint Paul's Magazine* in 1867. He edited it himself until relieved of his duties by his partners in 1870. With some bitterness he wrote in his *Autobiography,* "I was too anxious to be good, and did not think enough of what might be lucrative." While the editor of *Saint Paul's,* Trollope contributed several stories, which he reprinted under the title *An Editor's Tales* (1870).

While it is now generally regarded as Trollope's most unified and ambitious collection as well as containing some of his best short fiction, the initial critical response to *An Editor's Tales* was at best cool. The 13 August 1870 *Saturday Review* found most of the stories "washy and spiritless sketches," lacking any real unity of effect, and the January 1871 *Contemporary Review* considered it as "Trollope only at his second best." *An Editor's Tales* includes six stories: "The Turkish Bath," "Mary Gresley," "Josephine de Montmorenci," "The Panjandrum," "The Spotted Dog," and "Mrs. Brumby." Abandoning the format of *Tales of All Countries*, Trollope uses a harried editor of a successful London magazine as the narrator of the stories, which recount his dealings with an odd assortment of would-be contributors. In the 13 August 1870 issue of the *Saturday Review,* one critic offered "the editor who deliberates is lost" as the moral of the collection. The editor, Mr. Brown, is another of Trollope's satiric self-portraits and is an amiable if somewhat pompous man, fond of the editorial "we." He prefaces "The Panjandrum" with the statement that once "the great *we* was not, in truth, ours to use," explaining, "we shall, therefore, tell our story, as might any ordinary individual, in the first person singular, and speak of such sparks of editorship as did fly up around us as having created but a dim coruscation, and as having been quite insufficient to justify the delicious plural." One might recall Trollope's portrait of Tom Towers, the editor of *The Jupiter,* throwing his thunderbolts in *The Warden, Barchester Towers,* and *Framley Parsonage.*

"The Turkish Bath" and "Mrs. Brumby" present another of Trollope's studies in opposites. In "The Turkish Bath" the editor is approached in a bathhouse by a loquacious Irishman named Michael Molloy, a down-on-his-luck writer who wants to write for the magazine. Against his better judgment the editor offers to look at a sample of the Irishman's work and even pays a small advance. When the work is delivered he is appalled to discover that it is neither coherent nor grammatical. Unable to resist Molloy's pleas, however, he accepts another sample that proves little better. Going finally to Molloy's house he learns that the Irishman is insane, but harmless, spending his days maniacally writing pages and pages of nonsense. Trollope claimed that the plot for "The Turkish Bath" was based on an actual incident, though the idea of the maniacal writer suggests a parody of Trollope's own methodical habit of composition. In "Mrs. Brumby" the editor again encounters an aggressive contributor. But where Michael Molloy was good-natured and harmless, Mrs. Brumby, a resurrection of Mrs. Proudie of the Barsetshire novels, is not. She forces her way into the editor's office, attempting to bully and browbeat him into accepting her manuscript. Since her work is almost as worthless as Molloy's, the editor refuses, whereupon she threatens a lawsuit. In the end the editor pays her a ten-pound quit fee and apologizes to her for an alleged assault by his clerk.

"Mary Gresley" and "Josephine de Montmorenci" explore the editor's susceptibility to young women. While the name Mary Gresley was based on that of his maternal grandmother, the character and some incidents of the plot look to Trollope's relationship with Kate Field. In the story the editor is approached by a charming young woman who has ambitions of becoming another Currer Bell (the pseudonym of Charlotte Brontë). Although Mary is engaged to an invalid curate who disapproves of novels and novel writing, the editor tries to nurture her limited literary talents. These efforts are largely in vain, and Mary finally promises her dying fiancé to abandon literature. The story ends several years later with the editor seeing her off as she sails to accompany a missionary husband in Africa. "We kissed her once, – for the first and only time, – as we bade God bless her!"

The editor's aid and advice to Mary resemble those that Trollope gave to Field, who published several books on the literary figures she knew, including *Pen Photographs of Charles Dickens' Readings* (1868), but she never achieved her ambition of becoming a great novelist and poet. When she sent Trollope some of her stories to criticize he advised her to avoid heavy didacticism. In a May 1868 letter he suggested that she "tell some simple plot or story of more or less involved, but still common life, adventure, and try first to tell that in such form that idle minds may find some gentle sentiment & recreation in your work. . . . Afterwards, when you have learned the knack of story telling, go on to greater objects." In an essay on the genius of Nathaniel Hawthorne, published in the September 1879 *North American Review,* Trollope made a similar point about his own writing practice: "It has always been my object to draw my little pictures as like to life as possible, so that my readers should feel that they were dealing with people whom they might probably have known." His advice and observations reveal something about Field's abilities and Trollope's own conception of the art of fiction.

The much-criticized lack of variety in Trollope's plots may be explained by the author's understanding of the importance of plot and its relation-

*Caricature of Trollope in* Spy, *1873*

els as *The Moonstone* (1868) and *The Woman in White* (1860), in the first category and placed himself in the second. The sensational novel, Trollope argued, depended on plot for its effect, in a sense, rendering the action independent of the characters. In his own work, plot emerged from the characters, suggesting an organic relationship between character and the unity of the story. The novelist (and short-story writer) should write "not because he has to tell a story, but because he has a story to tell." The young author is moved by some person or experience. From this he or she imagines how the character might act in certain circumstances. "Some series of events, or some development of character, will have presented itself to his imagination, – and this he feels so strongly that he thinks he can present his picture in strong and agreeable language to others." Without a clear link between the action and the character the characters become merely puppets to be moved about in interesting patterns. Thus, in both his novels and short stories Trollope tried to imagine his characters and how they would react and behave under circumstances that they would likely encounter. In this way Trollope generated his plots either by putting a series of different characters into the same set of circumstances or by putting similar characters into a series of modified circumstances.

While Trollope primarily constructed "Mary Gresley" out of his actual or imagined dealings with Field, he also worked an homage to Charlotte Brontë into the story. In addition to the reference to Currer Bell, Trollope put Mary into a set of circumstances that reworked the relationship between the young Jane Eyre and the Reverend Mr. St. John Rivers, who wished Jane to join him as a missionary in India. Trollope saw in Brontë an author who felt her characters intensely and drew her plots out of her characters. "I know no interest more thrilling than that which she has been able to throw into the characters of Rochester and the governess," he wrote in his *Autobiography*. "She lived with those characters, and felt with every fibre of her heart, the longings of the one, and the sufferings of the other." Because "the men and women depicted are human in their aspirations, human in their sympathies, and human in their actions," Trollope predicted that *Jane Eyre* would still be read long after many other novels were forgotten.

At first "Josephine de Montmorenci" seems in the spirit of "Mrs. Brumby." Mr. Brown, the editor of the *Olympus Magazine,* receives a peremptory letter from a Josephine de Montmorenci, demanding that he publish her novel, *Not So Black as It Is Painted.* In-

ship to character. Surveying the state of English fiction in his *Autobiography*, Trollope distinguished between two types of novels – the "sensational" and the "anti-sensational" or realistic. He classified his friend Wilkie Collins, author of such mystery nov-

terested by such an imposing name, Brown invites the author to call, only to discover that Josephine de Montmorenci is not as imposing as her letter suggested. The charming young woman who arrives, Mrs. Puffle, reveals that the name is merely a pseudonym and that the true author of the novel is her sister-in-law, Maryanne Puffle, known to her friends as Polly. It further turns out that Brown is an old smoking companion of Polly's husband, Charles Puffle, an official in the post office. As in "Mary Gresley," "Josephine de Montmorenci" combines Trollope's personal experiences with literary homage. The game of pseudonyms, as R. H. Super points out in *The Chronicler of Barsetshire: A Life of Anthony Trollope* (1988), makes playful reference to Trollope's friend George Eliot, the pseudonym for Maryanne (or Marian) Evans, also nicknamed Polly. In turn Trollope and Lewes, Polly's companion, were frequent smoking companions. As part of the joke, however, Trollope reverses roles, making Lewes, the editor, an official of the post office, and himself an editor. (Lewes's son, Charles, worked in the post office, thanks largely to Trollope's good offices.)

"The Panjandrum" pokes fun at the business of founding and editing a magazine. The events of the story perhaps look back to 1840 and 1841, when Trollope was involved in various literary projects not long before he went to Ireland. It may also look more immediately back to his experiences on the editorial board of the *Fortnightly Review* and its tone of earnest seriousness. In the story a group of literary friends plans to start a review called the *Panjandrum*. (Trollope borrowed the title from a nonsense word coined by the Irish playwright Samuel Foote to designate a self-important local magnate. It also puns on pandemonium.) The project finally collapses after months of meetings, when each founder rejects everyone else's proposed contribution. The story is of interest for its satire of intellectual literary circles, especially of the figure of Mrs. St. Quinten, a popular novelist who proposes to contribute an essay on Berkeley's theory of matter, and her cousin Churchill Smith. "It was his own specialty to be an unbeliever and a German scholar; and we gave him credit for being so deep in both arts that no man could go deeper."

The story probably indicates something of Trollope's method of dealing with writer's block. When the young editor is desperate to come up with an idea for his contribution he resorts to following an old woman and a child one rainy night in order to overhear their conversation. Taking this seed from experience he imagines a scenario and

from that builds a short story. "These wondrous castles in the air never get themselves well built when the mind, with premeditated skill and labour, sets itself to work to build them," muses the editor, anticipating Trollope's remarks in the *Autobiography*: "It is when they come uncalled for that they stand erect and strong before the mind's eye. . . ."

In "The Spotted Dog," frequently cited as Trollope's best short story, the editor takes pity on a desperate and destitute scholar named Julius Mackenzie. In "Trollope as a Short Story Writer" Stone describes Mackenzie as "the embodiment of the human death wish," a man who has cut himself off from friends and family. The editor observes "an intensity and a thorough hopelessness of suffering in his case." Like Fred Pickering, Mackenzie has married against his family's wishes. Mackenzie's wife, however, is an alcoholic prostitute, subject to violent bouts of jealousy and rage. After much deliberation the editor decides to let Mackenzie edit and index the manuscript of a friend who is a reverend, a life's work of classical scholarship. So that Mackenzie might have a safe place to work the editor sets him up in a room at The Spotted Dog, a pub owned by some friends of Mackenzie. The work seems to be progressing until Mackenzie's wife appears one day at the pub. In the ensuing row the proprietor of The Spotted Dog expels both Mackenzie and his wife. When the editor goes to the poor scholar's lodgings to recover the manuscript he discovers to his horror that the wife has burned most of it in a rage and that Mackenzie has drunk himself into oblivion. The following day Mackenzie commits suicide.

Trollope's story presents an affecting picture of poverty in the nether regions of London, anticipating George Gissing's work by twenty years. As in "Aaron Trow" and "Malachi's Cove," Trollope is especially interested in imagining the limits to which passion and despair can drive ordinary people and in exploring the subtle gradations of jealousy and generosity. "The Spotted Dog" may be read, as Stone suggests, "as a Victorian fable of the Romantic will-to-freedom turning inevitably into a suicidal urge." Trollope's fable, however, resists a simple moral, eschewing the reassuring formulas and artificial sentiments of his Christmas tales or a Dickensian appeal to pathos. Instead, he constructs his fable with deeply felt sympathy for the subtle shades of human weakness, portraying his characters in a spirit of charity and tolerance. While the subject and outcome of the story seem foreign to the world of Mr. Harding and Lily Dale of the Barsetshire novels, Trollope's treatment is in concert with these gentle beings. As the editor says of his reverend friend, who shrugs off the loss of his life's work, "I never thought very much of the Doctor as a divine, but I hold him to have been as good a Christian as I ever met." And it is indeed in that spirit that Trollope imagines the sad story of Julius Mackenzie and denizens of "The Spotted Dog."

With the publication of *An Editor's Tales* in 1870 Trollope turned his attention more fully to writing novels, biographies, and travel books. The period between 1870 and 1880 saw the completion of the great parliamentary novels or Palliser series with *The Eustace Diamonds* (1872), *Phineas Redux* (1874), *The Prime Minister* (1875–1876), and *The Duke's Children: A Novel* (1880). Other noteworthy novels Trollope wrote during this period include *The Way We Live Now* (1874–1875), regarded by a growing consensus as his masterpiece, *The American Senator* (1877), and *Is He Popenjoy? A Novel* (1878). In May 1871 Trollope and Rose sailed for Australia to visit their son Fred. The immediate product of this trip was another travel book, *Australia and New Zealand* (1873). A trip to South Africa in 1877 led to *South Africa,* which was followed quickly by *How the "Mastiffs" Went to Iceland,* the result of an expedition to Iceland shortly after his return to England from Africa. Both books were published in 1878. Trollope also published *The Commentaries of Caesar* (1870) and *The Life of Cicero* (1880). While both of these works are limited in their contribution to classical scholarship they were satisfying to Trollope as a confirmation of his intellectual credentials as a classically trained gentleman, redeeming his dismal experiences at Harrow and Winchester. During this busy period Trollope also managed to complete his *Autobiography* and a short biography of his old friend Thackeray. Thackeray's daughter, Lady Richie, was cordial but not forthcoming with letters and information. The biography appeared in 1879 as part of Macmillan's English Men of Letters series. The *Autobiography* appeared posthumously in 1883, edited by his son Henry.

While Trollope remained prolific in the production of large works, he published only nine short stories during this period. Of these he reprinted only five in the last collection published before his death, *Why Frau Frohmann Raised Her Prices, and Other Stories* (1882). Part of the reason for this was that Trollope and his publishers felt that the market was becoming saturated with his novels and stories, and indeed, publishers and editors backlogged some of his works. In addition many of the stories of this period were strictly business and had little sense of personal investment. The four he

chose not to collect were "Christmas Day at Kirkby Cottage," "Harry Heathcote of Gangoil," "Catherine Carmichael," and "Never, Never, – Never, Never." The last was a burlesque of *The Small House at Allington* and *The Last Chronicle of Barset,* caricaturing Lily Dale as Mary Tompkins, Johnny Eames as John Thomas, and Mr. Slope as the Reverend Abraham Dribble. Writing to Susan Hale, the editor of the short-lived *Sheets for the Cradle,* the Boston-based magazine where the story appeared in December 1875, he wrote, "as Bret Harte says I have no sense of humor, and won't laugh at me, I must try to laugh at myself, and make fun of the heroine I have loved best."

*Why Frau Frohmann Raised Her Prices, and Other Stories* loosely reprised the format of *Tales of All Countries.* In addition to the title story, it included "Christmas at Thompson Hall," "The Telegraph Girl," "The Lady of Launay," and "Alice Dugdale." The collection received mixed reviews when it appeared. The 11 March 1882 *Saturday Review* found the stories readable but thought that Trollope had been slovenly, putting in little effort. While the 1882 *Literary World* was dismissive, the 14 January 1882 *Athenaeum* was brief but sympathetic: the tale, as one reviewer put it, "is a pleasant little parable upon political economy." In a letter to the publisher of the *Athenaeum,* William Isbister, Trollope wrote, "The Frau Frohmann is a good story, though I say it who ought not." Frau Frohmann, the owner of a Tyrolean inn, believing that prices should always remain the same, tries to coerce the local peasants into selling her meat and produce at the old prices for her hotel. She finally relents when she learns that the incomes of all her guests have also gone up over the years.

"The Telegraph Girl" is a slight tale of selflessness rewarded, which Trollope originally published in *Good Cheer* (1877), the annual Christmas issue of Donald Macleod's *Good Words.* Writing to Macleod in January 1877 Trollope explained the genesis of the story. "Some weeks since I went to see these young women at work [the London Central Telegraph Office], and being much struck with them, my imagination went to work and composed a little story about one."

"The Lady of Launay" first appeared in *Light* at the invitation of Robert Buchanan. Buchanan, famous for his October 1871 attack in the *Contemporary Review* on Dante Gabriel Rossetti, "The Fleshy School of Poetry," wrote to Trollope, "I don't presume to dictate, but we strongly desire a tale with great sexual interest." The plot in part reprises "La Mère Bauche" and in part anticipates *Ayala's Angel*

(1881). A domineering Mrs. Miles, the wealthy owner of Launay, wishes her son to marry a wealthy cousin. He, however, wishes to marry the orphaned Bessy, Mrs. Miles's foster daughter. To prevent difficulties Bessy is sent away from Launay, but Philip, unlike Madame Bauche's son, remains true, following her into exile. The story ends on a note of reconciliation. In a similar fashion, "Mary Dugdale," the most satisfying story of the collection, repeats the story of "The Parson's Daughter of Oxney Colne." In this version, however, Major Rossiter decides against the wealthy heiress for the homely but solid Mary.

Despite deteriorating health Trollope continued a heavy literary output, publishing five more novels by 1882. He also managed a final trip to Ireland to research *The Landleaguers* which appeared posthumously in 1883 along with *Mr. Scarborough's Family* and the *Autobiography*. During this period Trollope also produced two more tales, "The Two Heroines of Plumplington," first published in *Good Cheer* in December 1882, and "Not If I Know It," first published in the Christmas annual of *Life* that same year, and he was negotiating with the owner of the periodical *Bow Bells* about a series of ten new stories just months before his death. Of these "The Two Heroines" is chiefly of interest for one last look at Barsetshire. On 3 November 1882 Trollope suffered a severe stroke that seriously impaired his faculties. He died on 6 December 1882 at the age of sixty-seven.

Trollope's output of novels and stories was vast, with the inevitable result that much of the good was lost amid the mediocre. As Trollope confessed in the *Autobiography*, "when the things were good they came out too quick upon another to gain much attention; – and so also, luckily, when they were bad." While Trollope's short fiction fails to achieve the greatness of the masters of the genre, it is always competent and stands well against the work of other Victorian practitioners. His stories retain an interest and appeal, not only as artifacts of Trollope and his world, but as astute, humane, and entertaining studies in the rituals and nuances of everyday life. Trollope's style, as one critic astutely observed in the 21 September 1867 issue of *Saturday Review*, "is simply the sublime of commonplace." His achievement is perhaps summed up best in an April 1882 review of *Frau Frohmann* in *The Spectator:* "Mr. Trollope is always amusing, but he is never more amusing than in his shorter tales, when he makes them turn, as he so often does, on his curiously microscopic knowledge of those little social tactics and maneuvers by which so many important positions are gained or lost, though no one but social microscopists like Mr. Trollope appreciate their significance."

**Letters:**

*Letters of Anthony Trollope,* edited by Bradford Allen Booth (London: Oxford University Press, 1951);

*The Letters of Anthony Trollope,* 2 volumes, edited by N. John Hall (Stanford, Cal.: Stanford University Press, 1983).

**Bibliographies:**

Mary Leslie Irwin, *Anthony Trollope: A Bibliography* (London: Pitman, 1926);

Michael Sadleir, *Trollope: A Bibliography* (London: Constable, 1928);

John Charles Olmsted and Jeffrey Egan Welch, *The Reputation of Trollope: An Annotated Bibliography, 1925–1975* (New York: Garland, 1978);

Anne K. Lyons, *Anthony Trollope: An Annotated Bibliography of Periodical Works By and About Him in the United States and Great Britain to 1900* (Greenwood, Fla.: Penkevill, 1985).

**Biographies:**

T[homas] H[ay] S[weet] Escott, *Anthony Trollope: His Public Services, Private Friends, and Literary Originals* (London: John Lane, 1913);

Michael Sadleir, *Trollope: A Commentary* (London: Constable, 1927);

Lucy Poate Stebbins and Richard Poate Stebbins, *The Trollopes: The Chronicle of a Writing Family* (New York: Columbia University Press, 1945; London: Secker & Warburg, 1947);

James Pope Hennessy, *Anthony Trollope* (Boston: Little, Brown, 1971);

C. P. Snow, *Trollope: His Life and Art* (London: Macmillan, 1975);

R. H. Super, *Trollope in the Post Office* (Ann Arbor: University of Michigan Press, 1981);

Super, *The Chronicler of Barsetshire: A Life of Anthony Trollope* (Ann Arbor: University of Michigan Press, 1988);

Richard Mullen, *Anthony Trollope: A Victorian in His World* (London: Duckworth, 1990);

N. John Hall, *Trollope: A Biography* (Oxford: Clarendon Press, 1991);

Victoria Glendinning, *Trollope* (London: Hutchinson, 1992; New York: Knopf, 1993).

**References:**

David Aitken, "Anthony Trollope on 'the Genus Girl,' " *Nineteenth-Century Fiction,* 28 (March 1974): 417–434;

Ruth apRoberts, *The Moral Trollope* (Athens: Ohio University Press, 1971);

Richard Barickman, Susan MacDonald, and Myra Stark, *Corrupt Relations: Dickens, Thackeray, Trollope, Collins, and the Victorian Sexual System* (New York: Columbia University Press, 1982);

John William Clark, *The Language and Style of Anthony Trollope* (London: Deutsch, 1975);

David R. Eastwood, "Romantic Elements and Aesthetic Distance in Trollope's Fiction," *Studies in Short Fiction,* 18 (Fall 1981): 395–405;

Elizabeth R. Epperly, *Patterns of Repetition in Trollope* (Washington, D.C.: Catholic University Press, 1989);

Peter K. Garrett, *The Victorian Multiplot Novel: Studies in Dialogical Form* (New Haven: Yale University Press, 1980);

James Gindin, *Harvest of a Quiet Eye: The Novel of Compassion* (Bloomington: Indiana University Press, 1971);

Mary Hamer, *Writing by Numbers: Trollope's Serial Fiction* (Cambridge: Cambridge University Press, 1987);

Hugh L. Hennedy, *Unity in Barsetshire* (The Hague: Mouton, 1971);

Christopher Herbert, *Trollope and Comic Pleasure* (Chicago: University of Chicago Press, 1987);

Walter M. Kendrick, *The Novel-Machine: The Theory and Fiction of Anthony Trollope* (Baltimore: Johns Hopkins University Press, 1980);

James R. Kincaid, *The Novels of Anthony Trollope* (Oxford: Clarendon Press, 1977);

U. C. Knoepflmacher, *Laughter and Despair: Readings in Ten Novels of the Victorian Era* (Berkeley: University of California Press, 1971);

George Levine, *The Realist Imagination: English Fiction from Frankenstein to Lady Chatterley* (Chicago: University of Chicago Press, 1981);

Blander Matthews, *The Philosophy of the Short-Story* (New York: Longmans, Green, 1901);

Juliet McMaster, *Trollope's Palliser Novels: Theme and Pattern* (New York: Macmillan, 1978);

J. Hillis Miller, *The Form of Victorian Fiction: Thackeray, Dickens, Trollope, George Eliot, Meredith and Hardy* (Notre Dame, Ind.: University of Notre Dame Press, 1968);

Jane Narden, *He Knew She Was Right: The Independent Woman in the Novels of Anthony Trollope* (Carbondale: Southern Illinois University Press, 1989);

Clara Claiborne Park, "Trollope and the Modern Reader," *Massachusetts Review,* 3 (1961–1962): 577–591;

Roger L. Slakey, "Trollope's Case for Moral Imperative," *Nineteenth-Century Fiction,* 28 (December 1973): 305–320;

Donald Arthur Smalley, *Trollope: The Critical Heritage* (London: Routledge & Kegan Paul, 1969);

Donald D. Stone, *The Romantic Impulse in Victorian Fiction* (Cambridge, Mass.: Harvard University Press, 1980);

Stone, "Trollope as a Short Story Writer," *Nineteenth-Century Fiction,* 31 (June 1976): 26–47;

L. J. Swingle, *Romanticism and Anthony Trollope: A Study in the Continuity of Nineteenth-Century Literary Thought* (Ann Arbor: University of Michigan Press, 1990);

Reginald Charles Terry, *Anthony Trollope: The Artist in Hiding* (London: Rowman & Littlefield, 1977);

Jerome Thale, "The Problem of Structure in Trollope," *Nineteenth-Century Fiction,* 15 (June 1960): 147–157;

Robert Tracy, *Trollope's Later Novels* (Berkeley: University of California Press, 1978).

**Papers:**

Collections of Anthony Trollope's papers are at the Bodleian Library, Oxford, and the Beinecke Library, Yale University.

# Checklist of Further Readings

Adams, Robert M. *The Land and Literature of England: A Historical Account.* New York: Norton, 1983.

Allen, Walter. *The Short Story in English.* Oxford: Clarendon Press, 1981.

Altick, Richard. *The English Common Reader: A Social History of the Mass Reading Public, 1800–1900.* Chicago: University of Chicago Press, 1957.

Altick. *Victorian People and Ideas: A Companion for the Modern Reader of Victorian Literature.* New York: Norton, 1973.

Beachcroft, Thomas Owen. *The English Short Story,* 2 volumes. London: Longmans, Green, 1964.

Beachcroft. *The Modest Art: A Survey of the Short Story in English.* London: Oxford University Press, 1968.

Harris, Wendell V. *British Short Fiction in the Nineteenth Century: A Literary and Bibliographic Guide.* Detroit: Wayne State University Press, 1979.

Keating, Peter, ed. *Nineteenth Century Short Stories.* Essex: Longman, 1981.

Kelly, Gary. *English Fiction of the Romantic Period, 1789–1830.* London: Longman, 1989.

Klancher, Jon. *The Making of English Reading Audiences, 1790–1832.* Madison: University of Wisconsin Press, 1987.

Orel, Harold. *The Victorian Short Story: Development and Triumph of a Literary Genre.* Cambridge: Cambridge University Press, 1986.

Rafroidi, Patrick, and Terence Brown, eds. *The Irish Short Story.* Atlantic Highlands, N.J.: Humanities Press, 1979.

Schirmer, Gregory. "Tales from Big House and Cabin: The Nineteenth Century," in *The Irish Short Story: A Critical History,* edited by James F. Kilroy. Boston: G. K. Hall, 1984, pp. 21–44.

Sutherland, Kathryn. " 'Events . . . Have Made Us a World of Readers': Reader Relations 1780–1830," in *The Romantic Period,* edited by David Pirie, volume 5 in the Penguin History of Literature Series. London: Penguin, 1994.

Thornburg, Mary K. Patterson. *The Monster in the Mirror: Gender and the Sentimental/Gothic Myth in Frankenstein.* Ann Arbor: UMI Research Press, 1984.

Wheeler, Michael. *English Fiction of the Victorian Period, 1830–1890.* London & New York: Longman, 1985.

# Contributors

Edward Ball ...................................................... *University of North Carolina at Asheville*
LynnDianne Beene.................................................. *University of New Mexico*
Thomas L. Blanton ................................................ *Central Washington University*
Natalie Bell Cole................................................. *Oakland University*
Thomas L. Cooksey ................................................ *Armstrong State College*
Martin A. Cavanaugh.............................................. *Washington University*
Mary Lou Fisk ................................................... *University of New Mexico*
Richard D. Fulton ............................................... *Clark College*
Tony Giffone..................................... *State University of New York at Farmingdale*
Ruth Glancy ..................................................... *Concordia College*
Betsy Gordon .................................................... *McKendree College*
David C. Hanson ................................... *Southeastern Louisiana University*
Leslie Haynsworth ............................................... *Columbia, South Carolina*
Gillian H. Hughes ............................................... *Manchester, England*
David E. Latané Jr. ............................................. *Virginia Commonwealth University*
Kathryn Ledbetter............................................... *Oklahoma Baptist University*
Deborah A. Logan........................... *University of North Carolina at Chapel Hill*
Toni Louise Oplt................................................. *Edwardsville, Illinois*
Richard D. McGhee............................................... *Arkansas State University*
Maureen T. Reddy................................................ *Rhode Island College*
James R. Simmons Jr. ........................................... *University of South Carolina*
Elton Edward Smith.............................................. *University of South Florida*
Kathryn West.................................................... *Bellarmine College*
Linda Mills Woolsey ............................................ *King College*
Jennifer L. Wyatt............................................... *Civic Memorial High School,*

# Cumulative Index

*Dictionary of Literary Biography,* Volumes 1-159
*Dictionary of Literary Biography Yearbook,* 1980-1994
*Dictionary of Literary Biography Documentary Series,* Volumes 1-12

# Cumulative Index

**DLB** before number: *Dictionary of Literary Biography*, Volumes 1-159
**Y** before number: *Dictionary of Literary Biography Yearbook*, 1980-1994
**DS** before number: *Dictionary of Literary Biography Documentary Series*, Volumes 1-12

# G

Cumulative Index

# H

# Q

# R